close relations

an introduction to the sociology of families

second edition

susan a. mcdaniel
UNIVERSITY OF ALBERTA

lorne tepperman
UNIVERSITY OF TORONTO

PEARSON

Prentice
Hall

Toronto

For Doug, my life's partner and kindred spirit—SM

To Sandra, my partner and closest relation—LT

National Library of Canada Cataloguing in Publication

McDaniel, Susan A., 1946-
        Close relations : an introduction to the sociology of families /
Susan A. McDaniel, Lorne Tepperman. – 2nd ed.

Includes bibliographical references and index.
ISBN 0-13-044933-4

1. Family—Canada.   I. Tepperman, Lorne, 1943-   II. Title.

HQ560.M28 2004   306.85'0971   C2003-903261-2

0-13-044933-4

Vice President, Editorial Director: Michael J. Young
Executive Acquisitions Editor: Jessica Mosher
Senior Marketing Manager: Judith Allen
Developmental Editor: John Polanszky
Production Editor: Mary Ann McCutcheon
Copy Editor: Karen Hunter
Production Coordinator: Heather Bean
Page Layout: Debbie Kumpf
Permissions Research: Sandy Cooke
Photo Research: Alene McNeill
Art Director: Mary Opper
Interior Design: Jennifer Federico
Cover Design: Jennifer Federico
Cover Image: Chris Windsor/gettyimages

6   08 07 06 05

Printed and bound in the USA.

Statistics Canada information is used with the permission of the Minister of Industry, as Minister responsible for Statistics Canada. Information on the availability of the wide range of data from Statistics Canada can be obtained from Statistics Canada's Regional Offices, its World Wide Web site at http://www.statcan.ca and its toll-free access number, 1-800-263-1136.

Photo Credits
Page 1, The Image Works; page 16, CORBIS/MAGMA; page 29, Glenbow Archives NA659-2; page 44, National Archives of Canada #C-038723; page 68, Taxi/Getty Images; page 86, Tony Freedman/PhotoEdit; page 106, Getty Images; page 140, CP Photo/Kevin Frayer; page 154, Getty Images; page 185, Zigy Kalusny/Getty Images; page 193, Andy Cox/Getty Images; page 224, Joel Gordon Photography; page 239, Ian Shaw/Getty Images; page 255, Dick Hemingway; page 286, Ariel Skelley/CORBIS/MAGMA; page 297, Toronto Star/Dale Brazao; page 329, Getty Images; page 350, CP Picture Archive; page 379, Getty Images; page 411, Marc Grimberg/Getty Images; page 427, First Light; page 457, David Burnett/Contract Press Images, Inc.; page 471, Brad Martin/Getty Images; page 494, Mark Richards/PhotoEdit

Contents

Chapter 3   How Families Begin:
Dating and Mating

Chapter 8   Family Dynamics:

Chapter 9   Stress and Violence:

Preface

As this second edition of *Close Relations* goes to press, family is very much in the news. There is discussion of what marriage is and should be, and whether gay and lesbian couples should be allowed by law and policy to marry. There is new information about families in Canada from the 2001 Census. And there is active discussion about how families can best be supported by shifting social policies in Canada and elsewhere. Family remains a hot topic. Talking about our own family experiences and relationships is endlessly interesting, and family is a popular theme on radio and television talk shows. Family is what we still say we value most in life (Vanier Institute, 2001). Yet families are rife with contradictions. Although we value our families, increasing numbers of us abandon them. Family is a place of love, in which we seek solace from the world; yet it is also a place where abuse and violence are prevalent. Politicians seem to value families, commonly using terms such as "family responsibilities" and "family values," and yet they blame families for social problems.

Family life is still a fundamental part of life throughout the world, and certain general features characterize most families: extended kinship ties, provision of resources and social support, relative stability and permanence, and a (fading) association with the sacred as revealed in the 2001 Census of Canada. However, marital, divorce, and childbearing behaviours, attitudes, values, and norms have changed rapidly and dramatically.

The Approach of This Book

As recently as 20 years ago, books on the family were often simple "how-to" guides to family life. Sometimes called "matching, hatching, and dispatching" books, they had subtitles such as "Dating and Courtship" and "Family and You." There are still books like this on family today. This approach was possible a few decades ago since the ways in which people lived in families tended to be less diverse than they are now, and the diversity that did exist was neither portrayed nor celebrated in family texts. These types of contemporary books on family tend to "sell" the traditional family way of life. But, of course, shifting patterns and demands of work in post-modern societies create new kinds of family relations and forms, as we explore in this second edition.

Far more interesting than the regularities in close relations, though, are the variations in form and structure. Modern families are remarkably diverse. It is largely in response to this fact that we wrote the first edition of this book, and then revised it substantially with updated data and new insights about families in this second edition. This book sets itself the task of being different from many other family books in use today. Its focus is on applications and theory: what works for families, for us as individuals, and for society. Several themes characterize our book:

- Families are immensely varied and characterized more by processes than by the forms they take.

- Family is becoming more, not less, important to us as individuals and to society as a whole. Recent research and theory has clearly shown that family health affects individual health and longevity, and the population health of entire countries (Evans & Stoddart, 1994; McDaniel, 1998).

- Old expectations about family may no longer work. New solutions to family problems, based on what is known from family research, are needed and are offered here.

- There is a constantly changing interplay among families, schools, and work. Family is both part of the problem and part of the solution, as shown in this book in a variety of ways.

- Historical changes and cross-national comparisons help us to better understand and interpret families today.

Throughout this book, we look at families as plural and diverse. We focus on families in terms of what they do rather than the shape they take.

Canadian Content

Speaking of diversity, this is a Canadian book intended primarily for Canadian students and classrooms. While some generalizations based on American data apply to Canadian situation, others do not. Our laws and policies are different, as are our histories, traditions, values, norms, and customs relating to family and marriage. At the same time, it is difficult to write a text based entirely on the findings of Canadian research. The body of available Canadian research is not only smaller than one might hope, but also uneven in scope. It must be noted, however, that both the volume of research on families in Canada and the scope of the topics covered have expanded enormously in recent years. That said, a Canadian text, to be useful, should rely on the Canadian research and then incorporate findings from abroad. Thus, what we attempt here is a careful triangulation, using research from Canada, the United States, and elsewhere. We try to offer international comparisons wherever we feel they are critical. On the other hand, we do not draw attention to the nationality of a finding if we think that doing so adds nothing to understanding of the research on families.

In this second edition, there are six key areas that we have emphasized and strengthened, largely in response to readers' and instructors' suggestions:

- We have deepened the discussion of theoretical and methodological perspectives that frame research and thinking about families.

- We have added more on historical and cross-cultural aspects of family and family change.

• We have enhanced consideration of "external" challenges that affect families such as class discrimination, poverty and racism.

• We have enlarged the attention we give to social, economic, and legal policies.

• We give more attention to sexual, ethnic, and other kinds of family diversity.

• We devote more space to ongoing debates within sociologies of family. Each chapter has a debate box that highlights key aspects of differing points of view on an important issue in that chapter.

Brief Overview

Chapter 1 begins with an exploration of the variety of interesting shapes and processes of families and family-like relationships. We explore competing definitions of family, and how families are seen through theoretical lenses. We also consider how different research approaches to family work, and what they enable us to see.

From here, we move on to an entirely new chapter (Chapter 2) that opens the door to what we now know about families in the past. It offers an exciting glimpse of family diversity from an historical perspective. This discussion provides context for today's debates.

Chapter 3 then explores how families begin by taking a look at dating and mating. A renewed emphasis on ethnic and other cultural differences is offered here; attention is also paid to same sex dating.

In Chapter 4 we examine the different ways couples form and live, including cohabitation, marriage patterns, and same sex partnerships.

There follows in Chapter 5 a discussion of ways of being close in which we consider points of satisfaction and dissatisfaction, particularly in relation to communication, trust, and sex.

People sometimes think of real family life as beginning with the entry into parenthood—a time fraught with many new changes and challenges. That is the subject of Chapter 6. In this chapter we also propose several approaches to parenting that are supported by research, and offer some solutions to parenting problems.

In Chapter 7 we discuss work and family life, including the division of both domestic work and paid work. Domestic work is a known source of family conflict, while paid work in relation to the family is a topic of strong interest in the early 2000s, as most adult members of families must balance family life with paid employment.

In Chapter 8 we consider families as systems—systems with boundaries, resources, skills, and interrelated problems that often seem to defy any solution.

An understanding of violence and stress in families, the topic of Chapter 9, is crucial if we are to solve or even ameliorate these problems. We describe some of the contexts in which stresses occur for families, including poverty, racism, alcoholism, and the particular challenges faced by First Nations families. We also give attention to policies that attempt to reduce the negative situations with which families must cope.

In Chapter 10, the trends, myths, causes and consequences of divorce are considered. We also look at the policies surrounding divorce including how some of these policies can have unintended consequences.

If couples divorce, some people remarry, and some experience step-parenthood. Other families, over the life course, go through the stages of children growing up and leaving home. Second (or more) families, in all their diversity, are the topic of Chapter 11.

Chapter 12 takes a glimpse at families of the future, emphasizing how families will create their own futures, influenced by both the opportunities and the constraints of society.

Chapter Features

Each chapter of the text begins with a chapter outline. Boxes throughout the text feature anecdotes and excerpts from the popular media and from scholarly works that highlight related attitudes, debates, and current features of family life. Each chapter also includes a special debate box outlining pro and con arguments on relevant controversial issues.

Study tools at the end of each chapter include a chapter summary, key terms with definitions, questions for review and discussion, suggested activities, and an annotated list of relevant internet sites.

Supplements

Instructor's Manual. An instructor's manual is available with this edition. Its features include chapter outlines, key terms and concepts, motivational activities, answers to review questions in the text, critical thinking exercises, debate suggestions, group activities, project suggestions, and film and video suggestions.

Test Item File. A comprehensive test item file, including approximately 50 multiple choice and 5 essay questions per chapter, is available in print and computerized formats. The Pearson TestGen is a special computerized version of the Test Item File that enables instructors to view and edit the existing questions, add questions, generate tests, and print the tests in a variety of formats. Powerful search and sort functions make it easy to locate questions and arrange them in any order desired. TestGen also enables instructors to administer tests on a local area network, have the tests graded electronically, and have the results prepared in electronic or printed reports. Issued on a CD-ROM, the Pearson TestGen is compatible with IBM or Macintosh operating systems.

Acknowledgments

It has been very satisfying to complete this new edition of *Close Relations*. Reactions to both the earlier full edition and the brief edition have been very positive; this reception by the sociological community has encouraged us.

However, we have been aware of enhancements and changes that would benefit this new edition. About 18 months ago, freelance editor Heather McWhinney provided a clear schematic outline of the changes we could make in this new edition. Based on a careful reading of the two earlier versions and on conversations with other sociologists and us, Heather crafted a blueprint that was intelligent and workable. This edition has followed that blueprint almost exactly. We want to thank Heather for her synthesis of comments and suggestions by readers as well as for her care and insights.

Next, we thank our publisher. Everyone connected with Pearson Education Canada has been quietly supportive and has stayed backstage, except when we really needed them. For their quiet but strong support, we thank acquisitions editor Jessica Mosher, development editor John Polanszky, production editor Mary Ann McCutcheon, and copy editor Karen Hunter. You all have done your work in a supportive and professional way, for which we are very grateful.

Susan, at the University of Alberta, thanks several students for their assistance and good advice. In particular Ph.D. student Stephanie Knaak deserves special thanks. Thanks also to Teresa Abada, Kwame Boadu, Kate Krug, and Amber Gazso-Windle for their encouragement, help and advice. A special thanks goes to the hundreds of students in Sociology 271 at the University of Alberta in the fall of 2001 and 2002 who helped "test kitchen" some of the new material for this revision. Thanks also to Naomi Castle, Uju Mollel, and Angie Gerrard of the Sociology Information Centre, University of Alberta, and to Doug Wahlsten. Thanks also to colleagues, Sharon Abu-Laban, Sara Dorow, and Amy Kaler for their kind comments on the first edition.

Lorne, at the University of Toronto, worked with a variety of undergraduate students in the work-study program. All had been fine students in one or more of Lorne's courses. They soon proved to be fine research assistants as well, providing criticism of the chapters, and helping Lorne to develop learning aids, boxed inserts, and other materials for the book. The students in this year's multicultural work-study group were Maja Jovanovich, Evan Kazolis, Iris Lazaro, Ha Luu, Nicola Torma, Victrine Tseung, and Michelle Wong. Banasa Williams deserves thanks too, for her brief participation in the project. Outstanding undergraduate Maria Karasyova helped us with the final paste-up of the book, bringing together text and additional materials, filling gaps in the learning aids, and seeking permissions.

As we authors delight in our work and this new edition, we are mindful of close relations who have recently passed away. Accordingly, Lorne dedicates this book to two particular friends—Toby Ryan and Jack Richardson—who touched his life in important ways. Susan dedicates this book to her dear friend and close colleague, Ellen Gee, whose sudden passing at far too early an age left a huge absence not only for her many friends and family members, but for Canadian sociology.

We have learned a lot in writing this book, and the experience has been fun too. All we can say now is read the book and let us know what *you* think. We want this book to make family life, your own and that of others, clearer and more meaningful. If you have any ideas how we can do that better in the next edition, do let us know.

Susan McDaniel, University of Alberta
Lorne Tepperman, University of Toronto
April 2003

CHAPTER ONE

Families and Family-Like Relationships:

Definitions, Theories, and Research

Chapter Outline

Introduction

Among our deepest and most abiding human needs is to have someone close who understands and loves us and in whom we can confide and trust. In an uncertain and insecure world, we seek solace and hope in close relations.

Families belong to a group of relationships we would characterize as "close," including intense friendships, love affairs, and long-term work relationships. These relationships are characterized by a strong attachment or bonding between the partners. Of course, not all family members feel strongly attached or bonded to each other. However, what people commonly imagine when they think of the word "family"—what the word "family" evokes in our culture—is attachment, sentiment, and emotional intensity. For most of us, families provide our most important relationships, our first connection to the social world, and one that remains important throughout our lives.

This book explores the changing dimensions of family relations and the ways in which they affect and are affected by school, work, society and perhaps most importantly by social changes. We examine the diversity of close relations and consider how families may be becoming more rather than less important in our lives.

The Importance of Family

Some people point to the upsurge in single-parent households, increases in the number of children born outside legal marriage (Statistics Canada, 2001 Census 2002a), and high divorce rates (Statistics Canada, 2002b) as evidence that the family is in trouble. However, public opinion polls consistently find that family life is tremendously important to Canadians (Angus Reid, 1999; Vanier Institute of the Family, 2000) and that if anything, family relations are increasingly important to Canadians. Young people are no less enthusiastic about families than older people, with 96 percent of women aged 20 to 29 wanting a child at some point in their lives (Vanier Institute of the Family 2000: 79). Most young adult men also wanted to be fathers at some time.

People continue to value families because they provide emotional support and economic benefits. Perhaps most importantly, families give us grounding in an otherwise uncertain and chaotic world. The familiarity of family can be reassuring and, throughout our lives, gives us the confidence to explore new things.

What Is Family?

Most people think of families as groups of people related through marriage, blood, or adoption. But is that description specific enough? Is it inclusive enough? Is it possible to delineate the boundaries between families, friendships, and other close relations?

To some people the answer seems obvious. They argue that the word "families" should be used only to describe "traditional families." But families have varied in form throughout history, still vary from one society to another, and are very different within societies like Canada and the United States. There is, in this sense, no traditional family. Families now regarded as traditional are themselves a significant departure from earlier traditions.

In this text we shall examine the ways in which families are now viewed and how these changes are closely tied to events in society and to what is seen as a social problem or concern.

Where, then, do we draw the line?

Defining the Family

People tend to think when they talk about family that everyone is talking about the same thing. "How's the family?" someone might ask, referring perhaps to one's spouse and possibly children. "I'm taking time now to have a family," says a woman to her co-worker. "My family came from the Ukraine," says another. An HIV/AIDS survivor says, "My family are those around me now who support me." Immigration policy refers to "family reunification," where the concept of family has shrunk recently to include only close blood relatives and spouses. What do these images of family have in common? How differently do we see family?

Defining the Family

family *n.* (*pl.* –ies)

A family is a place where minds come in contact with one another. If these minds love one another the home will be as beautiful as a flower garden. But if these minds get out of harmony with one another it is like a storm that plays havoc with the garden.

—Buddha

A family is but too often a commonwealth of malignants.

—Alexander Pope

A happy family is but an earlier heaven.

—John Bowring

I think the family is the place where the most ridiculous and least respectable things in the world go on.

—Ugo Betti

The family is our refuge and springboard; nourished on it, we can advance to new horizons. In every conceivable manner, the family is a link to our past, bridge to our future.

—Alex Haley

The family is a court of justice, which never shuts down for night or day.

—Malcolm De Chazal

The family is the nucleus of civilization.

—William James Durant

The family is one of nature's masterpieces.

—George Santayana

Call it a clan, call it a network, call it a tribe, call it a family. Whatever you call it, whoever you are, you need one.

—Jane Howard

The answers to these questions regarding family are not merely academic. How family and other close relations are defined matters to us personally—to our values, our dreams, our aspirations as individuals, and our identities.

How family is defined also decides whether we get time off from work to attend to a family emergency, who is entitled to benefits under workplace policies, who can immigrate with us, whom we can marry, and the list goes on. These definitions are important in regard to our rights under the law and to our entitlements to pensions, schools, and many other social resources. Debates rage about common-law spouses having the same rights as married spouses, about spousal rights for gays and lesbians, and about the financial responsibilities and the rights (to custody, access, etc.) of divorced people. The Law Commission of Canada has consulted recently with Canadians about changing family relations and how government can or should recognize and support the variety of adult close relationships that Canadians form. As this book goes to press, consultations are occurring with Canadians on intergenerational relations and how they are seen in law and policy (see Law Commission of Canada, www.lcc.gc.ca). The Province of Alberta is preparing a bill that would redefine what they call adult interdependent relationships (Alberta, 2002). These relationships are defined as "a range of personal relationships that fall outside the traditional institution of marriage." Let's look now at some definitions of family.

Murdock: Three Relationships

For many years, sociologists used as a benchmark George Murdock's (1949: 1) definition of family as

> a social group characterized by a common residence, economic co-operation and reproduction [including] adults of both sexes, at least two of whom maintain a socially approved sexual relationship, and one or more children, own or adopted, of the sexually cohabiting adults.

Note that by this definition, three basic relationships—co-residence, economic co-operation, and reproduction—must all be present to qualify a social group as a family. Murdock's definition excludes many groups that most of us would consider families: childless married couples, for example, and single parents and their children. Same-sex unions are excluded, as are married couples who are separated. Celibate couples, according to Murdock, cannot be a family even if they have children, live together, and share other kinds of intimacy. (This means questioning a couple about their sex life to determine whether they and their children constitute a family!) Two sisters who live together cannot be a family, according to Murdock. Thus, Murdock's definition does not seem to allow for the variability that exists among families living in Canada today.

Census Family

Because the approach to defining family discussed previously is so limiting, Statistics Canada (2002c), the official census and survey agency for Canada, takes a much more inclusive approach. Statistics Canada defines family, for the Census,

> as a married couple (with or without children of either or both spouses), a couple living common-law (with or without children of either or both partners) or a lone parent of any marital status, with at least one child living in the same dwelling. A couple living common-law may be of opposite or same sex. "Children" in a census family include grandchildren living with their grandparent(s) but with no parents present.

This definition is better, since it includes a wider variety of people. In fact, Statistics Canada broadened its definition in September 2002 to be more reflective of how families see themselves and how society has changed in its views of families. However, it still misses a large number of groups that would consider themselves to be families, and would be considered families by others outside of their household. This being so, many researchers have changed their focus to households for practical purposes.

Household versus Family

Market researchers and census-takers often try to sidestep difficulties of definition by focusing on "households" as though they were "families." Doing so allows us to talk about changes in households and imply changes in close relations without necessarily addressing changes in families or family life. But this approach also presents problems. As pointed out clearly by Eichler (1997), many families live in separate households but maintain ongoing family relationships. The prime example is divorced families in which custody is joint or shared (Smart and Neale, 1999); the divorced parents and their child(ren) constitute at least one family and maybe more. This is, in fact, a growing trend in Canada, with 37.2 percent of divorced families with dependent children now being awarded joint custody (Statistics Canada 2002b).

A "household" may contain only one person or many unrelated members—roommates, boarders, or residents in a group home. Or it may contain a **nuclear family**, an **extended family** or multiple families (for example, communes or families sharing living space to save money). Sharing living accommodations among generations is, as we shall see, a growing trend in Canada. Sometimes, these arrangements involve multiple families—parents, for example, with their parents, or with their adult children's families. Conversely, a family may spread across many households, even households located in different countries. However, usually families and households coincide, giving rise to "family households."

In the United States, family households are officially defined by the Bureau of the Census as married couples with or without children under 18, or one-parent families with children under 18. Family households also comprise other households of related individuals (for example, two sisters sharing a household or a parent living with a child older than 17 years). By contrast, non-family households contain unrelated individuals or people who live alone. Canadian definitions from Statistics Canada and other official data-gathering organizations are similar.

Process-based Definitions

The United Nations (1991), by contrast, prefers to define family by the important **socioeconomic functions** it performs such as emotional, financial, and material support to its members, care of each other, transmitting cultural values, and serving as a resource for personal development. In doing so, the UN is defining families in terms of their main shared processes, rather than in terms of structural features that they may not—increasingly, do not—share. The Vanier Institute of the Family (2000) uses this function or process-based definition of family in Canada.

In Canada, serious consideration has been given to the question of what family is and what families are. The question has been taken up by family researchers, the Vanier Institute of the Family, and the Canada Committee for the International Year of the Family on which one of the authors of this book (McDaniel) served. The conclusion is that ultimately families are defined not by the shape they take but by what they do (Vanier Institute of the Family 1994: 9). As Moore-Lappe (1985: 8) puts it:

> Families are not marriages or homes or rules. Families are people who develop intimacy because they... share experiences that come... to make up their uniqueness—the mundane, even silly, traditions that emerge in a group of people who know each other... It is this intimacy that provides the ground for our lives.

To acknowledge the diversity of family and close relations, broad inclusive definitions are needed that encompass the dynamics of family and close relations over time. Consistent with much of family research, it is process rather than form that defines families.

Over the past two decades, a broad process-based definition of family has become generally accepted by most Canadians (see Angus Reid, 1999; Vanier Institute of the Family, 2000). Much of current Canadian family law and policy reflects the move toward inclusion of families that are diverse and similar in their processes, if not structures (see Law Commission of Canada, 1999).

However, some groups continue to oppose such inclusive definitions. The diversity of families is controversial and has become a highly political issue, with some "family values" groups pushing to have these issues placed at the forefront of the national agenda or some provincial agendas (see Stacey, 1996, for examples). Gay and lesbian families, for example, have become a touchstone in many contemporary debates about what is and is not a family and what rights and entitlements those who are deemed family ought to have. Remember that Statistics Canada, in its recently modified definition of Census family mentioned above, includes same-sex families. Similarly, immigration and

Debate Box 1.1 IS FAMILY BEST DEFINED BY THE SHAPE IT TAKES?
Which side of the debate do you fall on?

I am FOR defining family by shape

- Families are ancient institutions, often having mother, father, and children.
- Nuclear heterosexual family is natural and God-given.
- Blood and legal ties determine what family is.
- Certain kinds of close relations are not considered family.
- Family is unchanging, which gives us stability and security.
- Nuclear families are easy to understand and distinguish from other close relations.
- Men and women are happiest in nuclear heterosexual families and children are best raised in them.
- Objective, clear definitions of family are important to us and to societies.

I am AGAINST defining family by shape

- Families have evolved over history and now take different shapes.
- We create our own kinds of families that suit our historical time and ourselves.
- Caring relationships determine what family is.
- Families change and evolve.
- Because they are easy to identify doesn't mean nuclear families are best for us or that we all want them.
- We know from research that nuclear families are not always happy.
- Attitudes and policies based on nuclear families exclude and devalue other ways to care.
- Shape of family (or structure) has nothing to do with what people do in families.
- Our subjective sense of belonging matters to us and our well-being.

growing ethnic diversity have challenged the ways we define, form, maintain, and connect in close relations. Definitions of what is family matter greatly when it comes to bringing family members to Canada. And, of course, these definitions may differ by cultural group.

How family is defined and thought about is a weathervane on social ideas and ideologies and the kind of research done on families reflects the concerns of the day. We shall explore this idea in more detail later on in this chapter.

Common Elements of Family Life

The social groups we think of as families typically share many features, and that commonality can help us begin to understand the nature of families. Because families are extraordinarily diverse, it is difficult to generalize about them. However, it is possible to focus our attention on their common processes.

Dependency and Intimacy

All close relations have in common attachment and some kind of dependency or interdependency. This is not unique to families; most close friendships and work relationships also include some degree of emotional dependency, based on familiarity and expectations of reciprocity. However, family relations are special in that they tend to include long-term commitments, both to each other and to the shared family *per se*.

Sexuality

Adult partners within families typically have, or are expected to have, a long-term, exclusive sexual relationship, whereas among co-workers and among friends, sexual relations are either absent or of short duration. In families, sexual relations are permitted and expected between certain members (e.g., spouses) but prohibited between other members (e.g., parents and children). Norms of sexual propriety are much stronger in families than they are in friendship or work groups. Taboos against sexual exploitation of children exist to prevent sexual relations with a family member other than a spouse. Nevertheless, sexual abuse of children and elders does occur within families.

Protection

Effective families keep their members under guard against all kinds of internal and external dangers. There is a clear cultural expectation that families will try to protect their members. Parents and relatives are supposed to keep children safe from accidents and household dangers, and away from drugs, alcohol, predators, and other forms of harm. As well, spouses are supposed to protect one another, and adult children are supposed to protect and help their parents. All this is an ideal, of course. In reality, family members often fail to protect each other sufficiently, and worse, some people neglect, exploit, or abuse family members. However, those who break the cultural rules tend to face criticism and disapproval.

Power

Households and families are small social groups whose members spend a lot of time together and depend on each other to fill both economic and social needs. There are large differences in power, strength, age, and social resources among members. Ideally, the more-powerful family members protect the less-powerful ones. However, it is this imbalance in power that makes **patriarchy**, control of the family by a dominant male (typically, the father), a central fact in the history of family life in most known societies. Simply put, men have dominated because they possessed and controlled more of the resources. And, in much of family law and policy, this domination over family by men was seen as a right, sometimes even an obligation.

Violence

Likewise, families—though ideally peaceful and loving—are also marked by violence, perhaps to a higher degree than any other groups based on "close relations." Although violence has always existed in families, in the last few decades there have been growing reports of violence within families. Some estimate that one woman in ten will be assaulted at some time in her life. In most cases the assailant is a spouse or boyfriend. As well, researchers estimate that one girl in four and one boy in ten is sexually abused before the age of 16, often by friends or relatives. Perhaps violence is more common in families than in other close relations precisely because for many, the family is a place of intense emotions. As well, some family members are young or otherwise vulnerable and cannot easily escape. Victims suffering similar violence at the hands of friends or workmates more likely than not would simply leave.

Kinship, Clan, and Community

So far we have focused on families as they exist normatively in our own dominant culture. However, families vary from one society to another, just as they vary within our own society. In many societies families exist within larger social networks—within kinship groups and clans—and we cannot really understand how these families function unless we also understand their place in these larger networks, and in the community at large. The members of the household—the husband and wife, parent and child, brother and sister—are thoroughly integrated into a larger web of kin—uncles, aunts, cousins, grandparents, grandchildren—and their lives cannot be understood without reference to this larger web.

A **kinship group** is a group of people who share a relationship through blood and/or marriage and have positions in a hierarchy of rights over the property. The definition of a kin relationship varies between societies; kin relationships may also determine where the members must live, whom they can marry, and even their life opportunities.

Some societies count relationships through the male line, so that any individual's relationships are determined by his or her father's relationships; we call such kinship systems **patrilineal**. Others count relationships through the female line; these are **matrilineal** systems. Still others count relationships through both lines; they are **bilateral kinship systems**.

If the kinship system is patrilineal, a person gains a position in the community just by being the child of his or her father. In a matrilineal kinship system, on the other hand, a person has certain property rights because of being the child of his or her mother. However, that kinship system is independent of which sex holds more authority in society; men can be the dominant sex even in a matrilineal society. In this case, the person whose kinship link is most important to a child is not the biological father but the mother's brother, as among the Ashanti in West Africa or a number of North American Aboriginal societies.

Western Europeans and North Americans have no special words to distinguish kin on the father's side from kin on the mother's side. For emotional purposes, it does not matter whether a first cousin, uncle, or aunt is on the mother's or father's side. However, our system is mildly patrilineal. For example, a woman has historically taken her husband's family name, not the reverse, and this name is the one that passes to the children. (It should be noted, however, that this is not the case everywhere in the West. In Quebec, for example, the law prevents women from taking their husband's name on marriage.)

Our family system follows the Western pattern, in which property is also typically inherited along the male line. Where families settle down is traditionally determined by the husband's job, not the wife's, although this too is changing. However, our society also has certain matrifocal characteristics. Because women have been defined as the primary **kin-keepers**—the people who maintain family contacts—children tend to have stronger ties with their mother's kin than with that of their father (Rosenthal, 1985; Thomson and Li, 1992: 15). Children also maintain closer contacts with their mothers when the mothers grow old (Connidis, 2001). When parents of grown children live separately, fathers are less often visited, called, and relied upon than are mothers.

New Ways to Understand Family Diversity

In this book, we will argue repeatedly that some of the older ways of understanding family life do not serve us well in a highly diverse and fluid society. As a result, we have adopted some new approaches to studying family life. We did not invent all these new approaches, however; they enjoy wide currency among many sociologists.

The life-course approach is one new way of studying family change. This approach follows the variety of social and interpersonal dynamics of close relations and how these change throughout our lifetimes (Elder, 1992; Klein and White 1996; Kohli, 1986). This approach focuses on the fact that, over the course of time, families change—they have to change—to meet new requirements, such as the arrival, care, or departure of children. These changes have effects on the entire family system: on relations between spouses, parents and children, and siblings; and on the family's relations with the "outside world," such as parents' changing relations with their employers and their careers (Kruger and Levy, 2001; McDaniel, 2001b; McDaniel, 2002).

Another new approach is to look at family relations from the perspectives of different family members. This approach recognizes that different family members have different interests and different experiences as members of any given family. Smart and Neale (1999) use this approach to study post-divorce families, for example. Because different family members often have different interests, it is often inappropriate to speak of "the family" as though it has a single interest and acts in a unified way.

Much family research up until the 1970s (and beyond) was done from a male perspective (Eichler, 2001; Giddens, 1992; Luxton, 1997). A popular phrase of the time that has stuck is "bedroom communities," which describes suburban communities in which families lived and women often worked at home. These were living communities and could be seen as bedrooms only from the point of view of men who worked elsewhere. Many other examples exist. What do family life and changes in close relations among adults look like from the viewpoint of children, for example? They look profoundly different, as we are now discovering (Marcil-Gratton 1993; Mason, Skolnick, and Sugarman, 2003). Children live in numerous and varied kinds of families while still dependent, and changes in family are happening earlier in their lives than those of children in times past. Looking at shifting close relations among adults from the viewpoint of children's living situations gives us a new and important vantage point on families.

Yet another new approach is to collect data in new ways so that family diversity can be studied over time. One example is Statistics Canada's Survey of Labour and Income Dynamics (SLID) (Statistics Canada, 1996), which builds a picture of the changes in people's work and family lives over time. Cheal (1997), for example, relies on SLID to examine the longer-term effects of being in a financially dependent family while young or at various life-course stages. He finds that the effects of both dependence and poverty of youth increase intergenerational inequities over time. Thus, families have different "life histories," and as these histories develop and change over time, they profoundly mark the future prospects of their members, especially the youngest members.

Another example is Statistics Canada's Longitudinal Survey of Children and Youth (Willms, 2002). This survey follows individual children through their growing up, interviewing them and their families every two years. Data are collected on family changes, schooling, health, and a whole range of variables that affect children's lives. A wealth of new insights is emerging about children's lives and how families and society can best benefit from these insights in the long run. Findings from this survey have already taught us that the effect on children of living with a single parent is more than the result of the low incomes often faced by such families. The good news from this longitudinal research is that good parenting can, to a large degree, overcome these detrimental effects. Much more is to be learned by following the same people (children or adults) for a long period of time and seeing whether they can, eventually, escape the disadvantages of a low-income childhood and, if so, how.

Of course, all families change, and the times change families. For example, Whitehead (1990, 1) reminds us that "Today's stay-at-home mother is tomorrow's working mother." Or, as Swedish social policy sees it, every married woman with children today is potentially a divorced or separated lone mother tomorrow. Whitehead points out that families change with the times: "One day, the Ozzie and Harriet couple is eating a family meal at the dining room table; the next day, they are working out a joint custody agreement in a law office (*op. cit.* 1)." Studying families in a context of change reminds us to stay away from any simple definitions of family, or theories about family life that assume that all families are the same, and stay the same, regardless of their historical context. We will return to this in a moment.

Combining this historical approach with recognition that different family members have different experiences gives us interesting results. Consider, for example, how family members may be differently affected by changes in the economy, for example, so that young adult children may be in schooling longer because they cannot find jobs, or cannot find jobs that pay enough for them to have their own apartments or homes. Similarly, children in families may be differently parented as a result of changing policies on parental leaves, enabling younger ones to have full-time parents for a period in their early lives, while older siblings experienced parents who had to return to work soon after birth.

In a study of the effects of economic restructuring on families in Hamilton, Ontario beginning in the 1980s, Luxton and Corman (2001) find that women and men were differently affected. Women moved from being largely full-time homemakers with husbands who were breadwinners in blue-collar work, to being workers as well as homemakers. The study shows how economic pressures on families ignited gender and ethnic tensions. Also changed was the politics of the working classes in Canada.

Theoretical Approaches to Understanding Families

A theory simply puts things together in an orderly fashion, assisting us to see and understand the social world. Theories are ways of seeing that help us to focus. Each theoretical approach is different, and each one may have a different insight to contribute to our understanding. Here, we will look at two things. First, we discuss how the thinking about families and the research on families has changed over time. These changes in thinking are closely tied to the events and climate in society at the time. Second, we will highlight some basic theoretical approaches to understanding families; however, these are not all the theoretical approaches that exist. Each one of the approaches presented hopefully will allow you to begin to see aspects of families that you might not be able to see without the use of the theoretical lens.

Theories of Family over Time

Our interest here lies in tracing the main threads of the sociology of families over time. These threads, as we shall see, sometimes tangle, sometimes follow, and sometimes lead social attitudes about families and political debates. This can be described as "double upheaval," as dramatic shifts are occurring in the way that families live and, at the same time, big changes are present in the way that families are seen and theorized (Cheal, 1991).

Thinking about families over time is challenging for sociologists for three linked reasons. First, there is new information, not only about families now but also about families in the past and how they lived. This new information challenges our understandings and shakes our beliefs about families and family change. Second, new ways to view families in society and through politics are connected to new theories about families. If you think theories are only academic, think again! Feminist and gay/lesbian theories of family have been hotly contested by society's interest groups and by some politicians. And the debate goes beyond family theory. New sociological and cultural studies theories and their proponents were blamed in part for the lack of simple political agreement on the causes of the September 11, 2001 events. Americans, and at times Canadians too, were asked not only to denounce terrorists and terrorism but also to refrain from post-modern social theorizing—theorizing which suggested that societies are complex, with many factors leading to the taking up of terrorism. Theories are very much alive and, as such, part of public debate. Third, changing family lives and changing ways to see families have risks and concerns that make us constantly question and revise our theories. Keep these challenges in mind as we outline how families have been viewed over time.

Family, as such, is a surprisingly recent social concept. Prior to the eighteenth century in Europe, for example, the term family was not used at all (Flandrin, 1979), even when people lived in groups that we would today see as nuclear families—parents with their children. More important at that time was the larger social grouping or the community. The focus, for example, lay in how people lived to survive, how they produced food and shared it. Therefore much of the study of communities, and indirectly of families, has been focused on sustaining life.

Some studies were anthropological, close-up studies of small, simply organized communities. It was found that in foraging societies (those that gathered food like berries or roots) childbearing was postponed to later in life more so than in early agricultural societies (Fox and Luxton, 2000). Since there were few assets to inherit in societies that foraged, it was argued in theory that there were less restrictions on how children were viewed in relation to their parents. Families *per se* may not have been seen to "own children."

A well-known theory developed by Friedrich Engels ([1884] 1972), the theoretical collaborator of Karl Marx, in the late nineteenth century, paints a picture of people living in a group without giving much importance to whose spouse was whose, or which children belonged to which parents. The children were "parented" by the entire community, Engels suggests. All children were welcomed, and even though their biological parents may have been known, it didn't change how people lived. There was some evidence that communities like this did, in fact, exist. Some still live much like this, even in urban neighbourhoods (see Stacey, 1990), with entire communities raising children with little focus on nuclear family structures as such.

Once an economic surplus was possible, however, people did not have to consume the food they gathered immediately but could save it and store it (bank it, if you like). Then, Engels says, it mattered much more who a child's parents were as inheritance was to follow bloodlines. How these bloodlines were decided is unclear, according to Engels' theory. Men began to control the food surplus, it was theorized. Women were expected to be sexually faithful to their husbands, to ensure that the children they had were, in fact, their husband's. Monogamy was born not because it was more moral than any other system of family or that living in families was a natural way to live. Monogamy was related, according to Engels' theory, to the economics of life at the time.

In part, some contemporary controversies and debates about family life are attempts to wrestle the family away from the effects of economic factors and forces. For example, some conservative groups argue that the family is more natural and fundamental than any economic change. Families, they argue, should respond to economic pressures and shifts by *not* changing. In this way, we are still engaging the theories about family from the late nineteenth century in this, the twenty-first century.

Another theory of family and family change parallels that of Engels' theory but follows a different thread at a different historical moment. The theory of Le Play in the nineteenth century suggests that families in feudalism were large and extended, with blood relatives and members of the community of the castle largely undifferentiated from each other. We have seen earlier in this chapter how large, extended families were not always happy families. However, with the development of towns and trades and markets, this kind of community "family" became awkward. It was certainly not easily mobile. So, the smaller "stem family" emerged, a family that runs the farm, or small shop, while the rest of the family moves on or stays behind. In fact, it was this development that led, in large part, to a massive out-migration from Europe to North America in the nineteenth and into the early twentieth century, as more people without access to family enterprises sought opportunities in the "new world" of North America.

Prior to the 1850s, sociology was only in its infancy as was thinking about family. Basically, family theory was Judeo-Christian religious belief, to a large extent. The Biblical "begats" of the Old Testament, mentioned in Chapter 2, characterized a patriarchal theory that saw an elder male as head of a community, clan, extended family, or even a realm. In many ways, monarchies are remnants of this system. It is only in rare cases in the absence of a male heir that women become the heads of state and spiritual leaders of the realm. The system of male headship was more than familial and private; it was a system of governing before public systems of law and democracy were invented. In fact, the Parliamentary system of government in Canada still parallels democracy with a ruling monarch who is Head of State. The extended kin, headship system was presumed to be natural and unchanging in both theory and practice. It was also, theoretically at least, presumed as a model for the emerging, urban working class to follow. With colonial rule in many parts of the world, this family system and the theory supporting it was exported. Many countries today in Africa and in other parts of the world that were part of the British Empire retain aspects of this family headship system, sometimes mixed with traditional cultural practices. Sociologists who study post-colonial societies work to sort out what is inherited from this system in today's policies and family practices and what is unique to that society. The study by Baker (2001) of Australia, New Zealand, and Canada is one example. She describes these three societies as "settler societies," in which we "can discuss the impact of colonial concepts of family on indigenous people, whose ideas about family structure and relationships differed from those of the colonizers in all three societies" (Baker, 2001:3).

In the middle of the nineteenth century, debates in society started to challenge old religion-based theories about family. This, of course, does not mean that religious beliefs or religious theories about family disappeared. They did not. In fact, they have continued to this day, some say even more actively as the twentieth century closed and the twenty-first century began. That is a story to which we will return momentarily.

The emerging debate in the 1850s occurred as societies were transforming rapidly with industrialization and the beginning of capitalism. Social unrest was apparent, as were social movements that challenged prevailing beliefs. One belief actively challenged at that time was the role of women in family and in society. New kinds of societies were springing up, based not on patriarchal authority, but on communal living arrangements where women and men were more equal and children could be raised collectively (Luxton, 2001: 34). This experimental approach, in fact, continued with the kibbutz in Israel, many of which are still communal. Other people lobbied for women's rights in both marriage and society. Married women at that time were not entitled to own property or to vote, or to have many other citizenship rights that women today take for granted.

Paralleling these changing social attitudes were sociologists and their theories. One was Émile Durkheim, known as one of the founding fathers of sociology. His theories about family had two aspects, and the two didn't fit together well. First, he argued in favour of "the law of contraction," or that families were, in the middle of the nineteenth century, being reduced in size at the same time as family ties were being intensified. Second, he then theorized that relations between husbands and wives were organized by society as monogamous and "near perfect" (Sydie, 1987: 19–20). The marriage relationship was seen by Durkheim as permanent, unequal, highly regulated by society, and, crucially, the means of moral organization of all of society. Family was theorized as both less and more important. Key to Durkheim's contribution was his understanding of family as a social creation, not as something given by nature or religion.

As industrialization continued in the nineteenth century, family and work became more separate. Work, which had been an integral part of family life, was moved out of the family and into the marketplace. In separating work from family, specialization of men in work and women in family began to emerge. Social theorists like Durkheim saw the bond between husband and wife as strengthened by the increasing specialization (Sydie, 1987: 22). The search began for biological differences between men and women that would parallel the growing social differences in family and in society. In hindsight, some of these

Émile Durkheim was one of the founding fathers of sociology. Durkheim saw family as a social creation, not as something given by nature or religion.

searches were rather amusing. A Dr. Lebon is quoted by Durkheim as reporting, "The volume of the crania of men and women, even when we compare subjects of equal age, of equal height and equal weight, show differences in favour of man..." (quoted in Sydie, 1987: 22). Of course, now we know that no such differences exist. That social theories about family were linked to presumed biological differences between men and women, however, was significant to later theories. It is also important to observe that sociological theories of the day were in response to the push in society for social change.

It may not be a coincidence that most of the sociological theorists of family of the nineteenth century were white, middle-class men. Many, it has been argued since, were keen to defend or promote the new capitalism and the new way to view marriage and family (Luxton, 2001). Some insisted that the birth rate would fall if marriage were changed, and if women were more equal to men. This way of thinking persists into the twenty-first century in some conservative circles. The argument is further made that the gender-unequal marriage is natural and based on both biology and God's will. Other theorists such as Herbert Spencer see this kind of family as a social construction that supports (and should support) capitalism. The patriarchal family was seen as the peak of social evolution (Luxton, 2001; Sydie, 1987). Had these social theorists been women, or working-class or Aboriginal or ethnic minorities, they might have viewed family very differently. Writings from some social movements of that time seem less content with the patriarchal family (Dua, 1999; Eichler, 2001; Luxton, 2001; Sydie, 1987).

As society changed, so did the preoccupations of family researchers. For instance, in the 1920s when the Roaring Twenties overtook the Victorian era of women being guarded in their appearance, dress and behaviour, sociologists turned their attention to dating and courtship. Women were dancing the Charleston in public, no longer wearing corsets, and showing not only ankles but also knees as they kicked up their heels! Speakeasy clubs became popular, where men and women could drink, socialize, dance, and listen to music and entertainers. Society, caught up as always in concerns about social and family change, worried. So, sociologists studied these changes by looking at relations among young people and changing dating practices.

The 1950s saw what many see still as the "golden age" of the nuclear family. The suburbs were created and nuclear families thrived, or at least seemed to. Moms did the childrearing and Dads commuted to work. Television programs such as *Father Knows Best*, *Leave it to Beaver*, *Ozzie and Harriet* and others reflected what was ideal in family life. The "Standard North American" family was born. As in previous eras, this kind of family had the support of family theory. Patterns of thinking sociologically not only about families but also about all of society were formed at that time and continue into the twenty-first century. Although the theory of the day, structural functionalism (which we will discuss in more detail in the next section) was largely an American creation, it was widely used in various parts of the world. This coincided with a high period of American prestige in the post–World War II period, when everything American was seen as good.

In terms of family theory, the basic concept was that the family was an essential social institution, well adapted to fit into society. Further, the nuclear family specialized by gender was seen as a universal, something good for everyone. Earlier work by Malinowski among the Australian Aborigines lent a credibility to the North American nuclear family form (Luxton, 2001). His views and assumptions about biological differences between men and women found their way into later theories of structural functionalists such as Talcott Parsons, one of the giants of family sociology. Key to Malinowski's theory was that the nuclear family specialized by gender was essential for societies to function smoothly.

The advent of the structural functional theory led to research on men as breadwinners and less so on women as housewives. Research was happy-faced. There was nothing until the late 1960s in the sociology of the family on family violence, or on women's dissatisfaction with their families or their family roles. This is surprising, given what we know now of the "mad housewife" of the 1950s, the very high teen pregnancy rate, the unhappiness of many men with the breadwinner role of that time. But, so it was.

Structural functional theories of family were not used only to study families; the theory became useful in workplace policies too. If women, for example, were theorized to specialize in family, and men in work, then women were presumed to be not good workers. Married women, for example, were often fired from paid employment upon marriage since it was thought that they were now to be housewives and dependent economically on their husbands. Women, who were, according to family theory at the time, emotional and centred on caring, were not thought to be appropriate candidates for jobs that required judgement or supervision. They were also excluded from jobs that involved risk, such as pilots, miners, soldiers, and much blue-collar work. That women had done a lot of this kind of work during World War II while the men who usually worked in these jobs were at war didn't seem to matter. Women were thought to be family specialists and unsuited by nature to working for pay, and certainly not suited to working for pay in high-paying jobs!

Research using this theoretical approach was intensely focused on family dynamics and interactions and on how families around the world were becoming more similar and more like the U.S. ideal. Not surprisingly, other theories developed that let us look at these aspects of family more clearly. One of these was *symbolic interactionism*. While not fully disputing structural-functionalist theory, symbolic interactionists looked at how individuals interpret social organization and expectations. They focused on how we change our behaviours depending on how others behave and treat us. This is an "in the face" look at family interactions. Mothers' interacting with children was a favourite subject of research. And in the period of the Baby Boom (1946–1962), there was no shortage of subjects for this kind of study!

The concept of "roles" became a central part of the vocabulary of sociology of family. Society assigned the roles, but all the roles were not the same in all aspects of our lives. So, a women could play the mother role with her kids, and then the wife role with her husband. Both became "scripted" by the childrearing and marriage experts who largely based the expertise they marketed on social theories of family. The role of the mother, for example, was scripted as caring, selfless, unassertive, always there for the child. It became an ideal, something to be carefully worked toward by women, no matter what their individual inclinations might be. The mother role also overshadowed everything else in its role demands.

Beginning in the 1970s and then in the 1980s, there was what Cheal (1991) and others have called a "big bang" in sociological theories on families. So big was this "bang," argue Cheal (2002), Giddens (1992), Fox and Luxton (2000), among others, that there was no turning back to previous ways of viewing families. All subsequent theories, states Cheal (2002), can be traced to this "big bang"— the feminist theories of families.

There is no single feminist sociological theory of family or of any other aspect of society. There are many. What is so different about feminist sociological theories of family is the opening of fresh new ways to regard families. Giddens (1992), in fact, is so taken with the freshness enabled by the feminist perspective that he remarks that the study of family used to be boring, but after feminist theories came into sociology, the study of family became among the most interesting of sociological endeavours. Feminist theories, like family theories before them, grew out of the times. There was political unrest in women's lives. The political push for day care, for reproductive rights, for equal access to jobs, promotions, and benefits, for rights in marriage, for rights not to marry, for gays and lesbians, for older women, for the disabled, for children, and for the poor and disenfranchised led to the posing of "why" questions. Why are all of these groups disadvantaged relative to straight, white, middle-class men with jobs? The answers called for new ways to see, new lenses by which to observe the social and political landscape.

Feminist theories have several dimensions in common. There is an acknowledgement of discrimination and disadvantaging of some, while others are advantaged by existing social arrangements, including those in families. There is a sense that no particular family form is God's will or written into our biologies. There is a feeling that things we create, we can uncreate and recreate. That gives an excitement and an involvement to feminist theory. Family, argues much of feminist theory, is an ideology as much as a way to live. Barrett and McIntosh (1980) were among the first to suggest that the ideal of the nuclear family as the *only* place to be loved sucks away from each of us the potential to care for non-family in society. We lurk in wait for the perfect family and resist loving friends and building caring communities because we see the nuclear family as the only site for that sort of caring.

A key insight of feminist theories of family is that the family is not private, but a very important public social institution. It coordinates our relationships to the economic system, for example, by seeing women as secondary workers who can be called upon when the economy needs them, but then sent dutifully back home when not needed. Feminist theories reveal how families are power-based. There are hierarchies of who has the money, who gets listened to, who is more likely to be abused; gulfs of silences in families are suddenly given voices: abuse survivors, the fact of family as work, the lack of equitable distribution of resources within families. The list is a long one, and we will explore many of these as we continue in this book.

Perhaps most fundamentally, feminist sociology opened new ways to do sociological research on families. Researchers look through the feminist lens at the multiple ways to live in families, for example. Gay and lesbian families were studied for the first time as families, whereas previously they had been studied only by sociology of deviance. Families were seen as in constant change, not as given. The ways in which the ideology of the nuclear family and the denial of other ways to live may compel heterosexuality could be explored. It is easy to see why so many see this theorizing as a "big bang."

Out of feminist theorizing of families, or perhaps because of it, in the latter part of the twentieth century and now in the twenty-first century, post-modern and post-structural theories of families have emerged (Cheal, 2002: Klein and White, 1996). With globalization, the focus on the development of international capitalism, and the growth in technologies, dissatisfactions grew with structural explanations. A central dimension of post-modernism and post-structuralism is in flux or constant change. Families today may live in multiple families and households that change in response to the changing circumstances around them. But, we also change our families and households and our ways of being women and men, which relates to big changes such as world changes or economic changes. Topics researched relying on this set of theories include sexualities, body images, cultural images, and representations including theories and ideologies of families. It is truly opening another window of opportunity for seeing families anew.

Some Basic Theoretical Approaches to Family

Structural Functionalism

Structural functionalism is a fancy way to say that everything in society has a structure and a purpose. It is up to us to see and understand what those purposes might be. Structural functionalism is a theoretical approach to families developed in the 1940s and 1950s in the United States by Talcott Parsons. It enables us to view families in how they benefit society, and how each member of a family fits in with the purposes that families serve.

Although much criticized in recent times, structural functionalism is and has remained the dominant theoretical approach to understanding families in North America. In fact, it has been found to characterize most contemporary family sociology textbooks (Mann et al., 1997). It is like a captivating child's game. We ask, what social purpose does the nuclear family serve? Well, the answers tumble out; it is useful in that it is small, versatile, and mobile. These features are useful when social change occurs because families can change easily. What purpose is served by a gender division of labour at home where women nurture children and men work for pay? Well, again the answer is simple and compelling. Women specialize in family and emotional relationships, while men specialize in work and relationships based on order and merit. That the two meet in family makes the family stronger, argue structural functionalists, since women and men complement each other. Competition between women and men, it is thought, would not be beneficial to families or to work.

The theoretical approach of structural functionalism has dominated family research for decades. Its spiderweb of common sense captivates even those who criticize it. Everything about families has a structure and a function. It is orderly and neat. This approach inspires us to find out how and why families act the ways they do.

The trouble with this theoretical approach is that it may be too captivating. It doesn't really allow for social change. When women work in the paid labour market like men, what then for families? Do they fall apart because there are no longer complementary roles in family and in society? Some might respond that "Yes, this could be a problem." Others would say, "Wait a minute. Societies change. Women and men change. Where is that change allowed for in structural functionalism?"

Still, this theoretical approach has dominated family research and thinking about families since World War II and it is still dominant today.

Symbolic Interactionism

This theoretical approach to understanding families depends not on structure or function but on sharing. The key to understanding families, this theory argues, is that family members share symbols and meanings. So, for example, the symbol "Dad" is not something that you alone understand, but it is a symbol shared by others. That the meaning is shared makes family experience more universal, more understood by others whose experience may be a little different than yours.

There is much about symbolic interaction that is like a stage. We play roles before the audience of society. Those roles extend our own experiences and meanings into the world beyond us. We become mothers, fathers, grandparents, aunts and uncles, not because we each figure out what these are, but because we depend on the labels to guide us, to teach us how to be. Some of these roles can be creative and problem solving, but always with an eye toward what the role is expected to be.

Nowhere is there more baggage than in the symbolic meaning of mother. Mother is… well, so much that is symbolic: selfless, sexless, caring, giving, nurturing and always there, no matter what. All this, in reality, is a tough order for ordinary women. We may fall short, but we know then that we are falling short on an ideal symbol.

Marxist Theory of Family

Many of you may know of Karl Marx as a political theorist or activist. In fact, Marx was a great thinker, a sociological theorist who conceptualized family in relation to economic systems. His thinking led him to see the nuclear family as specialized so that women would have to be faithful to their husbands to benefit economically. The story is like a fairy tale. Once upon a time, Marx and his collaborator, Friedrich Engels, contemplated, women and men lived together freely in groups. They had sex and children, but didn't worry much about whose children they were. Then, the economic system changed so that there was more to eat than could be eaten in one generation. Who would get the leftovers? Well, men had to know who were their own children so that only those children could inherit their rightful surplus of food (dried root crops, dried animal meat, etc.). The only way men could know who their own children were was to demand sexual faithfulness from women. Thus, it is theorized, women traded free and open sexual relations for economic benefit for themselves and their children. The notion of women's sexual faithfulness to men in monogamous marriages was born. Notably, it was not individual preference or religion or anything else that created this system, but the economic system.

Feminist Theory

Feminist sociological approaches to family see family as a place of discussion and negotiation. Men and women come to family with different resources and power. Therefore, they negotiate from those different places.

Women, feminist theorists argue, do not enter family with full resources comparable to men's. They, therefore, suffer inequality in close relations and, if the relationship breaks down, are more likely to be in poverty.

Feminist theory suggests that women are taught to see family work as based on love and expectation. It may, in fact, be based as much or more on the need of society and of men for cheap labour to keep the society and men going. So, women take on the major responsibilities for childcare and for housework, thus freeing men to focus more fully on paid work. Similarly, women's preoccupation with childrearing and unpaid housework compromises their capacity to work for pay outside the home.

Post-modern Theory

Post-modernists see that numerous ways to understand and see family co-exist. This is not a crisis in any way, but something natural and vital to understanding life and society in the late twentieth and early twenty-first centuries.

Key to the post-modernist theoretical approach to family is that nothing can be taken for granted. Instead, all must be subject to being taken apart (deconstructed) to be explained. Families and men's and women's relations to families are seen as social creations and subject to constant change and re-examination. The family members become part of the process. They re-create themselves and their ways to relate as they examine and re-examine what they are doing and why. Their senses of self form in response to this constant process of reflecting, responding, and re-examining.

Variation Despite Convergence

As we have seen throughout this chapter, changing economies and societies, as well as changing approaches to seeing family, play a major role in changing the form and content of family life, both in countries just becoming industrialized and in the western world, where economic change continues. Many social scientists perceive these changes as part of an inevitable and universal progress toward a single worldwide culture of modernity, in which families have a distinct and different form, compared to traditional families. This approach has several pitfalls. First, it assumes that all modern families are similar to one another and different from all traditional families. Second, and equally important, it assumes that all modern families "choose" their new forms, and these forms are necessarily better.

Convergence theory presents a rosy picture of family modernization, as though families and individuals are choosing to change and are all changing effectively. In fact, however, modernization forces families to change. William Goode (1984: 57–58) has pointed out the following reasons that families change when societies industrialize precisely because industrialism "fails to give support to the family":

1. The industrial system fires, lays off, and demands geographical mobility by reference to the individual, ignoring the family strains these actions may cause.

2. The economy increasingly uses women in the labour force, and thus puts a still larger work burden on them; but few corporations have developed programs for helping women with childcare, or making it easier for men to share in these tasks.

3. The industrial system has little place for the elderly, and the neolocal, independent household with its accompanying values in favour of separate lives for each couple, leaves older parents and kin in an ambiguous position.

4. The family is relatively fragile because of separation and divorce, but the larger system offers little help in these crises for adults and their children.

Industrialization produces not only great opportunities but also great perils for families and family life. Some societies, and some families, respond better than others. In some industrial countries, families receive much more support from the state than do families in other countries. By its laws and policies, a state influences the costs to individuals and to society associated with marriage, divorce, childbearing, childrearing, and elder care. In this way, the state influences the patterns of family life in that society. That is, in part, why industrial societies do not have identical family forms.

There is no evidence of a single evolutionary path in family life—from simple to complex, extended to nuclear family. Even nuclear families, thought to be the most distinctive feature of modern family life, are not a linear product of industrialization. Because the effects of industrialization have been so all-encompassing, social scientists have been tempted to search for the origins of the Western family with industrialization. But, as Goldthorpe (1987, 10) points out, many features of the Western family—neolocal residence, bilateral kinship recognition, and possibly monogamy—go back to pre-Christian history. Nuclear families were common in England long before industrialization. English adults apparently never had an overwhelming desire to live with their parents, with their grown children, or with uncles, aunts, or cousins. Like modern-day Canadians, the pre-industrial English preferred to set up their own households, containing only spouses and children, and did so whenever they could. A similar pre-industrial pattern was found in pre-Confederation Newfoundland (McDaniel and Lewis, 1997).

Major forces of change like industrialization, urbanization, and education certainly affect family life; yet the relationships are not simple, nor are the outcomes predictable. Indeed, in two of the most industrialized countries, Japan and Sweden, we find very different family forms. In Japan, traditional family and gender norms persist. In Sweden, by contrast, there are very high rates of cohabitation and women working in the paid work force (although mostly in traditional female sectors). Throughout this book we argue that many family forms are not only possible but also desirable, and, indeed, work well—in Canada and throughout the world.

No simple conclusions can be drawn about what a family is, what causes families to change, or whether family life is getting better or worse. Those who want simple answers may find this ambiguity disappointing. Those who want to understand the modern family will find that the many open questions make for an exciting and intellectually challenging area of sociology.

Concluding Remarks

It seems that everywhere, family relationships are in flux. Around the world, industrialization and urbanization are destroying extended kinship networks and drastically changing the nature of family obligations. In North America, people value family life, but they are spending a smaller fraction of their lives in anything resembling a traditional family. At the same time, North American families today show more signs of stress and conflict than ever before. What, if anything, is the connection among these facts?

Current family trends are the result of long-term worldwide changes in social life. New laws and new contraceptive technology have given rise to new sexual permissiveness. Fertility has continued to fall for more than a century. Divorce rates have reached historically high levels everywhere, especially in the United States. These long-term trends have been boosted by rapid increases in the labour force participation of mothers of young children. In turn, women's behaviour is the culmination of a struggle for equality with men that began in earnest almost two centuries ago.

As we will see, the process of industrialization has set in motion irresistible, irreversible social forces that transform the content of close relations in everyday life. These social forces include the development of a consumer culture, market economy, welfare states, and a mobile, urban social structure. As well, new technology prolongs life, prevents unwanted births, and creates life outside the womb. In future, many scientists expect that it will even create new sentient creatures through genetic engineering and artificial intelligence.

The sociological study of family life offers a good illustration of the relationship between social structures and social processes, between choices and constraints, similarity and diversity. Some aspects of family life—for example, the norm of marital fidelity—are slow to change. The family as a cultural ideal exists outside and beyond individual people, in the ways that people of a particular society think about love, marriage, parenthood, the domestic division of labour, and so on. What is amazing about family life today is the contrast between people's idealization of family life "in the old days" and people's never-ending creativity in the face of a rapidly changing everyday reality.

Family life is constantly being constructed, and every family bears the unique stamp of its members. No two families enact love, marriage, parenthood, or domestic work in precisely the same way. If anything, the study of families makes clear that social life is a process of continued uncertainty, variety, and negotiation. We get the families we struggle for, although some family members have more power than others do in the struggle.

Families *have* changed dramatically in the last 30 years. Accepted ways of thinking, speaking, and behaving have changed because dozens, then thousands, then millions of family members have changed their way of relating closely. We should not conclude that we are in the midst of a breakdown of the family, in which a mate is no more than erotic property, and a child no more than a consumer durable. The way most people continue to struggle and sacrifice for their spouses, children, parents, and siblings suggests that the family means a great deal more.

In the chapters that follow, we study a variety of families as they form, develop, grow, and, occasionally, dissolve. We begin with a discussion of dating and mating.

CHAPTER SUMMARY

In this chapter, we have discussed what families are and how they are viewed. We have explored how defining families is a challenge, as both families and how they are seen are constantly changing. Families, for most of us, are our most important social relationships, defining who we are, and providing us with emotional attachment.

This chapter examines the complexity of what families are, why they are interesting to study sociologically, and how they have changed and are still changing. Family is now as important to people as ever but it has changed. Even the Census of Canada has, as the twenty-first century began, broadened its definition of family to include all common-law unions including same-sex unions, and adult children living with parents.

We have seen that sociologists are moving away from defining families by the shape they take. Instead, families are more often now defined by what they do for us and for society. The common elements of family living—dependency and intimacy, sexuality, protection, and power— are explored.

The key to understanding families is how families are theorized. In this chapter, we take a brief journey through the major changes in theorizing families from the early days of human living, to post-modern media imagery.

This chapter sets the stage for an in-depth examination of family change and family diversity in subsequent chapters.

KEY TERMS

Bilateral kinship system Kinship through both the male and female lines.

Extended family A family system in which three or more generations of family members live together and have social rights and obligations.

Kinship group A set of people who share a relationship through blood and/or marriage and have positions in a hierarchy of rights over property.

Kin-keeper The family member who maintains and nurtures family contacts.

Matrilineal kinship system Kinship through the female line.

Nuclear family A family group that consists only of spouses, or spouses and their children.

Patriarchy A system in which family decision-making is dominated by males, most typically by fathers.

Patrilineal kinship system Kinship through the male line.

Socioeconomic functions Functions that offer emotional, financial, and material support to a members of a group.

SUGGESTED READINGS

Baker, Maureen. 2001. *Families, Labour and Love: Family Diversity in a Changing World.* Vancouver: University of British Columbia Press. This is a book about families in Australia, Canada, and New Zealand and how they have been and are shaped by history, policy, and social change. Families and family changes are examined in the contexts of the colonial experience, industrialization, globalization, and large-scale immigration.

Cheal, David. 2002. *Sociology and Family Life.* London: Palgrave. This book pegs itself on some key questions: Who are considered family? What do families do? How do families connect with other groups in society? In answering these questions, changes in family expectations, behaviours and structures are revealed.

Mason, Mary Ann, Arlene Skolnick, and Stephen D. Sugarman (Eds.). 2003. *All Our Families: New Policies for a New Century* (2nd edition). New York: Oxford University Press. The focus in this collection of articles by different authors is on family change in the United States. A hard look is taken at myths about family disintegration. Trends such as divorce, single-parent families, stepfamilies and dual-income families are examined with a specific look at the challenges these trends pose for social policies.

REVIEW QUESTIONS

1. Provide two different definitions of family and indicate why each is useful or not.

2. Describe two different approaches to defining family and indicate why one is preferable to the other.

3. Identify and give examples of the main differences between families and other kinds of close relations.

4. List a problem with Murdock's definition of families.

5. What is the difference between family and household?

6. Why is family so important to us today?

7. Give an example of what kind of families the 2001 Census of Canada definition misses.

8. What are two new ways to observe families and family lives? How do they differ?

9. Provide two examples of how family theories are political.

10. Give an example of how changing the way that we theorize the family changes how we research families.

DISCUSSION QUESTIONS

1. Why do family relations matter to us and to society so much?

2. If emotional intimacy is central to what families are, then why do we rely so much on our friends at times? Is this related to life course?

3. Why is family and family theory so hotly debated in society?

4. Given the close link of family life with economic life historically in society, what kinds of changes do you foresee in the future for families as economic life changes?

5. Why is the marriage relationship so often seen, even today, as the central moral relationship in society?

6. In this chapter, it is suggested that if the main theorists of family had been other than white, middle-class men, family might have been differently seen. Look at family as it might be theorized by women, working-class people, immigrants or Aboriginal people.

7. Can we think in terms of a "golden age" of the family? For whom is it a golden age and for whom is it not?

8. What did the "big bang" in family theory open for us to see about families?

9. What is the best theoretical lens to study family diversity? Why?

10. What is the best theoretical lens to study family convergence? Why?

ACTIVITIES

1. Look around at yourself and at your friends. How many have families where family members do not correspond with the household?

2. Conduct a media study about the types of families that are represented on TV, in print ads, and in movies. What did you learn from this study about what constitutes family?

3. You are asked to take a family portrait. Whom do you include? Whom do you not include?

WEBLINKS

www.vifamily.ca
The Vanier Institute of the Family
This Ottawa-based independent organization has a wealth of information, new studies, and data on families in Canada. The site has many links to other sources of information on families.

www.bccf.bc.ca
British Columbia Council for Families
This site provides news, resources and links for researchers, practitioners, and families. Issues highlighted include balancing work and family, caregiving, connecting generations, couple relations, and parenting. Content is regularly updated.

www.cprn.org
Canadian Policy Research Networks—
Family Network
This site has information about families, and debates about family related policies. Recent research and theory is posted regularly. Recent postings are on housing policies and on childcare policies.

www.cfc-efc.ca
Canadian Child Care Federation
This public education site about families has a large library of resource materials.

europa.eu.int
The European Observatory on the Social Situation, Demography, and Family
The site lists recent conference papers on family and on changing policies in Europe and beyond.

CHAPTER TWO

Historical Perspectives on Canadian Families:

Demographic, Social, and Economic Origins and Trends

Chapter Outline

To understand contemporary family patterns, trends, and challenges, it is good to have some idea of how we got to where we are today in family life. Some view families as determined by our genes or by our social practices and as largely unchanging. Of course, sociologists see families as constantly changing in relation to social and economic situations.

Others see the contemporary challenges families face as brand new, a break from the past where families were thought to stick together, care for each other, and where they seldom experienced the ups and downs of modern-day families.

Here, we examine some historical aspects of family lives in Canada. We discover that many of the trends and challenges today's families experience are not new at all. We also discover that what we may think families were like in the past is not necessarily the way they actually were. We are helped in this examination by the richness of recent research on families in the past, both in Canada and elsewhere.

We focus in particular in this chapter on looking at families in the past with a sociological lens. We emphasize the big changes in society such as the contact and ongoing relations between Aboriginals and settlers, industrialization, large-scale immigration waves, wars, how families in the past connect to some of today's patterns, and how contemporary socioeconomic changes have altered families and our perceptions of them. We also focus on the multicultural families that have been part of Canada since its beginnings. Historical dimensions of families are explored more specifically in the chapters that follow.

A Historical, Cross-Cultural Perspective

Before we consider some of the contemporary changes in family life, let's step back and look at what families were like in the past. The vast majority of people who ever lived have farmed the earth, herded animals, hunted, fished, or harvested wild plants. In such economies, activities tend to be gendered: women do one thing and men another. It should be noted, however, that the exact division of labour has varied from one time and place to another. As well, children and the elderly tend to have a clear place. Since an extra pair of hands is always useful in subsistence societies, training in economically productive activities starts at an early age.

In these societies, kinship relations are very important. Families succeed by multiplying and prospering, increasing the number of cows or camels or sheep, or improving the yield of rice, wheat, millet, or sorghum in their fields. Families die out if no children survive and none are adopted. For societies on the edge—which still includes many peoples in the world—survival of the group is the central aim. People tend to seek happiness collectively, if they consciously seek it at all. Personal freedom and individualism are not as highly valued.

Indeed it may be difficult even to explain our notions of individual freedom to people in many other societies. We find far more ideas about property than ideas about freedom and happiness. Virtually all societies have customs regulating the ownership of animals, the use of certain areas of land, the right to harvest wild plants in a given location, and the practice of certain trades. Tellingly, these rules are often defined for families, clans, or descent groups, not for individuals *per se*. As children reach adulthood, they can inherit property under certain conditions, not others. And when young adults marry into another family group, they take limited property with them. They also take on rights and duties as part of the family they marry into. In these cultures, marriage is seen more as a union of groups or families than of individuals. Romantic love does exist, but is not considered an important goal or a foundation of marriage.

In some cultural groups in Canada today, there is a greater tendency to focus on the family instead of the individual. Recent refugees, for example, from the former Yugoslavia and various parts of Africa rely greatly on family networks to find employment in Canada and to gain access to needed services (Lamba, 2003). Calliste (2001) shows how racism, sexism, and class inequalities have shaped the importance black Canadians place on families. And Man (2001) reveals how the economic situations many recent middle-class immigrant women from Hong Kong face in Canada force them into greater dependency on the family than they had in the country of origin.

The most familiar example of a traditional culture may be ancient Israel, as described in the Old Testament. Have you ever wondered why the Old Testament contains such long lists of people begetting other people? It is because these genealogies establish the membership of descent groups. This is enormously important, since kinship is what justifies people's claims to land ownership, and land ownership is the means of survival. It also gives people a clear sense of belonging to a group, a family, a tribe, a culture.

Issues of kinship are critically important. Kinship affects the right to choose a marriage partner, the adoption of potential heirs, and the legitimacy of children. The position of the family in the community and the individual within the family determine people's ability to participate in the society's economic activities. We see some of this system in hereditary monarchies such as the royal family in the United Kingdom.

It is not easy to know about the families of the past. We cannot be there to interview the people that came before us, and some of them did not leave much in the way of written records or diaries. Traditionally history was not thought to be about what occurred at home or in private, but about big, public events like wars, political battles, and religious crusades. Lately, however, there has been a growing interest among both historians and sociologists in what families and their lives were like in the past. There is also strong interest among individuals to find out about their own family histories. "Genealogy is a budding industry in Canada. Half the population shows an interest in researching their ancestors and their roots" (National Archives, 2003: A6). The resulting evidence is both fascinating and immensely informative. It dispels myths about what families were like in the past and, interestingly, once the door of possibility for research is opened, all kinds of records have been discovered.

Extended Families

As agriculture becomes less important, so does the larger kin group. Over time, kin life shades into family life as we know it. An important example of this is what the nineteenth-century sociologist Frederic Le Play called the "stem family." Over the centuries, the stem family maintains a small farm as a family-run enterprise, and only one of the children (often the eldest son) inherits ownership of it. The rest move out upon marriage or remain unmarried. At some times in the family life cycle, several generations of the family may be living under the same roof. At other times, they are off on their own living independently.

Most cultures have a saying equivalent to "Many hands make light work," and peasant families have traditionally borne large numbers of children. Many family sociologists have believed that big, complex families are happy families. Le Play described the "ideal typical" household of such a family as follows:

> The heir and his wife, aged 25 and 20; the father and mother, the heads of the household, married for 27 years and now aged 52 and 47; a grandfather aged 80; two unmarried kinsfolk—brothers or sisters of the head of the family; nine children, of whom the eldest are nearly as old as the brother who is the heir; and the youngest is a baby, often still at the breast; finally, two servants living on terms of complete equality with the other members of the family (cited in Flandrin, 1979: 52).

This ideal, however, was probably attained only rarely. Stem family households were only possible under certain conditions. In rural European communities of the Middle Ages, a wealthy man might have a large number of relatives, servants, and apprentices living in his household. In general, the richer the household, the larger it was. But for the most part, peasants remained poor, died young, and lived out their lives in nuclear families. Maintaining this kind of family in industrial society or in the kind of highly mobile society Canada has become today is significantly more difficult.

Recent research has found that the two-generation family—parents with their children—characterized much of human history. Peter Laslett, the Director of the Cambridge University Group for the History of Population, has this to say based on his extensive historical research: "It is simply untrue… that there was ever a time or place where the complex family was the universal background to the ordinary lives of ordinary people" (Coontz, 1988:18). The explanation is simple, really. Life expectancy was low, so parents often didn't live long enough to see their children grow up, let alone become grandparents. The image of the multi-generational extended family of the past is simply a myth or based on fictional accounts of very well-to-do families.

Aboriginals and Settlers: Contact and Conflicts

Aboriginal families in what became Canada have always been diverse (Dickason, 2002). Some, like the Iroquois Confederacy of which the Mohawk Nation is part, were matriarchal, with women making the important political decisions while men were the warriors. This is similar to the political powers of today making decisions about going to war or peace-keeping while it is the soldiers and the officers who lead them who go into battle. This matriarchal decision-making was apparent a few years ago in the Oka crisis in Ontario, where Mohawk people protested the building of a golf course on what was their ancient burial ground. At one point, television crews captured images of the Mohawk women sharply ordering the warriors to back down from confrontation. And the men did, much to the surprise of some viewers and commentators. This is consistent with the Iroquois traditions and customs. Other Aboriginal groups are more patriarchal in family and social behaviours. There is much variability among the Nations as multiculturalism has always been a part of Canada, even before Canada existed.

Contact with explorers, fur traders, settlers, and missionaries changed Aboriginal family practices, as did the practices of some of the settlers. Early settlers in Canada developed strong relationships of mutual aid with their Aboriginal neighbours. Blood Nation women helped homesteading women in the prairies with childbirth and with house building so as to stay warm in the harsh winters. The settlement of New France (now Quebec) and Upper Canada (now Ontario) brought the families of Aboriginal groups together with those of the colonists. In the early days, children born to unmarried settler women were often adopted out to Aboriginal families. This is in sharp contrast with the more recent (1950s–1970s) practice of white families adopting Aboriginal children.

First contacts between Aboriginal peoples and foreigners were with male explorers, followed by the fur traders and missionaries, and ultimately women and families who settled in Canada (Dickason, 2002). The relationships in those days cannot be characterized as necessarily good or bad. Some explorers and fur traders married or cohabited with Aboriginal women (Van Kirk, 1980). Some of these relationships were committed and long-lasting, and others took advantage of the difference in culture and status between the men from afar and the local women (Brown, 1980), engaging in short-term, sometimes exploitative sexual relationships. It is a common story of colonialism, occurring throughout the world, leaving a legacy of combined racism and sexism to native women.

From the point of view of the native women, however, the story has not been fully told. It took until 1980 to tell the story at all from the women's point of view. History, including family history, is written by those who have the power and time, and who *can* write their stories. A modern-day Aboriginal comedian says that if the ancestors had known what was coming, they might have had a better immigration policy!

Imagine what some Aboriginal people in the early days of contact thought. Suddenly, after thousands of years of living in an area, along come some odd-looking foreigners, all men with no women and no children. They must have seemed like Martians! Relations between the men from afar and the local women were not sanctioned by the church or society, or the fur trading companies, notably the Hudson's Bay Company. The relatives of the women, however, sometimes did support the relationships (Brown, 1982). The Huron, for example, perceived ties between French men and Huron women as a way to develop kinship alliances, much as we describe above, cementing trust and good will through family connections. What the women themselves thought is impossible to know. Some fell in love that lasted a lifetime. Others tolerated or endured the situation. Many thousands of Canadians today can trace their ancestry to the British and French fur traders of the seventeenth to the nineteenth centuries and Aboriginal women.

But the story of contact and of "country wives," as the Aboriginal partners of the fur traders were called, is even more complex. Missionaries were keen to convert Aboriginals to Christianity. They were very committed indeed, as we shall see when we discuss residential schools. Their interest was in saving souls and promoting what they saw as moral virtues. Imagine their dismay at finding the ongoing relationships among fur trader men and Aboriginal women, without church sanction and sometimes without the accepted courtship patterns of European society. Relationships in Aboriginal cultures often were considered to be formal only once children were born, and pre-marital relationships were not seen as a problem by many Aboriginal peoples at the time of initial contact (Brown, 1992: 45).

These events were also the opposite of what the missionaries sought. Souls of "their" people, the European men, were "going native," the term used in the period to describe men who converted to native ways of life. This inclination on the part of some of the fur traders was added to by the policies of the fur trade companies. The Hudson's Bay Company, for example, prohibited the men from taking their country wives and families back home with them on retirement

Love in Early New France

...[T]he main business focus of New France (beyond saving souls) was the fur trade. And to the dismay of the Jesuits, this uniquely North American endeavour was soon converting substantial numbers of young Frenchmen to Algonquin or Wendat or Ojibwa ways rather than the other way around. Life in *le pays d' en haut*, the vast "upper country" inland and upriver, was seductively free of colonial constraints and religious authority, and captivatingly full of nubile young maidens who had all the skills a fur trader could possibly need as well as important connections to the very people who provided the furs. Little wonder that despite myriad dangers and colonial censure, the lure of life as a free trader, or *courier de bois*, enticed many to abandon the land and form lasting relationships with native North American women.

Source: Huck, Barbara. 2001. "Love in Another World," *The Beaver,* February/March: 13. Published with permission of Barbara Huck and The Beaver magazine. Barbara Huck, an award-winning writer and editor, is managing partner of Heartland Associates, Inc., a Winnipeg publishing company.

(Van Kirk, 1980). To solve this, several tactics were used. Some men simply abandoned their Canadian families and returned home to their original European wives or married European women at home. Others, however, decided to remain in Canada with their families, adapting to and being adopted by Aboriginal societies. One couple, William Hemmings Cook and his wife Agatha, made a fresh start by marrying, after living together according to the "custom of the country" for a long time. Van Kirk (1992: 79) cites one of the guests at the wedding as observing, "old Cook had stood manfully forth... bringing his 35 years courtship to an early close." Still others provided for their country wives in their wills, or organized to find new husbands for their country wives to ensure that they would be provided for once the fur trader had departed.

The children of these relationships suffered a strain. Some, particularly boys, left their familiar lives at a young age, sometimes to go to their father's relatives abroad to be educated. Daughters more often stayed with their mothers and the mother's culture (Brown, 1992). Attempts were made at various points in history, notably in the 1820s, to organize and to "civilize" what were seen as mixed-race families and communities. This resulted in officials making new laws, and in missionaries working to sanction relationships. One outcome was a sense of *in loco parentis*, whereby family life was controlled by others who largely saw those they were regulating and governing as like children who needed discipline and order.

An extreme version of *in loco parentis* was the residential schools for Aboriginal children, which operated in Canada from the late nineteenth century until the last one was closed in the 1980s. We will discuss residential schools and their long-lasting negative legacy for Aboriginal communities and families in Chapter 11. The teachers, often members of religious groups or orders, served as "parents" to the children, who often did not see their own parents for up to 10 months a year. Some children never saw their parents. The residential school parents, however, were harsh disciplinarians. Children were forbidden to speak their own languages, wear their own clothes, or maintain cultural traditions or religions. Harsh punishment was meted out to children reluctant to obey their masters in the schools (Bradbury, 2001).

An important component of the assimilation of Aboriginal children was imposing upon them European ideals of marriage, sexuality, and the elevation of husbands above wives (Bradbury, 2001: 71). The priests/teachers/school authorities sometimes worked out arranged marriages for the children when they grew old enough (Fiske & Johnny, 1996). Essentially, these children were being resocialized for assimilation into mainstream society. This "experiment" in cultural domination has long since been declared a disaster—not only for Aboriginal families, who lost cultural traditions and often did not have or could not learn the skills needed to parent their own children, but for the entirety of Canadian society (Bradbury, 2001; Dickason, 2002). Claims for abuse and compensation are being made by the now adult children in Canada (see the Assembly of First Nations' Web site at www.afn.ca for details on the latest on these claims).

Other family issues arose with early contact between Aboriginal peoples and Europeans and conflicts resulted, some of which are ongoing to this day. Neither the multiple Aboriginal cultures nor the multiple European cultures, which were part of early contact, were static or unchanging. All the cultural beliefs and practices around family and family issues had been developing and changing for hundreds of years and were widely divergent. Among Europeans who came to Canada in different roles there were sharp differences. For example, the French who came to the St. Lawrence area differed from the English and Irish who came to Newfoundland, and the ethnic groups—Americans, Ukrainians, and others—who settled in western Canada had very different attitudes with respect to kinship, descent, and gender. Similarly, Aboriginal groups differed on these aspects of family too. For example, kinship was the basis for assigning rights and duties in some Aboriginal groups, but kinship was defined more flexibly than in European culture to include adopted children and adults, friends and people engaged in mutual aid. Kinship regulated relations with others in the absence of courts and states *per se*. Decisions about justice and about compensation were often worked through kinship systems and had very different outcomes than they might have had in a European court of law, creating consternation and conflict on both sides.

A large area of difference between the early Europeans and Aboriginals was in gender roles in families and in communities. Work, responsibilities, and entitlements always seem to be organized by gender, but the ways in which gender is a factor in these differs widely. "In most Aboriginal societies women appear to have been able to exercise greater power than their European counterparts…" (Bradbury, 2001: 72). In some west-coast cultures, women were chiefs, and among the Huron, women appointed leaders of their communities had the major power in families. This led some European observers to horrified reactions. In the U.S., one observer reported his dismay at the "petti-coat government of the Cherokees" (Coontz, 1988: 52). To Victorians who saw women as decidedly inferior to men, it must have been a shock to see women with power.

Aboriginal peoples and early Europeans also had very different views on relations of family and community, and of both to property. Property, whether land or money or goods, to the colonial settlers was private, to be traded in a market economy. Assets belonged to individuals and nuclear families. Not so with Aboriginal groups, whose extended kinship groups might determine who would get the benefits of a hunt. This created a clash of values, which posed some difficulty in the fur trade since the concept of furs for sale was a new one to many Aboriginal peoples at that time. Ritual exchanges among family groups such as the potlatches of the West coast were seen as dangerous by the colonials both to their economic values and to their sense of what was right. In fact, potlatches were outlawed by authorities, and in some villages all the goods to be exchanged were symbolically burned (Dickason, 2002). This would be similar to a foreign authority coming into our homes and communities and abolishing Christmas and burning all our gifts and decorated trees in front of our eyes!

The Daughters of the King

Interestingly, there are parallels to conflicts experienced with Aboriginal peoples over family and kinship values and systems and conflicts between the English and the French settlers. Many of these issues also continue to this day, as we shall see in subsequent chapters. English Common Law, from which many of the understandings of marriage, family, inheritance, and property rights came, tended to concentrate power, authority, and property in male heads of households. For women, marriage meant the "suspension of the independent existence of the wife…" (Bradbury, 2001: 74). Married women for a long time (until the early part of the twentieth century) in Canada could not own property, sign a contract, or sue anyone. They were similar to children in having no rights under law. In contrast, in New France, which became Quebec, rules governing marriage and family were guided by the Custom of Paris (Bradbury, 2001: 75). This set of legal codes was much more egalitarian than English Common Law. Property was seen as shared between husbands and wives, even if controlled by husbands. And children, regardless of gender, could share in inheritances.

After the Battle on the Plains of Abraham in 1760, known in Quebec as The Conquest, the English attempted, as all conquering peoples tend to do, to impose their version of family law and practice on the French. It didn't work immediately and it never has since. The reasons are more political than related to family preferences or values. The English in Canada had to have the support of the French in their stand with respect to the American Revolution. It was thus agreed as early as 1774 that Quebec would have its own legal code covering families but all criminal law would follow the English practice. Thus, in Quebec in the 2000s we see different approaches to family than in the rest of Canada. For over a hundred years—1840s to 1960s—Quebec's elites saw family as a major place of resistance to English domination. We shall see in a moment some aspects of how this worked. One major family difference at present in Quebec is that Québécois/Québécoise (Quebec men and women) are very much more likely to live common-law than other Canadians. Another is that Québécoises do not take their husband's name on marriage. Both will be discussed in the chapters that follow.

Les Filles du Roi (the daughters of the King) was a name given to about 770 young women imported to New France from the streets of Paris in the 1663–1673 decade (Landry, 1992). Many were orphans, some were illiterate (although a lesser proportion than the men of the new colony), all were poor, and none were even remotely related to royalty! In response to the gender imbalance in New France and the wish to colonize the new territory (Huck, 2001: 12–13), this remarkable chapter in Quebec history was written.

The women were imported expressly for the purpose of providing wives for the single men of New France. Most agreed to be sent to the new colony across the sea out of poverty and lack of any other options. However, some were true adventurers. They were under contract to marry as soon as feasible upon arrival and most did within six months after setting foot on the soil of what is now Quebec. Most, remarkably, seem to have made wise choices in their husbands, asking first whether the prospective suitor had a farm. Only 15 percent of the marriages were annulled, the equivalent of divorce in Catholic New France at the time (Huck, 2001: 14). Of those, most remarried, and seven even married for a third time. There is nothing new in multiple marriages it seems! Thirty-two of the women never married and most of these women returned to France.

One woman of *Les Filles du Roi* was particularly remarkable and ahead of her time. She is Madeleine de Roybon d'Alonne, who remained single her whole life but did not return to France (Landry, 1992; Huck, 2001). She made an independent life for herself in New France and lived to a ripe old age for the time, an estimated 72 years.

The story of *Les Filles du Roi* has been, as might be imagined, much romanticized in the telling and retelling over centuries. Likely, it was not romantic at all for many of the women. The image of coming down the gangplank of a ship after crossing the North Atlantic to be ogled by a bunch of sex-starved lonely men, each with an eye toward making a match with the best one of the group he could, is not entirely alluring. It must have been somewhat like the modern "meet market" where a group of women walk into a bar largely populated by single men, however, the difference being that those modern women can just walk out again. The *filles du roi* were expected to marry the guy, and soon, or face a long, expensive return ocean voyage to France!

All this said, many Quebeckers today can trace their ancestry to the unions of the original settlers and the *filles du roi*. Can Canadians think that our history is in any way dull with a past such as this?

The Transition to Industrialism

Before industrialization, the family unit was the primary unit of production. Most families were rural, and were either agricultural workers or connected directly to people who were. Work and family were found in the same space. A spouse primarily responsible for one activity could see and appreciate the work that the other spouse did. Since work and family occurred in the same place, the two were not separate, or even separable. Even children helped to run the family business and keep the home running smoothly. Each person, old or young, had a role to play and society defined each person's role. The husband was usually responsible for representing the family in public to the rest of the world. However, people accorded the wife respect for the work that she did within the home.

Agricultural work also lent itself to the formation of extended families. In the first place, agricultural work—based on land and animals—was difficult to move, so people more often stayed put. Exceptions, of course, were non-inheriting children, who often migrated or emigrated in search of their own agricultural land. People who stayed formed strong bonds among neighbours and generations.

This lent itself to the formation of a **gemeinschaft** type of community typical of pre-industrial rural life: that is, one in which everyone knows everyone else and people share common values. Since limited social safety nets existed, families largely had to take care of their own. Aging grandparents helped busy parents to provide care to the many children of the family and often provided housing and money when needed (McDaniel & Lewis, 1998).

Since work time and family time overlapped, people had no sense of "quality time," only of "quantity time." Meaningful discussions might have taken place as the family pitched hay or sowed the seeds for next year's harvest. Quality time, as we know it today in family life, was likely less important then. It certainly didn't occur as much, we suspect. Shared tasks and hardships helped to cement the bonds within the family, but also dictated that these bonds are different from the ones we are used to today. Think about it. Every family member was around the others twenty-four hours a day, seven days a week. By today's standards, this arrangement might seem claustrophobic, with other family members always in your face. Nevertheless, people in pre-industrial societies accepted it as normal, perhaps even desirable, but certainly necessary for economic survival.

Not only did people have no sense of quality time, they had no sense whatever of time budgeting in the ways that we experience it today. Efficiency was not a major concern, nor was punctuality, conciseness, or brevity. The clock of the seasons and the weather determined agricultural, and sometimes human, timing. Predicting how much time people would give to any task was impossible. Too many factors were involved. People did what was necessary. People valued dedication, sociability, and the satisfaction of working together for the common good.

Industrialization changed all of this. First it drove many individuals and families out of the countryside and into the new towns and cities. Some families became migratory, following the work. As this was almost impossible to do with an extended family, the nuclear family became the more common family form. This type of family was smaller and more compact, thus easier to move. It was also more specialized. Everyone had a role to fill, although the roles were different from those in an extended family.

Many nuclear families could not survive with only one or two members of the family working for pay. Typically, children worked in the factories or on the streets selling papers, shining shoes, or picking rags, or they took care of the younger children so that the mothers could work (Parr, 1990). In the early industrial period a significant portion of family income came from the work of children. However, factory work posed new problems for families. For example, children who were working in the factories with their parents often did not want to give their entire wages to their parents. They might even choose to move out. If they moved out, they would still be poor, but they would have control over their wages. Stay or leave, they had more independence from their parents' wishes than children had in an agricultural society. This meant a significant change in relations between older and younger generations, and a new image of childhood. Increasingly, children became a liability. Parents, behaving sensibly, started to have fewer children.

The Industrial Revolution, which began in Canada only in the mid-1850s, moved the productive activity of men outside the household. Increasingly, people began to work *with* strangers and *for* strangers. Their family life became more of their private personal business, none of the boss's business. Their work life was, if they wished, not their family's business. There are those who argue that the private family is payment for selling one's labour in an alienating work environment. This relates to the concept of the home as a working man's castle, a concept with important negative consequences, as we shall see in Chapters 8 and 9. In any case, a clear line between work and family life, in the way that we perceive them today, appeared only with industrialization.

Our images of life on the home front before industrialization, however, need some further discussion. We romanticize, perhaps too much. Typically, we picture young women by their spinning wheels before a bubbling pot of stew on the open hearth, or mothers tending lovingly to their children while they toil in sumptuous kitchen gardens or fields. Men are thought to have been occupied as craftspeople, hunters, or farmers. Division of labour is imagined to be clear, sharp, agreed upon and happy, but incontestable. However, the realities of domestic divisions of labour in pre-industrial times were much more complex. In fact, after industrialization women lost market ties and the independence that those ties permitted.

Men's and women's work were largely separate in pre-industrial times, and the female sphere was more often confined to the domestic arena, more broadly defined than it is now to include farm animals, some manufacturing, social services to others in the community, and so on (Cross & Szostak, 1995). Men also had domestic responsibilities such as farm work, child discipline, and some provisioning of the larder. It was in many ways a partnership of women and men. The division of who did what was crossed by both women and men. This was a function of necessity. Because resources were limited, both men and women had to work to be able to clothe and feed themselves and their children.

In North America the pre-industrial division of labour was coloured by contact with the new land and its long-time Aboriginal inhabitants. Among many First Nations people, women were more often in positions of power than they tended to be in Victorian society, as we have seen. These differences made some settlers question the traditional sharp division of labour they had brought with them from Europe.

Early settlers may have preferred a more strict division of labour at home than they, in fact, could manage. Land was sometimes owned and worked by unmarried women, for example, a practice unheard of in the "old country" of England and most of Europe. The motivation was less an interest in gender equality than in increasing the output of agricultural lands. The ongoing demands of provisioning required children, elders, and women to participate in work.

Because men often had to leave homesteads, farms, and early crafts shops to work at other jobs or to obtain supplies, women often ran domestically based businesses. The high mortality rate, particularly of men, meant that married women could anticipate being left as widows, usually with dependent children still at home. This is a topic to which we will return in a moment. This gave some women considerable power and autonomy in both their families' enterprises and in the wider society.

Pre-industrial homes involved a lot of work too—hard work. Although much of what women did in pre-industrial times was domestic, it involved direct production. Remember that the home and work were not separate then. Such activities as spinning yarn, making butter, keeping chickens and collecting eggs, making jams, baking, and sewing were the means by which women and their families entered market activity. Many of these goods and services were sold to others.

Women, left alone with children to care for, resorted to age-old reliance on small-scale agricultural production, something they knew and understood, and for many, their only economic option. This provided some incomes to the women, which were an important contribution to the family and a source of pride.

The trouble was that some women did this small-scale agricultural production in the rapidly growing cities of Montreal, Toronto, and Hamilton. Keeping pigs, cows, and chickens in city yards proved perplexing to authorities (Bradbury, 1984). In the interest of health, **"sanitary reformers"** began to work on bylaws prohibiting the keeping of farm animals in cities. Campaigns with such evocative names as "Death to the Pigs" (Bradbury, 1984: 14) began. It was poor women's pigs (and cows and chickens) that were first outlawed. Bradbury reveals that one-quarter of the pigs kept in Montreal in 1861 were in one particularly poor ward, among cramped houses and factories where the pigs roamed alleyways and streets. No doubt the banning of farm animals from cities did improve hygiene, but it further limited the means by which women on their own could access market activity and have some degree of autonomy. Later, the same restrictions to women's market activities occurred with zoning bylaws that prohibited non-family homes in some neighbourhoods, preventing separated, divorced, and widowed women from taking in boarders.

The industrialization of household technology brought some new and unexpected dimensions to family life, particularly the expectations for women. Vacuum cleaners, for example, brought the possibility of cleaning a house more readily than by sweeping or taking heavy area rugs out to the yard to be beaten with brooms or paddles. Yet, expectations about cleanliness also escalated with the capacities of a vacuum (or a Hoover, as the early vacuums were generically called) to suck up every bit of dust and dirt. Similarly, refrigerators replaced wells, cold storage areas, and iceboxes (which were kept cool by blocks of ice—brought by an iceman in towns and cities, or taken from lakes and creeks in the countryside). Fridges saved the worry and the trouble of food storage in homes but created the necessity to shop longer and with greater care because meals were expected to be more complex and elegant than they had been.

The availability of "labour-saving devices" increased time spent in shopping as the new devices had to be purchased, along with their accoutrements. Homes quickly shifted from small-scale production units into showplaces of consumer goods. Women's roles in the domestic division of labour were reshaped from producers of goods to sell on the market, to consumers of goods to make houses and living spaces "homey." This shift sharpened the domestic division of labour by gender. It was a precursor of the modern "domestic goddess" movement, spearheaded by Martha Stewart.

Campaigns to promote the new household technologies recognized the love component of housework in working against the fear that women might abandon their domestic work with the **"mechanization" of housework** (Fox, 1993: 151). Home economists worked to elevate the esteem of homemakers by promoting the idea that the new home technologies required skilled operators. Health came to be associated with extreme standards of cleanliness. Homemakers then were charged with technical work and health promotion, noble causes indeed but unpaid and immensely undervalued. The scientization of housework was complete, and women were cast into the role of maintaining the home as their central life work, with limited access through their homemaking skills to the markets they had enjoyed prior to industrialization. They had been transformed into domestic engineers, responsible for all things related to family and the household.

Immigration

When we think family change and family transitions, we often see this phenomenon as something recent that rarely or never happened in the past. In reality, making family changes is nothing new. With massive flows of immigrants out of strife-torn, and in some cases poverty-stricken, Europe throughout the first half of the twentieth century, many people started families afresh as best they could in Canada and the United States. Immigrants and refugees from Europe are still coming, as strife and economic difficulties recur, and have now been joined by people from Africa, Asia, and Latin America fleeing an old life or seeking new opportunities in Canada, Australia, and the United States.

Immigrants built new families in various ways in their new situations. They may have brought families with them as well as maintaining family ties with those left behind. But life in the new country never allows all the ways in which families live, or the ways their children form their own families, to remain totally unchanged. Family changes are necessitated by the process of immigration and the contact with new ways to live in close relations.

The American Revolution brought to Canada the United Empire Loyalists, including significant groups of African Americans. The latter settled largely in

Nova Scotia and in southern Ontario (Calliste, 2001). Many black families did not fit the public/private model of family and work based on the experiences of white middle-class families. Black women often worked and had to work outside the home to earn enough money to get by. "[F]or African-Nova Scotian men in the early 1800s, many families practised gender interdependence and reversals of traditional gender roles in the division of labour" (Calliste, 2001: 402). This reflects, in part, necessity as a result of discrimination. But, it is also reflective of the West African cultural tradition where women are both more economically and sexually independent of men and of families.

Later, in the early twentieth century, African-American families settled as homesteaders in central Alberta (Hooks, 1997). Gwen Hooks, the daughter of original homesteaders in that area, describes how they banded together in families and communities to make a new and happy life on the prairies. She also states how homesteaders of all ethnic groups tended to band together to build community facilities such as schools. Later immigrants to the west of Canada, of course, have included peoples from all regions of the world who are seeking a better life and who bring with them rich family traditions and strong beliefs. With time, some of their family practices change in the new situation and others enrich the traditions of those with whom they have contact.

Another more recent historical example of a family transition related to immigration is evident in the story of Maria, who came to Toronto in 1956 from a peasant farm in southern Italy to join her husband, Eneo, who had come a year earlier (Iacovetta, 1992). Within two days, she had a job as a steam press operator, for which she was paid $37 a week. She worked for the rest of her life at various low-skill, low-pay jobs to help support her family in their adopted country. The marriage of Maria and Eneo represents the new kind of couple relationship she and others like her made with their husbands in the new country, where men and women both contributed economically to their families and yet women had no prescribed public role. The almost constant supervision of women, prevalent in southern Italy in the 1950s and earlier, had to be abandoned in part in the new situation, according to Iacovetta (1992: 286). New ways to be familial were developed by couples in the new country, with varying degrees of success and difficulty. Other examples are provided by Howell (2001).

For other immigrants to Canada, restrictive policies and laws prevented the building of families, new or old. During the early periods of Chinese immigration to Canada, for example, racially discriminatory laws were applied. One is the requirement of a head tax, a fee to be paid to get a relative into Canada, imposed in the 1885–1923 period (Man, 2001). This tax made it impossible for working men to bring in their wives, although it does seem that some wealthier Chinese traders did manage to bring in their wives and families. However, the Chinese Exclusionary Act strictly forbade Chinese workers, who built the railroad in Canada and worked in the early mines, from bringing in their wives or fiancées or families. As late as 1941, Man reports (2001: 435), there were 20 141 "separated" Chinese families,

Wars can have major impacts on families. Pictures like this one, of families seeing their loved ones off to combat, have become emblazoned in the minds of Canadians over the years.

where the man lived in Canada but his wife remained in China. Many people living on the Prairies and in British Columbia know or remember the Chinese "bachelors" who worked hard but never had a family in Canada. Some of those men have only recently passed away. Their lives must have been immensely painful and lonely.

Wars

Wars, without doubt, shape and change families. Soldiers die in combat leaving widows and children, sweethearts do not return or find someone else to marry during the war, and extended families are relocated and disrupted. The stories of war have shaped generations of Canadians and Americans, and still are in the 2000s. It seems as if there is always another armed conflict somewhere, and pictures of families seeing their loved ones off on a ship or a plane are emblazoned in our minds.

The effects on the homefront of what Canadians refer to as The Great War (World War I) have been captured in print by Sandra Gwyn (1992). She relies on archival records from real people to reveal how families in Canada and the peoples of Canada can never be the same after the First World War.

One example of how lives are transformed comes from Gwyn's research (see the box below).

Picking up the Pieces after World War I

After the war, Ethel picked up the pieces of her life as best she could. Now that she was coming up to forty, marriage, children, and a real home of her own were no longer in prospect. There were, of course, countless other women like her: so many potential husbands had died in the trenches that middle-aging spinsters constituted a distinct post-war social phenomenon.

Source: Gwyn, Sandra. 1992. *Tapestry of War: A Private View of Canadians in the Great War.* Toronto: HarperCollins, 201–202.
© 1992 by R. & A. Gwyn Associates.

Variation in Family Life Course

One of the most significant changes in family life over the past century and a half has been in the ages at which major family life events take place and the years spent in various family life-course stages. The higher mortality rates of the past often meant that families experienced the death of one or both spouses/parents while the children were still young, creating family change. Remarriage after the death of one's first spouse was frequent, as were stepparents, adoption, and fostering of children. Family size was much larger than at present too. Couples spent a much longer period of time having and raising children than they do now, as shown in Table 2.1 below.

The scale of these changes is vivid in Table 2.1, where three cohorts of women born in very different periods (the mid-nineteenth century, the 1930s, and the 1950s) are compared. Age at first marriage was higher for the oldest cohort, then dipped for the middle, and went up a tiny bit for the third. Age at first birth is lower for the cohort born most recently, which may surprise many of you. We sometimes think that in the past couples had children early and lots of children. The first part of our assumption is clearly a myth.

Table 2.1 **MEDIAN AGE AT LIFE COURSE EVENTS AND YEARS SPENT IN LIFE STATES, CANADA**

BIRTH COHORT			
	1841–50	1931–40	1951–60
MEDIAN AGE AT EVENT:			
1st marriage	26.0	21.1	22.5
1st birth	28.0	22.9	24.5
Last birth	40.0	29.1	26.3
"Empty nest"	60.1	49.1	46.3
Widowhood	59.5	67.2	69.9
Death	64.3	79.4	82.2
MEDIAN YEARS SPENT:			
Raising children	32.1	26.2	21.8
Married with no child at home	0	18.1	23.6
In widowhood	4.8	12.2	12.3

Source: Gee, Ellen M. "The Life Course of Canadian Women: An Historical and Demographic Analysis." *Social Indicators Research*, 1986, vol. 18, Table VI, p. 273, Abridged. Permission given by Kluwer Academic Publishers.

When we look at last birth across the **cohorts**, we start to see a fundamental change in family lives. Women born in the 1950s had their last birth at an earlier age than women a hundred years before had their first birth! Even more striking is the huge difference in when the last birth occurred for women born in the mid-nineteenth century (age 40) and women born in the mid-twentieth century (age 26.3). This means that over a hundred-year period, families reduced the time spent having and raising children by over 10 years. And, this occurred at a time when life expectancy was increasing substantially. The result is that the portion of life spent as a parent with dependent children has been sharply reduced. By contrast, the portion of life spent married with no children at home, or at least no juvenile children, has sharply increased from 0 to almost a quarter of a century. We shall see in Chapter 11 that in the early 2000s there is a huge difference between when children become adults and when they leave home.

Hardly any family change we could outline over recent history would be as dramatic as this. The average woman in Canada born in the mid-nineteenth century could expect to be a widow before her kids were grown up, with her own death following not long after. But for women born in the mid-twentieth century, the kids are grown long before she is likely to be widowed and even longer until her own life is over.

It may not be surprising given these trends that having second or even third families was more characteristic of families in the past than we sometimes acknowledge today. In some ways, widows in the past were similar to single mothers today in the economic vulnerability they and their children faced, and in the social challenges they posed (Gordon & McLanahan, 1991). Widows often fell into poverty and had to rely on charity or the beneficence of the state or other family members to survive. In Chapter 10, we will see the differences in children's lives between the loss of a parent to death and the loss of a parent to divorce. We do know that poverty, in the nineteenth, twentieth, and, yes, the twenty-first centuries has negative consequences for children and for adults in families. And poverty is strongly related to family dissolution by one means or another.

In the past, people expected a certain sequencing of family-related events. They expected, for example, young people to complete their education before marrying, to marry before having children, to get old before becoming a grandparent, and so on. So predictable was the pattern that sociologists spoke confidently about a normal life cycle of family events. Today, the timing and sequencing of events are too varied to be easily categorized. A woman can be a grandmother and a mid-career professional at the same time, or a new mother at midlife while starting a career. Patterns of family life have become more complex: for example, a child whose biological parents have joint custody may call two houses "home" and claim four (or more) sets of grandparents. Some middle-aged adults have to cope with the anxieties of dating again after becoming newly single. A woman can safely have a first child, with or without a long-term partner, after age 40. It's interesting to remember that women born in the mid-nineteenth century, without the medical technologies available for childbirth today (Mitchinson, 2002) were having their last birth, on average, at age 40.

Changes in Family, in Canada and Worldwide

Struggles to define and redefine families are ongoing throughout the industrialized world (Baker, 1995). Indeed, industrialization, as we have seen, had a huge impact on family living. The separation of public and private domains took place as men left the household or farm to earn a living in the new factories. In the last hundred years, more and more societies have industrialized.

A number of changes in close relations seem to accompany modernization. These consequences of modernization for close relations are especially evident in Eastern Europe, Asia, and Africa, where the nuclear family has not had the same historic prominence as it's had in Western Europe. For example, with opportunities for paid employment, **neolocal residence**—a pattern in which adults live in nuclear families apart from their own parents—becomes more common. They may continue to live near their parents, but may be drawn away to wage employment in urban centres.

Urbanization has had as great or greater an effect on family life than industrialization, although the two typically go hand in hand (see Finlay, Velsor & Hilker, 1982). That is mainly because households—or who lives with whom—are determined by property ownership arrangements, which vary between urban and rural areas. Typically, households are larger (i.e., extended) and family life is more psychologically important to people in rural than in urban areas—or so we have been taught to think. That history has some surprises for those who look closely is clear in this chapter and will recur in subsequent chapters. In many parts of the world, people still spend substantial parts of their lives in extended households, though they increasingly spend significant parts of their lives in nuclear families.

Prospective brides and grooms become less willing to accept a mate their parents have selected for them, although arranged marriages still occur with considerable regularity, even in Canada among some ethnic groups. We discuss this in Chapters 3 and 4. Where **polygamy** existed before, even if only as an ideal, it tends to diminish. **Endogamy** may persist, but it does so in a modified form. For example, people may continue choosing mates from within their group (village, county, region, ethnic group, tribe, etc.), but not from among their kinfolk.

Changes in Gender and Family Relations

Throughout the world, women increasingly seek more education with industrialization and modernization. Families have changed dramatically as women have become more able to control their childbearing and to support themselves economically. Attitude change has also had a lot to do with changing patterns of intimacy. This trend parallels delayed marriage, and delayed (as well as restricted) childbearing. Men tend then to value and to seek more educated wives and wives closer to them in age. In general, marriages tend to become somewhat more egalitarian, in that family power is shared between spouses more equally than in the past.

This is not to say that all marriages become equal and fair; they have not. But marriages used to be even less equal and fair than they tend to be today. Despite the desire to imagine a "golden age" of family life to which we might someday return, families in the past had a great many shortcomings, especially for women and children (Bradbury, 2001; Coontz, 1992). In truth, there never was a golden age of the family against which we should compare modern families.

Even in small rural areas, where traditional family forms persist most strongly, parent–child relations are changing (Caldwell, Reddy & Caldwell, 1984). Children, on average, are gaining more autonomy and power in interactions with parents. These changes demonstrate the pervasive influence of Western cultural notions, specifically notions about childhood and adolescence, but also, more generally, notions about the life cycle. They also show the growing importance of education and media even in rural areas, and the socialization of new generations in preparation for an urban, industrial lifestyle.

Everywhere, a modern industrial economy means people earn wages that their families cannot control (see Melikian & al-Easa, 1991, writing about Qatar, in the Persian Gulf). Young people rely on schooling and the media for more of their knowledge and information than generations before them, and they learn to value a high material standard of living. These changes may conflict with traditional family norms, values, and expectations. They certainly have the potential to set up conflicts between the parental generation and their children and, often, between religious and state institutions. These changes may be particularly challenging in countries in which the state and religion are not separate, such as Iran or Israel. Yet outcomes are not preordained; there is no certainty, for example, that the family in a modernizing Muslim region will be identical to the modern Christian, Hindu, or Jewish family.

Another factor that changes family life is political will and ideology. China, for example, has attempted to mobilize families in support of social development. Planned change of the family has gone hand in hand with economic and political change. In research by Kejing (1990), both the hardship and the progress along this road are apparent. Many conditions of life in China remain difficult, yet there is no doubt that family life is improving, especially for women. Despite a lack of prosperity, state efforts to regulate marriage, fertility and the rights of women are starting to pay off with smaller families and increased gender equality, though at the expense of personal liberty.

In the West, where industrialization occurred a century or more ago, economies have continued to change to a pattern sometimes called "late industrial," "post-industrial," or "the information age." Along with these changes have come

Debate Box 2.1 WAS FAMILY LIFE BETTER THEN OR NOW?
Which side of the debate do you fall on?

I am FOR thinking family life was better in the past

- Childhood was a better life in times past. Back then, you didn't have to worry about drugs or gangs, violent television, unsafe streets, or AIDS. Childhood was safe then.
- Children have too much stress today. A child's life was much easier in times past. Today, homework starts in early elementary school. There is so much pressure to be good at everything—sports, music, and academics. Plus, so many kids have to deal with divorced parents or grow up with only one parent. Families move around more. Lots of kids change schools in the middle of the year because their parents got transferred. Childhood depression is becoming more common all the time.
- Children are not respected today. Child abuse and child neglect is everywhere, and "latch key" kids are commonplace. What happened to the days when parents actually cared about their children, when they weren't so busy and stressed that they could actually take care of them properly?
- In times past, families were much more stable. Divorce was virtually unheard of. Cohabitation was considered "living in sin." People got married and stayed married. That is the way families are meant to be.
- We had stricter rules about marriage and divorce in the past. Families are the backbone of society, so these kinds of laws are needed to keep the family stable. The world used to be much more orderly.
- Family networks used to be a lot stronger. Children grew up surrounded by grandparents, aunts, uncles, and cousins. These people all lived in the same community and helped each other out. Today, families are so fragmented and spread out. It's hard for the whole family to get together. There is no more sense of community.

I am AGAINST thinking family life was better in the past

- Childhood has never been safe. The dangers have just changed. In times past, there was so much more life-threatening illness and disease that many children didn't even live past childhood.
- Childhood today is a time of leisure and play compared to times past. In the past, many kids didn't even get to go to school. They worked on farms and in factories, often for 12-plus hours a day under hazardous conditions.
- Children today are considered priceless and precious. Parenting is a child-centred, self-sacrificing endeavour. Everything is done in their best interest. Children are put first. In times past, children were meant "to be seen, not heard." Also, corporal punishment was standard practice. Children did not enjoy the same level of indulgence, freedom, and affection from the larger society and parents that they do today.
- Just because the rules about marriage and divorce were stricter in the past doesn't mean families were more stable. High death rates also meant lots of family change.
- Social stability comes from people being happy and having choices rather than having to live in a straitjacket. Formal stability isn't the same as actual stability.
- Technology allows for geographically distant families to stay connected and in touch. Extended family is still an important network; it just has a modern twist to it.
- In times past, when there was no such thing as retirement, for example, children probably couldn't have the same kind of easy, bonding relationship with their grandparents and other extended family members that they do today.

shifts in family. Families have become both smaller and less stable, and have been affected by the changing role of women, who have entered the labour market in large numbers. This is a function of changing economies as well as changing opportunities for women in society. It also relates to the demise of what was known as the family wage, the payment of a wage sufficiently high to enable an entire family to live on it. With the end of this notion, families had little choice but to send out an additional worker to make ends meet. Interestingly, early in this century it was more often children who entered the market to earn the extra money families needed to survive. Now, it is more common for both spouses to work while the children do not. But there are hints in the 2000s of a strong tendency for families once again to be relying on the earnings of adolescent children—as well as both parents' earnings—in order to manage.

Changes in Sexual Attitudes and Courtship

In the Victorian era, the banishing of sex from public view reached its now famous apex. Legs on tables were covered for fear that, in their naked state, they would make people think of sex! Pregnancy was disguised, hidden, or denied. Women were not expected to be seen in public while pregnant, certainly not naked on magazine covers as occurred in the early 1990s. Feminine ankles were thought too alluring for men to observe. Nonetheless, during this period a world of men's pubs, clubs, and male occasions such as hunting flourished, as did a thriving prostitution trade and some lurid novels. Sex certainly did not cease to exist.

By the late nineteenth century, sex began to be seen as a central part of marriage and sexual attraction a crucial part of courtship. Ward (1990: 9–11) relies on the diaries of George Stephen Jones, a young Quebec City clerk who between 1845 and 1846 kept note of his growing feelings for Miss Honorine Tanswell, whom he describes as "that most amiable young Lady Miss Tanswell." George describes himself as feeling the first stirrings of romance but being uncertain of his newfound emotions. He learns, after making his feelings known to Honorine, that her parents intend for her to marry a Monsieur Gingras. Poor George, not certain what basis for marriage he is dealing with now, tells his diary, "If she dose [sic] I will be the most mesirable [sic] man on earth and I will never marry. No never" (Ward, 1990: 11).

In the 1920s, it's been said that sexuality "came out" (Dubinsky, 2001) heterosexuality in a married relationship, that is. Having culturally sanctioned "sexual papers" permitted a married couple to go to Niagara Falls for their honeymoon, filled with expectations about supreme sexual bliss (Dubinsky, 1999). In an older period, newlyweds had no privacy. They were accompanied into the matrimonial bedroom by relatives and friends, and, of course, rude jokes. In some cultures, the bloodied sheets of a virgin "deflowered" would be tossed from the window to the cheers of crowds of relatives and friends below.

Will the New Mr. and Mrs. Check In at Your Hotel?

Historians have identified the 1920s as the era in which heterosexuals "came out." Sexuality and sexual attraction began to occupy a more central place in modern ideas of personality and identity, and sexual happiness came to the fore as a primary purpose of marriage. This is why doctors and other experts turned their attention to the honeymoon... the "bungling groom" was almost as inept and nervous as the "blushing bride." Marriage was too important to be left to the bride and groom alone. So while privacy was still expected, honeymoon companions, everyone from service-industry personnel to sex and marriage experts were never far away.

Source: Dubinsky, Karen. 2001. "There's Something about Niagara," *The Beaver*, February/March: 31. Published with permission of Karen Dubinsky and *The Beaver* magazine.

The Victorians, by contrast, in the nineteenth century "de-sexed" the honeymoon. Isobel March, a newly married young woman in 1871 in Niagara Falls, cited by Dubinsky (2001: 30), "did all she could to avoid the horror of being an 'evident bride.'" Soon, sex experts and romance filmmakers found Niagara Falls and invented the sexual honeymoon. Identities, personalities, and family beginnings had their origins in this emergence. Honeymoons became a rite of passage into adulthood, and very importantly, consumerism. What was (and is) consumed were not only sexual holidays but also a lifestyle with promises of lifetime sexual fulfillment. Niagara Falls' status as the honeymoon capital was cemented with the 1953 release of the Hollywood film *Niagara*, with Marilyn Monroe (who else!) and Joseph Cotten as the newlywed Cutlers, "an obsessive, out-of-control couple, the perfect foil for the happily married newlyweds..." (Dubinsky, 2001: 31). After the film's release, but still in 1953, a record thirteen million people visited Niagara Falls! In the ad for the film, Monroe is lying across the Falls seductively; the caption reads, "A raging torrent of emotion that even nature cannot control." (Dubinsky, 2001: 32). In 1955, when Cary Grant declared to young Grace Kelly, in *To Catch a Thief*, "What you need is ten minutes with a good man at Niagara Falls," the future of both Niagara Falls as a honeymoon capital and of sexual bliss through marriage were sealed.

At the beginning of the twenty-first century, images remain of pure, virtuous women who search for knights in shining armour. Romance writers grow rich describing these images, as do others in the romance trade. Wedding planners and coordinators love it. Marriage is seldom considered clearly by dewy-eyed youth who are engaged often not in planning lives together, but in planning romantic—and increasingly costly—white weddings. Interestingly, in weddings today, all but the most ultra-modern brides still look like fairy princesses and grooms remain one step short of riding in on white chargers. Brides are still "given away" by their fathers (or both parents) to their husbands. And the important ritual of uniting the couple sexually as well as socially is shared by families brought together for the wedding.

Changes in Attitudes toward Marriage

Traditionally, marriage was viewed largely in terms of rights, duties, and obligations to each other's families. Throughout the West, a major attitude shift has placed greater emphasis on the personal or emotional side of close relations.

Even in 1981, only one in five North Americans surveyed expressed "traditional" family attitudes (Yankelovich, 1981). Likely, this number has since shrunk, although with the "family values" movement, particularly in the U.S., there is some evidence that the tendency toward traditionalism has been reborn. In 1981, however, another one in five believed life is about self-fulfillment, not duty to others in either family or society. This likely has not been reversed since. Marriage and family life may be valued so long as they complement—or at least do not interfere with—personal aspirations and self-fulfillment. The remaining three in five North Americans, the majority, fall between these two extremes. For most, the quality of a relationship is more important than its structure (e.g., married versus common-law). The important question for three-fifths of people is "What makes an intimate relationship satisfying?" not the legal or societal arrangements under which the relationship exists.

Why, then, do people still keep up the old forms? Why do so many still get married, many of them in churches or religious places, dressed in immensely expensive white bridal gowns and formal black tuxedos with cummerbunds, or all the glitter and gold of the Hindu wedding? We shall discuss these questions in detail in Chapter 4. In short, formal weddings and going through the legal ceremony of marriage have more to do with marking a life transition and/or gaining social approval than with emotional commitment. Many people still find the idea of legal marriage compelling, despite what they know about the realities of marriage and divorce. Enormous numbers of North Americans are neither rejecting the family or other long-lasting, close relationships nor accepting family in a traditional form. Most are hoping to revitalize and reinterpret family (Scanzoni, 1981a, 1981b, 1987), making families suited to themselves and their needs.

Yet in some parts of Canada and the world, and in the future, marriage may no longer be the close relationship in which people spend most of their adult lives. People are already less inclined to marry than they were in the past. They are more likely to view cohabitation or singlehood positively, as we shall explore in Chapters 4 and 11.

One significant change in family life in the Western world has been an increase in cohabitation—people living together without being legally married. Living together, also called cohabitation or common-law union, used to be more prevalent among working-class people. It also used to be seen as a lesser form of relationship than marriage—"living in sin" or "shacking up." Now, however, it has lost some of its stigma, and is much more accepted. In Quebec, cohabitation has become the norm for younger couples, with legal marriage decidedly less preferred. This is discussed based on the 2001 Census of Canada in Chapter 4.

Increasingly in the 1990s and 2000s, couples in cohabiting relationships have children. In 1993 to 1994, 20.4 percent of all Canadian children were born to women living in common-law unions with the child's father (Vanier Institute of the Family, 1994). Legal and religion-sanctioned marriage is decreasing as the basis of family formation and childbearing. The old stigma of illegitimacy, or birth "out of wedlock," is largely gone, particularly when the parents are in a stable, caring relationship. Especially in Quebec, people now see cohabitation as a lifelong way of family life, a close, committed relationship in which to have and raise children. We will explore this more in Chapter 4.

It may be coincidental that the growth in cohabitation has coincided with later marriage (since the 1960s and 1970s), higher divorce rates, and lower rates of childbearing. More and more often, people think of spousal relations as being about love and sexual attraction, as we have seen in this Chapter, not childbearing and creating family alliances. People have come to expect more satisfaction of their emotional and psychological needs in their close relationships. Women, particularly, are less economically dependent on their partners than they used to be. These shifting norms, opportunities, and expectations have all contributed to a decline in the stability of married and cohabiting life. But both continue, and for the majority seem to work and work happily.

Declining Fertility and the Value of Parenthood

One of the most profound changes in family life has been a change in family size. Since the 1870s, fertility in the West has declined steadily. Today, most European and North American countries are at, or just below, population replacement levels. This means that, unless there is a radical shift in fertility or immigration, Western populations will get smaller and older during the next century. This process is already well underway in Sweden and France, as well as in Japan. Whether this is a problem—for families and for societies—depends on who is deciding and how the situation is defined. It is a topic to which we will return as we proceed.

A significant blip on this downward fertility curve was the post-war "baby boom." The baby boom, however, was only a temporary reversal of the long-term trend and was largely confined to North America. The "boom" was also misnamed. Higher birth rates, in fact, were the result not of increasing family size but of compressing two decades of births into a decade and a half (roughly 1947–1962). In other words, it was the result not so much of increased fertility but of postponed fertility due to World War II. Several different age groups then had their desired number of children within a short time frame, leading to a dramatic increase in birth rate for those years. By and large, however, the long-term downward trend in fertility over the course of the twentieth century has never really stopped.

Family size and birth rates in Canada have always been political issues, as we mentioned earlier. The term used to describe Quebec's historically high birth rates (before they fell sharply from the late 1950s on) was "**the revenge of the cradle**," an image reflecting the belief that Quebec's long-standing sense of political injustice might be countered by having more Quebec (French-speaking) citizens (see Henripin & Peron, 1971). Quebec's birth rate remains a political issue in the 2000s. Family researchers who study birth rates—known as **demographers**—are household names to Quebeckers; not so in the rest of Canada. Early birth-control promoters, such as A.R. Kaufman of Kitchener, Ontario, were concerned about the French in Canada "outbreeding" the English (see McLaren & McLaren, 1986: 124).

Children in New France were the basis of settlement of the St. Lawrence valley (Landry, 1992) in the late 1600s and early 1700s. Wives and children were necessary to run farms and businesses. All were expected to work. Men who did not marry often left the colony. The basis of the legendary high birth rates in Quebec is traced to this period when girls as young as twelve were chosen as wives by the men of New France, and became mothers of many children.

Moogk (1982: 26–27) has shown that all was not entirely well, however, with high fertility in New France.

> Illegitimate births were an increasing problem in eighteenth-century New France, indicative of the breakdown of communal social restraints. In the villages of the Christian Amerindians, [were] observed numerous illegitimate children of the French colonists ... adopted by the native peoples and they fully accepted the Aboriginals' way of life.

Eighteenth-century New France may not have been so different from the world of today in Canada or the United States, except that teens today would likely have been older when they got pregnant than the unmarried mothers of New France. And fewer of them would get pregnant.

The Quebec Government awarded prizes in the 1930s and 1940s to women who bore many children. Their photos would appear in newspapers, the television of the past. Both the church and the government encouraged families to have more children. This policy was formalized with baby bonuses, which increase with each additional child born. The present Prime Minister of Canada, Jean Chrétien, is one of a family of many, many children. The shift from large to small families in Quebec has occurred rapidly indeed, leaving many Quebec families with older and younger generations of vastly different sizes.

Native peoples in Canada also had high birth rates in the past. In the 1970s and into the 1980s, births to native peoples were just starting to decline. Recently, however, First Nations birth rates have increased and are now the fastest growing group in Canada (Statistics Canada, 1998). As a result, 12.4 percent of the Aboriginal population are in the youngest age group (0–4 years old) compared to only 6.7 percent of the Canadian population at large (Statistics Canada, 1998). The prime working-age Aboriginal population will grow by 41 percent by 2006, according to the best estimates, with the numbers of Aboriginal children and teens swelling considerably in the immediate future. Enormous diversity in family size exists among various Aboriginal peoples, however, as well as between those who live on reserves and those who live in cities.

Aboriginal entry into parenthood occurs in a radically different family form than it does for many other Canadians. Approximately one-third of Aboriginal children under 15 live with a single parent compared to less than 20 percent for all Canadians. The proportions are close to one-half in Winnipeg, Regina, and Saskatoon. Nearly a quarter of Aboriginal children live with parents who are common-law, compared with 10.5 percent of all Canadians. And about 11 percent of Aboriginal children under 15 live with neither parent, compared with 2.1 percent of all Canadian children. This group includes children living in a variety of situations; foster care is the most common, but some live with relatives, often grandparents or aunts or uncles.

It is not only that Canadian families are now having fewer children than previously. It is also that expectations about marrying and having children have changed dramatically. When asked by family researchers today, most young people say that they expect to get married and have children (Vanier Institute, 2000). Interestingly, few expect ever to be divorced! In the late nineteenth century and the early part of the twentieth century, many more people than now never married at all. For example, Gee (1986: 266) finds from historical records that in 1911, 12 percent of Canadians never married. This compares with only 5.8 percent in 1981. It has dropped to less than 2 percent today. Not marrying in the past generally meant not entering parenthood. So, in fact, parenthood in the past was not part of as many people's lives as it is now. In the past, a lower percentage of the population got married, but those who did had many more children, on average, than couples do today.

The First and Second Demographic Transitions

The demographic transition from high mortality and fertility to low mortality and fertility transformed the social meaning of children, childrearing, and women's place in the family. We shall have much more to say about these never-ending changes in later chapters. This transition to low fertility in the West, which began around 1870, is called the *first demographic transition*. It brought births into line with a sharply reduced death rate, so the theory argues. Since 1965, we have seen a new force for lower fertility in the West. Demographers have called this new phase the "second demographic transition" (Van de Kaa, 1987). This contemporary transition has brought birth rates into line with new lifestyle goals and family practices. Wherever we find the second demographic transition well advanced, we find a profusion of new ("non-traditional") family styles, women working in the paid labour force in large numbers, and people seeking autonomy and fulfillment in their personal lives.

The second demographic transition is particularly advanced in Northern and Western Europe. Renewed concerns have been expressed in these regions about depopulation and a shortage of young people in the future. In Europe, the fertility rates needed to replace the population—about 2.1 lifetime births per woman—are found only in Ireland, Malta, Poland, Albania, Turkey, and some new countries in Eastern Europe. None of these countries is a highly industrialized, Protestant country. All of them have made a virtue of large family size or limited access to birth control. It must be remembered that Canada did this as well until very recently.

In most Protestant industrial countries, fertility rates hover around 1.5 children per woman. Japan's fertility rate has dropped too, from an annual level of 2.1 in 1973 to 1.4, the lowest ever recorded there. A continuing decline in fertility will leave Europe's population with a growth of only 6 percent between 1985 and 2025, while the world's population overall nearly doubles. As a result of low fertility, by 2025 one in every five Europeans will be 65 or older.

The effects of this transition are profound and subtle. A long decline in fertility, together with increased life expectancy, has led to an aging population. People have fewer young kin today than they did in the past. Many of us have (or will have) fewer sons and daughters, nephews and nieces, grandsons and grand-daughters than did our parents or grandparents. On the other hand, we are much more likely to have many generations alive at once than at any previous time in history, with some families having as many as five or even six living generations (McDaniel, 1996b). Remarried, step, and blended families also expand our kin networks into stepchildren and stepgrandchildren, as well as his-and-hers extended families. And, largely because of urbanization and industrialization, more people today live alone or outside conventional families than their parents or grandparents would have done. In general, domestic lives are becoming more varied and complex.

Several explanations exist for these recent fertility declines. We are hard-pressed to assign priority to one or another factor. Women have been taking advantage of more access to education and employment. Couples have delayed marrying. When people delay marriage, they are somewhat less likely ever to marry (although this is less so now than in the past) and, if they do marry, likely to have fewer children. At the same time, the costs of raising children, both economic and social/personal, rose dramatically during the twentieth century. Children are particularly expensive if they need daycare by someone other than the mother (whose childcare was in the past presumed to be costless), or if caring for them means forgoing a parent's income and career aspirations for several years. And, of course, who among us would not want our children to have "quality" lives? This term may be defined differently by each of us, but may include such costly items as hockey, ballet, and music lessons. As well, children today remain in a state of economic dependency for longer than in the past, sometimes for surprisingly long times, as we shall see in later chapters. Finally, children often contribute less to the family economy than they used to in pre-industrial times and in the early part of the twentieth century.

The number of people who remain childless has also grown in many Western countries; only, however, in comparison to recent decades. Among women now in their eighties, approximately 25 percent are childless (Rosenthal, 1999), a higher proportion than among younger women or than is likely in the immediate future. A small number of childless couples are desperately eager to make use of new reproductive technologies or to adopt a child. Most childless women and men and couples are, however, content to be childless. For some proportion (it is not known how many), childlessness is a chosen option, one they enjoy. In short, people think about parenting and having children in different ways today than they used to in the 1950s and 1960s.

Contraception, Childbearing Choice, and Abortion

In the past, women found a major source of identity in having children and being mothers. This was the case in such different situations as urban Quebec in the seventeenth century, and the early frontier societies in the West of Canada. Silverman (1984: 59) tells us that giving birth and raising children was the answer often given to the question, "What are women for?"—an answer given by women as well as by men (also see Mitchinson, 2002). Until recently, both women and men agreed that childbearing and childrearing gave women's lives meaning. Entering parenthood was also vital to populate Canada, particularly in settling the West, and, as we have seen, in the earliest settlements in Quebec.

The popular belief that couples in the past would accept however many babies God gave them is not quite true. There have always been attempts, some of them successful, to regulate pregnancy and births. Although officially illegal in Canada until 1969, some couples used birth control to choose how many children they would have and when they would have them. As now, not all birth control worked.

Among the most common birth control methods in the past were abstinence and prolonged breastfeeding. One woman who homesteaded on the Prairies tells in her diary, "A woman I knew when I was quite young nursed her baby until she was four years old so that she wouldn't have another one" (Silverman, 1984: 60). The woman reporting this adds, "That wouldn't have worked for me at all." Other popular birth control methods used in Canada's past include barrier methods, timing or rhythm approaches, withdrawal, abortion, and as one wise advisor to young married women suggested in her 1908 marriage manual, "twin beds" (McLaren & McLaren, 1986: 19–20).

Abortion was common in the past in Canada, with methods of "bringing down the menses" routinely advertised in daily newspapers and early magazines (McLaren & McLaren, 1986: 33–35). There were ads for Radway's Pills for "female irregularities," the New French Remedy, Sir James Clarke's Female Pills, Dr. Davis' Pennyroyal, and on the list goes. Cook's Cottonroot Compound was argued to be "used successfully by over 10,000 ladies" (McLaren & McLaren, 1986: 33). It is only in recent decades that abortion has come to be seen as an important public, moral issue. Interestingly, several of the well-known nineteenth-century **abortifacients** (herbs or potions that brought on a miscarriage) are still in use today for inducing labour.

Family planning and abortion may have been the means by which women could have identities apart from being mothers, and lives outside motherhood. Information about birth control and abortion was commonly shared among women, along with important information about parenting and caring for their own and their children's health. The beginnings of schools and health-care provision, often with emphases on maternal and child health, were ways that women created communities in frontier societies.

A very important factor in fertility decline may be technological. During the 1960s, safe, reliable contraception became easily available. The first **demographic transition** was accomplished through a combination of strategies including late marriage, abstinence from sex, awkward methods of birth control, and dangerous, illegal abortion. The second demographic transition has occurred in the midst of a liberalizing sexual revolution and new accessible means of contraception. Thanks to the Pill and other relatively readily available forms of contraception—including IUDs (intrauterine devices), spermicidal gels and foams, and higher-quality condoms—more and more women and couples are able to choose if and when to become pregnant.

Women are extending their education, entering careers, and postponing marriage and/or childbearing to do so. Many are not ready to begin parenthood before their thirties and few are willing, or able, to take much time off work to do so. The result is a late, brief explosion of births among women who, by world and historical standards, are "older" first-time mothers. In the last 20 years, we have seen an overall decrease in the numbers of children born to women aged 30 and over, but an increase in first births among these same women (Statistics Canada, 1992). These statistics represent changing preferences of women, including planned delay.

Sterilization and abortion also play important roles in fertility reduction today. Overall, abortions have had less impact on the North American fertility rate than contraceptives (pills, condoms, and the like). However the same is not true everywhere. For example, legal abortions have had strong effects on fertility in Eastern Europe and Latin America. Not enough is known about the effects of abortion on fertility in China and in other less developed regions of the world to be able to make claims with any certainty. Eastern European women, however, have an average of 1 to 2.5 legal abortions in their lifetimes, in contrast to .2 and .6 in other parts of Europe.

Contraception has been generally scarce in Eastern Europe. The average woman in the former Soviet Union and Romania in the mid-1960s would have had seven abortions during her lifetime. Van de Kaa (1987) notes the dramatic rise in third and higher-order births after the repeal of legal abortion legislation in

Romania, while the Ceausescu regime maintained an iron-fisted stance against birth control in a deliberate attempt to increase the birth rate. What this shows is that abortion had been playing a large role in controlling fertility where other means of birth control were unavailable. Once abortion was ruled out, people abandoned their babies to the care of the state. The net result was a huge number of Romanian babies and children crammed into orphanages under appalling conditions.

Though less dramatically, easier access to legal abortion has also influenced fertility in the West (Krannich, 1990). Up to the 1890s, abortion was tolerated in many jurisdictions, including in Canada. Women who wanted to end their pregnancies could do so with the assistance of surgeons, herbalists, or midwives. Abortion was in fact legal in most North American states until the 1890s. Then it became illegal for 70 years as a result of pressure exerted by social purity movements. Legalizing abortion once again made the process safer and more medically controlled. The (legal) abortion rate rose briefly after the mid-1960s, with a more liberal interpretation of the laws, but the rate soon tapered off (Krannich, 1990: 368).

The most important factor promoting a decline in the incidence of abortion is the use of contraception, which enables avoidance of unwanted pregnancies. As in so many areas of life, preventing problems is easier, safer, and surer than remedying them after the fact. So as contraceptive knowledge and use have spread, abortion has become a less often relied-upon means of limiting fertility. However, the debate over abortion has not ceased, nor is it likely to. All pregnancies are not planned or wanted or safe for the health and well-being of either the woman or the fetus. The need for abortion as an option is not likely to disappear anytime soon.

This revolution in birth control has had profound effects on relations between women and men. Before effective antibiotics and birth control methods existed, there was a strong prohibition on male–female relationships, even friendships, outside of marriage. People were afraid they would lead to sexual intercourse, loss of a young woman's virginity, and pregnancy or killer venereal diseases such as syphilis. (Ironically, the prevalence of contraceptive pill use may have contributed to the spread of HIV/AIDS as well as some of the newer venereal diseases such as chlamydia.) Where sexual purity was an issue, a double standard has always been applied. Moreover, sexual prohibition or abstinence was enforced more or less strongly in different times and places. We'll discuss sexual mores more fully in the next chapter.

Family and Household Size

As fertility has declined, the number of people in the average household has become smaller. The average Canadian household has shrunk by 50 percent, from around six people in 1681 to now 2 or even 1 in 2001. What's more, complex family households, containing a variety of people who are not part of a nuclear family, have almost vanished. The proportion of two-family households dropped by 75 percent since 1981. The proportion of households with lodgers also fell, from 14.9 percent in 1931—more than one household in seven—to nearly zero now (Bradbury, 1984). All these trends, however, may be changing slightly with tough economic times, as families double up more to share expenses (Mitchell & Gee, 1996). This is a growing tendency, as we shall learn in subsequent chapters.

At the same time, a major change in family life has been a rise in the proportion of single-person households (Statistics Canada, 2002c) —the proportion has more than tripled since 1931, when they made up 7 percent of all households. Since 1971 alone, there has been an 88-percent increase in non-family households (Vanier Institute of the Family, 1994: 29), while the proportion of people overall living in families declined since 1981 (Vanier Institute of the Family, 1994: 29). Today, more people prefer to, and can afford to, live alone, something to which we will return in a later chapter.

Curiously, while households have been growing smaller, houses have been growing bigger. Victorian-era houses were intended to serve as single-family homes with space for one or two live-in servants. When immigration was at a peak, as many as 15 people occupied these houses (Iacovetta, 1992). In pre-industrial times, even more people shared living quarters. But today, most single-family houses are occupied by couples with fewer than three children, or none at all. Yet suburban middle-class houses of the 1930s that were big enough for raising four children now seem too small for raising two children (Rybczynski, 1992). As families have shrunk, desires for space and privacy have increased.

In North America, home life and family life imply intimacy but also privacy. Intimacy and privacy demand a suitable physical environment. In practice, this means enough room (and rooms) to separate the household from the community and family members from one another within the household.

Social Support and Regulation: The Role of the State in Families

Around the world, both families and states provide social support for dependent social groups: children, old people, the infirm, and others who may need support. However, demographic changes associated with modernization have significantly reduced the size of the kin networks most people have. Increased longevity and decreased fertility have meant lesser portions of our lives spent parenting, smaller families, and fewer siblings. These changes have also lengthened pre-childbearing and "empty nest" periods for intact couples and extended parental survival and the probability of dependency in late life. In turn, this has reduced the potential quality and quantity of the family support that dependent people can obtain (Keyfitz, 1988; Matras, 1989). A study done by one of your authors analyzing the pre-Confederation censuses of Newfoundland, reputedly the most familial society in North America, found that even in the early part of the twentieth century families were largely two generations (McDaniel and Lewis, 1998). If they lived in three generations, it was most often because need forced them to, or that the older generation was supporting the younger.

As families have changed and evolved with respect to meeting people's needs for support, state support also developed, changed, and now shrunk. Major cycles of change in state support for families have occurred through recent times, with sharp reductions occurring at present. As well, gaps in service exist and there is wide variation from society to society.

In a small way, **family allowances** begun in Canada after World War II were to give women compensation as well as recognition for childrearing. The monthly payments, based on the number of children at home, went to all women with children—but only to women, never to men. For many women who worked solely at home, this was their only independent income. Quebec alone now continues with some form of family allowances (LeBourdais & Marcil-Gratton, 1995). The federal program of family allowances was discontinued in 1992, replaced by the Child Tax Benefit program, which targets low- and middle-income families. The Quebec program of baby bonuses is intended both to increase the numbers of births and to provide support for women raising children. The amounts paid in no way compensate for the costs involved in raising a child.

Marriage dissolution is very much in the interests of the state and policy. In fact, at the turn of the twentieth century, divorce in Canada could only be granted by an Act of Parliament. Marriage was considered a crucial part of the social fabric, not to be tampered with by the parties involved.

Nor did marriage failure and divorce, however, begin recently, as some might think. Men deserted their families; some women deserted too; and couples agreed mutually to separate (Gordon & McLanahan, 1991). Some Canadians went to the U.S. to seek divorces when divorce was not as attainable in Canada (Bradbury, 1996: 72–73). In some provinces, such as Quebec, where divorce was almost

Where Will This Country Be?

...Parliamentary divorces [divorces granted only by an act of Parliament] were defended as right and proper. Perhaps most articulate in this general sentiment was E.A. Lancaster, a lawyer and Conservative Member of Parliament for Lincoln, Ontario, 1900–1916. Divorce was a serious issue and had a "bad effect on the country," he claimed.

"Where will this country come to in twenty-five years if we are to grant divorces simply because some woman has been disappointed in regard to her husband, and comes here and asks for dissolution of her marriage because she made a mistake when she married? The whole social fabric of the country would go to pieces."

Source: Snell, James G. 1983. "The White Life for Two...." *Social History* 16: 114, www.tandf.co.uk.

impossible to obtain until well into the mid-twentieth century and was frowned upon strongly, some women slipped into Ontario and declared themselves widows.

Sometimes the women had been victims of spousal abuse or found themselves in intolerable marriages from which there was little escape. Because family was seen as largely women's responsibility in the past, women were more often trapped in difficult marriages. They felt that if they left they would be stigmatized, socially and legally, as the deserters of families. This was, indeed, the case under the law too. Escapes for women included close friendships with other women, charity and community work, sometimes illnesses or frailties that were seen as romantic, and often drugs and alcohol. It is not well known that in nineteenth- and early-twentieth-century Canada, as well as in the United States, middle-class women were the most common drug addicts. Failed marriages and attempts to make new starts are not only a modern-day phenomenon.

The greater access to divorce rates made possible in 1968 led to a fivefold increase in divorce between the late 1960s and the mid-1980s. Immediately following the 1985 Act, divorces again rose sharply, but much of this increase appears to have been accounted for by people who put off divorcing in 1984 and 1985, in anticipation of the revised legislation, and then initiated proceedings once the new law was enacted. By the late 1980s the rate was declining.

These changes did not come to all parts of the English-speaking world at the same time. For example, divorce remained illegal in Ireland until 1995. A referendum on the topic in that year defeated existing laws by a narrow margin. The pressure to liberalize Irish divorce laws contributed to a wide-ranging discussion of **secularization** (a move away from religion as an organizing principle of society) and the nature of social and familial change. People have also been forced to reconsider the relationship between moral and constitutional matters, or church and state. Ireland is not yet a secular society. However, Ireland is more pluralistic and tolerant than it was a decade ago. Individual Catholics, in Ireland as elsewhere, no longer embrace completely all the doctrines of the Church (though it may well be that, in practice, they never did so entirely).

Family violence has had a long recent road to recognition as a social and family problem. We will return to this in much more detail in Chapter 9. Here, we outline in table form the historical milestones along the road to recognition of the problem (see Table 2.2).

One reason policies do not meet the needs of Canadians is that they are often based on outdated assumptions. Canadian sociologist Margrit Eichler (1997) provides three models (patriarchal, individual responsibility, and social responsibility) and three conceptual models of the work–family relationship (separate sphere, spillover effects, and interactive). Thus, her starting point is to recognize the fact that families and work–family relationships vary widely. So must models of the family and state responses to family life.

Pre–World War II legislation perpetuated female dependency on males, signifying the change from a family-based to a socially based patriarchy. After World War II, the state began to promote gender equity with policy and legislation

Table 2.2 MILESTONES ON THE ROAD TO STOPPING FAMILY VIOLENCE

1965   Ontario became the first province to require reporting of child abuse

1970   First Royal Commission report on the Status of Women (no mention of violence)

1970   First women's studies course offered (University of Toronto)

1972   Canada's first shelter for abused women opened in Vancouver

1973   Canadian Advisory Council on Status of Women (CACSW) established

1973   Newfoundland's Neglected Adults Welfare Act became the first North American adult protective legislation

1976   House Standing Committee held hearings and issued a report on child abuse and neglect

1980   National Advisory Council on Aging established

1981   Media reports of laughter in House of Commons over report on prevalence of wife abuse prompted public outcry

1982   National Clearinghouse on Family Violence established

1982   Canada's Solicitor General urged police to lay charges in cases of wife battering when they had reasonable grounds to believe that an assault had taken place

1983   Broad amendments made to Canadian sexual assault legislation including an amendment making sexual assault in marriage a crime

1984   Speech from the Throne included wife battering as a priority concern

1984   The Committee on Sexual Offences Against Children and Youth (Badgley Committee) released report

1986   Health and Welfare Canada created Family Violence Division

1987   CACSW released report, *Battered But Not Beaten: Preventing Wife Battering in Canada*

1989   Eight women killed in Montreal in what became known as the "Montreal Massacre"

1989   First major Canadian survey on the extent and nature of elder abuse

1990   Special Advisor on Child Sexual Abuse to the Minister of National Health and Welfare released report, *Reaching for Solutions*

1993   Canadian Panel on Violence Against Women released report, *Changing the Landscape: Ending Violence, Achieving Equality*

1993   Statistics Canada conducts Violence Against Women Survey

Source: "Stopping Family Violence: Steps Along the Road." 1995. *Transition*, a publication of the Vanier Institute of the Family, September: p. 6. Reprinted with permission.

designed to reduce inequality in the marketplace (Boyd and McDaniel, 1996). However, the "equal opportunity" package, focusing as it does on the rights of individual workers, is inadequate to deal with aging, changing family structure, economic restructuring, and immigration. We cannot hope to make satisfactory progress until we have adopted the right model for change, as has been done in other industrial societies (Burstein, Bricher & Einwohner, 1995).

CHAPTER SUMMARY

Historically, families have been important bases for identity and for resource allocation. In many cultures, broader family structures such as kinship groups and clans have played a large role in determining relationships and social position.

We have seen in this chapter that families are always and have always been changing, in response to changing societies, changing attitudes and expectations of women and men, and changing roles and views of and toward children. We have seen that contact with new cultures, either when they come to you (as in the case of Europeans to North American Aboriginal communities) or when you go to them (as in the case of immigrants) brings change for everyone touched.

We have seen how politics shapes families and family change, and how long-term pain and suffering can be the outcome.

We have also seen how consumerism and state interests and policy shape families and our lives in families.

KEY TERMS

Abortifacients herbs or potions that bring on a miscarriage.

Cohort A group of people who experience some major demographic event, typically birth or migration or marriage, within the same year or period.

Demographic transition The transition to low fertility in the West, which began around 1870, is called the first demographic transition. This brought births into line with a sharply reduced death rate. A second demographic transition, more contemporary, has brought birth rates to a very low level, and it is theorized into line with new lifestyle goals and family practices.

Demographers Those who study population changes such as births, deaths and migrations.

Endogamy Choosing a mate from within one's own group.

Family allowances Started in Canada after World War II as a way to give women compensation as well as

recognition for childrearing; the monthly payments, based on the number of children at home, went to all women with children, not to men.

Gemeinschaft A type of community typical of pre-industrial rural life; that is, one in which everyone knows everyone else and people share common values.

Mechanization of housework The introduction of new home technologies. Home economists worked to elevate the esteem of homemakers by promoting the idea that the new home technologies required skilled operators.

Neolocal residence A pattern in which adults live in nuclear families apart from their own parents.

Polygamy Having more than one mate at a time.

Revenge of the cradle An image reflecting the belief that Quebec's long-standing sense of political injustice might be countered by having more Quebec (French-speaking) citizens.

"Sanitary reformers" In the interest of health, these authorities began to work on bylaws prohibiting the keeping of farm animals in cities.

Secularization A move away from religion as an organizing principle of society.

SUGGESTED READINGS

Baillargeon, Denyse. 1999. *Making Do, Women, Family and Home in Montreal During the Great Depression.* Waterloo, Ontario: Wilfrid Laurier University Press. This is a fascinating story of what women did in families during a major period of economic crisis in Canada.

Bradbury, Bettina (Ed.). 2000. *Canadian Family History: Selected Readings.* Toronto: Irwin. A sampling of original, engaging looks at aspects of families in Canada's past.

Coontz, Stephanie. 1992. *The Way We Never Were: American Families and the Nostalgia Trap.* New York: Basic Books. A myth-shattering book about American family life in the past. Coontz shows, for example, that teenage pregnancy peaked in the 1950s, that marriages in pioneer times lasted less long than in the 1990s, and that families have always faced troubles and sometimes crises.

Dubinsky, Karen. 1999. *The Second Greatest Disappointment: Honeymooning and Tourism at Niagara Falls.* Toronto: Between the Lines. This book explores the concept of the honeymoon as the launching place for modern marriage. It looks at how the growth in honeymoons paralleled the promotion of tourism at Niagara Falls.

Parr, Joy (Ed.). 1990. *Childhood and Family in Canadian History.* Toronto: McClelland & Stewart. An exploration of childhood in Canada from the early days of the fur trade into the twentieth century.

Special issue of the *Journal of Family History* (April 2001); based on the findings from the 1901 Census of Canada explored in The Canadian Families Project, centred at the University of Victoria.

REVIEW QUESTIONS

1. What is the origin of family as a unit?
2. How is it that families worked as groups to protect us?
3. Under what circumstances in the past was there a dispute or debate about women's power?
4. What is the link between the economic interests of the fur trade and the fur traders' intimate associations with Aboriginal women?
5. In whose benefit is childbearing? How has it been political?
6. What is the revenge of the cradle?
7. What is a "country wife"? Why is there no equivalent "city husband"?
8. What is one aspect of family lives changed by war?
9. How does immigration change families?
10. What are some future challenges to states with respect to families, based on what we now know about families in the past?

DISCUSSION QUESTIONS

1. Why is a historical understanding of families essential to explaining and understanding family challenges today?

2. Why has there been so little historical analysis of families?

3. What would the story of the fur traders' intimate associations with Aboriginal women look like from the women's point of view?

4. If the law had permitted divorce in the past, do you think that couples would have divorced to the extent they do today?

5. What has changed compared to the past with respect to family attitudes and practices of dominant social groups in societies such as Canada in relation to minorities?

6. Why is it that women are seen as familial, while men are seen as work-centred?

7. Why have families that are different been such a touchstone of heated debate over time?

8. Why do Canada and Quebec have different family laws and policies? If they had the same laws and policies, do you think that families would be more similar in Quebec and outside Quebec?

9. Why is fertility and sexuality control such a never-ending societal debate?

10. Has the concept of family changed related to economics and consumerism? How and why?

ACTIVITIES

1. Take a look through some old family photo albums. Imagine the feelings and views your mother, father, or grandmother, grandfather might have had about families when they were your age. How do you think their feelings and views would be different from yours?

2. Spend some time talking with older relatives or older people about their family lives. How does their experience connect with yours today? What's different? What's similar? Do any of their experiences surprise you?

3. Imagine writing a short description of family life today as if you were looking back on today in 2023? What do you think you might see about families today that we miss when we are busy living?

4. Imagine what early contact between explorers and fur traders in Canada looked like from the point of view of Aboriginals. How do you imagine that they might have seen the family lives of these foreigners?

WEBLINKS

www.afn.ca

The Assembly of First Nations Web site has resource material on residential schools, legal claims related to residential schools, and a wealth of information on Aboriginal peoples. It also has many links to other Web sites related to Aboriginal history.

www.globalgazette.net

The Global Gazette, Canada's Family History Magazine
The Global Gazette contains helpful "how-to" articles for everyone from the beginning family history researcher to experienced genealogists and historians.

www.members.shaw.ca/rempel

This Web site concerns itself with Mennonite family history/genealogy—especially those families that spent a period of time in Tsarist Russia.

web.uvic.ca/hrd/cfp

The Canadian Families Project is an interdisciplinary research project based at the University of Victoria. The project team is studying families in Canada historically, and has completed a national sample of the 1901 Census of Canada, which is now available to anyone who wishes to do analyses of it. Many publications have come out of this project, which reveals what family life was like at the turn of the twentieth century in Canada.

CHAPTER THREE

How Families Begin:

Dating and Mating

Sooner or later, most people end up in a serious, intimate relationship. About 90 percent of Canadians will marry at least once. Research suggests that the key to a happy relationship or marriage is not—we repeat, *not*—a matter of finding the perfect mate; we discuss this issue at length in Chapter 4. No method of selecting a life partner, however sound, will guarantee the survival or the happiness of your relationship. This is because, throughout your lives, you and your mate will continue to change, and so will the world around you. But some choices may produce more relationship satisfaction than other choices and some choices are riskier than others. It is worthwhile to examine what social science knows about mate selection and about the results of better and worse choices.

We will soon argue that the very idea of "mate selection" is misguided, in the same way that "job selection" inaccurately describes how people find work. But for the time being, we'll use the metaphor of mate selection, since most people think of finding a mate as a selection process. Theoretically, people bring their attributes and skills to the "mating game" and offer them in hopes of an exchange. Failure to make a fair or balanced exchange causes disappointment and resentment. In any relationship, the partner with the greater "resources" has more to offer and, therefore, more power (Blood & Wolfe, 1960; Scanzoni, 1972; 2000). For this reason, we should expect to find that people mate with others of similar social "value," since both stand to gain equally from the relationship. That may explain why most mating takes place between people of approximately equal physical attractiveness (Hatfield & Sprecher, 1986). When mates are not equally attractive, the less attractive person usually brings other valued attributes—wealth, power, or social position—to the relationship.

This somewhat cold-blooded process is surrounded by romantic notions of discovery: finding oneself, finding one's soulmate, finding one's destiny, and so on, and all of this is based, in turn, on the idea of **romantic love**. Most Canadians believe that love is the foundation on which families are built. And, in order to find love, we must search out "the one" who is right for us. In theory, that's why we date. But before we look more closely at dating and mating, let's look at how the idea of love has developed.

Love and Sociology

Curiously, love and sociology are linked almost as closely as love and marriage are thought to be. Émile Durkheim, one of the founding fathers of sociology, discovered in the earliest sociological research that close social ties make a difference to survival (married people are less likely to commit suicide, for example), and that ceremonies and symbols (such as weddings, and wedding rings, for example) tend to bring communities together for common purposes (Durkheim, 1915/1957). We will talk more about the importance of symbols and rituals in the following chapters when we focus on the effects of close relations on well-being, both individual and social.

Durkheim saw the marriage partners and their dependent children as a freeing family form that evolved as the **extended family** retreated in importance (Sydie, 1987: 17). Along with the reduction in family members, according to Durkheim, was an intensification of ties between marital partners, as well as between parents and their children. It is in the attachment of husbands and wives that the basis of societal solidarity is found, argues Durkheim. This view was echoed in the slogan chosen for the International Year of the Family—"The family is the heart of society."**Attachment** is characterized by common sentiments and shared memories, as well as shared purpose in work and life.

Max Weber, another founding father of sociology, reveals the centrality of marriage in his exploration of feudalism (Sydie, 1986: 73–77). The chivalry of knighthood required personal bonds and unity among knights. Women of feudal nobility were often the managers of estates and huge feudal households in partnerships with their husbands. Marriages were the means to cement clans or family groups, so that in some instances, men marrying women who owned fiefdoms took the woman's name on marriage.

Friedrich Engels, who along with Karl Marx is also a father of sociology, outlined a theory of marriage (Sydie, 1986: 96). With the availability of additional resources, Engels argues, women and men became **monogamous** (married to only one partner for life). The link between economic production and marriage is that men would be able to pass their wealth to their offspring with some certainty about their role in fatherhood. Women's faithfulness in marriage then becomes part and parcel of an economic system. Here, argues Engels, is found the origin of modern marriage. Here is also found one basis of inequality between men and women in marriage, and one way in which marriage gives men power over their wives.

Love and sociology go together in another sense too. It was often in courses in sociology of marriage and the family that men and women sought their future spouses, or at least did some scouting around for possibilities. Even if they did not succeed in this quest, students learned how to propose, how to date, and what weddings were all about; so the sociology of family was, in those days, truly an applied science. It may still be.

Love: A Recent Invention?

There is nothing natural about the connection of love and marriage, although many people today think that they have always gone together. In fact, traditionally, most people in the world have thought that the purpose of marriage was to benefit the family group, not the individual spouses. For this reason, marriages were arranged that were mutually advantageous to their families. Historically, this has mattered more than whether the couple loved each other romantically in the way that we think of love today. But, as we shall see, neither marriage for love nor

A Girl Like Diana

Not selected by the Royal Family, as is widely believed, Diana was coldly thrust forward by her own family, when efforts to interest Charles in her older sisters failed...Earl Spencer...was not averse to the chance for the Spencers to condescend to the House of Windsors....

Everyone involved knew that Diana was no match for the moody, sensitive Charles. But the Spencers pressed on with their dynastic designs, just as the Howards placed not one, but three, Howard girls in the King's bed (Henry VIII).

Source: Miles, Rosalind. 1997. "A Girl Like Diana," *Saturday Night*, November 18 (abridged).

marriage by arrangement is necessarily certain to produce happiness and a durable marriage.

The idea of romantic love is a social construction, the product of a particular culture in a particular historical period, although some argue that it has a biological basis (Fisher, 1992). It is not that love itself is a new concept; ancient myths and age-old stories have love at their core. For example, Krishna, one of the popular gods of Hinduism, is often shown as a flute-playing suitor of a maiden (Coltrane, 1998: 36). In Krishna, erotic and romantic love are combined with the quest for salvation. Ancient legends of Japan also have themes of love. Greek philosophers wrote about love. In all these instances, love is the focus. However, it is not the kind of love that we today think of as linked with marriage, or the basis on which most Canadian families are formed today.

Morton (1992) tells of how the idea of love as a basis for marriage grew out of questioning the traditional social and economic grounds for marriage. As feudalism ended and the market economy began to grow around the fifteenth century, Western European households began to shrink. The number of family-only households increased rapidly, and the traditional bases of marriage came into question. Ultimately, marriage as it was then known was transformed. Love came to be the basis on which families began. Divisions of labour emerged between the marriage partners, including different standards for sexual behaviours and for sharing and passing along family resources. Power differentials sharpened between men and women on the domestic front, as they were no longer equal partners in work.

The emergence of the concept of romantic love greatly changed social roles, especially for women. Women had to transform themselves from workers into love objects. In this role, adornment and looks mattered more than their actual contributions to the family's overall well-being. Women went from being partners in work to being weaker, passive, decorations (Abu-Laban & McDaniel, 2001). The differences between men and women became more exaggerated, as social and economic power in society and in marriage shifted more to men—a process that reached its peak with industrialization in the nineteenth and twentieth centuries.

Courtly love, the likely origin of romantic love as we know it today, emerged in Europe in the Middle Ages. Many images of romantic love in the late twentieth century still retain aspects of this period. Think of finding one's "knight in shining armour" or serenading one's love. Knights sometimes wore a token from their ladies, such as a scarf or handkerchief, as they entered into battle. No wonder that on Valentine's day each year one sees images of romantic love, many of them medieval in origin. Even in the weddings of today, most brides still look like fairy princesses and are still "given away" to their husbands.

Courtly love affairs were not simple, as the story of Romeo and Juliet illustrates. With the emergence of courtly love the woman, as the object of male affections, was placed on a pedestal. She was to be won, though she remained, in a fundamental sense, unattainable. These ideas, too, exist in our modern thinking about love and sex. Along with them goes the well-entrenched idea of a **sexual double standard,** which places a high value on women's limited sexual experience before marriage and their fidelity afterward. Men's sexual experience prior to marriage and fidelity afterward was seen as less important. However, both men and women seem to strongly discourage any previous same-sex experiences, and this sharply decreases both male and female desirability in marriage, regardless of the number of partners (Schwartz & Rutter, 1998). Attitudes towards female chastity are not limited to North American men and women. For example, in Sunni and Shiite Muslim American families, the need for Muslim women to maintain modest in their interactions is also highly valued (Carolan, 1999).

At least three important elements figure in our contemporary notions about love, and all have historical antecedents. First, romantic love is a leisurely activity possible only in societies that have leisure time. Second, romantic love is a private activity. It assumes that people have access to free time and private spaces, which implies a reduction in the overall influence of the extended family. Third, romantic love is a youthful activity that has become more important as the period of youthful dependency and "adolescence" has lengthened.

Expressive Exchange as the Basis for Romance

Whether we are examining heterosexual or same-sex couples, a central feature of couple relationships in Canada is commitment to the ideals of romantic love. In our society the arrangements—geographic and economic—of marriage are framed through the ideological rhetoric of romance. Though practical concerns always play some part, more in some relationships than in others, most people who get married do so because they believe they love their partner. And often, people feel they have discovered the best—even perfect—mate.

The ideal of romantic love plays a small role, if any, in selecting a marriage partner in many parts of the world. Instead, marriage is usually seen as a practical arrangement, in which love is beside the point or a matter of luck. What is relevant is whether the likely husband will be a good provider, whether the likely wife will be a good homemaker and mother, and whether the union will supply the family and kin group with sons.

However, in our culture, people generally expect—and are expected—to marry for love. Canadian marriages are ideally founded on expressive exchange, not instrumental exchange. The term "exchange" refers to a process of ongoing interaction between spouses. The exchange perspective sees marriage as a give-and-take process, in which each spouse both gives and gets. The stability and well-being of a relationship is thought to depend on how well a balance is struck and sustained in this exchange between spouses.

Expressive exchanges in marriage are exchanges of emotional services between spouses. They include hugs and kisses, sexual pleasure, friendship, a shoulder to lean on, empathy, and understanding. Expressive exchanges affirm the affection and love each spouse has for the other. By contrast, **instrumental exchanges** are non-emotional. They maintain a household in practical ways and include such services as sharing the housework, paying the bills, and looking after the children.

In our society, people are urged to marry someone they love, not just people who would help them in practical ways. Yet no matter how much two people may love each other, married life always involves practical matters and economic concerns. This is the central dilemma of modern married life. Romantic love may be central to our ideal of married life, but in the last three decades, most families have needed two incomes to support a middle-class lifestyle that one income would have supported in the past. Economic and cultural influences have led many people to delay marriage, forgo intimacy, or cohabit instead of marrying. The conditions of modern marriage are often not very romantic or love-enhancing.

Despite the interests of the early sociologists, remarkably little research exists on love in marriage and families. One Australian study tries to define the love that supports marriage and families (Noller, 1996). Love is found to be socially constructed and shaped by cultural beliefs. Love has a behavioural, an emotional, and a cognitive component; it can exist in a mature or an immature form.

Mature emotional love involves passion and companionship that can begin with young people and extend throughout life. *Immature* emotional love is exemplified by love addiction and infatuation, which are not, according to Noller (1996), the best bases on which to build strong marriages and families. Mature love, she finds, is best conceptualized as creating an environment in which both the lovers and those who depend on them can grow and develop. Part of the key to creating such an environment is peer marriage, finds Schwartz and Rutter (1998: 157–159), where partners feel free to explore and be themselves. This is consistent with falling in love with someone who is part of your community and of whom both families approve, so that love will be nurtured by others who love you as well as the lover.

So, the modern family still has both instrumental and expressive functions, but in our ideal culture the family is mainly expressive, directed to fulfilling emotional and psychological needs. In large part, it is this idealization of the marriage and family, and the conflict between ideal and real family lives, that leads to high rates of frustration, divorce, and sometimes violence.

Meeting and Mating

With love as a goal—for better or worse—Canadians of all ages look for intimate partners. Meeting a potential mate is not what it used to be. Yet some older traditions remain, and some new traditions emerge as the older ones are updated. When Ann Landers ran, in 1997, a series of letters on "How We Met," some readers expressed frustration and boredom with the old-fashioned stories of how couples met. The implication is that none of that sort of thing happens anymore, which may or may not be true.

The range of ways to meet one's life partner has certainly widened in recent years. Many meet in the usual places of shared activities—schools and universities, workplaces, religious places, neighbourhoods, sporting groups, or events. Others meet through common friends or relatives. Still others are put together by relatives or traditional marriage brokers in arranged marriages or semi-arranged marriages.

Arranged Marriages and Love Matches

A society that practises "arranged marriage" puts parents or kin in the control of making matches between people. In most societies for most of history, marriages have been arranged in this sense, not based on love but on the needs, beliefs, or desires of the couple's relatives. In Western Canada, there were a large number of arranged marriages in the 1860–1945 period (Millar, 1999), when partners were

---

The Way We Met

On a late January evening in 1941, I arrived home to find a strange guy sitting, fully dressed, in my bathtub. His company had sent him the wrong day to tile our bathroom and my roommate had let him in. I had a bridge party scheduled for that night and he knew I would be angry at the clutter in the bathroom, but he stuck around anyway. He had made quite a mess, and I was furious.

Then days later, he called me. He apologized profusely for his behaviour and asked me for a date. I reluctantly accepted his apology and agreed to have dinner with him the following evening. After six months of a romantic courtship, he paid a preacher $15 to marry us in the funeral parlour chapel.

Our romantic date lasted 50 years, including four years separation during the war. We had one son and four grandchildren. He is gone now, but our life was never dull. He kept me entertained for a lifetime.

Source: "Ann Landers Advice," *The Edmonton Journal*, October 18, 1997: G7 (abridged). Permission granted by Creators Syndicate. By permission of Esther P. Lederer Trust and Creators Syndicate, Inc.

scarce. And today in Canada, there are arranged marriages among some ethnic groups. Some of you may know or be from families where arranged marriages are preferred. Arranged marriages, however, are most common in societies where we find close extended families.

In cultures that have arranged marriages, rights to land are typically passed from one generation to the next (usually, from father to son). Since marriage is an arrangement between families, it makes sense to arrange marriages in a way that protects family assets such as land, grazing rights, or animals. Parents also want to minimize potential conflict between the families that will be joined by the marriage. For these reasons, the choice of marriage partners is considered far too important to be left to the whims of youth. Spouses are chosen because the union is economically advantageous or because of friendship or kinship obligations. Sometimes people marry people they have never met.

In the West today, few marriages are "arranged" in the traditional sense. In multicultural Canada, arranged marriages do occur among young people. An article in the University of Toronto's student newspaper *The Varsity* (January 25 1993, 7), reported that

> Most second generation Canadian-Pakistanis grew up expecting and accepting the concept of an arranged marriage—an arranged marriage was inevitable and the social norm. And yet the definition of an arranged marriage today differs from the definition of one 20 years ago...In Toronto today, most individuals actively participate in selecting their partners. The couple meets first with their families. If they are interested in each other, they can speak to each other on the phone and go out with or without a chaperone, depending on the values of the families... It's not an individual decision but a collective [one], involving six family members at least.

Arranged Marriage Goes Modern

When the time comes to marry, it will happen something like this: Boy meets girl. Boy likes girl. Boy tells his mother; Mother calls the girl's mother: The two families arrange to meet. The courtship begins. Both parties can back out if the courtship goes badly.

"This is the modern way, actually,"...Hamed Madani, a professor of political science at Tarrant Junior College Southeast Campus. "The traditional way, the boys and girls know nothing about it." Mitra Madani [Hamed's daughter] said she is entrusting her marriage to fate and to her parents with whom she has a close relationship.

"Even for me, it is confusing. The ideal situation would be: I'll get my degree [in Computing Science at the University of Texas], I'll have a lot of people asking for me and I'll get to pick."

Source: Brady, Matthew. 1998. "Finding a Mate in Texas Often a Matter of Faith," *The Edmonton Journal*, February 8: A2. Reprinted with the express permission of Edmonton Journal Company, a CanWest Partnership.

We don't know how common this practice is in North America. In Canada in the early 2000s, however, with the changing ethnic population of Canada, arranged marriages remain popular among several ethnic communities, for example some South Asians and some Orthodox Jews (see Howell [with Albanese & Obosu-Mensah], 2001; Weinfeld, 2001). As an indicator of increasing diversity, the 2001 Census of Canada (Statistics Canada, 2002), finds over 100 different languages spoken in Canada, with Chinese as the third most commonly spoken language in Canada after English and French.

Arranged marriages are very much present in industrial cultures, such as Canada. A 1995 study of urban Japanese young people (Applbaum, 1995) finds that 25 to 30 percent of all marriages are arranged. The couple typically meet through a "go between" or matchmaker who later will arrange a meeting of the couple's families, if things go well.

A popular media account by a woman from Calcutta who as the twenty-first century opened agreed to an arranged marriage is insightful (Pal, 1999). She sees her agreement to an arranged marriage as part of preserving her cultural heritage. But then she adds, practically, that marrying an Indian is also simpler, "Marrying an Indian means a lot less explaining. Why don't my parents call each other by their first names? Why do they eat with their hands? What is that red dot in my mother's forehead?" (Pal, 1999: 12).

Students often consider, in family courses or among themselves when a friend is experiencing an arranged marriage, what the differences are between so-called love matches and arranged marriages. We debate the matter here in a debate box.

Personal Ads and Internet Dating

Personal ads have grown both in popularity and acceptability in the latter part of the twentieth century. What used to be called "lonely hearts ads" for the truly desperate are now mainstream, appearing in respectable newspapers and used by respectable people. One U.S. study (Merskin & Huberlie, 1996) discovered that mate finding is becoming more a matter of mediated information rather than traditional selection. More people than ever are turning to the want ads or to Internet dating services to meet that someone special.

In personal ads, it has been found that men tend to emphasize looks and physical attributes (weight, height, ethnicity, even eye and hair colour) more than women do. For example, terms such as "attractive," "slender," "petite," or "sexy" are used much more often by men in their ads to describe the person they seek (Coltrane, 1998: 47; Smith, Waldorf, & Tremblath, 1990). For women, common keywords include "secure," "professional," "successful," or "affluent" along with terms to describe physical features and age in the man of their dreams.

Of course, this does not mean that mate selection is any more random than it ever was, only that the pools of potential mates within the socially preferred categories have been enlarged by reducing the factor of distance, via Internet and advertising. Maybe this is yet another dimension of globalization!

Debate Box 3.1   **ARRANGED MARRIAGE VERSUS LOVE MARRIAGE**
Which side of the debate do you fall on?

I am AGAINST arranged marriage

- In an arranged marriage, the decision about who you are going to spend the rest of your life with is made by your family. Brides and grooms to-be have no choice in the matter. It is a form of social coercion.
- The particular marriage mate your parent chooses is about finding someone from the same social class, ethnic and religious background. It is not about choosing the best love match.
- Arranged marriage views women negatively and is harmful. There is a long history of "child brides" and the tradition of dowry is a way of paying off another family to take your daughter off your hands.
- Arranged unions are not based on love, which is the cornerstone of marriage.
- You need to know that you love someone before you get married. You can't love someone you hardly know or don't know at all. How can the marriage survive?
- Marriage is between two people who love each other. Their family and the larger community have no business in the affairs of the couple.

I am FOR arranged marriage

- Parents care about their children more than anyone else does. They are going to choose the best person possible.
- Even if the final decision rests with the family, many brides and grooms to-be are allowed input into the arrangement.
- In love marriages, most people choose a mate from their own socioeconomic class and ethnic background. In this way, a love marriage is no different from arranged marriages in their homogeneous tendencies.
- Law now prohibits both child marriage and the exchange of dowry.
- Love is an important part of arranged marriage, it is just viewed differently. It is said to come after the marriage; love is something that grows over time.
- Arranged marriages have lower rates of dissolution than love marriages (although cultural sanctions against divorce are also a factor). Just like love marriages, there are both successes and failures.
- Marriage is not just individuals. The purpose of marriage is to build alliances between families and with the larger community. People need to rely on each other. Arranged marriage keeps entire families strong and connected.

A study of personal ads in a Canadian newspaper between 1975 and 1988 found a sixfold increase in the number of ads placed (Sev'er, 1990). The ratio of males to females placing ads was about 4 to 1. A stunning finding is that although the means used in the mate market has changed, the gender expectations of meeting and mating have not. Women still present themselves in terms of physical attractiveness, and men still seek women with specified physical attributes. It may be that in this method of mate-seeking, gender stereotypes matter more than in more conventional mate markets. Or, it could be that people placing personal ads are particularly "consumer"-oriented: they want a good "product."

Sev'er (1990, 76) concludes "Even in this unconventional market, the rules of the mating game have remained extremely traditional. Women (especially older

Pretty Woman, Pretty Dog

PRETTY WOMAN, 53, WILL EXCHANGE SEXUAL favors and affection for routine dog walking. Large poodle likes Maine, Mozart, and mysteries. Owner/food source like same, plus hiking, biking, and kayaking. Both are blond.

Source: Personals. 2001. *New York Review of Books* XLVIII(4), March 8.

women) are at a disadvantage, both as choosers and as potential chosen. The personal ads market seems to be a traditional market in disguise, a new bottle for the same old wine."

Social Aspects of Finding a Mate

Exposure to potential mates is a first step in the meeting and mating process as practised by most people in Canada today. This process, far from being random, is structured or arranged by our social characteristics. There is a range of possibilities extending from the more constrained choices of arranged marriage systems to the more open, but still constrained, process of falling in love with someone you meet at school, in your neighbourhood, or at your church, temple, or mosque.

The term "marriage market" may seem too rational or cold-blooded a description of a process we tend to view as largely emotional. And yet, there is much that is market-like about finding a mate. For example, we can think about mating in terms of exchanges. Each potential partner brings to the potential relationship something that is of value to the other: personality, skills, physical attractiveness, earnings potential, and so on.

Whether participants admit it or not, rating and ranking is part of the mate market. Meeting, mating, and marrying involve a giant sorting process whereby our "market values" are matched with the market values of others. It can be a cold calculation, as when, for example, a man seeks a wife who will "look good on

For Sale

(Under a photo of a smiling youngish man in a tuxedo)

50-year old classic. Well-worn, high mileage, rusty, leaks from bottom, poor exhaust with bad emissions, soft seats, no options, dull, guzzler. Needs lift kit, muffler, and TLC. Comes with a spare tire. Not exactly as illustrated. VERY CHEAP. Call G.H. anytime after February 14th.

Source: Announcements. 2002. *The Edmonton Journal*, February 17. Reprinted with permission of the Edmonton Journal.

his arm." We even have a name for such wives, although interestingly not for the men who seek them. "Trophy wives" are typically sought by men climbing the rungs of success in business or politics. These wives are visible at country clubs and in some elite social circles, beautiful as well as being well-groomed, well-coiffed, and well-dressed. Sometimes their husbands match them well in terms of appearance and style, but sometimes they do not. The husband's allure is his earning power, not good looks. We can all bring to mind numerous examples of these kinds of couples.

More often, the rating and ranking is less calculated. Watch people at a singles bar or a campus event. Both men and women eye those they wish they might have. But in the end they woo people more like themselves. Each of us constantly compares our self-perceived market value, sometimes based on testing the "mate market" in high school, in university or college, or in the work world, with what we think we can achieve in the marketplace of love. Confidence in one's ability to "strike a deal" often determines how far one can reach. Popular movies notwithstanding, princesses and billionaires seldom wed worthy but plain commoners or street prostitutes.

As we noted earlier, a central part of the mate market is the politics of attractiveness. Good looks make a difference, for men and women, heterosexuals and gays, in getting attention in the mate market. For women, attractiveness is a life's project (Abu-Laban and McDaniel, 2001). Immense amounts of time, effort, and money go into the construction of female attractiveness. Women pluck, wax, and shave unwanted hair, carefully groom the wanted hair, shape and flatten unwanted bulges, and enhance wanted ones. All this is packaged in the latest fashions after being "worked out" into the shape of the day, sometimes called "body sculpting." Impression management also matters in the attractiveness project; it must appear as if "the look" is achieved effortlessly.

Even aspects of the dating script contribute to the decorative potential of women. Often, gifts from the adoring man are decorative to the woman. Certainly, engagement rings have this decorative purpose. The well-entrenched concept is that the ring should cost X percent of the man's earnings, the latest being about two months' salary. The woman then wears the ring as a symbol with dual meanings: that she is desirable on the mate market, and that her intended makes sufficient money (or comes from sufficient family money) that she can be decorated well. This suggests that she will be "kept well" during their married life and announces to all who see her ring that she has made a "good catch." Among younger people, token gifts are often adornments as well. They include anything from scarves to hats, to shirts, to friendship or "pre-engagement" rings, to lockets, bracelets, or temporary tattoos.

In the mate market, flirting matters. However, the flirting script, like the dating market, has been considerably updated. Sexually aggressive women are still considered off-putting to most men (Coltrane, 1998: 33). Yet, flirting—by women as well as by men—is still an important part of the meeting and mating scenario.

Women are expected to flirt with a blend of innocence and interest; the mix must be exact so as not to convey unintended messages. Flirting prior to the 1990s was heavy on the innocence, light on the sexual innuendo. Now, the content is reversed, with women expected to be sexual in flirting, though not too aggressive (Coltrane, 1998: 34).

With greater equality between men and women in the present, perhaps the image of the woman waiting for the man to ask her out is outdated. Yet women were never entirely passive in this process, mastering many ways to convey interest in particular men. Among the most popular was to "put out the word" that you were interested. Some women, of course, still wait for men to take dating initiatives. The patterns of dating are different, however, in the 2000s; groups of young people of both sexes often go out together. The cues of who likes whom are hard to read for any but the initiated. It is the special look, the holding of the door only for you, the talking to you more than the others that must be read like tea leaves for signs of interest beyond friendship.

At times, the reading of the signs is so complex that both women and men ask others, sometimes even strangers, to help them interpret what meanings lurk in behaviours. One teenaged girl who worked in the local grocery store asked the advice of one of the authors in interpreting the behaviour of a young man she "really, really liked." Did his holding the door especially for her but not for the other girls in the group mean that he actually "liked" her?

The question of whether wooing is more equal remains. In some ways it is, since both sexes take initiatives in singling out the person they particularly like. However, a gender imbalance remains. Several studies of first-date initiation find that men tend to evaluate woman-initiated first dates in more sexual ways than do women (Mongeau & Carey, 1996). Those women who initiate dates are seen by a group of impartial observers as being more sociable, more liberal, but less physically attractive than the person being asked. Despite a welcome tendency toward more equality in dating initiatives, it could still be that women who initiate dates are viewed differently than men, who are expected to initiate dates.

Dating Scripts and the Double Standard

A traditional sexual double standard was the premise for dating rituals (or "scripts") that existed in North America from about the 1920s through the 1950s and most of the 1960s (despite popular images of that decade as the era of "free love"). **Sexual scripts** saw boys as initiators, calling girls for dates and often paying for the date. Though less widely accepted today, this double standard persists in many cultures around the world, and in Canada among immigrant families that come from these cultures. The same scripts expected girls to be chaste and virginal until marriage. This game was a difficult one for women. Schwartz and Rutter (1998: 79) note that girls were cast as "good" if they were chaste, and "bad" ("loose," "easy," and worse) if they followed masculine rules of sexuality.

Laumann et al. (1994), relying on data from the United States' National Health and Social Life Survey, find that the sexual double standard is shifting dramatically. They focus on people on their eighteenth birthday: in particular, what proportion have not had sexual intercourse as yet, and what proportion have had five or more partners. Comparing results over four decades, the 1950s through the 1990s, not surprisingly they find fewer 18-year-old virgins today than in the 1950s. However, the big change occurs in the proportion that has had five or more sexual partners by age 18. Almost four times as many women in the 1990s fall into this category than did in the 1950s. In contrast, the proportion of young men who had more than five sexual partners by age 18 has not changed much.

For both boys and girls, a dramatic shift has occurred in the age at which sexual activity begins. Brumberg (1998) notes that the average age for first intercourse for girls in the United States is now 16 years old. Today's girls, notes Brumberg, are sexually active before the age at which their great-great-grandmothers had even begun to menstruate.

This is not surprising when we think that in our grandmothers' time, the standard—although not always the reality—was abstinence until marriage. Now, the "love standard" (Hobart, 1996) usually prevails: sexual relations are fine as long as the couple love each other. Some cultures are even more supportive of unmarried sex. For francophone young men in Canada, for example, Hobart (1996, 149) found that the "fun standard" takes priority over the love standard.

Many discrepancies exist between what people do privately and what they say they do. Nowhere is this truer than with sexuality, whether premarital, extramarital, or marital. People underestimate, overestimate, and misrepresent their own sexual activity. It is challenging for family sociologists to sort out what is really occurring from what people say is occurring. From multiple studies

Abstinence, Inc.

Virginity has become a marketable commodity in the United States with hundreds of thousands of students being sold each year on the benefits of saving themselves for marriage

Abstinence education is the only government-approved sexual schooling children in the United States receive. Abstinence-only programs have increased during the past five years because of the 1996 Welfare Reform Act, which committed half a billion dollars to them and prohibited discussion of the benefits of birth control.

Earlier this year, the President [George W. Bush] renewed the federal sex education program and bolstered spending for it...It has created a need for..."the abstinence entrepreneurs." Companies... have made abstinence a marketable commodity that kids seem to want. They like talking about their desire to remain virgins. They make virginity pledges. They think it's cool.

Source: Richer, Shawna. 2002. "Abstinence, Inc.," *The Globe and Mail*, June 8, F7. Reprinted with permission from The Globe and Mail.

Table 3.1 RELATIONSHIP ATTITUDES AND EXPECTATIONS AMONG CANADIAN TEENS, AGE 15–19, 2000

	%
Approve of sex before marriage if couple is in love	82
Have been involved sexually	60
Approve of living together without being married	86
Approve of unmarried couple having children	63
Expect to marry	88
Expect to have children	92
Expect to stay with partner for life	88

Source: Bibby, Reginald W. 2001. "Canadian Teens: A National Reading on Family Life." *Transition Magazine* (The Vanier Institute of the Family). Autumn 31(3).

The Mojo Competitors

...[Y]es *Maclean's* really does want to know about your sex life. First of all, it should be pointed out that many of you are what is politely known as "unreliable narrators." Keeping that...in mind, 42 per cent say they first had sexual intercourse between the ages of 16 and 19 (though people in Saskatchewan and Manitoba seem to have had more control over their hormones, generally holding out longer). Seventy-four per cent say they were single when they lost their virginity.

The real shocker, however, comes in the crucial category of frequency. Throughout the history of our year-end poll, Newfoundlanders, perhaps attesting to the aphrodisiac qualities of Lamb's Palm Breeze rum and Diet Pepsi, have reported themselves to be the most active lovers in Confederation. But in a stunning reversal, it is now Quebecers who are Masters of the Mattresses, with a total 76 per cent of respondents in that province claiming they have an active sex life (well ahead of Newfoundland's 66 per cent).

Josey Vogels, a Montrealer who writes the sex advice column *My Messy Bedroom* and hosts a television show of the same name, says she isn't surprised that Quebecers have risen to the challenge. "I definitely think there is more of a sexual vibe in Montreal than, say, Toronto," she says. "There is a pride in having a sort of European attitude about the body and life in general. People here work to live, not live to work."

For their part, Newfoundlanders and Labradorians are professing shock and amazement at their collective loss of mojo. "Frequency isn't the issue, it's the quality of the experience," Seamus O'Regan, host of CTV's *Canada AM* and a St. John's homeboy, says defensively. But true to the can-do spirit that characterizes the Rock, there is already talk of mounting a comeback. "We'll embrace the project and regain our rightful crown," says O'Regan. "And I, for one, am ready to go back and do my part."

Source: Gatehouse, Jonathan. 2002. "Why So Cranky? The Year-End Poll," *Maclean's*, December 30, p. 28, abridged. Reprinted by permission from *Maclean's* Magazine.

(Hobart, 1996: 150 summarizes the Canadian studies), it is known, however, that the majority of unmarried youth today report having had sexual experiences and the vast majority do not think premarital sex is wrong.

A counter to sexual intimacy in uncommitted relationships has been the threat of AIDS and venereal diseases in the latter part of this century. The threat has been controversial and misinformation abounds; many young people mistakenly believe that heterosexuals are not vulnerable to AIDS. Nonetheless, the lethal threat of AIDS has affected the enthusiasm of some young people for sexual intimacy, at least unprotected sexual intimacy. In some quarters, celibacy outside marriage, even including pledges of virginity, has become a popular option.

Table 3.2   PERCENTAGE SAYING THEY FIRST HAD SEX BEFORE THE AGE OF 20

Most likely

Quebecers	65
Men	63

Least likely

Saskatchewanians and Manitobans	45
Ontarians and women	51

Saying they were married at the time

Most likely

Quebecers and men	82

Least likely

Saskatchewanians and Manitobans	65
Women	66

Describing themselves as sexually active

Most likely

Quebecers	76
Men	71
Newfoundlanders	66

Least likely

Women	53
Ontarians	54
British Columbians, Saskatchewanians, and Manitobans	58

Source: Gatehouse, Jonathan. 2002. "Why So Cranky?" *Maclean's*, December 30, p. 28. (vol. 115, no. 52). Reprinted by permission from *Maclean's* Magazine.

Sexuality is still seen differently for women than for men. Some of these differences are apparent in approaches to contraception. For example, a women-centred approach to family planning services and research is slowly being replaced by one that encourages male responsibility and participation. Russell-Brown (2000) determined that, given the strong influence of the husband's beliefs on the couple's sexual activity, male knowledge of contraceptive use might be more effective (Russell-Brown, 2000). Female participation is still necessary, however. A 2000 study investigating women's status and negotiation of sex in Uganda found that women's ability to negotiate the timing and conditions of sex with their partners is central to their ability to control a variety of reproductive health outcomes. Though men generally have more influence over the timing and frequency of sex, women can and do refuse sex under a variety of circumstances—such as city dwellers and more educated women (Wolff, Blanc, & Gage, 2000).

The age of a young person's first sexual experience depends on cultural as well as social factors. Belgrave et al. (2000) determined that for African American girls aged 10 to 13, girls with higher school interest, family cohesion, religiosity, and behavioural self-esteem would engage in less risky sexual attitudes. In addition, ethnic identity and gender role orientations contributed to explaining differences in sexual behaviour. Higher levels of ethnic identity were associated with less risky sexual attitudes (Belgrave, Van Oss Marin, & Chambers, 2000). Similar findings were found in Espiritu (2001) with Filipino-American girls. Anglo Americans were generally delineated as morally inferior to Filipino Americans and immigrants. Filipino wives and daughters were represented as models of morality compared to Anglo-American girls. Espiritu concluded that immigrant communities constrain women's lives in order to combat racial discrimination, but these restraints have also created generational conflict (Espiritu, 2001).

Age of sexuality also seems to depend on the influence of the family on the child. Family structural variables such as family income, parental education, and maternal marital status do not determine age of sexuality as much as process variables like maternal monitoring, mother–adolescent general communication, mother–adolescent sexual communication, and maternal attitudes about adolescent sexual behaviour in black and Hispanic families (Miller, Forehand, & Kotchick, 1999). Fingerson (2000) also discovered that parents do affect their teens' sexual behaviour, but in terms of the teens' perceptions of parents' beliefs about sexual behaviour, not parents' own reported beliefs. In addition, having a good relationship and communication with their mothers is associated with both greater probability of teens not having sex and also having lower overall numbers of partners if they choose to have sex, controlling for mothers' sexual permissiveness (Fingerson, 2000).

The concept of exchange in sexual interactions seems to mean that women are expected to provide sexual favours in exchange for dinner, movies, etc. In the 1990s, the old sexual double-standard takes a new form: some men perceive that women who dress in styles they consider provocative—tight, short dresses, skin-tight jeans, halter tops, even dangling earrings—are "asking for it." The young women themselves, in contrast, typically do not see their fashion statements as anything but trendy. Communication between men and women remains as imprecise and inadequate as ever. In inadequate communication about sexual expectations can lie the seeds of sexual and dating violence, as we will discuss later.

Dating in a Multicultural Society

As Canada and other countries around the world become increasingly diverse, one must acknowledge the different meeting and mating habits of the different cultures within a country. What is considered an acceptable dating practice can differ greatly for a Canadian youth and one from another country. Also, who is considered an acceptable spouse can be very different.

While every culture has its own ideas regarding acceptable mating practices, many cultures have a few beliefs in common. One is the maintenance of the culture through marriage. As we will see in other chapters in this book, the transmission and maintenance of culture is important for many immigrants living in Canada and the U.S. Yet, maintaining cultural traditions is difficult in a new land with different ways of doing things. Norms of the cultural tradition may be at odds with the pressures of Canadian society for young people to date and to select their own partners (Howell (with Albanese & Obusu-Mensah, 2001: 135)). For many immigrants, attitudes towards women and dating are seen as indicators of a successful transmission of culture (Dasgupta, 1998). Children are expected to date and marry someone of their ethnic group, and display traditional gender attitudes within the marriage. After all, marriage within one's ethnic group is a way to preserve that ethnic identity. As a result, many parents try to foster a sense of cultural identity early, through home activities and organized events.

This parental tactic is successful in some cases. For example, Portuguese men and women in the U.S. who are highly concerned with the ethnicity of their dating partners are also strongly committed to a particular Portuguese identity and have a predominantly Portuguese social network (Reich et al., 2000). This is also the case among Jews in Canada (Weinfeld, 2001). Similar findings can be found across most ethnic groups.

However, not all children respond as expected when entering the dating world, and intergenerational conflicts can occur. A comparison of Asian Indian women raised in the U.S. and women born and raised in India shows that the women born in the U.S. are considered "not Indian enough" on issues regarding marriage and dating, due to assimilation of U.S. beliefs (Srinivasan, 2001). Similarly, among Asian-American college students, intergenerational conflicts regarding dating and marriage are more common among immigrant families than U.S.-born families (Gim Chung, 2001).

Growing up in a multicultural society widens the number of available cultures one can date, and interracial dating is on the rise in Canada and the U.S. A 1995 study of black, Latino, and white individuals found interracial dating in over 50

One effect of growing up in a multicultural society is that interracial dating is on the rise in Canada.

percent of each ethnic group, which is only getting higher (Tucker & Mitchell-Kernan, 1995). While interracial dating was most associated with being male, black, or Latino, this dynamic seems to have changed over the years. In the 2000s, it seems that younger, more educated, less lonely, individuals and those perceiving more mate ability are engaging in interracial dating.

Like much of dating, engaging in an interracial relationship usually entails some sort of trade-off. This is probably not a conscious decision on the part of the individuals, but an unconscious response to how others may perceive the relationship. As interracial dating is still not always looked upon favourably, both parties will want to portray characteristics in the other to make the relationship more acceptable to critics. For example, many whites who enter interracial relationships trade their racial status for some other relational capital such as physical attractiveness and financial security. Conversely, racial minorities are likely to trade such assets for higher racial status (Yancey & Yancey, 1998). As interracial dating grows and becomes more mainstream, this effect may be lessened.

Same-Sex Dating

Much like interracial dating, same-sex dating is becoming more mainstream. As a result, many of the misconceptions surrounding gay and lesbian couples have been lifted (Oswald, 2002). One study showed that gays and lesbians desire the same things in relationships as heterosexuals, and are concerned with many of the same concerns as heterosexual couples, such as emotional pleasure between lovers, maintaining their circle of friends, and caring for children and aging parents (Herrell, 1997; Lehr, 1999).

Another misconception surrounding same-sex unions is that the majority are egalitarian and completely equal. Research has shown this is not necessarily the case. In fact, more than 50 percent of gay men were seeking relationships founded on domination and subordination and only 40 percent were seeking egalitarian partnerships (Gutierrez, 1997). Thus, the sexual double standard applies to gays, but in a different form: personality traits apply more than simply gender.

Where gays and lesbians meet and mate has changed somewhat over time. In 1990, gay bars were the most common initial meeting place, regardless of whether individuals were looking for a short- or long-term relationship (Berger, 1990). Today, there are many other avenues open to gay and lesbian youth, including well established subcultural institutions (bars and nightclubs, theatres, comedy clubs, gay travel tours, etc.) and, of course, Internet dating.

Romantic Love over the Life Course

A popular perception is that love and romance are for the young. With age, so the belief goes, romance—or at least the day-to-day experience of it—wanes. That this is not necessarily so has been shown in recent research (see Abu-Laban & McDaniel, 2001, for example). Happy marriages remain happy into old age. And happy couples remain sexually involved with each other, too.

Marriages or relationships that survive long-term are more often (but not always) based on shared interests, humour, respect, and friendship. Adams and Jones (1997) find, in a study of marital commitment, that three primary dimensions exist: attraction based on devotion, satisfaction, and love; a moral imperative component based on personal responsibility for maintaining the marriage; and the belief that marriage is an important social and religious institution accompanied by fear of the costs (social, emotional, and financial) of ending the relationship. These three dimensions are found to correspond well with couples' personal accounts of what it feels like to be in a committed relationship.

Many couples that reach their fiftieth wedding anniversaries are clearly and visibly in love with each other. People who have known close couples in their own families recognize the glow they have when they look at each other. Television and radio, on special-occasion programs, sometimes allow us a glimpse of long-term married couples where it is apparent that they love and respect each other deeply. A lifetime of sharing can bring comfort with each other and shared memories that pull them even closer. These relationships exemplify the supportive transactions that sustain solid relationships.

At the same time, marital duration is not always indicative of happiness. We all know couples, or know of couples, that stay together not because they are in love or happy with each other but for practical reasons: the children, too much shared to separate, too much invested to leave the relationship, or fears of the consequences of leaving.

Romantic love can be discovered later in life too. Some whose first marriages have ended in divorce or widowhood find love the second time around. Their attitudes may be more mature but are no less romantic. Few studies have focused on love in mid life or later life, but what exists offers hints that love can indeed be sweet and long-lasting when people find each other after having some life experience. Among the most romantic of scenarios is the couple that loses each other when young, marries others and then, when widowed, finds each other again and renews their love. These stories are almost epic in the feelings they evoke of love discovered. The struggles and separation from each other sweeten the sense of romance once they find each other at long last.

Mate Selection

The term "mate selection" may seem like an odd one. However, it does seem that we really do "select" whom we shall love or marry. Every society, including ours, has rules or laws about whom we can marry or with whom we can have sexual relations. We cannot legally decide, for example, to marry a sibling or to have sex with a child.

However, our society is relatively permissive; traditional societies have more numerous and specific rules about who can marry whom. Some societies practise **endogamy**, which is the requirement common in small, traditional societies that people marry within their own social group (such as their own class, caste, or ethnic group). Other societies practise **exogamy**, which means marrying outside one's social group. Exogamous societies are occasionally small and based on extended kinship, like the !Kung bushmen of the Kalahari desert.

Marriage rules always aim to ensure a kin group's advantage. Wherever land or other immovable property might be lost through marriage, the pressure toward endogamy is strong. Endogamy is also likely when a group is suffering discrimination by outsiders and has to strengthen its social bonds by stressing group boundaries in marriage. By contrast, exogamy gives the members of a small society more chance to survive by increasing the size of the group they can call on in the event of a famine, war, or other trouble. It is a good survival strategy where group resources are few and the group does not feel threatened by (all) outside groups, or where there are few if any family properties to be lost (or gained) through marriage.

Our own society has no explicit rules of endogamy or exogamy, but it sometimes seems endogamous, since most people tend to fall in love with and marry people who are like themselves in important ways. This should not be entirely surprising since we interact most with those with whom we have things in common. **Propinquity** (or proximity) theory says that people are more likely to find a mate among those with whom they associate. The theory of **homogamy** takes this further, proposing that people tend to fall in love within their own social group, as defined by class, educational level, religion, and race or ethnicity.

Homogamy

Given the importance of similarity in interpersonal attraction, one expects that people will marry others like themselves. People meet others like themselves, find them relatively more attractive than others they have met, and then marry them, or at least form a household.

This tendency of like marrying like—assortative mating or homogamy—is found for a wide variety of characteristics. Important variables on which mate similarity is evident include age, geographic location, various physical traits and overall physical attractiveness, and mental traits, including attitudes, opinions, and personality (Buss 1985). So, where in the past people married others from the same town and background and were similar to their mates on a great many dimensions, today we marry others to whom we are similar on a few of the most important dimensions.

There are good reasons why people tend to be homogamous. First, they are more likely to meet others who are (at least socially) like themselves than to meet people unlike themselves. This results from the social circles within which people move and interact with others. Second, we usually like people who think the way we do and act the way we expect them to; we feel comfortable in their presence. Third, instrumental and expressive exchanges are easier to balance when like is marrying like. That's because people are bringing similar, hence more equal, qualities and resources to the marriage.

As we will see shortly, homogamy promotes marital satisfaction and happiness. Thus, homogamy has a survival value: couples who are similar are not only more likely to meet and marry but also more likely to remain together and produce children than couples who are less similar. The resulting children of these homogamous marriages themselves enter the marriage market looking for marriages like those of their parents—namely, homogamous marriages.

Homogamy is promoted in some environments more than others, and the degree of similarity of one's mate will depend on where one meets him or her. Schools promote most forms of homogamy, whereas neighbourhoods and family networks promote religious homogamy (Kalmijn & Flap, 2001). Thus, institutionally organized arrangements can determine what kind of mate one will meet.

Educational and Other Status Homogamy

Some characteristics of prospective mates are more important than other characteristics in determining mate selection, and education is one of the most important in our society. For example, education—an achieved status—is a more important criterion in the selection of marriage partners than social class origins, which are ascribed (i.e., inherited at birth). Moreover, educational homogamy has increased over time (Kalmijn, 1991). More people are marrying spouses with the same or a similar level of educational attainment.

From the 1930s onward, the norm has been, and is, increasingly educational homogamy (Mare, 1991). There may be several explanations for this, including the increased importance of educational attainment for upward mobility, and the increased numbers of young people who prolong their education through secondary school, college, or university, and even post-graduate programs. Though a shift to achieved status over ascribed status, the increase in educational homogamy may not indicate a significant change in the pattern of social stratification in modern industrial societies (Jones, 1987). Educational homogamy may be important for the couples involved, but it holds no necessary implication for the way the class structure operates.

Age Homogamy

One of the most consistent and persistent facts of marriage is the age gap of the partners involved. Men tend to marry women a little younger than they are. This pattern is clear and persistent—a stable finding of sociological research.

In the days when marriage meant financial security, women may have looked for a financially secure man who could provide for them. That often meant an older, established man. Nevertheless, now, when marriage is more than security for women, the age difference persists. It could be argued that with the gender gap in earnings potential, marriage is still a matter of security for many women who cannot earn as much by their own labours in the market as they can by marrying someone with higher earning power. However, this is not likely the best explanation.

Age difference can reflect different power and experience, although, of course, this is not always true. It can mean that men exercise greater financial leverage in marriage. The younger partner may be in a weaker bargaining position. It is also possible, even probable, that if the man is a little older, it is his career that is more established and that sets the course for the marriage in terms of who is likely to follow whom for a job or a promotion, or a transfer. These differentials tend to widen further with the birth of a child.

The **marriage gradient**, a well-known sociological concept, takes unequal marriages one step further. First discovered by Jessie Bernard in the 1970s, the marriage gradient reveals that we sort ourselves into couples not only by age but also by differential status. Men, on average, tend to marry women with a little less education or a slightly lower occupational status than their own.

There are two interesting consequences of this. First, when taken together, the unequal matches form an off-centre parallelogram, of higher-status men linked with slightly lower-status women. Since the world comprises men and women of all statuses, there are bound to be some men and some women prevented from making marriage matches. But, they are not the same kinds of people. Men who are left out of the marriage gradient are those at the bottom, for whom there is no one of lower status to marry. Women who are left out of the marriage gradient are those at the top, for whom there is no one of higher status to marry. Thus, one must be wary when comparing the married with the unmarried: unmarried men and women are likely to be profoundly different.

It may be that this imbalance is resolved by outmarriage, such that highly educated women of lower-status ethnic groups marry equally or less-educated men of higher-status ethnic groups. In short, additional variables need to be tossed into the exchange process to solve this marriage-gradient problem.

The second consequence is just as interesting. When men and women pair off unequally by status and age, the impression is created that differences between men and women are larger than they actually are. It works like this: We see couples in which she is younger, and lower in status, than he is. Some people might conclude from this that there is a natural sex difference. In fact, social choices in marriage partners tend to exaggerate existing sex differences. By the marriage choices we make, we reproduce cultural prejudices about the natural abilities of women compared with men, in relation to education, wealth, and status. (Following these rules, if all that a Martian sociologist knew about Canadian women came from interviews with the wives of wealthy Canadian men, the Martian might conclude that all women are young, beautiful, and well-dressed.)

Despite this marriage gradient, research shows considerable age and educational homogamy. Indeed, it points to increasing age homogamy among people in their first marriages, and a parallel, though smaller, increase in the same direction in subsequent marriages. Age—like education—has become more relevant in mate selection (Vera et al., 1990; Qian & Preston, 1993). Other characteristics have become less relevant, among them ethnicity and religion. The increasing age homogamy suggests a reduction in women's reliance on men as "breadwinners."

Ethnic Homogamy

At the turn of the century, endogamy was strong for all North American ethnic groups. Ethnic homogamy was strongest for the new immigrants from southern and eastern Europe, with weaker endogamy in the second generation (Pagnini & Morgan, 1990). Today, ethnic intermarriage is more common for all groups. Second-generation European Canadians and Americans marry increasingly into the native stock and increasingly out of their national origin group. The ethnic boundaries that separate potential mates have weakened over time (Kalmijn, 1993). That's likely because people from different ethnic backgrounds are, during adolescence and early adulthood, attending educational institutions where they meet and mate with others of similar educational attainment.

Religious Homogamy

The data also reveal weak and diminishing barriers to religious outmarriage. Even among the Jews, a group that is particularly concerned about its group survival, the fairly high degree of homogamy is achieved largely by religious conversion (before or after marriage). Overall, for Jews and other religious groups, the data show a strong continuing trend toward secularization of the institution of marriage, meaning less religious homogamy over time (Glenn, 1982).

Intermarriage between Protestants and Catholics has increased dramatically since the 1920s, indicating that the social boundaries separating educational groups are stronger than religious (or ethnic) boundaries. In addition, interfaith marriages have become increasingly homogamous with respect to education, showing that education has replaced religion as a key factor in spouse selection (Kalmijn, 1991).

Religiously homogamous marriages are more satisfying, however. A survey of Seventh-day Adventists shows that family worship, common religiosity with spouse, and church attendance are strong predictors of marital satisfaction (Dudley & Kosinski, 1990). In other research, couples of the same denomination, couples who attend church/temples/mosques with similar frequency, and couples with strong religious convictions have the most successful, stable marriages. It appears that religious homogamy is important only where one or both spouses are actively observant.

Similarity and Couple Happiness

The literature consistently argues that social similarity of partners promotes marital satisfaction. Homogamous couples are significantly more satisfied than dissimilar couples (Weisfeld et al., 1992). This applies not only to age and religion but to common attitudes as well.

A study of long-term committed couple relationships finds that agreement on a wide variety of issues is one factor that contributes to the longevity of the marriage, marital satisfaction, and overall happiness (Lauer et al., 1990). Men and women whose attitudes diverge from those of their spouses are less satisfied with their marriages (Lye & Biblarz, 1993).

Marital happiness is positively related to the accuracy of perception of a spouse's motivational state; that is, to spouses' abilities to correctly identify and interpret each other's thoughts and moods, and generally associated with the frequency, positiveness, and effectiveness of spousal interaction (Kirchler, 1988). Main causes of marital dissatisfaction between partners are a lack of shared attitudes toward moral standards and sex, with moral standards being the predominant factor for women and sex the predominant factor for men (McAllister, 1986).

Ross et al. (1987) investigate the relationship between marital satisfaction and communication of sexual behaviour preferences in a sample of married couples. They find agreement on sexual matters is significantly related to the couple's marital happiness. Wives tend to have a better understanding of their husbands' sexual preferences than the husbands do of their wives' preferences.

The Gender Difference in Attraction

Some believe that mating and marriage are about the capture and possession of erotic property (Collins, 1983). This view is quite consistent with what we have said so far about the role of romance in the mating process and can account for the complicated and unreal beliefs people hold about mating and their mates.

Experts who provide premarital counselling note a variety of unrealistic beliefs that are common among people when they choose mates. They include the beliefs that

- people will find the perfect partner;

- there is only one good partner for each person;

- love is enough to smooth over the rough patches in a relationship;

- when all else fails, the mates will try harder and succeed; and

- opposites complement each other (i.e., heterogamy is better than homogamy).

People tend to hold such beliefs because, for many, mate selection is indeed the capture of "erotic property," and people's ability to reason is often clouded by passion. This is clear when we examine differences between men and women in their mating preferences. Women and men are not alike in certain key ways, and this difference is the basis of attraction. One overwhelming difference between men and women is men's placing a higher value on physical attractiveness and a lower value on earning capacity than women (Buss 1985, 1989; de Raad & Doddema-Winsemius, 1992).

Cross-cultural surveys using data from 33 countries confirm that women value the financial capacity of potential mates more highly than men do. Across cultures, women also value ambition, industriousness, financial status, and prospects more highly than men do.

What Men Want

Although the gender difference is larger in self-report data than in observed social behaviour, men's preference for physical attractiveness, youth, and reproductive value in a mate is documented in many studies (Feingold, 1990). For example, analyses of published personal advertisements for mates confirm the difference, with men asking for a photo and a sexual relationship and women looking for older mates and financial resources (Wiederman, 1993).

The results are similar no matter how we obtain the data: whether by survey, experiment, or otherwise. Surveyed undergraduates of both sexes express a desire for physical attractiveness, earning potential, and expressiveness in a mate; but, compared with women, men more often emphasize the first of these three qualities

(Sprecher, 1989). Similar patterns emerge in data drawn from the National Survey of Families (Sprecher, Sullivan, & Hatfield, 1994).

Some of this gender difference may be a matter of mere self-presentation. An experiment by Hadjistavrolous and Genest (1994) finds that women intentionally under-report the impact of physical attractiveness on their preferences. Connected to a lie detector–like apparatus, women undergraduates admit a more extreme influence by the physical attractiveness of potential male dating partners, and give more extreme dating desirability ratings to physically unattractive men. So, some of this gender difference is cultural, a result of what we are taught to say that we want, and not a biological difference between men and women.

Besides attractiveness and youth, men want vulnerability or submissiveness in a mate. In an undergraduate experiment, both men and women rated dominant men and vulnerable women consistently higher as prospective mates than dominant women and vulnerable men (Rainville & Gallagher, 1990). In a questionnaire study, though both sexes valued kindness, consideration, and honesty, men also preferred a submissive and introverted romantic partner (Goodwin, 1990).

In terms of sexual purity, the results are mixed. Both men and women may value relatively inexperienced marriage partners, regardless of their own experience level (Jacoby & Williams, 1985; Williams & Jacoby, 1989). However, Oliver and Sedikides (1992) find strong evidence of a double standard. Men prefer low levels of sexual permissiveness for committed partners, and they rate permissive potential mates lower on marriage desirability. For men, permissive partners may be attractive as dates but are less attractive as potential marriage partners.

What Women Want

For their part, women prefer low levels of sexual permissiveness for both low- and high-commitment partners, rating permissive potential mates lower than non-permissive ones on both dating and marriage desirability. In casual mating opportunities, and when considering how to choose a long-term partner, undergraduate women are more selective than men overall. Particularly important are status-linked variables and the anticipated investment of a partner in a relationship. Men have lower requirements for a sexual partner than women but are nearly as selective as women when considering requirements for a long-term partner (Kenrick et al., 1990).

In a study of strategies used to attract mates, women try to attract "investing" mates, who are willing to consider eventual parenthood, by acting chaste and emphasizing their fidelity. Men who show relatively more interest in eventual parenthood than other men attract women by emphasizing their own chastity, fidelity, and ability and willingness to invest (Cashdan, 1993). (By contrast, non-investing men, and women who expect non-investing men as partners, flaunt their attractiveness and sexuality to draw in as many partners as possible.)

No wonder, then, that survey data find men (but not women) of higher social status acquire more mating partners, showing that men's status is an important criterion in women's choice. Women's (but not men's) number of partners decreases linearly with age, showing that a woman's reproductive potential is an important criterion in a man's choice. Women (but not men) also become significantly more promiscuous after the dissolution of their marriage. This suggests that women's sexual exclusivity, an important criterion in men's mating choice, operates more weakly once a marriage is over (Perusse, 1994).

Though one might expect that women's attainment of higher education—and more direct access to their own economic resources—would reduce such gender-based differences in mate choice, survey results indicate the opposite. Rather, higher education increases women's socioeconomic standards for mates, thereby reducing their pool of acceptable partners (Townsend, 1989).

Many efforts have been made to account for the seemingly universal and persistent tendency of men to seek young and beautiful wives, and women to seek older and successful husbands. Evolutionary psychologists or socio-biologists provide one explanation. They argue that such matches have survival value. Dominant and successful ("alpha") males try to pass along their genetic materials by marrying and impregnating the youngest and healthiest females. Young and healthy females, for their part, seek dominant male partners to ensure that their relatively small opportunity to produce offspring (compared to men's) is afforded as much protection as possible during the period of pregnancy and childrearing. Offspring with the youngest, healthiest mothers and most powerful fathers stand the greatest chance of survival, hence the pattern of mating survives.

Why People Do Not Optimize

The metaphor of a mating or marriage "market" in which people rationally seek "perfect mates" is wholly fictional, however. In fact, finding a mate is much like finding a job—it is socially structured but largely unplanned and unconscious.

Reasonable people shop carefully for cars, television sets, and apartments, but they do not shop for mates. That is because rational people do not seek the ideal or "**optimal mate**" solution to their most important personal concerns. They do not try to optimize; rather, they "satisfice": they seek a "good enough" solution, within the constraints life has handed them (March & Simon, 1958). For most purposes, whatever satisfies us is ideal.

According to March and Simon, most human decision-making aims to discover and select satisfactory alternatives. "Only in exceptional cases is it concerned with the discovery of optimal alternatives. To optimize requires processes several orders of magnitude more complex than those required to satisfice" (1958, 141). The difference between optimizing and "satisficing" is the difference between searching a haystack for the sharpest needle and merely searching for a needle that is sharp enough to sew with.

Think of it another way: The human race could not reproduce itself and survive if people were romantic optimizers. We would have died out as a species years ago.

Consider the arithmetic of the problem. Suppose that, as an idealistic teenager, you had listed ten qualities you felt you absolutely must have in a mate. Your mate must be attractive—at least in the top fifth of all possible mates, by your own standards of attractiveness. Your mate must be fun—again, at least in the top fifth of all possible mates. He or she must be interesting to talk to—again, at least in the top fifth of all possible mates. Then add seven more qualities. This is the probability that your ideal mate actually exists, and that she or he would find you ideal.

If the qualities you are looking for in a mate are uncorrelated, only one person in five to the tenth power—one in 9.8 million—will meet all your requirements. That may be less than one adult person of the right sex, aged 20 to 60, in all of Canada. Equally, there is only one chance in 9.8 million your "perfect mate" will consider you the perfect mate. So, by this scenario, the chances of meeting and marrying the perfect mate are one in 9.8 million squared (or nearly zero).

Even more modest goals cannot be optimized. Suppose that, instead of requiring your perfect mate to be among the top fifth in attractiveness, you require him or her to be only in the top half. You similarly lower your standards for your other requirements. This makes your mating problem more manageable: now, you only need to look for that one "perfect" person in a thousand (that is, two to the tenth power). The probability of meeting and mating with an ideal mate who is making similar calculations has improved: now it is only one in a thousand squared, or one in a million. (There are likely to be nine or ten of your ideal mates in all of Canada. Some, of course, may be already married or in a committed relationship.) At most, you know only a few thousand. The chance of meeting and mating this way is quite unlikely.

With this in mind, you may try to solve the shopping problem by reducing the number of qualities you require in a mate. Suppose your potential mate has to excel in only one respect and satisfy you in four others. Now you and your perfect mate are each looking for someone who is in the top fifth in one quality and in the top half in just four other qualities. The probability of finding a person with the qualities you seek is one in 1250. The probability that you will satisfy his or her requirements is also one in 1250. Even so, the chance of meeting and mating is still well below one in a million (that is, one in 1250 squared).

If you try to optimize you will fail to solve your mating problem, even by lowering your original standards. Some people therefore adopt the strategy of trying to meet more potential partners. After all, if you knew 6000 people instead of 2000, your chances would triple. But getting on a first-name basis with 6000 people is very difficult and time-consuming, and the odds are still stacked against you. Besides, all this time spent mate-shopping leaves less time for education, good grooming, and all the other attributes required to make you an attractive mate!

Carefully expanding your network of acquaintances seems to be one way around this. By joining certain kinds of groups or perhaps placing or answering personal advertisements, you will more quickly meet new people with the qualities you seek. These mating techniques have become much more popular in the last few decades, especially among middle-aged people, whose opportunity to meet a large number of new, and possibly unmarried, people is seriously restricted. (Take note: You will meet more potential mates at college or university than at any time in the future.) Still, many people hesitate to look for mates in this way. They find it demeaning, fear the unpleasantness of blind dates that do not work out, or worry about getting sexually transmitted diseases from a new sexual partner.

However you revise the shopping list and extend your range and number of contacts, the chance of finding the perfect mate this way is nearly zero. Most people cannot and do not find a mate in this way. Rather, people fall in love with those who are close at hand. As in so many areas of life, we come to value what we know best and have available: people like ourselves. We become satisfied with the possible, not the ideal; then we come to love the person who satisfies us.

Whether we choose homogamy or heterogamy (intermarriage) depends on what kinds of people are close at hand. That explains why our chances of mating with people of other religious, ethnic, and racial groups increase when we have more contact with them. To illustrate this, a study of major language groups concludes that "endogamy [within-group marriage] varies positively with the number of available potential mates belonging to the same group; negatively with the average distance to them; negatively with the number of available potential mates belonging to different groups; and positively with the average distance to the latter" (De Vries & Vallee 1980, 168). Said more simply, people usually marry others who are socially and geographically near at hand, even if slightly "better" mates can be found much farther away.

This process of "satisficing" may sound very unromantic, but in practice the feelings of love are genuine. People in love believe that they have discovered the one perfect mate. In a sense, they have. But they have not (and could not have) done it by following a shopping list of the "right" characteristics. Instead, they have decided, after the fact, that their mate is perfect—and that is what's so amazing about falling in love.

Dating Violence

Unfortunately, and ironically, every discussion of dating and mating must include a discussion of interpersonal violence. This is ironic because, as we said at the beginning of this chapter, dating in our society is charged with romantic illusion and emotional intensity. There is an element of choice that is lacking in most other cultures, and a sense that the choice—though reversible through separation or divorce—is nonetheless enormously consequential. We need to examine the possible relationship between our pattern of romantic mating, on the one hand, and the high rate of violence between dates, mates, and lovers, on the other hand.

Abuse of women in dating relationships is relatively widespread but underreported and, until recently, understudied (DeKeseredy & Schwartz 1994). There may be a pattern of perpetuation of violence by men and acceptance of violence by women that starts as early as elementary school.

A national Canadian study of 1835 girls/women and 1307 boys/men (DeKeseredy & Schwartz, 1994) found that girls who experience violence while in elementary schools are more likely to be victims of dating violence in high school and colleges/universities. And boys who are violent while young are more likely to perpetuate violence in dating relationships. These men are also more accepting of rape myths (such as the myth that women enjoy sexual assault, or that sexual assault can be perpetrated only by strangers, etc.) than are non-violent men.

The 1993 Violence against Women Survey in Canada found that 16 percent of women in Canada had experienced some kind of violence in a dating relationship (Statistics Canada 1993, 2). Violence was found to be widespread, with over one-half of Canadian women experiencing at least one incident of physical violence since age 16. The survey addressed only behaviours such as hitting, threatening, and so on defined as crimes in the *Criminal Code* of Canada.

Women aged 18 to 24 and women with some post-secondary education were the most likely to have experienced violence in the 12 months prior to the survey, suggesting that dating violence is relatively widespread. Interestingly, about 20 percent of the women interviewed for this survey said that they had never before told anyone about the violence they had experienced. The Canadian survey, the first of its kind anywhere, is being replicated in other countries in the late 1990s and early 2000s.

Let's relate these findings to domestic violence. One survey of self-reported domestic violence in Canada shows that (1) younger people are more violent to their spouses than older people; (2) unemployed people are more violent than employed people; but (3) lower income and less-educated people are no more violent than higher income, highly educated people. There is also a relationship between a belief in patriarchy and spousal abuse. Husbands who believe men ought to rule women are more likely than other husbands to beat their wives. In turn, a belief in patriarchy appears to depend on educational and occupational level. Specifically, the belief appeals to lower status, less educated men.

It stands to reason, then, that violence against women will be particularly common among young, relatively uneducated people—people who aren't married or in a committed relationship and are dating. Thus, "date rape" is a growing concern among sociologists. But in this area of research, getting good data is difficult; young men and women tend to disagree about what happens on dates. A survey by sociologists Walter DeKeseredy and Katharine Kelly, conducted on 44 college and university campuses across Canada, found four women in five saying they had been subjected to abuse by a dating partner and nearly as many men admitting having acted abusively toward their dates.

The validity of the findings was questioned because the study listed a very wide range of behaviours under the heading of "abuse." These behaviours included insults; swearing; accusations of flirting with others or acting spitefully; as well as using or threatening to use a gun or knife; and beating, kicking, or biting the dating partner. So it may be best to separate the violent from the less violent abuses before we interpret the results. When we do, certain patterns fall into place. Where violent abuses are concerned, women are more than twice as likely as men to acknowledge their occurrence. Where less violent abuses are concerned, men and women acknowledge them equally often.

For example, 65 percent of women report being insulted or sworn at by a date, and 63.6 percent of men report having done that to a date. On the other hand, 11.1 percent of women report being slapped by a date, yet only 4.5 percent of men report slapping a date. Likewise, 8.1 percent of women report being kicked, bitten, or hit with a fist, yet only 2.4 percent of men report having done any of those things. This consistent discrepancy leads to one of three possible conclusions. Either (1) violent and abusive men date a lot more women than gentle, non-abusive men, (2) women tell a lot of lies about their dates, or (3) many men are ashamed to admit the things they have done to their dates. The third option seems the most probable based on what we know as sociologists.

The data also show that violent abuses on dates are not only physical, they are also sexual. As before, male respondents are only about one-half or one-third as likely to report initiating the abuse as women are to report experiencing the abuse. Bear in mind that most instances of forced sexual activity occur between people who know each other. The result is, too often, that women blame themselves for the experience. Because they know the assailant, they react passively to the sexual assault. Because they react passively, they blame themselves for not reacting more forcefully. A few even continue the dating relationship.

Date rape grows out of common practices of sexual harassment, another form of sexual assault that is especially prevalent in schools and workplaces (McDaniel & van Roosmalen, 1991). In the halls of our high schools, Canada's female students regularly experience harassment ranging from unwanted staring and rude or embarrassing remarks to unwanted touching. The result for girls is a frequent, if not constant, sense of discomfort—even dread—about being at school.

Part of the problem is that perceptions of sexual harassment vary by gender. High-school boys may have little idea just how much their actions upset the girls. College-aged men are much less likely to label such behaviour as "harassment" than their female peers. But after exposure to the work force, men's awareness grows and they, too, come to see certain behaviour as harassment. Overall, women label more behaviours as harassment than men do, but this discrepancy decreases with men's experience in the work force.

Concluding Remarks

It is apparent that the quest for a close, committed intimate relationship has changed dramatically in recent times in North America. What has not changed is the importance that a relationship has in our lives and to our sense of well-being. In fact, some sociologists think that having a close relationship matters more in times of rapid social change than in times of social stability.

Mating, and especially marriage or a long-term committed relationship, gives people the chance for both greater life satisfaction and deeper dissatisfaction than the single life normally does. If you marry, you will probably increase your standard of living and longevity, especially if you are a man. Marriage has riskier, less predictable outcomes for women, particularly when there are children involved or when women lack skills that would allow them to earn a living. Men gain the most from a marriage that works, and women—especially mothers and poorer women—lose the most when a marriage fails.

If you are a woman, deciding whether to marry means assessing your relationship realistically. If you think that there is too much fighting and not enough hugging in your relationship, marriage will not solve the problem. As we will see, the "enchanted" newlywed period is normally followed by many years of declining satisfaction, particularly if children are present. The typical marriage may worsen before it starts to improve. Certainly, the stresses any marriage is likely to experience will not disappear.

When you marry, avoid having children until you are fairly certain that your marriage will survive. Married women must develop the skills and self-reliance that they will need to support themselves. Most women have already changed their conception of marriage in significant ways, by equipping themselves for independence. Married women who continue to work for pay see their marriage more in balance with the overall scheme of their lives than married women who do not work in the paid work force (Baruch, Barnett, & Rivers, 1983, 294).

Most important, flee a relationship that is marked by physical or emotional violence. The violence is likely to recur. You are not to blame, and your partner is not likely to change. Message to men: Seek professional help if you tend to express your relationship frustrations in a physical or violent way. Doing so is not inevitable, normal, or acceptable in modern close relations.

Do people get what they want from mating and marriage? On the one hand, the range of possible choices is wider than ever: people are increasingly free to marry or not to marry, to have the kinds of relationships they want to, and to choose their own mate. On the other hand, what we want is patterned by our social experience. People learn to want marriage as the preferred form of adult life. We mate with people who are nearby and socially like ourselves, not with "ideal" mates. However, we can grow to think our partner is, in fact, the "perfect" mate.

In the end, we discover that there are no simple answers to dating and mating, no easy ways to select a mate who will ensure a happy, long-lasting relationship. However, as we will see in Chapter 5, there are better and worse ways of conducting close relations, and some approaches can lead to genuine happiness and fulfillment; so, in the end, mate selection is not the crucial issue we often think it is.

In the next chapter, we discuss some of the forms of early marriage.

CHAPTER SUMMARY

This chapter discusses mate selection as an exchange process in which a fair or equal exchange is most likely to avoid disappointment or resentment of either partner. The way in which we date to choose a mate has changed from when romantic love was created during the Middle Ages to present-day Internet dating services. However, in the game of love some things have not changed: love is still a deeply important construct in our society; a loveless marriage is still considered a tragedy. Although marriage is still a valued relationship, its consequences have changed. In the past a failed marriage was a disgrace for a woman. In recent decades women have fought to alter this and often retain economic independence by continuing to work outside the home after marriage.

As we looked at the origins of our dating and mating rituals in the courtly love tradition, we saw the origins of the sexual scripts of men and women. These dating rituals contributed to a sexual double standard in which boys were the initiators and girls were the receivers. Although love is the ideal basis of a marriage in the Western tradition, in other traditions a material exchange is more important. The process involved in arranging a marriage is quite different than the marriage market of modern singles bars, although in both cases an exchange is the basis of interaction.

We compare our marketability on the basis of physical attributes, earning potential, and personality; we search for "the one" on campus, in workplaces, among friends, on the Internet, or on holiday. As we select our mates it is clear that there are rules of whom we may date and whom we are most likely to date and mate with.

Like marrying like, or homogamy, is one way that the exchange process of dating becomes apparent. Similarity seems to play a large role in whom we choose to date and mate with. Educational homogamy has increasingly become an important factor in dating. Couple happiness is deeply connected to the social similarity of the partners in the marriage.

Nevertheless, dating and mating sometimes ends in violence, the irony of a love-based exchange. Sociologists face many problems in getting reliable data regarding violence; men and women are unlikely to report violence, whether as perpetrator or as victim. Sexual harassment, although perhaps a new term, is not a new experience for many Canadian women.

One problem is the definition of sexual harassment and dating violence. Although hitting and threatening could never be called acceptable romantic behaviour, there is a fine line between what one person may call persistent flirting and another may call sexual harassment. One characteristic of romantic love is that it is done in relative privacy, so when dating violence occurs there is less chance of a witness or an observer.

KEY TERMS

Attachment The close relationship that develops between individuals with strong emotional ties.

Endogamy Under rules of endogamy people are expected to marry people who are members of their own tribe or group.

Exogamy Under rules of exogamy people are expected to marry outside their own tribe or social group.

Expressive exchange An exchange of emotional and sexual benefits.

Extended family A multigenerational family in which grandparents, parents, children, and perhaps other relatives (aunts, uncles, cousins, etc.) share a household; or a description of such relatives even if they do not live together.

Homogamy A theory of mate selection that people are more likely to select mates with similar social attributes such as class, education level, religion, race, or ethnicity.

Instrumental exchange An exchange of practical and useful benefits, such as unpaid work or financial support.

Marriage gradient A systematic difference between mates, such that men are typically older and of higher social or economic status than their female partners.

Monogamous Married to one person for life.

Optimal mates The idea that people will find a "good enough" solution to the problems of choosing a mate.

Propinquity theory A theory of mate selection that people are more likely to find a mate among people who are geographically nearby.

Romantic love An idea of love that is influenced by idealistic concepts of mating, like chivalry and a search for one's soulmate.

Sexual double standard The application of different rules, or standards of sexual behaviour, to men and women.

Sexual scripts Attitudes and activities that a culture links to each gender, or that are typically expected of members of a particular gender in regards to dating.

SUGGESTED READINGS

DeKeseredy, Walter S. 1998. *Woman Abuse on Campus: Results from the Canadian National Survey.* Thousand Oaks, California: Sage Publications. This book focuses on abuse and violence against female college students, based on research carried out by Canadian sociologists on Canadian college and university campuses.

Foucault, Michel. 1979. *History of Sexuality.* London: Tavistock. An older but seminal sociology book. Foucault holds that knowledge and language form the basis for power in the social construction of reality, and this in turn shapes the way people view sexuality over the course of time.

Singer, Irving. 1984. *The Nature of Love: Courtly and Romantic.* Chicago: University of Chicago Press. This book offers a penetrating look at love from a historical perspective. The rituals of love seem rather timeless when looked at over centuries of change.

Whyte, Martin King. 1990. *Dating, Mating and Marriage.* New York: Aldine deGruyter. This text focuses on three topics that are key to a deeper understanding of our modern dating and mating rituals. The book looks at dating as a set of social customs and rituals. It also addresses marriage and mate selection, and asks whether more dating leads to better mating.

Wolfe, David A. 1997. *Alternatives to Violence: Empowering Youth to Develop Healthy Relationships.* Thousand Oaks, California: Sage Publications. This book puts forward a series of suggestions for avoiding violence. It contains a section on the relationship between youth and dating violence.

REVIEW QUESTIONS

1. What is "marriage gradient," and what are its consequences?

2. What are "age homogamy," "ethnic homogamy," and "religious homogamy"?

3. What are the qualities that men and women look for when it comes to mate selection?

4. What do we know about "dating violence"?

5. How do resources affect intimate relationships?

6. What is a "sexual double standard"?

7. What are "the love" and "the fun" standards?

8. What is expressive exchange? How is it different from instrumental exchange?

9. What is a "flirting script," and how has it changed?

10. How does the text define "mate selection"?

11. How do propinquity (proximity) theory and homogamy differ?

DISCUSSION QUESTIONS

1. "Men tend to marry women a little younger than they are; women tend to marry men a little older." Discuss how age difference can put the younger partner in a weaker bargaining position in marriage.

2. Some people believe in finding the perfect mate. Why do people hold such a belief?

3. When it comes to mate selection, why do people seek the "possible" and not the "ideal"?

4. How do different ages, ethnic backgrounds, and religious beliefs affect one's strategy of mate selection?

5. Dating violence is a growing concern. Discuss how dating violence can be stopped. What government policies and programs might contribute to such a change?

6. Discuss the development of romantic and courtly love.

7. There have been significant changes in the sexual scripts of both sexes over the past 50 to 60 years. Discuss how these scripts have changed and what positive and negative effects these changes have had.

8. Discuss what sexual standard is healthiest and why (e.g., abstinence

until marriage, the love standard, the fun standard). If you deem none of these healthy, discuss why.

9. Parental or familial involvement in the dating and mating process varies widely among Canadians (e.g., arranged marriages have high familial involvement). Discuss the possibilities for mentorship by parents or families to dating couples.

10. Why do men tend to emphasize appearance and women financial viability when looking for a mate? Discuss possible explanations. Do you see any connections between this tendency and socialization or cultural influence?

ACTIVITIES

1. In a group, discuss how different ages, ethnic backgrounds, and religious beliefs can affect one's strategy of mate selection.

2. Dating violence is a growing concern. Discuss how dating violence can be stopped. Examine the current government policies on date rape. What policies and programs might contribute to such a change?

3. Test propinquity theory and homogamy theory by conducting a personal survey of any past dating relationships (or using dating relationships you know of firsthand). Compare your significant personal data to that of a partner in your group. Are they similar? Different? This can be done as a group or individuals.

WEBLINKS

http://web.uvic.ca/~oursac/date_and_ac quaintance_rape.htm
University of Victoria Sexual Assault Centre
This University of Victoria site is operated by the university's sexual assault centre. The site is designed for people seeking basic information about date rape, date rape drugs, sexual harassment, child sexual abuse, stalking, and legal information. It provides useful links for more information.

http://www.newdirections.mb.ca/
New Directions
This is a non-profit agency funded by the United Way. New Directions provides information on families and parenting.

http://www.Asarian.org/
ASARian, Inc.

This is a free service to survivors of sexual abuse or harassment. This server provides anonymous accounts to increase users' sense of security.

http://www.stormi.com/luv.html
The Language of Love
This is a very entertaining and informative Web site that shows how our dating practices differ from courtship practices at the turn of the century by listing interesting facts and trivia.

http://www.secondwivesclub.com
Second Wives Club
This site provides an array of articles, information, and discussion for remarried women, stepmoms, and generation X. It provides similar information to other family

and women-oriented advice and information sites.

http://www.matchmaker.com/
Matchmakers.com
This site is a fun, less traditional dating service. You can participate in a trial match without spending money or giving away personal information. The site categorizes its participants by gender, sexual orientation, expected level of commitment, and ethnic and religious backgrounds. Ironically, the site does not sort its participants by occupation or interests/hobbies.

http://members.aol.com/_ht_a/ cohabiting/index.htm
All About Cohabiting Before Marriage
The goal of this Web site is to help couples build strong quality relationships that will grow into marriages that last a lifetime. The site includes articles, suggestions, and stories.

CHAPTER FOUR

Types of Intimate Couples:

Marriage, Cohabitation, Same-Sex Relationships, and Other Forms

Chapter Outline

Intimacy: Fast-Growing Area of Research

Intimacy is one of the fastest-growing areas of theory and research in sociology (see Giddens, 1992; Hanson, 1997). In intimate couple relations, it is argued, the family is being redesigned. Intimacy involves emotion, caring, and often inter-dependency—none of which are very well understood by sociology.

Why are intimate couple relationships of such interest in sociology now? Clearly, most of us are interested in having that special someone in our lives. That is not new, but there is much that is new about how we see and what we expect from intimate relationships. Sociological interest in intimate couples springs from family research waking up from "its drowsy fixation on the nucleus of the family" (Beck & Beck-Gernsheim, 1995, 147). We now find ourselves in a confusing modern world of rapid changes and worrisome risks and uncertainties. This gives power and possibility to love and intimacy as an anchor in the world (Giddens, 1992). It is also an important way for us to find ourselves and to find meaning in our lives.

Change and More Change

The importance of having a long-term intimate relationship may be both greater and lesser than it was historically. Personal need and social pressures continue to push us to find a close intimate partner with whom to share our lives. Most young people consider this a top (or near the top) priority in life goals (Bibby, 2001a; Vanier Institute, 1994), and 88 percent of today's Canadian teens expect to find a partner that they will stay with for life (Bibby, 2001a). People are very interested, as we have seen, in finding a long-term intimate relationship. Less emphasis, however, is placed on helping the partnerships work well once matches are made, as we saw in Chapter 3. At the same time, it is easier and more socially acceptable in this twenty-first century to live without an intimate partner, or to live in some other form of close relationship than the traditional legal marriage for life.

We live longer now, so making a lifetime commitment to one person is more serious and for a much longer period than it was for your grandparents. When **marriage** for life often meant 20 to 30 years, most of which were spent having and raising large families, couples had a different kind of intimate relationship. Now, couples may spend years childless, then have children, and find that they have what used to be a lifetime together after the children leave home. Being a close couple for a lifetime is a different prospect now, one that continues to change.

Now, more people live in families without an ongoing close personal relationship. Long life expectancy and family changes increase the likelihood of spending a significant portion of one's life, perhaps at different periods, without being part of a couple relationship.

Official definitions of family, as discussed in Chapter 1, rely on some concept of an ongoing intimate relationship. For example, Statistics Canada defines family (for the Census and other official surveys) as a husband and wife (either legally married or living in a *de facto* or common-law relationship), with or without children who have never been married, living in the same dwelling (Statistics Canada, 2001). Similar definitions are used by the Australian Bureau of Statistics and Statistics New Zealand (Baker, 2001). Government definitions still see families in terms of legal or semi-legal relationships and shared residence despite the immense changes that have occurred in families. Governments do not define families in terms of what they share and what they do for each other.

Twenty years ago, the *Tax Guide for Canada* had no definition of spouse; none was needed to guide people in preparing their tax returns. By the end of the 1990s, however, a full page in the *Tax Guide* was devoted to defining a spouse. Most company pension plans spend considerable time defining a spouse. An example from the University's Academic Pension Plan, University of Alberta (2000, 23):

> *Spouse*:
>
> a) A person to whom you are legally married and who is not separated from you, or if separated, is substantially dependent on you financially, or
>
> b) If there is no person under a), a common-law spouse of the opposite sex who has lived with you for five years, or has lived with you for two years if there is a child born of that relationship, or
>
> c) If there is no person under a) or b), a person to whom you are legally married but from whom you are separated, whether or not the person is financially dependent on you.

This seemingly thorough definition has expanded even further to incorporate the different types of unions that are not traditionally classified as "partner." This reflects society's adaptability and malleability with regard to recognizing intimate relationships.

More Diverse and More Complex Too

Rates of traditional marriage are declining. In 2001, the proportion of married-couple families was 70 percent, down from 83 percent in 1981 (Statistics Canada, 2002a). However, if we sum up those people in legally married, remarried, cohabiting, or *de facto* partner relationships, including same-sex unions, the proportion of people who are in intimate couple relationships is as high as ever (Baker, 2000, 14; Statistics Canada, 2002a).

Close relations are becoming more complex too. There are many more households in Canada than in the past, for example, but fewer are family households (Statistics Canada, 2002a). This means that more Canadians live alone or with others in what they, and the 2001 Census, see as non-family households. Some of those living in non-family households maintain close intimate relationships with someone not in their household such as in commuter marriages/relationships or young adults or seniors whose significant other does not share their home. After a long-term decline in multiple family households in the post-war period, since 1986 there has been an increase (see Peron et al., 1999, 27; Mitchell, 2000; Statistics Canada, 2002a). This could mean that more kinds of close relations among family members of different generations and in different nuclear families may exist. These relationships may substitute for intimate couple relationships, at least in part.

Relationship Trends and Patterns

Two trends characterize contemporary marriage: decline in marriage rates and the continuing popularity of marriage. These two trends seem contradictory but actually are not. More people in Canada now marry at some point in their lives than did in the 1910s, when an estimated 12 percent of women never married (Gee, 1986, 266). But at the same time, there has been a decline in rates of marriage since the 1970s. This trend continues in the most recent data available (Statistics Canada, 1998b; 2002a), which show a lesser proportion of all families are married families. The crude marriage rate was 5.1 in 1998 for every 1000 population, compared to the most recent peak of 7.0 in both 1988 and 1989 (Statistics Canada, 2001).

In the decade from 1981–91, first-marriage rates declined by 25 percent in Canada and 42 percent in Quebec (Nault & Belanger, 1996, 2). Put another way, the proportion of Canadian men who ever get married dropped from 80 percent in 1981 to 70 percent in 1991 (Nault & Belanger, 1996, 32, 36), where it remained in 2001 (Statistics Canada, 2002a). For Québécois men, the comparable proportions of men ever marrying fell from 71 percent in 1981 to 50 percent in 1991. By 2002, the rates of cohabitation in Quebec reached the highest in the world, a rank dominated by Sweden for many years (Statistics Canada, 2002). For women in Canada, 83 percent in 1981 would marry, compared to 75 percent in 1991; for Quebec women, the proportions are 74 percent in 1981 and 56 percent in 1991 (Nault & Belanger, 1996, 38, 42). Comparable calculations have yet to be done with data from the 2001 Census. While these are large declines, the fact remains that the majority of both men and women, even in Quebec, do marry at some point. Before we conclude that marriage is going the way of the dinosaur, we need to consider, however, what else is happening with the formation of couple unions.

Age at Marriage

First, people tend to marry later now than they did in the 1960s and 1970s. Even though the sixties was supposedly a time of "free love," the age at marriage during that period was lower than it had been for a long time and lower than it has been since (about 22 years for women, 25 for men) (Ram, 1990, 80). The long-term trend toward postponement of marriage continues; by 1998, the latest data available, women were 27.6 on average at first marriage, and men 29.6 (Statistics

Canada, 2001). The tendency is slightly greater for women than for men to postpone first marriage.

The reasons for later marriage are complex and related to social and economic opportunities and expectations. One factor is today's uncertain job prospects for young people. Young people in the 1990s, compared to young people in the 1980s, seemed to have lower cumulative earnings (Statistics Canada, 2002b), leading to speculation that postponement of union formation may be, in part, economic. Another factor seems to be people's interest in pursuing non-family interests such as education, travel, or work. Young people still seem to value marriage and family, as we have seen, although marriage is valued considerably less by younger than older people. Younger people seem to prefer not to jump into marriage early.

Types of Marriage

Broadly defined, marriage across the world is a socially approved sexual and economic union between two or more people that is expected to last for a long time. People often enter this union with public formalities or a ceremony, such as a wedding.

Single by Choice

Single by choice—it's an empowering statement, and for a growing number of women, an accurate description of their lifestyle too. Single women, once written off as outcasts or spinsters, are gaining acceptance as part of a major societal and cultural shift.

In 1960, about 30% of all adult females in the United States were single. Today, that number has jumped to over 40%. Focusing on women of the most marriageable age, the statistics are even more significant: between 1963 and 1997, the percentage of women aged 25 to 55 who were married dropped from 83% to 65%.

The rise of the single woman is due in large part to the greater collective power and independence that the group now wields. A Young and Rubicam study released recently labelled single women the yuppies of this decade, the consumer group to whom retailers are paying the most attention, even in consumer markets traditionally dominated by men. Women now fuel the home-renovation market and account for half of the customers at hardware stores. Auto manufacturers have begun to train their salespeople to target softer sell pitches at women. One in five homes sold in the United States in 1999 went to unmarried women. With their greater financial freedom, it isn't surprising that in a Time/CNN survey, over 60% of women ages 18 to 49 said they would consider raising a child on their own.

The shift away from marriage is also evident in popular culture and the mass media. Recent fiction, like Melissa Bank's *The Girls' Guide to Hunting and Fishing* and Helen Fielding's *Bridget Jones's Diary* and *Bridget Jones: The Edge of Reason* all feature single, strong-minded women, as do television shows like *Sex and the City*, *Judging Amy* and *Providence*.

Source: Edward, Tamala M. 2000, August 28. *Time* (Canada), Vol. 156 No. 9. © Time Inc., reprinted by permission.

In Canada, traditional forms of marriage and the family are experiencing dramatic change. Some people find such change disturbing. Because the family is such a basic institution, and marriage is such an intimate relationship, change can seem very threatening. Yet there is no particular form of couple relationship that is universal or necessary. In order to understand the change in our own society, and what it may predict for the future, we will take a larger view of the institution of intimate couples and the many ways societies organize "marriage-like" arrangements.

After all, societies vary in their patterns of marriage, family, and kinship. For example, societies are diverse in the range of choice given to would-be marriage partners, their reasons for marrying, rules about premarital and extramarital intimacies, and whether the same rules apply to both men and women. Even the desired age at marriage and the desired age difference between partners varies from one society to another.

In some societies, people wed more than one mate at a time. **Polygamy** is the generic name for this arrangement. Within this general category, **polyandry** is the marriage of one woman to more than one man, and **polygyny** the marriage of one man to more than one woman. Polygamy was common in most pre-industrial societies and is still permitted in a few. But polygyny is banned in all industrial societies.

Polyandry, on the other hand, has always been a rare form of marriage. It occurs in societies like Nepal, where living conditions are harsh, and few men are able to support a wife and children on their own. A woman is therefore "shared" by a group of men—usually, brothers—and she is a wife to all of them. Female infanticide is practised, justified by the argument that the number of women "needed" in such a society is much less than the number of men. Anthropologist Marvin Harris (1997) suggests that societies with low population pressure (the relation between population density and arable land) favour polygyny; societies with high population pressure favour polyandry.

Even Within Religions, There Are Intermarriages

And what if an Orthodox and non-Orthodox Jew fall in love? The thing resolves itself one way or another. If the family of the Orthodox Jew is not satisfied, then perhaps, to keep the peace, the other partner will embrace Orthodoxy with an Orthodox conversion if needed. If not, maybe the Orthodox family will grudgingly accommodate themselves to the marriage, which may produce a blended religious lifestyle some call Conservadox. Or the lovers will decide not to marry and break, at least temporarily, with one or both sets of parents. Sad, but not the end of the world. This happens often, for all sorts of reasons, to all sorts of couples.

Source: Weinfeld, Morton. 2001. *Like Everyone Else...But Different: The Paradoxical Success of Canadian Jews*. Toronto: McClelland & Stewart, 313. Used by permission of McClelland & Stewart Ltd. *The Canadian Publishers*.

Monogamy—marriage between one woman and one man—is the marriage form most familiar in Canada. However, variations on monogamy, too, are becoming more common. One of these, which is rapidly increasing in incidence, is **cohabitation**, or non-marital couples. Also increasing are same-sex couples. The 2001 Census of Canada asked about same-sex couples for the first time, finding that 0.5 percent of all couples reported themselves as same sex (Statistics Canada, 2002a). Sociological research (e.g., Sarantakos, 1998) shows that stable same-sex relationships are similar in many, but not all, ways to stable opposite-sex relationships. Another form is what sociologists have called **serial (or sequential) monogamy**. Serial monogamy is the marriage of a person over the life course to a series (or sequence) of partners, though only one at a time. In a society with high rates of divorce and remarriage such as ours, a growing number of people practise serial monogamy.

Is Marriage Still Valued?

Despite changes in timing and permanence, marriage continues to be central to interpersonal life in North America. See, for example, the popular book *The Case for Marriage...* by Linda J. Waite and Maggie Gallagher (2000). Cultural stereotypes and supports favouring traditional family life have not changed. Beaujot (2000) reports that Canadians typically see marriage as "natural," and believe it to be the foundation of family. Also, the vast majority (85 percent) felt that marriage provided more advantages than singlehood (2000: 108–9). Ganong, Coleman, and Mapes (1990) found that Americans view married people more favourably than unmarried. They also view parents more favourably than those who have not had children, and children with married parents more favourably than children whose parents are divorced. It is not clear that the same would be true in Canada, since Canadians have higher rates of cohabitation than the U.S. (Statistics Canada, 2002a).

Marriage shapes identities of men and women, and provides a support system for raising children. Social policy, tax structures, and the law support the institution of marriage. Increasingly, common-law status is being seen in Canada as either equivalent to marriage or carrying many of the same responsibilities and entitlements. Despite many doubts and obstacles, the great majority of people value the institution of marriage and want to marry. However, as we shall see, all of this is changing rapidly.

Zheng Wu's (2000) study of cohabitation and marriage reveals that Canadians place less importance on marriage than they used to: "there is clear evidence that people now place less emphasis on marriage than they did a decade ago...the centrality of marriage seems to have weakened (71)." For example, the percentage of Canadian women who felt it very important to be married in order to be happy in life has dropped from 41 percent in 1985 to 35 percent in 1995 (Wu, 65). Even though attitudes towards marriage are changing, most men and women still value the institution and feel it is important to be married. Wu also notes that Canadians have become more accepting of non-marital sexual behaviour and non-marital cohabitation. Common-law unions in the 2001 Census of Canada represented 14 percent of all couples, up from 6 percent in 1981 (Statistics Canada, 2002a). In Quebec, the proportion was 30 percent of all couples.

Thornton and Young-Demarco's (2001) U.S. study, which measured changing attitudes to family issues in the post-war period, had similar findings. Americans felt lessening pressure to marry or to have children, or to restrict intimate relations to marriage. Also, people are more accepting of alternative family forms and are more promoting of gender equality in family relationships. Nevertheless, there remains a "strong emphasis…on marriage, children and family life in America today" (Thornton & Young-Demarco, 1030). For Thornton, this implies an important shift in norms and values concerning intimate relationships. "Marriage may now be less important as a sanctioning institution for sex and cohabitation" (Thornton, 1989: 889). At the same time, fidelity in both marital and cohabiting relationships has increased in importance.

People have individual reasons for choosing to live common-law rather than getting married, but the question remains whether the chosen difference ceases if law and policy make the two equivalent. A similar question occurs with respect to gay and lesbian unions. The differences that may be valuable to gay and lesbian partners could be lost if their unions are defined as equivalent to common-law heterosexual couples, or married couples. Yet, it may be important to society to make gay and lesbian relationships equivalent to heterosexual relationships in terms of responsibilities and benefits. However, equivalence also could diminish ways in which heterosexual relationships might benefit from being more like gay and lesbian couples, particularly in terms of partner equality. In this and subsequent chapters, we will consider gay and lesbian couples in various ways as vital family forms.

Changing Attitudes that Affect Marriage

Into the 1960s, marriage was a social ritual by which young people were expected to declare their adulthood. Parents of "baby boomers" (children born between 1946 and 1964) epitomized this sentiment. These couples married in their early twenties, and had lots of children—about twice as many as the generation before and the generation after! There were good reasons for the strong interest in early marriage and family life. In the aftermath of World War II, North Americans were anxious to return to "normal" by refocusing on marriage, childbearing, and home life. The economic boom of the 1950s ensured the availability of jobs and housing and a "family wage" by which a family could live on the wages of one member, typically the man.

The sexual revolution and the women's movement paved the way for changes in attitudes to sexuality, and to women's place in the family and the economy. These attitudinal changes are reflected in changes in the timing, structure, and

Table 4.1 **THE CONTINUING IMPORTANCE AND POPULARITY OF MARRIAGE**

	1997	1998	1999	2000	2001
	NUMBER OF MARRIAGES				
Canada	153 306	153 190	153 380	153 697	156 340
Newfoundland and Labrador	3 227	3 117	3 043	3 001	2 940
Prince Edward Island	876	866	866	871	898
Nova Scotia	5 177	5 125	5 102	5 063	5 187
New Brunswick	4 089	4 044	4 013	3 993	4 120
Quebec	23 958	23 746	23 884	24 063	23 908
Ontario	64 535	64 536	64 533	64 704	66 167
Manitoba	6 261	6 218	6 211	6 199	6 344
Saskatchewan	5 707	5 730	5 752	5 739	5 740
Alberta	17 254	17 651	17 986	18 099	18 758
British Columbia	21 845	21 788	21 630	21 605	21 912
Yukon	167	161	153	150	141
Northwest Territories	144	142	141	144	140
Nunavut	66	66	66	66	85

Source: Data adapted from Statistics Canada website, CANSIM II, table 053-0001. Accessed May 22, 2002.

permanence of marriage. Marriage rates began to decline in the 1960s, declined rapidly in the 1970s, and have continued to decline at a slower rate since 1980, as mentioned above. The proportion of adult years spent outside marriage is higher than ever before. It began to rise as the average age at first marriage increased after 1960, a trend which continues today, as noted above.

Changing Attitudes to Marriage

Traditionally, marriage was viewed in terms of rights, duties, and obligations. Marriage in the past was as much an economic union as anything in the couple's own interest. In the West, a major attitude shift has placed greater emphasis on the personal or emotional bonds of close relations.

In 1981, only one in five North Americans surveyed expressed "traditional" family attitudes (Yankelovich, 1981). Likely, this number has since shrunk, although in the United States in particular there has been a resurgence of traditional family values. One in five, in 1981, believed life is about self-fulfillment, not duty to others in either family or society. Marriage and family life may be valued so long as they complement—or at least do not interfere with—personal aspirations and self-fulfillment. The remaining three in five North Americans, the majority, fall between these two extremes. For most, the quality of a relationship matters more than its structure (e.g., married versus common-law). The important question for three-fifths of people is "What makes an intimate relationship satisfying?" not the legal or societal arrangements under which the relationship exists.

Why, then, do people still keep up the old forms? Why do so many still get married, many in churches, dressed in expensive white bridal gowns and formal black tuxedos with cummerbunds? In short, formal weddings and going through the legal ceremony of marriage have more to do with marking a transition and/or gaining social approval than with emotional commitment. Many people still find the idea of legal marriage compelling, despite what they know about the realities of marriage and divorce. Enormous numbers of North Americans are neither rejecting the family or other long-lasting, close relationships, nor accepting family in a traditional form. Most are hoping to revitalize and reinterpret family (Baker, 2001; Beaujot, 2000; Scanzoni 1981a, 1981b, 1987, 2000, 2001), suiting their families themselves and their needs.

Attempts to reinterpret the family are the recent Ontario marriages of a lesbian couple and a gay couple. The rituals caused a predictable uproar, focusing as they did the clash between traditional and non-traditional conceptions of marriage. Those who view marriage as a sacred arrangement whose main purpose is procreation were upset by the use of marriage vows to legitimate same-sex cohabitation. Those who view marriage as an enduring close bond whose goal is love, companionship, and sex were pleased to see marriage vows exchanged between people who clearly cared for each other deeply.

Marriage Timing

> First comes love
>
> Then comes marriage
>
> Then comes Mary [or any girl's name] with a baby carriage.

So goes the skipping song. These days, however, there is less of a set sequence. Baby carriages may come first, with or without love, and marriage may never come, or may come along more than once. Still, people tend to live their lives

It's Never Too Late to Be a Virgin

No more sex till [sic] the wedding, some brides say.

Ms [X] said she hopes that a period of abstinence will ensure that the sparks fly during her honeymoon..., and help clear her conscience about having strayed from the expectations that her church and family hold about premarital sex.

These days, a period of "secondary virginity," as it is sometimes called, is increasingly the norm for many brides-to-be across the South, an accommodation to the modern reality of premarital sex and the traditional disapproval of it in the Bible Belt.

according to some sense of the appropriate timing of life events. Where this sense comes from is not entirely clear; it may be simply a sense of what is appropriate, or it may be pressure from parents, peers, the media, or some other source.

There are hints that the pressure some women feel to have children at, or by, a certain age comes from fears that infertility may set in or that risks to the pregnancy and/or the baby increase with age. This is the familiar "ticking biological clock." There *is* some slight increase in risks (of, for example, Down's syndrome) but the risks are not nearly high enough to account for the fears women have about not having children "on time." That these fears are often not particularly well grounded has little effect on the deep sense of the appropriate timing of life events people seem to have (Hanson, 1992).

A famous example of this occurred a few years ago when the media reported, falsely as it turned out, that women's probabilities of marrying after age 30 were abysmal based on an unpublished study by sociologists Neil Bennett and David Bloom (see Faludi, 1991: 9–14 for a summary of this story). The story was carried in a wide range of media for months, although the researchers whose work was reportedly being quoted denied that this was their conclusion. The result was massive fear by women that if they did not marry by that age, they would probably never marry.

The possibilities that this media-propagated fear might induce are difficult to imagine—settling for the next available man, perhaps. The story would be only an amusement were it not still cropping up in classes when age at marriage is discussed. Even though the media reports were not based on true research findings, the consequences of the reports were real nonetheless.

For Better or Worse, and for Fun

It was a beautiful June day... a perfect day for a wedding.

But as soon as the bridegroom appeared— wearing a bear costume—accompanied by a best "man" (who was actually a woman)... it became obvious to the few who may not have known that the wedding was not real.

It was an elaborate mock wedding, entirely fabricated by the bride, bridegroom and some close friends.

Across [the U.S.], whether for artistic expression or just to have a good time, perhaps dozens of men and women in their late teens and early 20s have been putting on costly pseudo-weddings, complete with a ceremony, reception, and festivities.

...the phenomenon of mock weddings among college-age students and recent graduates [may be due to] a new attitude toward marriage. Students' parents wed as soon as possible after graduation day. But now, a generation later, the marrying age has been pushed back. It may be that marriage is so far off that people want to have the marriage experience now.

Gee (1990) shows in a Canadian study that women measure the success of their lives, in part, on how closely they approximate the internalized ideals of family life events. This standard contradicts the increasing diversity of people's life courses. Women, for example, may get married or establish their first conjugal relationship in their teens or in their forties or older. The social rules are more flexible than ever, but people's internal sense of timing remains.

Most North Americans today tend to postpone marriage or establishment of a long-term committed relationship until they have completed their education. For a small minority, this is high school. For most, it is something beyond high school such as technical training, college, or university. This means that most people marry in their mid-20s or older, a pattern that is similar to what it was a century ago. In both Canada and the United States, many young people come to marriage with considerable experience with dating and sexual experimentation; many have lived with someone, either the new partner or someone else. This generally adds a maturity to the beginning of a marriage that can be important for its strength and survival. Older age and higher levels of education are also good predictors of marriage success and survival.

Living Solo

Marriage is not for everyone. Over the last two decades, one-person households have increased substantially in Canada. Approximately one-quarter of all households in Canada consist of a person living alone (Statistics Canada, 2001). Although elderly Canadians constitute the majority of single households, more and more younger Canadians are now living alone (Ram, 2000; Statistics Canada, 2002a). For example, 8 percent of women and 12 percent of men aged 25 to 34 are living alone. And for 35- to 44-year-olds, many more are now living alone than they were two decades ago. From 1981 to 1996, the proportion of people living alone in that age group increased from 7 to 11 percent for men, and from 4 to 7 percent for women (Ram, 2000). The proportion overall of one-person households in Canada increased from one-fifth of all households in 1981 to more than one-quarter in 2001. Among the reasons for living alone: never marrying, separation or divorce, widowhood. Some may be married and in a commuting relationship.

The growing popularity of living alone may be, in part, a function of people having sufficient money to indulge their preferences. It also reflects the divorce rate, in that more people at any given time may be between relationships and thus living alone. In part, the growth in living alone is due to an aging population containing more widowed people. However, it is also clear that some singles have made clear choices to live alone, and to develop a single lifestyle that they fully enjoy.

To live without a life partner is not new, nor is it even more common now than it was in the early part of this century, though more concerns are expressed about it now. Alone, however, need not mean lonely. Many who live solo are not isolated at all from their communities or circles of friends. People who are devoted to their work may prefer not to have a life partner; many great artists and writers have remained unmarried and some unattached in any permanent way. And the need for marriage for security and acceptability for women has declined, even though it is not gone.

Commuter/LAT Relationships

However, many people still feel a very strong urge to marry. Indeed, some people would prefer (or decide) to marry and live apart than postpone or avoid marriage. Consider so-called "**commuter marriages**," or what is now called a living apart together (LAT) relationship. A LAT is a marriage or other intimate relationship between partners who live in two separate households (Borell & Karlsson, 2002). Typically, couples take up separate residences after having shared a common one. More often now, couples live in two different homes from the beginning of their relationship, which is why some European sociologists call this arrangement "living together apart." Nault and Belanger (1996) also note committed long-term relationships in which both partners live with their parents. This is an aspect of the growing "cluttered nest" phenomenon that occurs when adult offspring return to the family home, or never leave it. In the 2001 Census of Canada, this pattern was observed as a growth pattern. Young adult Canadians in their early 20s, some 41 percent of them, live with their parents (Statistics Canada, 2002a). This will be explored in more detail in Chapter 12 when we consider fresh starts in family.

For some couples a LAT marriage is only a short-term arrangement. For others, it becomes a long-term lifestyle. Though LAT relationships remain a minority, nothing illustrates so well people's continued commitment to close involvement with a partner despite enormous odds and the conflict between the cultural values of living together versus pursuing career success. In addition, LAT relationships force couples to create intimacy differently than couples that see each other every day. Bawin-Legros et al. (1998), Skirboll and Taylor (1998), and Borell and Karlsson (2002) explore how long-distance couples maintain intimate connections without the ritual of everyday practices in a common place. While couples living in LAT relationships tend to have an enhanced appreciation for their spouse or family, it remains a complicated way to live (Groves & Horm-Wingard, 1991; Forsyth & Gramling, 1998; Borell & Karlsson, 2002).

Economic, cultural, or even policy pressures may be part of why couples choose this path. The main reason for keeping up a LAT relationship is career advancement. Today, more women in committed relationships are entering professional occupations that make it hard for them to move when their husbands move, and vice versa. Laws and policies also make relocating to another country as a couple challenging. For example, if your partner is offered a job in the United States, you as his/her partner may not be entitled to work at all there. At the same time, tighter job markets are forcing more people to relocate.

People in commuting marriages are usually well-educated and affluent professionals. As Forsyth and Gramling (1998) note, "commuting couples are making choices based on their career needs and ambitions both as individuals and as a couple" (95). According to Gerstel and Gross (1987), over half are academics, and the vast majority have completed some graduate studies. Most commuting partners are in their late thirties and over half have been married more than nine years. About half of commuting couples also have children.

The Falling Marriage Rate

More Canadians, as well as Americans, are postponing marriage. Fewer people are ever marrying, those who do are spending a smaller proportion of their lives in spousal relations, and marriages last a shorter average time than in the past (Espenshade, 1985; Wilson in Baker, 2001). These trends inevitably lead to a decline in the numbers of those experiencing marriage. Let's examine two theories to explain this: an economic explanation and a demographic explanation.

To Love, Honour and E-Mail: Net Helps Partners Stay Connected in Long-Distance Marriages

In commuter marriages, the loss of physical proximity to one's spouse can put a serious strain on the relationship. But thanks to the globalization of communication technology, long-distance couples who can't be together in the same physical space can at least interact with one another in cyberspace.

Career demands in our modern economy have forced many couples—over 2 million in the United States alone, according to one estimate by psychologist Karen Shanor—to live in separate households, at least for a period of time.

To keep phone bills from skyrocketing, many are turning to e-mail communication as a way to remain in constant contact with one another. It's also a convenient way to get around pesky time-zone differences, and it allows one to carefully sort out one's thoughts before constructing the message. This technology-based form of interaction between commuter spouses has become so common that it's even developed its own nickname: an "e-marriage."

Of course, e-mail does have its downfalls, not the least of which is its inability to effectively communicate emotions. To combat this, veteran e-mailers offer the following advice:

To convey anger: Use bold-face or upper-case lettering, or lots of exclamation points.

Affection: Use X's and O's, or pet names, or romantic text art, such as flowers.

Surprise: "Gasp! ... thud"

Finally, there's always the ubiquitous emoticons, in which letters and punctuation marks are combined to create smiley (and not-so-smiley) faces.

IRC (Internet Relay Chat) and other private cyberspace chat-rooms allow commuter couples to communicate over real time. And, with the growing popularity of scanners, microphones, and digital cameras, spouses can now send pictures, sound bites and live video feeds to each another, half way around the world.

Source: Matchan, Linda. 1998, September 25. *The Spectator* (Hamilton), Final Edition, F1. Reprinted courtesy of the Hamilton Spectator.

A leading economic argument is that marriage rates have fallen in recent decades because marriage is less necessary for both men and women, and the alternatives to marriage are more attractive. For women, financial independence and reproductive control have begun to tip the balance in favour of cohabitation or singlehood. Combining marriage, parenthood, and labour force participation is hard work, particularly for women.

Economist Gary Becker (1991) argues that lowered "gains to marriage" are primarily due to a rise in female earnings and labour force participation, along with a decline in fertility rates. Women have less to gain from motherhood, and more to gain from paid work, than they did in the past. Although this theory, which has been sharply critiqued (see McDaniel, 2000 for example), seems to suggest a greater equality of women's occupational opportunities and incomes than actually exists. It also takes a rationalistic, decision-making stance on emotional issues such as falling in love and marrying.

This theory could explain why African-American families have become even less stable than white families. Compared to African-American men, who have suffered enormous discrimination in employment and from the criminal justice system, African-American women are better educated and hold positions of higher status. On this argument, black women have even less to gain from marriage (and more to lose) than white women. More generally, data show that anything that provides a measure of independence and support to women, or puts them in a more nearly equal economic position (compared to men), reduces marriage rates.

An interesting demographic explanation comes from Richard Easterlin (1980, 1987; Easterlin et al., 1993), an American economist/demographer, who attributes low marriage rates and high divorce rates to rises in **cohort** size. Easterlin argues that relative income is tied to the size of a birth cohort (a group of persons with a common demographic statistic, such as date of birth, which determines job opportunities). The smaller the cohort, the more easily people in that age group will find jobs and promotions since the supply of labour will be smaller than the demand. So, North American baby boomers, born between 1946 and 1964, experience more financial insecurity and earn relatively less than their parents because they belonged to a particularly large birth cohort.

Baby boomers' marriage prospects would also be reduced because some of the large numbers of men in this cohort would not find suitable mates when ready for marriage, because fewer women were born in the last few years of the boom. And, if married, they may be more likely to divorce since they would see possibilities in that large cohort for new mates. This means that, on Easterlin's argument, the increase in divorce over the 1960s and 1970s may give a misleading idea of the long-term divorce trend. That is, "the traditional family may not be going down the drain quite so fast as some think" (Easterlin, 1980, 231). If smaller cohorts experience better economic conditions (and they usually do), they ought to feel better off than their parents and divorce less often. So, with smaller families, the divorce rate in the future might be lower than it was in the 1970s. Balakrishnan et al. (1990) and Wu and Balakrishnan (1995) argue similarly for Canada, and note that divorce is reduced when men earn higher incomes.

Guttentag and Secord (1983, 231) propose a different kind of demographic explanation that focuses on sex-ratio imbalance to account for changing rates of marriage and divorce. "When sex ratios (i.e., ratios of men to women) are high," they suggest, "men are in excess supply and women are in undersupply. Young adult women are highly valued because of their scarcity, and traditional sex roles are common." But when there is an "excess" of women, women feel more powerless and devalued by society. Men in this situation will have a weaker commitment to women, and women will in turn develop a weaker commitment to marriage and less willingness to depend upon men.

Guttentag and Secord note a greater sex-ratio imbalance among African Americans than whites. The reasons for this include a disproportionate number of African-American men in the armed forces and penal institutions, lower sex ratios for African Americans at birth, and higher than average death rates among African-American men due to homicide and suicide, among other health risks. This would account, they argue, for the lesser participation in marriage by African Americans.

Decline of the Traditional Family

The decline of the so-called traditional family is causing upheaval in Quebec and children are paying the price, suggests a Province of Quebec government study.

The increasing number of Quebec children born out of wedlock are four times more likely to face the separation of their parents before they reach their sixth birthday than are those born to a married couple, the study says. This conjugal instability places them at greater risk of developing behavioural problems, even before they enter elementary school.

"It seems that young people having children today have lived with many partners before they start having children," said Richard Tremblay, an expert in child development at the University of Montreal and one of the study's researchers. "There has been a habit of changing partners ...

and it's worrisome, because it leads to family break-ups and very complicated lives. It also leads to a lot of poverty, because single mothers are put in a more difficult position afterwards." Fellow researcher Nicole Marcil-Gratton, a demographer at the University of Montreal, said "unbridled conjugal mobility" might suit Quebec adults but has a negative impact on children.

Commissioned by the Quebec Health Department, the study is bound to raise the ire of some common-law couples and single parents, who know they're raising their children responsibly. The researchers conceded they were unable to gauge the impact of conjugal instability on childhood behavioural problems.

Poverty and a poor education might have a stronger negative influence, they said.

Source: Edmonton Journal. 2000, June 18. Final Edition, p. A3.
Material reprinted with the express permission of Edmonton Journal Company, a CanWest Partnership.

Unfortunately, none of these explanations tell us much about the changing nature of personal relationships. In spite of marriage rates being currently in decline, we cannot conclude that people are avoiding stable, emotionally committed relationships. In fact, when we look at the increased numbers of cohabiting couples, it is hard to conclude that North Americans avoid forming intimate couple relationships or avoid commitment.

Cohabitation

One significant change in family life in the Western world has been a sharp increase in cohabitation—people living together without being legally married. Living

Figure 4.1 COMMON-LAW AS A PERCENTAGE OF ALL COUPLES, CANADA, 1986, 1991, 1996, 2001

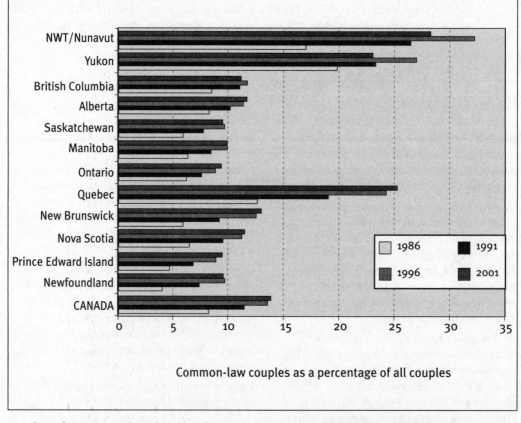

Common-law couples as a percentage of all couples

Source for 1986 to 1996 data: Adapted from the Statistics Canada website. 1999. "Age, Sex, Marital Status, and Common-law Status," Table 5.10. Source for 2001 data: Statistics Canada. 2002. "Distribution of Families by Structure, Canada, Provinces and Territories, 2001," page 24 in Profile of Canadian Families and Households: Diversification Continues. 2001 Census Analysis Series. Catalogue no. 96F0030XIE2001003.

together, also called cohabitation or **common-law** union, used to be more prevalent among working-class people. It also used to be seen as a lesser form of couple relationship than legal marriage. Now, however, cohabitation has become more common among all social classes, and is much more accepted. In Quebec, cohabitation has become the norm for younger couples, with legal marriage decidedly less preferred. Rates of cohabitation have increased dramatically in all provinces in the past two decades (Statistics Canada, 2001).

Cohabitation is, not surprisingly, a less stable form of union than legal marriage. It describes many different kinds of relationships, including some that may be less serious from the outset (Marcil-Gratton et al., 2000). Some sources have found that there may be more costs to cohabitation than benefits when compared to marriage. Cohabitating couples were found to have less involvement with extended families, less responsibility to the other partner during crisis, and a rejection of the union by religious institutions (Waite, 1999, 2000) and at times by policy in some provinces such as Alberta. Domestic violence rates were also higher in cohabitating relationships, as well as lower levels of psychological well-being. However, many cohabitating couples may disagree, as the numbers of long-lasting, happily cohabitating couples are growing rapidly. The 2001 Census finds a large growth in cohabitation among Canadians (Statistics Canada, 2002a).

Figure 4.2 **PROPORTION OF COMMON-LAW FAMILIES GROWS WHILE IT DECLINES FOR MARRIED FAMILIES, CANADA**

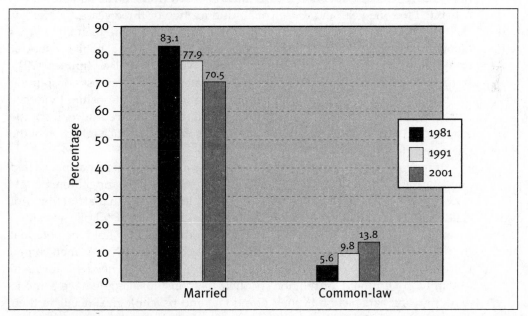

Source: Adapted from the Statistics Canada website. 2002. 2001 Census of Canada: Profile of Canadian Families and Households: Diversification Continues. Catalogue Number 96F0030X1E2001003. www.statcan.ca; accessed on October 22, 2002.

Some people may prefer cohabitation precisely because it does not have the same expectation of permanence, but others see cohabitation as permanent, a deliberate choice not to marry. Cohabitation gives people many of the expected benefits of family life—emotional and sexual satisfaction, mutual dependency, and support, for example—while they retain (or at least perceive) a greater degree of choice. Cohabitation may be a personal "vote" against the restrictions, legal and often religious, of traditional marriage.

Increasingly, couples in cohabiting relationships are having children, another indicator of their degree of commitment and permanence. In a 1995 study, almost half of cohabitors indicated they intended to have children (Wu, 2000). In 1993–94, 20.4 percent of all Canadian children were born to women living in common-law unions with the child's father. This is considerably different from the picture in 1963, when fewer than 5 percent of children were born to cohabiting parents. (Marcil-Gratton et al., 2000; Vanier Institute of the Family, 1994.) The old stigma of births "out of wedlock," once known as illegitimate births, is largely gone, particularly when the parents are in a stable, caring relationship. Especially in Quebec, people now see cohabitation as a lifelong way of family life—a close, committed couple relationship in which to have and raise children.

Increasing evidence suggests that cohabitation is an alternative form of family union, not trial marriage, for increasing numbers of people. If, however, cohabitation is seen as trial marriage, one might predict that the longer the cohabitation period, the more stable the subsequent marriage might be. However, not much difference is found in divorce rates between women who had previously cohabited for one year and those cohabiting for two or three years. One study, though, shows that women who cohabit premaritally for more than three years before marrying have higher divorce rates than women who cohabit for shorter durations with the man they eventually marry (Wu, 2000; Halli & Zimmer, 1991). It may be that it is not cohabitation *per se* that relates to the higher risks of splitting up, but the social risk factors that people bring into the relationship. Evidence shows that often people who cohabit may be already divorced once. If so, the difference in divorce rates may be not a result of cohabitation but a reflection of the characteristics of a self-selected group.

It may not be coincidental that the growth in cohabitation has paralleled later marriage, higher divorce rates, and lower rates of childbearing. More people now think of spousal relations as being about love and sexual attraction, not childbearing and cementing families together. The emergence of "plastic sexuality," sexuality freed from its close connection to reproduction, may hold the potential for democratization of personal relationships (Giddens, 1992). Women can be more like men in having sexual freedom. Fewer people today need the approval of family, government, or religion for their relationships. People have come to expect greater satisfaction of their emotional and psychological needs in their close relationships. This is the companionate relationship or marriage. Women, particularly, are less economically dependent on their partners than they used to be. These shifting norms, opportunities, and expectations have all contributed to a decline in the stability of married and cohabiting life.

In most Western countries, the same factors that have discouraged marriage have encouraged cohabitation. At the same time, the sexual revolution has removed the stigma that used to go with "living together" outside marriage. And women's greater access to education and jobs has reduced the incentive to marry, as we have seen.

Reflecting a need for new strategies, rates of first marriage have fallen to an all-time low in Canada. The falling national rate has been led by large declines in Quebec, which has one of the lowest marriage rates in the world. The trend of younger people opting for common-law unions over marriage partly explains this decline. Most people are merely delaying, not rejecting, marriage, so the average age at first marriage is increasing. Both increased common-law cohabitation and delayed marriage reflect at least a temporary flight from marriage, and predict lower percentages of people ever marrying. Likely the family will survive as an institution but not in the form we have grown up idealizing.

Increase in Cohabitation

In Canada, the growth in common-law unions has been dramatic, up nearly 40 percent in recent decades (Nault & Belanger 1996, 19). The proportion of adult Canadians living in common-law unions increased from 3.8 percent in 1981 to 6.9 percent in 1991. In the 2001 Census, the number of common-law *unions* had increased to 14 percent of all couples from 5.6 percent in 1981 (Statistics Canada, 2002a). And in Quebec, common-law unions represent 30 percent of all unions, up from 13 percent in 1986 and from 24 percent in 1996 (Statistics Canada, 2002a). For those aged 20 to 29 in 2001 in Canada, there is less inclination to form unions of any kind than in previous decades, but the popularity of common-law unions has increased (Statistics Canada, 2002a), with 56 percent of couples living in common-law unions. In the 25 to 29 age group, common-law relationships have risen from 17 percent to 32 percent in only one decade (Statistics Canada, 1999). Among Canadians, from the 2001 Census, the proportion of children (0–14) who live with common-law parents was 13 percent, more than four times the proportion in 1981 (Statistics Canada, 1998, 5; 2002a). The longest-duration common-law unions occur in Quebec, but time spent in common-law unions is on the rise across Canada.

There is surprisingly little variation in the rate of living in cohabiting family situations across the population subgroups. Between 1 percent and 2 percent lived in short-term cohabiting situations, whereas 3 percent to 5 percent were in cohabiting households six or more months of the year. The major exceptions are young adults, who had higher cohabitation rates; older people, who had lower rates; and members of single-parent families, among whom about 13 percent lived in a cohabiting situation at some time during 1990. Overall, three-quarters of those who cohabited at any time during the year (3.84 percent out of 5.13 percent) were in cohabiting situations that lasted six months or more.

Why is there a move away from traditional marriage (though it is still the majority choice) and toward common-law unions? (Mills, 2000). Some see the trend as a result of greater opportunities for women, enabling them to rely less on marriage as a kind of occupational choice (see, for example, Turcotte & Bélanger,

Table 4.2 PEOPLE LIVING IN HOUSEHOLDS WITH COHABITING AND NONCOHABITING HOUSEMATES, 1990 SIPP DATA

	Number of People (in millions)	HOUSEHOLD WITH A COHABITANT		HOUSEHOLD WITH A NONCOHABITING HOUSEMATE	
		1 to 5 Months (%)	6 Months to 1 Year (%)	1 to 5 Months (%)	6 Months to 1 Year (%)
All	241.5	1.29 (0.09)	3.84 (0.18)	1.20 (0.08)	2.96 (0.14)
Male	117.1	1.38 (0.11)	4.02 (0.20)	1.23 (0.09)	3.39 (0.19)
Female	124.5	1.20 (0.10)	3.67 (0.19)	1.17 (0.09)	2.56 (0.19)
Under Age 6	19.1	1.25 (0.22)	3.38 (0.43)	1.18 (0.23)	1.82 (0.28)
Age 6–17	41.7	0.93 (0.16)	2.88 (0.26)	0.67 (0.10)	1.60 (0.21)
Age 18–24	24.1	3.55 (0.43)	6.54 (0.55)	3.63 (0.35)	6.38 (0.49)
Age 25–44	79.9	1.77 (0.15)	5.48 (0.30)	1.38 (0.12)	4.24 (0.24)
Age 45–64	46.8	0.39 (0.07)	2.32 (0.22)	0.75 (0.15)	2.00 (0.24)
Age 65+	30.0	0.14 (0.05)	1.34 (0.22)	0.21 (0.07)	0.93 (0.18)
White	186.8	1.29 (0.10)	3.50 (0.18)	1.15 (0.09)	2.76 (0.16)
Black	27.0	1.38 (0.32)	5.68 (0.75)	0.74 (0.16)	2.66 (0.36)
Hispanic	19.6	1.24 (0.26)	4.23 (0.40)	2.37 (0.40)	4.80 (0.63)
Asian and Other	8.2	1.00 (0.33)	4.65 (1.01)	1.03 (0.28)	4.18 (0.86)
Single-Parent Family	16.3	3.27 (0.43)	9.80 (0.76)	2.65 (0.30)	6.04 (0.68)

Note: Numbers in parentheses are standard errors.

Source of table and interpretation: Bauman, Kurt J. "Shifting Family Definitions: The Effect of Cohabitation and Other Nonfamily Household Relationships on Measures of Poverty." *Demography*; Washington; August 1999; vol. 34 issue 3.

1997). Similar reasons are used to explain higher divorce rates, as we shall see in Chapter 11. It is not at all clear, however, that this is actually a factor (Le Bourdais et al., 2000; Oppenheimer, 1997). An alternative explanation focuses on men's deteriorating employment and income prospects. Men are seen by women as less stable providers (see, for example, Beaujot, 2000, 101; Easterlin & Crimmins, 1991). Changing values about traditional marriage also may play a role, as could distrust of traditional institutions.

The rise in cohabitation seems to show that people want intimate relations that are more flexible and less socially binding than legal marriage (Mills, 2000). For people of all ages, cohabitation offers many of the usual benefits of marriage, with fewer socially imposed expectations and fewer legal obligations. It is more of an individually created intimate relationship.

In both Canada and the United States, much of the early increase in cohabitation was accounted for by young people, particularly college and university students. In the mid-1970s, a national U.S. survey (Clayton & Voss, 1977) found 18 percent of young men had lived with a woman for six months or more. A study of college students discovered that nearly four respondents in five would cohabit if given the opportunity. And another study in the same era (Hobart & Grigel, 1992) found 71 percent of the men and 43 percent of the women expressing a desire to cohabit. A more recent study revealed that fully 86 percent of Canadian youths aged 15 to 19 approve of cohabitation and 63 percent approve of a cohabiting couple having children together (Bibby, 2001b). Perhaps interestingly, these approval levels are somewhat lower than they were a decade ago.

In the 1970s, students said the main advantages of cohabitation were convenience, testing for compatibility, love, hope of establishing a more permanent relationship, and economic considerations. Reasons for not cohabiting included parental disapproval, disapproval of partner, conscience, and fear of pregnancy (Huang-Hickrod & Leonard, 1980). Hobart & Gringel's (1992) Canadian study found that students favoured cohabitation as a way to gain independence from their family. Students who were more likely to favour cohabitation tended also to have positive family relationships and parents who held more liberal attitudes towards sexual relationships.

For many, living together was a practical way of splitting expenses. For others, cohabitation was a part of the dating and mating process—a prelude to marriage. For women, cohabitation was a part of the courtship process, not a long-range lifestyle. For others, particularly in the 1990s and 2000s, cohabitation is a long-term alternative. It is a marriage-like commitment without the wedding, and with obligations to each other, often spelled out in law.

Another group of cohabitors is older, previously married people. Over 40 percent of women cohabitants are previously married (Statistics Canada, 2001). These women had their own reasons for living together instead of marrying. Some were separated but not yet divorced from a partner, so they couldn't legally remarry. Religious beliefs prevented others from divorcing and remarrying. Finally, some widows did not want their pension benefits reduced by remarriage (Connidis, 2001).

International Comparisons

In North America, Australia, New Zealand, and most of Europe, cohabitation has increased, marriage rates have declined, and divorce rates have also increased (Baker, 2001, 116). Baker notes that "a growing percentage of the population lives outside the male breadwinner/female caregiver family that was prevalent in the 1950s and 1960s." Gay and lesbian cohabitation has also become more prominent as more countries grant these couples more legal rights. These countries have become more liberal in their attitudes towards sexuality and close relationships. Such changing attitudes are lowering the significance placed on marriage, making cohabitation or "de facto" relationships increasingly important (Baker, 2001).

Meyer and Schulze (1983) compared several European countries and the United States and found that the most important reason for the increase in cohabitation was the growth in female labour force participation; women with strong commitments to employment are less committed to marriage and family life and more receptive to alternate living arrangements. Women in cohabiting relationships are more educated than the average and are materially less dependent on their "mates" than less educated women. This is a big change from the past when it was the less educated who cohabited most often.

In Canada, Wu (2000) found that the number of people in cohabiting relationships increased by 158 percent over the 15-year period from 1981 to 1996. The increase in Quebec is particularly striking, where the rate of cohabitation increased by 231 percent over the same period. The Quebec rate of cohabitation is now equal to that of the Scandinavian countries (Statistics Canada, 2002a). The Family History Survey (Burch, 1989) found about one adult Canadian in six had cohabited at one time or another. Among young people (aged 18 to 29), the proportion was higher: about one man in five, and one woman in four. On Census Day 1981, about 6 percent of the couples enumerated were in a cohabiting relationship. On Census Day 1996, 11.7 percent lived in a cohabiting relationship; one in four in Quebec. On Census Day 2001, it was 14 percent in Canada, and 30 percent in Quebec (Statistics Canada, 2002a). The Canadian rate of cohabitation is about twice as high as in the United States.

Cohabitation, perhaps surprisingly to some, is more common in Quebec than in any other Canadian province—even than in any of the American states—despite Quebec's history of strict Catholicism (Balakrishnan et al. 1990, 8; Le Bourdais & Marcil-Gratton, 1996; Wu, 2000). By age 35, 44 percent of Quebec men and 40 percent of Quebec women will have cohabited, compared to only 28 percent for either sex in the rest of Canada. In each census year since 1981— when information on cohabitation first started being collected—Quebec had the highest rate of cohabitation (Wu, 2000). This shows that religious sanctions on cohabitation and non-marital sex have been seriously weakened since the sexual revolution of the 1960s. Some argue that it is the very strictness of those sanctions that has resulted in a backlash against them, and a reluctance to marry.

Since the 1970s, there has been a dramatic increase in cohabitation in the United States. Between 1970 and 1980, the number of cohabiting couples tripled to 1.6 million couples. By 1981 the number had risen to approximately 1.8 million, about 4 percent of all couples (Spanier, 1983). And this number has continued to rise. The U.S. Bureau of the Census projects that the number of cohabiting couples will reach approximately 6.5 million by 2006 (Shaw Crouse, 1999). More than one in every three ever-married 25- to 34-year-old Americans lived together before their first marriage (Cherlin, 1989). To take just one example, in Lane County, Oregon, premarital cohabitation increased from 13 percent in 1970 to 53 percent in 1980. Gwartney-Gibbs (1986) estimated this increase by noting addresses on marriage licence applications. Cohabiting couples were those who had identical addresses prior to marriage.

Canada, in 2000, introduced legislation in Parliament that would give same-sex partners the same social and tax benefits as heterosexual partners. This federal bill, Bill C23, does not, however, give gay and lesbian couples the right to marry. Extending marriage rights to same-sex couples is an issue of significant political debate. In a 2002 landmark case, the Ontario Superior Court ruled that restricting marriage to opposite-sex couples was unconstitutional. The court then gave the province and the federal government a total of two years to change their laws and to allow same-sex couples to wed. Ontario has not appealed the Superior Court ruling, but the federal government has. Interestingly, the federal government submitted this appeal to the Ontario Court of Appeal only three days after it released the results of a national public opinion poll that showed most Canadians favouring the extension of marriage rights to same-sex couples (religious tolerance.org, 2002). As of the time of writing, marriage continues to be defined in law in Canada as the union of a man and a woman. However, this opportunity has allowed more gay and lesbian couples to acknowledge their relationships as recognized by the government.

In Australia, cohabitation has increased, although the rates are lower than in North America (Baker, 2001; Khoo, 1987). An Australian Bureau of the Census study found that nearly 5 percent of all couples living together in Australia in 1982 were unmarried. The majority of cohabitors were young people, 70 percent under the age of 35. One-third of the cohabitors were separated or divorced from earlier partners. Over one-third of the cohabiting couples were living with dependent children. Since then, the cohabitation rate in Australia has doubled. In the mid-1990s, approximately 10 percent of couples were cohabiting (Baker, 2001).

In Europe, the trend to increased cohabitation had already appeared by the end of World War II (Festy 1985; Kamerman & Kahn, 1997). Cohabitation is most commonly found in Scandinavia, particularly Sweden, where it has a long history. In 2000, the rate of cohabitation in Sweden was 30 percent of all couples and in Norway 24.5 percent, compared to Quebec at 29.8 percent, Canada at 16.0 percent, and the United States at 8.2 percent (Statistics Canada, 2002a).

Because of its history, there are interesting differences in cohabitation practices in Scandinavia compared to the rest of Europe and the United States. In Scandinavia, cohabitation has long been accepted as an alternative or prelude to marriage. Indeed, in Sweden, a country historically with the world's highest rates of cohabitation, it is unusual for people to marry without living together first. But even in Sweden, rates of cohabitation have increased since the mid-1960s. This increase results from couples living together at younger ages and after a shorter period of acquaintance than previously. Hoem (1986) argues that these cohabiting unions are more like extended dates, or going steady, than they are like traditional marriages, but there is likely variation among couples.

Others (see, for example, Bracher & Santow, 1998; Duvander, 1999; Kiernan & Estaugh, 1993), however, suggest that few differences exist between cohabitation and marriage in Sweden today. According to Fawcett (1990), Swedish cohabitants are known as "sambor," a term that carries a sense of dignity and that gives legitimacy to the relationship. There is no equivalent word to "sambor" in English.

Increases in cohabitation are reflective of a shift in recent decades in the life-course trend that Swedish couples follow. Swedish couples in the 1960s would typically cohabit first, then marry, then have children. By the 1970s, however, this trend had already changed. Today, it is more typical to cohabit as an alternative to marriage or to marry only after children are born into the cohabiting union (Bracher & Santow, 1998). In her study of cohabitation and marriage rates in Sweden, Duvander (1999) found that whether or not cohabiting women decide to marry their partners depends on various factors, such as the perception of economic gains from marriage, life course stage, and family socialization. The increase in cohabitation is also related to a decline or delay in remarriage among divorced people. In Norway and Sweden, cohabitation is by far the preferred type of second union (Bracher & Santow, 1998; Blom, 1994; Hoem & Hoem, 1992; Blanc, 1987).

Swedish social policy (Benoit, 2000) may provide part of the reason; since 1955, paid maternity leave has been available to all Swedish women, regardless of their marital status. Other Swedish policies include no-fault divorce, free birth control, access to abortion, good childcare, state-paid children's allowances, and state-protected child support payments. Even the income tax system is organized in such a way that marital status is all but irrelevant. Sweden's policies focus on individuals and the well-being of children, not the legal arrangements of intimate couple relationships. In effect, such laws and policies make the decision about marrying or cohabiting unimportant.

Spain has a relatively low rate of cohabitation compared to most European countries, but cohabitation is still generally accepted. Legally, the rights of cohabitating partners is also being recognized (Tobio, 2001). Many European countries have also acknowledged gay and lesbian couples. For example, Denmark has legally accepted gay couples since 1989. Since then, all Scandinavian countries, Switzerland, The Netherlands, and Belgium have legally recognized same-sex unions. Germany, Italy, and Spain all have jurisdictions in which same-sex couples are legally recognized.

The dramatic increase in the incidence of cohabitation has attracted considerable interest. As a result, research has been directed at discovering the characteristics of those who cohabit, the nature of cohabiting relationships, and the subsequent impact on marriage.

Legal Implications

The major difference between marriage and cohabitation is that the former is an explicit legal commitment and the latter is not in quite the same way. In some provinces, such as Ontario, cohabitation may also mean differences in rights to spousal support or property acquired during the relationship. In other provinces, such as Alberta, cohabiting relationships are as yet not recognized as comparable to legal marriages. A proposal for recognizing cohabiting relationships in law was developed in winter 2002, however, in Alberta. The proposal includes same-sex couples and people sharing committed responsible relationships, such as sisters who live together or an adult child sharing a home with an aging parent. Couples who are cohabiting would be wise to check what rights and obligations they have where they live. They might be surprised! Even so, law and policy increasingly regard a cohabiting relationship that lasts for more than three years as a legally binding relationship, a "common-law" partnership. Long-term cohabitants are legally expected, in most jurisdictions in Canada, to support each other in the relationship and after a breakup. The degree of this expectation, however, varies from province to province, state to state in the U.S. One thing is clear, however: the difference between marriage and cohabitation is blurring.

Confusion and ignorance are so widespread on these issues that the province of Ontario has published a pamphlet called "What you should know about family law in Ontario" (August 1999, 7). Here is some of what it says about "living together:"

> Common-law couples do not have the same rights as married couples to a share in the value of property that their partner bought while they were living together. Usually, furniture, household belongings and other property belong to the person who bought them.

> Common-law couples also have no special rights to stay in the home they have been sharing while living together.

> However, if you have contributed to property your partner owns, you may be able to claim a share in it. Unless your partner agrees to pay you back, you will have to go to court to prove your contribution.

The pamphlet goes on to say that couples in common-law relationships can sign a cohabitation agreement to protect their rights and spell out who owns what in the event of a breakup. The point is, we should not assume that arrangements that prevail in one jurisdiction prevail in another or that the frequency and acceptance of common-law unions have made them equal to marriage in the face of the law.

Most provinces in Canada treat common-law unions that last for some specific period, typically more than two years, the same as married unions; the obligations of the partners to their children are the same, and the split of property if the union ends may be the same as it would be for married couples, although this varies. Putting into writing each person's understanding of the relationship can be helpful in sorting things out should the relationship end or one partner die. It is also a good protection to have a contract to protect them, their property, and their children.

For example, if an older couple of similar means decides to share a home, but wish for their estates to go to their adult children rather than to each other should one die, it is wise to have this in writing. Wills should also deal with occupancy arrangements. Otherwise, a surviving partner could be evicted by the government or by the partner's children from a house in which he or she has lived for years. New types of unions require new and sometimes careful steps.

The years 1999 and 2000 marked a major step forward in the recognition of the rights of lesbian and gay couples. Quebec, Ontario, and the federal government adopted omnibus bills granting same-sex common-law partners almost all the same rights as heterosexual couples under the tax system, social security programs, and family law (Rose, 2000). Others are moving forward with some recognition of same-sex couples in 2002. While this policy change is a great advancement in the acceptance of homosexual relationships, gay and lesbian couples must take the same precautions with their assets as heterosexual common-law unions.

Some argue that legalized same-sex unions are beneficial to the institution of marriage, for they eliminate stereotypical gender roles that generate sexist legal treatments when dealing with heterosexual couples (Bolte, 1998). One can examine this phenomenon as gay and lesbian couples continue to be recognized.

Births in Common-Law Unions

Births to unmarried people are increasingly common in Canada, and especially in Quebec. In the 2001 Census of Canada, about 13 percent of all children under age 14 lived with common-law parents. This is more than four times the proportion in 1981 (3.1 percent) (Statistics Canada, 2002a). The rate in Quebec in 2001 is 29 percent (Statistics Canada, 2002a). This suggests clearly a change in the historical belief that baby carriages follow marriage and not the other way around.

Some people might assume that such births would produce deserted women and lone-parent families, but as is often the case in sociology, the reality is quite different. As unions and marriages become less based on gender specialization and economic dependence of the woman on the man, choices emerge on how families can be created by those in them. The growth in childbearing in cohabiting relationships may be an indication of that kind of change in both attitude and behaviour. In the majority of cases of births to legally unmarried people, the parents are living together. Parents who cohabited before marrying are more likely to separate than parents who married without cohabiting (Marcil-Gratton, LeBourdais, & Lapierre-Adamcyk, 2000). They are, however, clearly less likely to do so than couples who remained in a cohabiting relationship (Marcil-Gratton, LeBourdais, & Lapierre-Adamcyk, 2000).

The image we have of teen pregnancies and young, unwed, deserted single mothers is largely derived from U.S. experience and is unparalleled in Canada and anywhere else in the Western world. Also, while it is commonly assumed that the experience of single, teenage motherhood is concentrated among young African-American women, Kristen Luker (1997) uses U.S. census statistics to show how this assumption is, in fact, a myth. In Canada, only 7 percent of births occur among single, non-cohabiting women (Beaujot, 2000). In most cases, there is no reason to believe that the feelings, promises, or the sense of family sharing are any less genuine because they are not formalized in law or religion.

As more countries accept or legalize gay and lesbian unions, the number of couples wishing to adopt a child or raise a child with two same-sex parents will naturally increase. Some individuals are concerned for the children of these unions, wondering if their development will be different from children of heterosexual parents. A common fear is that a child growing up in a homosexual household will also be homosexual. This fear is largely unfounded. Among lesbian couples, either mother's sexual orientation does not determine the child's gender development or increase the likelihood of psychological problems (Mooney-Somers & Golombok, 2000). Rather, the quality of family relationships makes more of an impact on the child's well-being. Similar findings are found for the children of gay male parents (Fitzgerald, 1999).

Effect of Cohabitation on Marriage

The majority of Canadians now live common-law in their first conjugal relationship (Statistics Canada, 1997; Wu, 2000). Common-law relationships are more often now the basis of long-term, sometimes lifelong, committed unions, in which increasing numbers of couples have children and even grandchildren. For example, 20 percent of all babies born in 1994–95 were born to parents living in common-law relationships. In Quebec, where cohabitation is most common, over 43 percent of births occurred in common-law relationships (Marcil-Gratton et al., 2000).

Surprisingly perhaps, the probability of divorce is greater, on average, for couples who marry after having lived together than for couples who marry without living together. Estimates suggest the probability of marital dissolution is two to three times higher among couples who lived together before marriage

(Le Bourdais et al., 2000; Marcil-Gratton et al., 2000; Wu, 2000). The reasons for this are complex and maybe even contradictory. Individuals who live together prior to marriage may have different characteristics than those who do not, in terms of religion, family supports, and perhaps class or ethnic backgrounds, so they may not be directly comparable to those who marry.

It may be, as well, that there is considerable diversity among those who live common-law, with many living in committed long-term relationships and others living in shorter-term, less committed relationships. When the two are lumped together and compared with those who marry, the result may appear that living common-law prior to marrying puts couples at greater risk of divorce than actually may be the case.

Zheng Wu's (2000) study on cohabitation in Canada sheds some light on this issue. Wu argues that the higher rate of marital disruption among couples who cohabited before marriage can—at least partially—be explained by individual characteristics and the self-selection process in deciding to cohabit:

> People who cohabited prior to marriage are generally less religious and conventional, they are probably less hesitant to end marriages when they encounter marital problems than people who did not cohabit before marriage. Moreover, the experience of living together may itself also be a factor. Living together without marriage can change a couple's views of marriage and divorce, and foster less conventional attitudes regarding marriage and family life. (Wu, 2000: 3)

Wu's empirical analysis supports this hypothesis. He found, for example, that people who have a history of cohabitation are at higher risk of divorce, suggesting that some people who cohabit may be less committed to the idea of life-long commitment. The length of cohabitation is also a factor, especially for men: those who experience longer periods of premarital cohabitation also tend to have more stable marriages. For women, having a job outside the home or being in school are associated with higher rates of divorce.

Wu also notes, however, that cohabitation itself is also more common among working women than among women who stay at home. This suggests that marriage sometimes is a less attractive option for women who are financially independent. Higher educational status is another characteristic more common to divorced couples who lived together before they married, while the presence of children tends to be a stabilizing factor. In terms of cultural factors, Wu notes that the risk of divorce is lower among Catholics and Protestants than those with other or no religious affiliation. Risk of divorce is also lower for foreign-born Canadians. Interestingly, the risk of divorce is no higher in Quebec, where cohabitation is much more common, than it is in other provinces.

Yet another possible explanation of the finding that couples who cohabit and then marry seem to have higher rates of divorce may be methodological. If all relationships are tracked from their beginnings, whether in cohabitation or marriage, then the finding that cohabitants have greater risk for union dissolution disappears. The idea is that here we are including *all* relationships, including those cohabitants who never marry but stay together. In the previously described study, the focus is only on those who cohabit and then marry, which may be a select group of couples, who might be under social pressures to change their relationship, pressures that could stress their relationships.

We know that cohabiting relationships are shorter-lived, on average, than legal marriages. But we don't know the effect cohabitation has on marriage and if cohabitation makes for stronger, more stable marital relationships. Unfortunately, the relationship between cohabitation and later marital success is not clear.

Often, common-law partnerships are a prelude to marriage, with just under half of the people ever in a common-law union ending up marrying their common-law partner. After five years of cohabitation, 44 percent of women and 41 percent of men end up marrying their partner (Wu, 2000). This suggests that common-law unions sometimes do still serve as trial marriages. However, as stated above, cohabiting before marriage does not make the marriage more likely to succeed. Prior cohabitation is found to be positively related to marital disagreement and an increased chance of divorce. We do not know why this is so. We have no sociological evidence that cohabitation itself causes a decline in the quality of a later marriage; but neither is there any clear evidence that cohabitation improves mate selection or prepares people for marriage. On the other hand, the finding may be simply a result of how the research is done, and therefore have no implications for cohabitation prior to marriage.

In Sweden, pre-marital cohabitation also increases the risk of divorce (Hoem & Hoem, 1992; Hoem, 1997). Women who cohabit premaritally have almost 80 percent higher marital dissolution rates than those who do not. Women who cohabit for three or more years prior to marriage have 50 percent higher dissolution rates than women who cohabit for shorter durations. Also, cohabitors and non-cohabitors whose marriages have remained intact for eight years have identical dissolution rates after that time. The evidence strongly indicates a weaker commitment to the institution of marriage on the part of those who cohabit premaritally (Bennett, Blanc, & Bloom, 1988). More recent research (e.g., Duvander, 1999), however, suggests that when union stability is prioritized, couples who cohabit premaritally are strongly committed to their marriage. This occurs, for example, among older couples, when children are born (where the risk of divorce declines as the number of children increases), or after a marriage search. Some Canadian studies like Le Bourdais and Marcil-Gratton (1996), and American studies such as Bumpass and Sweet (1989), for example, have found that couples that had previously cohabited were more likely to be divorced after 10 years than couples who had not cohabited. In Canada, the divorce rate after 10 years of marriage is 26 percent for those who cohabited before marrying and only 16 percent for those who did not (Wu, 2000).

Although Canadian research (e.g., Ambert, 1998; Lapierre-Adamcyk & Charvet, 2000; Le Bourdais & Marcil-Gratton, 1996; Wu & Balakrishnan, 1995;

Wu, 2000) suggests that couples who live together before marrying have higher rates of dissolution, White's (1987) study of a large sample of ever-married Canadians found that premarital cohabitation has a positive effect on staying married. This remains when length of marriage and age at marriage are controlled. Also, Watson, and DeMeo (1987) find that the premarital relationship of the couples, whether cohabitation or a traditional courtship ending in marriage, has no long-term effect on the marital adjustment of intact couples.

One would think that people who have cohabited would know when they were ready to commit themselves to a long-term relationship. But cohabitation seems to be no better a "screening device" for mates, or preparation for marriage, than traditional courtship. The data hint that people who are willing to cohabit are also willing to divorce. Along these lines, Canadian sociologist Zheng Wu states that "people who cohabitate tend to have less conventional views towards marriage or see themselves as poor risks in terms of a long-term relationship" (2000: 3). Similarly, Hall and Zhao (1995) and Balakrishnan (1987) find that people who cohabit are less stability-minded, or conformist, than people who marry legally. This makes sense, since by cohabiting, the couples may be carving out their own sense of relationship and responsibilities to each other.

Teachman and Polonko (1990), on the other hand, argued that the effect of cohabitation on marriage duration must be assessed more carefully. If cohabitants have spent more time in a relationship than non-cohabitants, then not only the total duration of the relationship should be examined but also the length of the marriage. When this is done, there is no difference in marital duration between those who cohabit and those who do not prior to marriage.

Some in cohabiting relationships have little desire to remain in a stable union. Nor may they plan to marry. In an early study, Glick and Norton (1977) reported that 63 percent of cohabiting couples in the United States remain together less than two years. Most of those staying together less than two years say they do not intend to marry each other, and in fact do not do so. More recently in Canada, some cohabiting unions may be short-lived because, in about half the cases, they are converted into legal marriage within a few years (Burch, 1989). But in the other half, some couples may continue to cohabit, while others break up.

Young People's Attitudes

Reginald Bibby's (2001b) recent study of Canadian youths found that the vast majority—almost nine out of ten—approve of cohabitation. Further, about 63 percent of teenagers feel it is okay for a non-married couple to have children together, and fully three-quarters think that homosexual couples should be entitled to the same rights as other Canadians. Interestingly, Canadian teenagers are more conservative in some of their views about intimate relationships than Canadian adults. For example, 14 percent of adults in Bibby's study approve of extramarital sexual relations, compared to only 9 percent of teens. Adults are also more likely than teens to approve of a non-married couple having children, and of same-sex sexual relations.

Another recent study, this one of white high-school seniors (Lye & Waldron, 1997), is revealing but certainly not the final word, since non-white students are not included in the sample. As expected, students who are more progressive, socially conscious, and/or sympathetic to gender equality, particularly males, were more favourably inclined toward cohabitation. Concerns about social fairness and the well-being of others may translate into support for gender equality and acceptance of cohabitation. By contrast, more conservative political beliefs were associated with traditional attitudes toward both gender issues and cohabitation.

An older study that uses various race/ethnic groups as its sample found that adolescents' expectations about family formation vary by race/ethnic group. Black adolescents are the most likely group to expect adolescent childbearing, the least likely to expect marriage at any age, and the most likely to expect nonmarital childbearing as teenagers or later in life. In addition, number of siblings has effects for black and Hispanic teenagers' expectations, but there are not significant effects for whites. Poverty also affects expectations somewhat more among black and Hispanic youth than among whites (Trent, 1992).

Elderly Couples

As the majority of baby boomers will soon be over 65, some attention should be paid to elderly couples. Martel and Legare (2000) found that 40 percent of Québécois seniors are involved in reciprocal relationships, most often with their partners.

Many elderly couples do not live alone—they live with extended families, especially children, which further contributes to the "cluttered nest" phenomenon. Elderly couples live with their children for many reasons: illness, limited income, loneliness, or unsuitable housing. Though many older people might prefer more independent living, shrinking social services make this independence difficult. For example, cluttered nests are more likely among older immigrants than Canadian-born elderly. A 1998 study showed that because older immigrants arriving in Canada are not eligible for government transfer payments or welfare benefits for up to 10 years, there is an 18 times greater chance that they will live with family than those elderly born in Canada (Basavarajappa, 1998). American research by Wilmoth et al. (1997) suggests that immigration policies, and not economic resources, functional limitations, or acculturation, influence the decision of elderly couples to move in with their children.

The 2001 Census of Canada, however, reveals that more seniors now live with their spouse or partner than previously (Statistics Canada, 2002a). This is not surprising since there has been an extension in healthy life expectancy among Canadians, enabling them to live independently and in an intact couple for a longer period of their lives. More men than women now live with their spouses until late in life. This is because men die earlier and more often leave widows. The 2001 Census also found a growing tendency for seniors, particularly women, to live alone: 35 percent of women aged 65 and above lived alone in 2001 (Statistics Canada, 2002a). For women over age 85, the percentage living alone in 2001 was 38 (Statistics Canada, 2002a).

Day-to-day caring for one's partner becomes an important factor in elderly couples, as they become more prone to illness. This task is carried out mostly by one's partner, which can put extra pressure on the relationship. Caring for one's spouse in old age is a key issue for current debates about Canada's aging society. Research (Keating et al., 1999) suggests that spouses are the least likely of all informal care providers to ask for assistance with caring, despite the fact that they often have high caregiving loads. Keating and her colleagues found that spouses may underreport the amount of care they actually provide. The future challenge for Canada "lies in finding ways to provide support to spouses who tend not to reach out for support" (Keating et al., 1999: 100). In addition to underreporting care and not asking for assistance, the responsibility of caring for one's spouse can put strain on the marriage and can also negatively impact the caregiver's emotional and physical health. These include feelings of guilt, insufficient personal or "me" time, increased stress, feelings of social isolation, and poor sleeping patterns. Women are usually more likely than men to experience these consequences and to suffer from "caregiver burnout" (Keating et al., 1999; McDaniel, 1999). Gendered roles and expectations reflect why older women feel more negatively about caring for ailing partners as opposed to men, who report more positive experiences (Davidson, Arber, & Ginn, 2000; McDaniel, 1999). We will discuss gender roles and marital wellness further in the next chapter.

Same-Sex Couples

Recent media attention and increasing social acceptance of same-sex couples may lead some readers to believe that these arrangements are new ways to live in intimate relationships; not so. Gay and lesbians have formed and lived in couples since the beginning of families. It is, however, a challenge to know how many gay and lesbian couples there are. One recent U.S. study (Black et al., 2000) systematically examines national data from the U.S. Census and from other national datasets. The conclusions reached are that gay and lesbian couples are considered underestimated in the U.S. Census, with perhaps only one-third self-reporting as such; that gay and lesbian couples concentrate in about 20 U.S. cities; and that many gay and lesbian couples have children (Black et al., 2000, 153). Much is to be learned sociologically about couplehood generally by looking at gay and lesbian couples.

Some sociologists, among them Anthony Giddens (1992), have argued that equality is not fully possible in a traditional heterosexual union; there are too many economic and social pressures toward inequality of the partners. Gillian

Figure 4.3 PERCENTAGE OF ALL COUPLES THAT ARE IN SAME-SEX
RELATIONSHIPS, CANADA, 2001

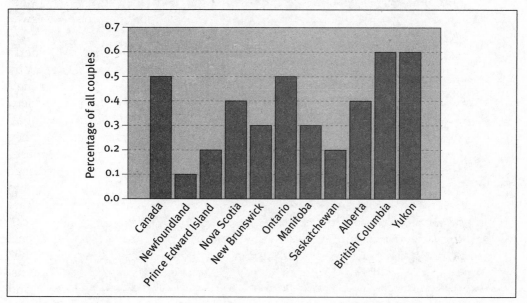

Source: Adapted from the Statistics Canada website. 2000. 2001 Census of Canada: Profile of Canadian Families and Households: Diversification Continues. Catalogue Number 96F0030X1E2001003. www.statcan.ca; accessed on October 22, 2002.

Dunne (1997) similarly argues that lesbian unions invite us to look more closely at heterosexual couples, because she sees heterosexuality as an institution that affects and regulates everyday social life. In looking clearly at how lesbians live in close relations, Dunne says we can learn about the links of intimate relationships to economic and social systems. Social constructionist theories in sociology argue that sexuality is socially created (e.g., Connell, 1987; Lorber, 1996; Namaste, 1994). These theories teach us that the very idea of people having a stable sexual orientation—heterosexual or homosexual—is maintained through a complex and powerful constellation of structural forces. Also, such theories argue that the very existence of heterosexuality is dependent on the existence of homosexuality. Indeed, a recent U.S. study of teen sexuality (Risman and Schwartz, 2002, 23) suggests that "Categories of gay and straight, queer or not, may be more fluid among teens today than ever before." In this way, studying the lives of gay and lesbian couples sheds light on the ways that heterosexuality as a social institution organizes intimate relationships and families, and how it maintains structures of power within those relationships.

Canadian sociologist Michelle Owens (2001), for example, examines how same-sex families disrupt or change our dominant views of what "normal" families are and what they do. Coming from a relatively new theoretical tradition known as Queer Theory, Owens argues that "families headed by same-sex couples signal

Some argue that legalized same-sex unions are beneficial to the institution of marriage, for they eliminate stereotypical gender roles that generate sexist legal treatments when dealing with heterosexual couples. In July 2002 an Ontario court ruled to allow same-sex marriage, finding that prohibiting gay couples from marrying is unconstitutional and violates the Charter of Rights and Freedoms.

both a 'normalization of the queer' and a 'queering of the normal'" (2001, 97). On one hand, many same-sex families want to be recognized as just like heterosexual families. On the other hand, the very situation of being a same-sex couple raising children resists the dominant model of family, because the dominant model operates on the premise of gender difference. Since conventional family norms don't apply in the same way, gay and lesbian couples must renegotiate and re-create for themselves how roles, responsibilities, and the balance of power will be distributed in their family. Thus, same-sex couples "normalize the queer" by forming families, by raising children, and in struggling to be recognized as being just like heterosexual families in their abilities to parent, to provide stability, and to be self-sufficient. At the same time, they "queer the normal" because their very existence signals that families are defined as being heterosexual. Therefore, same-sex families force us to examine in new ways how we think of family, what we do as families, and what we want the family to be.

Fiona Nelson (1993), in her study on lesbian parenting in Canada, makes a similar point. She argues that because lesbian families need to re-define who a mother is and what she does, they throw into question the very concept of motherhood. Forcing us to re-think our understanding of motherhood and families in this way is, according to Nelson (2000, 137), a revolutionary turn that "has implications for family-focused policies and programs."

Policy Challenges and Debates

Generally, the involvement of policy or the state (with all of its agents and agencies) in marriage has been limited to laws about who cannot marry whom and what procedures must be followed to enter legal wedlock. There has been some resistance on the part of governments to involve themselves closely in what is largely seen as a private family matter.

Of course, the reality is that the state and state policies have actively shaped the ways in which we form and live in families, as well as our sense of family. Ideas about individual responsibility, about the vulnerable dependent, about sex and morality, about life chances and choices, are all reaffirmed through our laws and policies. Therefore, it is not surprising that changes to these basic ideas cause concern and debate about family policies.

Two factors propelling the re-evaluation of policies on marriage and mating are recent concerns about family poverty, particularly the poverty of children in mother-headed lone parent families, and the rapid growth in women's labour force participation. Another factor at the forefront is the debate concerning gay and lesbian marriage and whether they should be legally recognized.

Poverty in Single-Parent Families

The issue of persistent poverty among female-headed single-parent families has raised questions about what policy steps might be taken to address the problem. Among the answers are improved subsistence for single mothers, more job opportunities, gender equity in pay and work opportunity, more child support from absent fathers, better access to affordable daycare so that single mothers can more readily seek work (see, for example, Davies et al., 2001; Eichler, 1996; Friendly, 1994; Palacio-Quintin, 2000; Phipps, 1998).

All of these are viable and reasonable policy options on which volumes have been written by sociologists as well as policy analysts. However, other solutions have been proposed. One is that governments, through policy, promote marriage continuity (Waite and Gallagher, 2000). The logic is simple: since it is divorce and separation that is behind most mother-only single parent families, the way to prevent the poverty so many of them subsequently face is to make marriages *more stable*. Davies et al. (2001) argue, in Canada, that since marriage is not so much an economic union as it once was, and since the evidence is clear that it is not going to be stable, promoting marriage is not a good policy answer.

Proposed methods to achieve this goal include making divorce more difficult to get, requiring conciliation counselling or divorce school for those who are seeking divorce or legal separation, and working to change attitudes, convincing women to expect less romance in marriage and men to value more highly their family roles (Richards, 1998; *The Globe and Mail*, 1993: A17). This approach suggests loudly that women's interests are secondary to those of families and society, something with which many would not agree.

Women's Labour Force Participation

The rapid growth in women's labour force participation has been repeatedly cited as a central reason for marriage not being as stable and secure as it was presumed to be in the past. The labour market is seen as competing with marriage for women's basis of security. "Once marriage provided a woman with the best guarantee of financial security. Now she can more easily escape from an unhappy marriage—even though the escape often leads to poverty" (*Globe and Mail*, 1993: A17). The exact means by which women's labour market participation is linked with marriage instability have not been well spelled out.

Oppenheimer (1997: 449) contributes by sociologically examining the presumption, carefully relying on existing research. Her conclusions bear sharing:

> Although the popularity of the women's economic independence explanation of marriage behavior remains strong in the 1990s, this review of the literature found little empirical support for the hypothesis...women's educational attainment, employment, and earnings either have little or no effect on marriage formation or, where they do have an effect, find it to be positive, the opposite effect of that hypothesized.

She adds two additional important conclusions. "The apparent congruence in time-series data of women's rising employment with declining marriage rates and increasing marital instability is partly a result of using the historically atypical postwar behavior of the baby boom era as the benchmark..." (Oppenheimer, 1997: 431). Then she makes a crucial point about presumed marital mismatches: "The frequent tendency to equate income equality between partners with women's economic independence and a lowered gain to marriage fails to distinguish between situations where high gains to marriage may be the result of income equality from situations where the result is a very low gain to marriage" (Oppenheimer, 1997: 431).

Focusing on the relative levels of couples' incomes ignores the contexts in which incomes are earned and the fact that those contexts are changing.

The Debate Over Gay/Lesbian Marriage

The political debate over whether gay and lesbian couples ought to be allowed to marry legally and in religious ceremonies is very sociologically revealing. On the one hand, some (but not all) gay and lesbian couples want to have the responsibilities and entitlements, as well as the social recognition, that legal marriage would provide. On the other hand, some worry that equating their unions with heterosexual marriages could rob gay and lesbian unions of their unique and valued aspects—among these, equality and sharing. Many gay and lesbian opponents of same-sex marriage see the institution as patriarchal and inequitable. They feel they have been lucky "to escape the strictures of gender roles and religious dogma about marriage and prefer not to be subjected to (it)" (in Schwartz & Rutter, 1998).

Some non-gay social conservatives who are against same-sex marriages make remarkably similar arguments. Essentially, if you make every couple relationship a marriage, then marriage as a unique social institution ceases to exist (Amiel 2000, 13). At the same time, some of the same conservatives worry that regulation of who is a couple and who is not involves too much government inference. This is what some cohabiting couples, gay or hetero, may be trying to avoid. Still others argue that encouraging individual responsibility for each other in an intimate union is a good way for individuals to support each other, who might otherwise call on government assistance. This argument was made in *The Economist*. A special issue dedicated to gay and lesbian issues argued that "permitting gay marriage could reaffirm society's hope that people of all kinds settle down into stable unions" (*The Economist*, 1996, cited in Owens, 2001, 87). The argument to allow same-sex marriage is based on the idea that marriage is beneficial to society because it keeps people from depending on social assistance and also keeps them healthier and happier. In short, that it functions as a "stabilizer" in society. This argument is the purely practical one of private support of people in families, no matter what kind of families they choose. It has the added advantage of taking the pressure off governments to help out when spouses of whatever type are doing the caring.

Are Policies Making Marriage Less Attractive?

It has been suggested that marriage laws may be disincentive to marriage. Laws may discourage couples from marrying if aspects of legal marriage are seen as bringing major, and possibly unwanted, changes in a couple's relationship.

On the other hand, if legal marriage is seen as changing nothing much they may not find it attractive as an alternative to living common-law. As common-law unions and legal marriages become more similar under the law, as they are in many jurisdictions, then marriage *per se* may seem less attractive.

In Quebec, for example, the province with the highest rates of cohabitation in Canada, there has been a seemingly progressive law on the books for 15 years that a woman may not take her husband's name. She can, if she insists, use his name in social contexts, but all legal documents will be issued in her maiden name. This was followed in 1989 by a law that specified that in case of divorce, all assets, even those acquired prior to the marriage, must be divided equally. There is no opting out. So, couples may feel, on the one hand, there is little difference

Debate Box 4.1 LEGALIZATION OF SAME-SEX MARRIAGE
Which side of the debate do you fall on?

I am FOR legalization

- Denying homosexuals access to this fundamental societal institution is a denial of their civil and human rights.
- Not legalizing their union is unconstitutional, as choosing whom to marry is a fundamental human right in the pursuit of happiness.
- Legalization ensures receiving spousal benefits such as health insurance, pension plans, and inheritance rights. These are rights that long-term domestic partners are entitled to regardless of gender.
- Legalization will strengthen a state's social fabric, and is not a threat to traditional marriage.
- These unions will continue to build community, to support children and families, and will promote the common good of a true democracy.
- The primary goal of marriage is love and companionship, occurring between people who care for each other deeply, with the likelihood of bearing and raising children together.
- If marriage and procreation must be linked, a state to be logically consistent would have to prohibit all unions in which one or both partners are sterile or impotent. What about women in menopause, impotent men, or the elderly? No one would disagree that they should not be allowed a legal marriage. The same should follow for homosexual marriages.
- A true democratic country, like Canada, separates the church and state and therefore religious values should not interfere with legal affairs.

I am AGAINST legalization

- Same-sex marriages challenge the authority of the sacred institution of marriage and should not be encouraged or supported.
- Same-sex marriages will do significant long-term social damage to one of society's most important institutions.
- Stretching the definition of marriage could open the door to further challenges to this fundamental institution.
- Limits must be strict or institutional authority will be undermined.
- Marriage is a sacred institution whose main purpose is procreation.
- Because children cannot be produced from gay marriages, they are considered unnatural and thus unacceptable.
- "If man lie with mankind. As he lieth with a woman, both of them have committed an abomination."—Leviticus 20:13.
- There is a strong objection to homosexuality rooted in such major world religions as Christianity, Islam, and Judaism.
- Homosexuality is a sin in the eyes of God and should not be condoned by the sacred union of marriage. Marriage is a covenant with God and should not be tainted.

between marriage and living together since both parties keep their own name anyway. On the other hand, they may feel that legal marriage compromises their preferences about property ownership and prefer to make their own personalized conjugal agreements. If societies value marriage, it is argued, then laws and policies ought to more consistently favour it.

At the same time, a strong argument is emerging from the family economy literature that many tax policies are based on an outdated view of what families are. Given that, increasingly, Canadian family policy is delivered through the income tax system, it does make a difference what model of family is used. Men are defined much more often as the economically dominant partner in a marriage or common-law union, and women as the subordinate partner. All kinds of tax options encourage husbands to purchase retirement plans in their wife's name, to assign income to the lesser paid partner. "Our tax system cannot achieve the modern social welfare and equity goals claimed for it so long as we continue to base policy decisions on an image of family that belongs to old reruns" (Phillips, 1995: 31).

Another policy debate involves the question of who should be entitled to the workplace benefits that marriage permits. Groups have lobbied for a broad definition of spouse in spousal entitlements. Access to such benefits, including health care, is especially important in the U.S. In Canada, public health care insurance makes the issue less pressing, but an incentive for being declared a spouse remains.

In both countries, common-law partners may wish to marry to take advantage of benefits packages, including access to pensions, to survivor's benefits, to bereavement and care leave. This has also been a motivator for common-law unions to be declared "as married" or "equivalent to married." It has also been the essential reason for homosexuals to lobby for access to legal marriage or to "equivalent to married" status. This position, however, is not without controversy among some gay and lesbian individuals, many of whom see their relationships as innovative and pioneering, and marriage as a heterosexual institution.

An Alternative to Traditional Marriage: PACS

New ways are emerging for gay, lesbian, and heterosexual couples to form intimate couple bonds. One is the *Pacte civil de solidarité*, or civil solidarity pact (known as PACS) in France (Daley, 2000). The PACS, available only in France, began as an effort to legalize gay and lesbian unions and was instituted into law only in early 2000, after intense debate and public protests. Experts had predicted that 10 000 couples would seek such unions in the first year. In the first four months, however, over 14 000 couples had made PACS unions. Interestingly, many were heterosexual.

Gay and heterosexual couples use PACS differently. For gay and lesbian partners, seeking a PACS is a big occasion with formal wear, invitations to attend, and big parties to celebrate. For heterosexual couples, it is often a kind of informal formal sanctioning of their relationship.

PACS is simply a kind of middle ground for couples, either gay or heterosexual, who want a legal partnership where each partner is responsible financially for the other, in both support and debts. After three years, the couple can file joint income tax forms and benefit from each other's work benefits.

A PACS, however, is easier to dissolve than a marriage and can be done without a lawyer. This compares to obtaining a divorce in France, which is a very long, involved process.

The PACS law made France the first traditionally Catholic country to recognize, in some legal sense, gay and lesbian couples. Fassin (1999) found this to be an interesting development, for France did not follow the more permissive attitude of the U.S. regarding same-sex marriage, even though they follow much

France Gives Legal Status to Unmarried Couples

The French Parliament passed a new law today giving legal status to unmarried couples, including homosexual unions. The Socialist Government proposed the law nearly two years ago, touching off protests by conservatives and the Catholic Church. The law allows couples, of the same sex or not, to enter into a union and be entitled to the same rights as married couples in such areas as income tax, inheritance, housing, and social welfare.

Legalization of the union, or "civil solidarity pacts", known here by the acronym PACS, stems from a promise that Prime Minister Lionel Jospin made to recognize gay relationships.

But during the idea's gestation, it grew to include virtually any two people sharing a home, be it brother and sister or event a priest and his housekeeper. Indeed, the Government has gone out of its way to say that PACS are not marriage but a new form of legal coupling that recognizes the needs of people today. Defending the new statute, the Justice Minister, Elizabeth Guigou said it would force "the retreat of homophobia" and offer "a solution to the five million couples who live together without being married."

The new law makes France the first traditionally Catholic nation to recognize homosexual unions. But even as the law proceeded through its last debate, protesters staged a noisy demonstration outside the National Assembly. Conservatives and the Catholic Church have denounced the legislation as an assault on the family, an unraveling of the moral fabric of society and a license for debauchery. Debates over the bill were among the stormiest the country has seen as impassioned legislators railed at each other.

Yet surveys showed that nearly half of the French people supported PACS for homosexuals ad even more wanted them for other relationships. Supporters of the law argued that it was a long overdue acknowledgement of modern relationships in a country where an estimated two million heterosexual people live together outside of marriage and 40 percent of the children are born to unwed parents. Supporter say the bill will help not only gay couples, but also young heterosexual couples, and older people and relatives who want to live together and pool their resources. "Voulez-vous PACS-er avec moi ?" became a joke here for a while.

In the end, however, the new law has not entirely satisfied gay organizations, who are unhappy that the PACS consign homosexual unions to a lower status than marriage and make no mention of adoption. Many people expressed disappointment that the law requires that they register their union and live together for three years before they can get the benefits of filing a joint tax return.

Source: Daley, Suzanne. "France Gives Legal Status to Unmarried Couples." *New York Times*, October 14, 1999.
© The New York Times. Reprinted with permission.

of what the U.S. does with regards to gender, sexuality, ethnicity, and race. Fassin argues that the PACS law is the French attempt to avoid an "American-style" attitude towards gay and lesbian unions, which is more mainstream in the U.S. than in France.

The use of PACS in France has not gone by without some controversy. Some argue that the family is defined by its status as a heterosexual unit and not a homosexual one (Scott, 1999). They also wonder about other legal implications of PACS, including adoption and child-raising. These issues will be discussed in more detail in Chapter 6.

The use of PACS also shows a paradoxical attitude towards gay and lesbian unions in France. On one hand, the PACS offer gay and lesbian couples a new opportunity to legalize their relationships. On the other hand, the PACS do not clearly define the state of the union, which makes it difficult to categorize. The PACS are neither a union nor a contract, neither private nor public (Martin & Thery, 2001). The result is an ambiguous response to the question of gay and lesbian marriage. However, the fact that this type of union is different than a traditional marriage may be appealing to some homosexual couples who wish to differentiate their unions from that of a heterosexual. Unfortunately for those who wish to be recognized in the exact same way as heterosexuals, this solution may not be satisfactory.

Marriage Policy and Canadian Immigrants

There may be a difference emerging between recent immigrants and the Canadian-born in terms of marriage policy. Immigration policy in Canada has long emphasized, along with market forces, family reunification. This is now less the case with the sharp focus on anti-terrorism in the legislation passed in late 2001. The definition of what is family is, of course, paramount in implementing family reunification.

Who exactly counts as family and is thus eligible for immigrant status in Canada has narrowed over recent years. The shrinking definition of family has excluded adult children of a couple, for example. A paradox emerges. Although in Canada, as we have seen, more couples are living common-law, for purposes of immigration a person does not qualifies as a spouse unless there has been a formal, binding, traditional marriage. Thus policy maintains a widening gap between new and other Canadians.

Other "Couple" Bonds

The image of people living alone with their cats or dogs or other pets is common. In Victoria, British Columbia, there is a hotel restaurant named the Parrot House, in honour of the pet parrot who resided in a mansion on the site where the hotel now is. The elderly woman who owned the mansion died, providing in her will that her pet parrot would live comfortably in her home until the end of its natural life. During that time the parrot lived alone in the big house, attended by servants. For this woman, her parrot was her significant other in a couple-like emotional bond.

> Life without Lucille? Unfathomable, to contemplate how quiet and still my home would be, and how much less laughter there'd be, and how much less tenderness, and how unanchored I'd feel without her presence, the simple constancy of it" (Knapp 1998: 6).

Lucille is a two-year-old dog. Approximately one-third of all people in the United States live with dogs (Knapp, 1998: 13). A sizeable proportion of these people regard their pet as part of their family (Coren, 1998). In Canada in the 1990s, over one-third of people age 45 and over had pets as part of their families (Statistics Canada, 1991). A neighbour of one of your authors (McDaniel), a man in his early 70s, married for a long time with grown children, was in tears for days over the death of his 14-year-old cocker spaniel. He says, "That dog was my companion, and I miss him more than some family members." Sometimes, as in the case of the Victoria parrot, pets are vital companions. Given this, "… it is amazing," suggests Sprey (2000: 30), "how few data on pet ownership appear in data banks that aim to document all aspects of marriage and family in our society." In Canada, questions about pets are rarely asked on surveys. And families are rarely conceptualized to include all those people, pets, and perhaps even objects that form part of our familial bonds.

Concluding Remarks

There can be no doubt that people worldwide are redefining what it means to be an intimate couple. The family remains the arena in which personal emotional and psychological growth can take place. But more than ever, couple relationships have come to be voluntary acts—choices made freely by individuals. As well, there is a sense that what's done can be undone. Intimate partners are not as closely dependent on one another economically as they once were, and they can opt out of couple relationships that do not meet their personal expectations.

In Western countries, people are less inclined to marry legally than in the past; more people view singlehood positively. Cohabitation offers many of the benefits of marriage, without the same social and religious constraints.

Yet, where marriage and divorce are concerned, variations persist among industrialized countries. For example, in Sweden reforms have eliminated many of the traditional incentives to marry. Marital-type property rights of married couples were extended to cohabiting couples in 1987. So, there are no direct economic policy benefits to Swedish women or men for being married. Even spousal support after divorce is uncommon, having been abandoned as early as 1973 (Fawcett, 1990). It appears that all Western countries are moving in the same direction, toward diversity of ways to form intimate couple unions.

From the data we have examined in this chapter, we see a continued increase in the acceptance of varied intimate partner forms. We see no decrease in the strength of commitment overall toward exclusive intimacy within a spousal relationship.

CHAPTER SUMMARY

Close relations in couples have become much more diverse and individualized, particularly in the last few decades of the twentieth century. At the same time, debate over who can be a couple and how couples should (or should not) be legitimized has intensified. In this chapter, we have looked at the variety and types of intimate couples. We have examined how couples are changing, and why; what the differences are, if any, in family experiences in relation to different forms of couplehood. We have seen that, around the world, cohabitation is becoming much more common and couples are redefining what they mean by a "close relationship."

Now, more than ever before, the decision to be a couple and the decisions of what kind of couple to be are left to the individuals. Additionally, there is an increasing sense that one can separate from one's partner and start again. Legal marriage is less popular and singlehood is seen as more respectable and positive. When we look at marriage as an exclusive contract of intimacy between two people, we see that marriage in all its forms is still a popular arrangement.

Living together or cohabiting has gone mainstream; it is more popular and much more often leads to a lifelong union. Ironically, the probability of divorce is greater for couples who lived common-law prior to legally marrying.

We discovered that first marriages are taking place later in Canada, and that many people wait to begin a committed relationship until after they finish their education. Most Canadians marry in their mid-20s or later. Marital homogamy, or like marrying like, is visible in marriages as well as in dating. However, men still tend to marry younger women, and women with less education and slightly lower occupational status than their own.

Many Canadians live alone, some as widowers or widows, some as divorcees, some as single persons by choice. The reasons for this vary; interestingly, one way some women solve their conflict between career and family is to choose career and independence by living alone. A commuter marriage, when partners live in separate homes, often for career-oriented reasons, comes about for similar reasons. Commuter marriages/relationships are not common but may increase for practical reasons, such as the scarcity of good jobs.

Common-law relationships affect our ideas about families. For example, births in common-law arrangements are increasing, and the stigma attached to children of such unions has almost disappeared. Another change that is occurring is greater societal acceptance of same-sex couples. Increasingly, same-sex couples are being granted rights and entitlements similar to heterosexual couples.

One practical argument for allowing same-sex couples the same rights and obligations as heterosexual couples is that the two partners are more likely to privately sustain each other, instead of relying on the state for support such as pensions.

KEY TERMS

Cohabitation A sexual relationship in which two people live together without being legally married.

Cohort A group of people who share similar life experiences as the result of a major common event (i.e., birth, marriage, graduation, or migration) in the same year or decade.

Common-law marriage A valid and legally binding marriage entered into without civil or religious ceremony, resulting from a cohabiting relationship that lasts for more than three years.

Commuter marriage A marriage between partners who live in two separate households for a variety of reasons.

Marriage A socially approved sexual and economic union between two or more people that is expected to last a long time.

Monogamy One rule of marriage in which one is allowed only one partner per person.

Pacte civil de solidarité **(PACS, civil solidarity pact)** An alternative form of couplehood in which a partnership is legally recognized and each member is financially responsible for the other, but that is easier to dissolve than a marriage.

Polyandry The marriage of one woman to more than one man.

Polygamy The marriage of one person to two or more partners at the same time.

Polygyny The marriage of more than one woman to one man.

Serial (sequential) monogamy The marriage of one person to two or more partners in a lifetime, though only one at a time.

SUGGESTED READINGS

Baker, M. 2001. *Families, Labour and Love: Family Diversity in a Changing World.* Vancouver: UBC Press. This study of families and their diversity in Australia, Canada, and New Zealand reveals with clarity the consequences of colonial experiences on how families develop.

Abbey, Sharon and Andrea O'Reilly (Eds.). 1998. *Redefining Motherhood: Changing Identities and Patterns.* Toronto: Second Story Press. This collection of essays explores the different ways that changing social and cultural conditions have influenced traditional views of motherhood. The articles present new views on motherhood, which are drawn from the lived experiences of women.

Dragu, M., S. Sheard, and S. Swan. 1991. *Mothers Talk Back.* Toronto: Coach House Press. Several mothers speak of their experiences with their own families. This book offers an insightful look into the life of mothers in the last decades of the century.

Graff, E.J. 1999. *What Is Marriage For?* Boston, MA: Beacon Press. This informative and enjoyable study of the history of wedlock argues that the rules of engagement have been so variable over time and across cultures that the concept of a "traditional marriage" simply does not exist.

Ihara, T., R. Warner, and F. Hertz. 2000. *Living Together: A Legal Guide for Unmarried Couples* (10th edition). Berkeley, CA: Nolo Press. This user-friendly book contains information on renting and buying a home, parenting issues, wills and estate planning, and sample living-together agreements for a variety of situations, and comes with a computer disk containing forms you can use and modify for your situation.

Pepitone-Rockwell, F. 1980. *Dual Career Couples.* Beverly Hills, CA: Sage Publications. This book contains several papers by different researchers delving into the issues of dual-career couples, such as its development, marriage, and family and career issues. These issues have changed somewhat in the last 20 years; however, the book is quite up to date for a 1980 title.

Slater, S. 1999. *The Lesbian Family Life Cycle.* Champaign, IL: University of Illinois Press. This book utilizes clinical research to examine how lesbian couples have formed their own richly diverse family patterns, coped with a homophobic culture, and extended the parameters of the very definition of what constitutes a "family."

Stiers, G.A. 1999. *From This Day Forward: Commitment, Marriage, and Family in Lesbian and Gay Relationships.* New York: St. Martin's Press. The result of a sociology doctoral dissertation, this book chronicles 90 interviews with lesbian and gay couples regarding their views on and concerns with commitment ceremonies and same-sex marriage. This title is current and applicable to an interesting debate in Canada.

Wu, Z. 2000. *Cohabitation: An Alternative Form of Family Living.* Toronto: Oxford University Press. This text traces the growing popularity of cohabitation in Canada, addressing the shifting cultural attitudes of the country, the current and future trends of cohabiting couples, and the sociological, demographic, economic, and legal implications of the phenomenon. It provides a current look at a long-term trend in Canada.

REVIEW QUESTIONS

1. Why are sociologists interested in intimate couple relationships?

2. How has the proportion of people who are in intimate couple relationships remained constant despite the decline in traditional marriage rates?

3. What two trends characterize contemporary marriage in our society?

4. Define "polygamy," "polyandry," "polygyny," "monogamy," and "serial monogamy."

5. Why does the institution of marriage continue to be central to relationships in North America?

6. How has the sexual revolution and the women's movement affected the institution of marriage?

7. What are some factors that account for the growing popularity of living alone?

8. What is a "commuter marriage," and why is it undertaken?

9. What economic and demographic arguments account for the decline of marriage rates?

10. What are the main advantages and disadvantages of cohabitation?

11. What social factors help explain why Sweden has the world's highest rate of cohabitation?

12. From the perspective of gays and lesbians, what are the pros and cons of legalizing homosexual marriages?

13. What distinguishes PACS from a traditional marriage?

Discussion Questions

1. Given the growing popularity of alternative types of intimate relationships, do you believe that a "traditional marriage" can still exist? Should it exist? Answer by first giving a definition of what you believe a "traditional marriage" to be.

2. In the past 50 years, the traditional model of couplehood in Canada has given way to a broader definition of what constitutes a loving, intimate relationship. Given this trend, what, in your opinion, will the typical Canadian couple be like in another 50 years? What social changes are likely to promote or impede this outcome?

3. Premarital sex, although gaining wide acceptance among the general public, remains a highly contentious issue among religious and ethnic groups. What are your thoughts?

4. People in commuter marriages are relying increasingly on electronic forms of communication to keep in contact with their spouses. What are some benefits and drawbacks of this practice?

5. Why are couples who cohabited prior to marriage more likely to separate? What pre-marriage conditions in the relationship could potentially increase the chances that the marriage will succeed?

6. "Essentially, if you make every couple relationship a marriage, then marriage as a unique social institution ceases to exist" (Amiel, 2000, 13). Do you agree with this statement? Why or why not?

7. In what ways are pets treated like part of the family? In what ways do others treat family members like pets? (Consider parents who bear children simply to show them off to others, and families who are obliged to care for their aging parents.)

8. It has been said that commitment is formed at a certain period in a relationship. In your opinion, should individuals date for a certain period of time before commitment is established, or is true commitment unrelated to the length of the relationship?

9. Throughout history, marriage has been intended not for the purpose of love, but for practical reasons. For instance, to pool resources to ensure economic stability or to ensure the continuity of family lines. In your opinion, is the general purpose or function of marriage much different today? Do you believe people still marry for the same reasons, or has marriage become something different?

10. Why do you think that, despite religious roots in Quebec, there are high levels of cohabitation in Quebec?

Activities

1. Take an informal survey of the attitudes of people your own age toward cohabitation, same-sex marriages, and other types of intimate couples. Contrast these attitudes with those of people from your parents' generation. Are there differences, and if so, what cultural developments can you think of that might account for the changes?

2. Spend some time monitoring the interactions between a pet-owner and his or her pet (either yourself or someone you know). Prepare a short video or journal documenting ways in which the pair interacts as though they are family members.

3. How are our views on marriage changing? Conduct a study of men's and women's magazines. How is marriage portrayed in popular culture media sources? Based on your findings, how is marriage cast in a favourable light, and how is it cast negatively? In what context is the "ball and chain" concept of marriage most popular? Why do you think this is so?

WEBLINKS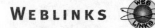

http://www.statcan.ca/english/Pgdb/People/famili.htm
Statistics Canada—Family, Households, and Housing
Statistics Canada—Family, Households, and Housing is the division of Canada's national statistical agency dealing with the latest facts and figures involving family life, including marriage and divorce rates, household composition, and living arrangements.

http://www.buddybuddy.com/toc.html
Partners Task Force for Gay & Lesbian Couples
Partners Task Force for Gay & Lesbian Couples is an information centre for same-sex couples, containing essays, surveys, legal articles, and resources on legal marriages, ceremonies, domestic-partner benefits, relationship tips, parenting, and immigration.

http://www.gwu.edu/~ccps/
Communitarian Network
In this site Linda J. Waite of the University of Chicago provides a more in-depth look at cohabitation. She discusses such issues as cohabitation as a "trial marriage," cohabitation and domestic violence, commitment, work, and much more.

http://www.unmarried.org
Alternatives to Marriage Project (AtMP)
This site is sponsored by the Alternatives to Marriage Project (AtMP), a U.S. nonprofit organization that promotes equality and fairness for unmarried and cohabiting people. It offers information, articles, tips, and links to a number of resources on cohabitation and alternatives to marriage.

http://www.dfwx.com/home.htm
Dallas–Ft. Worth Wedding Exchange
A business Web site with information on various wedding ceremonies (religious and secular) and other related offers. This is an entertaining site that shows the diversity of marriage ceremonies and encourages the celebratory aspect of marriage.

http://www.duhaime.org/family/famcentr.htm
Duhaime's Canadian Family Law Centre
This Web site, sponsored by Duhaime's Canadian Family Law Centre, provides general legal information about different areas of Canadian family law, such as marriage, divorce, child support, abortion, spousal support, and family violence.

CHAPTER FIVE

Ways of Being Close:

Interaction, Communication, Sex, and Trust

"All happy families are alike but an unhappy family is unhappy after its own fashion," begins Tolstoy's classic Russian novel, *Anna Karenina*. This ironic statement catches our attention, but is it true? Is there really only one way for a family to be happy but *many* ways for families to be unhappy?

Most social scientists would disagree with Tolstoy. Research suggests many ways to be happy, both individually and within close relations, and many ways to be unhappy. Still, there are only a few recipes for increasing the chance of a happy relationship, and we will explore them in this chapter. We will consider the reasons why some people have closer, more fulfilling relationships than others and why people in committed long-term relationships are, on average, happier and healthier than unattached people; that is, why close relations are good for people.

Close Relations, Good Health

This chapter makes a few simple but very important points. First, close relations are good for people. Second, good committed relationships can do people a lot of mental and physical good; bad ones can do them a lot of harm. Third, people can choose to form close relationships, and they can take actions to improve their relationships. So, in the end, the benefits of a close relationship are available to everyone.

Research shows that committed relationships are good for people. From this standpoint, marriage is better than a dating relationship, and dating is better than nothing. Other things being equal, married people are healthier than unmarried people are. Compared with married people, separated and divorced people are more likely to report poor health and less satisfaction with life. Compared with married people, unattached people are less happy, less healthy, more disturbed, and run a higher risk of early death. Researchers disagree about the relative benefits of cohabitation. Cohabiting people are typically less stable and satisfied than married people. However, on the whole, people in committed cohabiting relationships are happier and better off than unattached people are.

Among attached people, happiness and health depends a lot on relationship success—on how a couple gets along. As we shall see, many factors contribute to the dissatisfaction and poor health of couples. They include poor communication, lack of respect, and an unfair division of domestic labour. In some relationships, the two partners are simply not compatible. In other relationships, they do not know how to solve their problems. This chapter will explore these issues and discuss the ways that couples improve their relationships.

The most health benefits come from a happy committed relationship. Because a good relationship produces happiness and health, we can gauge the quality of a relationship from a couple's mental and physical health. In fact, we may be able to make a better guess about the quality of a relationship by looking at the health of the people in it than by listening to what those people tell us about the relationship. To take an extreme example, a battered wife may give all the "right" answers on a survey about relationship happiness, but signs of poor health such as depression, lack of sleep, and poor eating—not to mention signs of physical violence—will prove the relationship is in trouble.

Relationship problems infect every aspect of a person's life. Couples who report being unhappy in their intimate relationship are more likely to report poor health than couples that report being happy (Xinhua, 1997). Conversely, a happy relationship can improve all aspects of an individual's life. A good relationship can increase a person's stability and improve their health and personal habits, especially if the couple has children (Mullen, 1996). Relationship satisfaction can also improve the health and socialization of children, particularly if the mother is satisfied with the relationship (Feldman et al., 1997).

As partners come closer to fulfilling their ideals for an intimate relationship, they experience increases in personal well-being and satisfaction with the relationship. They report more enjoyable sex, less anxiety, and more overall happiness (Frieband, 1996). Thus, good intimate relationships produce both mental and physical happiness. A good close relationship is particularly important to people who are sick, weak, or otherwise vulnerable. For example, pregnant women benefit particularly from being in a good relationship with a supportive and understanding partner. The quality of the attachment between a pregnant woman and her partner increases the woman's sense of well-being (Zachariah, 1996). Moreover, this effect continues after the child is born.

Figure 5.1 HIGH STRESS BY HOUSEHOLD TYPE, AGE 18+, CANADA, 1994–95

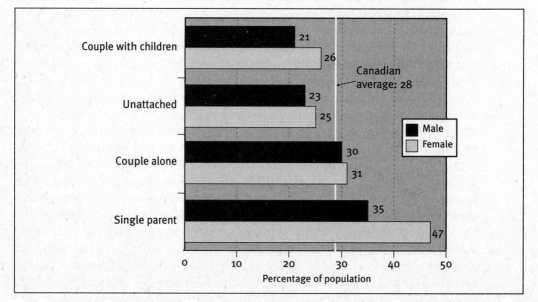

Source: Data adapted from Statistics Canada website, www.statcan.ca/english/freepub/82-570-XIE/01_11.pdf; accessed October 22, 2002.

Intimacy gives both partners health protection within a stable and caring family environment. Intimacy may also promote coping strategies in dealing with stressful life events (Xinhua, 1997). Many people cannot handle stress all by themselves. A partner or family can provide support during these difficult times.

We need to examine why a good relationship increases life satisfaction, health, and longevity to such a degree. One can speculate there are evolutionary advantages to close relations: where couples bond more closely, multiple offspring are more likely to survive to adulthood. This is because the children receive more protection, more attachment, and more investment in their "human capital." As a result, the habits of maintaining a close relationship, passed from parent to child, are more likely to survive than the habits of maintaining a weak or conflictual relationship.

On the other hand, the correlation between relationship closeness and happiness may be a mere result of social construction. Since we have structured society to enforce the idea that relationships are good and there is something wrong with people who never commit, the problems associated with singlehood may be purely social—a result of cultural bias and social prejudice against people who are single. At present, we can only speculate on these issues.

One Piece of Research

To illustrate these points, we briefly examine an important piece of recent research. For the moment, imagine that there are four (and only four) kinds of current relationship statuses: single, dating, cohabiting, and married. Let us take "**dating**" to mean being involved in an intimate, sexual relationship with someone who lives in another household, while "**cohabitation**" means being involved in an intimate, sexual relationship with someone who lives in the same household. We will ignore the statuses of "divorced" and "widowed," which for our present purposes are merely ways of being formerly married. Sociologists are trying to determine how being in one of these statuses compares, in health terms, with being in another of these statuses, and if it matters how a person got into one of these statuses.

These are questions that sociologist Edward Laumann and his team at the University of Chicago addressed to data collected from adults aged 18 to 59 who were part of the National Household Survey of Life Styles (NHSLS). The team cross-tabulated answers to questions about health, happiness, and physical and emotional satisfaction with the respondent's most recent partner against information about the respondent's relationship history and current relationship status.

The findings for women are clear-cut and convincing. On every dimension, women currently in their first marriage are better off—healthier, happier, more physically satisfied, and more emotionally satisfied with their partner—than any other women. After women who are currently in their first marriage, women who have never married and are currently cohabiting are the next healthiest, happiest, and most satisfied women.

On almost every dimension, the opposite is true for women who, after divorce, separation, or widowhood, are currently single. They are least likely to report they are happy and physically or emotionally satisfied with their most recent partner. The only women in poorer health than these single women are cohabiting women who have formerly divorced, separated, or been widowed.

According to these data, being single is not always a recipe for unhappiness. For example, single women who have never been married before are relatively happy, healthy, and satisfied, compared with single women who have been divorced, separated, or widowed. Being married is not always a recipe for happiness. For example, women who are currently remarried are slightly less healthy, happy, and satisfied than women who are currently in their first marriage. However, they are consistently happier, healthier, and more satisfied than divorced, separated, and widowed women who are currently single.

Finally, cohabitation is not always a recipe for well-being. Never-married women who are cohabiting are consistently less healthy, happy, and satisfied than women in their first marriage, but (with one exception) more likely to be happy, healthy, and satisfied than never-married women who are dating or single. Formerly married women who are cohabiting are (with one exception) less healthy, happy, and satisfied than currently remarried women, but (with two exceptions) more healthy, happy, and satisfied than formerly married women who are currently dating or single.

However, for women, the patterns are as clear and persuasive as they ever get in social science, allowing for human variability and sampling error. Close intimate relations are very good for women's health and happiness.

The patterns for men are far less conclusive. The healthiest men in this sample have never married and are currently dating. The happiest men are currently in their first marriage. The most sexually and emotionally satisfied men have been divorced, separated, or widowed, and are currently cohabiting. However, men who are currently in their first marriage are consistently closer to the top scores in health, happiness, and satisfaction than any other group of men. Men who have been divorced, separated, or widowed and are currently single are consistently closer to the bottom scores in health, happiness, and satisfaction than any other group of men. So, in the end, the patterns for men and women are not completely unrelated.

These survey data argue that relationships stretch along a continuum of closeness. Consequently, well-being decreases from first marriage, down through cohabitation, to dating, to singlehood. Earlier close relationships are more beneficial and satisfying than later close relationships; first marriages are "better" than second ones. Generally, people who have gone through a relationship breakup are less happy and healthy than people who have not.

However, since these are cross-sectional data, we cannot be certain about cause and effect. For instance, we cannot be certain that close relationships confer good health and happiness; perhaps, good health and happiness produce close

Table 5.1 **PERCENTAGE DISTRIBUTION OF QUALITY OF LIFE OUTCOMES BY MARITAL, COHABITING, DATING, AND SINGLE STATUS: AMERICAN ADULTS 18–59, NHSLS**

			PERCENTAGES	
Men	**Excellent or very good health**	**Very or extremely happy**	**Very or extremely physically satisfied with partner**	**Very or extremely emotionally satisfied with partner**
Never married, single	90.6	44.8	71.7	46.2
Never married, dating	95.3	60.7	81.7	72.6
Never married, cohabiting	88.3	55.0	82.8	84.5
Currently in first marriage	91.5	70.4	89.1	88.4
Divorced/separated/ widowed, single	87.5	31.4	67.5	47.5
Divorced/separated/ widowed, dating	85.9	42.7	84.3	69.5
Divorced/separated/ widowed, cohabiting	79.0	63.2	97.4	92.1
Currently remarried	87.1	68.3	89.2	84.9

			PERCENTAGES	
Women	**Excellent or very good health**	**Very or extremely happy**	**Very or extremely physically satisfied with partner**	**Very or extremely emotionally satisfied with partner**
Never married, single	88.5	54.2	65.3	56.0
Never married, dating	87.8	51.3	83.9	74.2
Never married, cohabiting	90.4	61.1	84.5	73.2
Currently in first marriage	90.9	68.8	86.2	83.6
Divorced/separated/ widowed, single	86.8	36.7	50.0	38.2
Divorced/separated/ widowed, dating	83.5	41.1	84.1	67.5
Divorced/separated/ widowed, cohabiting	76.8	50.9	85.5	74.6
Currently remarried	80.3	66.2	85.2	80.1

Source: Laumann, Edward O., Jenna Mahay, and Yoosik Youm. "Sex, Intimacy and Family Life in the United States," Presented at the ISA Conference, Brisbane, Australia, XV World Congress of Sociology, July 8–13, 2002, Plenary Session, Symposium III, Table 4.

relationships. Another possible interpretation is that the injuries associated with relationship breakdowns (divorce, separation) and widowed make it difficult for people to experience the same levels of satisfaction in later relationships. These data are not fully conclusive, then. However, they support and strengthen a large body of existing data that shows a link between close relations and well-being.

Relationship Health and Sociological Findings

Sociologists have measured the link between close relations and well-being for over a century, in at least three ways: (1) by examining the suicide rates of attached and unattached people, (2) by asking people to report their feelings of happiness or satisfaction with life, as in the Laumann study reported above, and (3) by looking for signs of poor mental or physical health, or changes from previous healthfulness, among people with different relationship patterns.

One of the earliest sociological studies, Émile Durkheim's (1957) classic work *Suicide*, discovered something that today we think of as almost common sense. In looking at the patterns of French suicide rates in the late nineteenth century, Durkheim found that socially integrated—that is, socially attached—people are less likely to kill themselves. The more attached they are—as spouses or parents, for example—the less likely people are to commit suicide.

People who are isolated and unregulated often suffer from a state that Durkheim called **anomie**, which increases the risk of suicide. Close relations reduce the risk, by providing attachment and care. Close relations also provide regulation. They set healthy limits on people's hopes and aspirations. Emotional ties connect married people to those they live with. Obligations to protect and support these people regulate their lives. Intimate partners typically agree to curb their sexual desires, for example. On the other hand, unattached people—especially people with no partner, children, or other close family (e.g., dependent parents, brothers, or sisters) to care for—are free to go where they want, when they want, and with whom they want. With less integration and regulation, they are more likely to commit suicide than attached people. Thus, freedom carries risks as well as benefits, according to this theory.

Today's statistics support Durkheim's theory. Suicide rates remain higher among unmarried than among married people, just as they were a century ago. In Durkheim's frame of analysis, there will be limited fulfillment and satisfaction unless we involve ourselves with others, in close relationships.

Durkheim's theory was difficult to test thoroughly until the second half of the twentieth century. Before then, structural barriers made it difficult for Canadians to divorce; divorce was possible only with a special act of Parliament. As well, Judaism and Christianity have historically opposed divorce, so Canadian society historically stigmatized divorced people. Cut off from membership in the religion and from religious members of the society, divorced people historically suffered a variety of social penalties. Thus, people who succeeded in obtaining a divorce were rare, unusual, and subject to intense social pressures.

However, with the growing social acceptance of divorce, divorce rates rose and stigmatization diminished. The association between suicide and divorce is now more clearly a link between suicide and anomie and isolation. That is why, as Durkheim's theory predicts, suicide rates remain consistently higher among the divorced and lower among the widowed and never-married.

However, researchers rarely rely on suicide statistics to measure people's well-being. Although suicide may be a sign of unhappiness, most people who are unhappy do not commit suicide. Some apparent suicides (for example, some drug overdoses) are accidents. Moreover, divorce and singlehood are not the only causes of suicide. Therefore, sociologists have developed a variety of other ways to measure the health, happiness, and satisfaction that a close relationship confers on people.

Types of Union and Relationship Quality

Though close relations are good in general, some close relationships are better than others. Research shows that the better the relationships, the better a person's health and happiness. Defining a "good" relationship is not as difficult as it might seem. Generally, people in "good" relationships manage to achieve a good fit between the partners' individual needs, wishes, and expectations, a fit that they regard as unique and irreplaceable (Wallerstein, 1996). Such couples believe that maintaining a good relationship throughout life means establishing and maintaining a good sex life and providing a safe place for expressing deep feelings.

As we have seen, reported well-being varies from one kind of relationship to another—for example, from marriage to cohabitation to dating. This is not necessarily because some relationship types are worse than others. More likely, people in different kinds of relationships bring different standards to bear when evaluating their relationships, and their lives within these relationships.

Researchers have long noted that cohabiting relationships last a shorter time and yield less satisfaction than marital relationships. As we have seen, the differences are not quite as marked as they once may have been. Recent research has found that people in different kinds of relationships may draw satisfaction from different things. Cohabiting couples appear to place more emphasis on spending time together and enjoying physical intimacy, while married couples place more emphasis on emotional stability (Cannon, 1999). Perhaps this is because many of the shorter-lived cohabiting relationships are still in their "honeymoon" phase, where sex and physical time together are very important. For the (on average) longer-lived marital relationships, physical intimacy has become less significant. Further research in this area controlling for length of relationship may illuminate this issue.

Just as researchers have sometimes oversimplified the differences between opposite sex couples, they have often oversimplified the differences between opposite-sex and same-sex couples. Without enough information, some researchers have assumed that lesbian couples are emotionally "fused" and that gay male couples tend to be emotionally distant (Green et al., 1996). Researchers continue to debate these views.

However, evidence supports another speculation about same-sex couples: namely, that it is essential for the health of the relationship that the parties "come out" to their families. Among gay male couples, "coming out"—i.e., revealing one's sexual orientation to one's family—predicts the onset of a long-term relationship (Eaton, 2000). Gay men who reveal their sexual orientation to friends and family are more likely to engage in a long-term relationship than men who do not. Among lesbians, women who "come out" to a wide group of people report more satisfaction in their relationship than women who do not (Jordan & Deluty, 2000).

"Going public" to friends and family and seeking same-sex supportive environments is especially important to gay and lesbian couples (Haas, 1998). In a society where gay and lesbian unions are still stigmatized, maintaining a strong network of supporters is important for the survival of the relationship. *Degree* of disclosure is also important. If one partner is openly gay to friends and family but the other is still hiding his or her sexuality, conflict can result and relationship quality can decrease. One partner may not feel he or she is getting the needed social support, or may be insulted that both partners are not acknowledging the relationship openly as a legitimate one.

Some researchers have also thought that relationship closeness and satisfaction depends on how similar the partners are. Partner similarity (i.e., homogamy) *is* important, as we said in Chapter 2. However, certain types of homogamy are less important than other types in determining relationship satisfaction. In fact,

Same Differences

Part of the changing face of Canada is all the same. As in same sex. The 2001 Census counts the number of gay and lesbian relationships for the first time. And the numbers are surprising. The survey looked at 11 million people, and discovered more than 34,000 were living in same sex relationships. That's roughly half a percent of all married or common-law couples in the country. And although 81% of them live in big cities, they're also represented in rural Canada and in large and small communities in every province.

And there may be even more than we know. Gay groups contend the numbers aren't accurate, because many people still fear repercussions if they reveal the truth about their lifestyles. "Ours is a community that has historically faced a great deal of discrimination, often at the hands of our own government," points out John Fisher of Equality for Gays and Lesbians Everywhere.

The census also provides one other sidelight: 15% of lesbian couples live with children, while only 3% of male partners reside with kids. The figures are a sign of the changes within the country. And more are likely when the next survey is taken in 2006.

Source: Pulse 24, www.pulse24.com/News/Top_Story/20021022-016/page.asp.

sociologist Robert Winch theorized, "opposites attract." Couples who are dissimilar, he argued, should be more satisfied with their relationships because their differences (in personality or skills) are complementary. Relationship is a series of exchanges, Winch reasoned. Therefore, couples ought to be more satisfied if each partner offers something that the other cannot provide for him or herself. A relationship between partners with dissimilar skills and aptitudes would be more "efficient."

Winch's (1962) initial qualitative study of couples supported his theory. However, this finding proved to be the exception. Typically, researchers have found that "like attracts like," not that "opposites attract."

This means that heterogamous relationships may be difficult in some situations. Other things being equal, partners in minority male/white female relationships are less happy than partners in same-race relationships, for example (Chan & Smith, 1996). Less family support, more severe problems with religion, and greater discrepancies in socialization mark some interracial couples and can lead to less satisfaction (Kahn, 2001). Cultural differences can matter too. For example, racially heterogamous couples in which the man is Nigerian and the woman African American consistently express more distress and dissatisfaction over finances, childrearing, and time spent together than (homogamous) African-American couples (Durodoye, 1997).

Homogamy increases relationship satisfaction by reducing the number of issues the couple may disagree on. Other things being equal, partners who think they are a lot alike voice more satisfaction with their relationship. They also speak to each other in more positive ways than partners who think they are very different (Thomas, Fletcher, & Lange, 1997). That may be because partners consider people like themselves to be more attractive and likeable than people who are different from themselves. They are also more willing to forgive indiscretions in partners they consider to be like themselves. As a result, an *assumed* similarity between partners may sometimes be just as important for relationship satisfaction as *real* similarity.

The Life Cycle of a Relationship

In many relationships, the expected sequence of events is courtship, union, children, and then possibly grandchildren. This "typical" sequence of events implies long-term stability in a relationship (Ravanera & Rajulton, 1996). Many couples also expect that their relationship will become even more satisfying as they enter each stage of life. Unfortunately, this is not generally the case.

Early Relationships

Sex is important to close relationships. The quality and frequency of sexual intercourse is an important indicator of relationship satisfaction and relationship quality, particularly in the early stages of a relationship. Factors affecting relationship sexuality include illness, aging, work-related stress, and frequent separation. Preconceived notions of sex and appropriate sexual behaviour can also affect sexuality in relationships. The choices couples make about their current sexual behaviours are as much a result of previous sexual experiences as they are of current ones. In many cultures—even our own—the sexual double standard heavily influences many sexual relations. Participants may not always recognize that the double standard is affecting their relationship (Greaves, 2001). Thus, if a husband expects his wife to be sexually timid and she is more "aggressive" than he expects, relationship satisfaction may decrease.

Bad sex, and other aspects of a relationship gone wrong, can result in worsened health, happiness, and satisfaction. So, we can measure the quality of this first stage of a relationship by the health of the couple. For example, researchers sampled young adults in New Jersey when they were dating and again seven years later, after they had married. Couples with marital problems were more likely to show signs of depression than couples with supportive relationships. Relationship quality affected the mental health of wives more than husbands (Horowitz et al., 1998).

Two reasons suggest why women are more depressed than men by bad relationships. First, women are more likely than men to experience depression under conditions of stress; in similar circumstances, men act out—drink or act in a violent manner. Second, as we saw earlier, for women more than for men, health, happiness, and satisfaction are more consistently related to relationship status. Conceivably, this means that stable, well-functioning relationships are more emotionally important to women than to men.

Children

Relationship satisfaction usually decreases over time, and the addition of children reduces satisfaction even more decisively. Willen and Montgomery (1996) call this fact the "Catch 22" of close relationships. Wishing and planning for children increases relationship happiness temporarily, but achieving the wish—actually parenting the children—reduces a couple's happiness.

Of course, this is not always so, nor equally so in every culture. Among people who view childbearing as a gift and parenting as the most important job in life, parental satisfaction is a major component of life satisfaction. For these people, parenting and parental satisfaction are highly correlated with life satisfaction. Among people who are highly focused on educational and occupational achievement, however, parenting and parental satisfaction may be uncorrelated with life satisfaction. Parenting may even reduce life satisfaction.

With the arrival of children, relationship quality decreases because children drastically reduce the time wives have for their husbands or themselves. This may cause resentment. The birth of a child reduces by up to 80 percent the proportion of activities wives do alone, or parents do as a couple or with non-family members, until the child is school-aged. This radical shift from spousal (adult-centred) activities to parenting (child-centred) activities creates an emotional distance that the partners find hard to bridge. Romance and privacy disappear. Sleepless nights increase. Mothers, the main providers of childcare, change their time use much more than fathers. Particularly after the birth of a first child, relationship quality and quantity of time declines immediately. Mothers report feeling more angry and depressed than before (Monk et al., 1996; for Canadian evidence on this topic, see Cowan & Cowan, 1992).

Parenting affects sexuality. Sex—from holding hands, cuddling, fondling, and kissing to the whole variety of physical pleasures—means as much to the young parents of infants as it does to newlyweds or people who are dating. So, the drastic reduction in sexual activity that often accompanies childbirth is likely to have a great impact on relationship satisfaction.

Even the closest, happiest couples feel distress after having a baby and, regrettably, few professional services are available to smooth this transition (Cowan & Cowan, 1995). After the initial euphoria of parenthood wears off, reality sets in. The partners are often too busy to spend even limited "quality time" with each other. This change to their relationship is long lasting. Sexual activity falls off dramatically and never returns to its original level. Researchers report that with preschoolers present in a household, sexual inactivity is likely and prolonged. It is amazing that couples with preschoolers have more children! Both husbands and wives become concerned about financial matters, leisure, and relations with family and friends. New sources of conflict emerge for the couple (Wadsby & Sydsjoe, 2001).

Having children also affects the mental and physical health of a couple, which in turn affects relationship quality. Children under eighteen take time and work, create feelings of overload, and lower relationship quality—all of which can cause depression (Bird & Rogers, 1998). Contrary to popular belief, there is no more conflict with sons than there is with daughters. Each brings a unique set of stressors into the family (Seiffge-Krenke, 1999). In this way, the burdens can overshadow the psychological benefits of children. A good relationship can decrease postnatal depression in first-time fathers and mothers and can also decrease couple morbidity. Many couples come to rely on their parents—especially, their mothers—for practical help and emotional support. A couple's health and relationship quality can come to depend on the new parents' relationship with their parents, especially their mothers (Matthey et al., 2000).

Canadian sociologist Bonnie Fox (2001) points out that the transition to parenthood often increases gender inequality in the relationship. With parenthood, the social relationships between husband and wife change. Wives, as mothers, devote more time to their infants and less time to their husbands. Husbands are often resentful of this change, and wives may adopt a new subservient way of dealing with husbands to reduce resentment and conflict. This often, and predictably, produces resentment on the wife's side. As Fox summarizes the evidence

> In short, how a woman defines mothering is partly a product of negotiation with her partner. Because intensive mothering requires considerable support, it is contingent upon the consent and active cooperation of the partner, which makes for all sorts of subtle inequalities in the relationship … [a] strong relationship between the father and his child … is partly contingent upon the woman's active creation of it. And in encouraging the relationship, women cater to their partners' needs more than they otherwise might. (Fox, 2001: 11–12).

The division of housework may affect close relationships as well. In dual-earner couples, early births coupled with a less traditional division of labour are more likely to produce conflict and lower relationship quality. Delayed-birth couples with a more traditional division of labour are also at risk, though not as much as the early-birth couples (Helms-Erikson, 2001). Perhaps this is because the delayed-birth couples have had a chance to know each other better, and work out some conflicts, before introducing another potential stressor. Early-birth couples are still dealing with other newlywed pressures, getting to know each other, and putting a lot of emphasis on sex in the relationship.

A husband's participation in pregnancy and parenthood is essential to helping keep the relationship healthy. Not least, husbands help to keep up the spirits of their wives. Wives in strong, supportive relationships are more likely to portray the fetus in a loving, warm, and joyful way, for example. These mothers are also more likely to report better relationship adaptation and less likely to feel abandoned

Figure 5.2 **CHILDCARE: MEN VERSUS WOMEN**

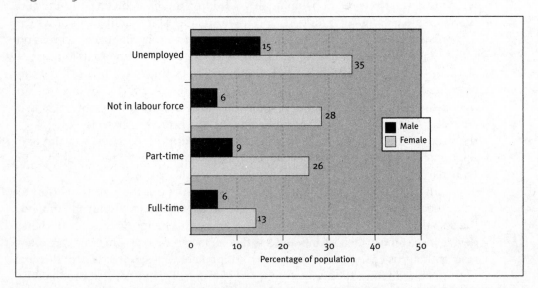

Source: Adapted from the Statistics Canada website, 1996 Census: Unpaid Work, The Nation Series.

by their husbands (Sitrin, 2001). Women with children have a harder time adjusting their relationship than men. Given the additional pressure for mothers, they often experience stress first (Graham et al., 2000). Thus, it is important that women receive social support from family to help with relationship adjustment.

Later Life

Typically, relationship satisfaction, which decreases with the arrival of children, reaches an all-time low when the children are teenagers. Then, as children approach late adolescence, relationship satisfaction may increase. The family members' perceptions of family closeness become more similar, and conflict decreases.

Once the children leave home, creating what sociologists call an "empty nest," many relationships improve to near newlywed levels of satisfaction. Parental (and other work) responsibilities decline, partly explaining this return of relationship satisfaction in later life (Orbach, House, & Mero, 1996). Many couples rediscover each other now because they have more leisure time to get reacquainted. So, compared with younger married couples, older couples report much less distress, less desire for change in their relationship, and a more accurate understanding of the needs of their partners (Rabin & Rahav, 1995).

Parenthood then is, in some ways, like a classic experiment conducted on naive subjects. Some well-functioning couples introduce the experimental condition, a child. Other matched "control" couples do not. In the experimental group, relationship satisfaction plummets; in the control group, it continues to decline slowly (if at all) as the relationship wears on. At a later stage, the experimental condition removes itself. The child grows up and leaves home. Relationship happiness returns to earlier levels. The conclusion is obvious.

Our first point, then, is that relationship satisfaction varies normally and predictably over the life cycle. It typically declines over time, and declines most rapidly and extremely with the presence of children. Then, satisfaction typically recovers when the children leave home. So, unless you avoid having children, this is likely to happen in your own relationship. Knowing this pattern, however, means that people can take extra efforts to keep the spark in their relationship.

Having children can be satisfying too. Remember that children are not the only causes of relationship problems, nor does the avoidance of parenting ensure happiness. In fact, couples that are involuntarily childless are unhappy as a result. We know less about couples who are voluntarily childless, but there are strong hints that they are satisfied.

What Makes a Relationship Satisfying?

Other relationship problems can also be predicted and avoided. We will now discuss separately, and in turn, several factors that affect relationship satisfaction.

Love

Many people consider love more important than anything else in keeping a relationship alive. For people in cultures that define a close relationship in romantic terms, this will necessarily be true.

However in many societies, relationships are not based on romantic love in the beginning: so-called "arranged" marriages are the norm. Arranged marriages in China, the Indian subcontinent, and the Arab world are often built on parents' perceptions of shared attributes between the partners. As a result, parents very often choose wisely—and homogamously—for their children. Arranged marriages tend, as a result, to be stable and sometimes immensely happy.

Folk mythology says that arranged marriages become, over time, even more satisfying than love relationships. Allegedly, arranged marriages "heat up" with time, while love marriages "cool down." However, research does not bear out that belief. Even in China, where the arranged marriage relationship has a long history, love relationships are more satisfying at every stage or duration (Xiaohe & Whyte, 1990).

In Canadian society, as we have said, most people marry for love. They see love as the basis of their union, without which the relationship would not satisfy either partner. However, this is not to say that people ignore practical considerations, like the earning power or social status of a potential mate. According to our ideology about marriage, people are not supposed to think about those things. They are supposed to fall head over heels. However, typically, love is associated with economic security. The more financially secure people feel, the more willing they are to indulge romantic impulses. People who must live hand to mouth cannot afford to think much about love. Wealth, of course, does not bring love, but below a certain level of income, romantic love may be an extravagance that few can afford.

Thus, our current preoccupation with love reflects economic prosperity that, ultimately, arises from the Industrial Revolution. By producing a material surplus and higher standard of living, the Industrial Revolution made romantic love more practical. That is why people pay more attention to romantic love in industrialized, or "westernized," societies. Paradoxically, material surplus also produces high divorce rates. Typically, people in nations with a high standard of living assign the most importance to love as a basis for a relationship and source of happiness, and have the highest relationship and divorce rates and lowest fertility rates (Levine et al., 1995).

In close relations, feelings of passion and companionship usually continue throughout life, yet some types of love are more common than other types at particular stages of a relationship (Noller, 1996). What some consider **immature love**—exemplified by *limerence*, love addiction, and infatuation—is characteristic of the first year or two of an intimate relationship. **Limerence** is that package of experiences that includes preoccupation with the loved one, wild fluctuations in mood, ecstatic feelings of well-being, and depths of despair. Lovers can't get enough of their mate and spend much time thinking about how they can win, please, and keep their beloved.

Mature love, on the other hand—the kind that allows the lovers and those who depend on them to grow and develop—provides constraint, stability, and certainty. This kind of love, less euphoric and less chaotic, supports marriage and family life, and it can continue throughout life. Mature love is more common later in a romantic relationship. It is, without a doubt, central to the relationship satisfaction, and life satisfaction, of contemporary Western people—the enactment of current notions of intimacy.

Intimacy

Most people would agree that feelings of intimacy are also very important in making people satisfied with their relationship. "Intimacy" comes from the Latin word meaning "inward" or "inmost." It signifies on the one hand "familiarity" and on the other hand "secrecy." Now, consider the connections among these three

Table 5.2 TIPS—SIMPLE CHOICES, POWERFUL CHANGES

Identify what you are feeling	Know what you are really feeling, not what you believe you ought to feel. Part of the value of quieting your mind with meditation or prayer is that it can help you pay greater attention to what you're really feeling. Paying attention to what you're really feeling can be a clue to what another person is feeling. Hearts tend to resonate with each other.
Feelings are true, thoughts can be argued about	When you tell another person what you are feeling, that is a true experience by definition. No one can argue with you; only you know how you feel. Thoughts like "I think you're a jerk" can be argued. The beginning of a real dialogue is to respond, "Why are you feeling that way?"
Healing may often occur even when curing is not possible	We can move closer to wholeness even when the physical illness does not improve. In the process of healing, you reach a place of wholeness and deep inner peace from which you can deal with illness with much less fear and suffering and much greater clarity and compassion. While curing is wonderful when it occurs, healing is often more meaningful because it takes you to a place of greater freedom from suffering.
Interconnectedness can be experienced in direct ways through intimate communication and connection, through meditation and prayer, but the experience of this human dimension of our interconnectedness can be quite profound and wonderful	As Henry Wadsworth Longfellow wrote: "If we could read the secret history of our enemies, we should find in each man's life sorrow and suffering enough to disarm all hostility."

Source: WebMD. Reproduced with permission of Dr. Dean Ornish.

words "inward," "secret," and "familiar." Each of us is uniquely familiar with our secret, inward thoughts, hopes, and fears. To become intimate with someone else means admitting them to our (largely) private, unique world, which in turn means trusting them with our most valued possessions. Building and maintaining this intimacy with a partner is the key to a mature, surviving relationship.

From these noble beginnings, the word "intimacy" in our culture has come today to mean little more than sexual intercourse. When we say that X and Y have been intimate, we often mean nothing more than that they have had sexual relations. This implies that our culture equates sexuality with trust, privacy, familiarity, and closeness. The reality is often different: Many couples who are sexually active are not truly intimate with each other, and many who are truly intimate have no sexual relations. Consider the peculiar status of friendship—especially, same-sex friendship—in our culture: Often, our friendships are far more intimate (in the original sense of the word) than our sexual relationships. However, in the best, most important, and most persistent close relations, people *do* pair intimacy with love and sexuality.

However, in this context some actions are considered a violation of intimacy, or "cheating." Typically, men consider cheating by their partner to mean sexual intimacy with another man. Women may also consider cheating by their partner to mean emotional intimacy with another woman, whether sexual relations occurred or not. We have more to say about this in Chapter 12, when we consider the new problems posed by cyberspace and "virtual cheating."

In good relationships, we find intimacy of both kinds, sexual and psychological. Satisfied partners are more sexually intimate with each other, as measured by how often they display affection physically, touch each other, kiss each other, cuddle, and have sex. These affectionate behaviours are mutual. Shows of affection by one partner usually prompt affectionate behaviour by the other partner. What is more, they prompt other positive actions. Often, they also prompt respectful behaviour (Gaines Jr., 1996).

Intimacy grows naturally in a supportive social relationship. However, intimacy does not come easily to everyone. Knowing how to be intimate with another person is something that we learn more by example and practice than by instruction. There are many potential causes of failure. A loving, committed couple can have problems with intimacy if one or both partners never learned how to be intimate. They may have trouble trusting or confiding in others generally or particularly in others of the opposite sex. They may have trouble expressing affection because they grew up in a family in which people never did so. Or, they may have trouble with sexual behaviour because of an earlier sexual trauma, or because they never saw their parents relate to each other as sexual beings.

Anglo-American (and Canadian) culture places a high premium on sex, both as a source of pleasure and as an indicator of intimacy and relationship happiness. Indeed, sexual satisfaction contributes significantly to relationship satisfaction (Kumar & Dhyani, 1996). Couples in which sexual activity is rare and one or both partners show little sexual desire may have problems getting along together. They can show signs of anxiety and depression. Usually, the partner with less sexual desire tends to be the wife (Trudel, Landry, & Larose, 1997), though this is not always the case. Little is known about couples that are not sexually intimate but still have strong and affectionate relationships.

People in different social and ethnic groups express intimacy in different ways and attach different meanings to sexual intimacy. For example, Spanish-speaking Mexican-Americans are less idealistic about sex than Anglo Americans (Contreras, Hendrick, & Hendrick, 1996). That is, they don't make such a big deal about it. In Anglo-American culture (and English-Canadian culture is similar in this regard), sexual satisfaction is correlated with greater self-esteem, positive regard, communication, and cohesion between the partners (Song, Bergen, & Schumm, 1995). In other words, sexual satisfaction is central to relationship satisfaction in an Anglo relationship.

Men and women experience sexual intimacy somewhat differently. When it comes to sexual and emotional intimacy in our society, women and men seem to want, need, and expect different things. Opposite-sex coupling is, indeed, a big experiment in **heterogamy** where opposites attract, but all the problems of difference are on display. There appear to be differences in the need for romance, fantasy, and foreplay. Women need to talk about their feelings, and they want their men to do the same. Some men often act as if the whole exercise is a big waste of time. As a society, we teach the sexes to talk to each other in different ways. It is no wonder that opposite-sex relationships have problems to solve.

This has consequences in every aspect of a couple's relationship, including sex. Wives report less sexual satisfaction than husbands. As well, the predictors of sexual satisfaction differ for husbands and wives (Song, Bergen, & Schumm, 1995). For women, sex occurs within a gendered or gender-unequal society. Many women have to find sexual pleasure within a relationship that also provokes feelings of powerlessness, anxieties about contraception, and exhaustion from childcare and outside employment.

For many reasons, including these power issues between men and women, sexual incidence and frequency decline over a relationship. Age, duration of relationship, and the presence of children all affect the frequency of sex. Allowing for age, duration of relationship, and the presence of children, happily married people have sex more often than less happily married people. Again, the cause–effect relationship is unclear. Perhaps it is that people who are happy together are more inclined to make love, that making love often helps a couple stay happy, or that other factors affect both happiness and sexual frequency. Perhaps it is some of each.

Coping and Conflict Management

How well a couple manages the conflicts that arise in their relationship determines their relationship satisfaction, and these conflicts and stresses come in many forms.

Financial strain, for example, increases the likelihood of depression in both partners. Depression leads the partners to withdraw social support and undermine the other. These behaviours, in turn, reduce relationship satisfaction and intensify the depression (Vinokur, Price, & Caplan, 1996). Health-induced strains also reduce relationship satisfaction. Taking care of a chronically ill partner puts an enormous strain on a relationship. This leads to dissatisfaction, especially for the caregiving partner. Dissatisfaction is more likely if a caregiver feels the ill partner brought on his or her own health problems, or has other reasons for feeling cheated in the relationship (Thompson, Medvene, & Freedman, 1995). Depressed partners can also strain a relationship by acting on irrational beliefs about communication and intimacy with their partners (Mullin, 2000).

As we said earlier, the birth of a child reduces relationship satisfaction by increasing conflict and parenting stress (Lavee, Sharlin, & Katz, 1996). The problem is worst if a couple has been unable to resolve important relationship issues before the birth (Heinicke & Guthrie, 1996). The death of a child also reduces relationship satisfaction, by reducing emotional and sexual intimacy for years afterward. Death itself may have less effect than the way each partner reacts to it and to the other partner's reaction (Gottlieb, Lang, & Amsel, 1996). Often, relationships fall apart after a child's death. Partners have a hard time thinking and talking about their suddenly changed lives, with their child missing. The grieving parents may need help to reorganize the ways they think and talk about themselves and their family (Riches & Dawson, 1996).

The stresses of work can also reduce relationship satisfaction. Often, conflicts resulting from a partner's employment cause distress. By producing hostility and reducing warmth and supportiveness between the partners, these conflicts reduce the quality and satisfaction of a relationship (Matthews, Conger, & Wickrama, 1996). Unemployment due to job loss also causes relationship conflict, either from the loss of customary ways of family living or an unwanted role reversal (particularly for males). Material deprivation and relationship conflict over financial issues also play a part (Lobo & Watkins, 1995).

Retirement from work can either increase or decrease relationship satisfaction. Leaving a high-stress job normally increases satisfaction. However, poor health and other changes that often cause or accompany retirement (which may reverse gender roles or reduce social support) reduce satisfaction (Myers & Booth, 1996). In general, people need to prepare for retirement and, often, adjust their close relationships to accommodate their new situation.

Married people cannot avoid conflicts, whatever their cause, and trying to avoid disagreements altogether is usually unwise. Relationship adjustment relies more on relationship skills and beliefs than on the presence or absence of hardship. So we are not arguing against confrontation, which means recognizing and dealing with interpersonal issues in a forthright way. As with much else in life, it's not what you do that counts, it's how you do it.

Though confronting disagreements is better than trying to avoid them, there are better and worse ways of doing this. In older couples, conflict resolution is usually less hostile and more affectionate than in middle-aged couples. With the passage of time, many couples figure out how to defuse and laugh at their disagreements. Styles of conflict resolution also vary by sex. Generally, wives tend to be more emotional than husbands, and husbands are more defensive and less expressive (Carstensen, Gottman, & Levenson, 1995).

Not surprisingly, people in unhappy relationships express more negative emotion than people in happy relationships. Though it is good to express emotion, expressing too much negative emotion may not be. Becoming quiet and withdrawn does more to keep the peace and maintain relationship happiness, providing this is not simply a means of avoiding the discussion of problems. Many new parents cope (effectively) with the increased stress that accompanies childbirth by adopting this strategy of quiescence (Crohan, 1996). However, this is only a short-term strategy, while the couple determines how to address their problem in a more constructive way.

Violence is never a satisfactory way to deal with relationship conflict. It neither makes the disagreement disappear nor improves the relationship. Partners in violent relationships often respond to each other's comments with one-up moves, and violence can escalate quickly. This interaction pattern, in which both partners assert but neither accepts the other's effort at control, may reflect poor skills in arguing constructively (Sabourin, 1995). In some couples, one or both partners excuse violence on the grounds of drinking or another extenuating circumstance. As a result, the violence has less impact on relationship satisfaction and thoughts of divorce (Katz et al., 1995). However, the violence problem does not go away and in the end it often becomes intolerable to at least one of the partners.

Scenes from a Relationship

A man's viewpoint is given in this article from a men's magazine. The article tells the story of a man and his wife who had very different ideas on how to spend their money. The feud springs from their old kitchen table, which Karen decided to replace contrary to what she and Bob had earlier decided. Bob thought the kitchen table, though old, was still in working order and did not need to be replaced, although Karen saw an aesthetic reason to purchase a new one.

The writer, Bob, goes on to talk about the differences of our parents' generation and today's marriages. He fondly recalls how his mother always seemed to wait on his dad and looked at him "with an adoring love." Bob points out that in today's marriage, the man and the woman try to "flourish individually" instead of one partner sacrificing for the other. He comments that his wife "in her opinion, never misses a stride." He supports her attempt for perfection.

The changing trend of attitude towards marriage is reflected in the writer's comment: "We got married not for security or sex or companionship or even kids, but as a way to come to ourselves."

Source: Adapted from "Scenes from a Marriage," *Dad's Magazine*, Sept/Oct. 2000.

Gender Role Attitudes and Equity

People are more satisfied with a relationship that meets their expectations of what a relationship should be, and how a partner should treat them. Increasingly, this means that, in our society, people, particularly women, are much more satisfied when their partner treats them as an equal in the relationship.

Over the past thirty years, we have seen an increase in the sense of injustice associated with an unfair domestic division of labour. In fact, this is often a greater source of relationship problems than disagreements over sex. The most dissatisfied wives today are younger mothers who are doing most of the household work—often, far more than their husbands are doing—as well as working outside the home (Stohs, 1995). When wives adopt less traditional occupations or careers, or more hours of work outside the home, often they still are expected to be the traditional "primary housekeeper." (We return to the division of household labour in more detail in Chapter 7, The Domestic Division of Labour: Gender and Housework.) This increasingly leads to marital conflict.

Couples today argue more about household work than about paid work or anything else. Conflicts about paid work usually revolve around the husband's working hours, with most wives preferring their husbands to spend less time at work (Kluwer, Heesink, and van de Vliert, 1996). Childcare is an area of particular contention when household work is discussed. Mothers who provide most or all of the childcare despite the demands of paid jobs are often stressed, resentful, and dissatisfied with the arrangement.

Whisman and Jacobson (1990) report an inverse relationship between relationship satisfaction and power inequality. Happy couples more often share a balance of power. Equality also brings couples closer together, so that partners are better able to perceive accurately the other's motivational state than moderately unhappy couples (Kirchler, DeLongis, and Lehman, 1989).

Mates who see themselves as equal partners are more satisfied with their relationship, and better adjusted, than are traditional partners, and report using fewer power strategies in trying to get their way (Aida & Falbo, 1991; Diez-Bolanos & Rodrigues-Perez, 1989). More-satisfied couples are apt to both give and take support, to be involved in each other's work lives, to have an equal commitment to the relationship, and to practise equal decision-making. Non-traditional gender attitudes, and husbands' approval of their wives' careers, promote higher relationship satisfaction (Ray, 1990).

In our society, close relations are better for men than for women. Indeed, men and women often even have different experiences of marriage. This insight led sociologist Jessie Bernard (1973) to speak of "his marriage" and "her marriage" as two very distinct versions of what many would suppose to be the same reality. Some critics (e.g., Glenn, 1975, 1978) have accused Bernard of overstating the differences. Evidence shows that close relations benefit both men and women. However, close relations do not benefit both equally.

As a result, members of the same family can have different, and even opposing, views about the quality and value of their relationship. For example, personal conflict at work is more likely to disadvantage women who are also experiencing conflict in their close relationships. Conflicts at work do less harm to men's well-being than to women's. They do less harm to women in good relationships than to women in poor relationships. This means that poor relationships are particularly consequential for women. Additionally, the pressures to get married, from society, families, and personal expectations, are stronger for women than for men. Thus, women may be more likely to marry for the wrong reasons and perhaps to have unrealistically high expectations. This too increases the likelihood they may gain less satisfaction than men from a close relationship.

Just as dating and mating choices are different for men and women, relationship "quality" means different things to men and women. Men, especially older men, most value the stability and constancy of "being married." Men don't look for emotional support so much as they look for practical, instrumental supports. Relationship closeness seems to dampen husbands' sense of well-being (Tower & Kasl, 1996). Among couples aged 65 and over, husbands are happiest when they have emotionally independent wives who don't need much attention. By contrast, wives are happiest and least depressed when they feel important to their husbands and feel they can depend on them emotionally.

Comparative measures of longevity show that women get less benefit from close relations than men do. We noted earlier that married people are healthier than unmarried people. Significantly, this is truer for men than it is for women. As a result, Canadian married men have a life expectancy five years longer than single men, while married women live only one and a half years longer in their already longer lives than unmarried women (Keyfitz, 1988). The precise causal connection between marriage and longevity is yet to be determined. All we can say is that, whatever biological benefit close relations confer, they confer more of it on men.

Men also gain more satisfaction from a close relationship because men and women hold different structural positions in society. Women, as a group, have less power. They get paid less, and society and employers discriminate against them in other ways. Because they do not as often occupy positions of social or political power equal to men, women are more vulnerable to exploitation. Thus, even before forming a close relationship, women are less able to achieve the same level of life satisfaction as men and, then, are less likely to derive as many benefits afterwards.

Even if close relations yielded women as much mental, emotional, and financial benefit, they would profit less than men because they had invested more. This is especially true where the partners have children to care for. As we will see in Chapter 7, women still do the lion's share of the housework, whether or not they also work outside the home. When the household division of labour is unequal (favouring husbands), wives—especially employed wives—are more likely to become unhappy and depressed (Pina & Bengston, 1995).

As gay and lesbian unions are more accepted in our society, the gender division of labour becomes blurred. There is no longer a clear distinction as to who "should" be doing what work. Bolte (1998) predicts "recognizing their relationships might eliminate stereotypical gender roles that generate sexist legal treatment by reducing heterosexism and homophobia and broaden and strengthen the legal and social concepts of domestic partnership." A move in this direction might reduce the housework-related stress for women and perhaps introduce a more egalitarian model of division of labour.

Often, relationship dissatisfaction and unhappiness take physical forms. The immune system weakens, we catch colds or infectious diseases, and recover slowly from whatever illnesses we might get. Symptoms of stress from relationship dissatisfaction occur in an apparently ever-widening range of illnesses. For example, people with cancer vary in their adjustment to the illness. Cancer patients in bad relationships report more depression and anxiety, less commitment to good health, and more illness-related family problems than patients in good relationships (Rodrigues & Park, 1996).

Moreover, people in unhappy relationships often show signs of psychological difficulty. The symptoms include a weaker will to live, less life satisfaction, and reported poorer health, compared to people in happy relationships (Shek, 1995a). A bad relationship may even lead to work loss, especially for men in the first decade of an unhappy relationship (Forthofer, Markman, & Cox, 1996). That is because our bodies show physically how we feel emotionally. Emotional suffering can make it hard to be productive in one's job.

A bad relationship is far worse, especially for women, than singlehood or divorce, which explains why many people divorce or avoid marrying in the first place. Yet despite all these gender differences, a relationship tends to be more satisfying for both men and women than never marrying or being single again after separation or divorce.

Leisure

The gender-based separation of labour reduces the free time of both parties, but especially the leisure time of women and mothers in close relationships. Firestone and Shelton (1988) found that women's paid work time has a negative effect on both active and passive leisure time, while household labour time has an estimated direct negative effect on total leisure time. This forces women to schedule their leisure time around both their work activities, and greatly reduces the amount of leisure time they have. On average, marriage increases a woman's total work time by more than seven hours per week. By contrast, the work time of husbands only increases by an average of 3.5 hours per week (Zick, 1991). This sharp, unequal increase of work for women can put strain on a couple and reduce their satisfaction with the union. If nothing else, it means there is less time for the couple to spend with each other and still have time for themselves.

Table 5.3 TIME SPENT ON LEISURE ACTIVITIES

	MEN	WOMEN
	(HOURS PER WEEK)	
Free time	6.1	5.7
Socializing	3.0	2.8
Restaurant meals	1.6	1.5
Socializing (in homes)	2.5	2.3
Other socializing	2.7	2.6
Television, reading, and other passive leisure	3.3	3.1
Watching television	3.0	2.7
Reading books, magazines, newspapers	1.3	1.4
Other passive leisure	1.1	1.1
Sports, movies, and other entertainment events	2.6	2.8
Active leisure	2.6	2.2
Active sports	2.3	1.7
Other active leisure	2.4	2.1

Source: Adapted from the Statistics Canada website, General Social Survey, 1998, www.statcan.ca/english/Pgdb/famil36c.htm.

The more unequal the incomes of the partners in the relationship, the more unequal will be the split of leisure time. Since men typically earn more than their female partners, they typically have more leisure time. To combat the problem of men having much more leisure time, women use many strategies to cope with conflicts over men's leisure time, with varying degrees of success. Collis (1999) found that women are "creative and resilient" in finding alternative ways of resisting the structures of male power. However, the outcomes of their action at an individual level are limited by the social, economic, and ideological structures of male power at the community level.

Communication

We have saved for last the most important factor in relationship satisfaction: it is good communication. Some of the problems we have discussed so far can be solved only by choosing a mate wisely, developing better coping skills, rekindling romance, or reorganizing the household division of labour and increasing equity. But most problems can be considerably improved by working on spousal communication issues. Both quantity and quality of communication are important in relationship dynamics. Quantity means how often partners talk with each other. The quality of spousal communication includes (1) how open partners are,

(2) how well they listen, (3) how attentive and responsive they are, and (4) whether and (5) to what extent they confide in each other. These are all important to the establishment of a good, satisfying, relationship.

Successful couples make lots of conversation, even if they have tight schedules and little time to spend together, or the topics of conversation are trivial. How much time partners spend in discussion influences their satisfaction with the relationship. More satisfied couples engage in much more communication than dissatisfied couples, who engage in little communication on most of the topics commonly discussed by relationship couples (Richmond, 1995). Lack of communication proves to be the most significant contributor to ending the relationships of gay men in long-term relationships (Alexander, 1997). Put another way, satisfied couples chitchat: they make small talk, banter, and joke around. Dissatisfied couples talk less, or mainly talk about weighty matters when they talk at all.

Couples do not all have to communicate at the same rate to be successful; it is the couples' *perceived* level of communication that contributes most to relationship satisfaction. The perceived accuracy, appropriateness, and effectiveness of communication contribute more to satisfaction than how much a couple may actually talk to each other (Glick, 1997). Length of cohabitation also seems to affect communication in married couples. Couples who cohabited before marrying display more negative and less positive communication and support behaviour than couples who did not cohabit (Cohan & Kleinbaum, 2002).

Communication and Gender

Communication is a gendered relationship challenge, in the sense that women sense more communication problems than men, and are more likely to see men as the source of these problems. Men, on the other hand, view the communication problem, if it is a problem at all, as mutually shared (Eells & O'Flaherty, 1996). Some supposed gender differences in language are stereotypical and have not been empirically confirmed. However, researchers have found gender differences in such dimensions as how much women and men talk, length of utterance, use of qualifying phrases, swearing, breaking of silences, and compliment styles (O'Donohue & Crouch, 1996; Tannen, 1993). There are also differences in the emotional content of the talk, with women typically expressing more emotions than men.

So, men and women speak differently, and this difference can become a problem. Consider an important form of relationship communication called debriefing—conversation about what happened during the day. Men view their debriefing talk as having an informative report function; that is, to bring their partner up to speed on current events. Women, for their part, see debriefing talk as having an equally important emotional or rapport function; that is, as chitchat and a way of keeping in touch emotionally (Vangelisti & Banski, 1993). In women's view, the talk may be about current events at home or at work, but the real purpose is downloading grievances, receiving and providing support, and renewing contact with the mate.

Homogamy between partners, which we discussed earlier, is one factor that notably increases the likelihood of more and better communication. People with a similar history, who grew up believing similar things and behaving in similar ways, have an easier time talking with each other. Members of homogamous relationships also have more similar expectations about the role that each is to fill in the relationship. So homogamy increases the likelihood each mate will satisfy the other by behaving in the expected ways. This advantage is especially valuable in the early stages of relationship, when both partners try to define their respective roles.

Encoding and Idioms

Communication is the transmission of information from one person or group to another. To transmit information successfully, the sender must present the message encoded as clearly as possible. That way, the receiver can understand the message with the least loss of meaning.

Sometimes, problems in communication arise from one person assuming that the other person is using the same codes (or shorthand). A word, phrase, or even type of body language can have profoundly different meanings for different people. It is partly to avoid these problems that many couples develop elements of their own private language to use with each other. Such a language involves the use of **idioms**.

Couples often create idioms to separate their relationship from others. By using a different language, they are defining themselves as a couple, both as a notice to outsiders and as a reminder to themselves of their special relationship. These idioms take a variety of forms: for example, special pet names for each other, "inside" jokes about other people, words or phrases that denote intimate activities (e.g., for sexual behaviour or parts of the body), special or ritual activities, occasions, or places, and so on.

Couples in the earliest stages of relationship report using the most idioms, and those in later stages use the fewest, for a variety of reasons. One is the appearance of children. When teaching children to speak, you want to teach them words that will help them in the outside world. Family idioms will not do that. Another reason is that, when a couple is close and secure, they do not need the public declaration of togetherness that idioms provide. So, long-established couples have less need for idioms.

The use of idioms also improves communication, because the couple has defined their meanings together. This vastly decreases misunderstanding. As a result, satisfied couples use more idioms than couples that report lower levels of relationship satisfaction. For interracial couples who may have grown up in different cultures, the use of idioms can reduce conflict and increase openness by creating a language that both parties are now familiar with (Shi, 2000).

Figure 5.3 FEELING RUSHED AND WORRIED ABOUT TIME WITH FAMILY

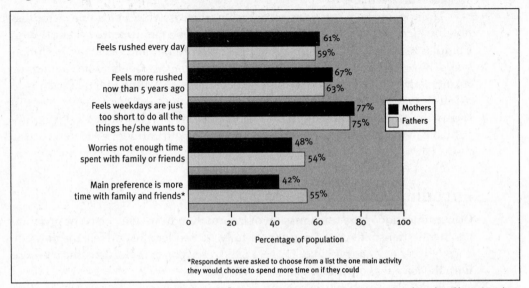

Source: The Vanier Institute of the Family, November 2000, press release, www.cfc-efc.ca/docs/vanif/o0008_en.htm.

Non-verbal Communication

Another important part of successful communication is the encoding and decoding of non-verbal information. Non-verbal communication includes posture, the direction of the gaze, and hand position. Researchers find that dissatisfied couples are particularly prone to misunderstanding each other's non-verbal cues. This lack of understanding can cause problems, especially when a person's non-verbal cues contradict the speaker's verbal cues.

For example, if one partner is apologizing sincerely, and the other partner misreads the non-verbal signals as insincerity, a simple miscue can turn into a full-blown argument. Long-term couples may also ignore each other's verbal cues and rely mostly on non-verbal ones, causing more misunderstanding. Older long-married couples tend to display lower frequencies of responsive listening than younger couples, which can increase conflict in a situation where a partner uses verbal cues (Pasupathi et al., 1999). Non-verbal accuracy increases over time in relationships, but it increases more for people who are satisfied with their relationships.

Styles of Communication

A common type of communication that can increase relationship conflict is the demand/withdrawal pattern of communication. Researchers have acknowledged three types of communication: mutual constructive, mutual avoidance, and demand/withdrawal (Bodenmann et al., 1998). Of the three, only mutual constructive communication is likely to be beneficial.

In the demand/withdrawal pattern, one party—the demander—tries to engage in communication but tends to nag, demand, or criticize the other partner. The withdrawer, on the other hand, tries to avoid such discussions through silence, defensiveness, or withdrawal (Walczynski, 1998). Partners with more feminine traits and more power in the relationship are more likely to be "the demander." However, women are not always demanders and men are not always withdrawers. In fact, the opposite may be true in many cases. In addition, the demand/withdraw pattern exists in heterosexual and gay/lesbian couples, so there is no intrinsic gender behaviour at work. Instead, socialization plays a greater role in what communication style the couple may engage in.

Like any behaviour that can reduce relationship satisfaction, the demand/withdraw pattern of communication has health consequences. Among married couples aged 23 to 71 years old, withdrawers had higher blood pressure and heart rate reactivity than the other groups. In addition, husbands who interacted with withdrawer wives had significantly higher blood pressure than the husbands of demander wives or wives who initiated conversation more often. Demander husbands with withdrawer wives experienced the highest blood pressure of all the groups (Denton et al., 2001).

Clearly, communication patterns must be effective and similar enough to maintain relationship health and couple happiness. If partners can interact with each other to determine what both parties want, the couple's commitment to their relationship will increase. This is harder than it sounds.

Rules for Successful Communication

Talking openly may be easier when we are already satisfied with our close relationship. Even so, good communication is hardly ever the automatic result of a good relationship. Couples who love each other intensely and are committed to one another may still have trouble learning to talk effectively. Like all our other social skills, communication is something we learn, and continue to learn, throughout our lives.

What counts as good, effective communication varies over time and across cultures. In our own society, however, most people agree that certain forms of communication harm the relationship because they undermine the listener's self-esteem. For example, personal insults, ridicule, questioning a person's authority or competence, or dismissing or belittling the person's achievements are negative, hurtful, even emotionally abusive forms of communication. Yet, not communicating is sometimes just as harmful as communicating negatively. Giving a partner the cold shoulder can sometimes hurt even more than a personal insult.

Some rules of successful communication emerge from sociological research on families. One purpose of communication is to convey information, either of a factual or an emotional nature. The first rule, then, is that communication must be clear if it is to be effective. This not only involves the encoding/decoding nature of communication discussed earlier but also suggests that both partners should say what they mean and mean what they say. This rule may seem self-evident. However, many partners regularly fail to observe the rule. Many learned at an early age that communication is not only a tool for making our thoughts and feelings known but also a powerful tool for hurting and controlling people. So, often, they speak in veiled ways, and listen for veiled insults, hints, or compliments.

The second golden rule of communication is: Be willing to hear and to respond to your partner's comments, complaints, and criticisms. A key to establishing and sustaining good communication in a relationship is recognizing our own deficiencies and trying sincerely to work on remedying them. Communication is important at all stages of a close relationship, but it can be especially important in the beginning. This is because during the so-called honeymoon period there is an increased sensitivity to the communication of a partner, as well as a strong desire to please and understand the other person. It is during this period that couples set up the basic interactional patterns of the relationship. Indicators of relationship quality, such as the methods that a couple uses in solving problems, are often first observed at this time.

Later, often during transition periods, other behaviours, such as the establishment of meaningful family rituals, can help a couple to build stability. Among couples with small children, relationship satisfaction is highest for people who have created family rituals and believe that these rituals are important. Such rituals may include regular daily events, for example, such as having dinner together, weekly events such as a Sunday afternoon outing, or seasonal events such as holidays together.

In lesbian relationships, family routines are of utmost importance for enhancing couple happiness. Caron and Ulin (1997) found that openness with a partner's family and friends is highly associated with the quality of the couple's relationship. For example, the couple's presence at family events and participation in the family ritual strengthens the relationship. As noted earlier, social support also increases relationship quality in gay male relationships (Smith and Brown, 1997). However, the benefits to this relationship succeed only if the family validates the partners as a couple. Otherwise, additional stress is introduced into the relationship. (Eyster, 2000).

Ways to Increase Relationship Well-being

Relationships are emotionally satisfying only if they are "good," which is to say that the partners *feel* the relationship is giving them something they value. It is important that both partners feel this way. A relationship must increase and maintain both partners' sense of well-being if it is to survive. Social science evidence shows that relationships that fail to satisfy—whether because of dissimilarity of the partners, absence of love, too little intimacy, too much conflict (or abuse or violence), or poor communication—are less likely to survive.

Ultimately, relationship quality depends on a couple's ability to adapt effectively in the face of stressful events, given their own enduring vulnerabilities (Karney & Bradbury, 1995). We discuss this at length in Chapter 8, which is about family dynamics. Every person, and every couple, has vulnerabilities. Every person and couple faces stressful events and must find ways of adapting or coping if the relationship is to survive. From this perspective on satisfaction, there are only three ways to increase relationship well-being: (1) by better adapting to stressful events, (2) by better avoiding stressful events, and (3) by reducing the couple's stock of vulnerabilities.

Many couples try to increase their relationship well-being on their own and do so successfully. Others seek help with their family-related problems from a variety of others. These include people such as family and friends, discreet and sympathetic (but unspecialized) advisors such as priests/ministers/rabbis/mullahs, family doctors or lawyers, or teachers. Little is known about the effectiveness of the advice these sources provide. Sometimes (perhaps a lot more often than we would suppose) people talk with wise amateurs: bartenders, cabbies, dental assistants, and hairdressers. And they talk to TV and radio talk show hosts increasingly, it seems, or write to newspaper advice columnists. Others, or sometimes the same people, consult specialized advisors, including psychologists, psychiatrists, and relationship and family therapists (MFT).

Does Relationship Therapy Work?

A survey of the outcomes of relationship and family therapy finds moderate but significant effects (Shadish et al., 1995). In short, yes, therapy does generally help couples. Of course, couples that seek **MFT** want to be helped, so this increases the odds that the process will help them.

One question to consider is whether the help couples receive from a therapist will guarantee they will stay together. In some situations, therapy may reveal that a couple is not best suited together and a separation or divorce would make more sense. While only a little over half are helped by relationship therapy, that does not mean that relationship therapy is not helpful for the couple. In some cases, therapy can indicate that two people are not suited for a relationship, which increases both individuals' satisfaction later on. In these cases, the relationship therapy was successful—it solved an ongoing problem—but the relationship did not survive. This is equivalent to a student taking an astronomy course to find out if she is actually interested in planets and stars. If she finds she isn't, that doesn't mean the course was a failure. On the contrary, it achieved precisely what it was designed to do: that is, provide information and insight.

....

Debate Box 5.1 **MARITAL COUNSELLING: DOES IT REALLY WORK?**
Which side of the debate do you fall on?

Marital Counselling WORKS

- When a relationship is in trouble, doing nothing makes people feel depressed and hopeless. Counselling at least gives them hope.
- It has statistically significant results. Whenever its effects are measured, counselling does better than mere chance. It works, though it needs to work better.
- It makes many people feel better about themselves even if it doesn't solve the relationship problem. Counselling can deliver needed help for one partner.
- Counselling may not work for everyone, but it definitely works for some couples, particularly if they have faith in the process and work hard at improving.
- Counselling clarifies problems, even if it can't solve them. No matter what the outcome, people should try to understand why they are having problems.
- It gives people a sense of how to work on their relationship. If people are motivated to improve their relationship, counselling can help them figure out how.
- Counselling can be used to gain more insight into each other, to learn new and more effective ways of communication, and to learn how to solve problems.

Marital Counselling DOES NOT WORK

- Counselling doesn't have a high success rate. Even if it works better than chance, its positive effects are small and uncertain.
- Counselling gives people a false sense of confidence. If they rely on it too much, they may fail to take more useful, appropriate steps to improve their lives.
- It takes people's money without providing expert advice. Counselling is no more deserving of payment than, say, palm reading or fortune-telling.
- It encourages people to keep trying to fix their relationship when they should probably give up. Many people would do better if they left their old relationships.
- It can't make partners love each other, or even like each other. Counselling only works on relationships with a strong foundation and good chance of improving.
- It increases the likelihood of conflict, depression, and violence at home. People are likely to lose their health by relying on counselling, which is unlikely to work.

Overall Assessments of Treatment

The findings on treatment effectiveness vary widely, but there is a general agreement that relationship therapy can be effective in reducing conflict and promoting satisfaction. Recent studies have found that slightly more than half of couples benefit from relationship therapy and about 60 percent of those couples maintained treatment in the follow-up period (Follette et al., 2000). While these numbers may seem disappointing, relapse into old behaviour is quite low and couples are generally satisfied with the treatment.

The findings on treatment effectiveness vary widely, but there is general agreement that relationship therapy can be effective in reducing relationship

Therapy can improve relationship satisfaction. To be successful, therapy must address the underlying issues that produce conflict.

conflict and promoting relationship satisfaction, at least in the short term (Bray & Jouriles, 1995). Research examining the long-term efficacy of couples therapy for the prevention of relationship separation and divorce is sparse but promising.

The treatment literature, like the research literature, shows that many couples do not know how to handle the bad feelings that are an inherent byproduct of the differences between people in close relationships. These bad feelings are unexpected and ironic: After all, the overwhelming majority of couples begin with true love and great hopes, yet divorce still claims more than one-third of all first marriages.

Many researchers have concluded that, instead of therapy, unhappy couples need to learn crucial psychological skills, called "psycho education," to help them avoid escalating conflict (Marano, 1997). Though bad feelings and conflicts cannot be avoided, they can at least be kept in check. Sometimes, the goal of the therapist, or of one or both parties, may be to eliminate conflict without solving (or even recognizing) the problem that is causing the conflict, due to issues of cost, immediacy, or tolerance of partner(s). However, if the underlying problem is spousal inequality, family poverty, or alcohol addiction, helping a couple to avoid escalating its conflicts may merely mask the problem temporarily. In the long term, therapy—if it is to succeed—has to address the underlying issues that produce conflict: the issues we discuss throughout this book.

Ideally, both partners will be satisfied with the outcome of therapy. However, in two-fifths of the couples that receive therapy, one partner is more satisfied than the other. In only one-third of cases are both partners satisfied (Follette et al., 2000). That leaves a lot of partners, and couples, who are not completely happy with the outcomes of therapy. Therapists must be aware of the demands of both parties so as to reduce frustration and possible deterioration of the relationship later on.

In a comparison of couples who divorced and those who stayed together after therapy, the divorced couples reported finding therapy just as useful as those who stayed together. In fact, these couples viewed the divorce as a positive result of therapy (Vansteenwegen, 1998). Thus, it is important for a therapist to determine whether a couple will work together or are better off apart, and to view either outcome as a success for the individuals.

Whom Does Relationship Therapy Help?

In short, whether a treatment program is "effective" depends on the treatment goal, such as avoiding divorce, reducing conflict, increasing understanding or helping a couple to break up in a friendly, peaceful way. Many of the "successes" of relationship therapy are partial successes in the sense that some goals are accomplished while others are not. Everything depends, then, on the defined goal of the treatment.

The goal, for example, can be to improve the well-being of the relationship as a whole, or of a particular partner. Increasingly, relationship therapists are seeing just one relationship partner, and the therapists need to consider methods of treating relationship distress within this mode (Bennun, 1997). It is not clear that helping one partner helps the relationship nor that helping the relationship helps either or both partners. Some partner-aided therapy with depressed patients leads to reduced depression and less dysfunctional thinking. However, there is no evidence that this treatment affects relationship satisfaction or communication and expressed emotion between the partners (Emanuels, Zuurveen, & Emmelkamp, 1997).

For some, couples therapy produces improvement in both individual psychological functioning and relationship satisfaction. This shows that couples therapy can accomplish both goals simultaneously, while individual therapy cannot (Hannah, Luquet, & McCormick, 1997). One study (Vansteenwegen, 1996a) finds that seven or more years after completing couples therapy, the individual changes were longer lasting than changes in the relationship itself. Thus, often, therapists must decide whether to apply psychological theories to help individual clients in a troubled relationship, or to apply sociological theories to help improve the relationship itself. Sometimes, it is impossible to do both.

Among distressed couples, some respond to therapy better than others. Gray Little, Baucom, and Hamby (1996) find that what they call wife-dominant couples improve more than any others from therapy. Egalitarian couples continue to function well before and after therapy, while anarchic (and to a lesser degree, husband-dominant) couples change little and continue to function poorly. Younger couples and those who initially believe therapy can help them are also more successful couples after treatment (Vantsteenwegen, 1996).

A couple's expectation of their therapist can affect success rates as well. Couples expect relationship therapists to be active, directive, and focused. They also expect a safe and empathetic environment. Couples identify poor therapists as those who waste time or are unclear in therapy. Both successful and unsuccessful couples think that safe environment and proper structure are important for therapy (Estrada & Holmes, 1999). Thus, ensuring the proper therapy for the couple is essential, and the right environment is key.

Concluding Remarks

There are no guarantees in life, and no fixed rules we can follow to ensure a satisfying relationship. Yet, one reason we place as much importance on our relationship and family life is that these are areas over which we can have a good deal of control.

In our culture, we choose our partners and decide whether to have children, when to have them, and how many to have. We may divorce if we no longer want to be married to our partner, remarry, perhaps encourage adult children to leave the house, adopt new children, and so on. It is because we think of our family lives as domains over which we have some control that we also expect that they will bring us great satisfaction. We assume this satisfaction will result if only we make the right choices and the right decisions.

As we have seen throughout this chapter, there are a few things we can do to increase our chances of finding satisfaction in a close relationship. The first is to excise the myth that happiness is all wrapped up in finding the perfect mate. No one is perfect—or not for long. Conflict is bound to arise, and a successful relationship is one in which conflict is managed well. As we've said before, the key to this is good communication.

Long before forming a close relationship, couples should start to discuss what they expect from it, what they want from life, what they are willing to give up, and what they are not. Most people who are about to get married, for example, discuss few of the important things that could lead to conflict in the future. They may discuss whether they are going to have children, when, and how many. They may devote less time to thinking through together the implications for each of them of this decision. However, they are unlikely to discuss the possibility that one of them may be infertile, and how they would deal with that. Nor do they often discuss the possibility of giving birth to a child with a disability, or of having one partner lose a job.

Couples who are planning to get married may discuss where they want to live. However, they rarely discuss what they will do if one of them gets a promotion that forces them to move to another city. Nor do they discuss the possibility that their parents will reach an age when they will no longer be able to take care of themselves. Then they will need to decide whether they will let their parents come to live with them or put them in a nursing home.

No one can anticipate—much less solve—all of their problems in advance. A close relationship is, in the end, a plan to try to solve problems together. People who can't solve problems together won't be married for long, or if married, they will be miserably unhappy. When it comes to any kind of close relationship, we can only regulate our expectations by communicating with one another. Only in that way are you likely to have some idea of what is in store when you say, "I do." At the same time, be aware that society has socialized you to pair off and marry without having even the faintest idea what is in store!

CHAPTER SUMMARY

In this chapter we have seen that achieving a satisfying relationship cannot be achieved by following a set of strict rules. We start by discarding some assumptions, such as the notion of perfection, which is impossible and probably dull. Couples should remember that conflict is inescapable and not as impassable as it seems. By relying on good communication many couples pull through.

Another inevitable outcome of life and living is the unexpected. Changes cannot always be anticipated, and mistakes will happen. We have learned that negotiation is key to working out problems in relationships. Interestingly, the fairer the distribution of power seems to the partners, the more satisfied they will be.

As we have seen, married people—and others in enduring close relations—tend to live longer, happier lives. Satisfaction in a relationship means different things to men and women. Men value emotional independence in their wives, while wives feel happiest when their husbands are "there for them" or emotionally available.

The life cycle of a family is fraught with difficulties; for example, planning to have a child, and then setting out to produce one increases relationship happiness, and yet relationship happiness usually decreases once the child arrives. Sexual intimacy seems to be a reliable sign of happiness throughout a relationship, although after children appear, sexual activity typically decreases, often for extended periods of time. The presence of children seems to lessen relationship happiness, as we have noted. However, parents would probably point to the immeasurable joys they have also gained from parenthood, and call attention to the other possible causes of unhappiness in a close relationship.

One factor that increases relationship satisfaction is homogamy, in attitudes, interests, behaviours. Not only do people date people like themselves but also do better to marry people like themselves. One of the most important criteria in homogamy is a similarity in attitudes toward gender roles. If partners disagree on a woman's role, the relationship is often less happy.

Intimacy is an important part of a close relationship. Both psychological and physical or sexual intimacies are signs of increased happiness in a relationship.

All relationships run into conflicts. Therefore, coping with conflict is a valuable and necessary skill. As couples age they often learn to defuse conflicts quickly. By joking about the conflict, they address the conflict directly and keep it under control. Conflicts about time are common; women who do most of the childcare and have paid jobs too are the most dissatisfied of all married women. Communication is the key to a successful relationship but, like many skills, it is easier to applaud than to acquire. Good communication may seem irrelevant to couples that choose to divorce and start afresh. They are likely to find the same problems with new mates. Others face their problems squarely, with the help of counsellors who may help them communicate and solve their troubles.

KEY TERMS

Anomie According to Durkheim, a lack of regulation, or a lack of norms.

Cohabitation Being involved in an intimate, sexual relationship with someone who lives in the same household, to whom one is not married.

Dating Being involved in an intimate, sexual relationship with someone who lives in another household.

Heterogamy A pattern of mating between people who differ in important respects, especially in their social characteristics.

Homogamy A pattern of mating between people who are like each other, especially in their social characteristics.

Idioms A variety of verbal forms, including pet names and inside jokes, that couples use to separate their relationship and define themselves as a couple.

Immature love Exemplified by limerence (below), love additions, and infatuation— is characteristic of the first year or two of an intimate relationship.

Limerence Infatuation or preoccupation with a relationship partner that is characteristic of the early stages of intimacy.

Mature love Love that allows the lovers and those who depend on them to grow and develop—provides constraint, stability, and certainty.

MFT Relationship and Family Therapists

SUGGESTED READINGS

Berg-Gross, Linga. 1997. *Couples Therapy.* Thousand Oaks, CA: Sage Publications. This book talks about the role adaptability and self-fulfillment play in a marriage. The author suggests that conflict and crises can be resolved by creating communication patterns and a spiritual connection.

Gottman, John Mordechai and Nan Silver. 1999. *When Partners Become Parents.* New York, NY: Basic Books. This book describes the natural history of couples' becoming parents, showing why this transition is a challenge for all.

Maslin, Bonnie. 1994. *The Angry Marriage: Overcoming the Rage, Reclaiming the Love.* New York: Hyperion. According to psychotherapist Bonnie Maslin, anger can be one of the most effective and constructive forms of communication. Since anger is inevitable in a marriage, how a couple uses that anger can mean the difference between an exciting relationship, and a destructive, painful one.

Weiner-Davis, Michele. 1992. *Divorce Busting: A Revolutionary and Rapid Program for Staying Together.* New York: Summit Books. There are four subjects in this book: marriage, interpersonal relations, communication in marriage, and relationship psychotherapy. Another self-help book designed to keep communication and hope up between the partners.

Weiss, Jessica. 2002. *To Have and to Hold: Marriage, the Baby Boom, and Social Change,* Chicago: Univ. of Chicago. Historian Jessica Weiss (California State University, Hayward) has written an enlightening book that examines the dynamics of American families past and present. She uses the lens of popular culture to decipher the myth behind familial roles. The book investigates topics such as gender roles in the 1950s, the baby boom, the role of fathers in American families, divorce, and the rise of feminism. Weiss provides analyses of her subject that are factual rather than emotive, and her use of family interviews furthers a strong presentation.

REVIEW QUESTIONS

1. What is meant by "relationship quality"? Contrast men's and women's perceptions of "relationship quality."

2. How does the birth of a child affect a relationship?

3. What role does homogamy play in relationship satisfaction?

4. What is the meaning of "intimacy"? What are the differences between sexual and psychological intimacy?

5. What are some of the "stresses" that a relationship may experience?

6. What are the ways married people can cope with and resolve conflicts?

7. How important is communication between partners? What are the "golden rules" of communication?

8. What are the three ways to increase relationship well-being?

9. How do comparative measures of longevity measure the benefits of relationship for men and women?

10. At what stage of relationship does relationship satisfaction typically reach its lowest point/highest point?

DISCUSSION QUESTIONS

1. Perceived happiness may differ from actual happiness. Discuss the importance of perception and how it affects our daily lives.

2. There is an increase in single motherhood. Discuss the significance of this trend. Postulate different theories for this trend based on the readings and what you observe.

3. Upon reading the text, we know that certain choices lead to a general decrease or increase in happiness. Would you then make choices in life that would always produce the higher level of happiness?

4. Durkheim's frame of analysis would state that relationship as an institution serves to socially integrate and regulate people so that there would be fewer unhappy people, fewer suicides, and therefore fewer relationship breakups. Would this theory apply to today's relationships? That is, according to Durkheim, are single people more suicidal because they are less integrated and less regulated?

5. What is your opinion of "communication and gender"? Do you feel that the proposed gender differences in the text referring to our use of language are stereotypical or accurate?

6. Discuss the following statement? "Married people tend to be happier...less disturbed, healthier, and live longer than unmarried people." Why does relationship affect mental health, physical well being, and life span positively? Why would widowhood, single life, separation, or divorce affect these things differently?

7. What is your opinion of "idioms" in relationships? Do you think having your own "private language" has advantages or disadvantages?

8. There is an obvious difference between males and females—how we think, how we are affected by relationships, and so on. What are some ways that we can make effective use of this difference in the home? In relationships?

9. Try to come up with ways to smooth a couple's transition into parenthood. What guidelines would ease this transition? What professional services might be useful?

10. Discuss the fact that couples who have mutually similar attitudes toward gender roles usually have better relationships. How could sharing the same attitude toward gender roles negatively affect a relationship? In what practical ways would a difference in attitude manifest itself?

ACTIVITIES

1. Assess the current views on parenting roles by collection of information from married and unmarried couples using gender to organize the views. Examine your data, and make conclusions on the differences and similarities in views.

2. Find couples who have been married for more than 25 years. What is their perspective on marriage? What do they think kept their marriage together? What are their methods of communication? Of conflict management? Summarize your findings.

3. Is there a difference between long-lasting relationships in heterosexual couples and homosexual couples? How are they different? How are they the same? What can you conclude about their communication patterns?

WEBLINKS

http://www.couples-place.com
Marriage Support/Couples Place
An on-line learning community for solving relationship problems, improving relationship skills, celebrating relationships, and achieving happiness with your partner.

http://www.americancomm.org/index.html
American Communication Association
The American Communication Association (ACA) was created to promote academic and professional research, criticism, teaching, practical use, and exchange of principles and theories of human communication. This is a resourceful educational site offering up-to-date information on communication.

http://helpin.apa.org/index.html
APA Help Center
A resource for families. This site offers suggestions on how to handle the problems facing today's families and maintain loving, healthy relationships. Articles that are provided by the American Psychological Association are a source for handling the social issues.

http://www.fotf.ca
Focus on the Family Canada
Focus on the Family Canada resource centre offers information for the newly married and for married couples (books and articles such as "Building Your Mate's Self-Esteem," and "Diffusing Anger in Relationships") as well as for teachers, physicians, families, parents, women, and men.

CHAPTER SIX

Parenting:

Childbearing, Socialization, and Parenting Challenges

Chapter Outline

In this chapter, we explore many changes: ways that becoming a parent have changed, the different ways people enter parenthood today, new reproductive and contraceptive technologies, the emergence of choices about entering parenthood, the implications of entry (and non-entry) into parenthood for individuals, families, and countries, and finally, the ways we enact parenthood— for example, how we socialize and discipline children in families.

Is Parenthood Family?

Entering parenthood, in our society as in many others, is almost synonymous with creating a family. Becoming a mother is often the definition of adult womanhood. Becoming a father can define manhood too, although in our society, men are more preoccupied with demonstrating their manhood through success in the workplace. In other societies and cultures, such as Latin America, fathering children matters more as a proof of manhood.

In many (perhaps most) cultures in Canada, marriage is mainly about having children. Many do not see marriage without children as marriage at all, although this view may be changing with recent generations. Historically, people did not consider a marriage "real" until sexual intercourse by the newlyweds had consummated it. In some African cultures, childbearing remains so fundamental to family life that only women who have already had a child (or children) are considered good candidates for marriage. In Canada, by contrast, women who have already borne children are *less* likely to marry or remarry than women who have not.

Decisions about Entering Parenthood

Several theories exist about the ways in which people decide to enter parenthood. One assumes that the couple has a plan that they carry out by starting and stopping contraception. Habitual, somewhat unexamined family and religious values are basic to the couple's decisions about parenthood, in this scenario.

An opposing theory sees the couple do a complicated cost/benefit analysis of childbearing. Into the equation would go such factors as the costs of having children, lost income opportunities for whoever takes on the largest part of childcare (typically the woman), and other goods (new house, car, travel, etc.) the couple may forgo to have a child, for example. We know this approach as the "new home economics." Likely, the process actually involved in deciding to enter parenthood is a combination of rational choices and irrational longings—life hopes for parenthood, background factors and influences, and estimated costs and benefits (McDaniel, 1996c).

A new, third approach to childbearing decisions focuses on mothers and their identities. McMahon (1995) shows how the effects of motherhood can be transforming of self and result in an enormous social power. Contrary to popular images of self-sacrificing mothers, the mothers McMahon interviewed do not see themselves as denying their own identities. Instead, they see motherhood as an opportunity for personal growth and development.

Entering Parenthood in the Past

Ellen Gee (1986, 269) shows from historical records how strong the decline in the Canadian birth rate was from the mid-nineteenth to the mid-twentieth century, in average numbers of children borne. Women born in Canada from 1817 to 1831, for example, had about 6.6 children, compared with 1.7 for women born from 1947 to 1961. In Quebec, an even sharper decline occurred over a much shorter time. For example, "Between 1959 and 1969 Quebec cut its crude birth rate (live births per 100,000 population) in half, accomplishing in ten years what had taken the rest of the country over a century" (McLaren & McLaren, 1986, 125). By the beginning of the 1970s, Quebec had the lowest birth rate in Canada and one of the lowest in the world, a distinction it maintains today (LeBourdais & Marcil-Gratton, 1994: 103–104).

Our grandmothers and great-grandmothers had more children, on average, than we do today, and they spent a much larger portion of their lifetime bearing and raising children. Said another way, today we spend less of our lives occupied with bearing and raising children. This is both because we live longer today and because our patterns of entering parenthood have changed. For instance, Gee (1986, 273) also found that Canadian women born between 1831 and 1840 spent

Figure 6.1 LIVE BIRTHS PER 1000 POPULATION, 1972–1996

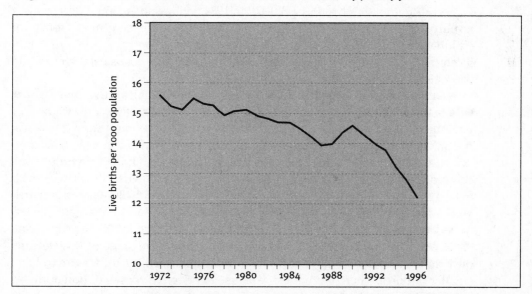

Source: Data adapted from Statistics Canada website, www.statcan.ca/english/freepub/82-570-XIE/01_11.pdf; accessed October 22, 2002.

an average of 14 years between their first and last births. This compares with an average of 1.8 years for women born between 1951 and 1960.

The decline in numbers of children born in families was largely due to the changing social and economic circumstances in which families lived. As society industrialized, people needed fewer children to work on the farms. Children in towns and cities were also more costly to raise than children on farms. Housing in towns and cities was more cramped, too. Children, thus, changed from a family resource to a family cost. Birth control had a role in fertility decline but not as large a role as is often thought, compared with changing perceptions about the value of children.

In the 1990s, people generally had fewer children than ever and had them closer together. Despite many ways of entering parenthood in the 2000s, most Canadians continue to enter parenthood in their mid- to late 20s. More people are parents than in the past, but they have fewer children overall, start later, and compress parenting into less of their lifetimes. This opens the door, along with other social and economic changes, for women to combine paid work with families.

Family Planning Today

Most people who are sexually active in the 2000s know something about contraception. Some use various methods regularly and reliably, others only occasionally. Why contraceptive practice varies remains to be fully understood, but family research provides some answers.

In Canada, knowledge about contraception is widespread (Balakrishnan, Lapierre-Adamcyk, & Krotki 1993, 197). In 1984, in the only nationwide survey of fertility and contraception ever done in Canada, about 68 percent of women of childbearing age were using one or another form of contraception, with only 5 percent of currently married women of childbearing age not using contraception (ibid: 198).

Of those not using contraception, most were not sexually active. Sterilization (where one or both partners have themselves sterilized for either contraceptive or other medical reasons) was the single most popular birth control approach in use in Canada in the mid-1980s, accounting for almost one-half of contraceptive usage (ibid, 200–1). Even more surprising was the discovery that sterilization was common (49 percent) among women as young as 25–29 when they had a birth before turning 18 (ibid, 45–46). Among women aged 35 to 39 who had a birth before age 17, the proportion sterilized is 79 percent.

Widespread use of contraception has been a vital factor in the decline in the Canadian **birth rate** and in family size—but it is not the cause of this decline, only the means. People have to want to limit their fertility, if they are to have smaller families. Then, the widespread use of effective contraception allows a separation of sexual intercourse from risks of pregnancy, which changes both the practice of sex and the perception and process of entering parenthood.

As a result, many people now see the entry into parenthood as a distinct choice, for good or bad. This perception, and the newness of it, has had serious social implications, particularly for single women who become mothers. The perception that childbearing is a choice may lead people to hold pregnant single women responsible for their presumed choice, with all its consequences and risks. However, pregnancy is not always a choice. It can still occur by accident or by sexual assault.

In other parts of the world, contraceptive use varies too. Europe, particularly Czechoslovakia and Western/Northern Europe, has the highest usage of contraception in the world (*Statistical Record of Women* 1991, 522–23). Japan also has high rates, as do China, Korea, and Singapore. Low contraceptive rates occur in Pakistan (8 percent), Haiti (7 percent), Senegal (11 percent), and Kenya (17 percent) (*Statistical Record of Women* 1991, 521). Typically, contraception rates are higher where literacy is higher and women receive more education, social and economic opportunity, and general empowerment.

The spread to women of literacy, education, and empowerment leads to a rapid change in contraceptive practices. Women who have more control over their lives and feel they have more control, are more likely to find about and use contraceptives. Contraception is even taking hold in traditionally religious high-fertility areas of the world. In Southern Italy, for example, widespread access to contraceptive measures and a rapid rise in the median age of marriage has caused a decrease in expected births (Dalla Zuanna et al., 1998). However, in Southern Italy as elsewhere, the number and fraction of unexpected births has risen. Often, the decline in expected pregnancies throws unexpected pregnancies into sharper perspective, and societies come to view *both* unplanned pregnancy and falling fertility as problems.

Entering Parenthood Young

One variation in life courses that has been the focus of public concern is "children having children." Until very recently, however, there has been a steady decline in births to adolescents in Canada. In the late 1990s, the rate increased a little, but it remains much lower than teen pregnancy rates in the United States (Baker, 1996a).

Teen pregnancy rates vary enormously across the industrialized West. Teen pregnancy, for example, is rare in Sweden, where childbearing among women below age 18 has almost disappeared (Hoem, 1988, 22). By contrast, the United States has the highest rate of unmarried teen pregnancy in the world. One-third of live births in 1990 were to teenaged mothers, for example (Baker, 1996a; Ryder, 1992). Teen mothers in the U.S. are more disadvantaged than their counterparts in Canada and Sweden, if only because of the absence of universal health care, the scarcity of good quality daycare, and the inadequacy of welfare in many parts of the United States.

Table 6.1 NUMBER OF CHILDREN THAT WOMEN AND MEN INTEND TO HAVE

Women aged 20–29	0	4%
	1	6%
	2	46%
	3+	32%
Men aged 20–29	0	6%
	1	5%
	2	50%
	3+	27%
Women aged 30–39	0	8%
	1	11%
	2	41%
	3+	26%
Men aged 30–39	0	8%
	1	9%
	2	45%
	3+	25%

Source: Adapted from Dave Dupuis. 1998 Spring. "What Influences People's Plans to Have Children?" *Canadian Social Trends*, Statistics Canada, cat. 11-008-XPE.

More of these young mothers have been keeping their babies and raising them alone, or with the help of their mothers. Both "shotgun weddings" and giving babies up for adoption have become less common. In the past, families and public authorities urged pregnant teens to give their babies up for adoption. A trend apparent in the 1980s and 1990s is for teen mothers to keep their babies, raising them themselves, or having relatives (most often mothers) raise them. An indirect consequence of teen mothers keeping their babies is that there are fewer babies for infertile couples to adopt.

Some people believe that the supports available to single mothers—social assistance payments, food stamps, Medicaid—contribute to teen pregnancies, because they make it easier for women to stay home with children. This seems unlikely, however, since stingier entitlement criteria for such benefits in the 1980s in the United States did not stop the rise in teen pregnancy rates. Comparative research (Jones et al., 1987) suggests, instead, that the source of the problem is cultural, not economic. We send North American teenagers very mixed messages about sexuality. The media bombard us with messages about the thrill of sexual

Table 6.2 THE COST OF RAISING A CHILD. CAN YOU AFFORD IT?

THE COSTS (IN DOLLARS) OF RAISING BOYS AND GIRLS TO AGE 18.

	Boys	Girls
Food	25 392	22 364
Clothing	15 270	16 801
Health care	5448	5448
Personal care Recreation Reading Gifts	2354	3064
School needs	14 020	14 020
Transportation	3060	3059
Child care Shelter Furnishings	52 029	52 029
Household operation	36 697	36 697
Total	**154 270**	**153 464**

Source: Vanier Institute of Canada, 136–37. Reprinted with permission.

love. Yet religious lobbyists make it difficult for governments and public schools to give children the information and contraception that would prevent unwanted pregnancies. In effect, we lead the horses to water and expect them not to drink it.

Researchers continue to debate the relative importance of different causes of teenage pregnancy. Some believe that teen pregnancy is a social problem that starts with insufficient parental support. They find that young people with less support from their families are more likely to involve themselves in risky behaviours, including unprotected sex (Hanna & Jones, 2001). However, other factors enter the equation. A study that interviewed pregnant or parenting adolescents found four factors that predict risky sexual behaviour that could lead to teenage pregnancy: presence of a family member with a drinking problem, physical assault by a family member, (early) age of first drunkenness, and (early) age at first wanted sexual experience (Kellogg et al., 1999). Thus, pregnant youth are found to have many other problems that contribute to their early pregnancy.

Not everyone shares this view of teenage pregnancy, however. Kristin Luker (1996) convincingly argues that teenage pregnancy in the United States is a scapegoat for seemingly insoluble social problems. In that sense, teenage pregnancy is a socially constructed problem, not a real one. She suggests that poverty, race, gender, and sexuality come together in a rich stew of mythology about teen moms.

Those who think that limiting welfare benefits will reduce teen pregnancy are wrong, given the evidence. The United States now has the highest rate of teen pregnancy in the developed world, and the lowest benefits for single mothers. These two facts, as we have said, are connected. Clearly, more education is crucial, not less money.

The children of teenaged parents are, often, the victims of inadequate funding and social stigma for young single mothers. However, the mothers themselves are also hurt. Many women who enter parenthood while teenagers *never* make up the lost opportunities for education and work. Having a baby while a teen disadvantages a woman, whatever her class background (Furstenberg, Brooks-Gunn, & Morgan, 1997). Similar findings have come out of Canadian research (Grindstaff, 1990).

We know far less about the fathers of babies born to teen mothers. One Canadian study found that many of these fathers are not teens! Using birth records, Millar and Wadhera (1997) found that more than three-quarters of births to teen mothers involved men who were older, by an average of 4.1 years. Twenty-four percent of fathers were six or more years older than the women they impregnated. These findings raise many questions about responsibility for pregnancy and contraception. Men in their twenties would likely have had more sexual experience and known more about contraception. A pressing question then is why no one translates greater knowledge and experience into pregnancy prevention with their younger girlfriends.

At the macro- or societal level, it is well understood that teen pregnancy is related to lack of education and lack of access to birth control and abortion services. At the micro-level, the problem of teen pregnancy may begin to be solved, or at least reduced, if we can enhance communication within families and communities, provide real opportunities to young women, and value them for their contributions rather than their sexuality.

Childbearing Alone

We no longer see childbearing as inevitably associated with marriage or even cohabitation. According to the 1996 Census, lone parents headed more than 1 million Canadian families with children. Of these, 83.1 percent were headed by a female parent and 16.9 percent headed by lone father. The proportion of Canadian families led by single mothers had steadily increased over the last 25 years, and now accounts for one in eight Canadian families. Data from Canada's Longitudinal Survey of Children and Youth reveal that when babies are born to single mothers, fathers are less likely to eventually move in. This pattern has changed in recent decades. In 1983–84, fathers came to live with more than half the children they had produced with single mothers. By 1992, however, movement was in the other direction. In more than half the births to women living apart from the baby's father, the parents had lived together when they conceived the baby, but the father moved out before the birth.

We need up-to-date information about whether the babies' fathers are continuing to move away from the mothers before the babies are born. Likely, this tendency is influenced by employment opportunities: fathers are more likely to stay if they can find a job to support the mother and child.

In Europe, the rapid growth of extramarital births mirrors that of Canada. For example, in Hungary, though traditional family life with marriage and children is encouraged, most of the mothers in 1995 were not married. However, many of them planned to marry in the future (Edit & Tiborne, 1998).

Single mothers are increasingly at risk for physical and mental health problems. Their children also have an increased risk of social, academic, emotional, and behavioural difficulties. Increases in divorce and non-marital childbearing have dramatically altered the daily lives of children in the U.S. According to Kesner and McKenry (2001), the increasing number of children who live in single-parent households can be linked to many of the nation's most serious social problems, including delinquency, teenage pregnancy, and welfare dependency. In fact, many believe that single-parent families represent a risk factor for children's development.

Childlessness, Voluntary and Not

The number of people who are childless has apparently been growing. However, this growth is evident only in comparison to recent decades. Taking a longer view, the proportion that is childless today is not very different from what it was in 1898. In Canada, experts estimate that the proportion that is married and childless has increased from about 14 percent in 1961 to about 23 percent now (Balakrishnan, Lapierre-Adamcyk, & Krotki 1993, 28). In the United States, there has been a comparable increase (United States Bureau of the Census, 1995). There is a challenge, however, in deciding the point at which we declare a person or couple childless. Some couples may be postponing their entry into parenthood, and ultimately will become parents.

We know a relationship exists between marital status and the choice of childlessness, however. Lapierre-Adamcyk (1987), for example, finds that of women who live common-law, approximately 30 percent expect to have no children. Among currently married women, only 5.5 percent expect to remain childless. The proportion of women overall who expect never to have children is 9.6 percent (Balakrishnan, Lapierre-Adamcyk, & Krotki 1993, 28).

While many would assume that people who decide not to have children feel less fulfilled than parents, this is not necessarily the case. Childless people have no fewer friends than parents do, though they tend to have fewer close relatives. In addition, childless people also experience less stress than individuals with children (McMullin & Marshall, 1996), as we noted in the previous chapter.

Adoption

By considering parenthood and family in terms other than biological reproduction, we pose a vital question about what "families" really are nowadays. The way the modern society answers this question lies at the root of today's adoption policies and practices. Not long ago in North America, officials handled adoption in secrecy and closed records on the child's adoption to the child, to the adoptive parents and to the biological parent(s). The intention was, as shown by Kirk and McDaniel (1984), to make the adoptive family as equivalent as possible to the non-adoptive family. This practice went so far as to alter birth certificates so that the adoptee would have the adoptive parents' name retroactively from birth. This "equivalence doctrine" was policy in North America for a considerable period

How Does a Child Get Adopted?

There are two ways:

1. Consent of the parent

The parent signs consent—that is, permission—to the adoption, any time after a baby is at least seven days old. Whether you have chosen a private or Children's Aid adoption, this consent must be signed in front of a Children's Aid Society person who has the authority to take consents. If the father is living with the mother, or has declared he is the father and helped to support her, he should sign consent too. You will be given a copy of the consent.

After this signing, the parents have 21 days in which they can change their minds and take back their consent. This reversal of decision must be made in writing to the Children's Aid or Court that was named in the consent form. The child may or may not be in an adoptive home at this point. It is then the responsibility of the person who placed the child to return the child to the birth parents.

The person arranging the adoption of your child must give you a chance to have your own legal advice and counselling before you sign the consent. If you, a parent, are under 18, the Official Guardian's office must have one of their staff explain your rights to you so you understand what you are signing. The Children's Aid or the private adoption person will make an appointment for you with an Official Guardian staff person in your area.

2. Crown wardship

The second way a child is adopted is by first having the child made a ward of the Crown.

The parents of the child go to court before a family court judge. The judge listens to all the facts, and then decides what is the best plan for the child. He may make the child a ward of the Crown. A Crown ward may be adopted. The responsibility for planning for a child who is a Crown ward is given to the Children's Aid Society. If the Children's Aid Society is suggesting Crown wardship for your child, the Society's social worker will carefully explain the reasons to you, and the way this is done.

In some cases, the judge may make the child a Society ward for a short time so the parents will be able to make a plan for the child. The child is usually in a foster home, and during this time the parents can visit the child. A Society ward cannot be adopted, because the parents still keep parental rights.

Source: Ministry of Community, Family and Children's Services. © Queen's Printer for Ontario. 2003. Reproduced with permission.

of time (Kirk and McDaniel, op. cit.). This adoption practice discouraged parents from telling their child that he/she was adopted, fearing that a sense of difference and/or alienation would affect the adopted child adversely. In reality, perpetrating such a fiction often led to problems if the child discovered the truth.

Most family researchers today agree that it is better to tell children that they have been adopted when they are old enough to understand what adoption means. By openly talking to the child about his or her adoption, parents make adoption a positive fact of the child's life. Now, if a child learns about the adoption from someone other than parents, he or she will not view the adoption as negative or shameful, because it was not kept a secret.

Dramatic changes in the perception of adoption, and of people's behaviour around it, are also a natural result of changes in the modern family. Today, adoptive parents, especially in Canada and the U.S., may belong to a racial or ethnic group different from that of their adopted child. In Canada, for example, Daly and Sobol (1993) estimate that there were about three international adoptions for every two domestic adoptions in 1991, and this tendency is increasing. For this reason, it is becoming more and more difficult to conceal the adoption fact from the child.

The increasing awareness of the value of the child's ethnical or racial original identity also encourages adoptive parents to go beyond their own community in quest of their child's original community. Such parents build up a blend of identities for their children, often involving representatives of the child's original community. Thus, the adoption ceases to be exclusively a family matter and acquires a broader social context, within which we see a gradual and continued movement towards openness and positive societal acceptance.

Homosexuals Becoming Parents

Until recently, most family studies ignored same-sex-couple families. Doing so resulted in an incomplete picture of what families are and do. Data are scarce on how many gay and lesbian couples are parenting children. Official definitions of family still often exclude gay/lesbian families, and some gay and lesbian couples are not "out," preferring to keep their sexual preferences secret.

Many official means of artificial insemination or adoption have not been, or are still not, available to same-sex couples. During the 1980s, lesbian access to clinic-based donor insemination was limited because such access was thought to threaten both the traditional family and the medical definition of infertility. Recent legislation regarding gay and lesbian unions has made lesbian donor insemination more acceptable, but only in a medicalized framework, not a familial one. As a result, people make many insemination arrangements privately (Haimes & Weiner, 2000). Some see this as a threat to medicine, because it is a practice outside medical regulations. However, for many lesbians who are unable to use medical channels due to stigma or other barriers, this is the only option. On the other hand, same-sex couples have unique opportunities as well. Aside from considerations of age, education, and health, lesbian couples have the luxury, for example, of deciding which partner may carry the child and how to create gender-unrelated parenting roles (Reimann, 1999).

Gay/lesbian families face immense challenges in being accepted by law and society. One well-publicized case, that of Ms. T in Alberta in 1997, brought to the forefront unspoken but strongly held attitudes toward raising children in same-sex-couple families (Abu-Laban & McDaniel, 1998, 82). The Province of Alberta deemed Ms. T, a woman who had successfully raised 17 foster children over many years, an unfit foster mother when authorities discovered that she had moved from a heterosexual to a lesbian relationship. They did not raise such questions about her capacity to parent when they saw her as heterosexual. Yet, notes Rosemary Barnes, former chief psychologist at the Women's College Hospital in Toronto, there are no visible differences between children raised by heterosexual mothers and those raised by lesbian mothers. To that end, many gay and lesbian parents are challenging the view that they are unfit parents. They do this by public acts of equal mothering, sharing parenting at home, and supporting each partner's sense of identity as a mother (Reimann, 1997).

Brave New Worlds of Reproduction

In a pronatalist society, people expect all women to bear children, and stigmatize those who fail to produce children. Drawing on Erving Goffman's stigma framework, an in-depth study by Remennick (2000) explored the experiences of 26 infertile Jewish women in Israel, a country with a strong pronatalist ideology. She found that women's coping strategies included selective disclosure, avoidance of exposing their "hidden disability," and other information management techniques. Infertility became a "master status" for these women, undermining any other merits and achievements they might have. Most women fully internalized and endorsed the pronatalist discourse, pursuing long-term and burdensome infertility treatments at high personal cost. Remennick concludes that resistance to the stigma of infertility is only possible where women dare question the motherhood imperative, which most Israelis do not do.

The stigma of childlessness is most devastating for less-educated women without career or other nonfamilial aspirations. Shame as a psychological response depends on the extent of an individual's conformity with the dominant norms.

Even in the United States, a less pronatalist society than Israel, infertility has negative effects on a couple's well-being. In a recent study, DeBoer (2002) finds that infertility is associated with lower levels of satisfaction with an intimate partner. It is also associated with lower levels of satisfaction with friendships. However, pessimism about the future varies with age and education. Infertile women over 30 have a more negative perception of the future than infertile women under age 30. Less-educated women with an infertility experience report a more positive outlook of the future and more control over their life circumstances than infertile women with higher levels of education.

Medically assisted procreation (MAP) is an aid to couples facing infertility or sterility (Romand, 2001). While MAP resembles conventional medical practice in some respects, it also creates relationships between doctor and couple (versus doctor and single patient), the gamete donors, and the legal system, and raises broader ethical questions. Methods of MAP include fertility restoration, artificial insemination, and "in vitro" fertilization, and lead to a variety of bioethical challenges. Among these are the medicalization of creation; the individualization and normalization of each MAP procedure; issues of confidentiality; the legal status of (frozen) embryos; and selecting the sex of the child.

A Finnish study by Malin et al. (2002) found that 16 percent of women surveyed had experienced difficulties in having a baby. Two-thirds of these had sought medical help, generally from private gynecologists. Less than half the women who sought help were satisfied with the infertility treatment, expressing less satisfaction than is generally found among health-care clients. Dissatisfied women were more often 35 to 39 years of age, in treatment during the study period, in treatment in public clinics, and not successful in having a baby. The most positive treatment experience was respectful, empathic, and personal care from the doctor. Unsatisfactory encounters with health-care personnel were the main reasons for dissatisfaction and were most often cited as the most negative treatment experience.

Birenbaum-Carmeli (1998) carried out participant observation of three in vitro fertilization (IVF) cycles in metropolitan national health care clinics in Israel and Canada. She reports that infertility treatments are the epitome of male domination and a means of objectifying women. IVF procedures in both countries are physician-dominated, highly technological, low in cost, and woman-friendly. Israeli doctors are more patronizing but also more personal and sympathetic than their Canadian counterparts. Organizational and economic differences result from the smaller size and lower affluence of the Israeli clinic. Uncritical acceptance of the control and dominance by male physicians reflects the greater marginalization of women in Israeli society. In contrast, Canada has more women on the medical staff, and paternalism is discouraged.

The relationship between patterns of disclosure and interpersonal support varies with the nature and type of disclosure, although overall, disclosure is associated with higher levels of perceived social support among women. The relationship between disclosure and couple adjustment is more complex.

A study by Martin-Matthews and Matthews (1994) examined patterns of perceived social support among couples undergoing treatment for infertility, focusing on patterns of support. They conducted intensive face-to-face interviews with married couples at their entry into a fertility clinic in Ontario, and again 18 months later. To marshal social support, the infertile couple must first reveal their status. Analysis shows striking differences between men and women in their general willingness to do this. Women are more likely to describe themselves as open on the topic, and to reveal their status to more people and to a broader range of ties within their social network.

Eichler (1989) notes that the new reproductive technologies (NRTs) have irrevocably changed the relationships between the state and the family and have dramatically increased intervention of social and economic factors in the reproductive process. Sociologists have not yet struggled with ethical issues presented by NRTs. They need to be involved in the critical assessment process. Eichler recommends research on the long-term consequences of intensive unsuccessful treatment for infertility, the type of information conveyed to clients, and the effects of anonymity of genetic parentage on offspring and others.

New reproductive technologies have allowed some people, who might otherwise have remained childless, to bear children. However, the "roller coaster" experience is more typical. The existence of new reproductive technologies raises hopes and expectations, and then often dashes them. The probability of success with many procedures is not high at all. In vitro fertilization, for example, succeeds in a healthy baby in only a small percentage of cases treated (McDaniel, 1988). Artificial insemination has a slightly higher rate of success.

For some women, the new technology succeeds only too well. They bear far more children than they had bargained for. Such was the experience of Bobbi McCaughey and her husband Kenny, of Carlisle, Iowa, who gave birth to septuplets after taking fertility drugs. Septuplets have since been born to two women in Saudi Arabia, one of whom was known to be taking fertility drugs. The year 1998 marked the first time a set of octuplets all survived birth. They were born to Nkem Chukwu of Texas, who had also been taking fertility drugs.

How Parenthood Affects Marriage/Relationships

The entry into parenthood has major effects on marriages/relationships, at least in North America. It can affect the career patterns of both parents, but it particularly affects the career patterns of women. It also affects patterns of household work, the distribution of power, marital satisfaction, and economic well-being within the household. The presumption that marriage and children go together, or that childbearing is women's natural destiny, may mask many important changes that occur in marital relationships with parenthood.

Research based on American data indicates that the presence of children in the family often has a negative effect on the mental well-being of adults. According to McLanahan and Adams (1987 and 1989), this relationship is explained by the temporal and monetary constraints associated with contemporary parenting. Parenthood puts particular strains on people who are particularly short of money and time—especially the poor and working-class people with little flexibility in their work patterns. In order to ease the problem, the authors urge public policy solutions such as child allowance and state-subsidized childcare.

Recent research by Savolainen et al. (2001) examines the relationship between parenthood and psychological well-being in Finland, a country that supplies the kind of support systems that McLanahan and Adams have in mind, yet where other conditions related to parental stress are very similar to the U.S. The results show that children tend to have no effect on the psychological well-being of Finnish women and a positive effect on Finnish men. This suggests that, in large part, the problem of parenting in North America is a lack of adequate financial and practical support.

As we said in the last chapter, the most consistent finding about the consequences of parenthood on marriage is that marital tensions increase (Glenn, 1990; Lupri & Frideres, 1981). Research on childless couples finds them generally happier than couples with children, and couples with children report being happiest before the arrival of their first child and after the last child leaves home (Lupri & Frideres, 1981).

The timing of childbirth may also add strains to a marriage. Increasingly, women are adopting strategies and plans about how to sequence education, career, marriage, and childbirth. Having a child too late may be risky for the mother and child, though it allows the mother to complete her education and establish herself occupationally. Having a child too early carries costs of its own. Women who have children early are more vulnerable to reduced wages than those who delay childbearing, though higher education reduces the impact of this result (Taniguchi, 1999). Women may find their career opportunities limited after bearing a child. This affects the way that some women see themselves and the role they have in the family. We will discuss this effect further in Chapter 7.

Figure 6.2   **DISTRIBUTION OF FIRST BIRTHS, BY AGE OF MOTHER, CANADA, 1976–1996**

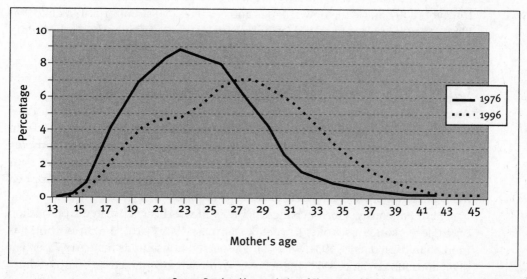

Source: Reprinted by permission of Clarence Lochhead. ISUMA Vol.1 No. 2, Autumn 2000.

As we saw in the previous chapter, new parents undergo a significant drop in the time they spend together as a couple. They worry about the child's safety or well-being, though these worries may not be shared equally or perceived in the same way by both parents. Last but far from least, there are the financial burdens of parenthood. Researchers estimate that the direct costs of raising one child are close to $150 000 (Scott 1996, 18). This can add immense stress for the couple.

The responsibilities of parenting become more onerous and the potential costs to marriages greater if people see children as vulnerable, easily damaged by stress, trauma, or poor parenting (as Freud argues), or as malleable by their environments (as behaviourism suggests). An alternative view is that parents are important to a child but are not the only factor. The child is an active social being who shapes his or her parents as much as they shape him or her. Other social actors also play vital roles in children's lives, such as other family members, siblings, the media, schools, and so on. Social structural forces also matter greatly, such as class, ethnicity, race, recent immigration, language, location, and, importantly, the support the parents have in entering parenthood.

However, not all the consequences of entering parenthood are bad for close relationships. Entering parenthood often gives the new parents a sense of meaning and direction that they might not have had before. Becoming parents can also enhance their status in the eyes of their families and society, and signify entry into adult responsibilities.

The research is clear on how best to have a satisfying entry to parenthood. Do not enter parenthood before you are emotionally, socially, and financially prepared. Have a child that both parents want and for whom both are willing to sacrifice. Talk openly with your partner about who will do what when the baby arrives, and how you will handle the new stresses and conflicts. Most important, realize that babies take up a lot of time and family resources. Start saving early for the baby's arrival and plan how you will deal with any forgone income.

Family and Household Size

As fertility has declined, the number of people in the average household has shrunk. The average Canadian household has decreased by 50 percent, from around six people in 1681 to less than three people today. What's more, complex family households, containing a variety of people who are not part of a nuclear family, have almost vanished. The proportion of two-family households dropped by 75 percent between 1931 and 1981, for example.

Simultaneously, a major change in family life has been a rise in the proportion of single-person households (Sweet & Bumpass 1987, 340). The proportion has more than tripled since 1931, when single-person households made up 7 percent of all households. Since 1971, there has been an 88-percent increase in non-family households (Vanier Institute of the Family 1994, 29), while the proportion of people overall living in families declined from 89 percent in 1971 to 84 percent in 1991 (Vanier Institute of the Family 1994, 29). Today, more people prefer to, and can afford to, live alone.

Socialization

Though parents are often unprepared for the changes that parenthood will bring them, the newborn infant is even less prepared. The baby arrives wholly unequipped to survive on its own, without care, love, and teaching. How parents provide this care, love, and teaching varies enormously from one culture and historical period to another. Today in Canada, it still varies from one social class, region, and ethnic group to another, though perhaps less markedly than in the past. Parents today have many of the same beliefs about how to raise their children, thanks in part to the mass media and public education.

Children do not arrive "ready to go" but must be carefully taught how to function in families and in society. Sociologists define **socialization** as the social learning process a person goes through to become a capable, functioning member of society. The process is social because it is through interaction with others and in response to social pressures that people learn the culture—the language, perspective, skills, likes and dislikes, the cluster of norms, values, and beliefs—that characterizes the group to which they belong. Socialization is one of the most important processes by which social structure constrains and transforms us, and also qualifies us to take full advantage of the opportunities society has to offer.

Primary socialization is learning that takes place in the early years of a person's life. The primary socialization of children is usually the responsibility of the child's family. It has a profound impact on the individual's life, by helping to set the child's future values, aspirations, and, to a certain extent, personality. It is in the family that a child first learns how to gain rewards by doing set tasks, how to negotiate to achieve a consensus on rules. Most important, children in well-functioning families learn that they are valued human beings. This lesson teaches them, by extension, that other human beings ought to be valued too.

Most children seem to follow a set pattern of growth, physically, emotionally, and morally, within a range. Cognitive abilities progress in a similar pattern. A baby learns to coo, then babble, and gradually progresses until he or she can carry on a conversation. The family environment affects these patterns by encouraging each step and by modelling for the baby how to communicate. Talking to children helps them learn to speak and understand language.

Gender Identities

Most children grow up securely attached to their family or other caregivers and able to take their place in society. It is in this secure family context that they begin to learn social roles, including one of the earliest and most consequential—their gender. People learn their gender-based habits of behaviour through **gender socialization**. The major agents of socialization—family, peer groups, schools, and the mass media—all serve to reinforce cultural and conventional definitions of masculinity and femininity. Gender socialization goes on throughout life and starts at birth. Young children learn gender identities when they experiment with hair and clothing styles, role-playing games, and body decoration, and by observing others at nursery school or daycare.

Parents routinely assign more household tasks to daughters than to sons. The tasks people assign to their sons are more usually "handyman" tasks, and less often cleaning, childcare, or meal preparation. Daughters get to do the latter. Not surprisingly, children often form traditional, gender-based attitudes toward housework before the end of high school. Men, older people, and poor people are particularly likely to hold and teach traditional, gendered, attitudes. As a result, fathers demand more help from teenaged daughters than from teenaged sons.

Socialization usually differentiates children by age as well as gender. A 1997 study that examined adults' role expectations found more positive role expectations for older siblings than for younger ones. The expectations also differed qualitatively for the siblings. For example, adults associate qualities like teaching, help, protection, and caretaking with older siblings. They associate learning, deference, and admiration with younger ones (Mendelson et al., 1997). Among older children, role expectations for siblings are more alike in important ways. However, often the early socialization experience creates resentments and identities that remain for life.

Gender socialization also affects the career paths children take in later life. Children are likely to follow in their parents' footsteps occupationally. Statistics Sweden finds that parents working or educated in a specific field increase the probability that a child will make a similar choice of educational program at upper secondary school (Dryler, 1998). However, this probability is stronger for fathers and sons. The connection between fathers and daughters, mothers and daughters, or mothers and sons is weaker. It follows that there would be a stronger influence on boys to become wage earners and providers. Girls, for their part, would receive less occupational mentoring and encouragement within their immediate family.

Learned gender differences in communication show up in our intimate relations, as we noted in an earlier chapter. For example, we generally teach women to behave in a demure, innocent, and disinterested fashion when sex is the topic of discussion with men. (Women are more forthcoming in discussions with other women.) Learned patterns of communication create and maintain distinctions between women and men, and reinforce social expectations between the sexes. Often, they complicate our understanding of what is really going on between the sexes.

We socially create differences in communication between the sexes. Often the different positions men and women hold in the occupational structure maintain these communication differences. Since bosses are more often men than women,

women often have to adopt "men's ways" of doing things if they are to succeed. Sometimes, women may adopt even tougher positions in order to remain in positions of authority.

For example, people resolve conflicts differently at home and at work, using more competitive styles at work and more accommodating styles at home. However, at work, at most managerial levels, men and women usually do it the male way, because that is the way in which women have achieved promotion in male-dominated workplaces.

Ethnic Identities

Many parents, especially those who raise their children outside their country of origin, want to ensure that later generations are aware of their culture and history. Parental involvement greatly affects the identities children take on in later life. For example, among Aboriginal people in Australia who are of mixed cultural heritage, children are more likely to call themselves Aboriginal if parents provide an upbringing rich in cultural life experience (Ramsay, 2000). Though other cultures are likely to figure in a child's ultimate conception of himself or herself, how strongly children hold on to their cultural heritage depends on the efforts of their parents.

Rituals and routines play an important part in the process of maintaining a family's ethnic heritage. McCarroll (2000) finds they have a great impact on children's developing racial attitudes. However, despite parents' best efforts, children still may choose to ignore ethnic traditions or identify with different groups. The child is an active participant in its development, not merely an empty vessel waiting to be filled with cultural information. The desire to stray from parents' cultural expectations may lead to conflict in families, as we will see in Chapter 8: Family Dynamics.

Parenting Processes

Family researchers have found better and worse ways of preparing children to participate in society. In saying this, we recognize that societies—and, within societies, subgroups—differ in their parenting behaviours. Some parents put a high value on obedience. Other parents value independence. Some parents want their children to be cooperative and adaptable, others, to be competitive and ambitious. However, good parenting typically produces children who are healthy, law-abiding, and successful at school. Poor parenting produces the opposite results.

When a child is failing, delinquent, or disturbed, this is not always the result of poor parenting. Genetic factors can increase the risks of childhood failure, delinquency, and depression. Outside social influences may also increase the risks. The best parenting in the world cannot prevent these factors from having a

Figure 6.3 PARENTING PROCESS

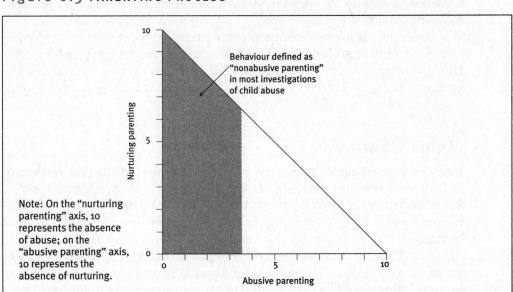

Source: Family Development Resources, www.nurturingparenting.com.

harmful influence. Moreover, poverty and other forms of bias put some children at higher risk than others of being labelled failures or delinquents in school. We have no way of telling, at this stage in the development of sociology, the relative sizes of the genetic, extra-familial, and parental influences.

The best we can do is look for trends in the research findings, while taking into account other factors. Doing this leads the open-minded observer to conclude that there really are better and worse parenting strategies, if our goal is to reduce the risks of childhood failure, delinquency, and depression—or, stated positively, to increase school success, good peer relations, and a healthy measure of self-esteem.

"Parenting" involves much more than taking care of a child's basic needs for food and shelter. It means helping mould that child into a functioning member of society. This, in turn, requires that parents create the right conditions for the emotional and cognitive development of their children. These "right" parenting conditions include providing love and attachment, emotional stability and family cohesion, protection and control, and fair and moderate discipline.

Love and Attachment

The vast majority of parents probably love their children, just as one would hope. Problems can occur, however, when parents do not know how to express love to their children (Perez, 1978), and when children who feel unloved by their parents suffer emotional damage. In addition, some parents and children might have higher relationship expectations than either party expects to give. Children usually remain closer to their mothers than to their fathers. Thus, more children may feel ignored by their fathers than by their mothers. These patterns and the relations between siblings as well, are subject to change over time, as children and their parents age (Burholt & Wenger, 1998).

There are many kinds of evidence of parental inadequacy, including juvenile delinquency. An early study, comparing delinquent and non-delinquent boys, found that delinquents are much more likely to have been deprived of parental affection (Bruce, 1970). Another found that delinquents received much less support and communication from their fathers (Cortex & Florence, 1972). A comparison of delinquent and non-delinquent girls yields similar findings (Riege, 1972). Delinquent girls are more likely to say that their mothers and fathers should spend more time with them. Often, they feel that neither parent gives them the right amount of love.

Explanations vary why children who feel unloved are more likely to break society's rules. Perhaps only delinquent peers are available to the unloved children, and they learn delinquent ways from these peers. Or, perhaps they are angry with their parents for (apparently) not loving them, so they deliberately choose friends of whom their parents will disapprove. By engaging in delinquent activity, they may also be seeking attention that they feel they do not get from their parents otherwise. Linden and Hackler (1973) find that a lack of ties to parents is associated with delinquency even among youth with no close ties to delinquent peers.

Criminologist Travis Hirschi talks about the importance of social bonds that keep people from resorting to delinquency. Research by Hirschi and others suggests that a feeling of attachment to one's parents is critically important. In turn, the three strongest influences on feelings of attachment are supervision, identity support, and instrumental communication (Cernkovich & Giordano, 1987). **"Control and supervision"** refers to the extent to which parents monitor their children's behaviour. **"Identity support"** refers to the parents' respect, acceptance, and emotional support for the adolescent. **"Instrumental communication,"** finally, refers to the frequency with which an adolescent talks to his or her parents about problems at school, job plans, and problems with friends.

Parental support and encouragement are important. Remember that children—indeed, people of all ages—form judgements about themselves by responding to how others treat them. That is the essence of what sociologists call the **looking-glass self**. People learn how to conform to rules, and how to obey authority, by generalizing from particular situations. We form our impressions of society, as we do of ourselves, from concrete, limited experiences. Many of these formative experiences occur within our family homes.

Children with more supportive, encouraging parents usually get higher grades at school, have more social competence, and get into less trouble with teachers. Other things being equal, these children see themselves as having more scholastic and athletic ability, take more pride in their physical appearance, and rate their overall worth more highly than other children. Feeling valued inside the home, they feel valued outside the home and conform more enthusiastically to the rules of social institutions like the school.

Parental involvement is another important form that love often takes. Parents who are more involved with their children spend more time with them, talk with them more, and think and talk about them more. Research shows that more involved parenting reduces delinquency among inner-city boys. Warm, supportive parenting leads to good social, psychological, and school adjustment. Even in adolescence, often a time of big changes and uncertainties, children whose parents are supportive do better. Adolescents with unsupportive parents are also more likely than other adolescents are to start smoking cigarettes. The health hazards of tobacco aside, cigarette smoking in adolescence also predicts a variety of substance abuses. The causal connections are complicated.

Emotionally responsive, democratic family environments are related to strategies of problem solving that more actively and directly address the stressor or its psychological impact. Enmeshed and conflictual environments, by contrast, are related to more avoidant strategies and use of alcohol or drugs (Harter & Vanecek, 2000).

Emotional Stability and Family Cohesion

Emotional stability ranks close behind love as a contributor to the healthy development of children. Anything that reduces the parents' ability to provide stable, consistent support runs the risk of producing school problems, delinquency, or depression in the child. These destabilizing factors can include spousal conflict, addiction, depression, or physical illness. Children whose parents are emotionally unstable are more anxious, less secure, and more likely to act out than children whose parents are emotionally stable. Similarly, instability often produces conflict, and as we noted above, children whose parents argue and fight a lot have lower self-esteem than those whose parents get along.

Family rituals are important for family stability and family cohesion. **Family cohesion** is a sense of attachment and relatedness among members of a family, both maintained and signified by shared activities, self-identification as a family member, and signs of familiarity and liking. Researchers report that children who live in families that have sit-down meals together at least three times a week are much less likely to become delinquents in their adolescence, or to turn to crime in adulthood. Family dinners are a sign of family cohesion and stability, which contribute to the healthy emotional development of children. Likewise, families that have recreational activities together are much less likely to produce delinquent children.

Protectiveness and Control

No less important than love and stability is parental control—how firmly, consistently, and fairly parents make and enforce rules for the child. Good rules guide and protect the child. They signify the parents' concern and attachment. Children are less likely to become delinquents if their parents keep an eye on what they are doing, offer them support, and give them a chance to discuss whatever it is that is bothering them. This is true of children in two-parent families, mother-only families, and mother–stepfather families. It is the quality of family relationships and family dynamics that counts in forming and socializing children. For example, successful completion of high school in Puerto Rican students is influenced by support for education from home, school, and community (Gonzalez, 1993). Youths who are supported at home develop identities conducive to success, while youths deprived of support at home, school, and community form identities that make school success much less likely.

Unhappy marriages often produce more troubled children, for two good reasons. First, an unhappy marriage can cause children to feel unloved. Unhappily married people often spend too little time with their children. The parents are depressed, stressed out, and self-absorbed. Second, marital conflict disrupts the normal practices of discipline, especially by mothers, who are typically the family disciplinarians in Canadian society. This, in turn, reduces the attachment between parent and child. (Rule enforcement is another form of attachment between parents and their children—a way that parents show concern for their children.)

On the other hand, too many rules enforced coldly or unfairly can be as bad as no rules at all. A survey of adolescents in Scotland identified four parenting styles, distinguished by their degree of acceptance and control of adolescent behaviour. (By "acceptance," the researchers mean that parents like and respect their children.) Researchers (Shucksmith et al., 1995) find these types:

- Permissive (high acceptances, low control; 37.8 percent of families);
- Unengaged (low acceptance, low control; 16.8 percent of families);
- Authoritarian (low acceptance, high control; 15.3 percent of families);
- Authoritative (high acceptance, high control; 23.7 percent of families).

The **authoritative parenting** style (high acceptance, high control) turns out children who achieve the highest levels of academic performance and mental well-being. They are also more likely than other adolescents to have a strong community orientation, are less self-centred, and are less likely to engage in deviant behaviour (Radziszewska et al., 1996 for African Americans, Taylor et al., 1995).

Other forms of parenting produce less desirable outcomes. For example, **authoritarian parenting** (low acceptance, high control) hinders the development of expressiveness and independence. This parenting style also increases the risk of adolescent drug use. Children whose parents are highly controlling but not as caring are more likely to become delinquents (Man, 1996), to become depressed, and to fail in school (Radziszewska et al., 1996).

This does not argue in favour of lax parental control, however. **Unengaged parenting** (low acceptance/low control) can also be harmful. For example, **latchkey youth** (who are home alone two or more days per week) are four times more likely to get drunk than youth who have parental supervision (five or more days a week). They are also more likely to smoke cigarettes, sniff glue, and use marijuana (Mulhall et al., 1996).

Permissive parenting produces poor results too. A study of high-school students in the San Francisco Bay area found that permissive (high acceptance, low control) parenting produces poor grades (Vergun, Dornbusch, & Steinberg, 1996). Poor students are more likely to come from families with permissive parenting styles (Bronstein, Duncan, & D'Ari, 1996; Radziszewska et al., 1996). What is more, differences in adjustment accumulate over time, and the harmful effects of neglectful parenting continue to take their toll as behaviour problems, internal distress, and poor school performance (Steinberg et al., 1994).

Thus, children whose parents are authoritarian, unengaged, or permissive are most likely to show problems of adjustment, poor academic achievement, or substance abuse. The authoritative parenting style offers the best mixture of love and control—not too much or too little of either.

Fair and Moderate Discipline

The issue of discipline is related to control. A desire for control leads to the creation of rules, and discipline is the enforcement of these rules. Overzealous discipline may wipe out the benefits of control, as may inattentive discipline. For example, Wells and Rankin (1988) report that delinquency is less likely when parental strictness is moderate, rather than high or low.

Hoffman (1979) distinguishes between three basic types of disciplining techniques: power assertion, love withdrawal, and induction. In **power assertions**, a parent or other caregiver threatens a child with punishment for non-compliance. Typically, punishment is to be delivered in a physical form. The child changes his or her behaviour to avoid punishment. However, they do not base this compliance on moral learning. The child's seemingly moral behaviour is externally, not internally, driven.

Similarly, in **love withdrawal**, a parent threatens a child. Instead of the punishment taking a physical form, it takes an emotional form—producing in the child anxiety over the loss of love. As with power assertions, the child complies with parental demands to avoid punishment. There is no moral learning—no internalization of ideas of good and bad.

Induction, on the other hand, emphasizes the possible benefits of the child's behaviour for others. Inductive discipline—teaching good behaviour by setting a good example, then rewarding imitation—is better for the child than power

Debate Box 6.1 SPANKING—SHOULD WE MAKE IT ILLEGAL?
Which side of the debate do you fall on?

SHOULD BE Illegal

- Spanking is cruel and unnecessary; it just makes the parent feel better. Parents should find ways to channel their aggressive impulses *away* from children.
- Spanking does not improve a child's behaviour. Other ways of disciplining children—by setting an example—are more likely to have the desired effect.
- Many progressive societies (especially in Northern Europe) have banned spanking. They are usually leaders in the fight for equality and social welfare.
- Our whole history as a society has been to move away from corporal punishment. Corporal punishment is a cruel, outmoded activity that privileges the powerful.
- Children are spanked only because they are defenseless to resist it. A comparable attack on an adult, to correct "misbehaviour," could result in criminal charges.
- Spanking is a carry-over—people who were spanked, spank. We cannot allow bad habits to be handed down from one abused generation to another.

SHOULD NOT BE Illegal

- Spanking tells a child the parent cares and loves him or her. Failure to spank indicates negligence and indifference, and children pick up on this lack of love.
- Spanking makes the child realize how serious his misbehaviour is. After all, if the parent did not get angry enough to spank, it probably wasn't very important.
- There is no concrete evidence a little spanking hurts anyone. The research has been on physical abusers who go to extremes, far beyond merely spanking.
- Spanking does not usually lead to more serious forms of physical abuse. Spankers are no more likely to become abusers than drinkers are to become alcoholics.
- Parents have a right to raise their children the way they see fit. Family life should be private and the parents should be left alone to raise their children.
- The government and courts should keep their hands off family life. The state already intrudes into, and messes up, too many aspects of our lives today.

assertions. When children break the rules, they become aware of contributing to another's distress and feel guilty. They also learn how to prevent that from happening. Feelings of guilt, unlike feelings of fear, exercise an **internal moral control** over our behaviour. Adolescents taught using inductive techniques make decisions more independently, for they have learned how to make moral judgements. Parental affection and inductive discipline foster moral internalization, while power assertions diminish moral learning (Hoffman, 1979).

Inductive techniques offer many benefits by, for example, forcing parents to explain and show good behaviour. Yet, 80 percent of American (and presumably Canadian) parents use some degree of physical punishment—a form of power assertion—as a disciplinary tool. Unlike inductive discipline, power assertions are quick and simple. Physical punishment, and power assertions more generally, appeal to parents who do not have the time, patience, or inclination to teach rules inductively.

To see discipline in a natural setting, researchers spent hundreds of hours watching parents threaten their children in indoor malls and other public spaces (Davis, 1996). They note that when parents use physical punishment as a form of discipline, usually they want compliance with some very simple demands. For example, the parent wants the child to sit still, be quiet, come with the parent, or stop touching things. Children typically respond by ignoring the parent. About half the adults making these threats also hit the children.

What we learn from this scenario is that parents use physical punishment routinely, and it is routinely ineffective! Seventy-seven percent of surveyed mothers of three-year-olds spank their children at least once in a two-week interval. They do so an average of 2.5 times per week. In the end, punitive discipline produces delinquency and low self-esteem (Peiser & Heaven, 1996).

Research also shows that the probability of physically punishing children varies with the age of the mother. Teenage mothers are more likely to punish their children physically, and the youngest adolescent mothers advocate the use of physical punishment more strongly. They also report less personal happiness than other adolescent mothers. Perhaps these two factors are related.

A broad range of studies has found that harsh childhood discipline produces harmful consequences for both sexes in adulthood. Among them are depression, alcoholism, low self-esteem, aggressive behaviour, suicide, and a tendency to physically abuse wives and children. As the harshness and frequency of punishment increases, so does the risk of delinquency. Perhaps that is because physical punishment leads children to think of violence as an effective means of solving problems.

Parents use physical punishment for a variety of reasons. Nonetheless, the single most important factor predicting physical punishment by an adult is violence that adults have experienced during their own childhood. People whose parents often yelled at and spanked are more likely to yell at and spank their own children (Barnett, Quackenbush, & Sinisi, 1996).

Runaways

"Runaways" are the most extreme version of children who stray from their parental homes, rules, and expectations. Short of a controlled experiment, nothing shows better the validity of theories about good parenting than the available evidence on runaway youth, or runaways. As first-hand observers, runaways have made a costly comment on their parents' parenting styles by leaving home to live on the streets. It is hard to imagine a more damning assessment of their parents, or their families.

Payne (1995) identifies five different kinds of young people who go missing: runaways, pushaways, throwaways, fallaways, and take-aways. Adams, Gullotta, and Clancy (1985) identify three categories of homeless adolescents: runaways, throwaways, and societal rejects. As the names suggest, young people have a variety of reasons for leaving home. However, runaways are a common element in any discussion of children who choose to live on the streets.

A review of runaway behaviour reveals different reasons for running, and changes in reasons with time or living situations. Industrialization increased the incidence of running in the nineteenth century, as did the Great Depression in the early twentieth century. During the 1960s, the counter-cultural youth movement had a similar effect (Wells & Sandhu, 1986). Recently, the population of runaway and homeless youth has changed. Today, most runaway youth have run away from abuse and neglect.

A variety of interpersonal and family relationships shape adolescents' decisions to run away. So do difficulties at school and problems with siblings (Spillane-Grieco, 1984). Most street youth are from families that suffer serious emotional, mental, or substance abuse problems. These youth are not necessarily on the street due to socioeconomic pressures (Price, 1989), though family financial difficulties increase the likelihood of physical abuse. Sexual abuse is different: it is more common in reconstituted (families comprising formerly married partners and their children) families that are financially stable, or in broken families that are financially unstable (McCormack, Burgess, & Gaccione, 1986).

The Family Problems of Runaways

In short, most runaways are young people fleeing dysfunctional families. Abuse aside, the children often come from "chaotic/aggressive families" and reveal a mixed pattern of youth aggression and parental skill deficiency (Teare, Authier, &

Figure 6.4 RUNAWAYS BY GENDER

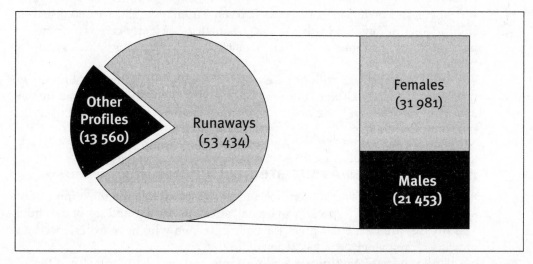

Source: Dr. Marlene Dalley, Research Officer, National Missing Children Service.
Figures extracted from the Canadian Police Information Centre (CPIC).

Peterson, 1994). Running away is usually, though not always, a response to neglect, abandonment, and physical or sexual violence (Cote, 1992). Abused runaways are even more likely than those who were not abused to describe their parents in ways that suggest serious antisocial personality and drug problems (Stiffman, 1989a).

Parents are often the villains in these stories. Powers, Eckenrode, and Jaklitsch (1990) report that, of New York runaways and homeless youth, 60 percent had suffered physical abuse, 42 percent emotional abuse, 48 percent neglect, and 21 percent sexual abuse. Biological mothers were the most often cited perpetrators of maltreatment (63 percent), followed by biological fathers (45 percent). Parents had pushed more than one-third of the homeless youth out of their homes.

A Canadian study concurs. Janus et al. (1995) estimate that 74 percent of runaway males and 90 percent of the females had been physically abused at least once. Most of these adolescents have been victims of chronic, extreme abuse, experienced at a young age, often perpetrated by the biological parents (most often the mother) and initiated before the first runaway episode.

Runaway males are much more likely to have been sexually abused than prior research has reported (Rotherham-Borus et al., 1996). Among adolescent runaways interviewed in a Toronto shelter, one in three males and three in four females report having been sexually abused. Many male victims of sexual abuse report a fear of adult men. Female victims report confusion about sex. Another Toronto study also reports high rates of substance use and abuse, attempted suicide (30 percent of runaways report having attempted suicide in the past), loneliness, and depression among the street youth population (Adlaf, Zdanowicz, & Smart, 1996).

Many chronic runaways grow up to be homeless adults. Homeless adults who display higher than average rates of criminal behaviour, substance abuse, and other forms of deviant behaviour often come from more abusive and deprived childhoods (Simons & Whitbeck, 1991). A history of foster care, group home placement, and running away is particularly common among homeless adults (Susser et al., 1991).

In short, happier, healthier parents who treat their children authoritatively produce happier, healthier children. Parents who are unhappy, unhealthy, or unaware of good parenting practices produce children who are more likely to run away from home.

Health Stresses Associated with Parenting

As we have already seen, parenthood itself causes stress. The most important predictors of parental (especially maternal) stress are the age and sex of the child. The stresses are particular great for young women who have experienced an unwanted pregnancy or physical abuse.

Under normal conditions, older infants and female infants are easier to handle (Sanik, 1993). Parental stress intensifies when children get older, or when they have special needs. Thus, one source of family stress that researchers have given much attention to is the need to care for a chronically sick child. This is a long-term stressor that cannot be fully eliminated by typically effective coping methods.

The effects of chronic illness vary from one family to another, partly due to variations in the illness itself. However, many similarities are also evident. Specifically, families with chronically ill children often suffer from a decline in the health of the parent who is most responsible for taking care of the sick child. Family members often experience a decline in the well-being of the family as a whole. This decline, caused by a chronic shortage of time and money, can show up in a variety of ways: physical exhaustion, irritability, depression, pessimism, seclusiveness, or a withdrawal of cooperation.

Two interacting causes of this decline are the *duration* of the illness and treatment, and the extent of *parental involvement* in caring for the ill child. The more severe the decline of the caretaker parent and the longer it goes on the more strain the entire family experiences, and the more difficult it is for the family to cope adequately.

Other family members suffer from emotional and psychic depletion too. Fully one-third of all children who become chronically ill by age 15 also suffer from serious psychological and behavioural problems as a result (Kashani et al., 1981). Moreover, the tensions caused by long-term care can be permanently damaging. Dysfunctional coping responses such as depression, blame, denial, and guilt are common in all family members, including the sick child (Bruhn, 1977). In such families, the members often grow estranged from one another and the risk of divorce is high (Field, 1982).

Immediate shock, anger, and helplessness (Valman, 1981), as well as hopefulness (Mattson, 1972), disappear. They give way to a dazed state, a deep sense of apathy, and isolation from other family members and society. Researchers also know this state as "pseudo-narcotic" syndrome (Anthony, 1970). It has some features in common with post-traumatic stress syndrome.

The isolation family members feel from one another intensifies as each member goes through the grieving process, experiencing different emotions at different times. Often, family members fail to talk about the child's disease or his or her fears of death (Taylor, 1980). The ill child also becomes isolated from friends and society (Burnette, 1975). Often, silence reflects the family's inability to cope (Turk, 1964). The family as a whole refuses to adjust to an abnormal or difficult situation (Kaplan et al., 1980). Many do not know where to begin.

When people take care of a chronically ill family member, the intensity of emotion is difficult to sort out or express in relationships with other family members. This produces some of the feelings of isolation. However, in some families, the illness also brings people closer. Thus, isolation and **enmeshment** can go hand in hand.

The presence of a chronically sick child also harms siblings in the home (Lademann, 1980). Just as fathers are often estranged from the mother–child relationship, siblings are left out of the intense relationship between the parents and their sick child (Larcombe, 1978). This provokes feelings of anger, resentment, and neglect (Valman, 1981). Children may try to compensate at school for lack of attention at home. However, lacking the communication skills of adults, they have a hard time giving voice to their feelings and desires; serious behavioural problems at school and at home may result. Adults and children in daily contact with these siblings often remain ignorant of the source of resulting behaviour problems.

Thus, many parents and siblings suffer uncommunicated fears, anxieties about the past and future, broken sleep, nightmares, bad eating habits, speech impediments, nail biting, accident-proneness, and more (Kanof et al., 1972). Most of the literature reflects a high rate of dysfunctional response to child illness. However, as we mentioned earlier, chronic or fatal illness sometimes strengthens family ties (Motohashi, 1978). In some families, members talk meaningfully for the first time (Valens, 1975). People occasionally discover unknown and creative personal resources (Anthony, 1970). Though the obstacles posed by a child's illness are phenomenal, these family breakthroughs prove that successful coping is possible.

The problems that families encounter in trying to cope with a chronically ill child are often closely tied to problems that existed before the onset of illness (Kalnins, 1980). In short, a family's ability to cope is correlated with its previous level of functioning (Steinhauer et al., 1984). We will have more to say about the related issues of family dynamics, stress, and coping in later chapters.

Variations on a Theme

Recent analyses of data collected as part of Canada's National Longitudinal Survey of Children and Youth (NLSCY) have focused on the identification of vulnerable children by measuring actual outcomes, such as physical and mental health, social skills, and readiness for school learning. This research has shown that relationships and activities within the family environment are the strongest determinants of childhood vulnerability. What this means, in practice, is that children benefit from good parenting skills, a cohesive family group, and parents who are in good mental health, and that these benefits can outweigh the negative effects associated with poverty.

There is no denying that socioeconomic status (SES)—the relative position of an individual family in the social class hierarchy, based on their access to or control over wealth, prestige, and power—affects both parents and their children. However, research so far finds that this effect is mediated through parenting practices, with the result that even though family income is related to childhood outcomes, we cannot claim that income supplements to poor families would necessarily reduce childhood vulnerability. Such findings present a serious challenge to the "culture of poverty" thesis, and to risk factor research that suggests childhood vulnerability stems predominantly from poverty or low SES. These findings do not suggest we should give up on efforts to reduce poverty, but present a strong case for universal interventions to improve the family environments of Canadian children. Interventions directed predominantly at poor families / communities will not substantially reduce childhood vulnerability, according to this research.

Gradients associated with family income and SES tend to be linear, though they are fairly weak for most childhood outcomes. Research finds that socioeconomic gradients (SEG) are evident in children's temperament even during the first two years of infancy, and they appear to get steeper as children get older. They have an especially strong effect on children's early vocabulary. Children are less likely to be vulnerable to this SEG effect if they are female and if their mothers have a high level of education. Single parents and young mothers are two groups whose children are particularly vulnerable to behaviour problems. The prevalence of childhood vulnerability varies substantially among neighbourhoods and cities, meaning that poverty is not only a family context that affects childhood—it is also a neighbourhood context (Willms, 2002a).

Well-intentioned, thoughtful parents can do a lot to create good conditions for their children. However, many things that can harm children are beyond parents' control. Desperate poverty, peer pressure toward delinquent or criminal behaviour, and single parenthood are conditions within which many parents raise their children. A complete discussion of parenting would have to consider the effects of economic, political, and structural variables on the lives of parents, and thus on their ability to care for their children. Workplace stress, unemployment, and racial discrimination, for example, all affect children directly or indirectly.

Diversity is normal and natural in family relations. Different kinds of parents can do an equally good job of raising their children if they provide the basics of "good parenting" that we have already considered. On this theme, we now consider a few variations.

Single Parents

Single parents—and especially, single mothers—constitute a group of particular interest since more children are growing up in families headed by single mothers. The research continues to indicate that single mothers are increasingly at risk for physical and mental health problems, and their children also have increased risk of social, academic, emotional, and behavioural difficulties.

Families headed by single mothers are characterized by multiple adversities that may include poverty and low levels of education. However, the distribution of these risk variables is not uniform, so we must be careful when we generalize about this group of families. Treating them as a single entity, as is often done, masks some of the important relationships. In fact, we can discern three distinct "types" of single-parent families—characterized by family income and whether or not the mother works outside the home. The first type has an income that is below the national average, but a level of education above national average; 90 percent of these single mothers work outside the home. A second type has an income of more than $21 000 and half of these mothers work outside the home. A third type, with incomes averaging $11 200— can be considered economically disadvantaged. Only one-fifth of these single mothers work outside the home, and a disproportionate number of them were teenagers when they first gave birth.

Research from the National Longitudinal Survey of Children and Youth (NLSCY) reports that children in the second and third types of single-parent family are more likely to exhibit behaviour problems, have lower vocabulary scores at ages four and five, and lower mathematics tests scores at ages six to eleven. In general, disparities in school-readiness outcomes between children in single-parent families and those in two-parent families are only partially attributable to differences in family income and other socioeconomic factors, according to this research. Boys who live in the second and third types of single-parent families tend to be particularly prone to behaviour problems, more than girls in these same families, and more than boys in the first type of single-parent families. These problems are both externalized (as trouble-making) and internalized (as depression) (Lipman, Offord, Dooley, & Boyle, 2002).

Concerns about adolescent single parenting continue to grow, even though the frequency of adolescent childbearing in Canada has declined steadily since the late 1950s.

In recent years concern about adolescent single parenting has increased. However the actual frequency of adolescent childbearing has decreased steadily since the late 1950s. For example, the childbearing rate among 15- to 19-year-olds has decreased in Canada from 34.8 per 1000 in 1975, to 20.2 per 1000 in 1996. The absolute number of teen births has declined by 50 percent (from 39 212 to 19 920). However, in contrast to the decrease in fertility rates, the rate of non-marital childbearing among teens has risen steadily over the last four decades—84 percent of teen births were unwed in 1997, 37 percent in 1975, and 19 percent in 1960.

Part of the reason for continued—if not growing concern—is that adolescent motherhood is generally associated with socioeconomic disadvantages for the mother and poor outcomes for the child. Research based on the National Longitudinal Survey of Children and Youth finds a clear pattern of improvement in children's outcomes as mother's age at childbearing increases. Teen mothers are typically characterized by disadvantages. For example, the average family income of mothers who had a first child as a teen was $25 000—half the national average. Their level of education was lower than that of older mothers. Teen mothers are much more likely to be single parents and not work outside the home. For these and other reasons, teen mothers report lower levels of family functioning than older mothers. One in four teen mothers reports being depressed—twice the prevalence of mothers who had their first child in their late twenties. Childbearing during older adolescence strongly influences the likelihood that the resulting child will display a behavioural disorder, especially during pre-school years, and have poor receptive vocabulary upon entry to school. These effects are only partly attributable to family background (Dahinten & Willms, 2002).

For generations, the folk wisdom has linked delinquency to "broken homes," and researchers continue to find an association between the two. Single-parent homes produce a disproportionate share of social problems such as delinquency, teenage pregnancy, and welfare dependency. However, studies have found that children from single-parent and two-parent families do not differ from other children in their social skills (Kesner & McKenry, 2001). These skills include conflict management, the lack of which could contribute to more serious social problems such as crime and violence, leaving us to wonder what these other reasons may be if the parenting itself is not the reason for so many social problems being attributed to single-parent families.

Some argue that it is poverty, not family disruption or single parenthood, that produces more delinquency in single-parent homes. Since single-parent families often live below the poverty line, they experience the same problems as other families with low incomes. Nevertheless, the presence of only one parent may heighten these problems. Evidence from the Canadian National Longitudinal Survey of Children and Youth supports the conclusion that economic problems are a large part of the issue. These data show that children in low-income single-parent families are much more likely than children in low-income two-parent families to show a variety of emotional, behavioural, and academic problems.

However, children in medium- and high-income single-parent families are much less likely to do so, and are only more likely to show these problems than children in same-income two-parent families (Lipman, Offord, Dooley, & Boyle, 2002).

This suggests that children in single-parent families are at risk for both social and economic reasons. More economic resources do not necessarily wipe out the social issues. For example, escaping from a shortage of money will not compensate for a persisting shortage of parenting time. However, with increased economic resources, the problems a family faces are reduced. Laub and Sampson (1988), for example, report that single-parent homes are no more likely to produce delinquents than two-parent homes, once we control for attachment, supervision, and discipline (see also Van Voorhis et al. 1988, who make a similar point).

More recently, the National Longitudinal Survey of Children and Youth supported these conclusions with Canadian data. It finds that quality of parenting and types of parental discipline and encouragement matter greatly to children's outcomes. Quality of family life is critical, reducing the harmful effects of poverty. The quality of the neighbourhood, and the neighbourhood school, also contributes to the outcome (Jones et al., 2002).

Overall, Jones's data confirm that long-term low income has harmful consequences for children. Persistent poverty, as well as workplace stress, increases parental stress and family conflict. It increases the likelihood of parental depression and hostile and ineffective parenting patterns—for example, yelling, smacking, providing no quality time or even time to assist a child with homework. Undesirable parenting behaviours tend to produce undesirable child outcomes: reduced mental health (e.g., more depression), worse physical health (i.e., more physical injuries), and poorer school performance (e.g., more school absences). Neighbourhood characteristics (such as social cohesiveness and social problems) are important for both parenting and certain child outcomes. Social cohesiveness can improve child well-being while social problems can worsen it. If parents and neighbourhoods can overcome the stresses and hardships associated with household poverty, child outcomes can be improved.

Other things being equal, however, single-parent families have a harder time than two-parent families maintaining a high quality of life for themselves and their children. A study of adolescents in Rochester, New York (Stern & Smith, 1995) finds that difficulties caused by single parenting are the result of lack of partner support, life distress, social isolation, and shortage of money. Even in families without economic hardship, the children of single-parent families still have more problems than the children of two-parent families. Likely, this is due to a shortage of time and social support.

Adolescent Mothers

Generally, people who enter parenthood unexpectedly are likely to find the parenting role stressful and their children difficult. Beyond this, adolescent women often have little understanding of the developmental milestones in their infant's behaviour. They may therefore fail to encourage their infant's development and may see their child as less competent, or more troublesome.

Outside support often helps an adolescent mother to handle the demands her child poses. Researchers (Luster, Perlstadt, & McKinney, 1996) report that adolescent mothers receiving an intensive family support program provide higher-quality care for their infants than mothers who receive less intensive support.

Teen Pregnancy

Despite the fact that the teen birth rate is slowly falling, there are still an estimated one million teen pregnancies in the United States alone. About 85 percent of these pregnancies are unplanned, which in any population can increase the risk for problems. The biggest risk for teen mothers is delaying prenatal care or worse; 7.2 percent received no care at all.

The reason for lack of prenatal care is usually delayed pregnancy testing, denial or even fear of telling others about the pregnancy. Most states have a health department or University clinic where prenatal care is free or low cost and patient confidentiality is very important, meaning no one can tell the teen mother's family.

Because the body of a teen is still growing she will need more nutritional support to meet both her needs and that of her baby. Nutritional counselling can be a large portion of prenatal care, usually done by a doctor or a midwife, sometimes a nutritionist. This counselling will usually include information about prenatal vitamins, folic acid, and the dos and don'ts of eating and drinking. Lack of proper nutrition can lead to problems like anemia (low iron), low weight gain, etc.

Another problem facing teen mothers is the use of drugs and alcohol, including cigarette smoking. No amount of any of these substances is safe for use in pregnancy. In fact, their use can complicate pregnancy even further increasing the likelihood of premature birth and other complications.

Premature birth and low birth weight create a wealth of their own problems, including brain damage, physical disabilities and more. The potentially lengthy hospital stay and increased risk of health problems for these babies leads to more stress on the teen mother.

While facing the grim realities of teen pregnancy is not pleasant, this is not the picture that has to be painted. Teen mothers are perfectly capable of having a healthy pregnancy and a healthy baby. With the proper nutrition, early prenatal care and good screening for potential problems the majority of these potential problems will not come to light. While some tend to think that you can't teach a teen mother anything about her body or baby, it's really a ridiculous notion. Many of the teen mothers who take active roles in their care do go on to have healthy babies, despite the other hardships that they will face in their lives. Support from the families and communities is a must for the young, new family to be successful.

Gay and Lesbian Families

Research finds stereotypical views about homosexuality even among young, highly educated people. These views include the beliefs that homosexual parents create a dangerous environment for the child, provide a less secure home, and offer less emotional stability. Such views are more common among older, rural, or less educated respondents, among people who are highly religious, and among people who are fearful about sex. Yet, research on same-sex couples does not provide any grounds for these concerns. As far as we know, and contrary to popular belief, gay and lesbian parents raise fine, healthy families as often as heterosexual families do.

Many studies support the finding that gay and lesbian parents are just as capable in childrearing as heterosexual parents. Children raised by homosexual parents do not have different behavioural and educational outcomes than children of heterosexual unions, nor do they feel any less loved or accepted by their parents (Mattingly & Bozick, 2001). Further, there is no more chance of children growing up gay or lesbian in a same-sex family than in a heterosexual family.

Some critics of homosexual parenting argue that lesbian unions lack a proper father figure, which could affect the growth of the child. This is not so, as many lesbian mothers include the fathers in the child's life in the cases where they know the donor. However, those who oppose homosexual parenting are often not as concerned about the role of the mother in parenting between two gay men. In addition, many lesbian mothers are challenging the idea that biological fathers should be involved as parents in their children's lives as part of normal development. Besides fighting for their right to raise children, many gay and lesbian parents also wish to dispel the notion that parenting be synonymous with gendered assumptions about mothering and fathering, and that mothers and fathers should share a household with their children (Donovan, 2000).

Many children of same-sex unions view their upbringing quite positively in the love and attention they received and their preparation to enter the adult world. Many feel they gained important insights into gender relations and broader, more inclusive definitions of family by growing up with same-sex parents (Saffron, 1998).

Custodial Grandparents

Grandparents in general are valuable family members. Many two-parent families (with both parents working) depend on retired grandparents for childcare. In this capacity, grandparents help to reduce stress for the parents, and in particular for the mothers—for example, the stress of daycare drop-off and pickup is reduced if children are left with the grandparents. Grandparents' homes usually have a good supply of children's needs, supplied by parents and grandparents. Family migration, however, impacts on whether grandparents are available to assist with grandchildren.

Grandparenting in the 2000s has increasingly become second-time-around parenting because of factors that include alcohol and drug abuse, teenage pregnancy, divorce, incarceration, and AIDS (Minkler & Roe, 1996; Minkler, Roe, & Robertson, 1994). Many cultures immigrating to Canada and the U.S. also place more value on custodial grandparenting and the use of extended families for parenting.

Caring for children again, especially at an advanced age, comes with a unique set of difficulties. Intergenerational conflicts may arise, as the grandparent and the grandchild grew up in different eras with different ideas of acceptable behaviour. Older grandmothers perceive themselves to have more information about grandchildren than younger grandmothers, and women who become grandmothers later in life perceive themselves to be stronger in teaching grandchildren (Watson, 1997). These "stronger" grandmothers may not be as flexible with grandchildren as needed, which exacerbates conflict.

In addition, the demands of custodial grandparenting can be taxing on older grandparents. One study warns that some grandparents may need mental health assistance for themselves, especially if they are caring for problem grandchildren (Emick & Hayslip, 1996).

Despite these difficulties, taking on a parent role is a valuable experience for both the grandparent and the rest of the family. Research by Harrison, Richman, and Vittimberga (2000) finds that grandparents report lower levels of parental stress than parents from both single- and two-parent families. The experience for grandparents is perhaps less stressed because they fulfill an important need in this respect, and their work helps to keep the family together. Lesbian women in the U.S. define the grandmother's role as providing emotional support to their grandchildren, providing varied experiences for their grandchildren, and providing support for the parents of their grandchildren (Whalen et al., 2000). Grandparents are particularly effective because they give their children an opportunity to learn from skilled caregivers. As a result, young African-American mothers who live in three-generation households with their own mothers give their children better quality care than other young mothers (Cox, 2000).

In Loco Parentis

As children spend more of their time away from family, in daycare centres, schools, and other public places, public institutions assume more responsibility for parent-like protection of children. This is what we mean by the term *in loco parentis*, literally, "in the place of parents." This has served to clarify and narrow the rights and duties of parents, and parent substitutes (such as guardians and grandparents).

In particular, schools and colleges have been forced to clarify their *in loco parentis* role in the lives of their students. Historically, the doctrine of *in loco parentis* gave teachers the right to act as parents would when responding to disciplinary problems. Corporal punishment was standard. The strapping of children in schools continued well into the middle of the twentieth century in many places in Canada. Now, in most jurisdictions, teachers are not allowed to hit a student under any circumstance.

Increasingly, teachers today are rejecting the *in loco parentis* role. Devine (1995) argues that the rejection of this role has contributed to the growing prevalence of urban school violence. However the questions remain whether schoolteachers should be held responsible for school violence and whether university or college administrators are responsible for regulating students' behaviour. The doctrine of *in loco parentis* originally permitted colleges to act as students' "parents" by enforcing both academic and non-academic codes of conduct. However, dramatic changes following World War II have resulted in schools losing the authority to discipline students without due process.

People also raise *in loco parentis* issues concerning children living in stepfamilies. Issues such as legal authority for stepparents to act for their stepchildren and stepparent obligations following the divorce, death, or incapacity/abandonment of the spouse surround the rights and obligations of members of a stepfamily. (On this topic, see Duran-Aydintug & Ihinger-Tallman, 1995.) Can we rely on them to provide satisfactory parenting, as though they are parents with all the rights and obligations of biological or adoptive parents?

Cultural Variation

Variations by culture and class go a long way toward explaining variations in the family experiences of different individuals. In North American culture, one common element is the work ethic, sometimes associated (as by sociologist Max Weber) with the rise of certain Protestant sects in the early days of capitalism. According to Weber, the Protestant work ethic is highly compatible with the capitalist drive for material success. Postponed gratification, ambition, and diligence are the keys to material success in this life and to reward in an afterlife. The strength of belief in this ethic varies from one cultural group to another.

The fact of cultural variation is evident whenever we look at a group that does not come out of the Anglo/Christian tradition—for example, the Chinese. In China, two compelling but sometimes contradictory ideologies face parents. Traditional Confucianism stresses large families and loyalty to family elders. Communism stresses small families and loyalty to the state. Chinese parents now worry whether they have what it takes to raise children or whether they lack needed insight into contemporary childhood experience. Interestingly, despite their concern with Confucianism, not Protestantism, Chinese parents usually teach their children a strong work ethic, nonetheless.

The difficulty Chinese parents face in changing over to Western styles of parenting is even more marked outside the People's Republic of China. For example, lower-class Chinese adolescents in Hong Kong report their parents are warm, but overly controlling. In Shucksmith's terms describing parenting styles, we would see the parents as somewhere between authoritative and authoritarian. As control increases and warmth declines, conflict between parents and children becomes more frequent and intense. The difficulty lies in Chinese parents learning to loosen the child–parent tie—to accept more permissive standards of parenting, which children raised in North America come to expect.

In many cultures, parents exert a high degree of close control for extended periods. We often stereotype Jewish mothers for this quality. Often, a high degree of control is associated with the use of shaming, guilt, or **love withdrawal** as tactics in exercising control. Research verifies that some groups—for example, Greek and Lebanese mothers—use this approach more often than other groups—for example, Vietnamese mothers. As with the Chinese parents we discussed earlier, these qualities—when kept to a moderate level—are not bad in themselves. However, they do run into conflict with the parenting standards that prevail in Canada, which are typically more permissive, child-centred, and aimed at preserving the child's self-esteem.

Class Variation

Cultural ideologies affect family process, and so does the family's social class. Even within the same cultural group, differences in social class can have a profound impact on the socialization of children.

In North America, parents holding blue-collar jobs often stress obedience and respect for authority and have been more inclined to use physical punishment. Though class differences may be narrowing, blue-collar parents are more likely to discipline according to the character of their child's misbehaviour. Parents holding white-collar jobs, by contrast, stress self-motivation and independence. They are also more likely to use reason or verbal threats to force the child to comply with household rules. However, these class differences continue to narrow as parents and children of all social classes are subjected to identical socialization by the mass media.

At the extremes, however, class differences will remain. Many poor parents do not have enough time for their children, and are too stressed to spend quality time with them when they are home. Time shortage, of course, is a problem not limited to the poor, but it may be more common among people who are struggling to make ends meet, perhaps working longer hours or multiple jobs. These parents often cannot take even a day off to care for a sick child without having their pay reduced or possibly their jobs imperilled. Poor families, particularly with single parents, are the most disadvantaged in terms of money, quality time spent, and stress for both parent and children. Often, the child is less motivated in school, and parents struggle with self-esteem issues while trying to balance all aspects of family life without adequate resources. They may feel left out of society.

Economic pressures can have many harmful effects for families, including parental depression and increased conflict. Hostile and coercive exchanges between parents and adolescents can lead to adolescent emotional and behavioural problems. Furthermore, children growing up in poverty are more likely to spend time by themselves or with their friends. They may feel neglected as a result, and are therefore more likely to become delinquent.

Concluding Remarks

We have seen in this chapter that parenting has changed and continues to change. The ways in which people become parents, the processes by which they begin parenting, and the kinds of families into which children are born and live have all changed and diversified in recent years. The needs of children for good parenting, however, remain.

Families are complex and important. How well families raise their children affects what kind of world we will live in, and what kind of adults those children

Figure 6.5 PARENTING STYLES

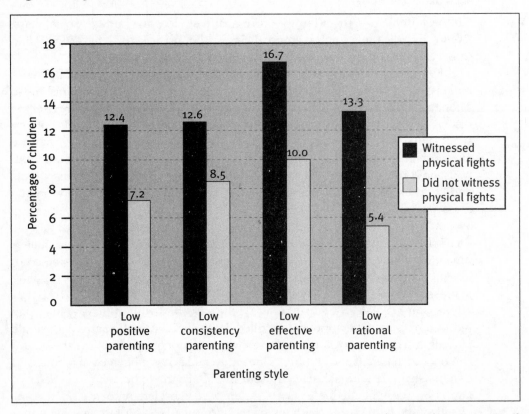

Source: Data adapted from Statistics Canada website, www.statcan.ca/english/freepub/85-224-XIE/0100085-224-XIE.pdf, page 21; accessed October 22, 2002.

will become. How well parents have managed to strike a balance between discipline and freedom will affect how the children act and feel when they become teenagers. In North America, teenagers who see their parents as accepting and warm, and as less controlling, have higher self-esteem than other children. In turn, parents with higher self-esteem are more likely to give their children freedom and acceptance, and to have better communication with the children as a result.

As we have seen and will explore in greater detail in Chapter 9, people exposed to family violence as children are more likely than others to end up abusing their own spouses and children. Childhood experiences resonate through adult life. Similarly, children punished physically by their parents are more likely to grow up to be aggressive toward other family members. A particularly explosive recipe is infrequent reasoning and frequent spanking. Treating children this way dramatically increases their potential for violence as teenagers.

Nevertheless, not all family difficulties (or lucky breaks, for that matter) are the result of parental influences and choices. Many important forces are not under parental control. Sometimes factors beyond the parents' control, such as the sickness of a family member or a sudden change in socioeconomic circumstances, interrupt the socialization process. We are only starting to understand the full effects of disrupted development and the problems that are likely to emerge later. Also, bear in mind that not only do parents socialize their children, but the children socialize their parents too. Children's influence over their parents is more powerful under some conditions than others. For example, a parent who feels guilty about neglecting the child or about divorcing a spouse, or who feels unloved or otherwise emotionally insecure and therefore depends on the child for important gifts of affection and attention, may change parenting styles to get the desired effect.

As we have seen in this chapter, parenting makes a tremendous difference to the ways that children grow up. Some turn out better than others in the family and society as a whole. Some are better-adjusted and more competent than others. Good parenting translates into good child and adult outcomes. Bad parenting produces the opposite. But parenting is not the full story either.

Parenting varies from one culture to another, because cultures vary in the ways they conceive of "good" and "bad" parenting. Yet, whatever the culture, good parenting demands resources. In our own society, people have unequal chances to be good parents, because they have unequal chances for a good income, good daycare, and good social supports. Most of these inequalities are socially structured, in the sense that they are a result of the way our society distributes scarce resources. Therefore, we can remedy most of these inequalities through social change, especially legislation to improve the social safety net for poor people, single mothers, and wives and children in abusive families.

In the next chapter, we further explore a topic mentioned in this chapter and one with much significance for both parent–child relations and the functioning of the family as a whole: namely, the domestic division of labour.

CHAPTER SUMMARY

In this chapter we have examined parenthood from the perspective of societies, parents, and children. We traditionally view the ideal order of events in one's life as marriage and then the baby carriage, although in some cultures, a marriage without children is considered hardly a marriage at all.

Today we have fewer children, reproduce at a later age, and compress our parenting period of life into a smaller timeframe than in the past, allowing more time for careers and family. We can plan our families in this way because of reliable contraceptive devices. Widespread use of contraception allows us to decide when and if to become parents. Unfortunately, despite the new role of contraception, pregnancies can still occur by accident and sexual assault.

The teen-pregnancy rate is quite low in Canada, compared with the United States. Given their relative access to reproductive control, however, some young men and women still "choose" to procreate. One theory states that teens are confused by the mixed messages of religious groups, which may discourage access to contraception and birth control. Meanwhile, the popular media show teens an exciting sexualized world where adult freedoms are associated with sexual activity. Some teenage pregnancies also help to fulfill the need to give and receive love, particularly when the teenagers have experienced a lack of family love. They may believe that the baby will replace love in their lives. The fathers of their babies are less important to them.

Despite, or perhaps because of this, there is still a large negative social stigma associated with single-motherhood. Many teenage mothers never make up their lost opportunities. Of course, some people choose to not have children. In Canada the numbers of married but childless people have increased by almost 10 percent since 1961. Finding accurate data on gay and lesbian parents is difficult, because of the social stigma attached to these groups. However, researchers have found no visible difference between children raised by heterosexual mothers and those raised by lesbian mothers, although as a culture we view the groups quite differently.

Once you have a child you must be a parent, and as a parent, you are responsible for the primary socialization that will take place during your child's first years. Gender socialization now begins as soon as the parent knows the sex of the child, perhaps *in utero*. One of the jobs of the parent is to ready the child for entry into society. Love and attachment, emotional stability, protection, and fair and moderate discipline are all conditions that aid this process. Runaways are children who appear to deem their parents' parenting styles inadequate to the extent that they prefer life on the streets to life in the home of the parent. Unfortunately, researchers back up the notion that awful, even criminally bad parenting leads children to leave their homes and live on the streets.

Stepparents are among the new groups of substitute parents. However, the legal and moral roles of the stepparent are still unclear. Class and cultural variation in styles of parenting is narrowing in many ways. Perhaps the identical socialization techniques of the mass media will decrease the variation further. However, though peers and mass media evidently play a large role in childhood socialization, parents have not yet lost their fundamental importance in moulding the child's personality.

KEY TERMS

Authoritarian parenting A type of parenting with low acceptance and high control, which can hinder the development of expressiveness and independence in children.

Authoritative parenting A type of parenting with high acceptance and high control, which produces the best outcomes in children.

Birth rate Number of births per 100 000 people in a given year.

Control and supervision The extent to which parents monitor and censure their children's behaviour.

Family cohesion A sense of attachment and relatedness among members of a family, both maintained and signified by shared activities, self identification as a family member, and signs of familiarity and liking.

Gender socialization The social learning process a person goes through to acquire gender roles and gender-based habits. This is usually done through family, peer groups, schools, and the mass media.

Identity support The parents' respect, acceptance, and emotional support for their adolescent.

In loco parentis Literally, "in the place of parents," where public institutions assume more responsibility for a child in parent-like protection.

Induction A form of discipline from the parent, where a child's good behaviour is focused upon benefiting others. For example, a child will be told not to be naughty for fear of upsetting her or his mother or father.

Instrumental communication The frequency of communication the adolescent has with his or her parents concerning personal problems.

Internal moral control An emotional feeling, such as guilt, that inhibits non-compliance.

Latchkey youth Children who are home alone two or more days per week.

Looking-glass self A sense of oneself formed through interaction with others, by assessing how they view us.

Love withdrawal A form of punishment to a child for non-compliance, where a child is anxious over the loss of love.

Parental involvement A form of love parents do by spending time with their child, talking about them, and thinking about them.

Permissive parenting A type of parenting with high acceptance and low control, which can produce poor results in a child's state.

Power assertion Occurs when a parent or guardian threatens punishment, usually in physical form, for non-compliance of a child.

Primary socialization Learning that takes place during childhood.

Socialization The social learning process a person goes through to become a capable, functioning member of society; to prepare for life in society.

Unengaged parenting A type of parenting with low acceptance and low control, which can result in delinquency in their children.

SUGGESTED READINGS

Crook, M. 2000. *The Face in the Mirror: Teens and Adoption.* Vancouver: Arsenal Pulp Press. Based on interviews with adopted and birth parents, this candid and sensitive book discusses the complex issues involved when adopted teenagers choose to explore their birth origins.

Dienhart, Anna. 1998. *Reshaping Fatherhood: The Social Construction of Shared Parenting.* Thousand Oaks, CA: Sage. What are the experiences of fathers who participate fully in parenting and daily family life? How do couples work out and maintain shared parenting? The lack of attention to the subtle dynamics between men and women was a clarion call for research on how couples lived and negotiated family relationships.

Dowd, N.E. 1999. *In Defense of Single-Parent Families.* New York: New York University Press. This book offers a lucid and convincing argument that the perceived inferiority of single-parent families is a result of bias and poverty and that legal change is needed to increase employment, income, and community support for parents raising children on their own.

Howey, N. and E. Samuels. 2000. *Out of the Ordinary: Essays on Growing Up with Gay, Lesbian and Transgender Parents.* New York: St. Martin's Press. This collection of short memoirs of adult children of gay, lesbian, and transgender parents explores the relationship between parent and child in these unique, alternative family situations.

Webber, M. 1999. *As If Kids Mattered: What's Wrong in the World of Child Protection and Adoption.* Toronto: Key Porter Books. This book discusses the issues involved in adopting through the child welfare system, and considers the unique concerns of single parents, lesbian and gay couples, and disabled families.

REVIEW QUESTIONS

1. At what level was the birth rate in nineteenth-century Canada? What changing circumstances over the century altered it?

2. What is socialization? What are the different kinds of socialization?

3. According to a survey of adolescents in Scotland in 1995, describe the four types of parenting.

4. What does the term *in loco parentis* signify, and what are the issues surrounding it?

5. What ideologies affect socialization of children and the family process?

6. What is the most common form of contraception used in developed and developing nations?

7. What is cultural variation?

8. Define "looking-glass self" and give an example or anecdote.

9. Define "internal moral control" and provide an example of it.

DISCUSSION QUESTIONS

1. "Secondary socialization" is the continuing lifelong process after primary socialization, when an individual is socialized into different situations by peers, work, the media, etc. Is one as important as the other? If so, is primary or secondary even necessary in one's life?

2. What are your standards for good parenting?

3. Is the "looking-glass self" relevant in the social development of children? Why or why not?

4. Why would some youth from abusive families run away to the streets instead of telling someone about the abuse?

5. In the chapter there is some discussion about parents who socialize boys in so-called "boy-type" ways and girls in "girl-type" ways. Do you believe this is an appropriate way of parenting? Is this changing? What are the long-term consequences of this difference in gender socialization?

6. Socialization is an integral part of becoming a capable, functioning member of society. In your opinion, do you feel a child's personality and behaviour is due more to their upbringing at home or certain external factors (friends, school, environmental surroundings, etc.)? Why?

7. Physical punishment is a topic that is getting more attention in today's society. In your opinion, what constitutes physical abuse or physical discipline? Where do we draw the line in terms of discipline? How can cultural variation be respected in these matters?

8. Do you think that the children of adolescent mothers will necessarily be socialized differently? Why?

9. Some parents dislike certain values being incorporated into the school curriculum. Do you think schools should be teaching a value system? How can the group choose the appropriate value system to teach? If schools try to avoid values in their methods and content of education, what would be the consequences?

10. What do you think accounts for the significant differences in the use of contraceptives around the world? Do we have a double standard in the West, advocating extreme forms of birth control in developing countries while encouraging different methods at home?

ACTIVITIES

1. Go to your local toy shop and observe the different ways parents react when their children want something that their parents refuse to buy. Try to match each parent's response to one of the discipline techniques discussed in this chapter.

2. While watching television, observe family-oriented shows that show at least one parent and a child. Does the television show illustrate a variety of parenting methods? Is the mass media presenting only one kind of family with slight surface differences in

accent, class, or culture? Or are the media showing total differences in family style on television?

3. Factors that affect a couple's decision to have children are often financial, religious, relationship dynamics, and ticking biological clocks. Discuss the validity and the weight of these factors in deciding whether or not to have children. Can you think of any other relevant factors? Why did people you know choose to have children?

4. Writing in *The Women's Quarterly*, Maggie Gallagher suggests that men and women now have entirely different goals in life: "To succeed, a man had best marry and have children. To be financially secure, a woman had best remain single and childless." Do you agree with Ms. Gallagher's thoughts? Give reasons for your position.

5. Author Judith Guest has written that: "All families are dysfunctional in some ways. How can they not be? They are made up of people, each and every one of whom is dysfunctional to a degree." Discuss these comments.

WEBLINKS

http://www.adoption.com
Adoption.com
This network offers guides, chat rooms, bulletin boards, on-line library, newsletter, and other resources for parents looking to adopt, parents considering giving their child up for adoption, and adoptees looking for their birth family.

http://www.allhealth.com/conditions/repro/
iVillage Health
IVF is the section of all health.com that provides information and resources on in vitro fertilization treatments, including articles, Q and A message boards, and a calendar of upcoming chats.

http://www.20ishparents.com
20ishparents.com
This informative and entertaining site includes articles, suggested links, and useful suggestions on coping with families as a young person.

http://www.parenting.com
Parenting.com
This site provides articles on parenting issues, such as "if your discipline method fails ... try another." It proceeds to offer four sure strategies of discipline, namely, Selective Ignoring, Redirection, Verbal Discipline, and Timeout.

http://www.lesbian.org/lesbian-moms/text.html
Lesbian Mother Support Society
This Web site is an Alberta non-profit group that supports lesbian parents and their children as well as lesbians considering having children. The site includes articles, links to other organizations, and bibliographical suggestions.

CHAPTER SEVEN

The Domestic Division of Labour:

Gender and Housework

Chapter Outline

Families need work to maintain themselves. "Housework" is not the best term to describe all the varied work needed to keep families going. **Family work** may be better because it includes far more than the chores that come to mind when we think of **housework**. A major part of family work or domestic labour in the 1990s is coordinating family activities and family with paid work. Another major component is childcare and childrearing.

The bargain struck by men and women today includes images of having children, but seldom does it ever include any (or much) discussion about division of household work. Most young couples seem to enter marriage in the hope that housework will do itself. Women in the paid workforce have less time and inclination to do all the household work as well. With the end of past presumptions about the domestic division of labour, housework and who will do what becomes a big problem, bigger than almost anything the couple might face, except money troubles or questions of marital fidelity.

Just Who Did What in the Past?

Housework and childrearing have not always been women's responsibility. Men took a more active role than women did in caring for and raising children in the past. The older idea of childrearing was that we should toughen children up for the real world, to earn a living to help the family, a task to which parents often put them at early ages. Children at age six were often working on farms and ranches, in the early factories and mines, and on the streets of towns and cities, selling newspapers, picking rags, or shining shoes. "The notion of 'home, sweet home' as a place of family togetherness, comfort, and refuge from the world of business and work was largely an invention of the industrial era" (Cross & Szostak, 1995: 41).

The pre-industrial family was a production site plus a consumption site, with women essential and central to early market production. Women also worked on farms and, as the first medical and nursing practitioners, they delivered babies, helped care for the sick, and cared for the disabled or chronically ill. Industrialization reduced women's involvement in the market economy and converted them into dependent homemakers with their home-based work confined to the domestic realm.

Women's reduced access to market activity undermined the previous partnership between men and women in marriage. Husbands and wives were no longer economic partners and co-workers in the same way. Women, as a result, became more vulnerable to desertion by their husbands. There was less economic incentive to stick together, and men often left to look for work in the new industrial economy. Women, alone with children to care for, resorted to age-old reliance on small-scale agricultural production, something they knew and understood, and for many, their only economic option.

The trouble was that they did this in the rapidly growing cities of Montreal, Toronto, and Hamilton. Keeping pigs, cows, and chickens in city yards proved perplexing to authorities (Bradbury, 1984). **"Sanitary reformers,"** in the interest of health, began to work on bylaws prohibiting the keeping of farm animals in cities. Campaigns began with such suggestive names as "Death to the Pigs" (Bradbury, 1984: 14). It was poor women's pigs (and cows and chickens) that were first outlawed. Bradbury reveals that one-quarter of the pigs kept in Montreal in 1861 were in one particularly poor ward, among cramped houses and factories where the pigs roamed alleyways and streets. No doubt the banning of farm animals from cities did improve hygiene, but it further limited the means by which women on their own could reach market activity and have some degree of autonomy. Later the same restrictions to women's market activities occurred with zoning bylaws that prohibited non-family homes in some neighbourhoods, preventing separated, divorced, and widowed women from taking in boarders.

In the 1930s and 1940s, society viewed women workers positively, for their contribution could possibly reverse the Depression. However, along with this positive view, there were more traditional ideas about the importance of home life for women (Honey, 1997). Thus, the image of women, and whether they belonged in the work world or in the home, was uncertain.

This trend is not limited to the North American experience. A Canadian study of Chinese-Vietnamese, ethnic Vietnamese, and Laotian refugees in British Columbia found that traditional domestic patterns involved much more sharing of tasks between partners than such tasks being primarily performed by the wife (Johnson, 1998). It is only when compared to present-day patterns that one sees a change from this original sharing.

Labour-Saving Devices and Household Work

Labour-saving devices have had one profound impact on women's lives. Although the devices make some tasks easier, they separate women from market activity. In the past, women sold some products of their labour to contribute to the family's income. However, as more devices became available, a woman's work became cleaning the house, cooking meals for her family, and no longer engaging in market activity. Cross and Szostak (1995: 50) put it well: "The unity of market work and domestic/family work was eventually sundered. With that separation came what we today call the 'traditional housewife' in her 'separate sphere' outside the workforce who was almost totally dependent on her husband's income."

People now expected women to make their homes attractive out of love rather than any interest in market rewards. The fusing of love with domestic consumerism and household duties for women changed forever the relations between the sexes on the domestic front. Campaigns to promote the new household technologies recognized the love component of housework in working against the fear that women might abandon their domestic work with the "mechanization" of housework (Fox, 1993: 151). Home economists worked to raise the esteem of

Figure 7.1 HOURS SPENT ON HOUSEWORK PER WEEK

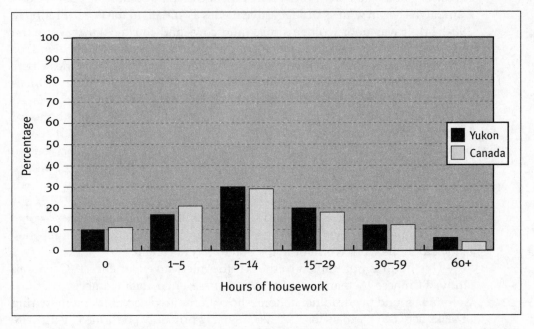

Source: Yukon Bureau of Statistics; data taken from www.gov.yk.ca/depts/eco/stats/census/UnpaidWork.pdf, © 2000, Government of Yukon.

homemakers by promoting the idea that the new home technologies required skilled operators. Health became associated with high standards of cleanliness. Society charged homemakers with the duty of technical work and health promotion, noble causes indeed but unpaid and immensely undervalued. The "scientization" of housework was complete, and women were cast into the role of maintaining the home as their central life work, with limited access through their homemaking skills to the markets they had enjoyed before industrialization.

The Worth of Housework

Attempting to assess the worth of housework is not a new idea. It has a long history going back, surprisingly, to Adam Smith. By the middle of the twentieth century, people generally agreed that it may be misleading or inappropriate to leave domestic work out of the economy, but they thought it impractical to try to measure its contribution (Statistics Canada, 1995: 3). Some argued, in contrast, that we could measure housework but it still should not be included as a market exchange since the work done by women at home ought to be freely provided. To make this point clearer, they suggested that confusion could arise, since if a man married his housekeeper or his cook, the national dividend would be diminished!

Shifting attitudes toward housework have resulted in serious attempts to measure the economic value of housework in market terms. In these efforts, Canada has been a world leader (see Statistics Canada, 1995). Some trace the work on measuring the worth of housework to a 1988 book by Marilyn Waring of New Zealand, *If Women Counted: A New Feminist Economics*, which argues that housework is real work and ought to be considered as part of a country's gross national product. Statistics Canada (1995: 2) agrees that unpaid work at home matters and suggests that putting a value on it can "… foster a greater understanding of the economy and of the links between its market and nonmarket sectors." When the calculations are done, they estimate those housework values at approximately $319 billion a year (Statistics Canada, 1995). This is about 30 to 46 percent of the gross national product (GNP) of Canada, an enormous portion of the economy.

Perhaps housework will someday be added to computations of GNP. Today, however, too many challenges remain in estimating its economic worth and making official records historically compatible.

Unpaid Work Comes of Age

People have acknowledged unpaid work in Canada in an important way—by including it for the first time in the 1996 Census of Canada. Canada is the first country in the world to include questions on unpaid work on its national census, although other countries will surely follow, giving housework and unpaid work new legitimacy.

In a small way, **family allowances**, begun in Canada after World War II, were a way to give women payment and recognition for childrearing. Ostensibly, they were meant to purchase needed items for children. The monthly payments, based on the number of children at home, went to all women with children—but only to women, never to men. For many women who worked solely at home, this was their only independent income. Quebec alone now continues with some form of family allowances (LeBourdais & Marcil-Gratton, 1995). The federal government stopped the program of family allowances in 1992, replacing it by the Child Tax Benefit program, which targets low- and middle-income families. Quebec intended the program of baby bonuses both to increase the numbers of births and to provide support for women raising children. The amounts paid in no way compensate for the costs involved in raising a child, however.

Many have argued that paying for housework would not be in women's interests since it would do nothing to change the existing division of labour. Women would continue to do most of the housework, but it would be paid work instead of unpaid. Eichler (1988: 250), however, suggests that if we could separate out the socially useful work from that which is privately useful, paying for the former might enhance women's status. She then argues that developing labour force re-entry programs for homemakers and displaced homemakers could aid in compensating women for the domestic work they do for the good of society. The debate is not yet over, although Eichler and others (e.g., Armstrong & Armstrong, 1994) hint that it is taking new and different forms.

Double Days, Double Toil

One characterization of today's paid and unpaid work is the 2000s workplace with a 1950s division of labour at home. The 1996 Census of Canada (Statistics Canada, 1998a) reveals that although women have made gains in occupations, women continue to cluster in traditionally female occupations while men continue to work in traditionally male, better paid, occupations. Data for 1998 (Statistics Canada, 1998e) show that among single people and young married people, the earnings of men and women are closer than ever before (women earn $0.93 for every dollar men earn). The earnings gap among married women and men, however, remains high: married women earn $0.69 for every dollar that married men earn. This gap shrinks when education, years in the paid labour force, and age are the same for women and for men. The gap is nearly zero for highly educated, young single men and women in professional or managerial occupations.

Families often need women's wages to keep the family from poverty. Without the contribution of the spouse with lower earnings, the number of families with low income in 1994 would have more than doubled to 400 000 from 184 000 (Statistics Canada 1996c: 1).

The invisibility of women's unpaid work at home and lower pay than men in the workforce underlines social attitudes toward women's roles. We see women as working at home out of love, due to the centrality of family in their lives, and as working for less pay in the workplace because of the priority they give to family. Armstrong and Armstrong (1994: 225) argue compellingly that the nature of women's work in the home and in the labour force reinforces and perpetuates the division of labour by sex. Because women have the primary responsibility for domestic work, they are undertaking a double burden when they enter the labour force. Their double day includes childcare responsibilities such as pick-up and drop-off, usually done by mothers; also, preparing meals and assisting with homework.

Their job in the home means that some women are unable to work continuously or full-time in paid employment and all women face constraints on their work in both spheres. Also, many women have little leisure time and have difficulty separating it from work time (Salazar & Clara, 1997). Though these tendencies are less pronounced in younger generation women who work outside the home, it is still a concern among women of all age groups.

Men contribute to domestic work too, most notably on household maintenance and repairs. Often, however, less time overall is spent on these kinds of tasks than women spend on day-to-day housework and childcare. Two additional factors matter in how men's contributions to the home play out in society. First, they can often postpone these sorts of household tasks until time permits. This means that men's work at home is less constraining than women's.

Second, and importantly, no one sees men's work at home as defining them in the way that women's does. Men who fix up and maintain their homes are less often defined by that work, whereas some people still define women as wives and mothers first and workers second. So, while both men and women often contribute to domestic work, they contribute in different ways and society sees their domestic work as less valued.

As we shall see, after the double day many women experience stress. "The ensuing exhaustion of women encourages dissatisfaction, especially when their partners do not share the responsibility of work in the home" (Armstrong & Armstrong, 1994: 227). Double days also produce depression in both spouses (Windle & Dumenci, 1997). Some studies, however, have shown that participation in the labour force can have benefits for some women, such as raised self-esteem, improved mental and physical health, and increased status and resources (Tingey, Kiger, & Riley, 1996). In addition, participation in the labour force can allow women to purchase housekeeping services and meals out instead of doing it themselves. Cohen (1998) found that in families where women had higher incomes and occupational status, the families spent more money on housekeeping services and dining out. Though this option is more popular among wealthier and white families, it is still one way that women can reduce the stress of the double day.

Baker, Kifer, and Riley (1996: 173) find, significantly, that "husbands are more satisfied with household-task arrangements than are wives." They quickly add, "The most obvious explanation for this finding is that wives continue to do the bulk of the household chores and husbands are satisfied with the arrangement."

Childcare: The Biggest Part of Domestic Labour

A study of the effects of parenthood on domestic labour (Sanchez & Thomson 1997: 747) using national U.S. data finds that "...there were no effects of parenthood ... on husbands' employment or housework hours." However, "motherhood increases wives' housework hours and reduces employment hours." The conclusion is sharp: "Parenthood crystallizes a gendered division of labor, largely by reshaping wives', not husbands', routine." A Canadian study (Lupri & Mills, 1987) comes to similar conclusions, as does a 1991 Canadian survey.

As the work lives of women and men become more similar (although, as we have seen, not yet by any means identical), childcare becomes the great divide on the domestic scene. As Baker and Lero (1996: 103) argue, "the gender-structured nature of the labour market, differential use of parental and child-rearing leave by men and women, and different gender expectations by families and communities preserve the unequal sharing of economic and social parenting."

It is not only that the presence of a child or children adds to the domestic demands; it is also that parents often take on particular roles. We see practical day-to-day parenting as women's work, while men specialize in economic responsibilities for the children. This is partly a reflection of the gendered labour

Table 7.1 TIME SPENT ON HOUSEHOLD ACTIVITIES[1], CANADA, 1998

	TOTAL POPULATION[2]	PARTICIPANTS[3]	PARTICIPATION RATE[4]
		BOTH SEXES	
	Hours per day		%
Paid work and related activities/unpaid work	**7.8**	**8.0**	**98**
Paid work and related activities	3.6	8.3	44
Paid work	3.3	7.7	43
Activities related to paid work	—	0.6	8
Travel	0.3	0.8	38
Unpaid work	**3.6**	**3.9**	**91**
Household work and related activities	3.2	3.6	90
Cooking/washing up	0.8	1.0	74
House cleaning and laundry	0.7	1.7	41
Maintenance and repair	0.2	2.5	6
Other household work	0.4	1.3	30
Shopping for goods and services	0.8	1.9	43
Primary child care	0.4	2.2	20
Civic and volunteer activities	0.4	1.9	18
Education and related activities	**0.6**	**6.2**	**9**
Sleep, meals and other personal activities	**10.4**	**10.4**	**100**
Night sleep	8.1	8.1	100
Meals (excluding restaurant meals)	1.1	1.2	92
Other personal activities	1.3	1.3	95
Free time	**5.8**	**5.9**	**97**
Socializing	1.9	2.9	66
Restaurant meals	0.3	1.6	19
Socializing (in homes)	1.3	2.4	55
Other socializing	0.3	2.6	12
Television, reading and other passive leisure	2.7	3.2	85
Watching television	2.2	2.8	77
Reading books, magazines, newspapers	0.4	1.3	32
Other passive leisure	0.1	1.1	9
Sports, movies and other entertainment events	0.2	2.7	6
Active leisure	1.0	2.4	40
Active sports	0.5	2.0	24
Other active leisure	0.5	2.3	22

— Nil or zero.

1. Averaged over a seven-day week.
2. The average number of hours per day spent on the activity for the entire population aged 15 years and over (whether or not the person reported the activity).
3. The average number of hours per day spent on the activity for the population that reported the activity.
4. The proportion of the population that reported spending some time on the activity.

Source: Adapted from the Statistics Canada website, General Social Survey, 1998, www.statcan.ca/english/Pgdb/famil36a.htm.

market, where women's paid work matters less to families because they are typically the lower earners.

Childcare is thus a central concern in the domestic division of labour. Working in the paid labour force is difficult for women if they are also minding young children. Even if they make adequate childcare arrangements, the plans often fall apart if the child falls ill, as most children do at some point. Such times reveal who is ultimately responsible for childcare. "Care of a sick child is still considered women's work" (Wylie 1997: 41). People expect women to take the time from work to do the caring, and do not expect the same of men. The great fear of having a child fall ill or suffer a crisis at school makes some employers reluctant to hire women with young children, particularly single mothers. The National Childcare Study in Canada (cited by Armstrong & Armstrong 1994: 106) found that each additional child lowers the probability that a single parent will be employed.

Even without sick children or crises, parents seldom share childcare equally (Wilson, 1996: 77). Statistics Canada data (cited in Armstrong & Armstrong 1991: 10) reveal that women are almost three times as likely as men to give physical care to children under the age of five, and 2.5 times as likely to provide care for children between ages five and eighteen. A 1990 study by the Conference Board of Canada found 76.5 percent of women reporting that they had primary responsibility for childcare, while only 4.1 percent of men reported this (Armstrong & Armstrong 1994: 110).

With most mothers of young children in the paid labour force, young children need care while parents work. The National Childcare Study (Baker & Lero 1996: 89) reports that care is needed for 64 percent of families with one child under age 13, 59.3 percent of families with two children less than 13, and 48.3 percent of families with three or more children. The gap between demand (estimated to be 2.2 million children age 12 and under) and supply of licensed childcare spaces (333 000) is huge. Only 15 percent of the children who need care have access to it (Baker & Lero, 1996: 91). Non-access to quality low-cost childcare creates stress for all parents.

Politicians have felt pressure for many years to address the childcare issue. At the end of its first mandate in 1997, the Liberal Government put forward a proposal for national childcare to be cost-shared with the provinces. Parliament did not pass the bill and has yet to reintroduce it. A 1998 study by economists Gordon Cleveland and Michael Krashinsky (reported by Philp, 1998) looks at the issue of childcare from the point of view of social problems and benefits. In essence, the economists estimate that a public program of childcare in Canada would be cost-effective if childcare were seen as an investment.

Researchers estimate the rewards of good childcare at $4.3 billion a year if lower school-dropout rates, higher future incomes, and larger tax revenues are considered. If benefits to the economy are added in, such as more women joining the workforce, fewer career interruptions, and more women with higher incomes, the overall benefits total $6.4 billion.

The More Things Change

Women still do most of the housework. Wives, whatever their employment status, consistently do about twice as much housework as husbands do (Davies & Carrier, 1998; Marshall, 1990; 1993; Statistics Canada, 1998, 16–18). This proportion has not changed much over time, despite the dramatic increase in women's paid work. A 1992 study found that self-employed wives devote the most time to household work, followed by part-time and full-time workers. Husbands whose spouses work full-time do more non-postponable tasks such as childcare than those with self-employed or part-time working wives, but not necessarily postponable tasks such as housework (Nagai, 1992).

There are hints of change in the air, but not all of them are positive! Nakhaie (1995) finds that when husbands' work hours increase beyond 30 hours a week, their contribution to housework decreases; but when women's work hours increase beyond 30 hours a week, their proportional contribution to housework increases. Though husbands with fewer working hours have more time to do the tasks, instead of participating in the housework, they wait for their spouses to complete those tasks—even if that spouse works longer hours! The males most likely to participate in housework are younger, white-collar workers employed no more than 40 hours a week (Gokalp & Leridon, 1983).

Domestic work is a mirror of what society expects of men and of women (see Oakley, 1974). Couples may, in fact, never choose who does what, but fall into expected gender patterns. Luxton, Rosenberg, and Arat-Koc (1990: 31) put it well:

> The most powerful myth surrounding housework is one that claims that a woman's place is in the home. This myth is based on the assumption that women's biological ability to bear children means that they are the best caregivers for children and that they are "naturally" inclined to cook, clean, and manage the running of a household.

Getting beyond the power of this myth is not easy for couples, even for New-Age post-modern couples. Power relations largely determine who does what on the home front. Davies and Carrier (1998), in a study of 2577 employed Canadians who have an employed spouse, find that gender inequalities in the paid work force matter to the domestic division of labour. They discover, for example, that the segregated nature of paid work into "male" and "female" jobs translates into doing male and female tasks at home. However, when the proportion of women in men's occupations increases, those men participate more in "female" housework such as grocery shopping, laundry, meal making, and housecleaning.

As gender is not a clear indicator of which partner does what task, gay and lesbian couples use different criteria to decide how housework is done. Unlike heterosexual couples, factors such as income, education, and time availability have little bearing on the distribution of tasks among homosexual couples (Illig, 1999). Instead, homosexual couples share the responsibility for the distribution of household labour more equally and use a different set of criteria to see who does what. The only time when a division of labour similar to a heterosexual form arises is when a pattern of primary breadwinner/primary caregiver emerges. Then, the primary caregiver will do most of the housework (Sullivan, 1996).

Though division of labour practices among gay and lesbian families do not use gender as their main criteria, Oerton (1998) warns against assuming that the division of household work is completely egalitarian and gendering processes have been eliminated. She notes that the gender differences may just be less obvious in lesbian household arrangements. This is an area of study that researchers will examine more closely in the future, as openly gay and lesbian couples become more common in North American society.

Though women still do most of the housework, children's participation in household labour has also increased, especially with Hispanic and black children. Blair (2000) found that Hispanic and black children did greater amounts of household labour than white children. However, even housework among children runs along gendered lines. Teenage daughters do much more housework than sons or children in other age groups, and father's employment is strongly associated with greater housework among all children. Thus, parents teach children from young ages which types of housework are acceptable for what gender.

Conflicts over Housework

Hoelter (2002) reports that perceptions of fairness about the division of household labour serve as significant predictors of changes in individual and marital happiness. Partners who feel that the domestic division of labour is unfair tend to show a decrease in positive sentiments and an increase in negative ones. In short, inequality makes people unhappy and dissatisfied with marriage. Note, however, that it is not just how the housework is divided in a family, but how the family members *feel* about that division of labour that is important.

Conflicts over housework can be problematic for couples. A Canadian study in a nationally representative sample (Frederick & Hamel, 1998: 8) finds that an unsatisfactory division of housework would be viewed as sufficient basis for seeking divorce among 17 percent of adults. Although much sociological research has focused on the division of household labour, surprisingly little has looked at the process of dividing the labour, or specifically on conflicts created by that process.

One Dutch study (Kluwer, Heesink, & Van de Vliert, 1997) finds that discontent with who does what in the family can be destructive to a marriage. Typically, in a conflict over duties, she makes demands and he withdraws. This does not bode well for maintaining strong marriages in the face of unhappiness about the division of housework and unwillingness to discuss it. In order to resolve such conflicts, Kluwer and his colleagues favour family education programs and therapy approaches that focus specifically on gender differences in conflict behaviours. This approach may help reduce the potentially harmful impact of trying to

Debate Box 7.1 **SHOULD EARNINGS OUTSIDE THE HOME DETERMINE WHO DOES THE HOUSEWORK?**
Which side of the debate do you fall on?

YES	NO
• It is rational for the better-paid spouse to work more hours for pay and fewer hours at home. To do otherwise makes no sense; the family economy suffers.	• The family should be a haven of equality in an unequal world. Partners should practise equality even if the rest of the world does the opposite. That is "love."
• The family prospers when more money comes into the household, and when the family as a whole prospers, all family members benefit.	• Just because women are victimized by low pay at work does not mean they should be victimized at home too. Families should set an example for societies.
• Society works best when the most efficient use is made of talent and energy. That is how the standard of living improves and, with it, our collective well-being.	• Couples who share the domestic duties equally get along better with each other. Marital satisfaction increases when partners are fair and equal in their treatment.
• People who earn more need to rest up at home, in preparation for the next day's work. They have a need for rest and they have a moral right to rest.	• If partners were paid fairly for housework, husbands would be more willing to share the work. The current situation reflects exploitation of unpaid housewives.
• It does not matter who does the work at home so long as both spouses work the same total number of hours per day. That is what "equality" really means.	• Equality in the sharing of housework sets a good example for sons and daughters. Otherwise, children grow up perpetuating the gender inequalities of the past.
• "Equality" is not as important as equity or fairness. So long as a couple feels the work is shared equally, that is all that really matters in the household.	

renegotiate the division of family work. As Kluwer and his colleagues note, "Issues of housework that are not resolved constructively are bound to lead to aggravation and conflict time after time" (Kluwer, Heesink, & Van de Vliert, 1997: 648).

Even in remarriages, housework is optional for men. Remarried women do about twice as much housework as their husbands. Only one in ten husbands in this remarried sample contribute equally to the housework. Furstenberg (1996, 38) notes, in discussing this study, that "Although many wives complain that their current husbands do not do enough of the housework, they often add that at least the men do more than previous husbands had done." First husbands who do little housework, beware!

Economic Independence and Domestic Work

Sociologists have found that women's increased paid work alters authority patterns between husbands and wives. Spouses more often make decisions about major purchases, for example, jointly in two-earner families (Baker & Lero, 1996: 97–98). Wives who work for pay see themselves as having more bargaining power in the relationship.

Personal resources theory holds that the person with the most resources exercises power in a close relationship. The resources in question may be money, social status, physical attractiveness, knowledge or social contacts—anything that would make one partner more valued by and valuable to the other. A partner with more earning capacity may initially have more power. However, if one partner is particularly attractive and the other sees him- or herself as less attractive, power will tilt in the direction of the more attractive partner.

Despite gains toward equality in marital or cohabiting relationships, there are strong hints in the research literature that women's growing economic independence does not translate into independence from domestic work at all. In part, this is because husbands typically remain the higher earners and can translate that into a sharp division of labour at home. "Patriarchal relations in the home are likely to be reinforced by the earnings dominance of the husband," argue Arber and Ginn (1995: 39–40).

A particular concern and focus of research has been the consequences for children of mothers working outside the home. Although people rarely question the effects on children of men's paid employment, many believe that women who work must necessarily be neglecting their families. The research evidence shows that fear is unfounded.

Consistent with earlier research, for employed mothers more occupational complexity predicts lower levels of child behavioural problems. Women with more challenging, interesting, and complex jobs have less troubled or delinquent children—perhaps because the moms are happier with their lives and work. The economic resources that grow out of employment, and opportunities for workplace autonomy that benefit parenting skills, overshadow any disadvantages that stem from decreased time working mothers spend with their children (Cooksey, Menaghan, & Jekielelek, 1997: 658).

The Effects of Domestic Work on Paid Work

Many Canadians assume women to be primarily responsible for work at home and therefore women are thought to have tentative connections with, and commitment to, the paid labour market. Whether this is true or not matters little to the commonness of the perception and the realities it creates. For example, Canadian federal policies allow certain categories of skilled workers to enter the country under special permits, but prohibit their spouses from working. Only recently have governments begun to recognize that this ban makes the program un-appealing to skilled workers (Church, 1998).

In no aspect of domestic work is the effect clearer than with reproduction and childcare. The International Labour Organization has a stark description of the effects for women:

In all parts of the world, working women who become pregnant are
faced with the threat of job loss, suspended earnings, and increased
health risks due to inadequate safeguards for their employment (F.J.
Dy-Hammar, Chief, ILO Conditions of Work Branch, International
Labour Organization 1998: 1).

Women, not surprisingly, take greater advantage of parental and family
leaves, **flextime**, and "family friendly" workplace policies than do men, largely to
care for dependent children. Women also more often turn down work that requires
travel, or decline transfers or promotions that mean a geographical move, because
of their responsibilities for children and families.

For men, the effects of domestic responsibilities on paid work are clear and
positive. Many think men work to support their families, so they see the presence
of family in men's lives as a stabilizing force. Men contribute to family welfare by
increasing their paid work rather than by increasing their contributions to domestic
work. That men's roles in family work remain largely economic is revealed in
their *increased* paid work hours after the birth of more than one child (Sanchez &
Thomson, 1997).

Displaced Homemakers

The assumption that women are primarily responsible for domestic work means
that women who spend their adult lives caring for families and homes do not
have equal access to economic resources through savings, pensions, contacts, or
status.

Some women who divorced in middle age argue that they deserve "severance
packages" and support from their ex-husbands after divorce. Others see this as
unrealistic and suggest that governments should provide support. Having no simple
answer, many jurisdictions have done nothing. After years of working as
homemakers, women whose marriages end in divorce all too often fall quickly into
poverty. Widows who spent their adult lives in family work—including, increasingly,
caring for a chronically ill or dying spouse—find themselves without any pension.

The landmark 1970 Royal Commission on the Status of Women (Wilson,
1996: 72) recommended that changes be made to the Canada/Quebec Pension
Plan to enable homemakers to contribute to it, but lawmakers never carried out this
recommendation. They have carried out some changes, enabling domestic work to
be pensionable. For instance, as of 1983, it became possible for women leaving the
workforce to care for small children (under age seven) to receive continuous pension
coverage. Since 1997, pension credits must be divided between married spouses on
divorce and can be divided at the end of a common-law union.

The challenge is to find an equitable way to provide pensions to women
who have spent their lives doing family work. Given that many women, and
some men, may spend portions of their working lives as homemakers or informal
caregivers, the question is whether pensions would also credit this work. And

there are the vast majority of women, and men too, who spend their entire adult lives combining paid work with family work. There are a number of thorny and unresolved issues here, such as contributions to pension plans for the unpaid work portion, and CPP contributions that can be made from the higher to lower-income partner, in this way protecting the (usually) lower-paid wife.

Elder Care: An Emerging Challenge at Home

Several factors come together to make the care of aged and frail relatives—which we will discuss further in Chapter 11—a growing challenge. Increased life expectancies, particularly among the old-old (those over age 85) have meant that the demand for care has increased. Dramatic cutbacks in both health and social services sectors have limited the options available for care (Fast et al., 1997). The fact that many middle-aged women are now in the workforce compounds all this, leaving few available for home-based care when needed.

Another factor contributing to the stress of elder care in families is that there is not much communication surrounding what may be an unpleasant topic. One study of independent mothers and their adult daughters found that almost 80 percent of mothers had not discussed and did not feel they needed to discuss future caregiving preferences. Instead, they felt their daughters already understood their preferences, either because the daughter knew the mother so well or had observed the mother providing care to an earlier generation (Pecchioni, 2001). Also, the mothers and daughters did not want to think about the mothers declining physically and mentally in later life. This lack of communication can lead to strain and unhappiness later, especially if the mothers and daughters have different ideas of what the mother prefers. Some mothers might want to move in with their daughters, which can lead to stress and resentment.

Additionally, family sizes have shrunk over the last few decades. As a result, there are fewer of us to share the responsibilities of caring for older relatives (Baker & Lero, 1996: 102; McDaniel, 1996b). In a great many situations, daughters/sons-in-law share the responsibilities of elder care.

McDaniel (1996b) finds that when asked why they took on caregiving for elders, many women reply that there was no one else to do it. Sometimes, the person who is left to do it simply does not want to. The problem is universal. For example, studies of elder care among children under the Chinese one-child policy find that there is a growing problem of finding suitable elder care among these families. The children under the one-child policy are less likely to live with grandparents and less willing to share the same household with their parents when they become older and perhaps more dependent (Zhan, 1998). If these children marry, they will become caregivers for as many as four elderly parents. Thus, it is little wonder that they are more interested in educational attainment and independent living.

Figure 7.2 CANADA'S AGING POPULATION

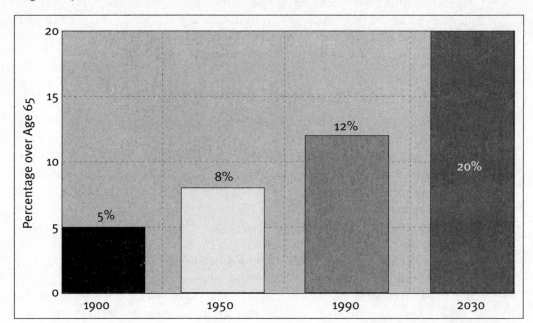

Source: About Canada Online Publication, Centre for Canadian Studies, Mount Allison University, www.mta.ca/faculty/arts/canadian_studies/english/about/aging/#friends-family.

Among reconstituted families with stepparents, the obligation of children to care for elderly parents becomes more difficult. Though there is general agreement that the adult children have some responsibility to help their parents, the guarantee of that help is dependent on several factors, such as degree of contact over the years. Also, the needs of the adult child and his or her children would rank more important than helping an elderly divorced parent or stepparent (Ganong & Coleman, 1998). Thus, it seems that biological ties play a role in determining the obligations to elderly care.

Most middle-aged women say they have considered quitting their jobs or turning down a promotion or a transfer because of family responsibilities. Besides economic loss, some personal drawbacks to elder care for women include feelings of fatigue, loss of personal time, and an expressed need for formal service support (Cooney, 1999).

Though men do perform elder care as well, women do most of it. One U.S. study found that while younger elders are more likely to live with their sons, older elders are more likely to live with their daughters (Schmertman, et al., 2000). This may be because as elderly parents get older and frailer, they wish to be cared for by the more traditional caregiver in the family—the wife. One Canadian study found that women showed greater engagement with caregiving and were more likely to travel to provide assistance (Hallman & Joseph, 1999).

With the large baby boom generation getting older, many families find themselves part of what we call the "sandwich generation"—they are caring for

People in mid-life who have responsibility for both the young and the old are sometimes called the "sandwich generation."

dependent children and elderly parents. In Canada, reduced public resources for the elderly make families view elder care as a private responsibility that they must carry out. This can greatly increase the stress and obligations of the family.

If even some of these women give up jobs to provide informal caregiving, the long-term societal consequences could be serious, with fewer older women having pension entitlements, and possibly more poverty among older women. Since poverty, on average, is a greater risk for women, particularly single mothers, than for men, the potential problems over the life course for women we ask to take on more caregiving for elders could be enormous.

Elder care is not always a negative experience. Some people expect or even prefer it. Research in Northern Ireland found that within farm communities, there is a strong expectation that the younger family members will care for older relatives (Hernan, 2000). Though government support is extremely limited, these families find elder care beneficial for the entire family. In fact, the reputations of these farm families depend on their treatment of older relatives. However, among women in careers or with other heavy responsibilities, elder care can pose problems. This is a global problem that is likely to increase.

Work and Family Life

In our society today, most adults work for pay. For a large portion of their lives, most people also live in families. Yet, often, these two major life activities fit badly; the demands of work are often hard to reconcile with the demands of family life.

The Problem: Balancing Work and Family Life

Both work and a family life make enormous demands on our time, energy, and emotions. Both form an important part of our identity, and both are the source of important rewards—financial, social, and psychological. In practice, life often calls upon us to make choices between work and family.

Two centuries have passed since this problem first arose. People in widely varying societies, doing different kinds of work, have tried to solve the problem in different ways. Nevertheless, today, for many the problem has worsened, as people have taken to working longer hours.

Of course, by historical and comparative standards, most workers are not working more. Lengthier education has delayed entry into the workforce, and retirement—both mandatory and voluntary—has hastened the exit. Workweeks have shrunk from 50 hours to 40 to close to 35 for many people who work for pay full-time. Yet the highly educated workers in full-time, primary labour market jobs are, often, returning from the 35-hour week to longer workweeks (Chafetz & Hagan, 1996).

Time Crunch

Sociologists disagree about the issue of why people work longer hours if it means shortening the time they can spend with their families. In her book *The Time Bind*, sociologist Arlie Hochschild (1996) suggests a reversal in the rewards of work and family, with work providing more credit and less stress than the family. In Silicon Valley, workplaces are turning into home-like environments. On the other hand, the demands of family life are, for mothers, less manageable and less egalitarian than the demands of paid work life. This, says Hochschild, accounts in large part for some women spending so much time at work. Many women fail to take advantage of corporate arrangements like part-time work and job-sharing that would allow them to spend more time with their families. They do not want to. Put simply, they like their jobs better than their families. More time off paid work would mean spending more time at home, doing more domestic work.

This appears to be a largely American phenomenon, however. What makes Americans unusual is their desire for *more* hours of work: U.S. workers are more likely than West German, Japanese, and Swedish workers to wish they could increase their hours (Reynolds, 2002).

On the other hand, long workweeks may not necessarily reflect employee preferences but may result from constraints and demands imposed by the workplace. The rising sense of a time-squeeze may stem from all-or-nothing assumptions about the nature and structure of work. There is pressure to put in long hours to be seen as committed, productive, and having the potential for advancement (Clarkberg & Moen, 2001). This is particularly evident in careers like law, where women lawyers experience particularly high levels of time-crunch stress (Leiper, 1998).

The debate on this topic continues. Voss (1998) contends that Americans are working longer hours because of inequality, a cultural shift in believing that people who are earning more are better than others, and coercive practices such as mandatory overtime. Fligstein (1995) sees the disempowerment of workers as the main reason Americans are now working longer hours.

Juliet Schor asserts that people are working more because of a great increase in potential profitability due to the technological revolution. In her book *The Overworked American* (1996), Schor reports that since 1970 Americans' annual time expenditure in work increased by 163 hours. She contends that employers are largely to blame for the increased length of the workweek, although she concedes that Americans also work harder to pay for consumer purchases. The quest to buy more consumer products could be a link between hours of work and the time crunch for a family. Lower-paid jobs would require more hours of work to accumulate the necessary funds to purchase more material goods. Housing costs and costs of higher education could also be factors; and yearly vacations, however attractive, may not be achievable goals without a time crunch to pay for them.

After the recession of the late 80s and early 90s, incomes became less secure for many workers. To get and keep a job, people had to sell, or give up, an ever-larger portion of their waking hours. To prove their worth to an employer, more people began to work overtime. Employers, for their part, preferred to pay full-time workers overtime wages, or get more work from employees for the same or less pay, rather than hiring more workers. As well, many women are working longer hours because, like men, they are now in jobs and careers where employers expect it. Many women value their careers and want to develop them, even if this means working longer hours. Finally, many women understand that earning an independent income increases the likelihood of equal treatment in society and within the household. It also provides security in case of marital problems.

Descriptions of the resulting problem fall into several categories we can name overload, culturally induced stress, and spillover. By **overload**, we mean the excessive amount of work many people—especially, mothers—have to do. They are physically and emotionally unable to keep up with the burden of demands. By **culturally induced stress** we mean that the workload, and the inability to get it all done, carry stress- and guilt-inducing meanings in our culture. Finally, by **spillover**, we mean that workers bring from the workplace strains and demands that the family struggles, often unsuccessfully, to meet.

Overload

As we have seen, the unequal division of domestic labour dumps a large amount of work on the shoulders of women who also work for pay. Results include stress, resentment, lack of self-esteem, and poor health.

The findings on occupational stress are confusing. Statistics Canada reports no difference in occupational stress by sex. Yet other studies show that paid work stresses women more and causes women more absenteeism from work than it does men (Jacobson et al., 1996). Women are more likely than men to hold paid jobs that are intrinsically stressful; many women's jobs combine heavy, continuing demands with a lack of decision-making authority (Karasek & Theorell, 1990). This combination causes higher than average risks of stress and cardiovascular disorders (ibid). Professional women, with more job autonomy, experience fewer harmful effects of work overload than female secretaries. However, compared with men, women are more likely to hold (high-stress) clerical and service jobs than (low-stress) professional jobs.

As well, most women have to work longer hours to earn the same amount as men, due to their lower overall earning power (the **wage gap**). Finally, the demands of single parenting stress many more women than men.

The problem of an overload seems to stem from the number of roles an individual has to play to survive. In one study of people who juggle the roles of employee, spouse, and parent, the overload was a significant predictor of stress for both men and women (Berger, et al., 1994). Too many working hours may also mean too many roles and difficult choices among them. Related to the number of roles a person must manage is the idea that living one role means abandoning others.

Because women spend more combined time on paid work and domestic work than men, they experience more overloads, especially during early

Table 7.2 WAGE GAP

ALL EARNERS	AVERAGE WAGES[1]		
YEAR[2]	WOMEN	MEN	EARNINGS RATIO (PERCENT)
1991	20 757	33 871	61.3
1992	21 459	33 665	63.7
1993	21 235	33 120	64.1
1994	21 432	34 555	62.0
1995	21 895	33 783	64.8
1996	21 678	33 633	64.5
1997	21 857	34 544	63.3
1998	22 832	35 649	64.0
1999	23 101	36 076	64.0
2000	23 796	37 210	64.0

1. $ constant 2000
2. Data before 1996 are drawn from Survey of Consumer Finances (SCF) and data since 1996 are taken from the Survey of Labour and Income Dynamics (SLID). The surveys use different definitions, and as a result the number of people working full-year full-time in the SLID is smaller than in the SCF.

Source: Adapted from the Statistics Canada website, CANSIM II, table 202-0102. Last modified: 2002-12-09; www.statcan.ca/english/Pgdb/labor01a.htm.

parenthood. However, the extent of the problem varies over the family's life cycle. Particularly when their children are young, women in dual-earner families report more symptoms of distress than men do. Women's jobs are still, on average, less satisfying and lower paid than men's. As we have discussed, in most households the domestic workload is both heavy and unequal. Mothers continue to do more of the work than fathers do. Mothers' and fathers' situations do not become similar until the children approach adolescence (Higgin, Duxbury, & Lee, 1994).

Dual-earner couples feel stress both at home and at work. However, husbands and wives do not feel stress equally. As they work more hours for pay, both husbands and wives feel more work stress, but only wives feel more family stress (Rwampororo, 2001). All forms of social support reduce the effects of work-related stress on husbands. Childcare support and family support reduce the effects of stress on both wives and husbands, but more so on wives.

The problem of an overload may diminish in time, as more people become adept at juggling their duties (Tingey, Kiger, & Riley, 1996). Time-management behaviour does not appear to reduce the effects of strain on feelings of *stress.* However, the use of time-management behaviours appears to reduce *strain,* in part because of increased control over time for those who "manage" their time (Jex & Elacqua, 1999).

We should not overstate the importance of total hours *per se,* since other related issues—such as sense of control over time—may be at the heart of the problem. Both women and men with low control either at work or at home have a higher risk of developing depression and anxiety. There is no interaction between low control at home and work. However, the risks associated with low control at home or work are unevenly distributed across different social positions, measured by employment grade. Women in the lowest or middle employment grades who also report low control at work or home are at most risk for depression and anxiety (Griffin et al., 2002).

Although many believe that reduced hours of work decrease distress, empirical literature relating distress to absolute number of hours worked is inconsistent. As well, the trade-off between giving up some aspects of work for more nonwork time may be more stressful for some employees than for others. Barnet and Gareis found that the *difficulty of trade-offs*—giving up some aspects of work for more nonwork time—is a more powerful predictor of quality-of-life indicators (i.e., symptoms of anxiety and depression, job role quality, and intention to turnover within one year) than is number of hours worked *per se* in a sample of reduced-hours physicians in dual-earner couples.

Culturally Induced Stress

Different cultures produce different patterns of work and stress. For this reason, we cannot ignore cultural context when discussing the family division of labour and its effects. For example, female Bulgarian and Israeli schoolteachers, who favour a traditional division of household labour, report higher levels of home–work conflict than American, Australian, and Dutch schoolteachers, who favour an egalitarian division of household labour (Moore, 1995). Both have similar amounts of actual work to do. The women who, for cultural reasons, continue to strive for high levels of homemaking experience the most conflict.

Often, the problems are most intense where men continue to hold traditional expectations while women change. The result may be role conflict or interpersonal conflict. For example, Argentinean professional women ages 20 to 45 do not have a clear definition of their roles as workers and mothers. Though they highly value both roles, integrating them is difficult (Garro Baca, 1995). This increases stress and conflict for the women and their families.

Men in Latin American countries have a different but reciprocal problem. Although to some degree the family in Costa Rica (for example) has always been an unstable entity and a source of stress for women and children, this is currently becoming a problem for men as well. Their traditional bases of power and identity in family units are being undermined by changes in the labour market and by legislative and policy initiatives in women's interests. Men's current "crisis" is strongly tied to their loss of power within families, and to the fact that decisions within and about households are increasingly being taken out of their hands (Chant, 2000).

In urban India, likewise, working women are expected to continue discharging their traditional domestic duties, often with the result of reduced well-being due to role strain. Husbands of working women may also experience pressures that harm their well-being. In a study of one- and two-earner urban middle-class parents in Bangalore, both groups of wives suffered poorer well-being than their husbands. Working wives felt more confident that they could cope than did nonworking wives, however. Husbands in two-earner families received better social support but less social contact, less mental mastery, and poorer perceived health than husbands in one-earner families. It appears from this study that women's employment may benefit wives, but adds stress to husbands (Andrade, Postman, & Abraham, 1999).

A comparison of Indian career women living in India and the West (England) finds few differences in stress, job satisfaction, and well-being. However, the Indian women in England report lower levels of anxiety and more spousal sharing of household chores. The data suggest that Indian women in the West may develop ideas of equality that differ from those of their husbands and family (Rout, Lewis, & Kagan, 1999).

Egyptian women in clerical jobs report taking pleasure in various aspects of their family life. The spousal role is central in their lives. Satisfying the needs and expectations of their husbands are most significant for them. Particularly important are the roles of creating harmony in the family and raising children. However, they complain of their husbands' demanding behaviour, the way the husbands express their demands, the husbands' abuse, and a constant feeling of *el masooliah*—

a "sense of overload from responsibilities." These women also see a gap in the values that they and their husbands hold. They appear to cope by enduring the stress (Hattar-Pollara, Meleis, & Nagib, 2000).

The expectations we place on husbands and wives, mothers and fathers, are different in North American society. Mothers are expected to hold two jobs: one at home and another outside the home. We view fathers who are employed full-time (versus part-time) as professionally competent, but we do not apply the same yardstick to mothers. Instead of viewing full-time employed mothers as more professionally competent, we view them as less nurturing. Mothers are popularly (and appropriately) perceived as being under more stress than fathers (Etaugh & Folger, 1998). Full-time employees are believed to experience more stress and to be less family-oriented than reduced-hour employees. Mothers are viewed as better adjusted but as experiencing more stress than fathers (Etaugh & Moss, 2001).

Our culture continues to hold women more responsible than men for the well-being of children and spouses, and for the avoidance or solution of marital problems. Wives typically report housework, not surprisingly, as unrewarding, monotonous, and boring. It is a major source of conflict and stress and a limit on their leisure time (Gill & Hibbins, 1996).

The conflict between economic aspirations and traditional duties affects the way women perceive their future life-course expectations. A study of female university students and their parents in Japan found that the women describe their futures as "changeable and ambivalent." There is a conflict between their hopes for an occupation and the responsibilities of the family. In addition, their parents give them conflicting messages about gender roles and what they expect of them (Muramatsu, 2000). Though many young people wish to please their parents, the internal (and external) struggles about what future is "right" for them can increase stress and unhappiness.

Husbands' attitudes may also contribute to wives' stress and unhappiness. Many studies find that paid employment improves women's mental health, and that multiple roles can have beneficial effects. However, when husbands oppose their wives' paid employment, marital conflict results, wiping out the potential health benefits of paid work.

Workload problems affect women differently, depending on their class or cultural group. Mothers in privileged social groups have a better chance to enter and stay in paid employment even if they have responsibility for children. Likewise, older and better-educated mothers are more likely to be in high-status occupations. They are also more likely to earn enough to pay for childcare, and to have their employer offer them on-site daycare, flextime, and other provisions for working mothers. In short, high-income women are generally better able to deal with the dual burden of work and marriage. Conversely, the problem of a work–family overload is greatest for women who are already the most socially vulnerable.

Spillover

The term *spillover* captures the idea that the products of one part of life intrude on another part. Work-to-family spillover is the tendency for stressful or difficult jobs to have a negative impact on workers' family experiences. As sociologists, we want to learn the reasons for this spillover, and its consequences (Skrypnek & Fast, 1996).

Factors causing work-to-family spillover include inflexible work schedules and high levels of responsibility with a low level of control over how work is conducted—characteristics generally found to cause health effects of stress among workers. Among transit workers, for example, family-to-work spillover results from lack of back-up childcare and inadequate social support systems (Reisner, 2000). More job flexibility improves the work–family balance, and benefits both individuals and businesses. Given the same workload, individuals with perceived job flexibility have a more favourable work–family balance. Likewise, employees with perceived job flexibility are able to work longer hours before workload harms their work–family balance (Hill et al., 2001).

One Stressful Job

More than a third of Ontario cancer care workers are considering quitting or cutting their work hours because of stress and burnout, a new study suggests.

The malaise, which hit all medical ranks from doctors to receptionists, is already hurting patient care. For example, one in five doctors reports a high level of depersonalization.

"They've really lost their ability to empathize with the human being who has cancer," says study co-author Dr. William Evans, vice-president of Cancer Care Ontario.

The survey of 1106 oncology staff, published recently in the *Canadian Medical Association Journal*, found roughly 50% of doctors suffered high levels of emotional exhaustion and low levels of personal accomplishment, while about 25% showed potential signs of mental health illness. Thirty-nine percent of cancer physicians said they would leave for a job outside the cancer care system, as did 37% of allied health professionals (including nurses, dietitians and pharmacists) and 30% of support staff.

The study says these numbers are worse than in prior studies of Canadian emergency room doctors and British medical oncologists.

The key problem cited in focus groups is the steadily increasing patient load. At the same time as a large portion of Canada's population is entering middle age, when cancer becomes more prevalent, provinces have cut or frozen funds to hire hospital staff.

Study co-author Dr. Eva Grunfeld says what bothers cancer care workers most is being too busy "to give the high quality of care that they want to give."

Research shows this kind of burnout can lead to mental and physical health problems, absenteeism, high staff turnover rates and diminished productivity. It may also make it difficult to work with people who are dying.

Source: Brad Evenson. 2000. "Burnout Overwhelms Cancer Workers: Ontario Study Finds They're Harder Hit Than Even ER Staff," *National Post* (National Edition), July 25, A5. Material reprinted with the express permission of "National Post Company," a CanWest Partnership.

A study of female hospital workers and their families finds spillovers from both paid work to the home, and to a lesser extent from the home to work (Wharton & Erickson, 1995). Simple exhaustion is one of the most important impacts of work on family life. Work-induced emotional exhaustion—along with work overload and mood shifts—profoundly affects a person's state of mind. Along with family conflict, emotional exhaustion increases the likelihood that work will interfere with family life by disrupting spousal and parenting relationships (Leiter & Durup, 1996).

The spillover of stress from work to family occurs in different ways for men and women. Mothers whose work has stressed them are more likely to ignore their children. By contrast, fathers whose work has stressed them are more likely to pick a fight with their children. Both child neglect and conflict increase the likelihood of adolescent problem behaviour. Parent–adolescent conflict is highest when work stresses *both* parents.

Since spillover produces a tendency for parental withdrawal from family activities after difficult workdays, parents reporting high work-to-family spillover are less knowledgeable about their children's daily lives. This applies only to fathers, however. Bumpus (2001) finds that fathers' (but not mothers') work-to-family spillover is associated with decreased knowledge about children's experiences. This relationship is mediated by marital love and father–child acceptance: When fathers report a high spillover, their marriages are on average less happy, which in turn is predictive of a less accepting father–child relationship and less knowledge about children's experiences. Said another way, parents are less knowledgeable when fathers' jobs are highly demanding and when they have younger boys or are less happily married. The negative effects of fathers' work stress are made worse by poor marital quality and having a younger son (Bumpus, Crouter, & McHale, 1999).

Spillover also affects children's perceptions of their parents' work. Adolescents have more respect for their parents' jobs when they perceive them as being less depersonalizing, less straining, and more satisfying. Adolescent perceptions of fathers' affect and work conditions interact with their respect for fathers' work to predict selected work values of adolescents (for example, the value they attach to human-centred work). No such relationship is found for mothers' work and adolescent work values (Galambos & Sears, 1998).

Spillover does not always have negative effects on individuals, nor does it depend on the number of hours worked in a particular job. Spillovers depend on other factors, such as interest in work and overload. A 1997 Canadian study questioned lawyers who worked 50-plus hours a week on whether they found their hours intruding on their non-work lives. Researchers conclude that although law firm workers do work long hours, work-related issues motivate them. They do not necessarily feel that work intrudes on other areas of their lives (Wallace, 1997).

Life strategies and work conditions are gendered, with workers in dual-earner couples most apt to be in neo-traditional arrangements—husbands in professional and/or long-hour jobs and wives working fewer hours, often in non-professional occupations. Life quality is gendered as well, with women in dual-earner arrangements reporting more stress and overload, as well as lower levels of coping/mastery than men do. However, the factors associated with life quality are similar across gender. Conditions at work predict quality of life for both men and women. Specifically, having a demanding job and job insecurity are associated with low life quality, while having a supportive supervisor is positively linked to life quality outcomes (Moen & Yu, 2000).

Among women who have parent-care responsibilities and who are also employed, higher levels of problematic interactions at work surrounding attempts to balance caregiving and work responsibilities are related to poorer well-being. Findings also indicate that problematic interactions with an immediate supervisor are generally related to poorer physical health, and problematic interactions with a co-worker with whom the caregiver works most closely are related to poorer psychological well-being. However, supportive interactions around attempts to balance caregiving and work responsibilities have no apparent effect on well-being (Atienza & Stephens, 2000).

Work hours and work-hour preferences matter as well, as we have seen. Men and women in couples where both spouses work regular (39–45) full-time hours tend to score high on indicators of life quality. People working longer or shorter hours than this are less likely to score high (Moen & Yu, 2000).

Spillovers in the other direction, from family to work, are also common and consequential, though research in this area can be contradictory. In one study, women with children under age 12 most often reported that their family responsibilities caused them to be absent, tardy, inattentive, inefficient, or unable to accept new work responsibilities (Crouter, 1984). Their most commonly cited reason for missing work, coming in late, or leaving early is caring for a sick child. However, in a later study, Canadian professional women with children reported more positive family-to-work spillovers than negative overall, and reported a greater use of coping strategies when they were parents (Kirchmeyer, 1993). In both studies, fathers describe *lower* levels of spillover from family to work no matter the age of their children (on this, see also Borden and Googins, 1987).

Family responsibilities also shape parents' perspectives on work. In a study by Galinsky and Hughes (1986), 21 percent of the male respondents and 27 percent of the females report seeking less demanding jobs so they can have more time with their families. Thirty percent of the men and 26 percent of the women also say they have refused a transfer or turned down a promotion because it would have meant less time with their family. The reasons why women decide to leave paid work are not only due to the care of the home and family needs. Women's perceived obligations to their partners and families influence their decision to leave the work force. Rosenman (1998) found that Australian women are more likely than men to retire from the work force due to family responsibilities and perceived obligations to their partners.

Work-Related Stress

As we have noted, paid work produces stress—sometimes a great deal of stress. Questionnaire data on nearly 80 000 employees from 250 work sites in the United States reveals that the greatest sources of stress in people's lives are (1) job, (2) finances, and (3) family (Jacobson et al., 1996).

Once they become parents, men and women approach the workplace in different ways. Fathers are more likely to work extended hours, when possible. Mothers work shorter hours and need more flexibility in their working arrangements. Full-time working mothers are more likely to ask for and receive parental leave from their employers than fathers or part-time working mothers. Family structure affects employee attendance either directly or interactively. For example, family demands moderate the effect of job burnout on absence frequency. A high level of burnout produces increased absenteeism if employees have children under six living at home, or report having difficulty with their childcare arrangements, for example (Erickson, Nichols, & Ritter, 2000); otherwise, it does not.

A combination of work-related and family-related stress can reduce job functioning. In a study of military personnel, both men and women were nearly twice as likely to report higher levels of stress at work than in their family or personal lives. However, women were more likely than men to experience high levels of family stress. Additionally, one-third of the women experienced high stress due to being a woman in the military. The effects of stress and depression on job functioning were similar for women and men. For both genders, higher levels of work-related stress, health-related stress, and number of depressive symptoms increased the odds of a lower level of job functioning. For men only, higher levels of family-related stress, use of a negative coping style, illicit drug use, and being a heavy drinker also increased the likelihood of lower job functioning (Bray et al., 2001).

Work-related stress is a major cause of marital problems in many families. When work increases the stress on a husband, it increases the likelihood of a hostile marital interaction. In that way, stress reduces the quality of both marital and family functioning (Larson, Wilson, & Beley, 1994). As work increasingly interferes with family life, both emotional and practical supports within the family deteriorate.

A study of police officers and their spouses asked couples to complete 30-day stress diaries and participate in four weekly laboratory interaction sessions. During interactions on days of greater stress, spouses were more physiologically aroused, husbands reported less positive and more negative emotion, and wives reported less emotion (both positive and negative). On days of greater exhaustion, husbands were more physiologically aroused. All of these findings indicate a heightened risk of poor marital outcomes and thus document an emotional mechanism by which job stress and exhaustion can negatively impact marriage (Roberts & Levenson, 2001).

Yet, for all the problems associated with working, unemployment and job insecurity hurt families even more. Both unemployment and job insecurity intensify family conflict and the risk of domestic violence. Unemployment harms the emotional health of the spouses, the quality of the marital relationship, the parent-child relationship, and family cohesion. Over time, job insecurity has a cumulative negative effect on women. For women, job insecurity in one year increases job exhaustion a year later, a negative effect that spills over into parenting (Mauno & Kinnunen, 1999). In turn, worsened parenting (in the form of neglect, short temper, absence of affect, or emotional or physical abuse) can hinder children's mental, physical and educational development.

The effects of unemployment on family life may vary from one culture to another, however. Where family life is valued particularly highly, unemployment may take on a different colour. So for example, in Israel, women are more likely than men to reject jobs because of conflict with family responsibilities or unsuitable working conditions. Both men and women mention gender-atypical characteristics of occupations as a reason for rejecting employment, although this tendency is especially prevalent among married women. Women also report more stress reactions and decline in health as a result of unemployment. When unemployed,

Figure 7.3 **INCREASED FEMALE PARTICIPATION IN THE LABOUR FORCE**

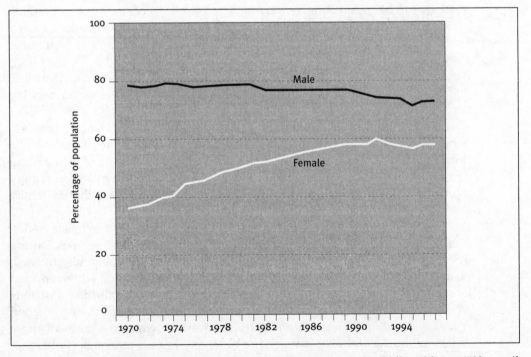

Source: Adapted from the Statistics Canada website, www.statcan.ca/english/freepub/82-570-XIE/01_11.pdf.

married men tend to seek jobs more intensively than respondents in the other research group, and single respondents of both sexes are more likely than their married counterparts to view unemployment as a personal advantage because it gives them more time to themselves. Moreover, married respondents of both sexes were more likely to reject job offers because of conflict with family responsibilities or unsuitable working conditions

A mother's paid work does the family a great deal of good when it makes up for a father's difficulties with work such as an inadequate or insecure income (Grimm-Thomas & Perry-Jenkins, 1994). Parental paid work is more likely to harm the children when fathers are heavily involved in their own jobs and mothers also work. Under those conditions, neither parent is paying the children much attention (Menaghan, 1993). Secure employment, on the other hand, generally benefits the family, even if it does increase people's overall workload. Research (Lamb, 1996) shows that maternal employment has little influence on a child's development, or on the quality of interaction between a mother and her (preschool) child, and may be beneficial to the child's achievement and aspirations.

Moreover, it is not maternal employment but parental employment that poses a problem for dual-earner families. We need to consider both parents' working conditions if we are to understand the effects of work on children's well-being.

Strain and Preoccupation

Another way in which paid work affects family life is by consuming the thoughts and interactions of the spouses. A survey of HIV/AIDS and cancer treatment staff in London, England found that one-third of the workers without long-term emotional relationships feel their work keeps them from becoming intimately involved with another person. Those in close relationships report spending much time discussing their work with partners. Work-related subjects lead to conflict for just under half the couples. As many as four respondents in ten report their partners complain regularly about their commitment to their work. One-quarter report the relationship has suffered as a result (Miller & Gillies, 1996).

Unlike many social conditions that change people's lives slowly, work-related emotional exhaustion produces harm almost immediately (Leiter & Durup, 1996). Strain and exhaustion due to job stress make parents more hostile and less responsive (Kinnunen, Gerris, & Vermulst, 1996). Work-related stress strains parents' relations with their adolescents and, in this way, increases the likelihood of adolescent problem behaviour (Galambos et al., 1995).

The major stressors affecting mothers of preschool children are lack of time, child-related anxieties (e.g., how is the child developing), and guilt (Rankin, 1993). Filling multiple roles does not necessarily cause stress. Whether a working mother feels she has control over her life is an important determinant of whether she feels stressed and whether the stress she feels has harmful effects for the family

(Tingey, Kiger, & Riley, 1996). In this instance, "stress" is a medical word for **structural powerlessness**.

For decades people have debated the question of whether maternal employment affects the emotional and psychological development of children, and the evidence is mixed. On the positive side, some research finds that school-aged children and adolescents with working mothers hold fewer stereotyped ideas about male and female roles, and daughters of these mothers are more achievement-oriented. On the negative side, some research finds that children whose mothers work for pay are more likely than other children to experience "insecure attachment" to their mothers. This implies that these children will grow up to be less secure in their social relations than the average person. Feelings of attachment also influence the chance of delinquent behaviour, as we said in an earlier chapter.

There is a likely correlation between insecurity and quality time spent with children from an early age. Bonding develops over time and is based on expressions of love, caring, and communication and active listening. Setting aside time for quality interactions with children is important, especially for working parents.

Children's overall adjustment, however, depends mainly on their parents' attitudes toward the mother working, not on her employment alone. Enjoyable features of work—such as the complexity of work with people, the challenge, and the stimulation—all contribute to good parenting (e.g., less harsh discipline, more warmth and responsiveness). That is because anything that makes the parent happier and more secure is likely to improve the quality of parenting and thus the well-being of the child.

Efforts to Solve These Problems

Strategies to resolve the problems that we have been discussing fall into at least two main categories: individual and familial (or micro) solutions on the one hand, and corporate and state (or macro) solutions on the other hand.

Individual and Familial Efforts

People use a variety of strategies to deal with the conflicting demands of paid work and housework (Paden & Buehler, 1995; Wiersma, 1994). One has been for a parent, usually the mother, to stay at home to look after the young children. Thus, women between the ages of 15 and 44 who have children are less likely than other women to work for pay.

Other strategies include one or both spouses working part-time, having fewer children, relying on extended family for support, and doing less housework. Some people redefine how much care their children really need. They rationalize that sending a three-month-old baby to daycare for a full working day is acceptable, since this teaches the child to be more independent, or gives the child a "jump-start on preschool," which may be the case. Many families buy more services: for example, paying someone to clean the house, buying prepackaged dinners, or hiring sitters to look after the children.

Another method of dealing with the problem is by restructuring the work arrangements of one or both parents. Self-employment is an increasingly attractive form of contingent work that offers schedule flexibility, particularly important for women (Carr, 1996). Education, age, and past work experience all influence parents' willingness and ability to become self-employed. Obviously, a physician or lawyer can exercise the option more readily than a teacher or factory worker.

The growth of home working makes it possible for women with few marketable skills, for example, immigrant women with an inadequate knowledge of English, to work at home making clothes for big clothing manufacturers. Though paid low wages, these women can organize their paid labour around the needs of their families (Gringeri, 1995). Unlike employment outside the home, the number of hours spent on home-based work does not significantly reduce the number of hours spent on domestic chores (Silver & Goldscheider, 1994). The result, argue some analysts, is that this home-based manufacturing reinforces women's lesser status both at work and at home.

Another adaptation is the home office. New technologies, such as computers, fax machines, and e-mail, have led to changes in thinking about work and home. Many duties can be done just as efficiently in either a public workplace or a private one. As well, working from home eliminates the need for an employer to pay overhead to supply its employees with a workplace.

Yet, despite hopes to the contrary, **supplemental work at home (SWAH)** does not solve the problem of a work/family spillover. Employed parents who do SWAH report more task variety and job involvement than other parents. However, SWAH adopters also report higher levels of role overload (too many simultaneous expectations—domestic, parental, work-related), interference, and stress (Duxbury, Higgins, & Thomas, 1996). We will have more to say about this in Chapter 12, where we examine the effects of technology on family life.

Real family life ends up intruding on the supposed advantages of new working technologies. Worse, new expectations associated with this new technology may even intensify stress. The scope for overload is larger than ever before. Fax, voice mail, and e-mail mean that colleagues expect a much faster response than in the past, and the volume of messages sent is greater. Since workers have access to these technologies at home too, home workers are not spared these new stresses. Employers may expect them to check for e-mail messages at night or even while on holidays.

The Daycare Debate

For obvious reasons, families today increasingly use daycare. The number of dual-earner families has almost doubled in the last 25 years. More than half of the families with incomes below the poverty line are single-parent families headed by women, and as we saw earlier, they usually do not receive adequate support from the child's father. The increase in single-parent families has led to an increase in demand for less expensive childcare, so that the single mothers can earn an income to support themselves and their children.

Today, 40 percent of Canadian children aged four to five spend part of their week in some type of care arrangement, while their parents study or work outside the home. Unregulated care outside the home (i.e., family daycare) is the most prevalent form of care arrangement. Children from low-income families who are cared for in facilities outside the home, either regulated or unregulated, have superior vocabulary skills to those who do not participate in care arrangements. Despite the importance of quality care for disadvantaged children, less than one-half of Canadian four-year-olds from low-income families attend licensed daycare centres or pre-kindergarten programs. The provision of kindergarten for five-year-olds varies by province, and is far from being universal.

Recent research based on the National Longitudinal Survey of Children and Youth has pointed to the importance of three factors in respect to the role of daycare in children's lives: low child-to-adult ratios, a highly educated staff with specialized training, and the availability of resources to provide stimulating

Figure 7.4   PROPORTION OF DUAL-EARNER FAMILIES, 1976 AND 1994

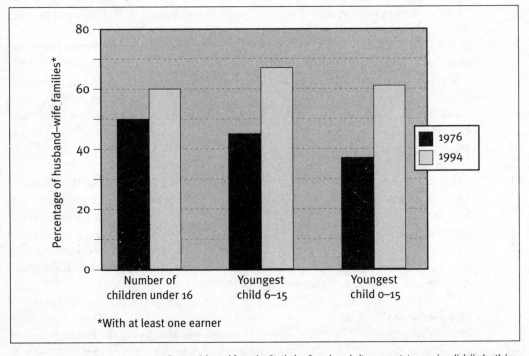

*With at least one earner

Source: Adapted from the Statistics Canada website, www.statcan.ca/english/indepth/75-001/archive/1995/pear199500700252a02.pdf.

activities. Where these qualities are present, daycare will contribute positively to children's development. High-quality daycare centres increase children's linguistic, cognitive, and social competencies, and this has long-lasting benefits for children from low-income families. As a result, investments in daycare for vulnerable children have large returns over time because they can result in less unemployment and dependency on social welfare, and increase tax revenue and decrease crime (Kohen, Hertzman & Willms, 2002).

As we noted above, the debate about daycare has continued for several decades. In the end, the daycare quality is what matters. Ultimately, the kind of care working parents can provide to their children depends on their financial, cultural, and educational background. Parents with the resources—perhaps the wealthiest 5 percent—may hire nannies to provide at-home childcare. About one-quarter of parents leave their preschool children with a non-parental relative (for example, a grandmother). Smaller proportions leave their preschooler in the home of the caregiver, who may or may not be tending her own infants and those of other parents as well. Corporate on-site daycare is typically of high quality but is still rare and few children—especially children from poor families—have access to it.

Daycare centres provide the most common form of childcare. These centres vary widely in cost and quality. They also vary enormously in the ages of children they accept, the staff-to-child ratio, the kinds of facilities that are available, and the quality of experience they provide for children. Some are more like preschools, with many educational activities for the children. Others are more like large babysitting services where the children do little more than play and rest. Poor quality daycare results in, among other things, children becoming ill frequently. This adds to lost paid time and adds stress to parents' lives.

Most research supports the benefits for children of good quality non-parental daycare. Typically, children have no problems and no attachment anxiety. They usually develop better social skills and generally develop more rapidly than other children. Children of impoverished mothers benefit most from daycare in cognitive performance. Children in daycare exhibit better social skills than their home-raised peers due to a more varied social world (Broude, 1996).

Dutch research finds little evidence to support the hypothesis that children in group daycare are more aggressive or less socially competent than peers with other childcare experiences (Goossens et al., 1991). Swedish research finds both girls and boys benefit from early daycare, especially boys who experience daycare early, at ages six to twelve months. Boys displaying learning or behaviour problems have usually been reared at home with no exposure to daycare or preschool (Andersson, 1996).

Perhaps the most decisive factor in the effectiveness of daycare is the degree of parents' and providers' satisfaction with the daycare situation (Van-Crombrugge & Vandemeulebroecke, 1991). Effective childcare provides a seamless fit between home and daycare. Children's adjustment to daycare, and their ability to benefit from it, depends on a cooperative relationship between parents and centre staff.

This relationship affects both family life and the children's self-development (Sommer, 1992).

Some research, however, raises concerns about the developmental effects of daycare on children. In the first year or two of life, children are apparently most sensitive to the use of non-parental care. Boys are more likely to be adversely affected than girls, as shown by behaviour problems in preschool, although, as discussed above, boys are also more likely to benefit. There is still debate about whether the child–adult ratio and daycare settings are important factors.

One study finds that children who experience 20 or more hours a week of non-maternal care during their first year of life run a much higher risk of disciplinary problems. Of all the parent groups studied, heavy daycare users report the most frequent defiance by their children. Resistance often explodes, with the child moving from passive aggression to active rebellion when parents try to control the child (Belsky et al., 1996).

Maternal employment may also produce acute problems when the mother experiences much stress at work and has little social support. Videotaped interactions show that when highly stressed mothers reunite with energetic preschoolers at the end of the workday, the mothers often withdraw emotionally and behaviourally. They speak less and offer the infant fewer signs of affection than less-stressed mothers.

Largely, however, the research to date seems to say, "No, children do not receive worse parenting when both parents are working for pay" (see, for example, Paulson, 1996; Beyer, 1995). True, parenting styles may change when women start to work for pay, but it is still the **parenting style**, not maternal employment, that may cause a problem. The research suggests that all children need rich and stimulating experiences, especially in early childhood, to support healthy development. This points to the importance of making high-quality care arrangements available to all Canadian children who need them, particularly as the numbers of dual-earner families continue to rise. At present, there are not enough spaces at high-quality daycares to accommodate all children, and waiting lists are common. Quality care arrangements need to be made accessible and affordable so that all children can participate, regardless of race, ethnic background, level of competence, or ability to pay. Canada will need to have a national standard of quality and universal access to childcare for those Canadian families who require or choose to use them and will need to coordinate the development and implementation of child services across the provinces. It will be necessary to establish a consistent training and education requirement for caregivers, require consistent licensing for high-quality care environments, and make a commitment to monitor programs and collect information in a coherent and coordinating way.

Individual and familial coping responses play a huge role in determining how the problems posed by work and family life will affect families. However, individual and familial responses can only respond to—not solve—problems that are societal and organizational. Only social change, explained below, can address these.

Corporate Responses

Large corporations have, over the last 20 or so years, become more sensitive to the needs of families. As a result, many have changed their policies, provided new employee benefits and services, and even reformed their organizational cultures—the way they think and talk about work issues. The changes have paid off. The more the organization supports employees with family responsibilities, the less strain employees will experience between paid work and family roles. Supervisor flexibility and the provision of family-oriented benefits also reduce the level of work–family strain (Warren & Johnson, 1995; Thomas & Ganster, 1995). The provision of on-site childcare and flextime helps workers, especially mothers, to deal more effectively with the real demands of work and family life. They also increase work satisfaction, which, in turn, increases life satisfaction (Ezra & Deckman, 1996).

However, employers do this not simply to increase employee satisfaction; they provide family benefits when they realize it is in their own best interest to do so (Seyler, Monroe, & Garand, 1995). Employers are more likely to provide these benefits to reduce per-employee start-up costs such as training or when work productivity is suffering because family life stresses too many employees.

A survey of 4400 families with children under age 13 finds that the availability of employer policies affects how quickly working mothers re-enter the workforce after childbirth (Hofferth, 1996). It is a combination of parental-leave laws, organizational policies, and the cost and quality of childcare that jointly determines how soon a mother will begin (or return to) working outside the home after childbirth. Mothers' family circumstances and their family's attitudes also matter.

Unions play a large part in pressing for more workplace benefits and gender equality. Overall, firm size and unionization are the most powerful determinants of family-responsive policies in North American, especially American, companies (Glass & Fujimoto, 1995). With large firms cutting back and union membership dropping in Canada, employers may reduce the prospects for family-friendly policies.

Since most people do not want the problems associated with home offices or self-employment, they increasingly value flextime. Flextime involves working the same number of hours but having some freedom to decide when to work these hours. Flextime does not involve a pay cut or diminish chances for a promotion, so it is popular among parents, particularly women. Flextime can be formal or informal. Informal flextime, common among professionals, may mean coming to work half an hour earlier to be able to take an hour and half lunch break to run errands.

Swapping shifts is another way of to create flextime, yet shift work, despite its flexibility, carries costs. It disrupts circadian (bodily) rhythms, sometimes leading to physical and psychological ill health and domestic unrest. There is no such thing as an ideal shift system. Nevertheless, organizations can develop more effective ones if they take the time to learn their employees' needs and preferences, and adapt their systems to fit these needs (Snyder, 1995).

Part-time work is a widely used policy, for many reasons. Organizations like to put people on part-time work because they do not have to pay full benefits and can fire the employee at will. Part-time status puts women who take it for domestic reasons on a **"mommy track."** Employers see the women on this track as less committed to their work and to their career and thus less promotable.

One popular family-friendly workplace initiative is on-site daycare for young children. This program does not change how parents have to work, but it relieves some anxieties. A quality childcare program is particularly critical for lower-income families. However, usually only large organizations can afford to provide it. Therefore, not only must employers integrate such policies but also existing programs should be more accessible to all families.

More workplaces are providing benefits packages for gay and lesbian families, including daycare for their children. Even the conservative Disney Corporation is doing so. However, many lesbian and gay couples are unable to take these benefits because they do not reveal their sexual orientation to their employer, for fear of losing their jobs. The challenge is to update social attitudes to fit contemporary family realities.

Tech Workers Aging

When Julie McMullin walked into her brother's workplace, she saw fun.

Young employees at bitHeads Inc., an Ottawa-based software development company, played pool and video games at the company bar while slamming back frothy drafts.

In their off time, they also watched hockey in the firm's movie theatre while munching popcorn.

When McMullin, 37, left bitHeads Inc., she had questions.

Companies in the information technology sector may cater well to a younger workforce but are they ready to handle their employees as they age?

Does the sector consist predominantly of young, white males?

McMullin, a sociology professor at the University of Western Ontario in London, Ont., is embarking on a four-year, national study to answer those and other questions. She was awarded $3 million from the Social Sciences and Humanities Research Council of Canada (SSHRC) earlier this week.

It's one of the largest grants the agency has ever given. McMullin will be one of the first researchers to tackle the issue of aging in the IT workforce.

"The whole nature of work has changed for everyone but it's especially dramatic for people in the IT business because that world just changes so fast," said Dominique Lacasse, spokesperson for SSHRC. "If we don't understand what is going on... then it's to our detriment."

McMullin said companies deal well with their employees' school-to-work life transition; however, she wanted to "explore how firms deal with other life course transitions" such as having children. "We expect to find in most small- to mid-sized IT firms, they won't have good pension policies and good maternity-leave policies in place," she said.

"There's a focus on stock options and making money—things that are important to younger people."

She expects most employees will be young, white males—with fewer older workers, females and racial minorities.

"There might be unintentional discrimination going on," McMullin said.

She speculated that there may be fewer women in the industry because women are "perceived as being less technically competent and they aren't as encouraged at a young age to engage in technical kinds of play."

Older workers face education barriers because the IT industry lacks sufficient retraining programs for them, she said. McMullin also added many don't want to go back to university full-time for a computer science degree.

McMullin, who's been a professor at the University of Western Ontario for five years, said she's been overwhelmed by the public response.

"I have been getting a huge response from older IT workers who are saying, 'I was fired five years ago and I haven't been able to find work in the IT sector.'"

Her research will also explore employment growth in the sector and the specific skill sets required for IT work.

McMullin hopes to use the data to develop policy initiatives for the IT sector.

"It will enable governments, employers and employees to deal more effectively with issues of aging workforces, diversity employment and life-long learning."

McMullin will be doing case studies of IT companies in: Canada, Australia, the United States and the European Union. "Australians seem to be ahead of us in terms of how they treat older workers and retraining issues," she said. "We can learn from their experience."

McMullin will be partnering with the SSHRC and the Human Resource Development Council of Canada.

They will be doing an IT survey across the country to determine the proportion of older workers, women and minorities in the sector. The study begins in January and will end with an international conference in 2006.

The study involves researchers at eight universities, along with various labour groups, technology organizations, government agencies and IT companies.

Source: Leong, Melissa. "Study to Examine IT Workplace: How Do Employers Cope with Change?" *Toronto Star*, Dec. 16, 2002. Reprinted with permission—Torstar Syndication Services.

Computerized Work and the Family

In this book, we have emphasized work's important influence on family life, and vice versa. Certainly, the spillover of stress from work to family life is a considerable problem for all spouses and parents, particularly for working mothers, who still carry the main domestic responsibility.

It follows, then, that changes in work life due to computerization and other information technology may have a large influence on family life. The computerization of work and its transfer to a home setting—what is variously called telework, telecommuting, or computer-supported work at home (SWAH)—is still at an early stage, and research on this topic is still developing. At this point, a few findings are worth considering. First, telework blurs the boundaries between work and leisure, which complicates both work and leisure. Second, telework does not reduce the work done, or the spillover from work life to family life. Nor, third, does telework appear significantly to change the gendering of domestic labour. Fourth, though telework may increase the time a parent spends near his or her spouse or child, there is no evidence that it improves (or increases) interactions between them.

The clearest conclusions we can draw are that telework reduces transportation time, passes the cost of workspace onto the worker, and makes worker visibility more difficult. Control over the worker can either increase or decrease depending on the telework to be done. For example, if it is routine clerical work, keystrokes can be monitored centrally, thereby increasing the employer's control. Other, more professional kinds of telework enable greater freedom and control by the worker. The effects on individual workers are mixed. For example, Duxbury, Higgins, and Thomas (1996) report that, on the positive side, teleworking gives workers more task variety. On the negative side, teleworking also gives them more role overload, interference, and stress. It has no effects, positive or negative, on marital or family satisfaction. Thus, it appears to do more for employing organizations than for their workers. No wonder newspapers and other media that put forward a management point of view strongly support teleworking. They claim that teleworkers gain productive time, are more efficient, and even bond better with their mates when they work from home together (*Globe and Mail*, 2000).

We are just beginning to realize that there are positive aspects to the distancing of work and family, and negative aspects. We need research to help us understand better the conditions under which telework will be a step forward or backward for workers, their families, and their work organization (Ellison, 1999).

Family Policies: A Cross-National Outlook

Family policies exist in many countries, in varying forms. Paid parental leave goes as far back as 1883 in Germany. From that time, industrialized countries have tried to incorporate policies because of their proven usefulness in helping correct the balance between family and work.

Maternity leave differs from one country to another. For example, Austria, Italy, and Sweden force employers to give all women employees maternity leaves without a precondition. In Canada, the United Kingdom, and Ireland, maternity leave is limited to full-time employees.

Paternity leave is not available in all countries. However, the participation of men in childcare and domestic work has grown with the struggle for equality of the sexes, and most industrialized countries have had to acknowledge the growing role that fathers play in the family. Among countries that have paternity leaves, Sweden, New Zealand, and Norway give fathers the longest leaves, while France, Spain, and Canada provide the shortest.

Sweden is an example of a country in which mothers are encouraged to participate in the workforce, through both widely available maternal leave and paternal leave. Sweden has a higher tax rate than Canada, so that more money can be spent on these policies. As well, Sweden has a century-long history of progressive policies on families and children. Sweden has also had many lone-parent and divorced families for longer than Canada has. Perhaps Sweden's history points to the road ahead for Canada.

Many European countries have more liberal policies than Canada, but they achieve their family-supportive goals in a variety of ways. For example, Australia allows low-income support even when a family owns a home and car, which would disqualify a family in Germany.

In Japan, the law seems to support corporate interests against family and individual interests. For example, the law often sides with the corporation when an employee resists a company's order to move. The husband must go, even if his family stays behind to sell the home, to maintain the continuity of the children's education, or to take responsibility for elderly family members. Such transfers lead to loneliness for the transferee, a huge burden for the spouse left to care for household needs alone, and a heavy strain on the marriage itself. It also destabilizes the children, who grow up without the presence of the father figure.

What cross-national comparisons show us is that we can solve any problem in a variety of ways. The ways selected will reflect historical, cultural, and social differences between societies. Comparison also tells us something about what the state can and cannot do to direct the interaction between families and work organizations. (For a useful comparison of organizational and institutional arrangements in six European countries, see Buchmann & Charles, 1995.)

Government Responses

Balancing work and family life is a huge burden for so many families and the source of both family and workplace problems. Many governments have stepped in to with policies designed either to give parents more time at home or to provide safe, affordable daycare.

A family issue of concern to every industrial state is population aging. As the Canadian population continues to be weighted toward the elderly (because of the decrease in birth rates), definitions of the family and of family policy are changing. Canadian companies and the Canadian government are witnessing an increase in pressure from various advocacy groups for better childcare and fairer policies that will benefit all types of families. As the policies expand and improve, Canadians need to realize that it will benefit them and their families to take full advantage of them.

As women enter the labour force, whether by choice or necessity, the work traditionally allocated to women—providing care to children, the infirm, and the elderly—will be done in other ways. Societies like Sweden *commodify* caring and domestic work to some extent, paying for it and providing it to those who need it. In market-driven societies like the United States, it has become more of a private service to be purchased by those who can afford it (Boje, 1995). However, it is still mainly women who carry out the caring work. They do so either as paid female service industry workers, or as female family members who must work a second (or third) unpaid shift at home (where the **second shift** is traditional housework and childcare and the third shift is elder care).

Many states are spending less money on public services such as health, education, and welfare that benefit families most directly. On the other hand, in many European countries, the state has recognized the double burden women carry by giving them paid parental leave and state-run daycare centres, for example. Corporations have followed suit. France, Germany, Hungary, and Sweden have all been concerned with promoting childbearing and helping parents to balance work and family responsibilities. In addition, they have increased national responsibility for the provision of care and education of children aged between three and five years and employer responsibility for parental leave (Hofferth & Deitch, 1994).

There are a variety of ways that the state can induce change in this area. Policy and lawmaking is one of these. However, policies are not effective unless we enforce them. Another effective way is to "lead by example" where policies are not legislated but are adopted by state-run agencies (in Canada, by Crown corporations).

At both the governmental and corporate levels, the United States and Canada lag far behind in responding to the plight of working women, particularly single mothers. Unlike France, where the state runs childcare, the United States has a market-based system. Middle- and upper-income parents make choices and are repaid by the state for some of their expenses. Low-income parents receive targeted subsidies. Parental leave legislation brings the U.S. only marginally closer to Europe because leave in the U.S. remains unpaid.

As we have seen, for women—the traditional caregivers—managing the dual role of outside employment and caregiving is often highly stressful. In the U.S., women rely on institutional (i.e., corporate) and domestic support. In Japan, they rely on social traditions. Governments in both countries are attempting to ease the strains, particularly through enacting tax exemptions, workplace training and support, and community partnerships, though they more thoroughly integrate projects in Japan (Lechner & Sasaki, 1995).

Sweden and the United States show contrasting approaches to integrating family and work (Lundgren-Gaveras, 1996). In the United States, private operators run most programs with this aim, while both the private and public sector are involved in Sweden. In both countries, they design programs to serve the labour market. Thus, in the United States, where single mothers make up little of the labour market, they often cannot take advantage of these programs. The United States is unique among industrialized countries in its lack of public assistance for childrearing mothers, its lack of state-guaranteed minimum payments, and its lack of employment policies that would help mothers increase earnings.

Recently debated in the United States was a "Help for Working Parents Proposal" (HWPP). Its goal is to get all poor mothers out working for pay, though most will be working in low-skill, low-wage jobs. The policy does this in two ways. On the one hand, it reduces the attractiveness of not working (that is, of being on welfare). On the other hand, it provides childcare, health insurance, and housing assistance for women who take these unattractive jobs. It guarantees health care and childcare for working parents, thus supplying benefits not available in many low-wage jobs. It also increases benefits for at-home parents beyond the current system, through vouchers. HWPP does not make more low-wage jobs available. However, it does enable parents to survive with the available jobs (on this theme, see Hartmann & Spalter-Roth, 1996).

The European, Canadian, and American approaches to thinking about work and family issues differ in many ways. However, they all point to the need for workplace culture to change in ways that incorporate the perspective of many interested parties (Lewis & Cooper, 1995). We need clear thinking on social policy. States must find some way to shape and predict the balance of housework (including childcare) and outside work, to ease the recurrent conflicts felt by the

Figure 7.5 LABOUR FORCE PARTICIPATION RATES BY SEX, 1980–2000

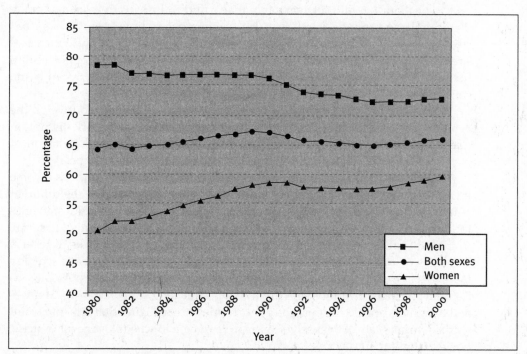

Source: Adapted from the Statistics Canada website, Labour Force Historical Review, 2000, catalogue no. 71F0004XCB, www.statcan.ca/english/freepub/89F0123XIE/13.htm.

general population. Doing so is in the national interest, and no one else is likely to do it. Private corporations have little interest in doing so, and overworked spouses are unable to do so.

Cross-national research on 15 industrial societies (Shaver and Bradshaw, 1995) finds that people commonly apply three models to the relation between family and work. In the *traditional* model, the wife is economically dependent on her husband. In the *modern* model, the wife remains outside the labour market but only while she has young children. In the *dual breadwinner* model the mother of young children is in full- or part-time employment. Welfare states typically embrace the dual breadwinner model. They provide support to women, whether or not they have young children and work for pay, though the levels of support vary greatly among welfare states.

Concluding Remarks

We end this discussion of domestic division of labour where we started. Domestic labour may be the most important arena in which gains in equality have yet to be made. Couples forming relationships need to talk openly about their wishes and aspirations with respect to housework, childcare, and elder care.

With North American workers putting in about 140 more hours on the job each year than they did 20 years ago, many find it difficult to relax and enjoy their family and friends regularly. Also, the increase in time spent at work has created a great deal of stress within the family. Financial insecurity also increases stress within the family, and the past 20 years have provided many opportunities for families to experience financial stress. We have already noted some consequences for mental and physical health.

For many individuals, the costs of family life are starting to outweigh the benefits. The consequences of family stress, bad parenting, and work disruption due to family concerns are significant public issues. Yet they are still, for the most part, problems for individuals to remedy in the privacy of their homes.

To meet the demands that work is putting on parents, family time has become increasingly regimented, with "quality time" scheduled between the different family members. Increasingly, dual-career couples develop behavioural strategies to solve work–home conflicts. These coping behaviours are cooperative or social, in the sense that they transform the way the family system works to reduce pressures on one or more of the family's members, but neither type of strategy involves state expense. Women-only gyms are gaining in popularity. As early as 7:00 a.m., women of various ages are walking, stretching, and exercising. Mothers and daughters are also seen in the gym. Women are realizing that it is important for them to take care of themselves, and are beginning to schedule time for exercise, however tight their daytime schedule.

The organizational and institutional standards in any society determine the context within which men and women make education, labour market, and reproductive choices. Currently in North America, irregular school schedules, limited shopping hours, and lack of childcare services reflect a social and political belief in the full-time homemaker. Women are forced to make a choice between family and work.

For most of this chapter, we have concentrated on the negative aspect of work, especially that of work causing stress in the family. We should not leave the topic without acknowledging that work can also be a profoundly rewarding experience, with benefits for the family. For example, many studies of single mothers show that if the mother is in a job that she enjoys, the child often grows up unaffected by the absence of a father. Other studies show that professionals can sometimes apply to their family the problem-solving skills learned at work. This is an interesting aspect of the relationship between work and home that researchers should explore further.

Women and men also need to establish a new domestic economy. Too many men still believe they are entitled to full domestic service from their wives. The whole question of what is fair in marriage—especially when both mates are working for pay and workers have children to care for—needs to be discussed. Men have had it their way for far too long. That's not only unfair. It can ruin a relationship.

CHAPTER SUMMARY

This chapter looks at the intersection of what are arguably the two most predominant aspects of an individual's life: family and work.

We show family work to be equally as important and valid as paid work, a major contributor to the socioeconomic fabric of Canada. We learned about the unequal sexual division of domestic labour and the "double days" that working women must often contend with. The consequences of this are commonly stress and marital conflict. We examined childcare, a major component of domestic labour. Again, we found that mothers, rather than fathers, more often do this work. Childcare for working parents in Canada is lacking, with only 15 percent of children who need care having access to it. We also examined the growth in unpaid elder care, in which family members care for their aged and frail relatives.

The basic problem facing working parents is that both work and family life take up enormous amounts of their time, energy, and emotions, and that it is difficult—but necessary—for adults to balance these often-conflicting demands. Secondary problems resulting from this dilemma fall into one of three categories: overload; culturally induced stress; and spillover. Work-related stress is a major cause of marital problems in many families because it creates other problems, such as preoccupying the thoughts and interactions of the spouses or intensifying arguments over domestic responsibilities.

The conflicts over work and family, and the secondary problems that it creates, are important enough for us to make efforts to solve them. Strategies so far fall under two categories: micro and macro. By *micro*, we mean personal and familial solutions, such as postponing work to become a homemaker, restructuring work arrangements and schedules, and opting for daycare. By *macro*, we mean corporate responses, such as setting up flextime policies and on-site daycare services for the children of employees, and state responses, such as expanding parental leave policies and offering economic and social support for single parents.

KEY TERMS

Culturally induced stress The stress and guilt people in our culture feel when they try to cope with the workload and their inability to get it all done.

Family work Tasks involved in maintaining a family, such as co-ordinating family activities with paid work and housework.

Flextime Working the same number of hours, but having some freedom to decide when to work these hours.

Housework Tasks involved in maintaining a home, such as cleaning and cooking.

"Mommy track" A term used to describe women who are seen as less committed to their work and to their career and thus less promotable.

Overload The excessive amount of work many people, especially mothers, have to do.

Parenting style The way in which a parent acts, expresses, or performs.

Personal resources theory A theory of marital relations that holds that couples will work out who has more power in any given situation, with the less-powerful partner deferring to the more-powerful partner.

Spillover The notion that the products of one part of one's life intrude on another part.

Structural powerlessness Actual lack of control over one's life that leads to harmful effects for anyone closely involved in that individual's life.

Supplemental work at home (SWAH) Work in the home office that is aided by technological advances such as computers.

Wage gap The differences between the sexes in number of hours spent working and average dollar earned per hour. Most women work longer hours to earn the same amount as men, due to women's lower overall earning power.

SUGGESTED READINGS

Coltrane, Scott. 1996. *Family Man: Fatherhood, Housework and Gender Equity*. New York: Oxford University Press. An in-depth look at the past and present roles of the male in the family, along with a discussion of current social trends and how they might affect the family in the future.

DeVault, Marjorie L. 1991. *Feeding the Family: The Social Organization of Caring as Gendered Work*. Chicago: University of Chicago Press. This book explores how women often actively subordinate themselves in the home through their interpretation of the domestic responsibility of cooking and feeding others as a form of service.

Gerson, Kathleen. 1994. *No Man's Land: Men's Changing Commitments to Family and Work*. New York: Basic Books. This book argues that men's lives are changing in both the workplace and in the home as a result of shifts in culture, social structure, and other conditions beyond their control.

Hochschild, Arlie R. 1997. *The Time Bind: When Work Becomes Home and Home Becomes Work*. New York: Metropolitan Books. Citing evidence from her study of a large corporation, the author suggests that many parents today prefer the rewarding and predictable world of work to the home, which is becoming increasingly stressful and devalued by society.

Williams, Joan. 1999. *Unbending Gender: Why Family and Work Conflict and What to Do About It*. New York: Oxford University Press. This book explores the issues women face in balancing work and family life from a feminist perspective and offers smart legal strategies and policy initiatives to restructure society's notions of work and gender.

REVIEW QUESTIONS

1. Define "housework" and "family work."

2. What one profound impact have labour-saving devices had on women's participation in market activity?

3. What is the approximate value of housework in Canada estimated to be? What percentage of the GNP does housework account for?

4. According to a 1990 study by the Conference Board of Canada, what percentage of women and men reported primary responsibility for childcare?

5. What is the "personal resources theory" of marital relationships?

6. What are the effects of domestic responsibilities on paid work for men?

7. Define "overload" and "spillover."

8. What is "SWAH"?

9. How does the "mommy track" affect the wage gap between men and women?

10. What are the differences between the United States' and Sweden's approaches to integrating family and work?

DISCUSSION QUESTIONS

1. Discuss the phrase "home sweet home." Does this phrase have the same meaning today as it did in the past? Explain your answer.

2. A major theme running throughout this chapter is that the gender differential in power between men and women in the workplace and in society has an impact on the division of labour. Explain and discuss the process by which the former has an effect on the latter.

3. Should housework be considered a part of the country's GNP? If so, what are the consequences for women, children, and families? Consider how

this may affect women's career options as well as community programs and workers. Also, consider how this would change the societal stigmas associated with being a homemaker.

4. How does the socialization of gender roles in our society contribute to workplace inequality and the domestic division of labour?

5. People use many strategies to help cope with conflicting demands of paid work and housework. Many of the strategies mentioned in the text are most applicable for middle- to upper-class families who can pay for additional help. What coping strategies, if any, do poorer families have to help them? What can community workers (counsellors, social workers, teachers) do to help these families cope more effectively?

6. Discuss the following statement: "The domestic problems of a family are private matters and should be solved internally by its own members. The state and the corporate world do not have an obligation to assist."

7. In pre-industrial times, the integration of production and consumption created a different organization of family work than ours today. How have things changed in terms of paid work, chores, and childrearing?

8. Consider a family structure where the husband is the homemaker and the wife is the breadwinner. Discuss how this may affect the couple's attitudes toward their marriage, the division of labour, and their decision to have children. What effects, if any, do you think this arrangement will have on children?

9. Nakhaie (1995) found that "when husbands' work hours increase beyond 30 hours per week, their contribution to housework decreases; when women's hours increase beyond 30 hours a week, their contribution to housework *increases* [emphasis in original]." What accounts for this seemingly counterintuitive finding? Discuss.

10. Discuss the pros and cons of family-friendly workplace polices. Are they the answer to the problems of "double days," or do they merely help to reinforce traditional conceptions of gender roles?

ACTIVITIES

1. Break into groups and attempt to come up with ways of remunerating each job performed by a homemaker (e.g., laundry, cooking, cleaning, childrearing, etc.). Would homemakers be paid per job, hourly, or monthly? What would be a fair wage? Who would pay these workers? As a class, compare ideas and try to come up with a national program based on your discussion.

2. Overload can be a detriment to personal health and family relations. In groups, design a half-hour seminar for a community centre targeted at helping people recognize, understand, and cope with overload. The seminar should include whatever information, exercises, and tools you believe are relevant in helping your audience to comprehend and use the information.

3. Spend several nights observing how families are portrayed on prime-time television. How do spouses relate to one another? How is the domestic division of labour divided? Identify any examples of gender-based prejudice and discuss how the media's portrayal of this affects the viewing audience at home.

WEBLINKS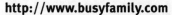

http://www.busyfamily.com
The Busy Family Resource Center
The Busy Family Resource Center is a referral service that provides users with verified information on professional family care services and agencies across Canada.

http://workingfamilies.berkeley.edu/
The Center for Working Families
The Center for Working Families conducts research on the experience of dual-income families, trains scholars to do research on working families, and offers information to the public through lectures, projects, and published papers.

http://www.theglassceiling.com
The Glass Ceiling
The Glass Ceiling addresses inequality and discrimination in the workplace, especially against women, and provides information on how people can balance work and family effectively.

http://www.momsrefuge.com
Working Mom's Refuge
Working Mom's Refuge offers articles, discussion boards, and advice columns on how married and single working moms can balance career goals and family needs.

CHAPTER EIGHT

Family Dynamics:

How Families Face Problems and Get Along

Introduction

In earlier chapters, we examined some of the problems parents face when they try to communicate with one another, raise well-adjusted children, and balance the demands of family life and work life. As we have seen, these problems are common and hard to solve. Often, the parents need help.

This chapter will further examine the problems that all family members face. These problems vary widely. Many are serious and hard to handle. Many are socially structured, in the sense that they arise out of the way that society as a whole is organized. For example, they may arise out of poverty, racism, sexism, or regional inequality.

Often, we keep our family problems secret because they confuse and embarrass us. Portrayals of family life on television and in movies lead us to believe that *good* families do not have serious problems. Therefore, families like ours, with sometimes serious and worrisome problems, must be bad families. This conclusion is unwarranted, however. In fact, all families have problems and they also have different resources for dealing with their problems.

Other things being equal, families that are more adaptable (or flexible) and cohesive are better able to solve their problems. However, other things are rarely equal. Families that suffer from poverty, racism or other types of hardship are hindered in their efforts to solve added problems like addiction, chronic illness, or domestic violence. Both the problems families face, and the resources they have available to solve these problems, are socially structured. This makes their problems public issues, not merely personal troubles.

The topic of **family dynamics** is concerned with how families solve their problems. What we mean by "family dynamics" is the sum of all the ways that families, as social units, cope with their problems and adjust to needs for change. The place to start is by noting that no family "naturally" gets along well. A well-functioning family is a social achievement, the result of hard work and sensitivity, as well as a supportive environment. To completely understand any family requires that we think about the nature of the family as a system, including the **assumptive world**—the internalized views of family relations—its individual members may hold (Kaye, 1986).

Problems and Secrets

Most of us are so deeply familiar with our own families that we find it hard to imagine any other kind of family. We know that our own family has problems, conflicts, and peculiarities. We feel we must not discuss family secrets with anyone else, and we are uncomfortable revealing certain things even to friends. Some people find it hard to imagine any family being stranger than their own. Yet, in fact, every family is peculiar and has problems, even strange, embarrassing, and secret problems. Some problems are persistent but mild. Other problems are much more dramatic.

Think of the family problems that involve alcohol or drug abuse, and family violence. The secrecy surrounding these family problems, great enough in heterosexual couples, may be even greater in same-sex couples. In one survey, for example, 39 out of 104 self-identified lesbian women report a past or present abusive relationship. Sixty-four percent report that alcohol or drugs were involved before or during incidents of battering (Schilit, Lie, and Montagne, 1990). Often, the secrecy that surrounds a same-sex lifestyle increases a victim's unwillingness to seek help with a family problem. There are multiple reasons for secrecy.

Whether heterosexual or homosexual, every family has its problems. In addition, every family has special ways of recognizing, containing, or dealing with its problems. Often, families work hard to keep their problems hidden from outsiders. To do this, family members may spend a great deal of effort keeping up an appearance of calm conformity to social roles and expectations. If they succeed, no one but the family members themselves will know about the hidden secrets, conflicts, and strains.

Figure 8.1 PERCENTAGE OF CHILDREN EXHIBITING DELINQUENT BEHAVIOURS, BY FAMILY STRUCTURE

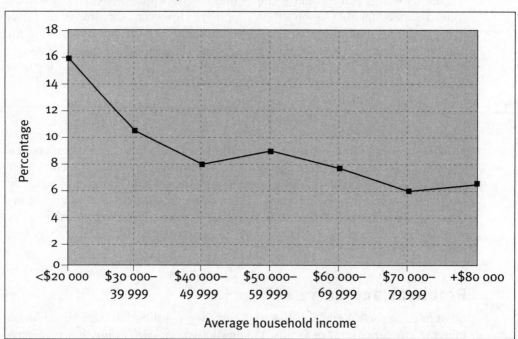

This figure illustrates that children in poor families are twice as likely to have scores within the top 10 percent in terms of frequency of delinquent behaviours compared to children in modest-income families, and they are nearly three times as likely to have high delinquency scores as children in high-income families. There is almost a 10-percentage-point difference in the likelihood of exhibiting delinquent behaviours when children from low- and high-income families are compared.

Source: Prepared by the Canadian Council on Social Development, using Statistics Canada Longitudinal Survey on Children and Youth, 1994–1995.

This impulse for secrecy may force family members to hide their true feelings, views, and tendencies. Many problems that a family tries to hide may result from changes a family is going through, changes they fear and do not know how to handle. The sources of change and conflict may be internal (e.g., an unexpected pregnancy) or external to the family (e.g., a war or economic depression).

Changes going on outside the family often create problems inside the family, and vice versa. For example, wartime conditions may increase the risk of juvenile delinquency by disrupting family authority (Shoham, 1994). Likewise, immigration often changes the power relations between husbands and wives, parents and children. Often, the new social and economic conditions require changes that family members find stressful (Haddad & Lam, 1994)—for example, the need for mothers to go out to work, siblings to share rooms, or extended family members to crowd together in a small apartment.

Often, changes pose particular problems for women. More than for men, life for women entails a struggle for equal power, both inside and outside the family (Allmendinger, Bruckner, & Bruckner, 1992). Changes in power relations, though often hidden, can lead to major changes in women's lives. Only in the last few decades have feminist theorists opened the door to discussing the power relations within families. As Diane Wolf writes, "feminists have cut through romantic assumptions about family and household unity, arguing that there exist instead multiple voices, gendered interests, and an unequal distribution of resources within families and households … Attention is slowly turning to intra-household relations between genders and generations" (1998: 43).

The existence of family secrets is so common that we must allow for the possibility that secrets contribute to family functioning—to the survival and well being of family members—in some strange way. Secrets, as Brown-Smith (1998: 31) points out

> enable the family to proceed in its development without feeling its identity is shamed or threatened. Moreover, intimacy related to love, closeness, and emotional commitment is created and maintained. Secrets shared among members also strengthen internal cohesion as the family is reinforced as a single unique entity. The family that shares a secret has a more clearly defined sense of self-concept than one that does not. As Simmel asserted long ago, secret keeping provides the family the advantage of protecting itself from outsiders.

However, family secrets can also harm families and their members. Under a veil of secrecy, some men carry out acts of violence against women and children. Women also perpetrate violence against children, and both men and women abuse elderly parents on occasion. As a rule, secrecy fosters a tolerance for deception and trickery in close relationships. Secrecy also opens up the possibility of blackmail. Power becomes unbalanced when one person knows more than, or something harmful about, another family member. Anxiety about the possible disclosure of a secret is likely to infect family relations.

Families are usually better off solving their problems than hiding them, but solving problems is usually harder than hiding them. Often, family members, and families as a whole, develop an investment in a problem. They learn to work around it. They define themselves and each other in terms of "the problem" and would have to relearn a variety of new family rules and "**scripts**" if the problem were to disappear. This fact helps to explain why it is often so difficult to solve problems, even when family members say they are committed to doing so.

Imagine, for example, a family in which one member has a "gambling problem." "The gambler" has lost large amounts of money over the years, is in constant debt to bookmakers, owes money to all his friends and relatives, and is on the verge of losing his job due to his obsession with "the horses." At home, when he makes a rare appearance, the gambler is a careless parent and thoughtless partner. He is depressed and drunk when he is losing money, which is most of the time. However, on those rare occasions when he has won some money, the gambler is a changed man: full of smiles, with gifts for everyone, plans for vacations, home improvements, and a better life. The family lives in hope of these rare happy times and in dread of the rest. As psychologists tell us, intermittent reinforcement is the strongest reinforcement. The pattern continues because people hope for the next return of good times.

A family that learns to live with these crazy alternations—the sudden wins and tragic losses, drunken tears and flattering compliments, the promises of repentance and pleas for mercy—may find it difficult to live an ordinary life, where people just go to work and school, save their money, eat meals together, and do everyday things. Some families may even fall apart when the daily excitement of risk and tragedy disappears.

Some Families Have More Problems Than Others

When we see families that have trouble coping with their problems, we should avoid "blaming the victim." Even when couples seem to collaborate in the continuation of a crazy life script—the French call this a *folie à deux*—or entire families turn a blind eye to the most outrageous antics by one of their members, there may be good reasons why they do so. People do not always deserve the problems they get, nor could they readily escape these problems if only they decided to change themselves or their families.

In fact, sociologists know that personal and family problems are socially structured: More problems beset some kinds of people than others. Typically, poor people have more problems than affluent people do. Likewise, people who are socially excluded or stigmatized, who suffer discrimination or contempt, have more problems than people who are accepted and even sought out. We like to say that "Money is at the root of all evil," and that "Power corrupts." However true these sayings may be, the only things worse than money and power are an absence of money and power. Consider poverty and its effects on family life.

The Culture of Poverty—Blaming the Victim

In sociology and anthropology there has been a long-running argument, carried over into the political field, over the origins of poverty and, particularly, who is to blame.

On the one side stand those who follow social thinkers of the last century, such as Herbert Spencer, who consider poverty a marker of human genetic "fitness" (or rather, unfitness). By this thesis, poor people are poor because they do not have the abilities to be anything else. A related argument known as the culture of poverty thesis holds that certain types of culture restrict people, prevent them from achieving their potential, and hence act to keep their members—groups, or even whole societies—in poverty.

Of course, definitions of poverty vary from one location to another, depending on what people do in their daily lives. Yet however we measure poverty, we find certain inconsistencies. People with less education, poorer health, or who live in economically depressed regions are more likely than average to be poor. Likewise, poor families are disproportionately found among Aboriginal Canadians or in families headed by female single parents.

There are reasons why we continue to blame people for their poverty, and they are linked to values that were important in the rise of capitalism itself. Max Weber, in his book *The Protestant Ethic and The Rise of Capitalism*, showed connections between the development of capitalist economies in Northwestern Europe, and religious attitudes influencing people's thoughts and behaviour. According to Weber, Calvinism and Catholicism emphasized different values: work for Calvinists, giving alms or charity for Catholics. For Weber, the attitudes expressed as part of Calvinist Protestantism were those that facilitated the development of capitalism and can explain why capitalism arose when it did, and where it did.

For the most part, these are the concepts most highly valued within North America. Capitalism could not have arisen without thrift and hard work, and the concept of investment. However, as Oscar Lewis, the anthropologist who coined the term "culture of poverty" points out, different cultures convey different values. For instance, where people do not learn to think of themselves as individuals, they do not act for themselves and may not try to rise above other family members.

Modern society requires work and initiative, the same values that were instrumental in the development of capitalism. Unfortunately, whole sectors of society have become caught in a series of poverty traps. Where children grow up seeing their parents dependent and ineffectual, they will absorb the culture of fatalism. People are socialized at an early age into the norms, values, and beliefs of their cultures, and the socialization may affect many of them for life.

The "culture of poverty" theory implies that people in poverty remain there and that the children of poor families themselves stay poor. However, many people's poverty cannot be accounted for by the theory. It is revealing to look at people who are poor today in North America. Some are unemployed and some of these are not seeking employment: the stereotypical "people on welfare." Many

Table 8.1 URBAN POVERTY IN CANADA: STATISTICAL PROFILE

	TOTAL	POOR	DIST. TOTAL	DIST. POOR	POVERTY RATE
All Persons	28 011 400	5 514 200	100%	100%	20%
Aged 0–14	5 737 000	1 344 500	20%	24%	23%
Aged 15–24	3 766 600	904 600	13%	16%	24%
Aged 25–34	4 400 800	895 000	16%	16%	20%
Aged 35–44	4 776 300	794 800	17%	14%	17%
Aged 45–54	3 650 900	511 000	13%	9%	14%
Aged 55–64	2 445 500	440 300	9%	8%	18%
Aged 65–74	2 000 300	334 100	7%	6%	17%
Aged 75+	1 233 900	289 900	4%	5%	23%
Females	14 235 700	3 015 300	51%	55%	21%
Males	13 775 700	2 498 900	49%	45%	18%

Source: Canadian Council on Social Development, 2000. www.ccsd.ca

others, however, are in the workforce and recent figures show a rise in the numbers of the "working poor."

Where people remain residents in areas where jobs are hard to get, we might expect them to move to other areas where jobs are more plentiful. However, moving may not be an option that appears to make much sense, particularly where people can contribute to their family economies in ways other than by directly earning a wage (such as by taking care of other family members, children, or elderly relatives). Moving may merely mean that the expenses for another household have to be found, somehow, with no guarantee of a job. If the only jobs to be found pay a minimum wage, earnings may actually fall below the poverty line for a household with one or more children to support, especially in an expensive city.

Rather than seeing poverty as a cultural phenomenon, we may better regard this as a reaction to the material situation of their lives, and to the ways that others treat them. It also seems odd that culture of poverty theorists stress familism as a problem when, throughout North American society, women are constantly being told that their first commitment should be to their children and other family members. However, many women on welfare say that they would welcome a chance to work—provided that they can find reliable, affordable childcare. Stories in the media tell of women who give up "good" jobs because they calculate that the financial costs associated with these jobs, particularly the costs of childcare, are so great as to make the job not worthwhile.

Middle-class, relatively well-off people often consider that poverty means simply being a bit short of cash and having to do some budgeting. However for many people in the impoverished areas of Toronto, Flin Flon, or Antigonish, being poor means not having enough money to pay the rent or power bills on a regular basis. "Budgeting" implies going to each company to whom the household is in debt and explaining, yet again, how much can be paid this month, so that power is not cut off or the family evicted.

Rather than look to the individuals for a reason for this incapacitation, we can look to the interaction between individuals and their society: How they are treated by officials and authorities, what rules are made concerning their employment and how much they can earn before deduction of benefits, what labels are applied to them by officialdom. Rather than blaming the victim, it makes sense for sociologists to ask how labelling comes about and how society is involved in it, how society constructs dependency in people so labelled, and how some groups have managed to break free of it.

Only by looking at the processes by which people struggle to make sense of, and overcome, their everyday obstacles can we hope to understand the experience of poverty. There is simply too much that this approach does not explain: such as how the same individual, given a change of circumstances, encouragement, and training, may behave in entirely different ways. We do far better to focus our attention on the role of capital: social capital, cultural capital, and of course, financial capital. We will do so in a later section.

Poverty and the Family

Poverty worsens virtually every kind of family problem, and some kinds of families are more likely to be poor. At bottom, poverty is rooted in the class structure. Unemployment often throws people into poverty. Poor health or addiction may throw people into poverty. Divorce may throw single mothers into poverty. Children born into poverty are more likely to grow up to be poor adults than comfortable, prosperous, or rich adults. People born rich are very unlikely to become poor, on the other hand. A number of factors ensure this: family connections, social and cultural capital, educational credentials, and inherited wealth, among other things.

Beyond these factors, family structure and age also play a part in impoverishing people. As we have seen in earlier chapters, female-headed lone-parent families are often impoverished. Other things (like education) being equal, old people are more likely to be impoverished than middle-aged people are. Children are also more likely to be impoverished than middle-aged people. In the United States, fully 34 percent of children (under age 17) will spend at least one year below the poverty line, and 18 percent will face extreme poverty (Rank & Hirschl, 1999). This problem will most significantly affect African-American children, children in nonmarried households, and children in households whose head received fewer than 12 years of education.

In Canada, we find higher than average poverty rates among First Nations families. Many impoverished Native families tend to be single-parent families with a large number of children and large households (Daly & Smith, 1996). In addition, compared to the Canadian average, the adults are younger, have lower education levels, and are more likely to be unemployed.

Racial discrimination can contribute to higher poverty rates among some families. In Canada, non-visible male and female immigrants have higher income advantages over visible minority men and women (Basavarahappa & Jones, 1999), suggesting racial prejudice against visible minorities. A similar U.S. study found that in 1995, whites had the lowest poverty rate of all racial/ethnic groups and Hispanics had the highest. In addition, the black and Hispanic poverty rates were almost three times those of whites (Sandefur et al., 1998). As we will see in the next section, issues of poverty often go hand in hand with racial discrimination, which can influence a person's earnings and the ability to support a family.

As we have said, education and unemployment also increase the risk of poverty within families, especially if the family depends on one family member as the sole source of income. A person who is highly educated is less likely to be unemployed and thus susceptible to poverty. This is reflected by statistics that show working-age adults with lower education being unduly represented in the poverty rates (Mcnamara & Ranney, 1999). However, a higher education does not guarantee riches in later life, as one can see by examining the poverty rates among immigrants to Canada. Other things being equal, immigrants coming from less-developed countries have lower incomes than native-born Canadians and immigrants from more-developed countries.

Poverty affects women more adversely than men, which has led some researchers to call the growth of poverty among women "the feminization of poverty." One study found that 50 percent of women do not earn enough to support a family at an adequate level even if they work full-time, all year round. Of these women, about half are supporting children and about 25 percent are the sole earners in the families (Spalter-Roth et al., 1990). A more recent though less systematic study of the same phenomenon, by Barbara Ehrenreich (2001), draws similar conclusions in a book titled *Nickel and Dimed*.

If one also considers the fact that women generally make less than men on average, the problem of poverty among single-parent families headed by the mother is more apparent. In addition, high rates of divorce and large numbers of single-parent families give rise to many women and children living in poverty. The feminization of poverty does not affect only younger women, however. Older women are largely excluded from pension coverage or have unstable pension plans at work (Farkas & O'Rand, 1998). This exclusion can increase the chance of living in poverty later in life, after retirement from work.

Nor are divorce and old age the only factors that interact with poverty to produce family problems. Chronic illness and disability also hinder many families. For example, poor mothers who care for children with disabilities experience more stresses than middle-class mothers caring for children with disabilities (Keller, 1999). In addition, poorer families face greater pressure to provide for extended family members. In Chapter 7 we discussed the increase of elder care among families. Poorer families who must care for ailing relatives experience more stress, because they have less money for the family (Glick, 2000). There may also be increased pressure on the elderly to share their meagre pensions with their children. Where poverty and unemployment are widespread, individuals may feel obliged to share their resources with their families, or else they might not be helped themselves later on when they are in need (Sagner & Mtati, 1999).

Living in poverty can affect the types of family unions people form. Generally, unemployment discourages low-income men from marrying (Testa et al., 1989). For example, among inner-city residents in Chicago, employed fathers are twice as likely as unemployed fathers to marry the mother of their first child. A rise in male joblessness, then, produces a rise in never-married parenthood in the inner city. This, in turn, increases the prevalence of single-parent families headed by mothers, and raises the risk of continued poverty in many families.

Poverty can harm families in other ways. For example, low-income parents may participate less often and less effectively in their children's schools than do middle- and upper-income parents (Diamond, 1999). Conversely, middle- and high-income parents exert a strong influence over their children indirectly as well as directly, by using the PTA and other methods to influence the school curriculum and school policies. They are also more likely to take actions to improve community and neighbourhood resources (policing, traffic patterns, parks, and recreation, for example). A classic work of sociology, *Crestwood Heights* by John Seeley (1958), documented these processes in a Canadian city.

Living in poverty can have extreme effects on the mental health of family members. A survey of households in Dresden (Germany) finds that repeated unemployment and the resulting poverty takes a toll on family relations. Levels of anxiety, depression, and conflict all increase, and marital relations worsen. In turn, bad marital and parental relationships, psychological distress, poor coping skills, and poor conflict management all make the effects of unemployment even worse (Nietfeld & Becker, 1999).

Poverty also has a harmful effect on the psychological health of children. Children whose parents are poor, or who have suffered severe economic losses, are likely to display higher than average rates of depression, anxiety, and antisocial behaviours (Samaan, 2000). McLeod and Shanahan (1993) also note that, among children, persistent poverty predicts feelings of anxiety, happiness, and dependence. It may not be the poverty *per se* that is causing these problems. In large part, the children are responding to their parents' anger or distress. A mother's low emotional responsiveness and frequent use of physical punishment, for example, may contribute to mental health problems in children living in poverty-stricken families (on this, see Jones et al., 2002).

Does Poverty Cause Mental Illness or Does Mental Illness Cause Poverty?

Poverty increases the level of stress in someone's life. The constant struggle to survive can take a great toll on their mental health, and bring about mental health problems. Clearly, it is easier to have good mental health if you have material comfort than if you live in poverty.

However, the causes of mental illness are varied and complex. It's hard to say that poverty alone directly causes mental illness. Mental illness occurs in all classes of society, and the great majority of people who live in poverty do not have mental illness.

Does mental illness cause poverty?

Having a mental illness can make it very hard to find a steady job. The chances of becoming poor are greater if someone is mentally ill. For instance, recent Canadian studies show that the numbers of homeless people with a mental illness are rising. Still, many people with mental illness hold down well-paid jobs. A key factor for many of these people is a strong support network of family and friends.

So we can say that poverty may contribute to mental health problems, and that mental illness can make it difficult to live above the poverty line. After that, the connections are not simple. Again, the support of family and friends is key. Poor people who don't have support networks are at higher risk of becoming mentally ill. Likewise, people with mental illness and no solid support networks are more likely to become and stay poor.

Source: The Canadian Mental Health Association (National Office) and the Canadian Mental Health Network.

These responses to adversity can vary dramatically from one cultural group to another. For example, African Americans, Native Americans, and Hispanics are less likely to report or be reported to have such mental health problems, compared with white Americans. A number of factors operate in poor communities to moderate the stresses of poverty: they include (perceived) social support, deep religiosity, spirituality, extended families, and maternal coping strategies. These all serve as buffers against psychological distress. Additionally, low expectations and an expertise in dealing with adversity may make it easier to cope with setbacks and hardships.

When combined with other social problems like crime and alcoholism, family relations under conditions of poverty can worsen sharply. For example, neighbourhood poverty has a more harmful effect on alcohol-related problems in black men than in white and Hispanic men (Jones-Webb et al., 1997). This racial difference is absent among more affluent men. Jones-Webb et al. conclude that neighbourhood poverty has more effect on alcohol problems for black men because they are more likely to live in neighbourhoods with low family incomes, high population densities, and easy retail access to alcohol. All the while, they are subject to social conditions (like poverty, discrimination, and low esteem) that increase the risks of alcohol-related problems.

Poverty and mental illness can create a vicious circle as poor people who don't have support networks are at higher risk of becoming mentally ill, while people with mental illness and no solid support networks are more likely to become and stay poor.

This may explain why the distribution of violent crime is heavily skewed towards younger, poorer, male minorities. A lack of legitimate job opportunities combines with beliefs and values that prevail in the neighbourhood to produce violent behaviour (Short, 1997). Violent cultural attitudes can also give rise to street gangs, which further concentrate poverty and destabilize conventional institutions, such as the family. Street gangs are more likely to resist and undermine adult authority, breeding the conditions for violent behaviour within communities and within families.

Nowhere are the effects of poverty and inequality on family relations as dramatic as they are among the homeless. Sometimes, adversity brings out the best in people. In the United States, some homeless mothers living in shelters report increased closeness and more and better interaction with their children. However, many others report the reverse: namely, that their parental roles as disciplinarians and providers, or caretakers, have been disrupted by homelessness. When adult parental roles—like the provider role—break down, discipline is hard to maintain. Other factors complicate parent–child relations among the homeless, including the mother's emotional state, the child's emotional state, and shelter conditions such as rules and interactions with staff and residents (Lindsey, 1998).

Poverty, unemployment, and homelessness have less harmful effects when family members are better able to cope with the difficulties they encounter. However, even the best prepared, best functioning family will suffer from poverty and unemployment.

Racism and the Family

If poverty is one source of family problems, racism is another affecting many aspects of a family's life. For example, U.S. census data indicate that, compared to white people, black people own homes of lower value regardless of their socioeconomic status or household structure (Horton & Thomas, 1998). Clearly, something is preventing black people from spending their money in the same ways as white people with the same incomes. That "something" is likely racism in the forms of prejudice, discrimination, and exclusion.

Housing wealth is arguably the most important form of personal asset, due to its considerable value and source of security for future generations (Flippen, 2000). The fact that black and Hispanic individuals do not own homes of the same value as whites contributes to residential segregation among the races and contributes to more concentrated low-income neighbourhoods and ghettos (Jargowsky, 1998). Multiracial families also suffer housing discrimination, contributing to the kind of homes these families will be offered and will eventually own (Dalmage, 2000).

Racism can impact the family in other ways, especially when combined with social problems such as crime and drug use. Among African-American youth, residence in underclass neighbourhoods contributes significantly to juvenile delinquency (Peeples & Loeber, 1994). Residence in an impoverished neighbourhood increases the risk of delinquent behaviour. Additionally, laws are enforced differently, for members of different races and classes. In juvenile court, minorities receive more formalized treatment, are detained more often, and are placed out of the home more often. Minority youth are also more likely to experience intrusive court interventions (Corley et al., 1996).

Higher delinquency, crime, and imprisonment rates are found among blacks rather than whites in the United States (Sampson & Lauritsen, 1997). Poverty interacts with family disruption to increase the risk of criminal behaviour. Since race is interacting with other social factors, it is hard to say how much of an individual's criminal behaviour is due to family disruption and how much is due to racial tensions.

Racism can also affect educational opportunities for children—including school quality and likelihood of school dropout—especially when combined with poverty. Race, along with poverty, is one of the key factors producing inequalities in school outcomes. No wonder, then, that Bankston and Caldas (1998) find low-income, minority-dominated schools show lower test scores than other schools.

A sense of mistreatment by major institutions may lead alienated minority children to abandon any effort to fit into conventional society. Many Aboriginal youth in Victoria, Australia, for example, prefer street life to the school setting as an alternative form of community. Other factors besides prejudice and lack of education and work opportunities may contribute to their dropping out—for example, abusive or negligent family life (Gardiner, 1997).

Racial issues can affect relations between individuals and so can affect the overall cohesion of the family. Consider the troubled relations between black men and women in the United Kingdom (James-Fergus, 1999). During the 1950s and 1960s, African-Caribbean women in the U.K. were the centres of family life, and they received little help from their male partners. By the 1990s, these women had achieved a degree of economic independence, but at the cost of added pressure on themselves and their children. Moreover, freedom meant that women were much more isolated from men. African-Caribbean males have been reluctant to recognize the new status of women, largely because they are under attack themselves—economically, culturally, and socially—from the larger society.

Racism increases the likelihood of joblessness for both minority-group mothers and fathers. This puts a strain on the marital relationship, which, many say, leads men to leave their families. In the United States, a similar problem—also unresolved—is increasing the numbers of "most disadvantaged children," children living in families that receive welfare and are headed by a jobless female. The fraction of children—especially young children—who live in such families is growing. Poverty rates miscalculate the extent of their disadvantage, its racial aspect, and the rapid rate at which an economic gap between the races is widening (Foster and Furstenberg, 1999).

Possible Solutions

Despite the problems that racism has posed for them, families still attempt to improve their situation and survive. Puerto-Rican families living in the U.S. survive through reliance on extended kinship and neighbourhood ties that are particularly helpful in times of crisis (Hidalgo, 1997). Similarly, African-American single-parent families develop strong extended kinship ties to survive (Battle & Bennet, 1997). Community, church, and family have always been important sources of strength for racial and ethnic minorities. In these ways, minority groups lessen the effects of racism, though they cannot eliminate them.

Some Problems Create Secondary Problems

Some families, especially socially vulnerable families, are forced to change rapidly and chaotically. This is often true of families in a war zone, of refugees, or of homeless people in our own society. To some degree, it is also true of families who are poor, unemployed, or socially excluded.

Often, the need for rapid change is a result of many problems building up and getting out of control. Domestic violence or poor parenting may result. For example, child neglect reflects stress, social isolation, and loneliness, although long-standing and pervasive character problems in both parents also contribute (Polansky, Gaudin, & Kilpatrick, 1992). Families in which parents neglect their children come disproportionately from minority groups, are often very poor and typically female-headed, and contain more children than similar non-neglectful households. Neglect is likely to be global rather than specific, and chronic rather than situational. Why do parents neglect their children? Usually, it is because the parents cannot cope with their lives: their disappointments, failures, regrets, and addictions. They lose their resilience and their ability to rebound from setbacks. They often lose the ability to care for themselves, so they can hardly care for children.

Some families, on the other hand, change very rapidly but intentionally. Sociologists are interested in learning why some families are better able to change, and control change, than other families. This is no simple question to answer. These families are able, for a variety of reasons, to seize new opportunities, as they become available. They migrate to the right places at the right times, see that their children get the right types and amounts of education, get into the right lines of work, and so on. They can prevent problems from accumulating and getting out of control. Change in families is moderated by the systemic nature of family relationships.

One important fact about families is that they are all "**social systems**." All systems—whether living or mechanical—resist change, but once change begins, any change sets off another. Families are social systems, and this means that each family member, each role, each activity, causes change and limits change in each other member, role, or activity.

Consider a common example: the inertia or sluggishness of family life. We tend to see other members of our family in fixed ways over long periods of time. We have trouble imagining them changing or accepting that they have changed even when others point out the changes to us. We feel sad or disoriented when our family gives up certain family rituals. Many of us oppose major changes in the domestic division of labour, especially if the new roles mean more work for us. More often than not, males—both younger and older—persist in teaching, learning, and practising traditionally sex-typed male chores around the household, for example (Record & Starrels, 1991). They may resist the efforts of mothers, daughters, and sisters to challenge and change the domestic division of labour.

What happens when Debby comes home from her Introductory Sociology class with new views about gender equality in the domestic division of labour? She questions the way things are done around her home and refuses to play the traditional female role. How will her family adjust to this new input? If Debby persists, and family roles are opened for discussion, decision-making and authority patterns—and the division of labour—will all be at risk of change. Many families resist such questioning and change. Conflict and opposition may result.

In living systems, however, changes are inevitable. One change leads to another, in unforeseen ways. For example, we know that when two divorced adults with children marry each other, problems often arise between the children of earlier marriages and their new parent and siblings. What began as a simple joining together of two partners in a committed relationship becomes the complex

Figure 8.2 DIVORCE BY DURATION OF MARRIAGE: 1998

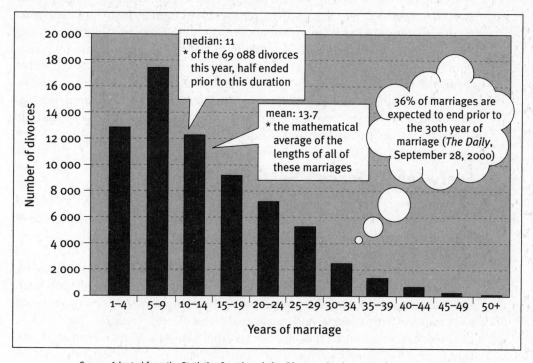

Source: Adapted from the Statistics Canada website, Divorces, Catalogue Number 84F0213XPB, Table 13, page 33.

joining of two social systems. Preventing a smooth and easy change are obstacles—system problems—like role confusion, conflicting family cultures, different ideas about child discipline, blurred family boundaries, and a feeling of unresolved grief over past relationships (Stern, 1984).

In turn, these system problems may create additional problems; for example, conflicts between the newly married partners. One study (Barber & Lyons, 1994) surveyed tenth graders from intact families and remarried families. It found that remarried families are more conflictual and less cohesive than intact families, and in both types of family, conflict affects adolescents' adjustment. Thus, the attempt to create a new, cohesive family through remarriage unintentionally produces conflict and problems for teenagers.

Family conflict increases the chance of delinquency by the children, for example (Downs & Robertson, 1991). Growing up in a family with divorced parents may even lead to a child running away, if family conflict deprives the child of an early close attachment (Tavecchio, Thomeer, & Meeus, 1999). As we note in our earlier chapter on parenting, runaways often come from disturbed, conflict-ridden families. Often, homeless teens are fleeing sexual and other abuse at home, and such abuse is more common where stepparents are involved.

Divorce and remarriage also affect sibling relations, and as a result child development. Two types of family change—foster-care placements and parental divorce—often separate siblings. Children separated from their siblings experience more instability than children who remain with their siblings. Children in foster care who have been separated from their siblings have a greater than average number of placements, suggesting that they get into more trouble. Children separated from their siblings by divorce tend to change homes more often, also suggesting a more troubled childhood adjustment. Overall, separating siblings cuts children off from a part of their social support system and has long-term effects on the sibling relationship (Drapeau et al., 2000).

Every Family Faces a System of Problems

As we've seen, family problems often mount up and lead to new problems. Further, these problems are interconnected, so that solving only one problem is difficult. We should, therefore, think about the systemic relationship between problems that a family faces.

Consider as an example, the problems associated with paid work. Paid work, as we saw in Chapter 7, The Domestic Division of Labour: Gender and Housework, can cause strains in the family, especially when one or more earners are in the early stages of a professional and managerial career (Mortimer, 1980). That's because paid work takes so much time and energy that many partners have a hard time keeping up their marriage, and many parents have a hard time caring for their children. All family members have to make do with less love and support than they might wish for. The adult family members often have more work to do and less free time to relax with one another than they require. More often than not, the burden of reconciling work and family life falls on mothers (Wolcott & Glezer, 1995). In the face of this, many adults—including mothers—retreat into their work, finding their workplaces more relaxing and pleasant than their homes.

These problems are connected. As long as the family members are chasing multiple career and family goals—including paid work, maintaining a household, and raising children—they will predictably face conflicting demands for their time, energy, and loyalty.

Or consider another systemic problem: the strains caused by adolescence and a teenager's needs to **individuate**, to separate psychically from one's parents. Family members often want to maintain their traditional patterns and ways of doing things, their *esprit de corps*. They want to continue thinking of their child in the old ways. Efforts by the adolescent to individuate put this *esprit de corps* at risk. Perhaps this is why problems arise at this time: they help to hide the real problem. For example, a problem such as anorexia, which may arise among adolescent women, hides the problem. Not eating delays the bodily changes associated with puberty. Eating too little is an easy way to stop this physical and sexual change. The family focuses all its effort on trying to get the adolescent to eat, thus increasing its cohesion and maintaining the illusion of a family group without conflict. Parents, then, have a chance to show their love and concern, as they did when the girl was younger. The daughter's "unacceptable" desire to individuate is hidden (Mille et al., 1996). Obviously, this is only a temporary, and dangerous, solution to the conflict caused by individuation, but it happens anyway.

Another systemic problem, unemployment, deprives a family of its income and deprives the wage earners of their status as "normal" upstanding members of society. Family conflict may result. Longitudinal research on 700 families finds that adolescents whose parents have lost their jobs report the highest levels of misbehaviour, financial anxiety, and conflict with parents, and the lowest levels of school adjustment. Adolescents whose parents find new jobs report a reduction in parent–child conflict when their parents return to work (Flanagan, 1988). In short, unemployment leads to more family conflict, more misbehaviour, and worsened school performance. What starts as "job loss" becomes a major catastrophe for the family.

The Generation Gap: One More Systemic Problem

The problem of anorexia that grows out of individuation, which we discussed above, is only one example of family conflict that can result from intergenerational differences.

Intergenerational conflict has been an interest of sociologists at least since the early twentieth century, when sociologists Thomas and Znaniecki (1925) studied the growth of conflicts between Polish peasants who had immigrated to America, and their children. With immigration, traditional norms, values, and roles started to break down. Authority and discipline were harder to enforce. Children were relatively more powerful in America than their immigrant parents.

Individual assimilation is common among immigrants, and especially among second and subsequent generations of those born in Canada. At the same time, ethnic residential communities and organizations persist for many immigrant groups (Darroch, 1981; Reitz, 1983). Conflicting pressures to assimilate and remain the same tug at immigrants. Ethnic assimilation, for reasons of size and organization, is more rapid in some communities than others, and as a result, intergenerational cultural conflict is greater in some communities than others. Many immigrants and their children also experience internal conflicts resulting from these opposing tugs.

For example, in Canada conflict arises between young South-Asian children and their immigrant parents, as the young people attempt to stay involved in their traditional community while also pursuing the types of leisure that are typical of Canadian young adults (Tirone & Pedlar, 2000). Family life remains a valued and central aspect of the young people's lives. However, conflict emerges within some families as the children begin to acculturate. Family conflicts then often emerge around issues of recreation, career choice, or cross-ethnic dating, for example.

Certain parenting styles produce fewer issues of ethnic conflict and generation gap than others. Better parenting—in the form of more attachment and more sensitive monitoring—often helps to solve the problem. Among low income, multi-ethnic adolescents age 10 to 14 in the U.S., better parenting moderates the link between family conflict and conduct problems (Formoso, 2000).

Some coping strategies unexpectedly produce more problems than they solve. A U.S. study of Chinese-American children, for example, found that parental teaching was the most important means of passing on (Chinese) language proficiency. Parents put the most pressure on first or only children, and children with fewer siblings, to learn Chinese (Cheng & Kuo, 2000). As a result, these children are more likely to rebel against the cultural traditions, making the problem of intergenerational differences worse and increasing family conflict.

Not only do intergenerational conflicts with children pose problems for families; so do intergenerational conflicts with elders. Williams et al. (1999) find a greater degree of stress and unhappiness in families where seniors are not consulted in family decisions. Often, the rest of the family views certain matters differently from their aging parents. To reduce conflict, adult children do not include the seniors in making major decisions. This practice generates a sense of worthlessness in the elderly. It deprives the family of valuable experience that the elderly might have contributed. Most important, it creates a conflictual, uncooperative atmosphere in which the elders may resort to passive resistance, complaining, or other means of registering protest.

Among immigrant families, intergenerational differences often create more conflict with daughters and sisters than with sons and brothers. This is because views about gender equality are changing so rapidly, and prevailing Canadian views may disagree with the views that prevailed in the immigrants' homeland. Traditional ideas about a gendered division of labour at home are particularly likely to cause conflict (Noivo, 1994), especially for women who have embraced Canada's more egalitarian view of the status and employability of women.

As mentioned earlier, intergenerational conflict can start with certain types of parenting styles. Many parents would like their children to maintain a sense of pride in their heritage and perhaps, in time, pass it on to their own children. However, some parents are ill equipped to teach ethnic values and skills to their children. Sometimes, they unwittingly show that they are ambivalent about the traditional culture or even prefer assimilation into the dominant culture.

For example, the immigrant Virasaiva community in the U.S. and Canada is at risk of rapid assimilation into the dominant culture. Parents are not adequately prepared to provide the religious, language, and cultural training that preserves their heritage (Chekki, 1996). Some solutions include improving the Virasaiva educational system and embedding the entire family in the culture. However, these solutions are hard to accomplish, requiring a great deal of what sociologist Raymond Breton (1972) called "institutional completeness" within the ethnic community.

Table 8.2   MEDIAN AGE BY CENSUS METROPOLITAN AREA (CMA), 1996 AND 2001

CMA	1996	2001	CHANGE
St. John's	33.3	36.3	3.0
Halifax	34.3	36.6	2.3
Saint John	35.1	37.9	2.8
Chicoutimi–Jonquière	36.1	39.8	3.7
Québec	36.7	39.5	2.8
Sherbrooke	35.5	38.1	2.6
Trois-Rivières	37.6	41.2	3.6
Montréal	36.0	37.9	1.9
Ottawa–Hull	34.6	36.6	2.0
Quebec Part	33.8	36.5	2.7
Ontario Part	34.9	36.7	1.8
Kingston	35.3	38.1	2.8
Oshawa	33.6	35.8	2.2
Toronto	34.6	36.2	1.6
Hamilton	36.1	37.8	1.7
St. Catharines–Niagara	37.6	40.2	2.6
Kitchener	33.5	35.3	1.8
London	34.7	36.9	2.2
Windsor	34.8	36.0	1.2
Greater Sudbury	35.2	38.9	3.7
Thunder Bay	36.1	39.1	3.0
Winnipeg	35.2	37.3	2.1
Regina	33.6	35.9	2.3
Saskatoon	32.7	34.4	1.7
Calgary	33.7	34.9	1.2
Edmonton	33.7	35.4	1.7
Abbotsford	33.5	35.4	1.9
Vancouver	35.5	37.4	1.9
Victoria	38.7	41.0	2.3
All CMAs	35.1	37.0	1.9

Source: Adapted from the Statistics Canada website, www12.statcan.ca/english/census01/Products/Analytic/companion/age/cmat.cfm.

Another Canadian study of Italian immigrants to Montreal finds similar problems. A majority of these immigrants became manual labourers when they moved to Canada. In coming to Canada, they hoped for upward social mobility and the creation of a vibrant local community. By raising their families in Canada, they have largely achieved these goals. However, in exchange they have detached themselves from their original Italian roots through prolonged contact with Canada's individualism and accelerated work pattern (Peressini, 1994). They have sacrificed community life to achieve upward social mobility. This has led their children to feel detached from the traditional culture, and has increased intergenerational differences. The children lack a community cultural base the parents have not had time to build. This makes them more likely to assimilate into the dominant culture, much to the chagrin of their parents, who still desire the local community of like minds.

Intergenerational conflict can have a number of consequences, including delinquent behaviour. For example, Laotian immigrants in California have entered the underclass and experience high rates of poverty. As a result, second-generation Laotian girls are exposed to ideas about gender and ethnicity that conflict with their community traditions and contribute to intergenerational differences. Attempts to keep the family cohesive, through family gatherings and other means, offer them a source of kinship and sense of belonging. Yet family relationships are filled with conflict and alienation. These competing cultural practices and beliefs have led some Laotian youth to involve themselves in risky behaviours, around sex, drinking, and otherwise (Shah, 2000).

Intergenerational differences are not always a source of conflict, however. In a highly cohesive and prosperous ethnic community, traditional ethnic ties may be profitable and benefit young people. For example, many Asian-American adolescents still exhibit Eastern values once they get older, though they showed some initial curiosity about Western values when they were younger (Ying et al., 1999). Among Portuguese-Canadians, members of the older generation influence the family life choices and contribute to the social mobility of younger family members. Cultural minority families help to ensure the economic survival of younger generations and maintain strong family cohesion by drawing on ethnic cultural traditions and sharing family resources (Noivo, 1993). Thus, there are fewer intergenerational conflicts among these groups.

Aboriginal families in West Kimberley, Australia, hope to reverse some of the negative aspects of assimilation, and in doing so instill cultural pride. The transition from gatherer-hunter to pastoral worker in this community has meant the replacement of meaningful work with welfare dependency and the culture of alcohol abuse. Reacting against this, many parents are trying to raise a generation of young people who protect the land and reproduce traditional culture, through socially useful activity (Shaw & Dann, 1999). It is harder to do this when traditional communities are smaller, less prosperous, and less institutionally complete than the dominant society or competing ethnic communities.

Stress and Burnout

Employers believe that stress is the basis of more than one-quarter of sick time reported by employees, a finding reported in a 1991 survey by the Canadian Institute of Stress. From 10% to 15% of Canada's work force is beleaguered by serious or chronic personal problems that affect job performance, estimates the Canadian Mental Health Association.

An individual's ability to tolerate stress depends on the frequency, severity and types of stressors confronted. It also depends on intrinsic or personal characteristics, including:

- Past experiences
- Personal values and attitudes
- Sense of control
- Personality
- Residual stress level
- General state of health

A number of external or organizational factors contribute to stress, such as:

- Work overload and family conflict
- Lack of autonomy or control
- Threat of job loss
- Role conflict or role ambiguity
- Interpersonal conflicts or external agency conflicts
- Organizational culture and environment
- Insufficient resources
- Inadequate job training or over qualification for current position
- Supervisor's attitudes
- Changes in organization structure

Source: Stress and Burnout, http://www.csc-scc.gc.ca/text/pblct/forum/e04/e041e_e.shtml, Public Service Commission of Canada, 1991. Reproduced with the permission of the Minister of Public Works and Government Services, 2003.

Other Problems

As we have seen through examples in the preceding sections, problems come in clusters and build on one another. Given the **inertia** in families, most attempts at change mean overcoming resistance. Any single change may set off as many as four different kinds of additional changes to the family system: new ways of earning an income and paying the bills, new ways of setting goals and making decisions, new ways of controlling deviance and resolving conflict, and new sources of belief and shared meanings. Without such extensive changes, there may be no way to solve the conflict between work life and family life, no solution to the problem of anorexia and delayed adulthood, and no reduction of intergenerational conflict, for example.

No wonder problems like work overload, anorexia, unemployment, and assimilation are so stressful, conflict-producing and sometimes even frightening for parents and children. They profoundly affect family life, by creating and maintaining other problems. Beyond that, many have a third common feature: they are linked to some fundamental problem in the way society is organized.

Public Issues and Private Troubles

The problems that families face often have structural origins and can be solved only by addressing these origins through public policy-making. Family policy is a way to put resources at the disposal of families so they can carry out their social tasks. In this context, a public discussion of family dynamics and the role of the state are crucial to effective policy (Meil & Landwerlin, 1992). Let us consider four problems that are in need of policies.

First, the **privatization of family life** since the industrial revolution has meant that we are all coping with our own family problems, often unaware that other families face these same problems. Given our seemingly unique family problems and conflicts, we may feel singularly, secretly deviant and inadequate. If only we knew the truth, we might help one another by pooling our ideas and resources. We would also feel empowered to seek changes in public policy that would help many families, including our own.

An example is the growing practice of commuter marriage (Gerstel & Gross, 1986), defined as a marriage in which employed partners spend at least three nights per week in separate homes, with both seeking to preserve the family unit while meeting career goals. Among immigrants from some countries, the commuting pattern is international and infrequent. Such immigrants are sometimes called "astronauts" because they are so far away and spend so much time in the air. The loss of proximity interferes with the performance of marital and parental roles. Policies may be needed to make travel and communication easier and cheaper for these commuters.

Or, consider the impact of population aging on care for aging parents. In many societies, children take responsibility for overseeing the care of elderly parents. This practice is far less common in industrial and post-industrial societies. In Singapore, the government has attempted to re-invigorate this traditional practice by underwriting part of the cost of new-home purchases for children who agree to buy homes near their aging parents. In Canada, governments have done nothing as imaginative to stimulate families to help themselves by rewarding children who care for their parents or making it easier for children and parents to get together.

Second, families are increasingly subject to the **influence of non-family institutions** like the workplace, school, government, and the economy. As families have lost traditional functions—especially education, entertainment, moral training, and job preparation—states and private organizations have claimed them. Whether for better or worse, families are acclimatizing to this large-scale change. Urbanization, opportunities for women, and changing family dynamics have altered social norms relating to multiracial marriage, divorce, abortion, and shifting family structures. In turn, these have altered the government's influence on family life (Imbrogno, 1989).

However, changes in the power and self-esteem of women and children have the potential to create conflicts within the family, as family members adjust to the new social order. Some refer to a crisis in men's family roles caused by the modern market economy, which has undermined men's traditional role as "breadwinner" (Soley, 1999). Highly educated women now earn more and have more influence in family decision-making. This change in the position of women is undermining patriarchy in one society after another (Saha, 1991). There is no question that thinner boundaries between the intimate, family sphere and the public spheres of work and state have forced families to adjust rapidly and continuously. The state and workplace have been far slower to change, for their part.

Third, the triumph of mass media as the chief definers of Western culture has meant a triumph of idealized, imaginary family life over real family life. Since all real families fall short of the imaginary families we see on television, many people live in a state of constant disappointment and misinformation. The mass media perpetuate stereotypical attitudes about family life. Too many people rely on the "dream factory" to teach them how to deal effectively with real partners, real children and parents, and real problems.

One of the jobs of a book like this, and the course in which you are reading it, is to bring some reality to the popular thinking, and debates, about family life. We cannot hope for changes that will make workplaces and states more "family-friendly" unless there is a general understanding that the family problems people face are systemic and widespread, not mere personal troubles. This means overcoming the fantasy trap produced by our media.

Fourth, industrialization and computerization have meant dramatic **changes in family relations**—in the relations between men and women, parents and children. Globalization too has meant dramatic shifts in the relations between older and younger generations, and between local and metropolitan family cultures. Throughout the world we find a struggle to balance traditional values and modern practices, and this struggle is shaping family dynamics, popular culture, education and the socialization of children, women's roles, and support for the elderly. The women's movement, among others, has played a key part in making these changes visible and political.

Such shifts in family relations have been going on in the West at least since the mid- to late-nineteenth century and they show no sign of abating. They provide the cultural and social context within which people today have to work out their sexual, social, economic, and domestic lives. There is no turning back to an idealized, fantasized past; even if we wanted to replay the past, this is never an option. The question today is how to solve the problems of today with solutions that will also work tomorrow. Moreover, our institutional and personal changes need to fit a wide variety of family forms and family stages.

Change and the Life Cycle

As we have seen in this book, families follow a "life cycle." The newly formed couple has certain problems to solve, which are usually different from the problems they will face five years later after bearing their first infant, fifteen years later when they have teenaged children at home, or thirty years later when they face an empty nest, retirement, and perhaps the start of failing health.

Change is often difficult. What makes social life regular and predictable, despite change and occasional turmoil, is that every family is largely self-anchoring. Like any organization, group, or society, a family is locked into certain modes of thinking and behaving. There are various reasons for this: among others, the strength of family culture, the dominance and interest of certain individuals (e.g., parent over child, husband over wife), and the use of routines to meet family obligations (e.g., to work every day to pay the mortgage). A change of patterns and routines can produce turmoil, even violence. For example, the risk of domestic violence increases when a woman is pregnant, especially if that pregnancy is unwanted. Typically, the child's father perpetrates this violence

Change can help or hinder a family, often unexpectedly. In predicting how a family will respond to the problems associated with childbirth, for example, a lot depends on the family, its organization, and its history. Different couples face the problems in different ways. Though relationship satisfaction changes in complicated ways with the birth of a first child, the types of changes that occur depend on whether the couple planned the pregnancy, the gender of the unplanned child, and the couple's problem-solving abilities.

After the birth of an unplanned child, partners often interact less positively, particularly if the unplanned child is a daughter. For all parents, good problem-solving skills are important. Better problem-solving skills result in more marital satisfaction before the birth of a child and less decline afterward. For marital satisfaction to stay high, at least one partner has to be good at solving problems. Couples particularly benefit if the husband has strong interpersonal skills and provides a lot of "relationship talk" after the birth (Coxet et al., 1999).

Not only do families change organizationally over time, but individual family members change too. They grow, mature, and decline in a variety of ways, socially, psychologically, physiologically, and otherwise, and these changes usually affect interactions with other family members. For example, as they approach adulthood, adolescents typically become more independent and develop a stronger sense of self.

Family rituals—complex, meaningful patterns of interaction—are often used to mark these changes in the lives of family members. Rituals and traditions are important to families as sources of strength, maintain a family's system of shared behaviours and beliefs, and convey its identity. Rituals also strengthen families by linking practices, beliefs, and values across generations (Newell, 1999). So, the collapse of family ritual is itself a new problem that needs solving.

Sometimes, the changes of individual family members are out of synch with one another. Some members may be changing more rapidly or radically than others. Such out-of-phase changes can cause conflict. For example, students leaving home for college may not only change their own lives but also those of their parents too (Holmstrom, Gray, & Karp, 1999). While often their departure improves relations between the parents, in some families it loosens the glue that has held a couple together for many years, and the parents separate.

Or, consider life cycle changes that are common among elderly people. Some older couples visit therapists to complain about their marital conflict or in hopes of gaining more satisfaction from the relationship. Some of their problems may date from the beginning of the relationship, while others may be of recent origin, following some change in the couple's situation, such as retirement. Some of their problems as a couple may relate to the development of a chronic illness or impairment, which upsets the balance of power and caring in the relationship. Others still may relate to the sharpening of conflicts, new or old, with their grown children (Florsheim & Herr, 1990: 40).

Or, consider the change in power relations within a family when married men approach retirement. They know that their income and social status will soon decline and they begin a process of anticipatory socialization that Kulik and Bareli (1997) call "anticipated dependence." The more a husband expects to become dependent on his wife to satisfy his emotional and social needs, and the more committed he is to his wife, the more he sees the balance of power tilting in his wife's favour. Many husbands begin this process of anticipated dependence well before they retire, very gradually changing the whole nature of the marital relationship.

These kinds of family life cycle changes are predictable; often they are gradual and progressive. Some families are better able than others to adapt to such changes over the life cycle. In part, their success depends on their cohesion and flexibility. In part, it depends on other resources we shall discuss later in this chapter.

However, some changes to families and their members are sudden, unexpected, unusual, and impossible to anticipate. These are usually the hardest changes to adapt to. During middle and later life, many emerging mental problems—sexual problems, substance abuse, psychosomatic problems, issues related to retirement or menopause—are a result of increased stress that is unmediated by social support or effective coping strategies (Kahana & Kahana, 1982). Elderly people experience many interpersonal losses—partner, siblings, and peers—and these losses have a direct impact on all the generations of the family. They call everyone's attention to mortality and the generational shifts occurring in the family (Brody, 1972).

Consider what happens when elderly parents experience a traumatic event—for example, the death of a partner. In these instances, many stay in their home. However, some move in with their children, sometimes disrupting their children's families. Some move away from their families to start new lives. For others still, a death or divorce leads to living alone. Often, the strategy adopted depends on income; elderly people with lower incomes are more likely to stay with their children, whatever the consequences, because they cannot afford to do otherwise (Chen, 1999).

However, despite all the problems we have considered, we should not despair. Not only do all families have problems, all families also solve problems.

Figure 8.3 HIGH LEVELS OF SOCIAL SUPPORT, BY HOUSEHOLD TYPE AND BY SEX, AGE 12+, CANADA, 1996–1997.

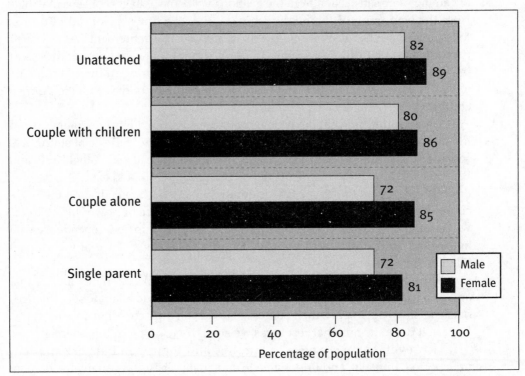

Source: Adapted from the Statistics Canada website, National Population Health Survey. 1996–97, special tabulations, www.statcan.ca/english/freepub/82-570-XIE/30_35.pdf.

Families Change in Patterned Ways

Each of us—each of the six billion humans alive today—is unique. Similarly, every family is unique, in the sense that no two families do things in the same way. However, most families are also very similar in that most experiences are repeated, many with tedious regularity.

It is within this context of similarity and predictability that all families are unique. Families, being little societies, all have their own history, culture, language, myths, pet peeves, irrational fears, and blind enthusiasms. They solve their problems within the context of their own unique history, culture, and language.

Each family has its own story, myth, or metaphor by which it sees and talks about itself. One family reveals, through both the content and the nature of its narrative, a thread of positive transgenerational relationships. For example, its members may emphasize that the family started in a foreign country and arrived in North America poor, isolated, unassisted. It survived and flourished through the gifts and devotion of its ancestors. Another family, asked to describe its history, dwells on a series of failed relationships, premature deaths—even suicides—and other sordid tales of abuse, violence, and humiliation. We may find such different family cultures in the very same ethnic group, class, and neighbourhood. These life stories do not merely reflect reality; they play a role in making it. Other things being equal, families with "survival myths" about themselves are far more likely to overcome adversity than families with "failure myths" (Khandelwal, 1999).

Likewise, every family has a point of view (or points of view) about different lifestyles. For example, some deplore homosexuality, others are indifferent, and some may embrace it. If a family has a negative view of homosexuality—its meaning, its origins, its consequences—and one family member has just "come out" (i.e., revealed his or her homosexuality), this poses problems that the family must confront in its own unique way, at its own pace. It must, in its own terms, make sense of this development and find a formula for accepting it.

Research on the coming-out process has investigated how family dynamics affected the experiences of both children and parents after the discovery that a child is homosexual. Many parents react with shock, disappointment and shame when they learn of a child's gay sexual orientation. A variety of factors may be involved in parents' decision to accept a child's homosexuality, including beliefs about the causes of homosexuality, the way that the parents view their pasts and futures, and strategies for minimizing disruptions to their lives (Aveline, 2000). Also, the parents' final feelings depend not only on their personal views, but also the perceived reactions of other relatives and people outside the family. A sympathetic, open, or welcome reaction is less likely to produce general family disruption.

Educating parents about homosexuality before the act of disclosure can prevent disruption. Ensuring that parents do not learn about homosexuality while finding out that their child is gay often eases parents' adjustment to the discovery, and even improves emotional dynamics within the family (Ben Ari, 1995). Lesbians and gay men need support as they struggle to cope with their parents' negative reactions. Family members need to talk non-combatively after the disclosure, even if contacts are brief and superficial (La Sala, 2000).

All Families Solve Problems

Amazingly, families, like other human groups, often become very good at solving problems and resolving their conflicts. In this respect, families—as complex systems of relationships and activities—are more like organic systems (e.g., living cells or ecosystems) than they are like mechanical systems (e.g., clocks or computers). Families can change themselves in response to changes in their environment and are capable of learning from their mistakes and changing by design, because they comprise human actors.

Human beings, though in some respects "programmed" or socialized to act in certain ways, are nonetheless able to change when necessary. All of us have changed dramatically over our lives, sometimes unintentionally or unwittingly.

Sometimes we have willed change, planned it, and carried it out to accomplish an important goal. Families do the same thing by setting goals and identifying strengths. Methods of changing family dynamics include changing beliefs, changing positions and roles in the family, building a sense of optimism, and developing social interest (Dinkmeyer & Sherman, 1989).

Many families also show an astonishing ability to bounce back from adversity. In the face of difficult situations such as isolation, hostile environments, lack of educational tradition, linguistic and cultural adjustment, conflict between home and school, and neglect, among others, the family was still able to survive. Coping strategies that make this possible include perseverance, resistance, friendly competition, faith and spirituality, putting an optimistic spin on the journey, creating distance, and adjusting (Phillips, 2001). These strategies help to avoid complete family breakdown in the face of adversity.

Solving problems is easiest if the parties to a dispute are like-minded. No wonder, then, that similarity is so important in an intimate relationship. Similarity in perceptions between partners is a crucial dimension of the family system. The members of better-functioning couples have more similar perceptions of their marriage and their family. This similarity between partners, which tends to be stable over time, supports family cohesion and is supported by it (Deal, Wampler, & Halverson, 1992). In turn, similar parents are likely to produce children who are also similar—in effect, reproducing their own views in their children. This shared similarity makes family life far simpler.

Seeking and achieving similarity with your environment is a way of simplifying your life and reducing personal stress. In research on people's responses to learning that they are HIV-positive, Behrens (1998) notes that people under stress restructure their network of friends so that they have frequent contact with people who are most similar to themselves. This similarity allows for more stable interaction, thereby helping them to cope with their stress. It makes sense, then, that married couples who are more similar have more stable interactions, since they are more likely to draw on each other for support in times of stress.

Well-functioning families set goals, plan for them, and accomplish them. Consider students reading this book: you, for example, may be the first member of your family to receive a post-secondary education. That is an accomplishment that required goal setting and planning, by you and maybe by your family. Transitions from adolescence to adulthood often involve much storm and stress, particularly if there is too little cohesion, caring, and quality family time to buffer the changeover. Where there is a support system in place, the change can go smoothly (Chen, 1999).

In well-functioning families, problem solving is an educative process of self-discovery. Families learn different ways to resolve conflict and change disabling ways of dealing with one another (Praetz & Eastman, 1980). Often, this is important in emotionally charged situations. Consider mothers' experiences of an adult child's HIV/AIDS diagnosis. Initial responses often include intense personal and emotional reactions. These mothers are inclined to lay blame, often on themselves. They must learn to face their feelings of guilt and personal responsibility for the adult child's illness before they can play an active role in supporting their children (Thompson, 2000).

What works well in family conflicts is largely the same as what works in courts of law: namely, openness and procedural justice. One study (Fondacaro, Dunkle, & Pathak, 1998) asked 240 participants aged 18 to 22 to recall an important family dispute that they experienced over the past year and rate how their parents handled the situation. Overall, respondents associated procedural fairness and specific aspects of fairness—neutrality, trust, and respectfulness—with family cohesion and psychological well-being. The same practices tended to reduce family conflict, psychological distress, and deviant behaviour. Disrespectful treatment was the single best predictor of deviant behaviour by these adolescents.

Said another way, this research shows that a family functions well if its members feel they can get a fair hearing, even if their views do not always prevail. The first steps toward changing and resolving conflict require laying down ground rules that everyone views as fair.

Some Families Need Help Solving Their Problems

We should not imagine that every problem—whether individual or familial—can be solved through therapy or counselling or by relying on relatives. Some problems are so widespread and inherent in the way society is organized that only a change in society can deal with them effectively. Without social change, family change may not reduce the number of problems family members face. Take one example: the problems that families face living in cities. For decades, urban decay and economic upheaval have been altering family relations and norms, particularly among people with the fewest resources (Farber, 1999). This is a source for concern because, paradoxically, in our crumbling welfare state, families continue to be a main source of social solidarity. Even unemployed family members continue to protect and care for many of society's most defenceless, dependent members (Moral, 1999).

People do not typically grow up knowing how to conduct their personal affairs, or family lives, in the best possible way. We all enter adulthood, intimate relations, marriage, and parenthood untrained and inexperienced, and we have to muddle through somehow. No wonder we have problems co-operating to change effectively. Yet, though all families change and solve problems, some families do so better, easier, and faster than others. There are reasons why families vary in this way.

Some of these are historic reasons. Some people have grown up with the benefit of experience in well-functioning families in which people co-operate to solve their problems. They know that it is possible to make plans, carry out plans, and achieve success. They know that this can be done without excess conflict, let alone violence.

There are also *systemic* reasons why some families solve their problems more easily. To set goals, make plans, and carry them out, families need leadership. Some families have stronger traditions of leadership than others. The stronger ones contain individuals who are willing to take responsibility for the family interest and attempt to mobilize support for a plan of action. Improvements in family relationships are more likely in homes where the parent(s) can describe strategies for fostering family ties, showing that he or she has spent time thinking about the problem. Improvements are also more likely in homes where a parent can describe ways of helping change in key areas of the residents' lives (Gibbs & Sinclair, 1999).

Families with stronger traditions of leadership, co-operation, and communication are more readily able to talk about their problems and their plans. They can sort out who is to do what, and why. The results are visible across many outcomes. For example, among the families of patients surviving bone marrow transplants and maintenance chemotherapy, strong family relationships are associated with better adjustment in every respect: physical, emotional, and social (Molassiotis, Van den Akker, & Boughton, 1997).

Besides benefiting from inner strengths, some families rely on the support of extended, even multigenerational kin. Grandparents, for example, can be important sources of wisdom and relative disengagement from many family conflicts. As mentors, grandfathers often contribute positively to the lives their grandchildren; they gain from the relationship too, through an opportunity to review and assess their own lives (Waldrop et al., 1999). Grandmothers give emotional support to their grandchildren and provide advice and guidance. They often continue to provide support as their grandchildren become young adults and remain an important part of their grandchildren's social support network (Block, 1999). As a result, grandmothers play an important role in developing competence and resilience in their grandchildren, under what may sometimes be difficult family conditions (Cox, 2000).

African Americans, among others, further increase their extended kin supports by using **fictive kin** relations. By giving and receiving fictive kin statuses, people who are otherwise unrelated by either blood or marriage assume responsibilities in each other's families and are rewarded by familial respect. African Americans expect fictive kin to participate in the duties of the extended family and view one another in kinship terms (Chatters, Taylor, & Kayakody, 1994). Like grandparents, these "uncles" and "aunts" and "cousins" can become important fixtures in family life, and important social supports in times of trouble.

Families that need outside help solving their problems, however, can often get the help they need. Some get it from friends or workmates. Some seek family therapy, counselling, or family mediation, which help different kinds of families to different degrees; often, anticipating what kind of help will work best is impossible. The role of a therapist—indeed, any helper—is, often, to help the family understand the situation in a way that enables them to act (Lyons, 1982).

Table 8.3 RESOLVING FAMILY CONFLICTS

The Problem-Solving Process

Families who successfully and quickly resolve problems have developed skills to manage their difficulties. They are aware of the steps in the problem-solving process and they consistently implement them to resolve problems. Problem-solving is a process skill that, like other skills, can be learned by the family. The following six steps will assist you in establishing a problem-solving process in your family.

Problem Identification and Agreement

Families may identify the instrumental problem but miss the affective side and wonder why the issue wasn't resolved. A family member may feel his or her feelings were not heard or addressed and will not agree to go along with the solution until the hurt feelings are dealt with. Therefore, families must practice problem identification and agreement as the first step in problem-solving.

Creating Options and Alternatives

Encourage brainstorming without evaluating the ideas until many options are on the table. The creative options step leads to effective solutions to problems.

Options should take into account both instrumental and emotional issues and should include all family members who are affected by the issue.

Evaluate Alternatives

Eliminate the alternatives that the family is unwilling to try. The goal is to find an option that each family member will agree to consider. Next, decide whether or not the family has the resources to carry out the alternative.

The goal is to find an alternative that each family member will agree to consider.

Choose a Solution

Putting the plan in writing enables everyone to better understand the plan and their part in resolving the problem or issue. A written plan is also helpful for monitoring your family's solution, which is the next step in the problem-solving process.

Monitoring the Solution

Monitoring the solution is critical to the problem-solving process. By monitoring the action plan, your family can keep track of their progress. This will remind you of what the family decided to do, which family member is going to do it, and when it will be done.

Evaluating the Success of the Plan

This stage involves reviewing what happened in order to learn from the situation. The review helps the family to make adjustments to the plan and to evaluate what worked and what didn't. Parents who teach problem-solving skills to their children promote resiliency in their children.

Source: www.ext.vt.edu/pubs/family/350-091/350-091.html. Authors: Rick Peterson and Stephen Green, Department of Human Development, Virginia TechPublication Number 350-091, posted June 1999.

Some people find discussing their problems in a group setting to be helpful. Family therapy and participation in a mutual support group can balance one another, giving relief from feelings of isolation and also treating complex issues of family dynamics (Goldstein, 1990). Think about the problems associated with providing long-term care to elderly family members: Although most caregivers say they are satisfied with their role, stressors such as lack of time and transportation are a persistent irritation. Ironically, some elderly people view their caregivers as less involved in their care than distant siblings, likely leading them to undervalue the caregiver's contribution (Shellenberger, Couch, & Drake, 1989).

Often, efforts to solve one problem spill over into other areas, generally improving family life. For example, behavioural couples therapy with alcoholics not only helps to reduce drinking but also generally improves family functioning, including better marital relations, reduced domestic violence and verbal conflict, reduced risk of separation and divorce, and reduced emotional distress in partners (O'Farrell & Feehan, 1999).

It is important to note that attempts to fix family troubles must be culturally sensitive to be effective. A Canadian example is the problem of alcoholism among First Nations communities. As First Nations people value and work within a large extended family, virtually everyone on the reserve or in the community is affected by alcoholism, whether because the problem of one individual is affecting everyone, or because many community members are suffering from severe alcoholism.

Some researchers feel that aboriginal alcohol programs fail mainly because the program is not sufficiently sensitive to cultural concerns (Lawrence, 2000). To remedy this problem, Dakota people are attempting to restructure treatment programs by first understanding the Native community and then examining how native individuals make sense of their world. A more effective treatment program would re-introduce traditional values and ceremonies such as the Sun Dance.

The Wagga Model, an attempt to reduce the number of Aboriginal youth in trouble in Australia, offers another example of culturally sensitive counselling. This method, based on Maori cultural traditions, uses shaming to control the youth and family conferencing to rehabilitate them. Critics warn that a method popular in New Zealand may not work as well in Australia, where a different aboriginal culture is involved. Indigenous people may not all be amenable to conference-style resolutions, nor respond in the same ways to shaming (Blagg, 1997).

Using the Native experience as an example, it is clear that the same methods may not work as well in every situation to repair families and reduce conflict, and one must tailor the counselling process to provide the maximum benefit to different groups of people.

Every Family Has Resources

Every family, like every group, organization, or society, has resources that help it address its system problems and system changes. These fall into three main categories: coping skills, systemic properties, and capital.

The members of a family vary in their **coping skills**. By that, we mean that some members can handle conflict and adversity more effectively than others. Take criticism: when criticized, some people collapse in tears or run away and

Debate Box 8.1 DO FAMILIES BRING AVOIDABLE PROBLEMS UPON THEMSELVES? Which side of the debate do you fall on?

YES	NO
• Most problems can be avoided if families develop better interaction and communication skills. Yet, few families take the trouble to develop them.	• Families can't entirely avoid problems like unemployment or illness. They befall even the best-organized, hardest-working families.
• Most problems can be avoided if family members avoid excessive drugs and alcohol. Yet many family members indulge excessively in drugs and alcohol.	• Poor people have to work much harder than rich people to avoid or solve problems. The fact that they fail in their efforts does not prove a failure to try.
• Most problems can be avoided if parents teach their children good values and behaviours. Yet many parents appear too busy or indifferent to do this parenting.	• Our society is organized in a way that causes problems for a large fraction of all Canadian families. Family problems will not diminish without societal changes.
• Most problems can be avoided if parents develop good parenting skills. Yet few parents take the trouble to read books or attend courses on how to parent better.	• Our culture encourages people to take advantage of others who are vulnerable. We are rarely helpful to the most vulnerable, and may even cause their problems.
• Immigrants are to blame when they fail to assimilate to Canadian society thus creating problems for themselves.	• The capitalist system stacks the deck in favour of rich and powerful people. This is why unemployment, poverty, and racism are prevalent and harmful to families.

hide. Others shout and scream and attack the critic. Others spend time quietly deciding whether, and to what degree, they deserve the criticism. They ignore the parts that are unwarranted and change themselves so that the other parts no longer apply. This, we would argue, is the most effective way to cope with criticism. This process does the least harm to social relationships and is least likely to lead to depression, alcoholism, violence, or other personal trouble. So, from one standpoint, an effective family—a family with good resources—is a family in which the individual family members each cope well with difficulties.

Second and more important, an effective family has good **systemic properties**. Specifically, it has a high degree of *cohesion* and a high degree of *flexibility*. That means the family roles and relationships can change when necessary, yet they are strong enough to stay put when no one needs or want change. This is different from personal coping: Families with strong systemic properties can even endure the weaknesses and poor coping skills of their individual members. As a result, family membership makes its individual members better able to deal with the adversities of life.

Yang (1999), for example, reports that, in Taiwan as in Canada and the United States, family differentiation helps the individuation of young people. For women particularly, it increases their self-esteem and interpersonal competence and reduces the likelihood of depression. Such individuation is one important type of family flexibility, which serves to increase the effectiveness and cohesion of the family in the long run.

At the same time, too much cohesion or flexibility is to be avoided. An excess of cohesion is repressive. It stifles individual development and may produce family members who are less competent and flexible than they need to be as individuals. An excess of flexibility is also undesirable, since it points to a lack of adequate normative support in the family. No wonder, then, that Durkheim found that, just as too little attachment (i.e., egoism) and too little normative control (i.e., *anomie*) predict suicide, so do too *much* attachment and too *much* normative control.

As we saw in an earlier chapter, attachment and supervision are particularly important for children. Research on immigrant teenagers, for example, finds that factors such as parental supervision, parent–child conflict, church attendance, frequency of prayer, and social support all act as protective influences. Despite the difficulties associated with immigration, they all help first-generation immigrants to maintain higher levels of well-being (e.g., less depression) than their native-born peers of similar demographic and family backgrounds (Harker, 2000).

Well-adjusted families, by definition, cope well with change. Poorly adjusted families hide problems, rather than solve them. For example, weak family relations drastically reduce the likelihood that gay and lesbian youth will "come out" to their parents, even indirectly (Waldner & Magruder, 1999). Poorly adjusted families cope badly and have a hard time changing. Families where trust is high and conflict slight react to the diagnosis of HIV/AIDS infection less negatively than families in which there is mistrust and partner conflict (Bharat & Aggleton, 1999).

To hide a problem is not to make it go away. Female partners of alcoholics, for example, may cope with the problem by trying to ignore or deny it. However, this method often produces depression, obsessive-compulsive symptoms, and hostility (Zetterlind, 1999). Some families, unable to deal with their problems— whether alcoholism, homosexuality, or critically ill or disabled infants—cope through a harmful form of religious denial, such as the eternal belief in a miracle (York, 1987). Since miracles are rare, the problems remain.

Generally, weak families indulge in unrealistic thinking, self-blame, distancing, and denial (Judge, 1998). However, cohesion and flexibility, and honest open efforts to solve problems, may not be enough. Strong families use their social supports and other types of **capital** they may have at their disposal.

The Three Types of Capital

Some families are more effective than others in dealing with conflict and trouble. Effective families are likely to have lots of capital: economic capital, social capital, and cultural capital. Changing or resisting change, as desired, is easier for families that have more capital on hand.

Economic capital is income, property, or wealth. Being poor is harder than being rich, because solving problems without money is harder. Throwing money at them can solve many problems. Poor people cannot elect that option, so they have more problems of many varieties. To take a simple example, affluent people are more likely to have good housing, and people with good housing are more likely to keep up frequent contact with their children than people with poor housing or none at all. This is true whether we are comparing homeless American women to other poor American women (as we did earlier in this chapter), or elderly people in a metropolitan area of Japan who vary in affluence (Maeda, 1999).

•   **Social capital** includes people the family can draw upon for support, influence, information, or aid. Again, being isolated is harder than being socially integrated, because solving problems without connections and supports is harder. All of us benefit, occasionally, from a shoulder to lean on, an advisor, a helper, and a contact. Nevertheless, some families and individuals don't have them, or the ones they have are themselves lacking in economic, social, or cultural capital. So, for example, as family dynamics change over the life course, family and friends become the major caregivers for the elderly and contribute to the quality of their

Figure 8.4 CHILDCARE SUPPORT FROM EXTENDED FAMILY MEMBERS, FOR EMPLOYED MOTHER, NOVA SCOTIA, 1999

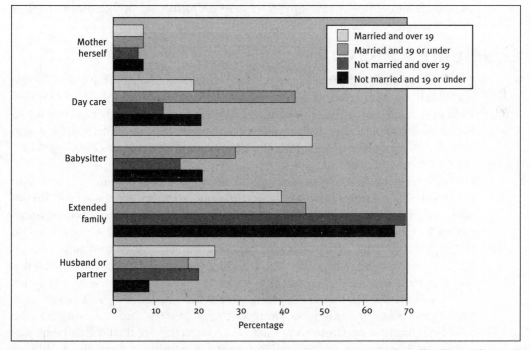

Source: Family Mosaic Research Project Report, www.gov.ns.ca/coms/files/files_pdf/family.pdf. Permission provided by Margaret K. Dechman, The Dynamics of Family Life.

lives (Wetle, 1991). By now, most of us have developed more equitable and flexible family ties in our intergenerational relations, caring, and transfers of family wealth (Bornat et al., 1999). However, we are still coming to understand the step-relationships that have proliferated with the divorce and remarriage explosion of recent decades.

Cultural capital includes all the kinds of intimate knowledge of culture—especially class-based culture—that make for social acceptance. It can hurt your career to show up at the boss's "black tie" retirement party wearing a glowing mint-green suit and a black tie with nude women on it. Knowing the culturally "right thing to do" in a thousand different situations will determine the standing of you and your family within the community. Ironically, people with high standing are more likely to attract other resources: help, co-operation, and advice—even money. Those that have, get.

Not only does the possession of these resources influence family functioning, the perceived possession also influences it. Thus, panel research on farming families in the American Midwest during the economic crisis of the 1980s found positive relationships between financial and emotional resources, decision-making, and family well-being (Rettig, Leichentritt, & Danes, 1999). Often, a belief that you can manage your problems—because of your financial and emotional resources, decision-making skill, and family cohesion—makes it easier to handle those very problems. This is not meant to argue in favour of irrational fantasizing, but to emphasize that our beliefs and attitudes can sometimes help get us through tough times.

Concluding Remarks

The study of family dynamics teaches us that we should celebrate the resilience and creativity of human beings who struggle to create and maintain families. Research findings testify to the ability of families to change themselves when they face a problem. Family processes (not structures) are all that matter, and "healthy" family processes—as we understand them in a modern society—produce "healthy" members of society.

Anyone who has ever tried to organize, run, or participate in a group for an extended period knows how hard group life can be. Many groups simply do not survive. For better or worse, group members go their separate ways. Some groups persist, but they give up their original goals and dreams; their members merely go through the motions of participating. These groups might as well have broken up. Other groups stay together but at a high price: conflict escalates, violence becomes more common. They ought to break up but cannot find the way to do so.

These are the boundaries of group experience, the failures, and just as there are failed groups, there are failed families. We discuss this problem further in the next two chapters, on stress and violence, and divorce. Against this backdrop of always-possible failure, we find millions of families trying, repeatedly, in millions of unique ways, to work out ways of staying together and working together. Or, breaking up and starting over in an optimistic way. Often, after divorce, mothers and their children are particularly close, and mothers become viewed as friends, especially by daughters. Divorced mothers often lean on their children for emotional support and advice. This contributes to a sense of equality, closeness, and friend status between them. The participants may value these qualities, playing as they do to family strengths, though some theorists continue to express concerns about boundary violation and its impact on adolescent development (Arditti, 1999).

Yet, "caring for and caring about other people is something that most if not all children are encouraged to do during childhood. It is part of their socialization and is a prerequisite for healthy psychosocial development. It is considered beneficial to both children and wider society" (Aldridge & Becker, 1999: 312). We are just beginning to acknowledge that children have an important part to play, from an early age, in caring for any parent, healthy or ill. A family, in the end, is a set of people constantly trying to adjust to the individual and collective needs of its members, within the given context of a culture, society, and economy—a remarkable social accomplishment.

CHAPTER SUMMARY

This chapter deals with family dynamics—the ways in which family members interact, deal with problems, and get along. Conflict, present to some degree in all human interpersonal relationships, is a normal aspect of family life, and in and of itself is not a sign of family dysfunction. Rather, it is how families respond to these problems that determines whether they will get along or fall apart.

All families have their problems. Often, these problems are the result of too many changes—or conversely, an inability to deal with change—inside and outside the family. Families differ, however, on the number and seriousness of the problems they face, which are often socially structured; that is, some problems are more likely to beset some social groups than others. Poverty and racism, also socially structured, also tend to create or exacerbate obstacles for families. These latter types of problems are so widespread and so inherent in our social fabric that they require major social changes to solve.

Problems also tend to create secondary problems, such that they often accumulate and snowball out of control. On a positive note, families are social systems that initially resist change but are inherently able to adapt when necessary. Problems, too, are connected to one another, in that families tend to face a system of problems rather than single isolated ones. It is very difficult, then, to attempt to solve one problem without solving all of them at the same time.

The types of problems that families face often have structural origins and thus require social policies to solve them. These problems include the privatization of family life, the increasing influence of non-family institutions, the dominance of mass media in individuals' lives, and conflicts resulting from changing gender roles and interfamilial relationships.

Also important in the understanding of family dynamics is the awareness of the **family life cycle**. Each family member faces different types of problems depending on the type and stage of relationship with other members. Sometimes, the changes of individual family members are out of phase with one another, leading to more potential conflict.

Well-functioning families are aware of the normalcy of domestic problems and solve them through open communication, like-mindedness, and fair judgement. Families also require the help of others, such as grandparents, fictive kin, and impartial therapists, in solving their problems. Furthermore, families often call upon resources to deal with conflicts. These include coping skills; systemic properties, such as cohesiveness and flexibility; and economic, social, and cultural forms of capital.

KEY TERMS

Assumptive world The internalized views of family relations and of individual members. This helps to inform how the family operates as a system.

Capital The resources that a family possesses, the amount of which can determine the types of problems a family will face and their ability to solve them. Also see: Economic capital; Social capital; Cultural capital.

Changes in family relations The relations between men and women, parents and children.

Coping skills An individual's or a family's ability to handle conflict and adversity in an effective and productive manner.

Cultural capital Beliefs and skills that help people get ahead in an unequal society. Teaching people that traditional upper-class culture (e.g., ballet, opera, polo) is "high culture" legitimates the maintenance of the status quo.

Economic capital The amount of income, property, or wealth that a family possesses.

Family dynamics The sum of all the ways that families, as social units, try to cope

with their problems and adjust to their needs for change. It should be noted that no family "naturally" gets along well.

Family life cycle The different phases that a family experiences throughout its lifetime, including the newly formed couple, the birth of offspring, retirement of the couple, and old age. In this cycle, individual roles in the family undergo several changes over time.

Family ritual Ritual action is present in almost all areas of social life. In the family rituals represent complex, meaningful patterns of interaction that are often significant only to its participants. They often strengthen and maintain a family's system of shared behaviours and beliefs, solidifying its identity.

Fictive kin People who are not related to a family by either blood or marriage but who participate and are perceived as kin through the endowment of familial roles, responsibilities, and status.

Individuate To form into a separate, distinct entity. Usually due to the strains in adolescence, one wishes to separate psychically from one's parents.

Inertia When no external force changes a system's movement, the system continues in the direction it is flowing. Any single change may set off many additional changes to the family system. Resistance often accompanies change.

Influence of non-family institutions Families are increasingly subject to the influence of the workplace, school, government, and the economy. As families have lost traditional functions—especially education, entertainment, moral training, and job preparation—states and private organizations have claimed them.

Privatization of family life Since the industrial revolution has meant that we are all coping with our own family problems, often unaware that other families face these same problems.

Scripts Sets of socially approved actions that embody the ideal form of a family and the roles of family members. New ones need to be incorporated when resolving familial conflicts.

Social capital Connections and contacts that the family can draw upon for support, information, influence, or aid.

Social system A social system basically consists of two or more individuals interacting directly or indirectly within a bounded situation. It also represents a complex whole of enduring, predictable, interdependent patterns of relations. All systems, whether living or mechanical, resist change, but once change begins, one change sets off another.

Systemic properties The degree of cohesion, adaptability, and flexibility that a family possesses in dealing with conflict and change.

REVIEW QUESTIONS

1. What is meant by "feminization of poverty"? Give specific incidences of how this affects women of all ages.

2. Describe some ways that poverty and racism affect family formation.

3. Where are the most dramatic familial inequalities found? Why?

4. Who are the "most disadvantaged children," and how does race factor into the definition?

5. Does paid work cause a strain on the family? Why?

6. What are some of the conflicts inherent to the "generation gap"? Give examples.

7. How does an awareness of a family's "life cycle" help to understand the problems it goes through?

8. How is a family "self-anchoring"?

9. Define "anticipated dependence."

10. What are the main categories of resources that families use to address their problems?

DISCUSSION QUESTIONS

1. "Family secrets are so common and so persistent that we must allow for the possibility that they contribute to family functioning, to the survival and well-being of family members." Do you think secrets are a healthy aspect of family life? Why or why not?

2. "All families are social systems." How does this fact create problems for families? Make sure to include examples such as intra-familial lawsuits in your answer.

3. Considering the types of problems that families deal with in our society, come up with some potential changes to current public policies that might help to improve family life. Do you feel that the government has a responsibility to maintain traditional family values? If yes, give examples, and if no, explain why.

4. How can a sudden change to a family (e.g., an unexpected pregnancy, diagnosing a family member with cancer) both help and hinder the family's dynamics? Research family therapy resources on the Internet, listing properties and characteristics common to all.

5. Do you think that problem-solving strategies vary according to gender? Why do you think it happens/why not?

6. "Families, being little societies, all have their own history, culture, and language." What implications does this statement have for family therapists attempting to solve a family's problems? Are family values universal? Discuss.

7. Outline some strategies that families use in solving problems. What conditions might optimize the successfulness of these strategies? Do you feel a specific coping skill is more commonly used than others? If yes, explain.

8. Discuss how a family's strong systemic properties can overcome an individual member's poor coping skills when dealing with family problems.

9. How can a family without a lot of capital gain more? What are some problems and paradoxes involved in this process?

10. "A family, then, is a set of people constantly trying to adjust to the individual and collective needs of its members, within the given context of a culture, society, and economy." Do you agree with this definition of a family? Is anything missing? Given what you now know about family dynamics from your reading of this chapter, compare and contrast the above definition with those in the book's Introduction.

ACTIVITIES

1. Select a common family problem, either from your own life or from society in general. Brainstorm on how this initial problem might create secondary problems on both a micro (individual or family) and a macro (society) level.

2. "As a little system or society, made up of interlocking emotional and social needs, each family has its own story, myth, or metaphor by which it sees and talks about itself." In a short essay or journal entry, describe your own family's "story, myth, or metaphor." Interview grandparents, parents, aunts, and uncles to learn more about your family roots. Did your family originate in Canada, or did they perhaps immigrate from elsewhere? This is a great opportunity to learn more about who you are and where you come from.

3. Assume the role of a couples' or family therapist. What recommendations and advice would you give to a family that was a) dealing with an ailing, elderly member or b) undergoing a divorce?

4. Using a mini-survey, what conclusions do you come to when you examine gender differences in solving problems? Are there any major differences? If there are, what are they?

5. Consider your own family rituals. How have they changed over time as you have grown up? How have they been affected by your transition into college/university? Discuss with reference to the "empty nest."

SUGGESTED READINGS

Aldous, Joan. 1996. *Family Careers: Rethinking the Developmental Perspective.* Thousand Oaks, CA: Sage Publications. This book uses the developmental approach to discuss how patterns of interaction change throughout the family's life cycle.

Anderson, Gordon L. (Ed.). 1997. *The Family in Global Transition.* St. Paul, Minnesota: Professors' World Peace Academy. This comprehensive book examines the changing forms and functions of the family in a global community. Discussed are major issues concerning the family, such as gender roles, homosexuality, abortion, and the ways in which families of various cultures are responding to the changing domestic landscape.

Coontz, Stephanie. 1992. *The Way We Never Were: American Families and the Nostalgia Trap.* New York: Basic Books. This book provides fresh insight into parenting, love, the division of labour, and other issues by attempting to dispel some popularly held beliefs and myths about "traditional" families.

Farrell, Betty G. 1999. *Family: The Making of an Idea, an Institution, and a Controversy in American Culture.* Boulder, CO: Westview Press. This book combines research from sociology, demography, anthropology, and cultural studies to discuss the history of American families, focusing on the growing differences between real and ideal images of childhood, adolescence, marriage, and aging.

Thorne, Barrie and Marilyn Yalom (eds.). 1992. *Rethinking the Family: Some Feminist Questions*, 2nd edition. Boston, MA: Northeastern University Press. This collection of essays provides a feminist perspective on issues concerning the family, such as abortion rights, household and sexual arrangements, and women's economic dependence.

WEBLINKS

http://www.aamft.org
American Association for Marriage and Family Therapy
American Association for Marriage and Family Therapy provides articles, resources, and an index of professional therapists in the United States, Canada, and abroad.

http://www.smartmarriages.com
Coalition for Marriage, Family, and Couples Education
The Coalition for Marriage, Family, and Couples Education runs a Web site that lists articles and links to organizations specializing in domestic relations and family counselling.

http://www.grandparenting.org
Foundation for Grandparenting
The Foundation for Grandparenting is a not-for-profit group dedicated to raising grandparent consciousness and the involvement of grandparents as agents of positive change for families and society through education, research, programs, communication, and networking.

http://www.wholefamily.com
WholeFamily.com
WholeFamily.com provides advice, articles, chat-rooms, discussion boards, anecdotes, and other resources for partners, parents, teenagers, and grandparents.

CHAPTER NINE

Stress and Violence:

Realities of Family Life

Introduction

In the mass media, families are havens in a heartless world, but in reality, families can be danger zones. Family life is the site of our closest, most intimate relations, as we have said repeatedly. In the intimate family setting, people reveal themselves, invest themselves, and leave themselves open to emotional, financial, and physical harm. As we shall see, violence occurs too often in this most intimate, vulnerable setting. The research on family life is full of attempts to explain why **domestic violence** is much more common than we would expect or hope.

Consider three sociological studies of the topic. In a nutshell, they contain most of the elements we will discuss in this chapter.

Study number 1: Qualitative methods were used (Freedman & Hemenway, 2000) to analyze the social and family histories of 16 men sentenced to death in California in terms of patterns of impairment, injury, and deficit at four ecological levels: family, individual, community, and social institutions. Family violence was found in all 16 cases, including severe physical and/or sexual abuse in 14 cases; individual impairments in 16, including 14 with post-traumatic stress disorder, 13 with severe depression, and 12 with histories of traumatic brain injury; community isolation and violence in 12; and institutional failure in 15, including 13 cases of severe physical and/or sexual abuse while in foster care or under state youth authority jurisdiction

Study number 2: A study of domestic violence in Korean-American families (Kim & Sung, 2000) concludes that male-dominance is part of the violence problem. In male-dominant immigrant Korean families, severe wife beating is four times more frequent than in egalitarian Korean immigrant families. The male-dominant couples Kim and Sung studied have been in the U.S. a shorter time, on average, and they adhere more strongly to traditional male-dominant cultural values. This recency of immigration may affect the stress level. Kim and Sung report that husbands who experienced higher levels of stress were more likely to assault their wives. Perhaps because they were less socially and financially secure, recent immigrants tended to experience more stress than less recent immigrants, and acted out their frustrations violently.

Study number 3: Researchers (Klevens, Bayon, & Sierra, 2000) in Bogota, Colombia carried out in-depth interviews with males reported to authorities for physical child abuse, and their female partners. The data reveal that abusive acts occur more often on a weekday, in the afternoon or early evening hours, with the mother present. Abuses are repetitive; occasionally, they involve alcohol abuse. The men who abuse their children are, more often than average, poorly educated stepfathers. They display, to varying degrees, signs of stress, substance abuse, mental illness, a history of childhood physical abuse, negative thinking, and unrealistic expectations of the child's behaviour. Typically, their female partners—the children's mothers—have no economic security, show a high degree of psychological dependency, and report histories of abuse (physical, sexual, and emotional) in both childhood and adulthood, including abuse by their current spouse.

Note the key elements in these stories. Husbands direct domestic violence against wives and their children; the reverse rarely happens. Male violence usually occurs in the context of patriarchal, male-dominant relationships. In this patriarchal context, stress and substance abuse often increase the risk of violence. Sources of stress contributing to violence are many, as we shall see. They include major family upheavals such as immigration, chronic stressors such as cultural dislocation, and recurrent stressors such as poverty, unemployment, and substance abuse. Dependent women in stressed, patriarchal relationships are additionally vulnerable due to their isolation from mainstream society (e.g., owing to a lack of English language skills, lack of job skills and income, or seclusion at home as caregivers) and lack of support groups based in friendship or kinship.

In this chapter we examine various forms of family stress and violence. We consider what it is about family life that often leads to stress, and the ways that stresses affect family relationships. Finally, we examine the common forms of intimate or familial violence, especially child abuse and wife battering. We are not claiming that stress is not the only or even the main cause of domestic violence. Stress does not always lead to violence, nor does violence always result from stress. In fact, stress is more often an effect than a cause of family violence. The main reason for including stress and violence in the same chapter is that both illustrate a gap between the idealized image of the family and the actual functioning of close relations in families.

Stress

Family stress is "a state that arises from an actual or perceived imbalance between a **stressor** (i.e., challenge, threat) and capability (i.e., resources, coping) in the family's functioning" (Huang, 1991: 289). To explain the effect of stressor events on families, most current researchers employ a version of the **ABCX family crisis model** first elaborated by Hill (1949). In this model, A, which represents the stressor event, interacts with B, the family's crisis-meeting resources, and with C, the interpretation a family makes of the event, to produce X, the crisis.

This ABCX model focuses primarily on pre-crisis variables that make some families more or less able to cope with the impact of a stressor event. Researchers originally developed the model to study family adjustment to the crises of wartime separation and reunion (Hill, 1949). Sociologists have since used the model to examine differences in the ways families cope with a wide variety of difficult problems.

One factor that always influences stress is the nature of the stressor event itself, as measured by its severity, intensity, duration, and timing. We can evaluate stressor events as *objective* and *subjective* phenomena. An outsider, such as a researcher, using agreed-upon standards of measurement, provides an objective evaluation of the stressor, which corresponds to *A* in the model. Thus, an objective evaluation of *unemployment* for a given family, for example, might take into account

Figure 9.1 WHAT'S STRESSING CANADIAN FAMILIES?

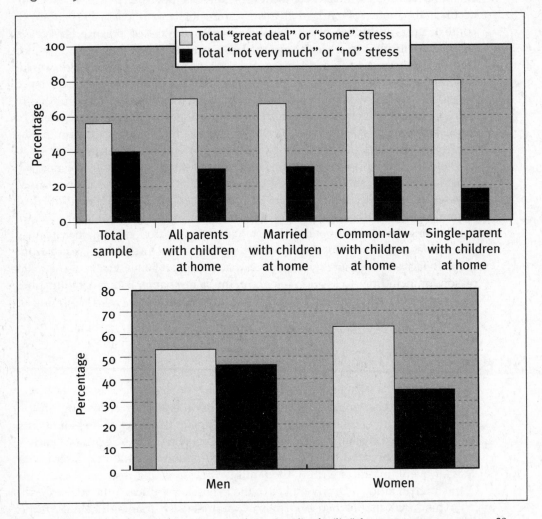

When asked to identify *"the most important issue facing Canadian families"* the most common responses, 30 percent in total, related to issues of household economies. A majority of Canadians (56%) report that balancing the demands of work and family causes them at least "some" stress, with 19 percent reporting "a great deal" of stress. Among parents with children at home 69 percent report "some" or "a great deal" of stress. Among single parents, that figure rises to 82 percent. Women experience "a great deal" of stress (24%) more frequently than men (15%).

Source: A Focus on the Family (Canada) and the Strategic Counsel, www.fotf.ca/family/facts/attitudes/execsummary.pdf.

the income-earning capacity of the other family members, the family's debt load, and the resources (e.g., property) the family has to fall back on. A researcher would measure the duration and timing of the stressor event: how long the unemployed period lasted, and the frequency with which it recurred. Typically, the longer a stressor event lasts, the more severe its effects. The more often it occurs, the more it strains a family's resources. Consequently, the harder it is for the family to cope successfully.

Family members themselves make a subjective evaluation, which corresponds to C in Hill's model. How family members view and define that event determines the way they react to it. Their subjective evaluation of an event may not correspond to the researcher's objective evaluation. In large part, how they evaluate it is largely a product of their own sense of whether they can likely cope with the situation. Like any self-fulfilling prophecy, a belief in their ability to cope increases the family's actual ability to cope.

When sociologists study families living under conditions of stress, they do so in different ways than psychologists and psychiatrists. Since sociology is the study of social relationships and social institutions, sociologists are interested in learning how stress changes the system of roles and relationships that make up a family. For example, they study how stress changes the ways that spouses relate to each other, parents relate to children, children relate to parents, or siblings relate to one another. They investigate the ways stress affects patterns of communication and interaction, marital satisfaction, or parental competence within the family. They also examine how stress changes the way that members of a family relate to extended kin, neighbours, community members, teachers, and employers. Finally, they investigate how stress changes a family's ability to socialize children, or provide a stable and healthy workforce.

Often, extreme stress reduces a family's ability to act well in these situations. For that reason, sociologists are interested in how family members cope and adjust to a long-term stressor. Some families and their members cope poorly by avoiding change as much as possible. Others cope better as individual members change their behaviours. Finally, others cope by changing their family relations. It is that change of family relations that interests sociologists most as they examine how families as a whole adjust their expectations and interactions to suit the new conditions of life and, in this way, reduce stress.

Ultimately, a family's success in coping with a stressor event will depend on the strength or quality of its crisis-meeting resources. As we will see, families that cope well with stresses are families that already had considerable resources— especially, cohesion and flexibility—before the stresses began. We will find systematic differences between the families that pull together and the families that fall apart under the strains of stressor events.

Causes of Stress

Common causes of family stress fall into at least four categories. First, they include **major upheavals** such as war and natural disasters (e.g., tornadoes, floods, and earthquakes) that affect many people simultaneously. Second, they include **major life transitions**—acute disruptions due to events that may affect some family members simultaneously, but not others—such as the birth of a child, the death of a parent, divorce, and retirement. Third, they include **chronic stressors** such as disability, chronic physical or mental illness, drug and alcohol abuse, occupational problems, unemployment, or imprisonment of a family member. Fourth, they include **occasional stresses**, which may be temporarily severe but go away without permanent change. Examples of this would include a car accident, a burglary, a sudden illness or death of a family member, or even apparently pleasant but stressful stimuli like a holiday trip.

Major Upheavals

For North American families, the Great Depression of the 1930s was a near-universal stressor causing widespread unemployment and poverty. A classic study of family dynamics during the Depression (Cavan & Ranck, 1938) concluded that coping ability rests largely on a family's previous organization. Families reacted to the Depression in the same way as they had reacted to earlier problems. Thus, families who had been well organized beforehand more readily recovered from the emotional strain caused early in the Depression. All families showed increasing strain as the Depression continued; however, the degree to which this strain was felt differed from one family to another.

World War II provided an example of a varied stressor. For many, the war reduced family stress by providing jobs for people who had been unable to find work during the Depression. It also allowed restless young men to leave home and join the military. Simultaneously, however, the dramatically increased wages that many teenagers brought home weakened parental control and increased delinquent behaviour. Also, the loss of a father to military service, or a mother's change of roles from homemaker to working woman, required all members of the family to adjust (Levy, 1945).

Recent studies of families in crisis conditions have highlighted other increasingly common sources of stress. Current research continues to examine the linkage between economic stress, poverty, and family dysfunction. Sociologists continue to find that economic pressure on a family increases parental unhappiness and marital conflict. It also increases parent–adolescent conflicts (Conger, Ge, & Elder, 1994). High levels of irritability, combined with arguments about money, lead parents to show greater hostility toward their children. In turn, these hostile exchanges increase the risk of adolescent emotional and behavioural problems.

Economic stress resulting from unemployment poses additional problems. Job loss can cause psychological depression—especially in husbands who have been living under economic strain for a long time and have an erratic work history (Wright & Hoppe, 1994). Generally, mental health worsens as economic problems increase. Wives are even more likely than husbands to stay depressed under these conditions (Friedemann & Webb, 1995).

Research also continues to examine the effects of war on family functioning. Families living under long-term war conditions suffer considerable stress. Consider the families in West Beirut, Lebanon. After 12 years of war, they show a variety of stress-related problems: depression, interpersonal and marital conflict, and psychosomatic symptoms (Farhood et al., 1993). In Honduras, symptoms associated with **post-traumatic stress disorder (PTSD)** due to civil war and repression are particularly common among the families of "the disappeared" (those who were arrested, taken away, and never again seen). Symptoms characteristic of PTSD include psychological numbing, increased states of arousal and anxiety, and a tendency to re-experience the trauma mentally. PTSD can be more debilitating than grieving the death of a loved one. An atmosphere of fear and isolation prolongs these stress-related disorders long after the disappearance of the family members itself (Quirk & Casco, 1994).

War, like unemployment, brings family members closer together if they were already cohesive. However, it drives them apart if they were not. During the 1991 Persian Gulf War, for example, residents of Haifa, Israel relied more on kin for immediate or direct aid than they did on their everyday networks of friends. Friends, by contrast, continued to provide comfort and advice. Thus, people who are not kin provide a specific form of social support, but people still turn to kin for survival (Shavit, Fischern, & Koresh, 1994).

As we have said, crises can make or break a family. Thus, in the early 1990s, Israeli and Palestinian couples with a strong, shared ideological orientation agreed more often and reported an increase in cohesiveness. Other couples reported a deterioration of their relationship. They disagreed more about the meaning of the peace process and its effects on the family (Ben-David & Lavee, 1996). Crises test families, and many are found wanting.

Family Life Transitions

Like war and economic difficulty, migration has been a continuing source of family stress throughout this century. Immigrant families face **acculturative stress**, due to the strains of adapting to a new society. These include a lack of local language skills, low employment and economic status, and limited educational background (Thomas, 1995). Prolonged stress tends to harm a family. Therefore, time spent in a new homeland may increase the anxiety and depression of both parents and children, as young Indochinese refugees reported after settling in Finland (Liebkind, 1993). Reportedly, women are particularly stressed by immigration.

Typically, the children of immigrants assimilate more rapidly than their parents to local standards of behaviour. This often produces conflict between parents and their children. For example, Southeast Asian adolescents in the United States report experiencing a lot of parent-induced stress about academic performance (i.e., studying for a test, pressure to get good grades) and parental expectations (i.e., high expectations to do well). They fear failing to meet family expectations. Adolescent women are particularly susceptible to stress of this kind (Duong Tran, 1995).

Chronic Stressors

Chronic stressors confronting families include poverty, racism, and alcoholism. In these and other respects, additional problems face certain types of families—especially Aboriginal families, lone parents, and older family members.

Poverty, economic hardship, and inequality are related aspects of a problem that increases stress, reduces resilience, and hinders every part of a family's well-being, even including its health. Taken as a package, economic stress—financial adequacy, perceived economic well-being, respondent's and partner's job instability, and respondent's and partner's job insecurity—strongly predicts a variety of measures of individual and family well-being. In a study by Fox and Chancey (1998), for example, for both women and men, perceived economic well-being was generally the strongest predictor of measures of individual and family well-being. Also for both, a spouse's or partner's job variables were important predictors of measures of family well-being. The respondent's own job instability and insecurity appeared more important to women than men, and more so for family than individual well-being outcomes.

Homeless people, for example, are particularly likely to suffer from mental and physical health problems, though perceived family support reduces distress levels (Wong & Piliavin, 1999).

Another group of economically vulnerable people are single or lone mothers. Employment changes do not hold the same costs and benefits for single and married mothers. Research in London, Ontario by Ali and Avison (1997) finds

Table 9.1 JOB CONDITIONS THAT MAY LEAD TO STRESS

THE DESIGN OF TASKS	Heavy workload, infrequent rest breaks, long work hours and shift-work; hectic and routine tasks that have little inherent meaning, do not utilize workers' skills, and provide little sense of control.
MANAGEMENT STYLE	Lack of participation by workers in decision-making, poor communication in the organization, and lack of family-friendly policies.
INTERPERSONAL RELATIONSHIPS	Poor social environment and lack of support or help from co-workers or supervisors.
WORK ROLES	Conflicting or uncertain job expectations, too much responsibility, too many "hats" to wear.
CAREER CONCERNS	Job insecurity and lack of opportunity for growth, advancement, or promotion; rapid changes for which workers are unprepared.
ENVIRONMENTAL CONDITIONS	Unpleasant or dangerous physical conditions such as crowding, noise, air pollution, or ergonomic problems.

Source: National Institute for Occupational Safety and Health
www.focusondepression.com/script/main/art.asp?li=GO&articlekey=21795.

that among women who left their jobs, single mothers experienced significant stress increases while married mothers did not. Stress-inducing factors were financial strains, low self-esteem, and lack of mastery. When transition involved a change of employment, stress levels were unaffected for both groups. Although married mothers' stress declined when they began paid employment, such declines were offset by stress increases concerning caregiving.

Lone mothers often pass heightened stress, anxiety, and anger on to their adolescent children, particularly when they spend a lot of time with their children and when they use psychological control in their parenting (Larson & Gillman, 1999). The psychological distress they induce apparently weakens a child's ability to form and maintain a satisfying marital relationship, and thus leads to higher risks of separation and divorce in adulthood (Clifford, 1998).

At the same time, closer and more frequent contact between a lone mother and her adolescent child are likely to reduce stress from other sources. Single mothers are reportedly aware of only half of their adolescents' stressors and not aware enough of the importance to their adolescents. During early adolescence when adolescent stress increases and family communication and monitoring change, monitoring by single mothers may increase awareness of adolescent stress, which in turn may buffer the negative effects of stress on adolescent adjustment (Hartos & Power, 2000).

Recent changes in the objective conditions of the poor—including deindustrialization, increased rates of divorce and single-mother families, and the retrenchment of the welfare state—have led to the feminization of poverty in the 1980s and 1990s and a worsening of the conditions of urban racial minorities (Roschelle, 1999; Wilson, 1988). Despite the insistence that the U.S. is a colour-blind society, the issue of race still pervades, highlighting how African Americans are perceived by mainstream society and its effect on their overall mental, physical, and emotional health. Historically, African Americans have been viewed as naturally deficient and pathological, leading to the subjugation of the African-American family. Few studies have examined how the legacy of slavery and continual institutional racism impact African Americans (Carroll, 1998).

Racial discrimination is not only a source of distress in its own right; it also intensifies other sources of distress. For example, Murry et al. (2001) find that when African Americans experience greater racial discrimination stressful life events produce more psychological distress than usual, and this distress worsens the quality of both intimate partnerships and parent–child relationships. A high quality parent–child relationship is particularly important for generating feelings of self-esteem and self-efficacy in African-American children (Jarrett, 1997). Conversely, factors such as maternal psychological distress, high family stress burden, and use of coercive parenting practices produce more problem behaviours and less resilience (Myers & Taylor, 1998).

Stresses of racism and tokenism are pervasive for black corporate managers and their families in America. Parents are concerned for their children who are growing up without regular contact with black people and feel greater isolation from the black community themselves. Successful black women suffer the additional problem of becoming estranged from single black men and facing sexism in their upward climb. Thus, the life experiences of these individuals are qualitatively different than that of their white counterparts. However, black corporate families also have much strength, based on better positive self-images, stronger family relationships, and informal networks of support (Tolliver, 1998).

Community resources can also help African-American families address stressful life events and maintain resiliency (McCubbin et al., 1998) In this respect, the black church has historically played an important role (Bagley & Carroll, 1998).

Community resources are also important among Aboriginal people in Canada and the United States. Major stresses such as alcohol use, family breakdown, inadequate tribal leadership, unemployment, and issues surrounding children's education place great demands on coping. Major family and tribal strengths include extended family support, spiritual values and religious practices, community generosity and support, tribal culture and traditions, and a determination of many tribal members to recognize and overcome their problems (Abbott & Slater, 2000).

Likewise, community resources are important for racial minorities who have recently immigrated. These resources include traditional roles, norms, values, and institutions: the family, community, and religion, in particular. For example, Somali families draw their strength from religious and cultural traditions that emphasize the importance of family solidarity. Beliefs in the sanctity of the family promote the sharing of resources for family survival, and require the unity of family members. Community solidarity, based on family solidarity, supports values of peace and harmony that promote psychological unity. Men and women, young and old, know the roles they are expected to play, and play those roles cooperatively and responsibly, according to religious customs. However, the host society has interfered in family disputes, challenging the stability of traditional roles and relations and undermining a system of dispute-resolution based on the authority of elders. Somalis describe these challenges to role functioning as "leaving traditions" and blame them for increases in stress in the new cultural setting.

Stress is known to increase the use of drugs, including cigarettes, alcohol, and illicit drugs (e.g., marijuana). In a one-year study of adolescents in California, the stress-related variables were low socioeconomic status, missing one's parent(s), family conflict, victimization, perceived stress, and stress-drug beliefs. Those who were lower in socioeconomic status, held stress-drug beliefs favourable toward drug use, and who had been victimized in the last year were more likely to be cigarette, alcohol, or illicit drug users. Those who had used drugs before the start of the study and had been victimized in the last year were particularly likely to use drugs the next year (Sussman & Dent, 2000)

Another study found that separation from parents, high levels of stress, and alcohol use by peers all predicted alcohol use by adolescents (Baer & Bray, 1999). Supporting this is a longitudinal study showing that the cumulative effect of stressful life experiences over time can lead to a steeper escalation of drug use in adolescence. This effect may be moderated by factors such as sex, income, family attachment, self-esteem, and mastery. Experiencing a high number of life events over time is related to a significant growth of drug use, even after controlling for such growth due to age or peer relations. High levels of family attachment significantly diminish this growth.

Alcohol and drug abuse are both causes and consequences of family stress. For example, Perreira and Sloan (2001) used four waves of the Health and Retirement Study to examine changes in alcohol consumption co-occurring and following stress associated with major health, family, and employment events over a six-year study period. They found that most persons (68%) did not change their use of alcohol over the entire six years, however, many did. Hospitalization and onset of a chronic condition were associated with decreased drinking levels. Retirement was associated with increased drinking. Widowhood was associated with increased drinking but only for a short time. Getting married or divorced was associated with both increases and decreases in drinking, with a complex lag structure. A history of problem drinking influenced the association between certain life events (for example, divorce and retirement) and changes in drinking. The size of these relationships, however, varied by gender and problem drinking history.

Interestingly, there is some evidence (Liu & Kaplan, 2001) that substance abuse under stress indicates a stronger commitment to conformity. Individuals who experience strain associated with marriage, parenthood, or single status are more likely to use illicit drugs only when they are committed to conventional values. The moderating influences of commitment to conventionality are consistent with the contention that individuals who experience role strain and are simultaneously committed to conventionality may find failure in valued social roles more distressing and that use of drugs may serve as a private and less disruptive stress-reduction mechanism.

The Care of Ill or Elderly Relatives

A new "demographic imperative" is upon us now (Keating, Fast, Frederick, Cranswick & Perrier, 1999). Gone are the days when people died at relatively young ages, surrounded by kin. A longer-living adult population increases the demand for care by family members, thus increasing family stress. Adult children in their 50s, besides being more likely divorced than in the past, are more likely to have a surviving parent. Compared with 30 years ago, more elderly people today live independently. However, a larger and growing fraction of the elderly require assistance because of long-term health problems (ibid., 99).

One result is the so-called "sandwich generation": 42 percent of Canadian women ages 40 to 44 balance parental care, childcare, and work outside the home.

Broader changes also include a shift from institutional to community-based care, a growing ideological commitment to elderly care by the state, and funding cuts by the federal government for such services (Rosenthal, 1997a). This Canadian trend to view eldercare as a private matter rather than a public responsibility may have many negative consequences in the future (Rosenthal, 1997b).

Because of cuts to the health-care system, Canada and other industrial nations with universal medical care appeared to slide back to the "non-system" that exists in the U.S. (Chappell, 1997). Yet public surveys repeatedly show that Canadians value public health care, want good health and longevity, and view health as a public good, even while electing governments that carry out cost-reductions and ill-considered health-care reforms (Chappell, 1999).

Social Support for Chronic Caregiving

Social support makes an important contribution to the health of elderly people and others (for example, the housebound disabled) who often suffer from social isolation. This tends to reduce family stress. The helpers in a social support network may include family members, friends, and informal community caregivers. As a result, network development and the establishment of support groups can be very important to people's health (Gottlieb, 1985).

Evidence suggests that 75 to 85 percent of seniors' total personal care comes from informal care arrangements (Chappell, 1996), and an equal proportion of

---

The Price of Eldercare

According to a joint study by the University of Alberta and Statistics Canada, the selfless people who take care of their elderly parents and grandparents have saved the national health-care system $5 billion a year. But the report goes on to conclude that the economic impact of those millions of hours of unpaid work runs deeper: the caregivers are silently causing hidden problems for themselves.

If the approximately 2.1 million Canadians who care for elderly at home or in another unpaid situation were replaced by full-time paid workers, it would cost the health-care system more than $5 billion annually. However, the workers themselves pay a harsh price. Not only do caregivers suffer from emotional and

psychological strain, but because many are in their prime earning years—their thirties and forties—they also sacrifice time when they could be earning an income and contributing to a pension or RRSP.

That raises the risk that they are causing a delayed form of economic damage to their own lives, running "a greater risk of becoming frail, isolated, and poor seniors themselves," the university says in a summary of the findings.

The study argues that better support for the elderly now—including more home care, more homes for the elderly, and more ways to help the unpaid caregivers—will save the taxpayer money in the future.

....

Source: Tom Spears. 2000. "Family, Friends Do 80% of Eldercare: Study," The *Ottawa Citizen*, January 2, A3.

Canadians report some type of self-care (Penning and Chappell, 1990). A study conducted in London, Ontario found that just over 9 percent of community-dwelling older persons are using or in need of community services. The vast majority of older persons manage without the aid of formal support services (Connidis, 1985). Need—specifically, functional inability—is the most important predictor of health service use (Chappell, 1987), though health, health beliefs, and marital status are also important predictors (Penning & Chappell, 1990).

Use of the formal system, along with informal care, appears to take place when seniors are in need and critical elements of their care network are lacking, or when they have an intact informal network but their health needs are extremely high. The data point to the complementarity of the two care systems, as for a sharing of overall task load (Chappell & Blandford, 1991). Among care recipients with more severe health needs, those who do not use services, and those using only in-home services, often have inadequate informal supports, more emotionally strained caregivers, and more functionally impaired care recipients, as compared with users of out-of-home or both in- and out-of-home services (Biegel, Bass, Schulz, & Morycz, 1993). The characteristics of caregivers account for much of the variation in whether or not services are used. Family enabling factors are the most important predictors of how much in-home services are used (Bass & Noelker, 1987).

Family composition features—specifically, number of children, number who are sons or daughters, and gender of the parent—affect whether a child will be the sole or primary helper for an older parent (Connidis, Rosenthal, & McMullin, 1996). Geographic proximity is the major influence on contact frequency and form. The greater the distance, the less frequent is contact and the importance of matters discussed. Sisters have more face-to-face and telephone contact, and are more likely to discuss important matters than are brothers and brother–sister siblings, for example (Connidis, 1989). Divorced and single people are more likely than married people, and the childless are more likely than parents, to rely on formal support and paid help, and less likely to rely on family (Connidis and McMullin, 1994).

Caregiver Burden

Long-term care for the elderly, disabled, or chronically ill can put great strains on a family's functioning. Often, the main caregiver has to add caring to other heavy responsibilities (Keating, Fast, Frederick, Cranswick, & Perrier, 1999: 105). As a result, caregivers frequently have to make changes in social activities, change sleep patterns, or give up holiday plans (op cit.: 69). Caregiving can also affect job performance (op cit.: 86). Typically, caregiving creates a bigger burden for women than for men (op cit.: 81). At some time in their lives, a large fraction of women in their 40s and 50s can expect to be sandwiched between responsibilities to old parents and their other commitments (Rosenthal, Matthews, & Marshall, 1989).

The "caregiving family" in our North American culture contains both people who provide assistance and people we perceive as having some obligation to provide assistance but do not. An idealized view of family caregiving is used to put pressure on families to provide more care, but is not justifiable in reality (Keating, Kerr, Warren, Grace, & Wertenberger, 1994). In fact, caregiving occurs in diverse household forms involving many men, employed, and multigenerational caregivers, most of whom express a permanent commitment to the role. Although caregivers often give elderly—and especially impaired elderly—parents many hours of personal care each day, caregivers vary widely in their incidence and severity of stress effects. Informal and formal supports, though present, seem to supply little hands-on care (Noelker & Wallace, 1985).

Often most of the care responsibilities, and attendant strains, fall on a single family member. Women are almost twice as likely as men to give personal care, for example, and this difference increases when care involves five or more hours of assistance per week. Working women experience important increases in stress when they are forced to alter their work schedule to meet home care needs of an impaired, elderly family member (Orodenker, 1990). Women continue to be far more likely than men to provide care, and to suffer consequent caregiving strain, work interference, income loss, and role strain (Fredriksen, 1996).

Women's disproportionate responsibility for elderly and other care has employment consequences, such as forced or premature exits from the workforce and postponement of promotion or career advancement (Matthews & Campbell, 1995). Elder care involvement interferes with work for women but not for men. Among women, family-related interference with work is more likely to reduce job satisfaction and increase absenteeism. Adult children in households shared with elderly parents experience much more activity limitation than those living in separate households (Deimling, Bass, Townsend, & Noelker, 1989). For example, men sharing households with their mothers-in-law are more likely to report interference in their social lives, family vacation plans, time with wives and children, and relationships with other relatives (Kleban, Brody, Schoonover, & Hoffman, 1989).

The extent, duration, and consequences of these family strains vary with the nature, severity, and duration of the illness. For example, informal caregivers for non-institutionalized parents with dementia report distress and heightened feelings of burden and depression because of the care recipient's aimlessness, aggressive behaviours, forgetfulness, and restlessness (Chappell & Penning, 1996). Strains also vary with the coping abilities and resources of the family, and with the disease sufferer, whether a parent or child, old or young, male or female.

When caregiving responsibilities are added to an income-earning woman's "double day," the dangers of caregiver burnout and family breakdown increase dramatically. The difficulty in balancing the demands of home and employment produces considerable stress that, taken to extremes, contributes to life-threatening health conditions (see, for example, Ginn & Sandell, 1997; Scharlach & Fredriksen, 1994).

Even after institutionalization, caregiving continues. Wives do a variety of personal, instrumental, relational, and recreational care tasks. This creates the need for collaboration between wives and staff to enhance the quality of care (Ross, Rosenthal, & Dawson, 1997). Spouses are more likely to report financial problems and the feeling that the staff do not listen to them. Children and other relatives are more likely to describe problems related to the wider family and to report conflict between competing role responsibilities (Rosenthal, Sulman, & Marshall, 1992). Rosenthal and Dawson (1991) find that, at first, spouses have negative feelings (e.g., guilt, anger, sadness, resentment, and loneliness). At the same time, they suffer ambivalence arising from feelings of relief over the cessation of arduous home-based care and the knowledge that the husband is receiving excellent care. In the early weeks following the husband's admission, wives display poor physical health, low morale, and high levels of depression.

Longer stays often have a negative impact on patient self-care and increased depression among caregivers (Sulman, Rosenthal, Marshall, & Daciuk, 1996). Overall, wives with better social support and better psychosocial health are more satisfied with the care their spouse is receiving (Dawson & Rosenthal, 1996). However, wives of husbands who are only physically impaired continue to be heavily involved in care. They are more likely to be moderately to severely depressed, and express dissatisfaction with aspects of institutional care (Ross, Rosenthal, & Dawson, 1997).

Coping with Stress

As we have seen, family life is full of stresses. However, many families deal with them successfully: family functioning returns to normal, though the stressor may still be present. Families learn to cope by taking advantage of the resources they have available and by organizing their lives around handling their problems. Support from family, friends, and community agencies buffers the impact of caregiving, work, and family role strain. A supportive work environment also reduces physical and emotional strains (Lechner, 1993).

Two types of resources ease the burden for caregivers: assistance from other caregivers, and support from people outside the caregiving situation. Overall, caregivers with larger support networks—especially of women and kin—report lower levels of stress. Close relationships with people who are both personal supporters and caregivers lighten the load of caregiving (Wright, 1994).

Two broad categories of resources—material and emotional/psychological—are key in deciding which families can withstand crises successfully. **Material resources** are easiest to define. They include money, time, and energy. Stressor events always use up large amounts of all these resources. When a family member develops a chronic illness, families have to pay for costly medication (even in Canada if the person is not in hospital, which happens more and more with health-care cutbacks) and family members have to take time off from work to look after the ill person. Time and money alleviate the strain. **Psychological and emotional resources** are more difficult to define. They include the ability to accept that the stressor event has taken place, talk honestly about one's reactions, begin the process of adjustment soon afterward, and acknowledge the need for help from others.

Family members commonly bring both resources to the family unit. Individuals bring their money and cooperation to the common pool of resources. Family members contribute to material resources, for example, by earning an additional income. However, they may drain resources by wasting time and money. Family members may build up the emotional resources of others by listening well and offering encouragement. This role is especially important in the spousal relationship. The most important resource for mothers of disabled children is marital satisfaction. It successfully predicts maternal coping 70 percent of the time (Freidrich, 1979).

Like other good things, good health is a product of social relationships. However, like other careers, a career in good health, or in sickness, is a social construction. Social support is important in accomplishing these careers. Social support includes information that diffuses through social channels, but it is more than that. To be useful, social support must give caregivers the right information and encouragement at the right time. Timeliness and a show of concern give the information its legitimacy, which leads to compliance by the patient and a reduction of the caregiver's burden. With an adherence to treatment rules, the patient can pursue his or her "illness career," more successfully.

It is social interaction, and positioning in a network of relationships, that bestows meaning and value on health information. The information gains its value by passing through social channels that have value and meaning. In the end, we cannot understand the value attached to information unless we understand the relationship that carried it.

Illness Careers and Network Ties

As Talcott Parsons showed in his classic paper on the medical profession nearly fifty years ago, we expect sick people in our society to play the "patient role." In return for being allowed to deviate from their everyday activities and neglect their social obligations, sick people have to appear ill, consult a doctor, and follow the doctor's advice. Failure to do so leads others to label the person a "bad patient" or even a malingerer. As a result, that person may forfeit the privileges accorded to sick people (e.g., time off work, relaxation, sympathy). Sickness in our society is an accomplishment that requires the successful, often long-term performance of role expectations associated with "patienthood."

Family and friends play an important part in this culturally scripted drama. It is through interaction in social networks that people recognize (or acknowledge) health problems, contact health facilities, and comply with medical advice. Pescosolido (1991) notes that three kinds of factors influence critical decisions people make while experiencing a health problem. They include the sick person's number, strength, and type of network ties; the advice, material aid, and emotional support that a sick person receives; and his or her attitudes toward illness and medical care. The key to understanding health and illness behaviours lies in understanding these social networks. Their stability and change over time contribute to a successful passage through the sick person's "illness career."

A key player in this scripted drama is the sick person's primary caregiver—usually, the sick person's wife, mother, or daughter. The caregiver may have a full-time or part-time paid job, besides domestic responsibilities. Whatever her other duties, the addition of primary caregiving drains a caregiver's time and energy. Caregivers differ widely in how well they adapt to caregiving demands. Also, some illnesses are more taxing than others. Often, however, the caregiver finds herself needing support.

Cancer patients and their caregivers have much respect for doctors—particularly, for their professional expertise. Caregivers want to tap that expertise. They also want doctors to recognize their role in helping to manage the illness. They want doctors to provide professional support, information, help in learning personal coping strategies, regular updates from professionals, and education about the nature of the disease they are caring for (Hill, Shepherd, & Hardy, 1998). However, often doctors are unable to provide this amount of information and encouragement.

Figure 9.2 PERCENTAGE OF MEN AND WOMEN PROVIDING CARE, BY AGE OF CAREGIVER

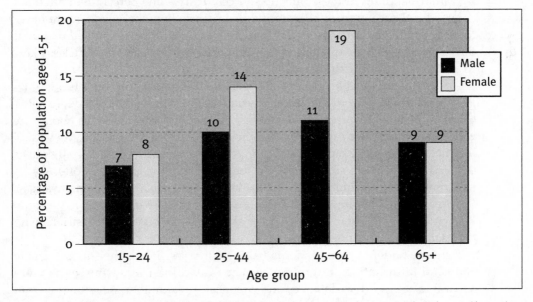

Source: Statistics Canada, 1996 General Social Survey, www.hc-sc.gc.ca/seniors-aines/pubs/unsorted/survey.htm.

Cancer patients want more information and more reassurance than their doctors have the time to provide. Their doctors realize this but can't do much about it; they're short of time. As a result, support groups grow up to provide information and reassurance to patients and their caregiving kin. These groups vary in size, and range from expert-led to peer-led, from mainly informational to mainly morale building, and so on. Whatever their structure, they seem to have adherents. Recently, the Internet too has become a support medium in cancer care, complete with on-line research libraries, discussion groups, chat rooms, and e-mailable experts.

To rate how this electronic provision of information works to inform and reassure cancer patients, Tepperman and Frydman (1999) administered a multiple-choice questionnaire through a Web site. They designed it to compare patients and family caregivers' perceptions of cancer information from Internet sources with information from their own physicians. They analyzed four hundred and twenty-three completed questionnaires. Outcomes assessed were subjects' interactions with their physicians, use of Internet resources to obtain information about their disease and care, and the relative values they place on information from both sources.

The data revealed that 72 percent of respondents contacted the Internet at least daily; 78 percent spoke with their doctors monthly or less. Respondents on-line gathered (medical) information 59 percent of the time and sought support (counselling and peer validation) 41 percent of the time. Physicians, it turns out, referred respondents for counselling or conventional support groups only rarely. They rarely encouraged, evaluated, or acted on information from outside sources (such as the Internet). Sixty-one percent of respondents had brought their doctors new information from these outside sources. Thirty-nine percent had attended conventional support groups or individual counselling; these were more likely to bring outside information to their physicians. Only 38 percent noted that their doctors were also users of Internet cancer resources; these patients were less likely to bring outside information to their physicians.

Respondents had an easier time finding information on the Internet than getting information from their own physicians. Physicians, however, were felt to be the more reliable information sources and respondents' decisions about care were based more often on information they received from physicians. They rated Internet sources more highly as having practical implications in daily living, as detailed, and as more supportive. On the other hand, respondents often had a hard time evaluating information obtained on the Internet and relied on physicians to resolve conflicts between information sources 60 per cent of the time. Respondents were particularly positive about interactions with physicians who themselves used the Internet.

Internet-adept cancer patients value their physician as their most reliable source of information and guidance. They rated Internet resources as more accessible, supportive, detailed, and practical in value than information from physicians. However, physicians remain primary advisors to resolve confusion over conflicting information, despite being somewhat averse to information from outside sources. As we can see from this study, information on its own is not sufficient to bring about a change of behaviour if the costs or the risks of a wrong decision are high, as they would be in this instance.

Their unavailability may have long-term effects on the relationship between patients, caregivers, and their doctors. For example, it may lead to the erosion of trust. Interpersonal trust depends on the degree to which patients see their doctors as competent, responsible, and caring. Continuities of care and encounter time that allows opportunities for response, patient instruction, and patient participation in the decision-making all encourage trust. Most medical leaders today believe that such trust is eroding. They blame the commercialization of medical care, conflicts of interest, media attention to medical uncertainty and error, and the growth of managed care (Mechanic, 1996).

As well, many doctors discourage their patients from becoming knowledgeable about their illness. Female physicians, in particular, express negative attitudes toward patients who show autonomy and take initiative toward their health care. This may be because female doctors hold a lower status in the profession than male doctors, so they feel more threatened by patient autonomy (Shuval, Shye, & Javetz, 1990).

Given the relative unavailability of their doctors, many patients and their caregivers look for help from *support groups*. These groups vary widely in size, composition, and activity. Medical professionals lead some, others are led by social service professionals, and others still are led by peers. They all share a desire to help patients and caregivers help themselves and one another.

What Social Networks Do

However, people get far more of the information and encouragement they need from their personal networks than from special-purpose support groups. Hundreds of empirical studies show that support from one's social network is a key factor explaining resilience in dealing with life stresses and adversity (Ganster and Victor, 1988). Social relationships give people a *sense* that they are receiving social support, and this *perceived* social support is important to their well-being (Gottlieb, 1985). Beyond that, social networks are also important for providing emotional and instrumental sustenance, and social regulation or control (House, Umberson, & Landis, 1988). Strong social networks get people to address their medical needs and use the health-care system regularly (Freidenberg & Hammer, 1998). As we will see shortly, they also increase compliance with treatment plans.

It is through personal and inter-organizational networks that individuals seek help with health problems (Pescosolido, 1996). Therefore, network characteristics make a difference to the care a sick person receives. Network size and cohesiveness are particularly important: large, cohesive networks are best for people's health (Tennestedt & McKinlay, 1987). Among mental health patients, network size predicts hospitalization and service use. As the patient's network size increases, outpatient service use increases and hospitalization decreases (Becker, Thornicroft, Leese, McCrone, Johnson, Albert, & Turner, 1997). Among old people, more resource-rich and diversified networks (of friends and neighbours) lead to more social support and, as a result, less activity limitation and better health (Litwin, 1998). Among people with AIDS-defining symptoms, large social network sizes lead to a greater longevity (Patterson, Shaw, Semple, Cherner, McCutcheon, Atkinson, Grant, Nannis, et al., 1996).

Large Networks Are Better

Typically, large, cohesive networks are associated with higher levels of social participation. Social participation, in turn, leads to higher levels of well-being and life satisfaction. Thus, membership in a social network predicts well-being (Wilson, Moore, Rubin, & Bartels, 1990).

Personal characteristics also make a difference: they interact with network characteristics to produce positive health outcomes. For example, a larger social network is more important for sick people who are less trusting than average; because they are distrustful, they use the resources available in their networks less efficiently. For people who are more trustful, and therefore better able to mobilize support from their networks, size is less important (Hibbard, 1985).

Because social networks can be useful in promoting good health, some health programs encourage the formation of new self-sustaining friendship networks. Women who participate in these programs improve their social networks and increase their quality of life and self-esteem (Benum, Anstorp, Dalgard, & Sorenson, 1988). In Quebec, two in every three elderly people (ages 65+) provide support to others, making them important actors in their own informal support networks. Old people living alone or having small kinship networks receive less support than others (Martel & Legare, 1998). Not having adult children as part of one's social network limits potential informal care (Havens & Chipperfield, 1990).

The processes of coping with chronic illness tend to damage social support networks. Often, after people become ill or become caregivers to the ill, their interaction with family and friends diminish. We need to learn more about why networks change when people become caregivers to Alzheimer's Disease victims, for example (Suitor & Pillemer, 1988). Key to helping chronically ill people and their caregivers is the reconstruction of social support networks (Pescosolido, Wright, & Sullivan, 1995). The provision of social support often reduces a primary caregiver's sense of a burden.

Dysfunctional Families

Certain kinds of families are better than others are at providing support. Other things being equal, flexible and cohesive families have the highest level of well-being. In **cohesive families**, members feel attached to the family, and to one another. In **flexible families**, members can change their ideas, roles, and relationships as the situation demands. Even families with adolescents (typically a predictor of diminished well-being) show high levels of well-being if they are cohesive and flexible.

Families in which cohesion and flexibility are weak have the least ability to cope with stress, because they can give their members the least support. Even with the support and assistance of others, many still have trouble handling the stresses life throws their way. Often, attempts at coping are unsuccessful. In these cases, the family situation deteriorates, communication worsens, and unhappiness increases. When the family's ability to cope breaks down, individuals in that family each try to handle the stress on their own. Their individual efforts often end up increasing the stress and discomfort of the family as a whole. Intense and prolonged stress of this kind can lead to the breakup of the family.

We can even see the decision to break up the family as a form of coping. However, this is personal coping. The family is unable to cope as a social unit of interacting individuals. That is why one or more members of the family decide they must separate from the unit to help them cope better. Precisely what we mean by a **dysfunctional family** is a social unit that works so badly that its members are better off on their own.

Families with chronically ill children often develop dysfunctions, indicated by social and psychological disturbances. These dysfunctional families are notable for chronic conflict, child abuse, medical neglect, psychiatric pathology, or alcoholism (White et al., 1984). Family communication worsens, and one or both parents fail to provide support for their children and other family members (Jurk et al., 1980).

Families under the strain of chronic illness and treatment often reproduce and magnify their most troublesome characteristics. Families that were happy and healthy continue to be happy and healthy. However, in families with histories of drinking, marital strife, sibling rivalry, or financial instability, problems that begin as minor ones may explode into major ones.

Violence

Violence among family members is probably as old as the institution of the family itself. However, the systematic study of family violence is a new branch of academic research. It only emerged in the 1960s, launched by the publication of the first detailed case studies of seemingly inexplicable physical injuries suffered by young children.

No one knows for sure how big a problem family violence is in our society. A large part of the difficulty in determining the extent or prevalence of family violence is methodological. To begin with, we have the problem of defining violence. Students of family violence come at the issue from a host of disciplines that include anthropology, sociology, psychology, social work, medicine, and criminology. Within each discipline, there are competing definitions of what

How common is family violence? Sociologists are limited in the study of intimate violence and abuse because it typically takes place in private as part of an ongoing intimate relationship.

counts as family violence, and a variety of ways of measuring its extent. Thus, the studies that they conduct are often hard to compare.

The term "family violence" did not even exist before 1930 (Busby, 1991: 336). People may have been aware that violence did occur within families. Almost certainly police, doctors, novelists, and nosy neighbours knew. However, an overwhelming social consensus sanctified family privacy, thus keeping researchers from asking, and victims from talking about, family violence. For a variety of reasons, that consensus broke down in the 1960s.

Family violence is an umbrella term covering a range of different kinds of violence, among different sets of family members. The oldest recognized form of violence is physical violence: the intentional use of physical force that one family member aims at hurting or injuring another family member (Busby, 1991: 335). It ranges from such acts as slapping, shaking, pushing, punching, and kicking to using (or threatening to use) a weapon, such as a knife or a gun or even a baseball bat, with the intention of scaring, hurting, maiming, or killing. It is estimated that family members, most commonly parents, carry out at least 20 percent of all physical assaults.

In addition, we need to include sexual violence, such as child sexual abuse, incest, and marital rape, which is likely to have a component of physical violence as well. Due to its qualitatively different nature, researchers categorize sexual violence separately from non-sexual physical violence and study it in its own right.

Researchers also study nonviolent forms of emotional and psychological abuse. These include anything from emotional neglect to psychological torture. The reasons for including nonphysical forms of abuse in studies of family violence

Table 9.2 ESTIMATED NUMBER OF SPOUSAL VIOLENCE CASES AND THE PROPORTION WITNESSED BY CHILDREN

	Total (No.) (000s)	%	Violence Against Women (No.) (000s)	%	Violence Against Men (No.) (000s)	%
Total violence by spouse	1239	100	690	56	549	44
Children witnessed violence	461	37	321	70	140	30
Children did not witness violence/ no child at the time	737	60	354	48	384	52
Not stated/don't know	40	3+	14	35+	26	65+

+Coefficient of variation between 16.6% and 33.3%. Figures may not add to total due to rounding.

Source: Adapted from the Statistics Canada website, General Social Survey, 1999, www.statcan.ca/english/freepub/85-224-XIE/0100085-224-XIE.pdf.

are twofold. First, emotional abuse often accompanies violent acts. Second, emotional abuse is often as painful or destructive of the self-esteem and healthy emotional development of its victims as physical violence.

As to neglect, it may seem that no attention at all is better than the excessive negative attention involved in abuse. However, neglect can be just as damaging to a family member, especially to a dependent child or elderly parent. Sexual abuse, neglect, and physical violence are different forms of violence and often stem from different causes. In the discussion that follows, we will focus on physical violence.

Sociologists see two additional problems in determining the prevalence of family violence. We generally lack access to hospital records and to cases gathered by social workers. These records and cases are confidential, and so they are off-limits even to researchers with the most benign motives. Moreover, adequate sampling and measurement is difficult. Family violence has, to a considerable degree, been dragged out of the closet. However, it remains a source of shame for most of its perpetrators as well as for its victims. Therefore, family violence continues to be hidden, to a large degree, from public view.

Even if people were completely forthright about what goes on behind closed doors in their families, measurement would still be complicated by the variation in what counts as violence, from one culture to another and often from one family to another. For example, in the early part of our century, many parents disciplined misbehaving children by beating them with a belt or ruler. For their part, the Sioux peoples considered the white settlers' slapping and beating of their own children as childish and reprehensible (Erikson, 1950). Some Muslim cultures still practise female circumcision. Most North Americans would consider this practice a severe form of cruelty.

If we consider female circumcision family violence then we must also consider infant male circumcision. This procedure, originally a Jewish religious practice, was at one time virtually universally adopted by North Americans, for supposed hygienic reasons, and is still routinely performed. However, many experts find no medical justification for this surgical procedure. When done without anesthesia it is undoubtedly painful and traumatic, but until recent research proved this fact, people doubted the infant's pain.

In spite of the difficulties in identifying family violence, sociologists have developed better techniques for estimating its prevalence. According to one such estimate, "(a)t least one form of physical violence (slaps and pushes) occurs in more than half the homes in the United States" (Busby, 1991: 374).

Most commonly used today in measuring the extent of domestic violence—especially for purposes of criminal justice intervention—is Straus's **Conflict Tactics Scales**, developed in 1979. The first reliable and valid scale for measuring family violence, the Conflict Tactics Scales measure verbal aggression and physical violence on a continuum. This, in conjunction with a checklist to identify high-risk cases, focuses on two specific criteria. One is whether there have been three or more instances of violence in the previous year. The other is the violence of the act or acts. Factors used to rate violence include the use of a weapon; injuries requiring medical treatment; the involvement of a child, an animal, or a nonfamily member; drug or alcohol involvement; extreme dominance, violence, or surveillance; forced sex; extensive or repeated property damage; and police involvement (Straus, 1996).

It is hard to determine how common family violence is. However, violence is sufficiently common to pose a problem for family researchers who need a nonviolent control group. Holtzworth-Munroe and colleagues (1992) report having collected questionnaire and scale data on over 550 respondents recruited through newspaper advertisements and from among couples seeking marital therapy, for example. Findings from five such studies suggest that husband violence has occurred in up to one-third of couples who do not report distress with their marriage and one-half of maritally distressed couples.

As we have mentioned, sociologists are limited in the study of intimate violence and abuse. Violence typically takes place in private, as part of an ongoing intimate relationship. We lack widely accepted and widely applied definitions of the key terms involved. Also lacking is a widely accepted definition of what is a family (Gelles, 1994).

Finally, recognize that much of what occurs between intimates within marriage also occurs between intimates outside marriage. Consider date rape: a survey was conducted on 44 college and university campuses across Canada by sociologists Walter DeKeseredy and Katherine Kelly (1993; 1995; Kelly & DeKeseredy, 1994). It found that four women in five claimed that a dating partner had subjected them to abuse. Overall, nearly as many men admitted having acted abusively toward their dates.

The validity of the findings was attacked because the study listed a very wide range of behaviours under the heading of "abuse" (Gartner & Fox, 1993). These behaviours included insults, swearing, accusations of flirting with others or acting spitefully, as well as violent and grotesque acts such as using or threatening to use a gun or knife, beating, kicking, or biting the dating partner. So it is best to separate out the violent from the less violent abuses before we attempt to analyze the results.

When we do this, certain patterns fall into place. Where *violent* abuses are concerned, women are more than twice as likely as men to acknowledge their occurrence. Where less violent abuses are concerned, men and women acknowledge them equally often. For example, 65 percent of women report being insulted or sworn at by a date, and 63.6 percent of men report having insulted or sworn at a date. On the other hand, 11.1 percent of women report being slapped by a date, yet only 4.5 percent of men report slapping a date. Likewise, 8.1 percent of women report being kicked, bitten, or hit with a fist, yet only 2.4 percent of men report having done any of those things. This consistent discrepancy leads to one of three possible conclusions. Either (1) violent and abusive men date a lot more women than gentle, non-abusive men, (2) women tell a lot of lies about their dates, or (3) many men are ashamed to admit the things they have done to their dates.

The data also show that violent abuses on dates are not only physical, they are also sexual. As with physical violence, male respondents are only about one-half or one-third as likely to report doing these things as women are to report having them done.

Bear in mind that most instances of forced sexual activity occur between people who know each other. The result is, too often, that women blame themselves for the experience. Because they know the assailant, they react passively to the sexual assault. Because they react passively, they blame themselves for not reacting more forcefully. A few even continue the dating relationship.

Sexual harassment is another form of sexual assault, and is especially prevalent in schools and workplaces. In the halls of their schools, female high-school students regularly experience harassment, which ranges from unwanted staring and rude or embarrassing remarks, to unwanted touching. The result is a frequent, if not constant, sense of discomfort, even dread, about being at school.

Part of the problem is that perceptions of sexual harassment vary by gender. High-school boys may have little idea just how much they are upsetting the girls. College-aged men are much less likely to label behaviour "harassment" than their female peers. But after exposure to the workforce, men's awareness grows and they, too, come to see certain behaviour as harassment. Overall, women label more behaviours as harassing than men do, but this discrepancy decreases with experience in the workforce, as women become accustomed to "the norm."

Causes of Violence

Violence between spouses may be the most perplexing form of violence, as it raises so many questions, such as why spouses abuse their partners and why the abused spouse stays with her or his abuser.

We use the term **spousal violence** in this chapter, but unmarried couples also inflict violence on each other. In fact, one study found severe violence to be five times more likely among cohabiting couples than married couples (Yllo & Straus, 1981). Other, more recent research confirms that cohabitors are still more likely than spouses to engage in violent relationships (Jackson, 1996).

Researchers debate the causes of family violence (for a text that reviews many controversies in the literature, see Gelles & Loseke, 1993). Possible contributors range from personal factors, such as stress level or a history of abuse, to cultural ideologies of families and "discipline." We are still unable to detect the relative contribution of any single factor. We can identify correlates of violent behaviour, but a correlate is not necessarily a cause.

Some argue that the same social conditions produce both domestic violence and violent crime outside the household: poverty, inadequate housing,

---

Debate Box 9.1 **WHO IS TO BLAME WHEN FAMILY VIOLENCE BREAKS OUT? Which side of the debate do you fall on?**

Usually the Men Are to Blame

- Men are trained by our culture to be aggressive and violent. The mass media are full of examples that encourage men to be brutal, physical, and dangerous.
- Historically law enforcement agents have not protected women and children from their male "loved ones." This has been due to faulty beliefs about family privacy.
- Male hormones increase the likelihood of violence whereas female hormones do not have the same effect. The problem is genetic, biological, and universal.
- Most male violence against women grows out of issues of possession, control, and domination. Women rarely pursue these goals to the same degree as men.
- Men do not start all the family fights, but owing to their size and strength they do more physical harm than women when they take part in physical fighting.

Both Partners Are to Blame

- You can't have a fight with just one fighter. Usually, the abusive incident grows out of an argument in which both partners have participated more or less equally.
- Family life is supercharged with emotional intensity, intimacy, and unfulfilled desires. This leads to frustration on both sides, which often leads to aggression.
- With the growing complexity of modern family life, it is to be expected that people's needs and desires will come into conflict more frequently.
- Though women are less likely to use physical violence to an extreme degree, they are likely to act in verbally abusive and provocative ways that inflame argument.
- Our society, in recognizing past inequalities suffered by women, has gone too far in the direction of forgiving all women's wrongs and blaming men for everything.

unemployment, and the social acceptance, even glorification, of violence. Others argue that a high crime rate fosters an acceptance of aggression and hastens the deterioration of the family unit, both of which increase domestic violence. The variables most strongly associated with domestic violence are age, income, work status, religion, urban versus rural residence, and ethnic group (Straus, Gelles, & Steinmetz, 1980). According to this research, the safest homes are those with fewer than two children, little stress, and a democratic system of decision-making.

Other variables likely to distinguish husbands who batter their wives are presence of alcohol abuse, low education, frequent arguments with spouse, and frequent drug use. Abusing husbands typically also have a (childhood) background of family violence and marital arguments (Coleman, Weinman, & Bartholomew, 1980).

Status inconsistency (inconsistency between one's education and occupation) is another risk factor associated with increased psychological and physical abuse, and an even greater risk of life-threatening violence. Perceived underachievement by the husband and overachievement by the wife are also factors. In contrast, overachievement by the husband decreases abuse risks (Hornung, McCullough, & Sugimoto, 1981). Violent men typically have lower levels of self-esteem than nonviolent men from either stressed or happy marriages (Goldstein & Rosenbaum, 1985). Violent men also consider their wives' behaviour toward them to be more damaging to their self-esteem.

The single best predictor of violent behaviour toward a partner is the experience of violence at the hands of a partner. If your partner hits you, you will likely hit him or her back. After that, having been the target of parental violence during childhood most increases the risk of violence in adulthood. Excessive use of alcohol is a significant, though modest, predictor of both intimate-partner violence and child abuse (Merrill, Hervig, & Milner, 1996).

Marital violence is a major predictor of physical child abuse. Men who abuse their wives often abuse their children as well; and the more often a spouse uses violence against a spouse, the more likely that spouse is to also use violence against a child. This relationship is particularly strong for men. The probability of child abuse by a violent husband increases from 5 percent with one act of marital violence to near certainty with fifty or more such acts (Ross, 1996). Thus, children in abusive households are likely to both witness and experience domestic violence firsthand. Witnessing violence between parents increases the likelihood that children will use violence against their own spouses when they grow up.

Children learn, by observation, to use violence to resolve disputes and vent frustration. We must stress the importance of early childhood experience in forming people's attitudes toward violence. Childhood experience doesn't explain all incidents of abusive behaviour, but it does account for many. According to Murray Straus (1992: 685), the more physical punishment a man experiences as a child, the higher is his probability of hitting a spouse. For it is in the family that children learn the normative legitimacy of family violence.

Some of the effect of childhood exposure is a reaction to the shock of witnessing violence. In this sense, it is due to the creation of mental health problems in the child—problems of shame, guilt, low self-worth, and depression.

However, many children who suffer or witness abuse never become abusive adults. Despite their violent histories, men who perceive threats from significant others (e.g., threats of rejection by their beloved) tend to be nonviolent if they are strongly attached to their spouse (Lackey & Williams, 1995). Thus, a strong adult attachment can often undo, or partly undo, the damage done by a violent childhood.

A second factor that affects whether a person will use violence against intimates is sex. The childhood experience of violence affects girls differently from boys. Girls typically internalize their problems, as depression and anxiety. Boys typically externalize their problems, as aggression and rule breaking. Girls who suffer abuse as children are more likely to become victims of abuse in adulthood, whereas boys who suffer abuse as children are more likely to become abusers.

Some view domestic violence as a defence of patriarchy by men who fear that women's increasing economic and social independence is eroding their dominance. So, for example, an income disparity between husband and wife predicts the occurrence of wife abuse (McCloskey, 1996). An income bias that favours women predicts more frequent and severe violence by men toward their wives. Since

Parental Substance Abuse a Major Factor in Child Abuse and Neglect

According to the Child Welfare League of America (CWLA), a major factor contributing to child abuse and neglect is parental substance abuse. The CWLA has recently published a new booklet which includes the following findings:

- More than 8 million children live with parents who are substance abusers.
- Substance abuse exists in 40 to 80 percent of families in which the children are victims of abuse.
- Children whose substance-abusing parents do not receive appropriate treatment are more likely to remain in foster care longer and to re-enter foster care once they have returned home.

- Children whose parents abuse alcohol and other drugs are three times more likely to be abused and more than four times more likely to be neglected than children from non-abusing families.

Parents' abuse of alcohol and other drugs can lead to a cycle of addiction, which is reflected by high rates of alcoholism and other substance abuse among children of addicts. Youth substance abuse can have a domino effect of problems in school, involvement in juvenile justice, teen pregnancy, and mental and emotional turmoil. The authors contend that the cycle can be broken by focusing on prevention programs and by having parents receive treatment from comprehensive programs.

Source: Adapted from "Alcohol, Other Drugs, and Child Welfare: Highlights" (fact sheet), © 2001 Child Welfare League of America, Washington, DC. Used by permission.

employment is a symbolic resource in relationships—a source of status, power, and economic resources—spousal violence against women is most common when the wife has a job and the husband does not. Risks are low when neither partner is employed, or only the husband has a job (Macmillan & Gartner, 1996).

Men are more likely to batter—or kill—to protect what they think of as their sexual property, whereas women are only likely to batter or kill to protect themselves. (For a contrary view, see Straus (1992), who argues that women too may be violent to men when they are not acting out of self-defence; however this is mainly characteristic of the less-serious "common couple violence.") Men are likely to kill themselves after killing their "property." Women are not. They only kill a partner who has battered them systematically and whom they fear will batter them even more. Compared with non-battered women, battered women in spousal conflict use more violence, receive lower levels of social support, and experience higher levels of self-blame. Battered women, therefore, are more likely to use violence on their spouse when they feel they are receiving little social support, and even if they feel they are to blame for the conflict (Barnett, Martinez, & Keyson, 1996).

Women's shelter records show five main types of battered women, determined by types of violence used and experienced: (1) women in stable low-violence relationships, who are likely to be violence instigators; (2) women in unstable relationships who suffer severe and often sexual violence; (3) severe and chronically abused women who have also seen their children abused; (4) women who were not abused but whose children were; and (5) chronically abused women who have grown to accept it. This last type is the most likely to return to the assailant after a period in the shelter (Snyder & Fruchtman, 1981).

The vast majority of battered women in jail for killing their partner share a few distinctive characteristics. Typically, they were sexually assaulted during childhood, dropped out of high school, have an erratic work history of unskilled jobs, cohabited with their partner, experienced a drug problem, attempted suicide by drug overdosing, and/or had access to the batterer's guns. These findings, based on in-depth interviews, help to explain why battered women kill their mates. After brutal, repeated assaults and death threats, and after failing in their attempts to escape through alcohol or drug abuse—even through attempted suicide—they see killing their abuser as the only way out (Roberts, 1996).

Women jailed for killing or assaulting their abusers are usually older, in the relationship longer, and have experienced a longer duration of violence in the relationship. They have also experienced more frequent and severe battering (including sex assaults) and sustained more injuries than a comparison group of battered women incarcerated for other offences. Furthermore, battered women who killed or seriously assaulted their partners were more likely to believe that their lives were in danger. They were less likely to use violence against their partners and less likely to have a prior criminal record or to have served time previously than battered women jailed for other offences (O'Keefe, 1997). In many venues, these cases are being reconsidered as self-defence.

Some researchers note that, on occasion, both husbands and wives are violent. They argue, in effect, that violence is an *interactional problem*—a result of marital dysfunctioning. For example, Brinkerhoff and Lupri (1988) state, on the basis of a survey conducted in Calgary, that husband-to-wife, wife-to-husband, and mutual violence occur in families at every socioeconomic, educational, and income level (see Figure 8.2 on page 301). The strongest predictors of violence are interactional— meaning that they arise from relationship processes such as marital conflict, customary modes of expressing aggression, and stresses induced by work. Accordingly, Lupri (1993) uses data from a representative national sample of Canadians to argue that male violence in the home is a widespread and, in that sense, "normal" element of marital interaction. Over the life course, partners negotiate and renegotiate their ways of interacting and dealing with conflicts, with the result that patterns of violence change with age. (On the importance of age and marital conflict, see also Lupri, Grandin, & Brinkerhoff, 1994.)

Indeed, Grandin and Lupri (1997) state that common couple-violence—the "normal" product of many U.S. and Canadian households—is characterized by gender symmetry. According to this research, and contrary to common belief, wife-to-husband violence is frequent, and Canadian couples are more likely to engage in domestic violence, both severe and minor, than are American couples.

Psychologically abusive women show the same personality profiles as abusive men, characterized by jealousy, suspicion, immaturity, and insecurity. As to physical abuse, researchers report that more than 70 percent of these women have been physical to the point of shoving their husband or boyfriend or destroying their partner's possessions in anger (Stacey, Hazlewood, & Shupe, 1994: 124). Their spouses' superior strength kept them from more direct forms of assault, but many women nonetheless punched, slapped, kicked, or used a weapon against their partner. In such relationships violence is two-sided. As Macmillan and Gartner (1996) have noted, "interpersonal conflict violence" is extremely common and symmetrical, with equal numbers of male and female perpetrators.

A woman may instigate the violence, for example, by hitting the man during an argument, to which he responds by hitting back. Though the man does more damage (up to five times more physical injuries) to his partner, both partners may be guilty of uncontrolled tempers. As we have said, some women also lash out in self-defence. Often, this occurs in the anticipation of violence from the man after long experience with his violence. Occasionally, it comes as retaliation after the fact, as with Lorena Bobbitt, who cut off her husband's penis, or Francine Hughes, who set her abusive husband's bedroom on fire while he slept, or the long-abused woman in Nova Scotia who shot her husband in his truck. (A National Film Board film was made about this very sad case.)

In a continuously and symmetrically abusive relationship, the line between instigation and self-defence blurs. Sometimes, the perception of women as victims and men as perpetrators is a false analysis of the situation. A better view might be the **circular causal model**, in which both partners contribute to the escalation of the abuse. But it still may be that the partners do not have equal power in the relationship or in society, generally making women more vulnerable. In these cases, therapy should focus on the treatment of both partners or on the peaceful end of the relationship.

Alcoholism and drug abuse are also important factors in explaining spousal violence. Many drugs (including alcohol) are disinhibitors, causing people to relax their inhibitions, including those against violent behaviour. Other drugs increase adrenaline levels and, in this way, may cause anger or frustration levels to get out of control. Thus, some people who would not otherwise resort to violence when they are sober may engage in it when they are under the influence of drugs. Macmillan and Gartner (1996: Table 5) show that drinking, for example, is a significant predictor of **systematic abuse** and of attempts at coercive control.

Alcohol and drugs may have different uses and different effects in different cultural subgroups. Jasinski et al. (1997) used data from the 1992 National Alcohol and Family Violence Survey to examine the impact of ethnicity on the relationships among several types of stressors associated with the workplace, heavy drinking, and wife assaults. The results show that Anglo and Hispanic husbands experienced different types of work stress and coped with those stressors differently. Among Hispanic husbands, all work stressors examined were associated with increased levels of both drinking and violence. Among Anglos, these same work stressors were associated with elevated levels of drinking, but not violence.

Alcohol is known to interact with poverty, stress, and other high-risk behaviours. For obvious reasons, alcohol and drugs are particularly attractive to people in pain or sorrow. Yet, alcohol use can also increase the likelihood of drug use and sexual activity that is connected with HIV/AIDS infection. A survey of American Aboriginal women in New York City, for example, found that 38 percent had used alcohol or other drugs in the last six months, and among the 59 percent who reported sexual activity in this period, 80 percent had had unprotected sex. The use of alcohol or other drugs also appears to have increased the likelihood of nonpartner sexual assault (Walters & Simoni, 1999). Alcohol does not cause violence per se, any more than it causes HIV/AIDS, but it increases the risk of being in a place where violence is apt to occur.

A lack of sufficient *coping resources* also increases the likelihood of violence in a family relationship. In one study, 90 percent of the violent families examined had serious problems such as financial difficulties and poor family cohesion. These families were also poorly integrated into society, showing a lack of social support (Bryant et al., 1963). **Social isolation**, or lack of social support, is a common predictor of physical child abuse. Mothers at the greatest risk of physically abusing their children are, typically, more socially isolated than others. Practical support from work or school associates and emotional support from supportive, nurturing people both help to decrease the potential for physical child abuse (Moncher, 1995).

Figure 9.3 PERCENTAGE DISTRIBUTION OF FORMS OF CHILD ABUSE IN CANADA

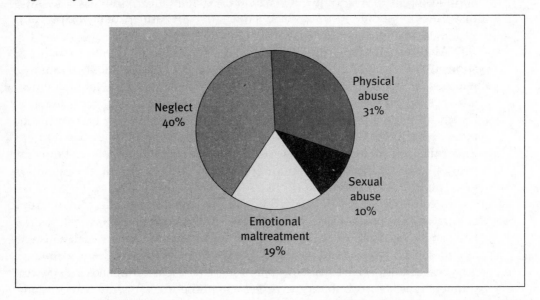

Source: Adapted from the Statistics Canada website, Family Violence in Canada, A Statistical Profile, 2001 Cat. @ 85-224-XIE, www.statcan.ca/english/freepub/85-224-XIE/0100085-224-XIE.pdf.

Cultural attitudes that support violence as a whole, or violence directed against women and children in particular, also contribute to domestic violence. A society that condones violent behaviours may end up encouraging them.

Hamby (2000) notes of American Aboriginals that native communities are extremely diverse and heterogeneous. Available evidence, while sketchy, suggests that male authority, male restrictiveness, and socioeconomic stress are associated with violence against women, but that the levels of these factors vary widely across native groups. For example, some native tribes practise matrilineal descent while others are patrilineal. This diversity has far-reaching implications for the community context in which domestic violence occurs. An approach that integrates both feminist and community approaches seems best suited to address the problem of domestic violence in Aboriginal North America.

On the other hand, acculturation may also contribute to violence by increasing the stress level. Findings by Firestone, Lambert, and Vega (1999) indicate that higher acculturation increases intimate abuse, and social support reduces it. Acculturation stress increases abuse only among immigrants. Abuse rates are higher among U.S.-born Mexican Americans than immigrants. There are no additive effects of education and income in explaining abuse in a multivariate model. Results highlight the need for improved understanding about how acculturation and acculturation stress processes are differentially related to intimate violence among immigrants and U.S.-born Mexican Americans.

Community violence generally—whether a result of patriarchal culture, substance abuse, warfare, poverty, or a combination of these—increases the likelihood of further violence. Al-Krenawi et al. investigated the well-being of Arab adolescents who live under the threat of ongoing blood vengeance, and to assess the impact of sociodemographic characteristics, cultural context, and family functioning as mediator factors. The participants of this study demonstrated higher levels of distress and symptomatic behaviour as compared to the Israeli norms. General family functioning emerged as the major predictor associated with mental health. Female participants reported a higher anxiety level than their male counterparts. Male participants, on the other hand, were more willing to continue the feud of blood vengeance. The findings suggest that there are similarities among children and adolescents who live in war zones and those who live under a threatening blood vengeance. Family functioning appears as the major mediator of well-being.

Among African-American children living in or close to an inner-city public housing development, exposure to community violence produces a sense of neighbourhood danger and family conflict. This feeling, in turn, may lead to symptoms of post-traumatic stress disorder (Overstreet & Braun, 2000). Exposure to actual family violence, however, affects development differently than exposure to community violence. Social support effectively cushions the effects of family violence, but not the effects of community violence (Muller et al., 2000). Of the two, community violence is likely to have effects that are harder to control and prevent. So, we need to invest in our communities, as well as our families, if we are to raise healthy children.

It is unclear whether societies that condone family violence have higher rates of violence than those that do not. However, these societies offer fewer options to abuse victims. In the past, cultural myths prevented Canadian society from accepting domestic violence as a serious problem, and therefore recognizing the need for laws and institutions to protect women. These myths included the belief that women typically provoke violence, and that family violence is a "private affair" and therefore police should stay out of it. The recognition of a "battered-wife syndrome" was a big step toward condemning wife abuse (Fineman & Mykitiuk, 1994).

Thus, to understand the prevalence of domestic violence in our society, we must understand ordinary people's attitudes toward intimacy, gender, and violence. Even those who are innocent of violent behaviour may unwittingly support violence by their ways of thinking.

In short, we note a variety of "causes of violence" in the literature. The reason for so many causal candidates is, mainly, that we are confusing three different types of spousal violence. Macmillan and Gartner (1996: 25) identify them as

> *interpersonal conflict* violence, that almost exclusively involves pushing, shoving, grabbing, and slapping; (2) *non-systematic abuse*, which involves a greater variety of violent acts, including threats, the

throwing of objects, kicking and hitting; and (3) *systematic abuse*, which involves a relatively high risk of all types of violent acts, including life-threatening violence such as beating, choking, and attacks with knives or guns.

In their analysis of data from the Canadian Violence Against Women Survey (Statistics Canada, 1993), Macmillan and Gartner (1996) examine the effects of such proprietary or "coercively controlling" attitudes on domestic violence. The jealous husband does not want his wife to talk to other men. He tries to limit her contact with family or friends, insists on knowing whom she is with and where she is at all times, and prevents her from knowing about or having access to the family income, even if she asks. We can say that a woman whose partner possesses all these traits has a coercively controlling husband.

Often, psychologically and physically abusive men fear the loss of their partner, whom they consider sexual and emotional property. These abusive men show a high degree of jealousy and always try to monitor their spouse or girlfriend. They insult and belittle her yet display an extreme fear of being left by her. Although they rationalize their behaviour by blaming their partner, alcohol, or various other sources for their rages, "[m]any men, particularly those at their meetings for counselling, were self-conscious, embarrassed, and ashamed" (Stacey, Hazlewood, & Shupe, 1994: 60). They recognize their behaviour as aberrant.

High levels of reported coercive control predict all three types of domestic violence and predict the most serious, systematic abuse most strongly (Macmillan & Gartner, 1996: Table 5). The more jealous and possessive a partner, the more dangerously and consistently abusive he is likely to be. In our culture, men can find justification for such pathological behaviour in the belief that it is appropriate for a man to protect his woman's purity and innocence (sometimes interpreted as ignorance). Today, the remnants of antiquated notions of chivalry do not protect women (if, indeed, they ever did); rather, they are used to justify gender inequality and hence domestic violence against women.

Also, because of cultural conceptions of masculinity, men are more tolerant of domestic violence than women. This too squares perfectly with the patriarchal model, which says that men are in charge and they use violence to stay that way. **Traditional family values** of male dominance, gender-based division of labour, and parental discipline of children are associated with high levels of family violence, including child sexual abuse (Higgins & McCabe, 1994). A review of previous studies finds that assaultive husbands are likely to support a patriarchal ideology, including positive attitudes toward marital violence and negative attitudes toward gender equality. For their part, assaulted wives usually hold more liberal gender attitudes than non-assaulted wives (Sugarman & Frankel, 1996). Usually, people in our society who hold egalitarian sex-role beliefs are more sympathetic to battered women than are traditionalists (Coleman & Stith, 1997).

Here's another window into our culture: researchers asked college students to assign verdicts to fictional court cases based on vignettes describing battered women who killed their husbands. They found some kinds of women guilty more often than others. Specifically, verbal aggression by the woman, and her characterization as a bad or dysfunctional wife or mother, increased the likelihood that the students would support a guilty verdict. The husband's use of a weapon against the woman did not much decrease the number of guilty verdicts (Follingstad, Brondino, & Kleinfelter, 1996).

The effects of traditionalism on beliefs about domestic violence are even more evident in recently industrializing countries. For example, residents of Singapore disapprove of wife beatings, even when extramarital affairs or child abuses by women are involved. However, beatings are more acceptable if people see the wife as violating her prescribed sex role, particularly in failing to be the "good mother" and the "loyal wife" (Choi & Edleson, 1996).

Women themselves have a hard time escaping from these traditional notions. For example, many Indian-immigrant women in North America show the effects of patriarchal training in their acceptance of domestic violence. Indoctrinated from childhood to believe that a good wife and mother sacrifices personal freedom and autonomy, they gain little sense of empowerment even from a professional job and economic independence. Further, they feel responsible for the reputation of their families in India and are eager to avoid compromising their families' honour by divorcing. As well, they operate under the added pressures of preserving traditions and presenting an unblemished image of their ethnic community to the North American mainstream (Dasgupta & Warrier, 1996).

Same-Sex Violence

Partner violence seems to be as prevalent in the gay and lesbian community as in the heterosexual community. This violence may take the form of lesbian battering, homophobic control, mutual battering, and violence associated with human immunodeficiency virus (HIV) status. Internalized homophobia is a particularly strong predictive factor associated with gay and lesbian partner violence. But other factors, such as violence in the family, substance abuse, dependency conflicts, and power imbalances, may also be associated with its incidence (West, 1998).

In a large American sample (n = 499) of ethnically diverse gay men, lesbians, and bisexual and transgendered people, physical violence was reported in 9 percent of current and 32 percent of past relationships. One percent of participants had experienced forced sex in their current relationship. Nine percent reported this experience in past relationships. Emotional abuse was reported by 83 percent of the participants. Women reported higher frequencies than men did for physical abuse, coercion, shame, threats, and use of children for control. Across types of abuse, ethnic differences emerged regarding physical abuse and coercion. Differences across age groups were found regarding coercion, shame, and use of children as tools. Higher income was correlated with increased threats, stalking, sexual, physical, and financial abuses (Turell, 2000).

In another American study, 283 white gays and lesbians, ages 18 to 79, reported on their experiences both as victims and perpetrators of gay or lesbian relationship violence by completing a modified version of the Conflict Tactics Scale. General results indicate that a same-sex partner had victimized 47.5 percent of the lesbians and 29.7 percent of the gays. Lesbians reported an overall perpetration rate of 38 percent, compared to 21.8 percent for gay men. In comparison to gay males, lesbians were more likely to be classified as both victims and perpetrators of violence and to have experienced a greater number of different victimization and perpetration tactics. When items were weighted to create an indicator of severity, no significant differences between lesbians and gay men were found (Waldner, Gratch, & Magruder, 1997).

Table 9.3 ABUSE IN SAME-SEX RELATIONSHIPS VERSUS ABUSE IN OPPOSITE-SEX RELATIONSHIPS

WHAT IS THE SAME	WHAT IS DIFFERENT
Abuse is always the responsibility of the abuser and is always a choice.	Very limited services exist specifically for abused and abusive lesbians and gay men.
Victims are often blamed for the abuse by partners, and sometimes even family, friends and professionals can excuse or minimize the abusive behaviour.	Lesbians and gay men often experience a lack of understanding of the seriousness of the abuse when reporting incidences of violence to a therapist, police officer or medical personnel.
It is difficult for victims to leave abusive relationships. Abuse usually worsens over time. The abuser is often apologetic after abusing, giving false hope that the abuse will stop.	Homophobia in society denies the reality of lesbian and gay men's lives, including the existence of lesbian and gay male relationships, let alone abusive ones. When abuse exists, attitudes often range from "who cares" to "these relationships are generally unstable or unhealthy."
Abuse is not an acceptable or healthy way to solve difficulties in relationships, regardless of orientation.	Shelters for abused women may not be sensitive to same-sex abuse (theoretically, shelters are open to all women and therefore, a same-sex victim may not feel safe as her abuser may also have access to the shelter). Abused gay men have even fewer places to turn for help in that there are no agency-sponsored safe places to stay.
Victims feels responsible for their partner's violence and their partner's emotional state, hoping to prevent further violence.	In lesbian and gay male relationships, there may be additional fears of losing the relationship which confirms one's sexual orientation; fears of not being believed about the abuse and fears of losing friends and support within the lesbian/gay communities.

Source: Education Wife Assault, www.womanabuseprevention.com/html/same-sex_partner_abuse.html.

Same-sex violence challenges contemporary feminist theory on domestic violence, and raises questions about the importance of patriarchal values and gender difference as sources of violence. Domestic violence theories that integrate a sociopolitical and a psychological analysis of battering are more inclusive of same-sex domestic violence (Letellier, 1994). Gay domestic violence parallels heterosexual domestic violence except that it can be understood in the more general terms of an imbalance of power in the relationship rather than difficulties in gender roles (Klinger, 1995).

Data from 52 gay male couples indicate that psychological abuse is more frequent in relationships with divided power (i.e., egalitarian in terms of decision making) than in those with power imbalances. The presence of abusive personality traits, usually in both partners, is also associated with intimate abuse. It is concluded that intimate abuse is not necessarily associated with power dominance and certain elements of intimate abuse appear to be similar for both hetero- and homosexual couples (Landolt & Dutton, 1997)

In a study of gay and lesbian cohabiting couples in three Australian states, most couples demonstrated a low degree of stability and commitment, and had experienced problems, conflicts, and interpersonal violence. However, their overall performance on these measures was not very different from that of heterosexual cohabiting couples (Sarantakos, 1996)

Stress

Finally, as we mentioned before, *stress* also contributes to violence. Perceived stress, verbal aggression, and marital conflict—all stressful—are all factors present in abusive relationships, according to an analysis of data from the 1985 U.S. National Family Violence Survey (Harris, 1996). High levels of marital conflict along with low socioeconomic status and a history of witnessed violence in the family of origin also increase the likelihood of long-term abusive behaviour (Aldarondo & Sugarman, 1996). High levels of depression and reported life stressors are among the significant predictors of male violence toward female intimates (Julian & McKenry, 1993).

Stress also increases the risk of child abuse by mothers. For example, child disabilities, such as we discussed earlier in this chapter, increase the risk of abuse (Ammerman and Patz, 1996). Mothers with disabled children and low levels of social support and coping skills score higher on child abuse potential than do other mothers. Likewise, in Hong Kong, abusive mothers demonstrate much more stress on a parenting stress index. They also have much lower levels of neighbourhood support, spousal support, community involvement, and emergency help (Chan, 1994). However, as we noted earlier, stress is also an effect of domestic violence, and it is only one of many causes.

Types of Abusive Relationships

In 1946, the case study of a child with a mysterious head injury led researchers to examine the external cause of the injury. Out of their investigation came the phrase

battered-child syndrome. Before that, people often merely labelled beating a child "strict discipline." In 1962, Kempe and colleagues watched hospitals and found 302 (known) cases of child abuse in one year. Of these children, 33 died and 85 suffered permanent brain injury. The syndrome could affect children at any age but mainly affected children under the age of three. This study led to the first legislation that required professionals working with children to report suspected cases of abuse.

As we mentioned earlier, abused children often grow up to be abusive adults. Also, child abuse contributes to the risk of delinquent behaviour. As shown in Figure 8.3 on page 312, the majority of young offenders had suffered childhood abuse of some kind, and among those young offenders classified as psychopathic (meaning that they are incapable of internalizing moral standards or forming deep attachments) the level of childhood abuse was even higher.

Even if the abused child grows up to be nonviolent, he or she is unlikely to be well adjusted. Elmer and Gregg's (1967) study found that, out of twenty abused children, only two measured normally in all five areas of interest: physical, emotional, and intellectual development, speech capability, and physical defects. Few of these children went on to become capable adults.

Unfortunately, it may not be possible to provide a valid estimate of the population affected by parent–child violence. Thus, saying whether this is a major determinant of the adult criminal or mentally ill population may not be possible. However, for speculation on this topic, see Lykken (1996).

Child homicide by parents offers an extreme but well-documented version of child abuse. In the first few weeks of a child's life, the risk of being killed by a parent is about equal for males and females. In the first few weeks or months, mothers are usually the perpetrators. The main causes of death are asphyxiation or drowning. It is only as the child's age increases that guns and knives become predominant. Then, too, fathers become ever more likely to commit the murder, committing 63 percent of all homicides among the 13- to 15-year age group and 80 percent for the 16- to 18-year age group. From one week to 15 years, males are the victims in about 55 percent of all parent–child homicides. In the 16- to 18-year age groups, this proportion increases to 77 percent (Kunz & Bahr, 1996).

Both child abuse and elder abuse arise from attempts by the caregiver to control behaviour they find problematic. Male abusers typically use physical violence, whereas female abusers tend toward neglect (Penhale, 1993). Both these kinds of abuse often pass from one generation to another (Biggs, Phillipson, & Kingston, 1995). In some cases of elder abuse, adult children are now abusing the parents who abused them in childhood. Note, finally, that children of lone mothers are punished less frequently and severely than children who have two parents, indicating that children in one-parent homes are not a risk group for harsh physical punishment or abuse. Indeed, in difficult circumstances partners might exacerbate mothers' stress and increase the chances of child maltreatment. Lone mothers are considerably more disadvantaged than partnered mothers yet did not punish their children more frequently or more severely. Among mothers with poor mental health, those with partners report having used more severe physical punishments (Nobes & Smith, 2002).

Though common in North America, this has often also been the case in rural China, where very young women traditionally move in with their husband's family after marriage (Gallin, 1994). Young women who are treated poorly by their husband's mother often become abusive when they must look after these women in their old age (Kwan, 1995). Research shows that **elder abuse** cases fall into three categories, determined by the type of mistreatment (physical, psychological, financial, or neglect), the relationship between victim and perpetrator, and the sex and race of the victims and abusers. Profiles include (1) physical and psychological abuse perpetrators, who are likely to be financially dependent on the victim; (2) neglect victims, who are likely to be dependent on the perpetrator; and (3) financial abuse victims, who are often lonely, with few social contacts (Wolf, 1996).

Unlike child abuse, elder abuse receives little attention in our society, partly because it is less common, and perhaps also because we have less interest in elders than in children. Most would acknowledge that children are our future; however, many see elders as burdens we must put up with until they pass on (Biggs, Phillipson, & Kingston, 1995). Another reason may be the economic prosperity of the past few decades, which allowed many seniors to provide for their own needs, instead of being dependent on their children. However, with the aging of the baby boom population and the decrease of available pension funds, we may see an increased interest in the well-being of elders.

The most common form of domestic violence is one that is considered natural, and therefore most acceptable in our society: namely, between-sibling violence (Steinmetz, 1977). We often excuse violence committed between children by saying they "don't know better." Or, we may see the injuries they inflict on one another as less serious than those inflicted by adults. For whatever reason, little research is done on **sibling abuse**. Future studies may discover it is a more serious difficulty than we have previously thought.

Effects of Violence

Both perpetrators and victims of violence are less likely to verbalize their feelings than are nonviolent people. Thus, for example, female victims are much less aware of their emotional states, and possess and express much fewer positive feelings than the average adult woman. Though some researchers may view this condition as a cause of domestic violence, we view it as an effect we spoke of earlier, called post-traumatic stress disorder (PTSD).

More than four in five battered women meet the criteria for a diagnosis of PTSD, as do two in three verbally abused women (Kemp, Green, & Hovanitz, 1995). Compared to other battered women, those with PTSD have been the victims

What Are the Possible Long-Term Effects of Child Sexual Abuse?

If child sexual abuse is not effectively treated, long-term symptoms may persist into adulthood. These may include:

- PTSD and/or anxiety
- Depression and thoughts of suicide
- Sexual anxiety and disorders
- Poor body image and low self-esteem
- The use of unhealthy behaviors, such as alcohol abuse, drug abuse, self-mutilation, or bingeing and purging, to help mask painful emotions related to the abuse

If you were abused as a child and suffer from any of these symptoms, it may help you to get help from a mental-health professional who has expertise in working with people who have been sexually abused.

Source: www.ncptsd.org/facts/specific/fs_child_sexual_abuse.html, National Center for PTSD Fact Sheet.

of more physical abuse, more verbal abuse, more injuries, a greater sense of threat, and more forced sex. Besides the battery itself, other factors contributing to PTSD are the experience of other distressing life events and a lack of perceived social support.

Battered women are three times as likely to suffer from PTSD as are women who are maritally distressed but have not suffered battering. Both groups have similar rates of previous traumatic experiences. However, women showing PTSD—whether battered or not—are more likely to report having experienced childhood sexual abuse. They also report more previous traumas than women without PTSD.

Though little research has been done on the linkage between spousal abuse and PTSD, a great deal of research has documented other symptoms of domestic violence that are similar to symptoms of PTSD. For example, women whose partners initiate violence or force them to have sex have more fear of future assaults than other women (DeMaris & Swinford, 1996).

Abused women typically have less faith in their own efficacy, are more depressed, and have less self-esteem than non-abused women. Further, as physical abuse increases in severity, so does the woman's level of depression (Orava, McLeod, & Sharpe, 1996). At a domestic violence shelter, more than four women in five are at least mildly depressed, and over half are still depressed six months later. Feelings of powerlessness, experiences of abuse, and insufficient social support all contribute to the persistence of this depression (Campbell, Sullivan, & Davidson, 1995).

Psychological factors aside, social and economic factors also conspire to make women fear their vulnerable and dependent condition. Typically, battered women live in an oppressive ("coercively controlling") environment. Powerlessness, social isolation, and economic dependency characterize their lives (Forte, Franks, & Forte, 1996). As we saw earlier, abusive husbands try to isolate their spouses and hide domestic conflict (Lempert, 1996a).

Jacobson, Guttman and colleagues (1996) find that only 38 percent of couples separate or divorce in the two years following an initial assessment of severe husband-to-wife violence. For the other 62 percent, in some cases, the abuse continues—particularly where the husband has been domineering, negative, and emotionally abusive toward the wife at intake.

Women remain in abusive relationships for a variety of reasons. For example, women are taught that they should forgive and forget, that they ought to help their spouses be better people and support them through stresses. Also, abuse that is coercively controlling creates feelings of powerlessness and hopelessness (Aguilar & Nightingale, 1994). Most women who continue to feel closely attached to their partners, even after leaving them, have a negative self-image and tend to feel fearful or preoccupied about the relationship. In turn, preoccupation with the relationship is associated with more frequent previous separations from the relationship, continuing emotional involvement with the partner after separation, and more frequent sexual contact with the partner (Henderson, Bartholomew, & Dutton, 1997).

Battered women have, typically, lost the ability to make decisions about their relationship in their own best interest. However, some research (e.g., Campbell, Miller, and Cardwell, 1994) rejects a "learned helplessness" model for most women experiencing abuse. In their view, most abused women just need practical help and advice to be able to break with their past. They argue in favour of supporting battered women seen in the health care and social services systems, so that they can more easily decide the status of their relationship.

Feelings of commitment to an abusive partner are strongest among women who have limited economic alternatives and are more heavily invested in their relationships. Thus, women with little education—and therefore little chance of achieving economic independence—are more "committed" to their abusive relationship. Likewise, women with preschool children are more "committed" since they have more invested in the relationship than women without young children. Level of commitment predicts which women will return to their partners immediately after leaving a shelter, although most do so many times before finally deciding to leave.

Witnessing Violence

Children also suffer from spousal violence, possibly even more than adults (Engle, Castle, & Menon, 1996). Witnessing violence between one's parents harms the emotional and behavioural development of children (Kolbo, Blakely, & Engleman, 1996). For example, exposure to family violence produces behavioural problems in girls and reduces self-worth in boys (Kolbo, 1996).

As we noted earlier, parent–child violence is common in families where parent–parent violence occurs. Both parent–child violence and exposure to interparental violence are significant predictors of adolescent behaviour problems (O'Keefe, 1996). Exposure to physical abuse produces open hostility in children and a tendency to flare up in anger without a specific provocation. (Exposure to *emotional* abuse is more likely to produce shame, hostility, and anger, both expressed and unexpressed.) Often, the outcomes of domestic violence are gender-specific. Females tend to internalize their emotions, reporting higher levels of shame and guilt. Males usually externalize their emotions, expressing higher levels of hostility and anger (Hoglund & Nicholas, 1995).

National U.S. estimates of the number of children who witness interparental violence annually are as high as 10 million. Telephone interview data obtained as part of the National Youth Victimization and Prevention Survey from a nationally representative sample of 2000 youth ages 10 to 16 indicate that witnessing interparental violence is associated with more post-traumatic stress disorder (PTSD) symptoms and depression even when controlling for demographic variables, quality of parent–child relationships, personal victimization, and other life stressors. PTSD symptoms and depression increase with the frequency of incidents witnessed, but not with the severity of the violence. These results contribute to the growing body of research that stresses the importance of treating exposure to interparental violence as a risk factor for youth.

Exposure to domestic (partner) violence appears to lead to a variety of behavioural and emotional problems among children. Various problems, including aggression, delinquency, feelings of anxiety and depression, and poor academic performance may all result from experiences or observations of physical danger. Additionally, high levels of maternal stress and paternal instability are indirect influences on children's well-being; children's responses to these influences appear to vary with age and gender. However, the stress factors are often interconnected, and researchers have had trouble separating exposure to partner violence from other stressful factors in a child's life. Our understanding advances slowly in this relatively new research area (Wolak & Finklehor, 1998).

Factors that appear to moderate the impacts of witnessing violence include whether the child was also abused, child gender and age, and time since last exposure to violence (Edleson, 1999). Among college undergraduates, witnessing marital violence is associated with other family mental health risks, childhood physical and sexual abuse, and adult physical assaults by strangers. Women who witnessed marital violence reported more symptoms of post-traumatic stress disorder than other women did, after family background and abuse variables were accounted for. The evidence also suggests that the effects of witnessing marital violence depend on the presence of childhood abuse in a woman's history (Feerick & Haugaard, 1999).

Like battered women, battered children show signs of post-traumatic stress disorder (Wind & Silvern, 1994). Motta (1994) suggests that a rise in family violence, violence within schools, and a variety of other stressors are leading to the characteristic PTSD symptoms increasingly observed among children.

A reported one-quarter to one-third of all female children suffer sexual abuse before their eighteenth birthday, and at least one-half of all the women with severe mental illness acknowledge such events. An even higher percentage of mentally ill homeless women have a history of childhood victimization (Rosenberg, Drake, & Mueser, 1996). Among adolescent psychiatric patients, family dysfunction and trauma are more marked in those who have been sexually abused (Wherry et al., 1994). Sexual abuse, parental assault, and kidnapping experiences are particularly strong predictors of depression and PTSD-related symptoms in 10- to 16-year-olds studied over a long period (Boney-McCoy & Finkelhor, 1996).

Parental substance abuse, family conflict, and exposure to both child and adult abuse set in motion a vicious circle that predicts substance abuse in later life. It also continues abusive family patterns into successive generations (Sheridan, 1995). In short, a **cycle of abuse** exists—a tendency for abused girls and daughters of abused mothers to become abused women, and for male children of abusive fathers to become abusive fathers themselves. The connection between childhood

Figure 9.4 THE WHEEL OF POWER AND CONTROL

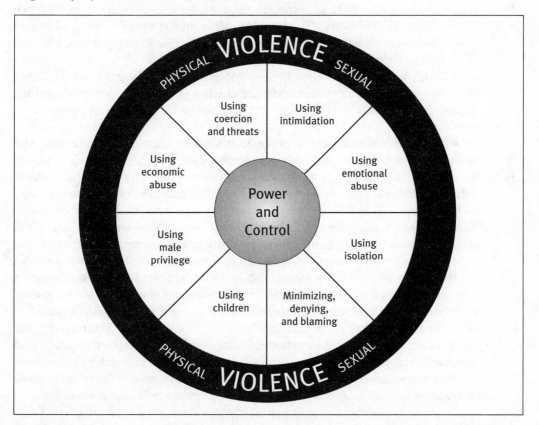

Source: Domestic Abuse Intervention Project, Duluth, Minnesota.

abuse and adult abuse may lie in interpersonal functioning. Children who grow up in abusive families don't learn how to conduct their lives, or their marriages, in non-abusive ways, or how to prevent the escalation of violence or abuse (Weaver & Clum, 1996). They may also have a history of depression and low self-esteem, both predisposing them to violence and victimization (Cascardi, O'Leary, & Lawrence, 1995).

Concluding Remarks

From research we have come to a several conclusions about the best ways to intervene to solve problems of family stress and violence. For reasons of brevity we will consider a few here.

First, we learn that violence is a major factor causing women to leave marriages. It often continues throughout the separation and divorce process, affecting negotiations for assets and custody (Kurz, 1996). Second, programs that attempt to address abuse directly—such as civil restraining orders, treatment programs for batterers, and policies requiring mandatory arrest and no dropped charges—are generally not effective in solving the problem of domestic violence (Davis & Smith, 1995). By contrast, treatments aimed at reducing alcohol and drug abuse may make a long-term difference to the likelihood of future violence (O'Farrell & Murphy, 1995; Brannen & Rubin, 1996).

Third, we must actively address problems like stress and violence. If we want to reduce family stresses, we must create a society that is family-friendly, with more social support and more practical assistance for working parents with small children.

Fourth, the health and social service professions are, sadly, far behind the times. To deserve the respect and rewards they seek, these professionals are going to have to do a better job understanding and intervening in modern relationships. Fifth, research also shows us that personal lives, and families, are increasingly diverse. This means that families have varied problems. Because of language, cultural, and immigration issues, for example, recently arrived immigrant and refugee women have needs that differ markedly from most battered women in the general population (Huisman, 1996). Along similar lines, lesbians have different needs from heterosexual women, and less reason to use traditional battered women services that were designed for male–female relationships. Workers in the health and social service professions have done little to make lesbians feel welcome and respected (Renzetti, 1996; Istar, 1996). Gay men face similar problems.

The recognition of domestic violence as an important social issue, and mobilization against it (e.g., the Zero Tolerance campaign, cf. Mackay, 1996), owes much to grassroots coalitions of feminist and other movements. Women established in relevant local institutions (e.g., the press, government) make a big difference, especially when support from local politicians is available (Davis, Hagen, & Early, 1994; Abrar, 1996). We must all be alert to new problems, and to new solutions.

In the end, however, we must recognize that there will be no major decline in the violence against family members until societies reduce the stresses on family members. Yet governments and corporations have been *adding* to the stress by downsizing (recall that a risk factor is men being unemployed while their wives are employed). Societies must also dismantle the cultural justifications for domestic violence, and deprive the violent of opportunities to hide or repeat their behaviour. Ending domestic violence must be a societal project, no less complex than dealing with unemployment, illiteracy, AIDS, or any of a dozen other recognized social problems.

CHAPTER SUMMARY

We have discussed two realities—stress and violence—that can result from a failure by families to deal with their problems.

Stress, like the other family problems we discussed in the previous chapter, is normal and a normal part of family life. However, stress is also the result of an imbalance between a stressor and the ability to deal with that stressor. Common causes of family stress fall into at least four categories: major upheavals, such as wars and natural disasters; major life transitions, such as the birth of a child or divorce; chronic stresses, such as chronic illnesses, drug abuse, or unemployment; and occasional stresses, such as a car accident or the flu.

Common sources of family stress include poverty, discrimination, substance abuse, demands of paid work, parenting, and caring for ill or elderly family members. Families cope with stress through two broad categories of resources: material and emotional/psychological. Cohesive and flexible families, as we saw in Chapter 8, Family Dynamics: How Families Face Problems and Get Along, are most able to deal successfully with stress. The members of families who fail to handle stress effectively—dysfunctional families—are often better off on their own.

Violence is another potential consequence of family problems. We learned that domestic violence is widespread throughout society and diverse in nature. Family violence can take the form of physical, emotional, or psychological abuse.

Researchers have yet to identify any single factor that conclusively causes family violence. Some suggest that violence is the result of social conditions such as poverty, unemployment, and the media's glorification of violence. Others argue that high crime rates promote aggressiveness and the deterioration of the family unit, both of which can lead to violence. The single best predictor of violent behaviour toward a partner is the experience of abuse at the hands of a partner. Marital violence is also strongly correlated with physical child abuse. Although the perpetrators of violence are often men, women also abuse their male partners, but the motivation of the violence is different for each sex. Alcohol and drug abuse are also important factors in explaining spousal abuse.

Other types of violence include child abuse and elder abuse, which arise from attempts by the caregiver to control behaviour they find problematic. The effects of violence are also severe and widespread. They include post-traumatic stress disorder, powerlessness, social isolation, and economic dependency. Also, children exposed to abuse are more likely to become abusers themselves, perpetuating the cycle of violence.

KEY TERMS

ABCX family crisis model In this model, A, which represents the stressor event, interacts with B, the family's crisis-meeting resources, and with C, the interpretation a family makes of the event, to produce X, the crisis.

Acculturative stress Stress originating from the challenges involved in adapting to a new society.

Battered-child syndrome Prior to 1962, people labelled beating a child "strict discipline"; however, after Kempe and colleagues watched hospitals and found 302 (known) cases of child abuse in one year the syndrome was identified. The syndrome could affect children at any age but mainly affected children under the age of three. This study led to the first legislation that required professionals working with children to report suspected cases of abuse.

Chronic stressors Events such as disability, chronic physical or mental illness, drug and alcohol abuse, occupational problems, unemployment, or imprisonment of a family member.

Circular causal mode A model of family violence that views both partners in an abusive spousal relationship as contributing to the escalation of the abuse.

Cohesive families Families in which the members feel attached to the family, and to one another.

Conflict Tactics Scales An instrument developed by Murray Straus to measure the extent of domestic violence based on frequency and severity of incidents.

Cycle of abuse A tendency for family violence to replicate itself from one generation to the next, as abused girls and daughters of abused mothers grow up to become abused women, and abused boys or sons of abusive fathers grow up to become abusive husbands or fathers.

Domestic violence Family violence; violence against any member of the household, including a child, spouse, parent, or sibling.

Dysfunctional family A social unit whose members are neither cohesive nor flexible, and who would be better off on their own.

Elder abuse Physical violence, psychological cruelty, or neglect directed at an older person, usually by a caregiving family member.

Flexible families Families where members can change their ideas, roles, and relationships as the situation demands.

Major life transitions A common cause of family stress. These are acute disruptions due to events that may affect some family members simultaneously, but not others— such as the birth of a child, the death of a parent, divorce, and retirement.

Major upheavals A common cause of family stress. Major upheavals, such as war and natural disasters (e.g., tornadoes, floods, and earthquakes) affect many people simultaneously.

Material resources They include money, time, and energy. Stressor events always use up large amounts of all these resources.

Occasional stresses Events that may be temporarily severe but go away without permanent change. Examples would include a car accident, a burglary, a sudden illness or death of a family member, or even apparently pleasant but stressful stimuli like a holiday trip.

Post-traumatic stress disorder Symptoms characteristic of PTSD include psychological numbing, increased states of arousal and anxiety, and a tendency to re-experience the trauma mentally.

Psychological and emotional resources They include the ability to accept that the stressor event has taken place, talk honestly about one's reactions, begin the process of adjustment soon afterward, and acknowledge the need for help from others.

Social isolation Lack of social support.

Spousal violence Physical abuse between spouses. It may be reciprocal ("common couple violence") or directed by one partner against the other, and may occur between cohabitors as well as legally married couples.

Status inconsistency Lack of congruence between the various indicators of social class, such as education and occupation, or wealth and prestige.

REVIEW QUESTIONS

1. Describe and give an example for each component of the ABCX model of stress.

2. What are the three main types of stressor? List at least two examples for each major type.

3. Name the two characteristics that are common to families that cope with stress well.

4. Name and elaborate on two kinds of resources that might help a family cope with a stressor.

5. What difficulties does a sociologist attempting to do a comprehensive study of family violence face?

6. Explain when and why family violence began to be publicly acknowledged as a social issue.

7. List some ways in which a child's development can be affected by experiencing family violence, whether as a victim or a witness. How do the effects on boys and girls differ?

8. The term "family violence" covers many different types of intimate relation violence. List the various types covered in this chapter and explain one thoroughly.

9. List three types of spousal violence and briefly explain the differences between them.

10. What social and cultural factors contribute to family violence, and how?

DISCUSSION QUESTIONS

1. Recall that the availability of certain resources much improves a family's ability to cope with a crisis; one of these resources is family structure. Why would certain family structures (i.e., those with the most flexibility and cohesiveness) allow for increased coping by the family unit? What sort of inhibitions to coping might an opposite structure impose?

2. Other than the direct physical effects of the illness itself, what sort of obstacles—inside and outside the family—stand in the way of a chronically ill child leading a "normal" life?

3. What particular stressors might accompany a family's emigration to a country very different from the one in which it originated? What stressors would be added with the coming of the first generation born in the new country?

4. As a researcher studying stress, you must weigh both objective and subjective stresses; your measurements must reflect their relative significance in the situation being studied. In studying, for example, unemployment's effects on family, what sorts of measurements might be appropriate? How might objective and subjective perspectives differ?

5. All abuse is, by nature, damaging to the victim. "Non-violent" forms of child abuse—psychological abuse and neglect—are usually considered less serious than physical violence and sexual assault. However, one might argue that they are equally damaging to a child's sense of self-worth and ability to cope in the world. Do you think the law should be paying equal attention to these two types of violence?

6. We are already changing the once commonplace opinion that grade school bullying is a far cry from criminal assault. Should we also be considering the impacts of sibling abuse more seriously? Should the legal system involve itself, or should sibling abuse remain an issue for parents to deal with?

7. Why might certain relationship conditions (such as cohabitation versus marriage) affect the rate of family violence?

8. We mentioned earlier that much intimate partner violence is more or less reciprocal. With this in mind, should we alter the way we approach domestic violence cases? Should men who have beaten their wives receive lighter (or no) sentences if the women were also physically aggressive? Should an abused wife who kills her husband in his sleep be able to claim "self-defence"?

9. Some people feel the traditional structure of some societies facilitates the abuse of women, children, or the elderly in that society. Others feel it is the breaking down of traditional structures, leaving a society trapped between ancient norms and modern realities, that causes family conflicts and violence. What arguments could you make for either side? (Give examples if you can!)

10. In what respects is violence between family members similar to violence between warring countries? In what respects is it different, and why?

ACTIVITIES

1. Interview someone whose family life includes a chronic stressor (e.g., a chronically ill relative, unemployment, etc.), identifying the daily stresses that the person undergoes in dealing with his or her problem.

2. Conduct a survey (males versus females). What does each gender consider to be child abuse, spousal abuse, and sexual abuse? Can you draw any conclusions about how different the opinion is among men and women? Prior to conducting your survey, make up a list of specific instances that you would like to evaluate (i.e., slapping, kicking, spanking). Make sure there is a varying severity of each act.

3. In small groups of three or four, come up with a definition of family violence. Then compare your answer to those of other groups. In what ways do they differ?

SUGGESTED READINGS

Baumrind, Diana. 1995. *Child Maltreatment and Optimal Caregiving in Social Contexts* New York, NY: Garland Publishing. This book reviews the literature on child abuse and normal family functioning to argue that maltreatment of children is directly linked to socio-structural rather than psychological factors.

Buzzawa, Eve S. and Buzzawa, Carl G. (Eds.). 1996. *Do Arrests and Restraining Orders Work?* Thousand Oaks, CA: Sage. A collection of essays by researchers and practitioners that discuss issues related to domestic abuse, including the proper role of the police, prosecutors, and other officers of the court. Also included are recent findings on differential arrest practices for victims of domestic and stranger assaults.

Cheal, David. 1996. *New Poverty: Families in Postmodern Society*. Westport, CT: Greenwood Press. Despite the myth that the modern welfare state is benevolent, state income supports in Canada and the United States do little to protect families with children. The least secure families are those with low, unstable incomes. Female-headed families are in a particularly precarious financial situation, with few savings and low rates of home ownership.

Ellis, Carolyn. 1995. *Final Negotiations: A Story of Love, Loss, and Chronic Illness*. Philadelphia, PA: Temple U Press. This personal account of the author's nine-year love relationship with a man dying of emphysema includes the intricate details and difficulties of caregiving. The author examines the emotional roller-coaster accompanying physical decline, negotiations with medical professionals, embarrassment, fear, and grief, and highlights the social processes of chronic illness and dying.

Fleisher, Mark S. and Robin F. Meier. 1995. *Beggars and Thieves: Lives of Urban Street Criminals*. Madison, WI: U of Wisconsin Press. Drawing on life histories and field observation of nearly 200 informants in jail, in prison, and on the streets, this book shows how street criminals are enmeshed in a life cycle that comprises running away from home, membership in a gang, serving time in jail, residence in a shelter or prison, and homelessness.

Gordon, Linda. 1988. *Heroes of Their Own Lives: The Politics and History of Family Violence, Boston, 1880–1960*. New York, NY: Viking. This book shows that family violence has been well known to social workers and reformers for a century but the realities of family violence have been concealed behind images that alternately pathologize or normalize it, making it seem the inevitable by-product of predispositions and stresses.

WEBLINKS

http://www.ama-assn.org/ama/pub/article/3342-3635.htm
American Medical Association
Published by the American Medical Association, this site contains information on alcohol, drugs, and family violence.

http://www.icfs.org/bluebook/si000052.htm
Interface—Children Family Services of Ventura County
A wide range of links to information on family violence.

http://www.acjnet.org/docs/famvidoj.html
Family Violence in Rural, Farm and Remote Canada
Publication of the Department of Justice Canada, 1995. Contains a wide range of information on family violence in rural and remote Canada.

http://www.cuav.org/
Community United Against Violence
Community United Against Violence (CUAV) is a 20-year old multicultural organization working to end violence against and within lesbian, gay, bisexual, transgender, and queer/questioning (LGBTQ) communities. This Web site shows the kind of help available to victims of same-sex violence.

CHAPTER TEN

Divorce & Ending Relationships:

Trends, Myths, Children, and Ex-Spouses

Chapter Outline

Introduction

Divorce is challenging for sociologists to understand. The factors leading to divorce are complex, as are the consequences for individuals involved and for society. Adding further challenge is that close couple relations have changed so much recently, as we saw in Chapter 4, with the growing popularity of cohabitation. Cohabiting relationships that end are not considered divorces, of course. So, the greater the numbers of couples cohabiting, the less the risk of divorce. Adding even more complexity, divorce rates are sometimes misleading, as we shall soon see.

It is often said that about one-half of all marriages end in divorce. That's scary, if people think that their own marriage stands only a 50-percent chance of surviving. However, this figure may be misleading. Researchers using 2000 statistics estimate that 37.7 percent of marriages in Canada are expected to end in divorce by the thirtieth wedding anniversary (Statistics Canada, 2002). This divorce rate is higher in some provinces (in Quebec at 45.2) than others (Newfoundland and Labrador at 23.2). The rate is also higher for second marriages, and higher still for third marriages. On the other hand, the overall divorce rate is generally falling, except for the 1997 to 2000 period where there were slight increases. Indeed, divorce rates and numbers of divorces have been declining in Canada since 1987 (with the exception noted from 1997 to 2000), and in the United States since 1980.

Divorce Rates

To explain why divorce rates are misleading at times, we must explain what the various indicators of divorce mean. There are several ways to compute divorce rates, and meanings depend very much on the method of calculation. The *crude divorce rate*, for example, is calculated as the number of divorces in a given year (say, 1998), divided by the mid-year population in 1998, multiplied by 100 000. This yields relatively low rates because the denominator includes everyone in the population, many of whom are not at all at risk of divorce, since they are children, single, or already divorced.

By contrast, another measure of divorce is based on the number of marriages in a given year. Here, the number of *divorces* in 2002 is divided by the number of *marriages* in 2002. This clearly overestimates divorce risk and lends itself to attention-catching statements (e.g., "One-half of all current marriages will end in divorce"), which titillate but do not really inform us. Those married in 2002 are *not* those generally at risk of divorce in 2002! As well, if the number of marriages in any given year goes down, as it has in the past decade in Canada, and the numbers of divorces stays the same, it may appear as if the risk of divorce is going up when it isn't. As you can see, this way of calculating divorce rate and risk is very misleading. It can be a "false fact" reported as if true and then interpreted by couples as a risk to them. This is inappropriate and needlessly frightening.

Better measures of divorce risk, though too rarely provided for public discussion, consider the population at risk of a divorce, and *only* that population.

Figure 10.1 DIVORCE RATE PER 100 000 POPULATION IN CANADA, 1961–2000

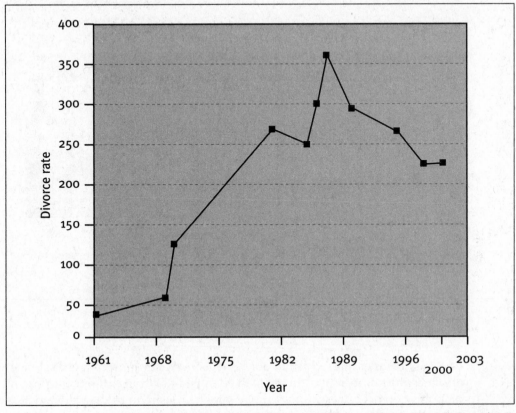

Source: Adapted from the Statistics Canada website. 2000. "Divorces." *The Daily*, September 26;
www.statcan.ca/Daily/English/021202/d021202f.htm.

Thus, the population at risk of a divorce in 2002 are those (and only those) who are married at the beginning of 2002 *and earlier*. This estimate can be improved by standardizing for age and other social characteristics that are known to influence people's propensity to divorce. Since older people tend to divorce less than younger people, for example, we would do well to compute divorce rates on a "standard population" with the same hypothetical age structure at two points in time. Only in this way would we know whether divorce-proneness was increasing, or changes in population make-up (such as population aging or immigration of more young people) were causing the appearance of more divorce-proneness.

Another approach is to calculate a rolling divorce rate, which measures the number of people in the population ever divorced as a fraction of the population ever married. This method has advantages and disadvantages. For example, one disadvantage is that this method is biased by cohort and period. Said more simply, large cohorts of people (like the baby boom generation) have a disproportionately large effect on this estimate.

Figure 10.2 TOTAL DIVORCE RATE PER 100 MARRIAGES IN CANADA, 1998–2000

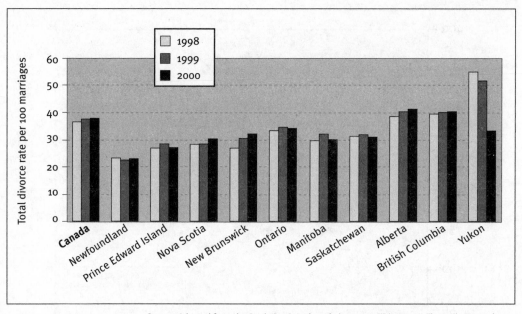

Source: Adapted from the Statistics Canada website. 2002. "Divorces." *The Daily*, December 2; www.statcan.ca/Daily/English/021202/d021202f.htm.

One final measure, which to our knowledge is never used in official data, calculates the number of adult years lived outside marriage. If our purpose in computing divorce rates were to gauge people's desire to be married and stay married, nothing would demonstrate the societal rejection of marriage more clearly than a continuous decline in the amount of time people actually spend being married. In the same way, increases in the population living common-law may be seen, by some, as a rejection of traditional marriage. However, the goal of computing divorce rates is not only to measure societal rejection of marriage. For sociologists, divorce rates also help us make and test theories about the factors that contribute to the survival and breakdown of marriages. In turn, this helps us understand something about the conditions that make for better and worse family functioning.

A lot more could be said about the challenges of divorce rates. Demographers spend a great deal of time perfecting these measures, and those who watch rates, like the readers of this book as well as policy makers, should be careful to know what is being measured and how. As a general rule, the best rate is one that correctly measures the risks of experiencing something such as divorce. It is wise never to rely on a rate without knowing what question you are trying to answer; equally, never accept a rate as valid unless you know how it was created and what it really indicates.

Divorce and Society

There are a number of questions involving divorce that need to be answered, as divorce is a situation that affects many people in society. The chances are high that your own parents may have divorced or that your friends' parents are divorced. You may have already spent time thinking about the reasons why divorce occurs. Many children think, deep down, that they are somehow to blame, for example. Or, they blame one parent and not the other. This can have important consequences for their self-esteem, life chances, and future relationship success, as well as their relations with one or both parents.

Maybe your parents didn't divorce, but you suspect they might have been happier if they had. This chapter may help you make sense of the reasons people *do not* divorce as well as some of the reasons they do.

Figure 10.3 DIVORCE RATE BY 30TH WEDDING ANNIVERSARY

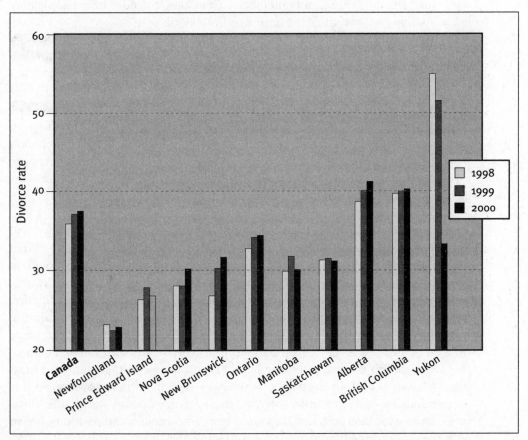

Source: Adapted from the Statistics Canada website. 2002. "Divorces." *The Daily*, December 2; www.statcan.ca/Daily/English/021202/d021202f.htm.

Finally, you may have questions about divorce because the chances are not negligible that, despite your best hopes and efforts, *you* may experience divorce. Or if not you, then your brother or sister or best friend may divorce at some time. Divorce usually solves some problems and creates others, problems between people and their children, their parents, siblings, or friends. You may have already witnessed some of these problems up close and want to understand them better and prevent similar problems from occurring in your life.

Sociologists are interested in divorce for similar (though usually less personal) reasons. They hope to gain insights from research on divorce about the nature of social bonding, the effects of economy and culture on personal relations, and the causes and consequences of divorce. At the micro-level, sociologists try to understand why individual couples get divorced. To do this, they examine family dynamics and interaction patterns, the expectations people have about married life, who they choose to marry and why, and people's subjective assessments of available alternative mates. They also examine the effects on divorcing spouses, their children, and other family members. Then, they consider how people may individually work to reduce the harmful effects of divorce.

At the macro-level, sociologists debate how to measure divorce, how to measure "a marriage or relationship breakdown," and how to find out the relationship between breakdown and divorce. Often relationships break down long before divorce occurs, so separation may be a better indicator than divorce of marital problems. With dramatic increases in cohabitation, divorce rates are no longer reliable indicators of relationship breakdown. But, even in the past, they may not have been good indicators. In one way, higher rates of cohabitation may lead to increased rates of divorce—since cohabitors who then marry are more likely to divorce (LeBourdais, Neil, & Turcotte, 2000). In another way, increased cohabitation can lead to decreased divorce rates, since cohabitors are not at risk for legal divorce.

Macrosociologists have examined the social, cultural, economic, and political forces that shape the institution of marriage. Their goal has been to find out what accounts for the long-term increase in divorce rates (until recently, as we noted) in all industrialized countries over this century. To find out, they examine such large-scale processes as industrialization and urbanization, the increasing participation of women in the labour force, and changes in the societal norms regulating marriage and family life. They also study the macro-level effects of high divorce rates on family and social life, on parenting, and on the distribution of income.

Despite high divorce rates, the family is still the most important and most fundamental institution in society, as we have seen in earlier chapters. So it is understandable that some may interpret high divorce rates as a sign of societal breakdown. This interpretation, favoured by political conservatives today, began with the work of the nineteenth-century sociologist Émile Durkheim in works like *Suicide* and *The Division of Labor in Society*.

Conservative sociologists note that, even today, high divorce rates are associated with high suicide rates, suggesting that the divorce rate relates to distress or disorganization in the general population (see Popenoe, 1996, for example). Positive correlations between divorce rates, suicide rates, and alcohol consumption per capita suggest a broad-based social characteristic: a **social pathology**, as early sociologists would have called it. This produces a variety of stress-related behaviours.

However, liberal sociologists deny that divorce rates necessarily show **social disorganization** (see Smart & Neale, 1999; Stacey, 1996, for example). High divorce rates can coexist with a healthy family and social life if clear norms specify what is to happen to the husband, wife, and children after a divorce. In societies that handle divorce well, such as Sweden, children continue to live with their kin: often, with their mother and her relatives. They do not suffer unduly from the separation of their parents. In this instance, divorce produces few stress-related consequences. There are examples of relatively smooth divorce arrangements in our own society. One study, for example, finds that some fathers may be more involved with their children after divorce than they were when they were married (Smart & Neale, 1999).

All too often in our own society, however, the problems supposedly caused by divorce, problems we associate with what thirty or forty years ago were called "broken homes," result from a lack of societal and policy support for those experiencing divorce. Modern North Americans don't handle divorce well as individuals, nor does our society. As long as that remains largely the case, divorce will likely continue to result in social and personal problems. Problems will diminish when we clearly define norms and customs to regulate the process of marital breakdowns.

It must be added here that it is not only divorce that causes problems for individuals and society. Unhappy, abusive, unequal marriages also cause great pain for individuals, for society, and for children. Sometimes, wars of words over divorce and what it means can also be harmful as individuals and societies try to sort out feelings about relationship breakdowns. The active media discussion that took place about sociologist Judith Wallerstein's book on the legacy of divorce for children (see Wallerstein, 2000) is an example. We invite you to engage in that debate with our Debate Box on page 386. Sorting out the causes of social and individual problems in relation to divorce is not an easy task. Often many problems go together, making it unwise to attribute any or all subsequent problems to the divorce in particular.

People in our society have trouble thinking about divorce in a calm, dispassionate way, sometimes viewing it in dramatic terms, as a "pathology" or "societal breakdown." There may be two sorts of explanations for this way of thinking. First, divorce is both an emotional and a religious and ideological matter. Religious advocates from many different religions argue that marriage is sacred and should not be dissolved. Politics enters the debate too, as socially conservative

Debate Box 10.1 THE EFFECT OF DIVORCE ON CHILDREN
Which side of the debate do you fall on?

I am FOR staying married for the sake of the children

- A recently published well-known study (Wallerstein, 2000) suggests that children of divorce have more emotional problems when they reach adulthood. They fear commitment, conflict, and change, and think they may be abandoned or hurt from a relationship.
- Wallerstein (2000) finds that, compared to those from intact families, children of divorce marry at younger ages, and are more likely to themselves divorce.
- The Wallerstein study is praised in the media and is a best-selling book. It tracked 93 children of divorce into adulthood—a study that took 25 years. The study's author is a clinical psychologist who works with children of divorce and has been studying this topic her whole career. Her co-author is an academic psychologist. The book has a lot of credibility.
- Parents who divorce are selfish. Kids need an intact family to grow up feeling safe and secure in this increasingly competitive world. They need both a mom and a dad. Parents who divorce are sacrificing their children's happiness for their own.
- Divorce often results in one parent—usually the father—being excluded from the children's life. Children growing up in a home with a single mother also tend to have less money, and mom usually has to work. It's much better to have two parents at home—even if they do have some problems—than it is to only have one parent and to be poorer.
- Just because the parents have problems, it does not mean that they have to share those problems with their kids. They can keep the problems to themselves and fight behind closed doors. Or they can get counselling. That is the best way.

I am AGAINST staying married for the sake of the children

- Wallerstein's findings are not consistent with the findings of other longitudinal studies (e.g., Amato et al., 1995; Amato and Booth, 1996; King and Booth, 2000). These studies show that relationship quality is a much more important factor than divorce *per se* in determining how emotionally healthy children will be when they reach adulthood.
- Because of the small size of her study samples, the findings cannot be generalized to the broader population. Also, the experiences of her study participants cannot be considered "typical" or representative, because the sample was not randomly selected. In fact, all her main study participants were patients she counselled.
- "Wallerstein really views divorce as a terminal disease. That's just not true" (Hetherington, 2002, professor emeritus, U of Virginia, quoted from www.healthyplace.com).
- "When kids move into a happier family situation with a competent, caring, firm parent they do better than they do in a nasty family situation" (Hetherington, 2002, quoted from www.healthyplace.com).
- Some divorced dads say divorce gave them the opportunity to become *more* involved in their children's lives (Smart & Neale, 1999).
- No child should have to grow up amidst constant fighting and conflict. Parents in a bad marriage are doing the best thing for their kids by divorcing. Divorce can actually be beneficial for kids when it takes them out of a highly antagonistic environment. It is high-conflict parent relations and poor quality parenting that is most harmful, not divorce.
- Parents do the best job of parenting when they are in a good situation and are happy. It is much better for kids to have two happy divorced parents than two miserable married parents.

politicians and journalists engage with more liberal people about what divorce means and how societies ought to respond. Second, we may have trouble being calm and dispassionate about divorce because we really never prepare for divorce as we do for other major adult life experiences like education, employment, and marriage. Most young people, for example, say that they expect never to be divorced (Vanier Institute of the Family, 2002). Most couples still marry with the expectation that their marriage will last forever. Although the odds still favour marriages lasting, many do not. People organize their lives and societal roles/policies operate around the belief that long-term marriage is the only reasonable expectation. Beliefs about marriage and divorce have not changed much, though historical and cross-national data show us that divorce practices surely have!

A Historical, Cross-National Overview of Divorce

In industrial societies, divorce rates hit a peak in the second half of the twentieth century. This peak occurred because of changes in the structure of social, economic, and legal institutions that shape family life and individual expectations of marriage. Divorce is nothing new, however, nor is it limited to Western industrial societies (see Phillips, 1988). What follows is a thumbnail sketch of the relevant socio-historical processes.

Table 10.1 DIVORCE RATES PER 1000 POPULATION. SELECTED COUNTRIES, 1996

COUNTRY	DIVORCE RATE
U.S.	4.3
Cuba	3.7
U.K.	3.1
France	2.7
Canada	2.6
Sweden	2.2
Germany	2.0
Portugal	1.4
Spain	0.7
Italy	0.5
Mexico	0.4

Source: United Nations, 1996. *Demographic Yearbook*. New York: United Nations publications, Sales No. E/F.96.X111.Z.

Social Changes

To understand the reasons for these social changes, we have to step back from our present lives. We must try to imagine life as people lived it for most of human history. In pre-industrial times, as we discuss in Chapter 2, most families were rural, land-based, self-sufficient units. They produced most of what they needed to feed, clothe, and house their own members. The division of labour was simple. Tasks and responsibilities were allocated according to age and gender. *Social differentiation* beyond that was slight, except for royalty and the aristocracies in some parts of the world.

With the onset of the Industrial Revolution about two hundred years ago (mid-nineteenth century in Canada), however, the modern Western family lost its function, to a large extent, as a productive unit. Many people were forced off the land, moving to towns and cities, where they took wage-paying jobs. Most economic production thus moved out of the household and into factories and (later) offices. Individual family members still worked to sustain themselves and their families; however, the family itself was not the basic social unit of production anymore. Work and family were no longer the same thing, and a sense of family separate from work began to emerge.

These changes affected the strength of family ties, and the family's ability to control its members. When people earn their living from wages paid for work done outside the family, they may (though they do not always) effectively escape control by the family. Their future no longer depends completely on getting a share of land or any other asset that is typically under the control of family elders. Jobs in the market economy allow people to earn a living as individuals, not family members. Workers receive their own wages. They may be able to spend them independently too, although not always. People's lives become more individuated and governed by market forces. People can begin to lead highly individualistic, independent lives if they want.

In the last hundred years, other functions of the family, such as the education and training of the young, increasingly have become the responsibility of the state. In Canada, compulsory education was the state response to unruly youth of the early industrial period, as discussed in Chapter 2. The interest was less in educating children than in controlling them. The state grew larger, taking responsibility for more of our lives—health, education, welfare. This meant that the family was no longer the major place of production or the only source of personal economic security. Of course, that period of state expansion is now at an end. With increasing job and policy insecurity (in pensions, social assistance, etc.), families may once again be becoming a crucial source of security for individuals (McDaniel, 2002).

To be sure, the family was always, and is still, important. In fact, throughout the industrial era the family continues to be a crucial economic unit. Even today, perhaps especially today, it is only by pooling their members' incomes that many families keep themselves out of poverty and off social assistance. Immigrant family members, in particular, tend to pool their resources to achieve upward mobility. Nonetheless, since the second half of the twentieth century, the family has been much less necessary for educational and some other purposes. As a result, people may invest less in the family. And, the looser their ties become, the easier it is to sever them when problems arise or attractive alternatives beckon. So, divorce rates tend to be high (South, Trent & Shen, 2001).

By this historical reckoning, higher divorce rates are the result of a change in the ties that bind family members to one another. Where family ties once rested on life-and-death economic dependence and co-dependence, today they rest more often on emotions of love and liking. Since emotional ties are by their nature more fragile than ties of economic dependence, we more easily sever them. However, not every couple that falls out of love gets a divorce, since divorce is a legal process and not simply a social or emotional one. Some couples, as we shall see, may not wish to end their marriages in the public realm at all.

Legal Changes

To understand divorce as a legal process, we must understand the laws governing divorce and how they have changed. Divorce laws in Canada and other Western

My Life Was Broken Apart

When his marriage of 27 years ended, lawyer Brian Watson was overwhelmed and numbed with shock. Although he'd worked on scores of divorce cases in his 25 years in practice, when faced with the end of his marriage, Watson initially had no idea how to cope.

"I was like a mechanic fixing cars before when I did divorce cases but when it happened to me it was like my life was broken apart." he says. "I needed help to get things back on track."

Unfortunately, society's casual acceptance of divorce causes many people to downplay the emotional, social and financial upheavals associated with it.

There are multiple losses suffered with divorce—the loss of love, affection, sex, and the role of wife or husband. The changing family structure can be very hard to adjust to, especially for children. When a divorce happens, the whole family may lose their home, neighbourhood and friends

Experts say that while society has formal routines and rituals for mourning death, there is no such structure for the grief that accompanies divorce.

"Though society has accepted divorce, it has not accepted responsibility for providing the support divorced families and single parents need," Jannie Mills, executive director of New Directions says.

By far one of the biggest problems for divorcing couples is our legal system, experts say. Lawyer Al Weisbrot has given up family law litigation and now works as a mediator in such cases.

"The system is no good," he says. At the end of one court case where we were very successful, I looked at the father. He said, "We won. We won!" I thought 'What did we achieve? I took every effort to destroy that poor woman.'"

Source: Harvey, Robin. 1997. The *Toronto Star*, December 6, l L1, L2. Reprinted with permission—Torstar Syndication Services.

countries have gradually liberalized over the past two centuries. For example, during the colonial period in North America, divorce was completely illegal in the southern United States and Quebec. It was granted elsewhere only under narrowly defined circumstances such as adultery or after seven years of desertion. Even then, it was nearly impossible to get a divorce granted. Canadian law up until fairly recently required an Act of Parliament for each divorce to be granted (Snell, 1983). Not surprisingly, divorces were granted most often to the well-to-do and the influential.

There was a strong sense in the early 1900s in Canada that divorce was a moral and political issue, with bad implications for the country. Snell (1983: 113) quotes E.A. Lancaster, the Conservative Member of Parliament for Lincoln, Ontario, 1900–1916: "Where will this country come to in twenty-five years if we are going to grant divorces simply because some woman has been disappointed in regard to her husband…? The whole social fabric of the country would go to pieces."

Increasingly over the twentieth century, North American governments granted divorces upon ever-widening grounds. A turning point occurred in the late 1960s and early 1970s with the introduction of **no-fault divorce** laws in Canada and some jurisdictions in the United States. In Canada, the 1968 Divorce Act first enlarged the "fault grounds" under which a divorce could be granted, but also allowed divorce without accusations of wrongdoing in the case of "marital breakdown," which required three years of living apart, or five if both spouses did not agree to divorce. The 1985 Divorce Act considers marriage breakdown to be the only ground for divorce, though the older grounds such as adultery or cruelty are considered evidence of breakdown. It is no longer necessary for one spouse or the other to accept moral blame for the breakdown of the marriage. As a result of this change in approach, society has gradually redefined divorce. No longer does divorce have to be a stigmatizing process where one party is held responsible under the law. On the contrary, we now may be more likely to look critically at marriages that survive even though they are emotionally dead. These are marriages that we now think could end, freeing their participants to find emotional fulfillment in another union.

No-fault divorce laws implicitly define marriages in which couples are "incompatible" or have "irreconcilable differences" as grounds for divorce. Divorce, according to no-fault laws, then, could end marriages that are "irretrievably broken." The grounds for **no-fault divorce** are not inherently adversarial; they are based almost entirely on the loss of emotional connections. In earlier times, many marriages may have broken down emotionally or may never have been emotionally based in the first instance. It is only recently that the legal system has come to view this as sufficient reason to end a marriage.

In December 2002, the Government of Canada announced a new approach to divorce in Canada (Canada, 2002). The purpose of the proposed changes to the 1985 Divorce Act is, according to Minister of Justice Martin Cauchon, to focus on children's needs first and foremost. To this end, the Minister is proposing that four amendments change the Divorce Act:

- providing a list of specific criteria for parents and judges to use in considering the best interests of the child(ren) on separation and divorce;

- eliminating the terms "custody" and "access" in divorce law and put in place a model of parental responsibilities;

- parents to decide how they will carry out their parental responsibilities either on their own or with help from a mediator, counsellor or lawyer;

- additional amendments to other acts to improve enforcement of child support and to the Criminal Code on child abduction.

In addition, changes are proposed to the court process, ensuring that it is simpler, less adversarial, and more efficient. We will consider these changes more fully when we discuss children and divorce issues.

Changes in divorce law and policy did not come to all parts of the English-speaking world at the same time. For example, divorce remained illegal in Ireland until 1995. A referendum that year defeated existing laws prohibiting divorce by a narrow margin. The pressure to liberalize Irish divorce laws contributed to a wide-ranging discussion of **secularization** (a move away from religion as an organizing principle of society) and of the nature of social and family change. People have also been forced to reconsider the relationship between moral and constitutional matters, or church and state. Ireland is not yet a secular society; however, it is more pluralistic and tolerant than it was a decade ago. Individual Catholics, in Ireland as elsewhere, no longer embrace all the doctrines of the Church (though it may well be that, in practice, they never did so entirely).

Experts' Advice to Couples: Get a Contract

At a time when a growing number of Canadians are settling in love without a wedding band, the Supreme Court has decided that matrimonial property law should not apply automatically to common-law couples who split up....[R]esolving who gets what becomes, potentially, a whole lot more nasty—a fight over the nitty-gritty details of ownership and contribution.

The advice then is to make the rules clear from the beginning with a legal contract—a step few couples in the first blush of love are even willing to contemplate.

"Take nothing for granted," said Alan Mirabelli, executive director of the Vanier Institute for the Family. "Be very clear ahead of time about the 'what if's.' You can't just enter an alternative agreement without defining it. Because it's like quicksand, it changes with the mood of one partner or another."

Source: Anderssen, Erin. 2002. "Experts' Advice to Couples: Get a Contract," *The Globe and Mail*, December 20, A9, abridged. Reprinted with permission from *The Globe and Mail*.

Cultural Changes

The liberalization of divorce laws has contributed to a steady increase in divorce rates over the past while—until recently, Where divorce is still illegal, or hard to get, couples who would otherwise do so cannot legally end their union. This doesn't mean, however, that their marriages will continue or that they will find workable solutions to live happily together. Sometimes, they separate and stay married on paper only. The divorce rate thus seems to be low, but the separation rate may be higher. When and where divorce is easier, more couples divorce. Rising divorce rates are correlated with easier divorce laws. Couples long separated will seek a divorce when the laws allow. Yet, in and of themselves, easier divorce laws do not *cause* the increase in divorce any more than the building of a McDonald's causes hamburger-eating, although consumption of both hamburgers and divorce may increase with the widening of opportunities.

The increase in divorce is largely attributable to economic development (industrialization or modernization) that stimulates individualism in every area of life. Culture, including religion, also affects divorce. Some parts of the culture accept divorce more easily than other parts. For example, Jews in Canada, on average, have more liberal views on divorce than some other ethnic groups (Weinfeld, 2001: 142–143). However, "the Orthodox rules of divorce penalize women routinely," suggests a comprehensive study of Jews in Canada (Weinfeld, 2001: 143). This more restrictive attitude on divorce is common among more conservative religions of all stripes. Legal changes may be faster than religious or cultural changes. In any event, culture does not seem to override the general increase in divorce brought by development. That is why we see a liberalization of divorce laws, and rising divorce rates, wherever societies industrialize, whether they started life as Protestant, Catholic, Jewish, Muslim, Hindu, Buddhist, or Confucian.

Today, the condition of the family includes a vast array of increasingly diverse and complicated relationships and values. Both men and women enter marriage expecting less from it in terms of financial security but much more in terms of interpersonal communication, intimacy, and sexual gratification. More people today think of a close couple relationship or marriage as a place for self-actualization and empathetic companionships. However, such aspirations have a downside. Wherever people put a strong emphasis on intimate partnership as the ideal behind marriage, they are slower to marry and quicker to divorce if necessary.

As well, women's economic independence, the growth of human rights and protections, and the availability of modern contraception have all led Canadians along with others to assess marriage in non-traditional ways. Each cultural change affects marriage in a different way. Taken together they have all made marriage more discretionary. Both men and women feel less compelled by parents and friends, social norms, or cultural ideals, to marry. If married, they feel less compelled to stay married. And certainly, women now have other avenues of activity open to them if they choose not to make a career of marriage and parenthood.

Divorce in the Internet Age

"This fella was into spanking. So he hooked up with a [like-minded] group on the Internet. Eventually, he met someone in a chat room." His wife found out and spanked him with a divorce.

The American Academy of Matrimonial Lawyers, which represents 1600 American lawyers, recently issued a report suggesting that 62 percent of its members participated in at least one divorce last year that involved the Internet.

E-mail on the sly may never replace lipstick on the collar as the leading cause of divorce, but Mr. Short [J. Lindsey Short, Jr., the recent President of the American Academy of Matrimonial Lawyers] believes that the Web is a breeding ground for trouble in a marriage. "If you've got an itch in a relationship, the Internet is an easy place to get it scratched," he says. "People might be too embarrassed to pick up a prostitute or go meet someone in a bar, but find it easy to click on a porn site...or [send off an e-mail] to a paramour."

Source: Cole, Stephen. 2002. "Divorce, 21st –Century Style," *The Globe and Mail*, December 7, F6, abridged. Reprinted with permission from *The Globe and Mail*.

Therefore, more liberal divorce laws and higher divorce rates both stem from the same sources. Changing values and norms in the larger society, alterations in economic opportunities, political ideologies, even the models presented by the mass media all play a part. Liberal divorce laws are merely tools for the ready user. As Goode (1993: 322) explains:

> Under any legal system, some people try to leave their marriages under the existing laws, but many will also press toward new laws with fewer restrictions. If we remove some barriers, some people get divorced who would not have done so before. But, if the deeper social forces that drive both actions become stronger, then still other people will try to dissolve their unions under restrictions they now consider hard and some will work toward even fewer barriers.

However, so many people have been propelled toward demanding and using more liberal divorce laws.

Causes of Divorce

A description of the social changes associated with changes in divorce rates may be taken to imply an explanation of those changes. However, a description should not be mistaken for an explanation. Let us consider the supposed causes of divorce, and changes in divorce practice, more systematically. (For a discussion of the causes of divorce, see Guttman, 1993; or Ambert, 2002.)

In the discussion that follows, we speak of "causes," but often as not we might as well be using the words **determinants** or **predictors**. That is because many supposed causes of divorce intertwine with other causes. Their distinct, separate influence is hard to discover. The most we can say with certainty is that these are predictors—correlates that typically precede divorce and influence the likelihood of divorce. In that limited sense, they are causes of divorce.

We also distinguish among three levels of causal explanation: the micro-, macro-, and meso-levels. By **micro-level** causes, we mean something close to the lived experience of people who divorce: attitudes, perceptions, sentiments, beliefs, and the like. We include the experiences of rejection, infidelity, and marital dissatisfaction in this category. By **macro-level** causes, we mean societal changes like social integration, women's involvement in the workforce, and changes in divorce laws. These are the kinds of variables that Durkheim and his fellow classical macrosociologists studied and first called to people's attention.

Finally, "middle-range" or **meso-level** causes of divorce are, typically, demographic predictors—that is, characteristics of people who are at a high risk of divorce. In this area it is unclear whether these characteristics are causes, determinants, or merely predictors. For example, people who marry at an early age, or after only a short relationship, run a particularly high risk of divorce, perhaps due to the stress, conflict, and dissatisfaction that arise when two immature strangers try to work out a life together.

Precisely what we call the "cause" in the situation will vary from one analyst to another. Let us begin with the microsociological causes of divorce. We have already discussed some of these at length in Chapter 5. They are the easiest causes to understand intuitively. But they may not be the major factors leading to divorce.

Microsociological Causes

We commonly cite two kinds of microsociological "reasons." The first are grounds that people use when they file for divorce. Depending on the jurisdiction, the most common are alcoholism or drug abuse, infidelity, incompatibility, physical and emotional abuse, disagreements about gender roles, sexual incompatibility, and financial problems. These "grounds" may have value in a court of law, but sociologists find them largely unrevealing.

We learn more from the personal "accounts" of individuals who have undergone divorce. "Respondents' accounts of their own divorces illuminate several factors that receive little attention in the empirical literature..." (White, 1990: 908). They tell us a lot about the state of mind of the divorcing people, and the ways they make sense to themselves of what has happened. However, people often do not really understand the reasons for their own behaviour. As well, "(b)ecause these studies only include divorced respondents, they can tell us little about the extent to which these factors predict divorce" (ibid).

The second kind of microsociological reasons people cite to explain divorce typically describe the dynamics of the marriage relationship. As we said in Chapter 5, the quality of a relationship largely determines the stability of a marriage. Marriages likely to end in divorce have a typical profile. Usually, they are characterized by poor communication and poor conflict-resolution skills as well as a lack of commitment to the spouse and/or to the institution of marriage. The spouses may have few shared values and interests, and there is often a perceived inequity between spouses, and less respect, love, and affection on the part of one or both spouses than one might wish or anticipate. These are overall average traits and, of course, will not characterize each situation. These dynamics help us explain why particular couples end their marriages. We can imagine people in such relationships wanting and getting a divorce. However, because these are common problems of relationships, they do not help us predict which couples are going to celebrate a fiftieth anniversary together and which ones are going to break up next week. Even those on the inside of the relationship often cannot make that prediction.

Consider, instead, some life-course (demographic) variables that make certain people more divorce-prone than others. These are better than microsociological variables at identifying conditions that produce tensions and unhappiness—which, in turn, increase the likelihood of divorce. That is, even if they do not seem to explain divorce as well, they are better at predicting it.

Mesosociological Causes

Not everyone who marries, divorces. In fact, the majority stays married. Moreover, the probability of divorce is spread unevenly throughout the population. Thus, to understand the causes of divorce we must look at who gets divorced and why. As Lynn White explains:

> A shift in the lifetime divorce probability from 10 percent to well over 50 percent cannot be explained at the micro level. In addition to asking why some marriages are more likely to fail than others, we also need to examine changes in the social institutions that structure individual experience. (White, 1990: 904)

Major life-course and demographic variables correlated with a high divorce risk include young age at marriage, cohabitation before marriage, second or subsequent marriage, parental divorce, premarital pregnancy and/or childbearing, childlessness or conversely having a large number of children, early stage of marriage, urban residence, residence in British Columbia or Alberta (or in Quebec), absence of religious belief or affiliation, and low socioeconomic status.

Age at Marriage

Age at marriage is probably the strongest predictor of divorce in the first five years of marriage. People who enter marriage at the youngest ages do so with the greatest risk of leaving marriage by divorce (Ambert, 2002). Risks are particularly high for people who marry in their teens. Various explanations for this have been ventured: young people lack the emotional maturity needed for marriage; and they have ill-founded expectations of what married life holds in store. They are more likely to become disappointed and disillusioned with marriage, especially when they come upon plentiful alternatives to their current spouse (South, Trent, & Shen, 2001). As well, some of the effects of youthful marriage on marital dissolution are the result of the harmful effects of early marriage on educational achievement. Young marriers divorce more often because they have less education, therefore a lower income, and perhaps fewer communication skills—which, in turn, can result in more marital conflict.

Ironically, though young marriers in our own society have high rates of divorce, young-marrying societies, in which the average age at marriage is low, have low rates of divorce. Typically, countries with low average ages of marriage have other features—for example, high rates of childbearing, strongly institutionalized religion, extended families, and restrictive divorce laws—that keep the divorce rates low for people of all ages. Latin American and Islamic societies share these features, as do some cultures in Africa and Asia.

Cohabitation

Cohabitation before marriage has, as we've said in earlier chapters, also been correlated with a higher risk of divorce. This finding runs counter to common sense, which suggests that people who marry after they live together should have a lower divorce risk. After all, they are basing their decision to marry on more knowledge about each other than people who marry without having lived together first. However, there are other factors in this puzzle, as we shall see.

Measurement and risk are important to interpreting what's happening with cohabitation and divorce, just as they are to interpreting divorce rates, as we have seen. What is not included in studies of divorce following cohabitation are two significant groups of couples: those who cohabit and break up before marrying, and those who cohabit and never marry. With respect to those who cohabit and split up without marrying, not much is known, except that cohabiting relationships tend to be more volatile than marriages. For some individuals, cohabitation involves less commitment and therefore a greater likelihood that the union may be unstable. That cohabiting relationships are more stable and long-lasting in Quebec, as well as growing in length and stability in the rest of Canada, as we have seen in Chapter 4, suggests that not all cohabiting relationships are the same (LeBourdais, Neil, & Turcotte, 2000). With respect to those who cohabit and never marry, again, not as much is known as about marriages. But, it seems that, increasingly, Canadians are choosing cohabitation as a permanent alternative to marriage. Of course, there could be a relationship to divorce; one sure way of avoiding divorce is not to marry in the first place! Taken together, these tendencies may add a strong note of caution to the interpretation that cohabitation prior to marriage is risky. Even without this caution, however, it is never wise to generalize from a statistical risk to one's individual situation.

Another factor possibly at work here is counterintuitive as well. Societal and familial pressures to marry for stability and in the hope that marriage brings good effects for couples, for individuals, and for society may in fact cause couples to marry to be accepted. In this sense, cohabitation may hasten marriage and hence increase the risk of separation and divorce (Ambert, 2002). Further, couples in happy cohabiting relationships who succumb to societal pressures to marry may find their relationship changed by the very legal and policy contexts that shape expectations about wives and husbands and supposedly encourage stability. Couples, in other words, may not be separating as much from each other as from the socially scripted roles and expectations that legal marriage entails. Much has been learned about this from gay and lesbian couples, some of whom see the reality that they cannot legally marry (in most jurisdictions) as strengthening their relationships (see Lehr, 1999). In other words, couples are creating their own ways to be couples rather than working to fit into legally prescribed roles and obligations.

Still another possible explanation for this finding is **adverse selectivity**. Historically, "the kinds of people who flout[ed] convention by cohabiting [were] the same kinds of people who flout[ed] normative marital behaviour, [had] lower commitment to marriage as an institution, and disregard[ed] the stigma of divorce" (White, 1990: 906). While not as true now when cohabitation, in Canada more than in the United States, is much more normative, cohabitation may still attract some who are less keen on commitment and stability. When the effects of selectivity are removed, cohabitation does not affect union stability (Lillard, Brien, & Waite, 1995; Ambert, 2002). What this means is that as more people—and more varied people— cohabit, cohabitation no longer predicts a high risk of divorce. So, cohabitation as a predictor variable for divorce risk is likely on the way out of sociological theories, although of course not all sociologists are of one mind in seeing it this way.

Second Marriages

Other things being equal, second marriages are more likely than first marriages to end in divorce. The risk in Canada is estimated to be about 10 percent higher than in first marriages (Ambert, 2002). The probability that third marriages will end in divorce is higher still. (As well, remarriages that end in divorce end more quickly than first marriages.) When remarriages work out, it is typically because the remarried people are older than average. Older people are less likely to divorce. Young people who remarry are more likely to divorce than older people who remarry.

Again, this violates our common sense. One would expect remarriages— like cohabiting relationships—to have a lower divorce rate. People who had already gone through one divorce would, we imagine, be more careful choosing their next mate. They would try harder to make their marriage work, to avoid the problems and costs associated with divorce. Some, in fact, do just this. When a second marriage endures, it often outlasts the first (Ambert, 2002). However, this is not so for all, clearly. Adverse selectivity may *again* be the explanation. People who get a first divorce may be more willing to get a second. They may more readily see divorce as a solution to marital problems. Of course, given the frequency of divorce, this includes more and more of us.

A competing theory argues that the stresses and strains of a remarriage are greater than those of first marriages. Second marriages may bring "unfinished baggage" from the first marriage/divorce, or the (difficult) integration of stepchildren into reconstituted families, or the challenges of ongoing interactions with ex-spouses. Furthermore, there are fewer norms that guide second marriages, although of course that is changing with their greater frequency. This makes remarriages more challenging and perhaps may be a factor in divorce risk. Both theories are compelling. We need more research to decide which explanation is better, or whether both sets of factors come into play, perhaps with other factors still not well-understood.

Parental Divorce

People whose parents divorced are also more likely to divorce. However, the mechanism that transmits this inheritance is unclear. Perhaps, people whose parents divorced are less likely to believe that marriages can last. That makes them more likely to opt for divorce when things get tough. They may have married before they were ready, out of fear that they would be alone (like their parents). They may have married before they really understood what marriage was all about, because their parents' marriage didn't last long enough for them to find out. Or they may simply be the victims of optimism. This does not mean, however, that if your parents are divorced your risks of divorce are automatically high. They are not. Many children of divorced parents marry well and live happily.

One Canadian study (Corak & Heisz, 1999) compares children whose parents divorced with those who lost a parent to death. They find, interestingly, that there are no consequences for children's subsequent marital behaviours if they lost a parent to death. These children, when adults, have the same likelihood of marrying and of divorcing as anyone else. However, children whose parents divorce have a slightly greater likelihood of divorcing as adults. They also have a greater tendency not to marry. It might be that one consequence of divorce, as hinted earlier, is to increase the rates of cohabitation.

The correlation of parental divorce with heightened divorce risk may be due again to adverse selectivity. People whose parents divorced were once a small minority. Today, they are not. Their parents' divorce stigmatizes them less and leaves them less ignorant about the variety of possible adaptations to marital conflict. They know that people survive divorce, and many people are better for doing so. If this explanation is so, we might expect that more people will have "learned how to divorce" from their parents. However, demographically speaking, as the average age of the population increases, and as older people remarry less often and cohabit more often, we may see a decline in divorce.

Childbearing, Before and After Marriage

Evidence documenting the relationship between premarital childbearing and likelihood of divorce is overwhelming. For people who marry after having a child, the risk of divorce is high. However premarital pregnancy does not, by itself, predict divorce. Couples who marry after discovering that they are expecting a child may marry under extreme pressure to legitimate the birth of their child. This is not the best motivation to marry. The good news is that shotgun weddings are less common than they used to be.

The relationship between the birth of children within marriage and the likelihood of divorce is strong, but not straightforward. Couples who divorce tend to have no children or have fewer on average than those who stay married (Ambert, 2002). The reasons may be unrelated to childbearing, but be due, in large part, to the fact that most divorces occur within the early years of marriage. On the one hand, people who have no children may see themselves as freer to divorce than couples with children.

Children are becoming less of a deterrent to divorce than they once were. Both the number of children affected by divorce and the proportion of divorces involving children have been increasing, however. Couples no longer, if they ever did, stay together because they have children.

An interesting finding from research on the demographic correlates of divorce is that the sex of the child or children influences divorce-proneness, at least in the United States. Data from the Current Population Survey in the U.S. show that sons reduce the risk of marital disruption by 9 percent more than daughters. Fathers apparently get more involved in raising sons than daughters, which creates more attachment and a stronger sense of obligation. Having at least one son also lowers the mother's perception of the likelihood of separation or divorce, as paternal involvement is higher with boys than girls. This increased paternal involvement fosters the idea that if fathers have more invested, they have more to lose as a result of divorce (Popenoe, 1996; South, Trent, & Shen, 2001).

However, some research suggests that child-related variables, such as the presence of a male child in the family, play no role whatever in predicting or causing divorce (Devine & Forehand, 1996). Like other variables we discuss, this apparent correlation may reflect a change over time, as divorce becomes more common. When divorce was unusual, it was relatively easy to pinpoint predictor variables. As divorce became culturally "normal," the characteristics of divorcing couples became more varied, and the predictive value of any particular factor diminished.

Stage of Marriage

Duration of marriage is strongly negatively correlated with a propensity to divorce. That said, the lowest risk of divorce is in the first year of marriage (Statistics Canada, 2002). The risks increase dramatically each year thereafter, from 5.1 percent after the first anniversary up to a peak of 25.5 percent after the fourth anniversary (Statistics Canada, 2002). After four years of marriage, the risks of divorce drop considerably. Most couples divorce, if they are going to divorce, during the first 15 years of marriage. The explanation is that the more time and energy people invest in their marriage, the higher the costs of abandoning the marriage and starting a new life. Couples are more aware of being badly matched early in the marriage since the factors responsible for divorce (e.g., emotional satisfaction) carry more weight in the early years. After about three years, relationships stabilize and many partners adjust.

On the other hand, the longer a marriage goes on, the older the spouses tend to be, and the more likely they are to have grown up with cultural values in which marriage had much greater normative pull than it does today. We must wait another few decades before we find out the strength of this **cohort effect.** A cohort effect is something that influences everyone of roughly the same age. World War II or the Depression might be such influences.

Place of Residence

Urban living is positively correlated with divorce, while rural living is negatively correlated. That is, people living in urban centres are much more likely to divorce than people in rural areas. One the one hand, these findings reflect a higher probability of divorce under the demands and stresses of urban life. However, in part these statistics also reflect adverse selectivity—specifically, the tendency for rural people to migrate to urban areas before, during, or after a divorce, or simply for younger people to migrate to cities for work or education and find themselves marrying there. A family farm or a rural small town can be a difficult place for divorced people, particularly divorced women.

The effect of urban living is sometimes confounded by the divorce-increasing role of migration. When we control for many possible explanatory factors, rates of union instability are strongly related to recent and lifetime migration experience. The weaker social ties of some migrants appear to provide less social support for their unions and fewer barriers to union disruption. At the same time, many immigrants come from cultures with strong family sanctions for lasting marriages. An alternative explanation is that when immigrants from countries in which marriage is seen primarily as a practical arrangement come to Canada and encounter the expectation that marriage should be based on passion and companionship, they look at their own marriage from a different point of view, and may become dissatisfied. A third possibility is that selectivity explains the finding. People who take the initiative of moving to a new country are risk takers, willing to confront challenges and make changes in their lives. They may be more willing to consider divorce than the more cautious people who stay behind. Or, they may experience greater stresses, which can cause even firmly based marriages trouble.

Divorce rates vary across regions in any given country, too. In both Canada and the United States, divorce rates increase as one moves from east to west. An exception is posed by Quebec, which has high rates of divorce (and also of cohabitation, as noted in Chapter 4). One factor explaining this east-west pattern is a difference in attitudes and values. Something of a frontier tradition that includes migration for work seems to characterize the West. The age distribution of the population also differs, with younger (and thus more divorce-prone) people being found in the West. People tend to move away from the stabilizing influences of extended families and family traditions in search of jobs as well.

Religion

Finally, the ethnic and religious composition of the population has something to do with the patterns of divorce. Religiosity is negatively correlated with divorce-proneness. That is, the more religious people are, the less likely they will be to opt for divorce, even if they are unhappy in their marriages. Religious affiliation also plays a part. Couples in which the spouses belong to different religions are more likely to divorce than couples who belong to the same religion. Couples in which neither spouse has a religious affiliation tend to have even higher rates of divorce (Goode, 1993: 320).

Related to this is the overall secularization of societies such as Canada. With the massive move away from religion as a dominant social institution in everyone's everyday lives have come new norms. Among these, individual choice and liberalization of sexual beliefs and behaviours loom large. Marriage has become, for many, an individual choice, sanctioned by government rather than a covenant taken before God. Even couples who marry in churches tend to believe less in the religious covenant aspect now. Divorce, then, is seen more as a choice rather than the breaking of a larger spiritual commitment.

Socioeconomic Status

Class, or **socioeconomic status** (SES), is strongly correlated with probability of divorce. The divorce rate increases as one moves down the socioeconomic ladder. Study after study confirms that, whatever the index of socioeconomic status used—income, occupation, or education—we observe an inverse correlation between SES and divorce rates.

The higher level of financial insecurities that people face may explain the relationship between social class and divorce rates, on the one hand. Economic stresses produce marital stresses. Simultaneously, the poor have less to lose from divorce and less to gain from staying married. In other words, compared to more prosperous people, their material investment in marriage may be lower, so divorce "costs" them less. However, differences in divorce rates by socioeconomic status generally tend to be decreasing. This is in part a function of an increase in the divorce rate among middle- and upper-class people.

Sociologist William Goode has an interesting explanation for both the finding that divorce rates diminish as one moves up the socioeconomic ladder, and that the divorce rate for middle- and upper-middle-class couples is on the rise. He notes that in the 1950s,

> lower-class women had relatively less to lose economically from divorce because they were more likely to be close to the wages of their husbands. Middle- and upper-class women, in contrast had a much greater economic stake in the stability of their marriages and

much more to lose from a divorce. There was likely to be a much greater discrepancy between their own income (which was often nonexistent since few middle-class women with children were employed in those days) and the income of their husbands. (Goode, 1993: 331)

If the relationship between class position and proneness to divorce has been changing, the change is likely the result of a shift in the strongest variable in this pattern: the discrepancy between the husband's and the wife's incomes. Now that more married women from the middle and upper classes are likely to be employed, and more likely to be employed in occupations and professions similar to their husbands, there is less discrepancy between their incomes. With less discrepancy (and with independent incomes), those women now look—sociologically—more like the lower-class women of the past in that they will not experience as great a loss of income if they divorce. The same variable may also account for part of the higher divorce rate among Afro-Americans, since it determines how great a loss the wife would experience if a divorce occurred (Goode, 1993: 331).

By suggesting that the divorce rate is higher because more women can afford to get divorced than once could, Goode assumes that women are more likely to want out than men. The more economically independent women become, the more likely they will be to leave their marriages when they want. We would have to look further, at who initiates separation or files for divorce, to confirm this hypothesis. The implication is that marriage, though seemingly about love or emotional union, is still a way for women to gain economically. Poverty that affects women is a social construction and women's needs for marriage work through their economic needs for support.

An unexpected finding is that when the members of a couple are considered as individuals, the inverse relationship between class (or income) and divorce rate holds for men but not for women. So, the higher the man's class or income, the lower the likelihood of divorce, but the higher a woman's income, the higher the likelihood of divorce. What do these tendencies mean, given that high-income women are generally married to high-income men? Obviously some tensions exist between these two opposing tendencies, in a substantial but unknown number of cases.

Some research finds that increases in wives' socioeconomic status and labour-force participation increase the probability of marriage disruption. We may know of situations where this occurs. Other research finds no support for this hypothesis. When the wife's work status is higher than her husband's, instability is more likely (Tzeng & Mare, 1995). However, improvements in wives' status usually *increase* marital stability, perhaps by reducing economic stresses in the family, or by increasing the wife's **autonomy** and fulfillment.

Couples with more education and a stronger attachment to the work force have more stable marriages, on average. It is also these couples who are most likely to be egalitarian. Given the importance of work in stabilizing marriage, it is no surprise that unemployed people have higher divorce risks than employed people. The receipt of family-support income also (slightly) increases the likelihood a married woman will become divorced (Hoffman & Duncan, 1995; Davies et al., 2001). This does not mean that social transfers cause marital instability, but only that economic and other instabilities may be correlated.

Finally, research has shown that African-American women are 1.8 times as likely to divorce as white American women (Kposowa, 1995). Being African-American in the U.S. is also strongly related to other important determinants of divorce, such as class and childbirth outside marriage. In Canada, although marriage is the dominant family form among blacks, "less emphasis is placed on marriage as a context for childbearing" (Calliste, 2001: 411). It is less known whether black families, which in Canada represent a huge diversity of cultures and length of time in Canada, going from very recent immigrants from the Caribbean and Africa, to seventeenth-century slavery in New France (Calliste, 2001: 404), have the same greater tendency to divorce. The black/white differential in divorce in the United States cannot be explained by controlling socioeconomic status and background factors such as fertility, sex ratios, and age at marriage. When these variables are controlled, the relationship between race and the propensity to divorce still exists, though to a lesser degree. This remains to be fully explained.

African-American spouses are much more likely than white spouses to think their happiness outside marriage is greater than inside marriage. This could be a legacy of the slavery period or colonialism. In this way, they are more similar to Latin Americans, Québécois, and Europeans than to white Americans or Anglo-Canadians. In addition, African Americans are more likely to feel that other aspects of their lives would not be as damaged by divorce. They also may feel less bound by middle-class propriety and norms than are many white Americans. Happiness may matter more than social image. This may explain, in small part, the higher rates of divorce and lower rates of marriage in the African-American community (Rank & Davis, 1996).

Macrosociological Causes

It should be clear by now that although the decision to divorce is one made by an individual couple, the decision is influenced strongly by large processes in the structure of society over which people have little, if any, control.

The institution of the family has changed a great deal over the past two centuries. The ties of authority and economic dependence that bind family members together have weakened considerably. In addition, the legal structure forcing people to remain together has loosened, making divorce an attainable option for many people. Other important macro-level determinants of divorce include wars and migrations, economic cycles, sex ratios, gender roles, social integration, and cultural values. We will look at each of these factors in turn.

Wars and Migrations

Sharp increases in divorce rates usually follow wars. Divorce rates usually then return to the prewar levels. This is likely because war separates many couples for long periods. Sometimes, couples who were formerly close grow apart—or are torn apart. Some migrate to other regions or countries, never to return to their home countries or their spouses. In other cases, wartime separation merely establishes separate lives for couples whose marriages had been held together only by inertia. In addition, war throws together many lonely spouses with people of the opposite sex under conditions that encourage involvement. Few people institute divorce actions while a war is in progress. Many do so when wars end and people readjust. Finally, the strains of postwar reunion themselves are often great. Some formerly stable marriages break under this additional strain.

Economic Cycles

People are less likely to divorce during recessionary periods than during periods of economic prosperity. People feel freer to strike out on their own when economic opportunities exist. They are more wary of leaving a familiar home or relationship, even if it is unpleasant, in times of economic uncertainty.

Moreover, divorce is costly. It requires establishing separate households, dividing the property, and establishing specific terms for the support of children. These requirements tax most people's financial resources even during prosperity and often become prohibitive in bad times. Great financial hardship may draw together some couples who might otherwise become isolated from each other. If this happens, apparently the effect is short-lived. Although divorce rates drop during depressions, they rise rapidly when the depression ends.

On the other hand, according to White's review of the sociological literature on divorce, "(t)he most sophisticated analysis of American time series data... finds that the effect of prosperity is to slightly reduce divorce" (White, 1990: 905). Although prosperity may make divorce more feasible, the *benefits* of prosperity outweigh this effect on personal relationships (South, 1985). Indeed, as we noted in the last chapter, financial insecurity places a great deal of stress on any marriage. It can add enough strain to break marriages that would otherwise survive under conditions of prosperity. Thus, divorce rates may fall because financial security adds stability to personal relationships. At the very least, the evidence on this is inconclusive.

One thing is certain. Divorce may be costly, but like environmental disasters, it is good for the economy. Divorce promotes spending on lawyers and separate household goods, and otherwise spurs the economy by consumer growth. Without divorce, the economies of Canada and the United States might not be as vibrant.

Sex Ratios

One of the more provocative and controversial findings in the literature on macro-level determinants of divorce is that the ratio of women to men in a given society affects the divorce rate (Anderssen, 2002; South, Trent, & Shen, 2001). Among non-Hispanic whites in the U.S., the risk of divorce is highest where either wives or husbands have the option of many potential mates. Despite strong cultural norms against extramarital relations, many people remain open to alternative relationships while married. The supply of spousal alternatives in the local marriage market seems to increase the risk of divorce. The jury is still out on how much of a factor this is, however.

Gender Expectations

The evidence regarding the influence of gender expectations is difficult to interpret. Researchers have examined two hypotheses. First, when social structures allow women more economic independence from men and families, women have more freedom to divorce (Hetherington & Kelly, 2002; Popenoe, 1996; Stacey, 1996). Second, a growing similarity of women's and men's lives and roles may produce less marital cohesion than complementary, reinforcing roles do. Both of these imply that the more women become financially secure, the higher the divorce rate will be.

Evidence from both time-series studies in the United States and in Canada and from cross-cultural studies overwhelmingly finds that as women's participation in the labour force increases, so does the divorce rate (Ambert, 2002). This may be more correlation, however, than causation. It is unclear whether the critical factor is extra-familial opportunities, economic independence, growing similarity of gender roles, the worldwide trend toward more modern marital relationships based on higher expectations, or some other factors.

Indeed, evidence suggests that the most satisfying marriages (for both spouses) are those in which gender roles are egalitarian, men are sensitive and nurturing, and husbands and wives share equally in making the decisions that affect their lives (Stacey, 1996). Antill & Cotton (1987) studied 108 couples and found that when both spouses are high on "feminine" characteristics such as nurturance, sensitivity, and gentleness, couples are happier than when one or both spouses is low on this cluster of characteristics. "**Femininity**" of both wives and husbands is positively associated with a smooth marital adjustment (Kalin & Lloyd, 1985). The explanation is that many qualities and characteristics that make up femininity are conducive to positive interpersonal relationships. Relationships that both spouses view as equitable have the best marital adjustment. The greater the perceived inequity, the poorer the marital adjustment, *and thus the higher* the risks of divorce.

The nature of the relationship between gender expectations and divorce-proneness is unclear. Historical and cross-cultural research is addressing the issues of 1) whether divorce rates and rates of female participation in paid work are intrinsically related; 2) if the observed relationship is a passing effect of the tension between changing social expectations and lagging societal understandings of *these* changes; 3) if the divorce rate is as high as in countries that have had a longer history of female participation in the labour force.

Social Integration

Another macro-level determinant of divorce is a society's degree of **social integration**. The higher the social integration, the lower the divorce rate. Aggregate-level studies in the United States and Canada uniformly find that community instability, as measured by **social mobility**, is the best predictor of aggregate divorce rates. In a stable, highly integrated community, consensus on social rules is strong and rule-breakers are punished. This happens especially when the rules broken bear on social institutions as central to the community life as "the family." The highly integrated community typically supports a variety of "pro-family" ideals bearing on marriage, premarital or extramarital sexuality, or child obedience. Social integration decreases the likelihood that people will divorce by increasing the costs of divorcing and divorce. By getting a divorce, people risk incurring a social stigma for flouting social norms and tearing the social fabric of the community. In these highly integrated communities, this is scary stuff and a definite deterrent.

Cultural Values

Researchers have given a lot of attention to the postwar shift in cultural values from an emphasis on community to the primacy of the individual. Today, it is argued, we invest less in familial commitments, whether to parents, spouses, or children, than was once the norm.

Since the 1960s, the cultural value placed on marriage has been declining. Many scholars argue that formal marriage has lost its normative support. This means it is no longer something that one *ought* to do, but is simply a matter of personal choice or preference. Distinctions between marital and non-marital childbearing, marriage, and cohabitation have lost their normative force. We have reduced marriage and divorce to mere formalities, or sets of family options.

Effects of Divorce

Divorce, like the breakup of any important relationship, is usually messy and painful. Most couples decide to divorce only reluctantly over a long period. For most of them, considerable trauma is involved. A minority experiences some discrimination and may be, for a time, almost without friends. Some, notably women, suffer considerable economic deprivation.

Effects on Both Spouses

One of the major effects of divorce is economic: for men and women, but especially women, incomes fall. For both men and women, patterns of credit use change and debt problems increase after divorce. The material effects of divorce should not be underrated. Economic distress is a large contributor to generalized psychological distress and to social-policy challenges (Davies et al., 2001).

Controlling for financially caused stress reduces the estimated effect of divorce or separation. However, economic distress is only one aspect of divorce and its aftermath. The other side is the emotional stress of interpersonal conflict. This begins well before the divorce, and may reach its peak then. In the years immediately preceding divorce, people experience higher-than-usual levels of distress. But conflict does not end with divorce. The effects of divorce on the divorcing adults, both material and emotional, can be surprisingly long-lasting for some (Mastekaasa, 1995). Elder women, in particular those with little education and employment experience, can be particularly disadvantaged for a considerable period of time afterwards (Ambert, 2002).

Some take longer than others to recover from the effects of divorce. For example, people who experience high levels of guilt have more trouble adjusting to their new situation following divorce, as measured by depression, role strain, and continuing attachment to the ex-spouse. However, continuing attachment may be the norm. A majority report some level of contact with their former spouses. This is particularly likely if they have children, of course. Also, those who have contact hold more similar views about the desirable level of contact and behave in conformity with these views, though their norms may conflict with perceived societal norms (Smart & Neale, 1999).

By contrast, former spouses often disagree on the involvement of non-custodial parents in co-parenting. An overwhelming majority of residential parents feel they have problems with the issue of visitation rights. A smaller but still substantial percentage of non-residential parents do too. Moreover, these problems don't go away quickly. For residential parents, usually the mother, visitation problems are connected to feelings of hurt and anger about the divorce. They are also connected with concerns about the ex-spouse's parenting abilities, child support, and sometimes about abuse of the child.

The process of changing role-identities during divorce and post-divorce interactions is different for initiators than for non-initiators, or what Hopper (1993) calls "dumpers" and "dumpees," although both pass through a series of predictable stages on the way to recovery (Duran-Aydintug, 1995). Each person's network of relationships, including the family and various organizations, helps to shape the effects of divorce and adjustments to it. Remarriage is more important, for reasons of economic security, for women than for men, especially if there are children and if the woman does not have a well-paid occupation. And yet, it is less likely for women, particularly women with dependent children. For men, cohabitation may be a more attractive option. Thus, divorced spouses are likely to find themselves in very different living arrangements immediately after divorce.

After divorce, the satisfaction people feel with their current family situation or (subsequent) marriage is influenced by a variety of things, including the contact they have had with relatives since the divorce. Participation in organizations and clubs also helps people feel that things are better afterwards than during the divorce. It may be simply that people feel that they have seen the worst and survived it.

Having acknowledged that men and women have some similar experiences during divorce, we will now focus on the different effects for each after divorce. Particularly, we will consider the difficulties women face with divorce, which tend to be greater than those for men.

Effects on Women

This section emphasizes the adverse effects of divorce. However, we will begin by acknowledging that divorce may also have benefits. For example, divorced mothers whose marriages were difficult, and sometimes abusive, are typically relieved that their marriages are over. However, even among those who are happy to be out of a bad or intolerable relationship, a majority express concern about the conditions they face after divorce. They tend to be angry about diminished opportunities and their perceived second-class treatment as divorced women (Kurz, 1995).

Because women and men have different experiences after a divorce, they behave differently. For example, separated men are six times more likely than married men to commit suicide (especially in the younger age groups). However, compared to married women, separated women do not have much higher suicide rates. After divorce, both male and female suicide rates rise. Thus, as Durkheim said, marriage protects both sexes, but it does so differently. Women with more children have lower suicide rates than women with fewer children, for example. It is possible that their childrearing responsibilities protect women against suicide. This protection erodes as their children become independent.

Though the end of a marital relationship, whether by death or divorce, is almost always traumatic, the way the relationship ends also makes a difference, particularly for women. German research suggests that, for women, the actual loss of the marital partner is not as important as the circumstances under which the partner was lost (Maas, 1995). Divorced women and World War II widows are financially worse off than recently widowed women. They also report more health problems.

Divorce depresses both women and men. However, women undergoing divorce show greater increases in rates of depression. Men whose marriages are breaking up typically show higher rates of alcohol problems but not of distress (Wu & Hart, 2002). Women report more distress but not more alcohol problems. These findings support the idea that men externalize their problems in response to circumstances that lead women to internalize. Women also show more symptoms of distress before the separation, whereas men display more symptoms after the final separation. In short, men and women respond to the stresses of divorce differently. Therefore, researchers must measure men's and women's well-being differently and therapists must help them in ways appropriate to the problems they face.

After divorce, women usually suffer a decline in their standard of living. A classic American study by Lenore Weitzman (1985) estimated a decline of 73 percent in women's standard of living, compared to a 42-percent decline for men in the first year after divorce. (For comparable Canadian data, see Finnie, 1993, which will be discussed below. For more recent American data, see Arditti, 1997. For a re-analysis of Weitzman's data and less dramatic findings, see Peterson, 1996.) This drop in living standard occurs even among less-advantaged subgroups, such as African-American and Hispanic low-income adults. Most young minority men fare poorly after divorce in absolute economic terms. However, young minority women fare even worse, a disparity that stems, either directly or indirectly, from women's roles as primary child caretakers (Smock, 1994).

Finnie's (1993) Canadian research also demonstrates that both men's and women's income drops as a result of divorce, but women's income drops twice as much, on average. Men tend to recover lost income more quickly than women in the aftermath of divorce. Thus, divorce is much more likely to plunge divorced women into poverty, and keep them there for longer. This is particularly true if they have children for whom they are solely or largely responsible.

Women usually experience a decline in their standard of living because women typically earn less than men in the paid labour force. Also, they usually get custody of the children, which means that fewer dollars have to support a lot more people. And women with children may have taken time out of paid employment to have or stay with the children while they are young, thus reducing their years of income and work experience. Low income is the cause of higher levels of life strains reported by separated women, according to a six-year longitudinal study (Nelson, 1994). On the other hand, "fathers are generally better off after divorce, for they can now spend most of their money on one person, themselves..." (Goode, 1993: 166). Some divorced fathers dutifully provide child support, however, for their children after divorce.

Women's economic disadvantage after divorce is largely due to the traditional practice of investing male human capital in the wage labour market and female human capital in the family and home. The latter greatly disadvantages women after divorce, when women are likely to receive inadequate compensation for time spent out of the wage labour market. Even women with almost the same educational background as men are at a disadvantage, leaving women, who had invested heavily in their families, vulnerable because of divorce (James, 1996).

This effect is even more dramatic as single women grow older. Elderly women who divorced twenty years ago or more are worse off than long-term widows, despite their (typically) higher education. This is in part because they have not had the benefit of much shared income. In the past—even the recent past—widows were treated with more respect by policy and by law than divorced women, having greater access to their deceased husband's pensions, for example, and greater rights to own property on their own and to get mortgages. Divorced women are also more likely to lack informal support systems and to rely on paid helpers (Ambert, 2002; Choi, 1995).

The gender-related problems we are discussing are nearly universal. For example, divorced people in India, Canada, and the United States experience similar problems with economic adequacy, social support, and psychological well-being. Furthermore, the predictors of divorce adjustment are similar in both societies. However, for a combination of cultural and economic reasons, Indian women suffer more hardship than North American women do. Three factors are responsible for this pattern: Indian women's traditional economic dependence on men, Indian cultural beliefs about women and marriage, and the patriarchal organization of the Indian family.

The impact of divorce is often lifelong; the healing process takes time. For divorced mothers, for example, stressful events and depressive symptoms heighten dramatically soon after the divorce. They then decline over the next three years. Healing is influenced by such variables as age of mother and child, potential for remarriage, coping skills, social networks, and income changes. Having a steady, satisfying job is associated with higher self-esteem and lower distress among divorced women. A good job provides meaning, social interaction and support, productivity, positive distraction, and, of course, income. Spirituality helps some women. Others change their behaviour to reduce stress. They may take up exercise or otherwise focus on nurturing a healthy body; they may take classes or take up hobbies to improve their mental well-being; they may revamp their personal appearance to give themselves a boost. (For more on this theme, see Wallerstein & Blakelee, 1990.) We will discuss more about life after divorce in Chapter 11 when we consider fresh, family starts.

Effects on Children

Traditionally, many couples avoided divorce and stayed together "for the sake of the children." Their concern was, in some respects, justifiable. Divorce may have harmful effects for the children involved. However, as we will see, recent research suggests that many couples might think in terms of breaking up "for the sake of the children." The research shows repeatedly that the effects of divorce for children as well as for parents depend very much on what is happening in the family before divorce and the quality of family relationships during and after the divorce (Amato & Booth, 1996; Amato, Loomis & Booth, 1995; Smart & Neale, 1999; Stacey, 1996). If the family is violent or family relationships abusive and hostile, for example, then divorce might provide relief.

Since the early 1970s, more than a million North American children per year experience parental divorce (Stacey, 1996; Wallerstein et al., 2000; Ducibella, 1995). Divorce has been associated with a variety of adverse psychological and health effects in these children. But, of course, tendencies or averages conceal diversities. The media pendulum has swung to the side recently of reporting research findings on *every* negative outcome on children of divorce as fact. Hetherington & Kelly (2002) suggest that the negative long-term effects of divorce on children may have become so exaggerated that it has become a self-fulfilling prophecy (Jacoby, 2002: 38). For example, children of divorced parents can display poorer social and

Parental divorce can increase the risk of adolescent depression by both acting as a source of many secondary problems and stresses that cause depression, and by altering the reactions to these stresses.

psychological adjustment than children from non-divorced homes (Kunz, 1992: 352). But, if schools and counsellors and parents are taught to look for these outcomes, that could account, in part, for why they find them more often. When the children grow up, they are much more likely than those from intact families to think their own marriages may be in trouble. The question arises as to whether there might have been other differences in these children prior to divorce, and whether their subsequent expectations about their own marriages are the result of hype about negative-outcomes research or something more.

Parental divorce can work to increase the risk of adolescent depression in two ways. First, it may be a source of many secondary problems and stresses that cause depression. Second, it can alter youths' reactions to these stresses, sometimes increasing the depressive effects. Economic hardships, a common outcome of divorce for children, also increase the risk of depression, thus accounting for the greater vulnerability of youths in single-parent families to depression (Amato & Sobeolewski, 2001; Aseltine, 1996). That these factors go together makes it challenging for researchers to sort out the independent effects of divorce *per se*.

Children of divorced parents show higher levels of depression and lower levels of self-esteem than children from intact families. In particular, children with irrational beliefs and feelings about divorce are most likely to develop behavioural and psychological problems (Skitka & Frazier, 1995). This shows the need for counselling that puts the divorce in perspective. As well, children who blame themselves for their parents' problems seem to have particular difficulty adjusting to the separation. The more recent the separation, the less likely children are to accept it and the worse they feel about it. As they settle into their new living arrangement, distress diminishes (Bussell, 1995; Carlson & Corcoran, 2001).

Adolescents from lone-parent and stepparent families generally suffer from lower self-esteem, more symptoms of anxiety and loneliness, more depressed moods, more suicidal thoughts, and more suicide attempts than children from intact families. Among adolescent children with divorced parents, boys appear to have more emotional problems in stepparent families and girls have more problems in lone-parent families (Garnefski & Okma, 1996).

To the extent that children do suffer from divorce, much of the ill effect stems from one of two sources. One is a diminished sense of personal security; the other is worse parenting. After divorce, some children living in relatively happy homes report no change in security and happiness, while others feel less security and less happiness. Much of the decreased sense of security may reflect a temporary decline in the parenting provided. This can be due to parental preoccupation or depression, or due to a reduction in the number of parents present.

Divorced parents may experience problems in raising their children. Research shows that children in homes where one parent is missing through divorce are more likely to display problems than children in two-parent families are. Partly, the reason is that separation and divorce commonly fail to end the conflict between parents.

Separated and divorced parents often have difficult problems to solve. They may become frustrated when they choose, or are forced, to make decisions that conflict with their own desires and beliefs. For example, the court may grant a father the right to visit his children periodically, though the mother deems the father incompetent or even dangerous. Because the mother opposes the visits, she may be extremely frustrated, especially if the children exploit parental differences. For example, children may tell their mother, "Well, Daddy lets us." This causes the mother to feel insecure about her parental practices or resources as she struggles to both fulfill the child's needs and be the "favourite" parent, or at least a liked parent. Given her often-reduced financial circumstances, she may not be able to buy the food or clothes or entertainment that the child's father can afford. This adds to the frustrations and the challenges in good parenting.

Because of these conflicts and frustrations, parents are often too preoccupied to meet their children's needs completely. Failure to agree on custody is a common source of problems after divorce or separation. The child can become a pawn in a never-ending war between the parents, sometimes making repeated court appearances. Some parents see the child as a prize to be won rather than a person with needs of his or her own. Visitation or access and child support are often the touchstone issues. Moreover, these problems tend not to improve much over time. Some of these issues as created or maintained by policy and legal terms and approaches are being addressed at the time of this writing by the Canadian government (Canada, 2002). We will talk more about this later in this chapter. And in the next chapter, we consider custody issues more when we discuss new family starts.

On the other hand, separation and divorce can improve family functioning, especially if custody rules are clear and agreed-upon, civility is attained, and peaceful order is beneficial to both parents. Compared with sole-custody mothers, mothers with joint custody report lower levels of parenting stress and better co-parental relations. But, of course, joint custody is known to be more probable as well as more workable for couples that get along better in the first place, and put their children's interests above their own (Smart & Neale, 1999). This produces a happier set of parents, which will no doubt lead to better parenting. Most important, divorce is better for children than perpetual conflicts in a family.

The effects of change in marital status vary by sex. For women, marriage and parenthood are distinct institutions, and women tend to provide for children's needs whether or not they are married to their children's father. For men, marriage tends to define their responsibilities to children. When men divorce, they may disengage from their biological children. Also, men are more likely than women to remarry quickly and have new children, whom they help to support. Thus, their first-family children are liable to feel rejected and neglected. However, for a contrary view on this topic, see David Popenoe's (1996) *Life Without Father*.

Some enticing research from a study of post-divorce parenting in the U.K. (Smart & Neale, 1999) finds that a significant proportion of post-divorce fathers become *more* involved than they were when they were married. Their reason is fascinating. The dads say that when they were married, their fathering was limited to earning money to support the family. They didn't feel as if they had to do anything more. Once they were divorced, however, they had to be involved with their kids to maintain contact with them since their physical presence in the home was no longer an option. They therefore worked out ways to be involved and responsible fathers to their kids for the first time. Mothers post-divorce tended to throw up their hands in wonder about why their ex-husbands didn't do this sooner! It may be a case where the normative expectations of the nuclear family are such that some men feel they cannot be active, involved parents until they leave!

Teens from divorced families tend to be, on average, less well-adjusted than teens from intact families (Muransky & DeMarie-Dreblow, 1995). Again, this does not apply to individuals directly. Many teens from divorced families are fine and very well-adjusted. And we all know some teens from two-parent families who are far from well-adjusted. Due to loss of access or reduced access, they may feel less intimately connected with their fathers. They may feel they have less social support (Carlson and Corcoran, 2001; Clifford & Clark, 1995). Also, they may have assumed more family responsibilities, which could cut into time they might spend with friends, on sports, or with school work (Gonzalez, Field, & Lasko, 1995).

However, it is not the process of divorce *per se* that shapes the children's adjustment but the family environment—the degree of parental conflict, paternal indifference, or lack of involvement (Weiner, Harlow & Adams, 1995; Willms, 2002). Children in divorced families are children from families that have experienced spousal conflict and dissatisfaction. So we should not focus too much attention on divorce as a cause of children's problems. Instead, we should emphasize what went on and what goes on between family members. The processes within a family matter more than what the family looks like. The previously mentioned problems suffered by children of divorced parents persist in adulthood. Rodgers (1994) notes that in childhood, few behavioural differences exist between girls from divorced and intact families. Later, large differences emerge in job-changing during early careers, premarital pregnancy, and marital breakdowns. A higher-than-expected incidence of "problems" is found among the adult children of divorce who are never married, divorced, or remarried.

Studies have shown an association between parental divorce and juvenile delinquency. However, the correlation may be with all forms of "broken homes": not just those broken by divorce, but also those that are structurally intact but emotionally broken. Parental conflict has at least as damaging an effect on children as does divorce (Stacey, 1996). Therefore, predictions of dire effects of divorce on children seem unwarranted. In fact, many studies on the topic imply that parental divorce may improve the well-being of children if it stops parental conflict (Jekielek, 1996).

To the extent that divorce is associated with health problems in children, it is the conflict between parents that is most harmful to their emotional and psychological development (Wu & Hart, 2002). Indeed, "parental conflict has a greater impact on the social and psychological adjustment of children than divorce" (Kunz, 1992: 353). The negative effect of parental divorce is eliminated once parents' past marital quality is considered (Cooney & Kurz, 1996). This suggests that living in a conflict-free home with one divorced parent is better for children than living in a conflict-ridden intact home.

Thus, the effects of parental divorce depend greatly on parental marital conflict before divorce. In high-conflict families, children have higher levels of well-being as young adults if their parents divorced than if they stayed together. However, in low-conflict families, children have higher levels of well-being if their parents stayed together than if they divorced (Amato, Loomis, & Booth, 1995).

Other things being equal, marriage or living in a stable long-term relationship is better for children than divorce. Children living in single-mother families with no parental conflict, and with much contact with the non-residential father, still have lower levels of well-being than children who live in two-parent families without parental conflict. However, the well-being of children living in peaceful single-mother families is higher than that of children living in two-parent families with much parental conflict. The degree of parental conflict after divorce is more important for the well-being of children than contact with the departed father. That is to say, it is better for the children of divorce if the father doesn't come around if parental arguments break out when he does (Dronkers, 1996).

Parental divorce, as we have seen, is correlated with a variety of mental health stresses in children, due mainly to the conflict that precedes divorce. The conflict-and-divorce process influences how children view the world and view their place in it. However, we must be careful not to exaggerate the size of that influence.

Beyond the effects on thinking and feeling, divorce is correlated with variations in children's behaviour. So, for example, in a family that is not abusive, divorce leads to deterioration in children's school performance; increased proneness to crime, suicide, and out of-wedlock births; adult work performance; and likelihood of the children themselves becoming divorced later in life (Galston, 1996). The experience of divorce may weaken trust in people and institutions, and impede the capacity to form stable, enduring relationships.

These claims have some support. For example, parental divorce and remarriage have strong effects on children's attitudes toward premarital sex, cohabitation, marriage, and divorce. These effects persist even after controlling for parental attitudes (Axinn & Thornton, 1993). Thus, children do not merely replicate their parents' values and attitudes toward non-marital sex, marriage, and divorce but develop an approach that incorporates their lived experience. Kozuch and Cooney (1995) note that results from studies using parental marital status to predict young adults' attitudes have been inconsistent. In their own survey of young adults from a variety of backgrounds, parental marital status predicted only two of five attitudes toward marriage and family. By contrast, level of parental disagreement predicted four of the five.

Children of divorce typically marry earlier, cohabit, achieve less economically, and hold more pro-divorce attitudes. All these factors account for some intergenerational transmission of divorce. However, holding these constant, interpersonal behaviour problems account for the biggest share of the transmission. It seems that processes related to parental divorce increase the probability that children will learn to exhibit behaviours that interfere with the maintenance of stable and mutually rewarding intimate relationships (Amato, 1996).

We can easily grasp the links between conflict, divorce, and behavioural outcomes. For example, increased interparental conflict and parental divorce predicts decreased self-esteem among children of divorce. This, in turn, predicts poorer peer-adolescent relationships, which predict poorer adult interpersonal competence (Armistead et al., 1995). Likewise, family disruption, marital conflict, and disengaged parent–child relations all greatly increase antisocial behaviour in childhood, though few of these effects generally continue into adulthood (Sim & Vucinich, 1996).

Divorce is associated with less formal schooling, possibly because young people with divorced parents may have less financial support for college from their family. The support they receive is much more likely to come from their custodial than non-custodial parent (Grissett & Furr, 1994). Thus, the lower educational and occupational attainment of children of divorce is more likely associated with reduced financial support than with a loss of confidence in higher education.

Despite all the information on how divorce negatively affects children, recent research on this topic provides little basis for concern that divorce will inevitably produce problem behaviour. Neither exposure to parental divorce nor exposure to parental conflict affects the quality of attachment to adult intimates, nor the quality of parenting (Taylor, Parker, & Roy, 1995). Adolescence and early adulthood may present many challenges—more to women than to men. Coming from a divorced family may contribute to those pressures. However, coming from a divorced family does not, in the end, diminish an individual's ability to cope with new challenges (Dunlop & Burns, 1995).

Relations with Parents

Since divorce often results in the departure of the biological father from the family, father–child relationships are often most affected. Increasingly, however, children and fathers maintain an ongoing relationship after the divorce. However, on average, adolescents in divorced families get less advice from their fathers and feel less satisfied with paternal support. Adolescents from intact families say they have more positive emotional relationships with their fathers than do adolescents from divorced or remarried families. Adolescents who live with both parents fight their fathers to achieve independence. However, this can be a good thing, related to the development of more self-esteem and a stronger ego-identity (McCurdy & Scherman, 1996).

Amato and Booth (1996) used data from a 12-year longitudinal study of marital instability to examine the effects of divorce on parent–child relationships. The quality of the parents' marriage has both direct and indirect implications for later parent–child affection. Problems in the parent–child relationship before divorce, and low quality in the parents' marriage when children were (on average) 10 years old, led to low parental affection for the children when they were (on average) 18 years old. Divorce continued to undermine affection between fathers and children, although not between mothers and children. Thus, the break in a father–child relationship after a long history of turbulence and indifference may predate divorce.

The father's departure in a divorce greatly reduces the likelihood his child will name him as someone to whom the child would go for help with a stressful event. However, this outcome is far from inevitable. Departure may reduce the child's access to his or her father. However, those fathers who maintain contact remain important functional people in their children's lives and an important source of support in times of stress (Munsch, Woodward, & Darling, 1995; Smart & Neale, 1999).

High marital quality predicts a similar relationship with both parents. However, when marital quality is low, children usually "choose a parent" to be close to. For example, the father–daughter tie is particularly vulnerable after divorce. By contrast, the mother–daughter tie is especially resilient (Booth & Amato, 1994). This suggests that the way in which poor marital quality and divorce affect adult child–parent relations is by polarizing children, forcing them to take sides when they are young.

Compared with those who grew up in two-parent families, the adult children of divorced parents perceive their relationships with both mothers and fathers to be of lower quality. The quality is generally two or three times lower for fathers than for mothers. Usually, memories of parental conflict or other family problems can explain the effect of parental divorce on relationship quality. Children of divorce also have much less current contact with their parents than adults from two-parent families (Webster & Herzog, 1995). Children generally evaluate their relationships with mothers more positively than those with fathers. They generally evaluate pre-separation relationships more positively than post-separation relationships, with some recovery after the passage of time. As already noted, a positive relationship with one parent contributes negatively to the evaluation of the other parent after separation, suggesting that separation typically polarizes loyalties (Hoffman & Ledford, 1995).

Stepfamilies

Stepfamilies, often formed by the remarriage of biological parents after their divorce, are multi-parent families that may give children as many as two full sets of parents (and siblings), and four sets of grandparents. Lots of loving parents and grandparents can be a real plus for a child, under the right circumstances. However, stepfamilies can pose problems too, for a variety of reasons. People form them after divorce, and marital conflict usually preceded the divorce. So, there are problems to solve—*usually* bad feelings between the former spouses—even before the new families begin. Chiefly, however, the problems associated with stepfamilies are due to the number and rapidity of changes a child must make. This is particularly true if the remarriage occurs within a few years of the initial divorce.

Adapting to new parent(s) and potentially more siblings may cause confusion and stress for the child. Even the child who likes his new siblings may feel in competition with near-strangers for the affection of his or her parent.

Moreover, remarriages are problematic if they create an unstable environment for the child. As we have seen, remarriages have a higher failure rate than first marriages. Research also shows that changes in parenting can significantly hurt a child. These changes increase the likelihood that a child will suffer poor grades, poor health, low self-esteem, drug abuse, peer rejection, and lower self-reported well-being. At the extreme is a succession of divorces and remarriages. This presents a very unstable environment for any child, especially since expectations change with each new parent. We'll talk more about remarriage and stepfamilies in Chapter 11.

Effects on Spouses as Parents

After divorce, most fathers and mothers are unprepared for the unique problems they will face, and the inadequacy of counselling and support services that are available. Separated parents often choose or are forced to make decisions that conflict with each other's desires and beliefs. Further, children can play to parental differences and parents' desire to be the favourite parent. Custodial parents often fail to realize the impact of a move on the other parent, and remarriage or new partnerships complicate interactions between biological parents (Weiss, 1996).

Remarriage is associated with less frequent co-parental interaction, less reported parenting support from the former spouse, and more negative attitudes about the other parent for both women and men. For men, remarriage predicts lower levels of parenting satisfaction and involvement in children's activities (Christensen & Retting, 1995).

Non-custodial fatherhood has increased due to trends in divorce and out-of-wedlock births. The standard divorce—the mother with custody, father with child-support responsibilities and visitation rights—is most common in cases of longer marriage, higher male income, and younger children. Visitation is essential to non-custodial parents and, as we have seen, the nature of visitation rights is crucial to the quality of the subsequent father–child relationship. Visitation and child support are complementary, and joint custody improves support compliance. Non-custodial fathers benefit from successful resolution of issues of autonomy, connections, and power that can confront men after divorce, and from social supports that encourage moving beyond gender and **role polarization** (Fox & Blanton, 1995).

Divorce has a variety of effects on fathers, and on their children. For example, it affects non-custodial fathers' views of their parental role. Common themes among non-custodial fathers include divorce-related emotional distress; dissatisfaction with custody, visitation, and child support arrangements; perception of divorce proceedings as unfair; and ongoing conflicts with former spouses (Dudley, 1996). The father often views himself as a victim of his spouse. Moreover, his disempowerment, loss of legal custody, and relegation to the role of an economic provider has a profound impact on his masculine identity (Mandell, 1995). This may be another way of saying that "real men" in our culture are not supposed to let themselves get pushed around by their wives or ex-wives. It has recently taken a decidedly political turn with father's rights groups actively pushing the government on custody and post-divorce settlements, with some nasty altercations between these groups and mothers' groups.

Fathers often have limited contact with their children after divorce, and this contact decreases over time. As fathers develop new relationships, they reduce the involvement with their children from their previous marriage. Not so for mothers. Their remarriage affects only the probability of fathers' having weekly contact with their children. For the most part, characteristics of the mother and of the children do not affect post-divorce contacts except that fathers are more likely to see preschool-age children every week than school-age children (Stephens, 1996).

Why the reduced contact and visitation by so many fathers? Researchers have offered many reasons. One is that non-residential fathers feel less competent and less satisfied in the role of father. Typically, fathers of all kinds who identify strongly with the role of father are more frequently involved with their children. Non-residential fathers identify less strongly with the role (Minton & Pasley, 1996). Overall, fathers who do not want contact with their children are more apt to have been less involved with childrearing, to feel indifferent about their children,

Modernization and Divorce: Contrasting Trends in Islamic Southeast Asia and the West

During the 1960s and 1970s, when Western divorce rates were rising sharply, divorce rates in Islamic Southeast Asia declined dramatically, despite rapid urbanization and industrialization. According to demographer Gavin Jones, several factors associated with industrialization increased the potential to break away from unsatisfactory marriages in the West, while in Islamic Southeast Asia these same factors allowed people to avoid unsatisfactory marriages in the first place, thereby lowering the divorce rate.

"Any argument... that development of an urban-industrial economy and improved educational and employment opportunities for women correlates with rising levels of divorce is stood on its head by the experience of the Malay-Muslim world" notes Jones.

During the 1950s, divorce rates in Islamic Southeast Asia had been at extraordinarily high levels. A crossover took place during the 1970s, with rates in Islamic Southeast Asia falling [far] below those in the West.

Many factors contributed to high divorce rates in the Malay world, [including] legal ease of arranging a divorce. Furthermore, the Islamic-influenced marriage system placed great emphasis on protecting family honor by ensuring that daughters were married off before they could disgrace the family, either by becoming pregnant outside marriage or by reaching an age where they could be considered "old maids." The Malay world of the 1950s to 1970s was unique in the high proportion of divorces occurring in the early years of marriage, Jones notes.

While there is no single key to understanding the decline in divorce rates in Southeast Asia, Jones suggests two proximate determinants: rising ages at marriage for females and greater self-arrangement of marriage. These trends were in turn related to socioeconomic developments, including rising levels of education, employment of young women away from the home, and greater influence of the media in changing traditional attitudes.

Source: Jones, Gavin. 1997. *Population and Development Review,* vol. 23, no. 1 (March 1997), pp. 95–114. Reprinted with permission of the Population Council.

or to have been in an abusive or violent relationship (Smart & Neale, 1999; Greif, 1995). But even involved, caring fathers at times lose contact with their children on divorce.

So far, we have been discussing how many—perhaps, most—non-custodial fathers deal with their children. Now, consider "best case scenarios." In contrast to the majority, nine fathers studied by Arendell (1995) have developed strategies more congruent with their aim to parent their children actively. Child-centredness prevails in their accounts and actions. Each of these men has established, with their former wives, some type of parenting partnership. They actively seek to create "best case scenarios" in divorce and are absorbed with family relationships, their maintenance, repair, and nurture. Unlike most respondents, these men are satisfied, even pleased with their parenting. Simultaneously, they see themselves as defying the norms of masculinity, which has led them on occasion to question their identity as men. Thus, self-confidence and uncertainty coexist for these innovative fathers.

In sum, for children, parents, and other relatives, divorce, like other major life events, can be stressful. However, we must be careful not to exaggerate the extent or permanence of harm done. With divorce, the stresses include economic hardship, parental adjustment, interpersonal conflict, or parental loss. Developing resources and protections can reduce the negative effect of these stressors. Higher levels of coping resources support a greater optimism about the future, fewer financial problems, more confidence in parenting ability, and a more satisfactory relationship with the former spouse (O'Leary, Franzoni, & Brack, 1996).

Factors that reduce the adverse effect of divorce on children include a strong and clear sense that both parents still love them, an understanding that they are not to blame for the divorce, and regular visits with the non-custodial parent. Children of divorce may need some help coming to terms with irrational beliefs about divorce and feelings of sadness, guilt, and anxiety (Skitka & Frazier, 1995). Involved and caring parents can produce a good child adjustment to divorce. Parental distance, on the other hand, is likely to produce maladjustment. Parental conflict, as we have said so often, has a bad effect in both intact and divorced families (Wiener, Harlow, Adams, & Grebstein, 1995).

The impact of divorce on children varies enormously, depending on many factors, including the responsiveness of parents, schools, and community adults. Overall, young adults are optimistic about marriage, and their parents' divorce has not had a large impact on their attitudes toward marriage and divorce (Landis et al., 1995).

Though divorce may sometimes cause problems, it sometimes also solves problems. Divorce spares many children serious problems. It may even bring benefits. People whose parents divorced during their adolescent years display a much higher level of moral development than those whose parents did not divorce (Kogos & Snarey, 1995). Underlying the development of moral judgement is an increased perspective-taking, necessary for children of divorce who witness differences in opinions between their parents.

Proposed Legal/Policy Changes

As discussed earlier in this chapter, at the time of this writing dramatic changes are proposed to the Divorce Act of Canada that would abolish the combative and possessive terms of "custody" and "access" (or visitation). The intent is to reduce divorcing parents' levels of conflict and confrontation, and encourage a refocusing on parenting, even during and after divorce.

Concluding Remarks

As we have seen, divorce is both a micro- and a macro-level phenomenon, with both micro- and macro-level effects. Little synthesis between macro- and micro-level analyses has been achieved. We are still far from having a comprehensive theory that predicts who will get divorced and why.

The past 25 years have not fulfilled legislators' objectives in adopting no-fault divorce. There is no improved family life, no expanded choice and happiness, at least in the eyes of critics (see, for example, Stanton, 1996). Some have remarked on how the combined effect of increased divorce rates and escalating levels of unwed childbearing have ensured that over half the children born in the 1980s will be raised in single-parent homes for all or part of their lives. The decline of marriage has also led to paternal disinvestments in children. Allegedly, unmarried men are less likely to support children financially. Increased maternal earning capacity or improved public investment has not compensated for the decline in paternal support (Whitehead, 1996).

The conservative approach to these problems of increased divorce rates, teen pregnancies, suicides, violence, and substance abuse is to blame the emerging culture of tolerance and the expanded welfare state, contending that they undermine the benefits of self-reliance and community standards. The conservative definition of family values is too narrow. However, the perspective rightly emphasizes the role of the family in childrearing education. Liberals do recognize that increased unemployment, rising competition, and the need for dual-earner households have threatened the family.

However, they overemphasize the extent to which government services can replace effective family bonds (Giele, 1996). According to conservatives, strategies to encourage the re-institutionalization of the family would include restricting the legal benefits of family life and of marriage, beginning tighter controls on entry into marriage, making divorce more difficult, protecting children from divorce, and changing the nature of family law so that we define marriage as a moral obligation between partners rather than a personal contractual decision (Schneider, 1996).

Though it is not the job of sociologists to favour one side or the other, it is part of our responsibility to collect and examine data that would support one side or another. Here, sociology has an important role to play in the process by which a democratic society makes the policies and laws that govern family life.

The evidence shows us that divorce is correlated with unhappiness and trouble. The question is, does divorce cause the unhappiness and trouble, or does unhappiness and trouble cause the divorce? Further, does divorce prolong unhappiness and trouble, or cut it mercifully short? While it is foolhardy to generalize about all divorces, certainly there is no evidence to show that, generally, divorce is the cause of most family-related unhappiness, nor that divorce tends to prolong unhappiness that might be otherwise cut short. Though it is true that people benefit from stable family lives when those families are functioning well, it is also true that people suffer from family lives when those families are functioning badly.

For better or worse, it is up to the participants to determine whether their family life is functioning well or badly. Outsiders' impressions count for little. Remember, as we have pointed out so often throughout this book, what counts is a person's perception. If the people involved think the family is working well, then to all intents and purposes, it really is. If not, and efforts to remedy the situation don't work, then divorce makes good sense—for the sake of the children as well as the spouses themselves. After all, a child can get good parenting without father and mother living together. On the other hand, conditions of stress, violence, unhappiness, and depression make good parenting almost impossible. We must assume, and probably can assume, that the vast majority of parents take these factors into account when they decide to stay together or divorce. This being so, the conservative viewpoint on divorce has little to offer us.

CHAPTER SUMMARY

In this chapter we looked at the rise in divorce experienced since the second half of the twentieth century in most industrial societies. As social scientists, we look at the nature of social bonding, and our discussions on divorce cover not only some of the reasons behind increased divorce rates, but also the effects this increase have had on individuals and society as a whole. Although these trends indicate a dramatic change in family structure and the functions the family plays in our lives, research has shown that our beliefs and attitudes regarding the role of the family have not kept pace. This makes the task of assessing the real impacts of divorce a bit more difficult, yet all the more needed.

Historically, divorce has worried social scientists and policy-makers alike. This concern has become heightened with the recent explosion of divorce rates worldwide. Social, legal, and cultural changes have all played a part in the development of these trends.

Generally, causes of divorce should more accurately be called predictors, since it is easier to note relationships between variables than to pin down a cause-and-effect relationship. Factors influencing the likelihood of divorce are found at the micro-, meso-, and macro-levels. Micro-level factors include poor communication, poor conflict-resolution skills, lack of commitment, lack of shared interests, and perceived inequity. Meso-level factors include age, marital duration, location, religiosity, class, and race. Macro-level factors include war, economic cycles, and cultural values.

The effects of divorce were then considered. Divorce is a time of distress for spouses and children. Both men and women suffer a decline in standard of living, but men's incomes drop less and rebound faster. This effect is particularly important for women, since they are most commonly the prime caregivers of the children after a divorce. Typically, fathers gradually disengage from children, though some do remain closely involved in parenting. Children are distressed immediately after a divorce, but gradually adjust.

The harmful effects of divorce are often talked about. Yet it is important to recognize that many of the harmful effects observed stem not from divorce *per se* but from poor family interactions prior to, during, and after the divorce.

We concluded with a look at some popular political viewpoints on divorce. There is a movement urging legal and policy changes to discourage divorce, in an attempt to alleviate some of the social burdens that divorce produces. We find many of the proposed solutions incomplete and ineffective because of the narrow interpretations of the problem, which labels divorce as the culprit rather than dysfunctional family interactions.

KEY TERMS

Adverse selectivity A tendency for people who choose to engage in a given behaviour to be, by nature of the kind of people they are, also at risk for a given outcome; selectivity may create the appearance of cause-and-effect relationships where they do not exist.

Autonomy Independence; ability to make choices and direct one's own life.

Cohort effect A cohort effect is the accumulated experience of going through life in the same set of years. Thus, everyone alive during WWII experienced the effects of war in one way or another. However, only people born in the period 1924–28 (say) experienced the war as teenagers, then experienced the postwar economic boom as young marrieds.

Determinant A factor that contributes to an outcome (such as divorce) without necessarily being the direct or principal cause.

Femininity A cluster of characteristics, such as nurturance, sensitivity, and gentleness, traditionally considered natural to women, but that can be found in men or women; couples where both spouses have these characteristics tend to be well-adjusted.

Macro-level The broad level of examining a social phenomenon, focusing on changes that affect society as a whole.

Meso-level A middle range at which a social phenomenon may be examined,

focusing on demographics the characteristics of the people affected.

Micro-level The smallest level at which a social phenomenon may be examined, the level of interactions between individuals and effects on individuals.

No-fault divorce Divorce granted on the basis of marital breakdown rather than of specific wrong-doing (e.g., adultery) on the part of one spouse or the other.

Predictor A characteristic that is correlated with and precedes an outcome but may or may not be a cause.

Role polarization A tendency to view male and female roles as fixed and separate.

Secularization A move away from religion as an organizing principle of society.

Social disorganization A breakdown of societal functioning.

Social integration The state of societies that are closely knit and stable, in which people hold similar world views and there is a strong consensus on social rules.

Social mobility The potential for an individual or family to experience significant change in their social status.

Social pathology A broad-based distress or disorganization within society.

Socioeconomic status Class; standing in society in terms of income, education, and prestige.

SUGGESTED READINGS

Ambert, Anne-Marie. 2002. *Divorce: Facts, Causes, and Consequences*. Ottawa: The Vanier Institute of the Family. The basic numbers and trends of divorce in Canada are provided in this readable report. Myths about the risks of divorce are discussed.

Friedman, Debra. 1995. *Towards a Structure of Indifference: The Social Origins of Maternal Custody*. Hawthorne, NY: Aldine De Gruyter. Between 1880 and 1920, in all Western countries that permitted divorce, there was a legal shift of huge importance: fathers ceded custodial rights to mothers. Responsibilities for children were split between mother (nurture), father (financial support), and state (schooling), indicating a growth of indifference towards children.

Kurz, Demie, 1995. *For Richer For Poorer: Mothers Confront Divorce* New York: Routledge, 1995. This book explores the impact of divorce on U.S. women, detailing the reasons women are leaving their marriages and the hardships they face afterward. It also discusses *benefits*, such as freedom from domination, violence, and destructive emotions. Thus, divorce is an experience with both good and bad aspects. Domestic violence and hardships due to poverty remain problems to solve.

Popenoe, David. 1996. *Life Without Father*. New York: Free Press. A deeply expressed concern about the state of U.S. families. Divorce is seen as a problem, and children in lone-mother families are seen as being at risk.

Stacey, Judith. 1996. *In the Name of the Family: Rethinking Family Values in the Postmodern Age*. Boston: Beacon. A critique of conservative worries about families and the high divorce rate with a focus on the benefits of diverse families and personal as well as family happiness.

Wallerstein, Judith S., Julia Lewis, and Sandy Blakeslee. 2000. *The Unexpected Legacy of Divorce: A 25-Year Landmark Study*. New York: Hyperion. A look at the longer-term consequences of divorce, with some unexpected results from children's viewpoints.

REVIEW QUESTIONS

1. Why is it that so many of us have a misunderstanding about the risk of being divorced?

2. Define no-fault divorce. How does it differ from what preceded it?

3. Outline the difference between macro-level and micro-level reasons for divorce.

4. Describe the changes in families (family structure, division of labour, functions of the family, etc.) that occurred as a result of industrialization and urbanization.

5. Define adverse selectivity.

6. What is the relationship between divorce rates and socioeconomic class, race, age, and religious affiliation?

7. Discuss the role that female participation in the work force played in the changing of the divorce rates.

8. What happens to the divorce rate after a large-scale war? Why?

9. What are some of the known consequences of divorce for children?

10. Describe the effects of divorce on women.

11. Give some reasons why many couples ought to break up "for the sake of the children."

DISCUSSION QUESTIONS

1. Individualism and secularization are seen as factors contributing to the increase in divorce rates. Do you agree? Explain your answer.

2. Describe the concept of social integration, how it affects divorce, and how it is affected by divorce.

3. What separate functions do the mother, the father, and school fill in a child's support framework? How does divorce affect each of these?

4. Some say that divorce is bad for children, and therefore for society as a whole. Others say that it is not divorce *per se*, but the family interactions before, during, and after divorce that harm children's healthy development. With whom do you agree? Why?

5. Traditionally, we have invested men and women's human capital in two different social spheres. How does this contribute to the difference in experiences women and men have of divorce?

6. Explain the concept of social mobility. How would divorce affect a person's social mobility? Contrast a divorced woman's chances and a divorced man's chances.

7. Men's masculine identity can be affected by divorce. Explain how, and the ways in which our culture fosters these attitudes.

8. The children of divorced parents tend to achieve less economically throughout their own lifespan. Give some reasons why this might be. What changes to social policies might prevent this effect?

9. Describe some of the characteristics of divorced fathers' parenting strategy that promote healthy involvement and attachment to their children. Why do you think that these are effective? What are some of the obstacles many men face in initiating and pursuing the strategies successfully?

10. What are some of the strategies both parents can implement to reduce the harmful effects of divorce on children? Describe the difficulties that parents might have in achieving these strategies?

11. What do you think the effects will be of the changes to the Divorce Act in Canada focusing on parental responsibilities rather than custody or access?

WEBLINKS

http://canada.justice.gc.ca/en/dept/pub/divorce/index.html

Divorce Law: Questions and Answers, a regularly updated sourcebook by Canada's Department of Justice provides the basics on getting a divorce in Canada. Included is how to set up living arrangements for children, child and spousal support issues, and sharing of property and of debt. The site also has links to useful contacts in each province and territory.

http://www.hc-sc.gc.ca/hppb/mental-health/mhp/pub/life/index.html

Because Life Goes On...Helping Children and Youth Live with Divorce and Separation. This site is a resource for Canadian families in need of information on helping children through the separation and divorce process. It has links to other Web sites.

http://www.divorceinfo.com/

An excellent source of information on a variety of topics related to divorce. The site has advice on helping children cope, coping with the pain of divorce, life after divorce, and the costs involved.

http://www.divorce-online.com/

Articles, general information, and psychological and professional help with regards to divorce. This site is also quite helpful as a search engine.

http://www.vifamily.ca

The Vanier Institute of the Family, in Ottawa, is an excellent source of the best and most recent data and analyses on divorce and related issues. The site also links to Statistics Canada data on divorce.

http://www.hughson.com/

General information on divorce, including information on U.S. law and divorce, and children and divorce, as well as a good reading list.

CHAPTER ELEVEN

Family Transitions & Innovations:

Second Families, Empty Nests, Cluttered Nests, and New Kinds of Families

Chapter Outline

Introduction

Transitions into parenthood are momentous and perplexing moments in one's life and the life cycle of families. Transitions to different family situations can be just as challenging and momentous. The term *transition* can mean a happy shift to a new family life. These transitions are fresh and new, reflective of learning from mistakes and regrets of the past. Yet some transitions are not fresh starts, but stale starts, or redoing the old start without much that is new. Some transitions prove impossible. Family transitions can involve reinventing close relations, customizing social ideals to best fit one's particular needs and situation.

In the previous chapter we explored the many challenges posed by family dissolution. In this chapter, we focus on life *after* separation or divorce, or widowhood. We also consider some of the ways people are inventing new ways to live as families. We look at the multiple ways in which people and families make transitions, as they experience family dissolution, as they age, as they discover and create new ways to be familial. We examine what is possible and what we can learn from the heroic efforts of many to make transitions from one kind of family to another and to create new kinds of families.

Family Transitions in the Past

When we think of family transitions, we often see this as something recent that rarely or never happened in the past. In reality, making fresh starts is nothing new, as we saw in Chapter 2. With massive flows of refugees and immigrants out of strife-torn and, in some cases, poverty-stricken Europe throughout the first half of the twentieth century, many people started families afresh in North America. Immigrants and refugees from Europe are still coming, as strife recurs, and have now been joined by people from Africa, Asia, Latin America, and the Caribbean fleeing an old life or seeking new opportunities in Canada, Australia, and the United States.

Immigrants built new families in various ways in their new situations. They may have brought families with them as well as maintaining family ties with those left behind. But life in the new country does not allow all the ways in which families live, or the ways their children form their own families, to remain totally unchanged. Fresh family starts are necessitated by the process of immigration and the contact with new ways to live in close relations.

In a historical study of Methodist missionaries in northern Manitoba from 1869 to 1876, Brown (1992) recounts the central and formative role played by a Cree nurse known as Little Mary, who cared for the boy Eddie. As the first white child born into the region, Eddie was largely raised by the indulgent Little Mary, who modified strict Victorian practices of childrearing to raise Eddie more as a Cree boy than as the son of the missionary. Eddie's life was given a fresh start by his introduction to her world view and culture. It led to hilarity and conflict when

Eddie danced for his parents dressed as a young Cree boy. When he was revealed by a stocking that would not stay up, exposing a white leg (his description in later life), his parents became dismayed. Eddie, in later life, attributes much that he valued in his character to the socializing influence of Little Mary, which softened his parents' strictness. His upbringing is an example of a new form of childrearing combining two cultural approaches.

Another example of a fresh family start also comes from early Canada where the voyageurs and fur traders lived with Native wives according to the customs of the Aboriginal people with whom they associated. This was called "**à la façon de la pays** " or "**the custom of the country**" (Van Kirk, 1992). Some of the men were already married and had left their first wives in France, Scotland, or eastern Canada. Once the Native woman became a country wife, she was treated with respect by other fur traders, who then referred to her as "Madame." What emerged was not only a fresh start in family for individuals but also a new family form (Van Kirk, 1992: 72).

Both the fur-trader men and the Native women made fresh starts, sometimes spectacularly so, as in the case of Robert Pilgrim's Native wife, Thu a Higon, who accompanied him when he returned to England, along with their infant son (Van Kirk, 1992: 72). One can imagine the adjustment challenges she must have faced in Victorian England, and wonder at the fresh starts their family made. Other fur traders were denied the possibility of taking their Native wives and families back to the old country by company policies. Many families were left behind in Canada, sometimes with pensions provided by the "husband" or the company (the Hudson's Bay Company or the North West Company). This may be the first known example of pensions for homemakers, discussed in Chapter 6.

Still others among the voyageurs/fur traders decided to solemnize their marriages on the retirement of the "husband" from active service. As mentioned in Chapter 2, one couple, William Hemmings Cook and his wife Agatha, made a fresh start by marrying, after living together according to the "custom of the country" for a long time. Van Kirk (1992: 79) cites one of the guests at the wedding as observing, "old Cook had stood manfully forth...bringing his 35 years courtship to an early close." Living together is not so new as a family form, and marrying as a fresh start after a long cohabitation is not so modern either.

Also mentioned in Chapter 2 is another more recent historical example of a fresh family start related to immigration evident in the story of Maria, who came to Toronto in 1956 from a peasant farm in southern Italy to join her husband, Eneo, who had come a year earlier (Iacovetta, 1992). Within two days, she had a job as a steam press operator, for which she was paid $37 Cdn a week. She worked for the rest of her life at various low-skill, low-pay jobs to help support her family in their adopted country. The fresh start for Maria and Eneo is the new kind of marriage she, and others like her, made with her husband in the new country, where men and women both contributed economically to their families and yet women had no prescribed public role. The almost constant supervision of women, prevalent in southern Italy in the 1950s and earlier, had to be abandoned in part in the new situation, according to Iacovetta (1992: 286). Fresh starts were made by couples in their new country, with varying degrees of success and difficulty.

The higher mortality rates of the past often meant that families experienced the death of one or both spouses/parents while the children were still young, creating the possibility or the need for fresh family starts. Remarriage after the death of one's first spouse was frequent, as were stepparents, adoption, and fostering of children. Fresh family starts were more characteristic of families in the past than we sometimes acknowledge today. In some ways, widows in the past were similar to single mothers today in the economic vulnerability they and their children faced, and in the social challenges they posed (Gordon & McLanahan, 1991).

Nor did marriage failure and divorce begin recently, as some might think. Men deserted their families; some women deserted too; and couples agreed mutually to separate (Gordon & McLanahan, 1991). Some Canadians went to the U.S. to seek divorces when divorce was not as attainable in Canada (Bradbury, 1996: 72–73). In some provinces such as Quebec, where divorce was almost impossible to obtain until well into the mid-twentieth century and was frowned upon strongly, some women slipped into Ontario and declared themselves widows.

Sometimes the women had been victims of spousal abuse or found themselves in intolerable marriages from which there was little escape. Because family was seen as largely women's responsibility in the past, women were more often trapped in difficult marriages, for if they left they would be stigmatized, socially and legally, as the deserters of families. Escapes for women included close friendships with other women, charity and community work, sometimes illnesses or frailties that were seen as romantic, and often drugs and alcohol. It is not well known that in nineteenth- and early twentieth-century Canada, as well as in the United States, middle-class women were the most common drug addicts. Failed marriages and attempts to make new starts are not only a modern-day phenomenon.

What Is a Family Transition?

A family transition can be a step filled with hope and dreams for a wonderful shared future. The strength of this hope is evidenced in social research, which shows that most young people expect never to be divorced. This may be indicative of their sense of commitment to a life-long relationship, but their hopeful expectations may blind them to the known risks of divorce. A fresh start at family can be any happy young couple on the brink of establishing themselves as a couple, whether married or not, gay/lesbian or heterosexual. That first kind of fresh start is discussed in Chapter 3, so we will not focus on it here.

Family transitions of interest in this chapter are second or subsequent starts at families or familial relationships. The processes through which transitions come about are various. It can be a flight from violence in a family of origin or a conjugal family/relationship, an escape from an abusive practice sanctioned by the prevailing culture, a mutually-agreed-upon separation or divorce, a death, or a myriad of other family changes over the life course. It can be a rediscovery of one's roots and a new basis on which to found and maintain a family, or even a discovery of cultural roots in a new setting or country. It can involve a personal reinvention of family to meet one's particular needs.

Family changes, transitions, and innovations are possible because things did not work out as planned, expected, or hoped for the first time around. Fresh family starts can be begun reluctantly as one's idealism about family is tarnished by family dissolution. In this way, new families reflect change, both individual and social, as well as personal learning and adaptation. It is an adventure to explore the complex ways in which people make families afresh, and the new ways for people to have close relations.

One of the themes in this book is that families are immensely varied. Perhaps at no point is this clearer than when families make transitions or innovations. The multiple pathways of transition include shrinking of family to its smallest unit, a single-person household with non-household-based families, or to a parent with a child. It can also involve non-residential parenting, and the development of intricate and large extended-kin or non-kin networks. Another theme highlighted in this book is that family processes rather than forms provide the rewarding focus of family studies. In considering family transitions and innovations, we observe families and individuals actively engaging in family as process, in designing families anew, in negotiating family, and in striking bargains with former family members on how to endure as family. It is family dynamics in process, active development of new solutions to family challenges.

Multiple Family Starts

In today's world of long life expectancies and rapidly changing families, people may expect to make not one but multiple transitions in family over the course of their lives. Think of those who marry or live together after having lived alone or as an adult in the parental home. They have already experienced two kinds of transitions, first the transition to new ways of being family when they became adults and continued to live with their parents, and then marriage. And the family transitions are likely to continue throughout their lives, with possible separation, divorce, cohabitation, perhaps remarriage, then possibly widowhood and maybe another later-life relationship or marriage.

Within each of these states of family life, there can be phases that mark other kinds of transitions: into parenthood, into or out of working parenthood, from being in a two-earner to a one-earner (or no-earner) family, to grandparenthood, stepparenthood, and so on. In families today, diversity is now the norm, with almost endless possibilities. The SNAF (standard North American family) no longer exists.

Living Solo

Most, or at least many, people who experience the end of a marriage or a committed relationship become single before becoming any other kind of family. Some may move directly from one relationship to another. And some stay single with no intimate relationship as part of their lives. Some wonder if singlehood is an aspect of family life and might respond that a single person living alone is not a family. True enough, but a single person is not necessarily without a family. A few rare people may be, but most of us have families even if we live alone, are living separated from our spouses or partners, or are between relationships. This raises an important dimension of family transitions and innovations, one to which we will return as a theme in this chapter: that family is not equivalent to household. Families and close relations can and do exist, and even thrive, across households.

Living solo is an option growing in popularity. The 2001 Census of Canada reveals a 26.6-percent growth in one-person households since 1981 (Statistics Canada, 2002c). The largest proportion living alone occurred among those aged 65 and over; 35 percent of women in this age group lived alone in 2001 compared with 33.7 percent in 1981. For men aged 65-plus, 16 percent lived alone in 2001. For both senior women and men, the proportion living alone increases with advancing years.

Significant proportions of those 30 to 44 (9.7 percent) also lived alone, a substantial increase from previous censuses. Among younger adults, preference for living solo dropped like a stone: only 6.3 percent lived alone in 2001 compared to 23.9 percent in 1981. Young adults aged 20 to 24 in 2001 had a strong tendency to live with their parents (58 percent of them did!). This continues when they are 25 to 29, with 23.7 percent still living with parents.

Living by oneself does not mean that one is isolated from family. Findings from a national survey in Canada (McDaniel, 1994) reveal that 35 percent of adult children live within walking distance of their mothers, while another 19 percent live within 50 kilometres. Visiting between parents, particularly mothers, and adult children is frequent, as is contact by phone or letter. Even among adult children who live more than 1000 kilometres from their parents, one out of five is in weekly contact, and fewer than 10 percent have limited or no contact with parents. Among siblings, there is even more regular contact. Family ties and connections continue across households and generations, regardless of the living arrangements of those involved.

However, a clear pattern emerges: single women have more contact with relatives than single men (Connidis, 2001: 86) at all ages, and have wider social networks in general than single men. And those living solo with more education tend to have more ongoing connections with their families (Connidis, 2001: 86). A U.S. study (Marks, 1996) of the Wisconsin Longitudinal Study (sample size of 6876) finds that unmarried men who live alone are more disadvantaged than unmarried women. Although the picture of living singly is complex, with advantages and disadvantages for both men and women, single women are found to score higher on personality characteristics associated with better psychological well-being than married women. Single men, however, do not compare so favourably with married men.

For some, living alone is a transitional stage to a new committed relationship. We will discuss that in a moment. For increasing numbers of North Americans, however, living alone is a life choice, a preference, or better than other alternatives. The diversity of solo living, however, prevents us from making many solidly based generalizations about it. People living alone include older people who are widowed, middle-aged professionals, and poor people who may have little prospect for marriage. Those living alone also still includes young people, although, as we have seen, the numbers of young people able to live alone have declined recently.

The growth in living alone may reflect, more than anything else, the capacity to do so. In the past, living on one's own was often not an option, particularly for women. Sociological research has found that even in a place as reputedly family-centred as pre-Confederation Newfoundland, there was a strong preference for living alone when old, if possible, but it was often not feasible (McDaniel & Lewis, 1997). One should *not* conclude, however, as some have, that the growth in living alone is indicative of disinterest in family or growing individualism. Research evidence does not support such a claim.

Lone-Parent Families

In the past, as we have seen in Chapter 2, lone-parent families were most frequently just that: one living parent with dependent children (Morton, 1992b). There was often no other parent living. Tough as it no doubt was (and still is) to be a widow or widower with dependent children, these families really were lone-parent families. Today's lone-parent families, created as they are most often by separation, divorce, or relationship dissolution, are often families where one parent lives with the children and one parent does not. In that sense, they are really two-parent families where the parents do not share a household.

We have seen in Chapter 10 that some fathers do not maintain family ties with their children once they are divorced or remarried after divorce. The reality that children have two parents who remain as parents when they no longer live together raises a number of complex challenges in determining who takes what responsibility for the children.

It also raises a crucial clarifying point about families, discussed in detail by Eichler (1997): *family* and *household* are not congruent. "One household," argues Eichler (1997: 96), "may encompass people who belong to two (or maybe more) family units that are not shared by other household members." An example would be a boy who lives with his biological mother and her husband and his two children from a previous marriage. The boy's biological father may continue to parent him, but does not live in the same household. A portrait of the boy's family, seen from his viewpoint, would involve at least two households. If he has a sister away at university who comes "home" to both his own principal residence and his father's, he might see himself as having a family that crosses three (or even more) residences. The assumption that a family is bound by the walls of a household may no longer be valid or appropriate. We have explored how this reality is being reflected by changing parenting practices and policies in Chapter 10. We will return to these changes and discuss them in more detail in a moment.

Marital or relationship dissolution can be the start of lone parenthood, but it is not the only pathway. There has also been growth in the numbers of people having children without being in a committed couple relationship. This, as we have seen in Chapter 3, can occur in a variety of ways. One of those, the deliberate seeking of parenthood on one's own, through biological parenting or adoption, will be considered in the next section as a kind of family innovation. Here, we will focus on the more common pathway to lone parenthood, as a result of marriage or relationship breakdown.

Before discussing lone parenthood as a family transition, it is important to shed some light on the perplexing problem of defining lone parents. Typically, estimates of the numbers of lone parents are based on a one-time sample, such as a census or a survey, and are looked at from the viewpoint of adults. The research question typically asked is: What proportion of adults at this moment are living in lone-parent families? Three problems, at least, are apparent in this approach. The first is that it often remains unknown whether lone parents of children are indeed living on their own and how many are cohabiting.

Approximately one child out of five in Canada lives in a single-parent family (Statistics Canada, 2002c). A U.S. study based on a sample from the 1990 U.S. Census finds that 2.2 million children (3.5 percent of all children) live in cohabiting couple families (Manning & Lichter, 1996). It is clear also from Table 11.1 that more Canadian women separating from their first union, whether marriage or common-law, are opting for common-law unions for their second union. This means, of course, that more children are living in a common-law family after separation and divorce.

Generally, children in common-law unions are less well off than children in married families (Manning & Lichter, 1996). This is a "chicken and egg" issue: do less well-off people prefer cohabitation, or does cohabitation lead to being less well-off? Research evidence favours the former explanation. But, with the rapid growth in living together in Canada, particularly in Quebec as discussed in Chapter 4, this may well be changing.

Second, without considering lone parenthood from a life-course perspective, it is not possible to see it as a process rather than a state, to see how the experience affects adults and children, and to distinguish between transitional and permanent arrangements. Third, and importantly, examining single parenthood in terms of adult relationships tends to overlook the ways lone parenthood affects children.

One innovative Canadian study (Marcil-Gratton, 1993) turns data collected from the Census and a social survey at single points in time into studies of

Table 11.1 COMMON-LAW UNIONS FOR SECOND UNION

More separated women in recent generations are opting for common-law unions rather than marriage for their second union.

AGE (YEARS) IN 2001	50–59	40–49	30–39
		%	
First union was a marriage:			
Second union was common-law	38.1	45.8	42.4
Second union was a marriage	38.0	35.4	24.2
First union was common-law:			
Second union was common-law	59.8	73.3	80.5
Second union was a marriage	12.5	12.5	5.6

Source: Adapted from the Statistics Canada website. 2002. "Changing Conjugal Life in Canada," *The Daily*, July 11.

children's family experiences by generations (or cohorts). This allows an important look at lone parenthood over time from the child's standpoint. Although the children followed are not the same children in this study, it is possible to observe changes in patterns of children's exposure to single-parenting. The findings are striking and worth summarizing:

- In 1975, the proportion of "out-of-wedlock" births in Quebec was lower than elsewhere in Canada, but the proportion boomed to 19 percent in 1980, climbed to 33 percent in 1988, and reached an astounding 38 percent of all births in 1990.

- More children than ever experience life in a single-parent family in Canada. By age 20, one out of four children from the 1961–63 cohort had experienced single parenthood; the same proportion was reached at age fifteen for the 1971–73 cohort. By age fifteen, 18 percent of the 1961–63 cohort had experienced single parenthood; the same proportion was reached at age six for the 1981–83 cohort.

Lone parenthood has increased dramatically in recent decades. In Canada, the number of lone-parent families tripled between 1961 and 1991, to 14 percent of all families (Lero & Brockman, 1993: 92).The number has continued to increase to 15.7 percent of all families with dependent children (Statistics Canada, 2002c). In the 2001 Census, all families include same-sex families as well as those living common-law and families with adult children in the family home (Statistics Canada, 2002c). In the United States in 1990, nearly 25 percent of all families were single-mother families (17 percent of white families, and 53 percent of African-American families) (McLanahan & Garfinkel, 1993: 16). The overwhelming majority of lone parents in both Canada and the U.S. are mothers, although the fastest growing family type in Canada over the 1990–2000 decade has been lone-father families (Sauve, 2002: 3).

The incidence of poverty remains high among lone parents, particularly single mothers. In Canada in 2000, 34 percent of lone-mother families were below the low-income cutoffs, making these families the group with the highest incidence of family poverty in Canada (Statistics Canada, 2002d: 3). Poverty among lone-mother families is most resistant to remedy (Dooley, 1993: 117). This compares with a poverty rate of 7.4 percent among husband–wife families with children under age 18 living at home (Statistics Canada, 2002d: 5). The good news part of this story is that low income among lone-mother families dropped by 10 percent from 1999 to 2000 in Canada, and among two-parent families with children by 2.6 percent (Statistics Canada, 2002d: 5). Lone mothers in the 1990 to 2000 decade experienced the highest increase in employment and are now more likely to be employed than are wives without children (Sauve, 2002: 3–4). However, among lone mothers still in poverty, the depth of their poverty may have increased.

But the news on lone mothers in poverty is not all good. Affordable housing shortages over the last decade have posed big problems. "Among the surging number of single mothers who have taken refuge in temporary shelters [recently] are an entirely new class of homeless—formerly secure career women," notes a recent report (Gadd, 1997: D1). Among the new homeless are lone mothers who have lost their jobs and are not able to find new ones.

Many women with dependent children tumble into poverty when their marriage or union ends. This occurs for a number of interconnected reasons. Marriage, in our society, still is a presumed economic alliance between a man who can earn more and a woman who is economically subordinate or dependent while devoting herself to childbearing and childrearing (Townsend, 2002). It's part of what Townsend calls "the package deal" of marriage. When the marriage ends, women find (as noted in Chapter 10) that the initial disparity in income and potential income has widened. As well, a woman with young dependent children and perhaps fewer work skills, less training or education, and sole responsibility for children, may not seem like a good prospect to an employer. And on separation, the considerable benefits of having the combined incomes of two earners no longer exist.

Housing is a further challenge for many lone mothers, as mentioned above, who may be unable to find reasonably priced housing. The upshot is that they quickly become poor, and tend to remain so, with disadvantages both for themselves and for their children (McDaniel, 1993). Not surprisingly, the consequences to men of divorce are seldom as financially bleak.

Children in lone-parent families are known to suffer both directly from the disadvantage of their family situations—particularly poverty—and from society, which stigmatizes them and expects less from them. The two forces work together to create lower achievement prospects that tend to become self-fulfilling. These factors, though powerful, are not deterministic. Many children from lone-parent families achieve at high levels indeed, among them Eartha Kitt and Charles Chaplin, to cite but two world-famous examples. Nonetheless, making opportunities for children from lone-parent families is often not easy for the mothers, the children themselves, or society.

The positive experiences of living in a lone-parent family, for both mothers and their children, are not to be discounted. Among other things, they may learn the value of interdependence, of invention and innovation, of self-reliance, of mutual interdependency, and how to value women in a world that too often fails to do so (Colllins, 1991; Ferri, 1993). Children from deprived situations where love persists can learn to persevere, to aim high in their expectations, to deny themselves for future gain.

These lessons can be beneficial in a world where many have so much that they do not see a need to struggle to succeed. A longitudinal study in Britain (Ferri, 1993: 289) finds that "[m]any of those who had grown up in lone-parent families had done as well, if not better, than their peers who had enjoyed more stable family lives." This is a hopeful and not-often-heard message that bears noting. Knowledge of this sociological finding by family research can go a long, long way toward encouraging children in lone-parent families to strive for success in life.

Latchkey children, children who are regularly left for some part of the day without adult supervision, epitomize both the best and the worst of resilience. Not all latchkey children are from lone-parent families. Many are from two-income families where no one is home when they return from school each day. Both good and bad consequences are found for latchkey children in one study (Leung et al., 1996). The positive outcomes include learning to be independent and responsible, as well as learning useful skills such as how to start dinner for the family or how to grocery shop. Among the negatives are loneliness, fear, boredom, under-achievement in school, and perhaps drug or alcohol abuse.

Lone parenthood after divorce or separation is a family transition plagued with perils, as we saw in the previous chapter. Not the least of the challenges is the stigma, both social and economic. It does not help that poverty and economic insecurity are generally associated with lone motherhood, but there is more to the stigma than economic deprivation and its labels. The negative attribution may start with the social sense of women's inadequacies as women and as mothers, and then move to the threat, both social and economic, that women having children without men pose to the society.

> [T]here is a tendency for minority arrangements like lone-parent families to be seen as something of an affront to established beliefs about the nuclear family. If they can be seen to "work," they undermine the credibility of the nuclear family, and this has subversive implications for the dominant economic and moral order which to a great extent depends on the nuclear family and in its turn endorses it. (Collins, 1991: 159)

The transition into lone parenthood can cause a woman in particular to question her identity as a woman, and her understandings and assumptions about family and the society in which she lives. This can also occur with men, but men less often have as much invested in their identity as spouse and parent as women do. Men withdraw from their children much more often on separation or divorce because they tend to see family as including a wife and children together (Townsend, 2002).

One transition to lone motherhood, not as often considered, is when the marriage or relationship ends because the husband "comes out" as gay. This is a more frequent occurrence than might be imagined, particularly with the societal encouragement of the recent past to deny same-sex attractions and marry anyway. Few marriage partners expect a change in sexual identity in their partners when they marry.

In one study of this experience, French (1991) finds that some couples agree to stay together after the "coming out," while others separate but maintain active parental involvement with the children. French points out how becoming a lone parent can be a means of problem-solving for women in this situation. She further reveals that sexuality, like family, is not static and given, but a process sometimes worked through in family as the means to new identities and lifestyles. Interestingly, French's study shows that as the men came to grips more and more with their gay identities, their interest in maintaining their father roles continues, sometimes even intensifying. Self-help groups for women married to gay men have formed and can prove helpful to women, if primarily to provide support and to indicate that they are not alone in their experiences. The study reveals that family is indeed a process and that husbandhood and fatherhood need not be synonymous, and need not be only heterosexual roles.

Lone mothers in the United States, and increasingly in Canada, have become the targets for cutbacks to social assistance (welfare in the U.S.) and vicious public labels. They are variously termed slothful, manipulative, inadequate mothers, irresponsible women, and selfish takers of public monies. Some are even labelled as women who use their sexuality and reproduction to get public subsidies. That little of this has any basis in fact does not seem to matter. It has a reality of its own in belief systems that favour more and deeper cuts to social assistance and so-called incentives to lone mothers to work outside the home, even there are no jobs and few childcare options for them. The campaigns against lone mothers also have a clear basis in efforts to preserve the nuclear family against other family forms, as we have seen earlier in this chapter.

Lone-parent families have posed perplexing problems for policy makers because of their persistent and deepening poverty. Many countries, including Canada and the United States, have had policies which explicitly or implicitly build in the belief that women and children are the responsibilities of husbands and fathers (Baker, 1995: 13). Only when this fails do states believe they must act, reluctantly and under pressure. State family policies have ranged from providing incentives to lone mothers to parent full-time, as in the Netherlands, to offering incentives for them to work in the paid labour force, as in Sweden and Australia (Baker, 1995), to apprehending children at risk in Aboriginal families (Castellano, 2002). Europe, on average, does far more for lone-parent families than does North America (Kamerman & Kahn, 1988), enabling them to balance work and family responsibilities by a variety of supports.

Behind social policies oriented to lone-parent families are three models. The first is the private family approach, characterized by the United Kingdom and the United States, where family is believed to be a private institution that ought to look after itself, with the state stepping in only on a casualty basis (Lesemann & Nicol, 1994: 117). This contrasts with the family-oriented model (France and Quebec), which sees the state as having a public interest in families. The third is the state-based model (Sweden), which sees state intervention as important not to help families but to promote socioeconomic participation as fully as possible. Canada is caught between these models, using a little of each in its approach to policies for lone parents.

Much attention has been devoted recently to how to move lone mothers away from social assistance. An interesting and innovative Canadian study of 150 single mothers on social assistance offers some important insights (Gorlick & Pomfret, 1993). Focusing on women's exit strategies from social assistance, Gorlick and Pomfret find that the main predictors of successful exits are social supports, including information, and the women's aspirations. The research finds that lone mothers on social assistance in Canada are actively involved in an extensive range of social and economic strategies to exit social assistance. They are realistic and hopeful about the possibilities, but feel that they could benefit from useful supports and information to assist them.

Seeking Parenthood on One's Own

The largest growth in childbearing outside of marriage or cohabiting relationships is occurring among women in their late 20s and early 30s (Ram, 1990: 33). Rates of non-marital childbearing, however, have increased for most age groups. The exception has been births to teens, which in Canada has been falling (Dryburgh, 2001). The teen pregnancy rate in the U.S. is also decreasing, but remains about double that of the Canadian rate (Dryburgh, 2001: 2).

If mature women are having births without being in couple relationships, several factors could be at work. There could be accidental pregnancies, as there always are. More women who accidentally become pregnant now choose to keep and raise their babies instead of giving them up for adoption. This is a deliberate choice in favour of motherhood, even if the conception itself may not have been planned. There is also evidence that some women are seeking motherhood on their own without the traditional step of marriage or being in a committed relationship.

Few studies have looked at unmarried lone mothers, women who *begin* single parenthood without being married or in a union at all. One study (Clark, 1993) finds that the social and economic costs of unmarried single motherhood are evident ten years after the first child is born. Although there are no effects on likelihood of marrying, the risks of poverty are greater than for married mothers (Dryburgh, 2001). As well, there is lessened opportunity to pursue education, thus further disadvantaging the unmarried mothers. As the children grow, however, the initial discrepancies between unmarried and married mothers decrease. Age at first unmarried motherhood matters greatly: the younger one is, the greater the disadvantage and the less likely one is to catch up later on. Children born to younger unattached mothers do less well in school and in IQ tests than other children.

In deliberately seeking motherhood on one's own, options exist today that did not exist previously. We introduced some of these options in the scenarios in Chapter 3. With the stigma lessened of having a child outside marriage, it may not be surprising that some women are going for it. This may be a generation of women who have been taught to get what they aim for in life, rather than waiting for all their dreams to fall into place by luck or chance. Some are successful, educated, thoughtful career women who know their own minds. Others may have become infertile earlier in their lives, but not given up their dreams of motherhood. Options now include new reproductive technologies including **artificial insemination** and **in vitro fertilization**, informal means to access sperm for conception, private adoptions, and foreign adoptions.

Let's look first at adoption, although in reality women often look at adoption only after considering the option of giving birth to a baby. Adoption not long ago was carefully controlled by churches and the state. For good or for bad, it was thought that adoptive parents should be married and matched in religion, region, and ethnicity/race as much as possible to the adopted child. This left out single women, single men, cohabiting couples, and lesbians and gays. It also often left out the non-religious. Adoption has opened up considerably in recent years, most notably in private adoptions whereby the birth mother (or parents) can know and sometimes select the adoptive family for the baby/child. More single people have been able to adopt children too, although the waiting lists are lengthy and the screening tight and sometimes unnecessarily judgemental about lifestyle.

A new option that has opened things up for couples and single women wishing to adopt—and some single men, too— has been foreign adoptions. These occur for numerous reasons. One is that strife and disruption in various world regions have created unwanted babies and children, either as war orphans or as a result of policies such as the forbidding of birth control and abortion in Romania a few years ago. The one-child policy in China has led to numbers of babies, primarily girls, being adopted by Canadians and others, as many Chinese choose, for cultural reasons, to have a boy if they can have only one child (Dorow, 2002). There is the concern that some babies or children may be taken from their parents for the lucrative foreign adoption market, or brought into the world for the purposes of the adoption market. It is not fully known whether this occurs and, if so, to what extent.

The opening up of foreign adoption has meant that more Canadians and Americans can adopt who may not meet, or do not wish to meet, the requirements of domestic adoption agencies. International adoption is costly and time-consuming, with lengthy screening and often frustrating international negotiations, but it is possible for a small minority of people to become the adoptive parent of a child born elsewhere.

The not-so-new reproductive technologies have also opened possibilities for single people, and to some extent gays and lesbians. For example, artificial insemination has been used for a long time by women and by doctors to inseminate their patients. It has not been so routinely discussed until recently, however. Surrogate motherhood can be found in the Old Testament, but has lately become more popular in North America, although regulation has lagged behind practice. In vitro fertilization, or test-tube conception, has a low success rate, but has been used to help women and couples conceive if one or both has fertility problems. These technologies have created new families and challenged the bases on which nuclear families have traditionally been built.

As a result of changing families, with multiple-family fresh starts as well as the new reproductive technologies, new types of fatherhood have been created. Eichler (1997: 72) notes that there are now nine kinds of fathers:

- biological, social, exclusive, full fathers

- non-biological but social, exclusive full fathers

- biological but not social fathers

- biological, social, exclusive, partial fathers (where the father is non-custodial)

- biological, social, non-exclusive, partial fathers (a non-exclusive father is one where the mother has a new partner)

- non-biological but social, exclusive, partial fathers

- non-biological but social, non-exclusive, partial fathers

- gay co-fathers, non-biological, social, non-exclusive fathers

- post-mortem biological fathers (where the man's sperm is taken for impregnation after his death)

Not much is known about men seeking fatherhood outside marriage or committed relationships. Some gay men who are single, as well as some in committed relationships, have been pushing for the option of adoption in several provinces in Canada. It is not known how many men on their own are seeking fatherhood. It might be anticipated, however, that as men's self-images with respect to families and fatherhood change, more men might seek to have children outside of marriage or a committed relationship. It also might be predicted that, even with contemporary social changes, fewer men than women would deliberately seek single parenthood (Townsend, 2002). Existing practices, such as surrogate motherhood (whereby a woman agrees to conceive and gestate a baby for a fee), are more readily available to men, given their greater average purchasing powers.

Parenting Without Living Together

When spouses separate, divorce, or part ways, the important question of who will assume responsibilities for the children in the new families that emerge arises. Custody decisions are often amicable and made by the couple without resort to the courts, but also can be the basis for immensely heated emotions, nasty court battles, and highly charged policy forums. The latter have been seen in Canada with the 1998 Senate committee hearings on divorce and custody. Successes of fresh starts in families following divorce or separation can depend on custody arrangements being satisfactory for all family members involved. Custody involves the children's entire well-being, including day-to-day care, control and protection, instilling of values, and future opportunities. Custody issues can relate to, and overlap with, issues of access to children by the non-custodial parent as well as issues of child support.

Short of King Solomon's solution—dividing the child in half—there is no simple solution to child-custody disagreements. Debates about the rights of mothers relative to the rights of fathers and the rights of grandparents often overlook what is in the best interests of the child(ren), and how those interests can best be achieved. Even the concept of "custody" itself might better suit families if it were abandoned in favour of something that indicates a child-centred focus. "Parenting responsibilities" is one alternative that is being proposed for the new Divorce Act, discussed in Chapter 10. "Primary caregiver" has been another helpful suggestion (Richardson, 2001). Others might be devised.

Joint custody (soon to be called co-parenting) is rapidly increasing in both Canada and the United States. Many think (Drakich, 1993; Eichler, 1997, for example), however, that it is unlikely to work successfully except in those cases

Tears, Sneers, and Accusations

There were tears, sneers and accusations in Toronto last week as advocacy groups for battered women, non-custodial fathers and grandparents unleashed pent-up resentments and complaints before the Special Joint Committee of the Senate and the House of Commons on Child Custody and Access. The hearings are part of a compromise reached last year when the Senate held up approval of a tough new bill to force delinquent parents—mostly fathers—to make good on their child support commitments....

Stories abound of lonely and distraught grandparents, of mothers leaving town with the kids to elude brutal former partners, and of fathers who have been denied visitation rights by mothers who wield access like a weapon to extort money.

... will only work if fairness to both parents is guaranteed. The way to do that is to ensure that children have open and ample access to both parents and to other family members.

Source: "Where Kids Sit When Families Split," Editorial, *The Globe and Mail*, April 6: A20. Reprinted with permission from The Globe and Mail.

Divorced Dads as "Non-Parents"

Separated and divorced families are a growing reality in today's society, [Ron] Kuban [past President of Children and Parents Equality Society] told a small audience. So, divorced families, including fathers, require more attention and support. If they don't receive it, the consequences will be costly to all levels of society...

Right now, fathers don't get much support, he said... "The courts are now saying to the one parent, who has traditionally been the mom, for whatever reason or for whatever bias, you continue to be the parent. The non-custodial parent suddenly ceases to be the parent in the traditional sense. He or she now becomes the access parent. But the access parent is a misnomer for a large babysitter."

Source: Arnold, Tom. 1997. "Divorced Dads Treated as Non-Parents," *The Edmonton Journal*, June 11: B4. Material reprinted with the express permission of "Edmonton Journal Company," a CanWest Partnership.

where the marriage breakdown was amicable. Joint custody requires negotiations in good faith by both partners, and the capacity of each to have the best interests of the children at heart. It has clear benefits in good situations, but can create problems, too. For instance, the child(ren) can continue to be socially parented by both parents, which can help their development and their adjustment to the disruption of the separation and divorce. However, if the mother and father have different standards of living (as they often do, as we have seen), the kids may blame one or the other for the relative deprivation the child endures in that household. If Mom and Dad live in different regions, there can be a lot of travel and shuffling back and forth, creating a sense of rootlessness for the child. And if the child has regular contact with both parents but the parents don't coordinate their parental roles well, the child can play one parent off against the other.

Some parents, as we noted in Chapter 10, effectively stop parenting once they live in a household separate from the child. Others continue to act as parents. A major challenge for divorced families is that there is no clear model for non-residential parenting. The relation of parenting with custody issues is, in part, what makes custody such a political hot button, particularly for men's rights groups.

Remarriage or Cohabitation

Most divorced people remarry (Baker, 1996; Richardson, 2001), or form a new union. In fact, the proportion of marriages in which one or both of the partners has been previously married is increasing. In Canada in 1967, for example, only 12.3 percent of marriages involved a previously married partner; by 1998, the proportion was 22 percent (Statistics Canada, 2001). Remarriage of divorced people is so common now that some see it as normative. Called "conjugal succession" or "recycling the family" (Richardson, 2001: 231), it seems here to stay. More than anything else, the extent of remarriage after divorce underlines people's desire to have committed, emotionally involving relationships. Divorce rates would only mark a decline in family if few divorced people remarried, or subsequently became involved in long-term unions. A trend is discernible toward a lesser rate of remarriage among younger cohorts than among older ones in Canada, as shown in Table 11.1 on page 435, but it should be remembered that marriage rates overall have declined. The preference is increasing for the second union to be common-law.

More divorced men than women remarry (Baker, 1996: 30), and the likelihood of remarrying following divorce is reduced if one has children, particularly for women. In the United States, more people marry, more divorce, and more remarry than in Canada (Richardson, 2001; Statistics Canada, 2002a). Although still popular, the overall rate of remarriage has declined a little in Canada recently, corresponding with the lower marriage rate.

Second marriages, as we noted in Chapter 10, have a higher risk of divorce than do first marriages. The reasons for this could be many. One is that those who are divorced may have fewer of the social supports and the values that keep couples together. For example, they may be less willing to tolerate unhappiness or violence to preserve the marriage. Another reason is more psychological; people entering a second marriage may not have resolved the personal problems that led to problems in the first marriage. They may thus bring "baggage" into the second relationship, or choose the wrong kind of partner again the second time. A third reason is that in some situations, conflicts between first and second families are too difficult to work out. We will talk more about the particular challenges of blended families in a moment.

Most explanations for the higher risk of divorce in remarriages are sociological. When couples marry or form a committed relationship, they begin a process of "social construction of marriage," by which they create together their own shared traditions and memories. Over time, they create together a shared new definition of themselves in relation to the world around them. When a marriage ends, this social construction of self-identity in relation to marriage becomes shaky but it does not get forgotten.

In remarrying, different and new social constructions must be developed through negotiation, agreeing to new social roles and divisions of labour. The imprints of the past relationship are shadowed by the new relationship, but always provide implicit comparisons. Since the former relationship is in the past, memories of it can be either overly rosy or overly bleak, with no reality checks. Both types of memories can have implications for the present relationship and make it more challenging to maintain. When children are involved, the increased number of relationships and the need to maintain an ongoing relationship with the ex-spouse can make remarriage even more challenging.

A study based on a national survey in Canada (Wu, 1994) finds that adaptation to a second marriage is related to the particular type of marital dissolution, age at marital dissolution, religion, and gender.

Less is known about remarriage after widowhood, but generally it is less common than remarriage after divorce (Connidis, 2001: 108). In large part, this may simply be that divorce tends to occur earlier in life than widowhood. One Canadian study (Wu, 1995), using event history analysis, has found huge differences between men's and women's probabilities of remarriage after widowhood. Remarriage is significantly higher for men (almost twice as high), and in particular for men who are better off financially. This is not surprising given that women tend to outlive men. Men who are widowed would have a larger pool of potential mates than women who are widowed. Prospects for remarriage of widows and widowers have dropped recently, particularly for young widowers (Nault & Belanger, 1996: 11). The drop was less for young widows. Nault and Belanger (1996: 13) conclude, "The chances of widowed persons remarrying are consequently much lower, in particular for women who at older ages find themselves facing a marriage market strongly slanted against them."

Little is known about the extent to which obligations to extended family members remain after divorce and remarriage. One of the few studies that have looked at this finds that the divorce of either younger or older generations in families tends to magnify the gendered nature of family responsibilities (Connidis, 2001). Contacts with extended family members continue but are maintained more by women than by men. Another study finds that among 190 women and 93 men who divorced and remarried, most feel that they are obligated to help family members in need, if possible (Coleman, Ganong, & Cable, 1997). They perceive their obligations to the younger generation as stronger than those to elders.

The majority of couples succeed in meeting the challenges of a second marriage (Richardson, 2001). What works is, not surprisingly, similar to what works in a successful first marriage: good communication, realistic expectations, honesty, a shared sense of humour. Meyerstein (1997) suggests that advance preparation is highly useful in a good second marriage. It helps to recognize that a second marriage is not the same as a first, and that the first marriage cannot be repressed and forgotten but should be mined for lessons learned. Beyond these sensible approaches, the couple needs to work to develop the marital relationship and to establish and maintain the new loyalties to each other (Kheshgi-Genovese & Genovese, 1997).

Assessing the degree to which cohabitation is a fresh start after dissolution of a first relationship is not easy. Cohabitation, unlike marriage, does not have a clear date of beginning and ending, thus errors in estimates of cohabitation are probable. Language is also elusive in satisfactorily capturing cohabitation arrangements, making accurate estimation even more challenging. Terms used include common-law unions, cohabitation, living together, persons of the opposite sex sharing living quarters (known as **POSSLQ**—or **PSSSLQ** for same-sex partners), and in French, "*union libre*," as well as street-language terms such as "shacking up," "living in sin," and "trial marriage." Whether these terms connote similar kinds of living arrangements is far from clear. No matter how definitions are spelled out on surveys and census forms, people's own self- and social definitions of what is and is not cohabitation come into play in their responses.

Despite these measurement challenges, data on divorce and remarriage suggest that there is a reduced tendency for men and women to enter a second marriage after the failure of a first relationship, as shown in Table 11.1 on page 435. This is not surprising. There is the sense that marriage may not be for them after all, or alternatively, there are the attractions of singlehood or lone parenthood, both of which offer some autonomy and independence—although a parent can never be fully independent. Nonetheless, "[c]ohabitation is replacing marriage as the framework to begin life as a couple, to give birth to children and start a family, and to reconstitute another unit when the first one has failed" (Marcil-Gratton, 1993: 89).

That said, there is a strong tendency to form new unions after a first one breaks up. Ninety percent of women aged 30 to 39 whose first marriage dissolved form a second union (LeBourdais, Neill, and Turcotte, 2000: 16). The likelihood declines with age. Notably, women who started conjugal life in a common-law union are no less likely to form new relationships than those who were married.

Growing proportions of Canadian children experience a family transition when one or both of their parents start a new family by cohabitation. "Three-quarters of the children from broken unions whose parents have ever engaged in cohabitation have at age sixteen experienced at least one new two-parent family and the integration of the new partner" (Marcil-Gratton, 1993: 87–88). The proportion of children born to at least one parent who has ever lived in cohabitation has risen dramatically in the last thirty years. The phenomenon barely existed in the early 1960s (2.5 percent of 1961–63 birth cohorts), increased to 9 percent for children born 1971–73, climbed to 32 percent for those both in 1981–83, and reached 43 percent for those born in 1987–89 (Marcil-Gratton, 1993: 76).

Second families based on cohabitation seem to be more fragile than those based on marriage (Desrosiers, LeBourdais, & Laplante, 1995). A cohabiting family in which one or both partners is divorced is less likely to break up if there is a pre-school child or children at the time of the formation of the new union, if a child is born to the newly formed couple, or if only the man brings children into the new relationship (Desrosiers, LeBourdais, & Laplante, 1995).

Fleeing into New Family

Some people, with immense courage and fortitude, create entirely fresh family starts for themselves after suffering not only marital disruption, but also family at its worst. Two of these kinds of second families are discussed in the readings on pages 447 and 448: fleeing from family abuse, and fleeing from abusive cultural practices. Both involve journeys of self- and family discovery. Other examples could easily have been included.

Fleeing into fresh starts at family and at life itself is not limited to the kind of pain Florence describes in the first reading.

Growth and Triumph

I am from the Peigan Nation. I was adopted out when I was an infant so I have never had the opportunity to live on my reservation. Eleven years ago I was reunited with my birth parents, and that is where my healing began...

I grew up in... an average, middle-class white family... In school, "squaw" was a label that was always applied to me. Sexual abuse, disruption in our home and my own longing to know who I was welled up inside me and I began to run away from home... I grew to be ashamed of who I was and remained so until I understood Canadian history, until I understood the circumstances of my birth, until I understood that I was loved and until I understood that racism was a reflection of ignorance...

I was suicidal and I either ran away at every opportunity or slashed my wrists in hope that someone would care. I spent the rest of my teens... in a haze of drugs, alcohol and all the evils that street life can offer to a teenager...

In Vancouver, I met the man I would stay with for twelve years; he was twenty-two and I was seventeen. We were both on the streets and we learned to exist together, but neither of us really knew how to love or respect each other because we were both searching for some part of ourselves. We had a daughter and eventually a son but our relationship deteriorated—fighting, alcohol and drugs were always present and we patterned our lives this way for many years until we separated for the last time.

If I were to sum up my lifetime, I would have to say that the first half has been about pain and the rest about healing... I am now in university and working on a degree in native studies. It has been a struggle with myself... I have had to give up drinking and drugs, kicking and screaming and it is hard to keep that commitment... It has taken a long time for the street to leave me but those survival skills have carried me through a lot of years.

Source: Shone, Florence. 1998. "It Became Important..." *Our Voice*, April 8. Reprinted with permission.

Do They Hear You When You Cry?

...[A] happy, spoiled little girl in the tiny West African country of Togo, Fauziya...is the favourite youngest daughter of a well-to-do businessman who is traditional enough to have stature in his community but progressive enough not to let his four girls be "circumcised" according to tribal tradition.

Then he dies... Within a year, the ambitious 17-year-old's education has been scrapped and she's been gift-wrapped as a fourth wife for an old man

who won't take delivery of his new bride until her "woman's parts" have been removed to ensure her "cleanliness" and fidelity.

... Fauziya flees the night before the butchers are to come for her... is delivered from her room by her eldest sister, who smuggles her out of the house and to the airport, where she boards a flight to Germany using papers provided by a shabby "fixer."

Source: Gadd, Jane. 1998. "A Harrowing Escape from Genital Mutilation," *The Globe and Mail*, April 4: D13. Reprinted with permission from The Globe and Mail.

Generational Dislocations

From the passing of the first Indian Act in 1876 until the protection of Aboriginal and treaty rights in the Constitution Act of 1982, Aboriginal societies were essentially under siege. While poverty, powerlessness, and breakdown of social order were taking hold in Aboriginal communities under the impact of colonial policy, Aboriginal children were simultaneously being removed to residential schools whose express purpose was to disrupt their ties with "savage" culture and, of necessity, their families.

Chief Cinderina Williams of the Spallumcheen band in British Columbia, writing of her community's experience with residential schools, reported:

Later when these children came home, they were aliens. They did not speak their own language, so they could not communicate with anyone other than their own counterparts. Some looked down on their families...They had formed no bonds with their families...

Consequently, when these children became parents, and most did at an early age, they had no parenting skills. They did not have the capacity to show affection.

Source: Castellano, Marlene Brant. 2002. *Aboriginal Family Trends: Extended Families, Nuclear Families, Families of the Heart*. Ottawa: Vanier Institute of the Family, www.vifamily.ca, accessed December 30, 2002, p. 17, abridged.

What comes through in both of these examples is the strength of survival, the skills and confidence that enabled both women to become stronger and to create new selves along with new families. These are truly inspiring escapes into new families.

Still another kind of second family is the recreation of family after the generations-long experiences of Aboriginal peoples in Canada with residential schools (Castellano, 2002; Fournier and Crey, 1997). Some Aboriginal professionals, according to Castellano (2002: 19), describe the impacts of residential schools on Aboriginal families in terms of "'post-traumatic stress syndrome' that not only haunts those who experienced the traumatic events but also establishes reactive partterns of behaviour that are incorporated into family life and passed on to younger generations."

Not the Brady Bunch:
The Challenges of Blended/Stepfamilies

The number of blended families is not fully known. **Blended families** are remarried or cohabiting families in which one or both partners brings children into the new relationship. In 2001, there were 503 100 blended families Canada, or 12 percent of all families with children, compared with 10 percent in 1995 (Statistics Canada, 2002a). Eichler (1997: 32) compellingly argues that this number could be doubled, since there is another person often (but not always) involved, a non-custodial parent who may still parent the children in another blended family.

In Canada in 2001, 50 percent of remarried families with children contain only the children of the female partner, 10 percent his children only, and 32 percent are "blended" after the birth of a child to the remarried or now cohabiting couple after one already has children from a previous relationship (Statistics Canada, 2002a: 6). There are not many like the Brady Bunch, where both partners bring into the second relationship a number of children.

From the perspective of numbers of children in different kinds of families, it is estimated that in 1994 in Canada about 5 percent of children lived in some sort of blended family (Peters, 1997). In the United States, it has been estimated that 20 percent of children will have lived in some kind of stepfamily by the age of 18 (Church, 1996: 82).

The total number of stepfamilies in Canada is about equally split between remarriages and cohabiting relationships (Statistics Canada, 2002a: 7).

The terminology of blended families is as challenging as that for cohabiting couples. The terms "blended" or "reconstituted" make new families sound almost strange, in contrast to "regular" families. One suggestion is the term "**binuclear family**" (Church, 1996: 83), which also has drawbacks. Using the descriptor "blended," "reconstituted," or "binuclear" highlights differences rather than similarities with other families that have not experienced divorce and remarriage.

Similarities are likely large, and when differences are found, the question must be asked whether the differences are due to the blended family experience, to the divorce experience, or to family problems that might have occurred anyway. These are not easy questions to sort out in research. However, the emphasis we tend to give to "blended" families as different may cause us to search there for the source of family or child problems, appropriately or not.

Making second families is not easy or straightforward. What to call non-biological parents is one challenge, for example, along with what to call the children of the stepparent. The terms can be perplexing for both children and parents.

Additionally, there are the mythologized images of the immensely happy Brady Bunch of TV fame, and the opposite but strongly compelling images of

---

Good-bye "Daddy" and "Mummy"

The terms "mummy" and "daddy" are to be banned from schools in Ireland as part of a drive by the Roman Catholic Church to... recognize the growing number of one-parent families.

A new church program aimed at four- and five-year olds in Catholic schools throughout Northern Ireland and the Irish Republic asks teachers to use phrases such as "the adults who live in your house" and "the people who look after you" instead of referring to mothers and fathers.

Source: "Good-bye 'Daddy' and 'Mommy'." 1997. *The Edmonton Journal*, October 17: A6.

Beyond the Wicked Stepmother

Stepmoms can still be called "wicked," but in today's slang it can mean they're cool or excellent. They've been transformed from fairy tales by a modern society where separation and divorce are common, and where the new families that rise from them include a growing number of stepmoms.

"When one of the stepchildren does something that I have to discipline, right away I get the wicked stepmother type of thing," Corinne says chuckling.... [Corinne is a mother of two and stepmother of two.] "Being a stepmom isn't scary. Parenting four teenagers at the same time, now that's scary," she laughs.

Source: Zbeb, Chris. 2002. "The New 'Wicked' Stepmother," *The Edmonton Journal*, January 15: E1. Reprinted with permission of *The Edmonton Journal*.

the wicked stepmother of folklore and fairy tales (Ackerman, 1996). Cinderella's stepmother (and stepsisters) are vivid images for children of what stepfamilies can be and what they would not want (Valpy, 1998). Stepfathers do not fare too well either in some children's literature, with images of stern taskmasters, of negligent men, or of propensities.

There is also the contemporary reality of biological fathers and mothers who are not only alive, but also often a continuing part of the child's life. The child may make comparisons between the two "mothers" or "fathers," or play one against the other, or deny that the stepparent is really a parent after all. Stepparents, too, may make comparisons, experience self-doubts about their parenting, or find that the necessary ongoing relationship with the absent parent is challenging.

With the trend toward joint custody—or, to use the new policy terminology, co-parenting responsibilities—there can be a shuffling back and forth between the homes of parents (Ackerman, 1996). This can create a sense of rootlessness for the child(ren) and possibly insecurity. It can also make for a mad rush as children fit in living in different homes along with all the other many demands of childhood (school, sports, music lessons, often language or religious classes, etc.).

Don't Expect the Brady Bunch

When Marianne Libertella married Ray Massi, a divorced father of three, she thought she was prepared for her new life and her new stepfamily.

But after two years' experience..."I was really going into it naive. I was 40. I had never had children. I thought this was going to be the family I had never had."

Reality hit at a family gathering that included both mother and stepmother. The child favoured her mother, ignoring her stepmother...Since then, Marianne Massi has become a close friend to her stepchildren, a role better suited to stepparents... say experts.

Source: Kadaba, Lini S. 1998. "Don't Expect the Brady Bunch," *The Edmonton Journal*, April 5: G3.

Children can also resent that one stepsibling gets to go off for what may appear a holiday for a period while he or she cannot. Or, the child may resent the presence of a stepsibling in what they consider "their" domain for the period in which the child is in their second home, a real example cited by Richardson (2001: 233).

A particular challenge of life in blended families is the sharing of children at special family events, such as Christmas or Chanukah or Ramadan. Children we may think of as ours are away at the other parent's place for some holidays, which creates the need for regular negotiations and close collaboration among the various parents and their other family members. Some parents, too, may deeply feel the absence of their children at important family times. Mother's Day and Father's Day can also highlight differentness and create longings amongst children and parents.

At the same time, living in a blended family is not all bad by any means. One little boy who lived with his mother, stepfather, and younger brother thought his situation much better than that of his younger brother since he had two Dads while his brother had only one!

Family research is helpful in identifying what works successfully in blended families. A popular research strategy is to compare second families with so-called "intact" families. This research design has its problems, in that the two kinds of families may not be comparable. Members of blended families may have been through family disruption and, for good or bad, have learned strategies for dealing with problems, while intact families may not have had such lessons. It may also be that in comparing intact and blended families, the implicit standard is set by the intact families, leading to inappropriate and prejudicial comparisons. In addition, step or blended families may be new territory for many, for which they make up the rules as they live through experiences. That is not so for many first families that often have many examples of how to parent before them, most notably their own families of origin.

Without Our Most Precious at the Holidays

This Christmas we'll be without our two of our most precious gifts. A daughter and a son.

The sting of separation is familiar to those in "non-traditional" families. There are more than one million children in this country living with one parent, or a parent and a stepparent, or dual-custody parents. Stepsiblings abound.

What it all adds up to for many families is a certain amount of confusion. A certain amount of anxiety. And a lot of pain.

At no time is this more evident than at Christmas. In this season of joy and sharing and coming together the pain of being apart is keenly felt...Since moving to this city eight years ago, our family has faced this painful reality every other Christmas. One year, the kids are with us. The next, they're gone. It never gets easier. Our three children are my wife's from her first marriage. Their father lives in Saskatchewan.

Source: Rick McConnell. 1996. "It's A Lot to Ask..." *The Edmonton Journal*, December 15: G1. Material reprinted with the express permission of "Edmonton Journal Company," a CanWest Partnership.

Nonetheless, the findings of what works well in blended families from such studies bears sharing. A significant predictor of success is the degree of focus on the children themselves as important. Another important factor is the consensus on parenting between the new spouse and the child's parent (Saintjacques, 1995). Preparation for the stepparent role is also important, including accepting the reality that both the new spouse and stepchildren had a previous family life that did not, and never can, include the stepparent (Richardson, 2001: 232). Stepparents also need to recognize that they ultimately have limited control over whether the child(ren) accept them.

Trying too hard can be a mistake. Since women face more obstacles and challenges in becoming stepmothers than men do in becoming stepfathers (Valpy, 1998), it is important that women prepare more and understand some of the particular challenges they face in advance (Morrison & Thompson-Guppy, 1986). For instance, Valpy (1998), in citing research done by David Cheal in Canada, notes stepparenting can be stressful, especially with the vivid wicked stepmother imagery that we all seem to have. This is clearly evident in the box example about wicked stepmoms. Added to this is the fact that women have traditionally borne the major responsibilities for childcare and childrearing, meaning more contact with stepchildren and more points at which to encounter tender feelings on both sides. This makes stepmothering more challenging than stepfathering.

In research that focuses on couples in mutual support groups as they make the transition from being lone parents to becoming blended families, Collins (1991) finds that there are both private, personal issues and social challenges. Unlike most research, Collins does not compare blended families with intact families but looks at second families as a process. He particularly examines the interplay between individual lives and dominant ideologies about marriage and families.

Two forces draw lone parents to remarry, according to Collins: first, there is the desire to escape from the "cheerless life" of the lone parent; and second, "the widespread view in Western societies that the nuclear family is the proper setting in which to bring up children" (Collins, 1991: 159), or what Church (1996: 87) refers to as filling the "kin vacuum." Recognition in the light of day that lone parenthood has distinct advantages, and that the nuclear family is not all that it is deemed to be for children or for anyone else, gets crowded out by the power of ideological beliefs that restoring "order" to what is seen as a deviant family form is to be desired. In deciding whether to make the transition to stepparenthood or blended family, lone mothers must balance the roles of mother and woman, and are influenced by the "herd" notion that marriage or being part of a couple relationship must be good because most people do it.

Negotiating the dilemmas of parenthood responsibilities, personal preferences, and ideological pushes is the basis on which families begin life as a blended family. Their success in working out these dilemmas will relate to the success of their new family (Church, 1996).

Research with 105 stepmothers in Canada (Church, 1996) finds that stepmothers define family in more fluid terms than members of other kinds of family. They do not see household and family as directly equivalent. And roles, including gender roles in family, are seen as more flexible. Church concludes that stepparents may not want to try to be parents to their stepchildren immediately but rather wait and see what new family relationships emerge. This is a theme we have mentioned before.

From the child's viewpoint, there may be a need to establish new relationships with the stepparent, and perhaps with stepsiblings, but also with both the custodial and non-custodial parent, as all the relationships adjust to the new family arrangement. Conceptions of who is family and who is not matters to how these relationships develop and to their ultimate success. Shared parenting can produce a broader and sometimes more accepting view of what family is, and can be. In situations where there is a distinct difference in level of socioeconomic status between the homes of the two parents, there can be ambivalence and even guilt, which can cause the child to wonder about families and gender, but can also expand the child's horizons.

A crucial, but under-researched, aspect of the success or failure of blended families is the degree to which they are socially institutionalized, or provided with everyday supports, guidelines, and societal acceptance. Some see step and blended families as "incomplete institutions," for which society has no clearly established norms (Richardson, 2001: 233). If, in fact, blended families are viewed, or see themselves, as less able to draw on society's resources and rewards, they may be disadvantaged. The judgement is self-fulfilling: if we expect less of blended families, we give less and get less in return. There is some evidence emerging that this may be the case (Richardson, 2001: 233). However, as marital disruption becomes more normative, or widely accepted as happening to many of us, it may be that the institutional supports for remarried and blended families will strengthen.

Discontinuity of relationships between children in blended families and their grandparents (the parents, usually, of the non-custodial parent) has not been the subject of much research. It is, however, of growing policy and legal importance as grandparents increasingly express their rights to have access to their grandchildren after divorce and after remarriages. One study (Kruk, 1995) discovers that grandparents whose adult children are non-custodial (mostly paternal grandparents) are at high risk for contact loss. The primary mediators in ongoing grandparent/grandchild relationships are the daughters-in-law. Disrupted contact between grandparents and grandchildren is found to have adverse consequences for the grandparents. It is not fully known whether the consequences are as adverse for the grandchildren.

Widowhood

Widowhood is now seen as an expectable life event. Given the difference between men's and women's life expectancies, a woman who marries or establishes a

Figure 11.1 MOST SENIOR MEN AND WOMEN LIVE WITH A SPOUSE, CANADA

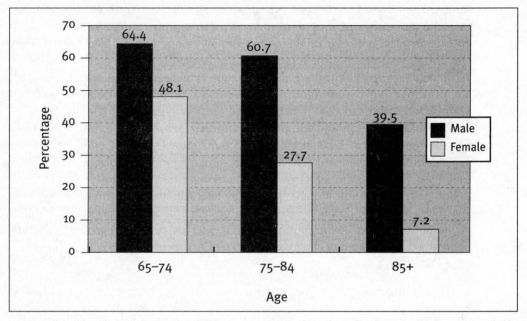

Source: Adapted from the Statistics Canada website. 2002. 2001 Census of Canada: Profile of Canadian Families and Households: Diversification Continues, Catalogue Number 96F0030XIE2001003, www.statcan.ca, accessed on October 22, 2002.

lasting relationship can realistically anticipate that she will be left a widow. The good news, however, is that widowhood is occurring later than it used to (Connidis, 2001: 93; Moore & Rosenberg, 1997: 31). In Canada, almost 80 percent of women aged 85 or over are widowed, while even at age 70 to 74, 40 percent are widowed. Since most men at advanced ages are still married (39.5 percent of men aged 85-plus compared to only 7.2 percent of women the same age) while most women are widowed at these ages, the gender differences are clear.

Older women, mainly widows, are much more likely than men to make a change in their living arrangements late in life. Usually, these changes are related to health status, but they also relate to family. A man with health problems more often has a built-in caregiver at home, his wife, while a woman with health problems, even at the same age, is less likely to have that benefit. Hence, she is more likely to move in with relatives or into an institution. Widowed women, as mentioned earlier, are less likely to remarry than widowed men (Connidis, 2001; Gee & Kimball, 1987: 89).

Myths abound about widows. Mainly they are seen as sad and depressed. Depression does strike some, and at times it is debilitating. But it is not the only reality for widows. Eighteen months or so after the spouse's death, most widows are ready to start life over for themselves (Gee & Kimball, 1987: 90). Most often this means reaching out to friends, siblings, adult children, and others such as clergy or even lawyers. Some develop active new hobbies or interests. Contact with their peers seems to provide the most satisfaction for widows. Some even note that this is the first time that they have felt independent and that they enjoy it (Connidis, 2001: 96).

The death of a long-term partner for gay and lesbian couples poses different problems. The sense of loss may be similar but the lack of institutionalized acceptance of gay and lesbian relationships may make for less strong support (Connidis, 2001: 96). On top of this challenge is the prevalence of AIDS among gay men, the stigma involved, and the reality that more bereaved partners will be left behind. There can also be losses of others in the gay network, intensifying the sense of loss and grief.

Family Transitions in Later Life

Most research on family transitions has focused on people under the age of 50. But with increasing life expectancy and divorce likelihood, the proportions of those over age 65 who are divorced has risen. In 1996, 7 percent of men and 6 percent of women aged 65-plus in Canada were divorced, compared with 1 percent of both men and women in 1971 (Connidis, 2001: 24). People older than 50 remarry with increasing frequency, and establish new cohabiting families as well. In France, for example, in 1992, 1.8 percent of all marriages involved a man over the age of 60 (Caradec, 1997: 47). In Canada, a relatively small percentage of older people remarry or enter their senior years remarried. However, among those divorced or widowed at younger ages, a majority of men and a substantial minority of women eventually remarry (Connidis, 2001: 111).

Some older couples who are alone after widowhood or divorce may choose to cohabit but keep separate households in order to maintain continuity in their living arrangements and to avoid fuss by their offspring about loyalties and inheritance (Borell & Karlsson, 2002). An unusual study in France (Caradec, 1997: 65) of conjugal arrangements among those 60 years and older finds "a great diversity of conjugal lifestyles: some couples live together in marriage, some outside marriage (showing that cohabitation is not reserved for the young in age), and others have adopted more novel forms of union, intermittent or alternating cohabitation." Borell and Karlsson (2002) find similar innovative living arrangements among older people in Sweden.

Living apart together (LAT) is not only for the high-powered couples but also for those who wish companionship without the traditional arrangement of sharing a home full-time. When LAT relationships were discussed in a large family sociology class by one of your authors (McDaniel) in fall 2002, several students mentioned that one of their parents had arrangements with a partner similar to those found in France and Sweden by researchers. And, the students thought that these were happy and clever ways to be a couple. LATs may catch on as the university-age generation ages.

This may suggest two things: first, as Caredec (1997: 65) argues, an **intergenerational contagion** whereby non-marital unions have become diffused from young to old; and second, the need for different people—in this case people at different stages in the life course—to customize relationships to fit their particular needs. It is notable, however, that available statistical data routinely collected by censuses, vital statistics, or most social surveys in North America may not truly capture the immense diversity possible in family living arrangements.

Gay/Lesbian Families

There have always been gay fathers and lesbian mothers, usually in the past those who have become parents in a heterosexual marriage or relationship, and then come out as gay or lesbian. What is newer is gay and lesbian families as such, increasingly accepted by society (Mofina, 2003), with policy entitlements and protections under family law. Gay and lesbian couples more often now decide to have children together and raise them as a family unit. What is also relatively new is for the gay and lesbian couples that form after the end of a heterosexual relationship or marriage, along with the children of one or both partners, to live together as family. Here, we will discuss gay and lesbian parents raising children in families, however they formed, as well as gay and lesbian couples in committed relationships, as new kinds of family.

The significance of gay and lesbian families as new kinds of families cannot be underestimated. They are transforming the ways families are measured, as witnessed by the change in definition of family for the 2001 Census of Canada to include same-sex common-law unions (Statistics Canada, 2002c). And family laws and policies of Canada, as well as workplace policies, have largely been widened to be inclusive of same-sex families.

It is not only that the ways gays and lesbians create and live in families have transformed how sociologists research families and changed the definitions of family, it is also that same-sex families have transformed thinking about families theoretically. An entirely new way to theorize close relations, *queer theory*, has grown out of this line of enquiry. Identities, relationships, even politics are seen as less fixed and more social, based on queer theory (Lehr, 1999). Queer theory takes theoretical thinking in sociology beyond notions of roles and fixed identities in families and society. It argues that gender is performed, like a concert by Michael Jackson or Madonna, on a social stage, and in doing so, we change ourselves and society (Walters, 1999: 250). This gives both power and insight to people and to family theorists and researchers. In this way, same-sex families are really an engine of both social and sociological change, and a way to see how the two are linked.

Diversity exists among gay and lesbian families, as among all families. With respect to gay and lesbian families, there are several added dimensions. One is whether or not they are "out" as a family, or in other words open about their relationship with all they know and meet. Miller (1996: 132), in describing his own gay family, has this to say:

The definition of family for the 2001 Census of Canada was updated to include same-sex common-law unions.

> The family I live in as a father is also the family I live out in as a gay man. I call it an "out family" for three reasons: its openness to homosexual membership; its opposition to hetero sexist conformity (the prejudicial assumption of heterosexuality as normal and proper); and its overtness within the contemporary lesbian and gay movement....Mine is a family that opens out, steps out, and stands out. It opens out to people traditionally excluded from the charmed circle of Home; it steps out beyond the police and policed borders of the Normal; and it stands out as a clear new possibility on the horizon of what used to be called...the Just Society. (Miller, 1996: 132)

Not all gay and lesbian families are "out" in this or any other sense. Some still remain cloaked in secrecy out of fear for the children or themselves. This is most likely among older gay or lesbian couples, however (Connidis, 2001).

Lesbian families with children have been seen as a contradiction: women having children without heterosexual relations. Or they are seen as threats, women without the need for men. Lesbian mothers became more visible in the 1970s and 1980s, according to Epstein (1996: 109) because they chose to claim their identities as both mothers and lesbians. She notes, with sadness, that the claiming often occurred in courtrooms in custody hearings, where lesbians were typically defined as unfit mothers. The risk of losing custody of their children still gives lesbian mothers a strong motivation to conceal their orientation. One example occurred in Alberta in the late 1990s, where a long-time, highly successful foster mother, referred to in media reports as Ms. T, was denied foster children when it was discovered that she was lesbian (Abu-Laban & McDaniel, 1998: 82).

Gay and lesbian families challenge the family *status quo* and thereby offer innovative models of family in several fundamental ways, according to recent family research. First, both gay and lesbian families may provide important developmental learning for children in the possibilities of resisting confining gender-role expectations (Epstein, 1996: 111). Second, lesbians can teach daughters, in particular, how not to compete with other women but to bond with them to work together. Third, both gays and lesbians force a questioning of the assumptions and values of heterosexist nuclear families. Fourth, gay families raise vital questions about the presumptions we make about masculinity in families and in society. And fifth, gay and lesbian families are an effective force of change in family policies.

Challenging family policies by gays and lesbians goes beyond gaining access to the same benefits that heterosexual couples have, although this is important. Epstein (1996: 108) asks readers to imagine what it is like to face the following situations:

- Your child is in a medical emergency and you are not allowed to make any decisions about the care the child is to receive.

- Your child's teacher will not speak to you about your child's progress at school.

- You are assumed to be a single parent even though you live and parent with your partner.

- The courts grant custody of your child to your mother because your sexual relationship with your partner is deemed immoral.

The challenges involve rethinking what families are, what spouses are and do, and what parenting is. These are profoundly important sociological endeavours

The Zoo

I can remember a time long ago when my father took me and my sisters to the zoo with "Joe" and his small children. Entering the gates my Dad could not help but see an ad stating that families could buy a pass that would reduce costs for he and "Joe" significantly. Delighted by this, he nicely asked the cashier for one family pass. She reacted by saying, "I'm sorry, sir but we only sell passes to families." Well, this infuriated my Dad and he demanded that he should be able to buy the pass. He and the cashier continued to argue over whether or not he could buy a pass. Then finally Dad stopped and yelled, "Listen, 'Joe' and I are gay lovers and these are our children." The cashier's face went bright red and she immediately handed my Dad the family pass while apologizing.

Source: Personal communication to one author from the narrator, now a teenager.

at reconceptualizing families. It was, in large part, this sort of rethinking that has led, in recent years, away from defining family by form and instead defining families broadly on the basis of processes: what families *do* rather than what they *are*.

Gay and lesbian families, in not reproducing the heterosexual model of family, tend not to be structured hierarchically by gender. They therefore do not have the same divisions of labour by gender that many heterosexual families have. They are chosen families, characterized by fluid boundaries, new roles, little institutionalized symbolism. They can be creative in making families and in devising new ways to be familial.

Lesbian couples deciding to give birth to a child must negotiate which one will become pregnant, and then agree on the process. This necessitates closeness in talking openly about their feelings and innermost desires and longings. Nelson (1996) reveals in her study of lesbian mothers, to which we referred in an earlier chapter, the intricacy and beauty of reproductive decision-making. Epstein (1996) refers to parenting roles in lesbian couples being based on personality attributes rather than gender, so one parent is the funny one, or the hard-liner, or the one pushing academics. One of Epstein's (1996: 119) respondents puts it well: "We're not modelling male-female power dynamics, we're modelling women doing everything that needs to be done in order to maintain life." Miller (1996: 155) talks about shared and solidifying humour when one of his daughters, Alice, "tactfully informed Jennifer (who was babysitting) that if she was looking for a husband at our house, she was 'barking up the wrong tree.'"

Yet, there are tensions in lesbian and gay families. These occur at several levels, emanating in part from the lack of acceptance of gays and lesbians in some of society and the reality of having no blueprints on how to be. One respondent in a study of lesbian mothers puts it this way:

> We don't presume that we are a family. And I think that has created
> a closer, ah, an opportunity for closeness that would not have been
> there if I had just assumed that we were a family and dammit behave
> like one! Because it gives you no choice. (Nelson, 1996: 105)

Epstein (1996: 122) cites homophobic behaviours of family members such as disowning family membership, or a lesbian partner showing preference for biological links by taking her own child somewhere for a special occasion but not her partner's children. And Miller (1996: 150) notes that his children endure taunts such as, "'We don't want you on the team because you're a fag like your dad.'" On the home front, Dad suggests the following comeback: "Come on, just because my dad's gay doesn't mean I am, and even if I turn out to be gay, what difference would that make to my pitching arm?" (1996: 151).

Post-gender families is a description of relationships in which gender forms no part of the household or the domestic division of labour. This kind of relationship raises important questions about the social concept of "coupledom" as well as about the ways in which gender determines much of what we are and do in families, and how a commitment to non-sexist principles as the basis on which to build families can create new kinds of families. Oerton (1997) explores these issues among lesbian couples in an article she evocatively entitles, "Queer Housewives?" Her conclusion is that gendering processes may so intertwine with all domestic labour and all that we are in family that inventing family without it is challenging, but not impossible. She argues that creative new solutions to family processes, particularly divisions of labour, might be found in closer study of lesbian and gay couples. Risman (1998) argues that some of these new solutions can be found among heterosexual couples as well.

Risman and Johnson-Sumerford (1998) examine heterosexual "post-gender" marriages in which the partners share equally in paid and unpaid family work without regard for gender. They find that there are four pathways to such relationships: a dual-career household, a dual-nurturer relationship, a post-traditional relationship, and external forces that open relationships to egalitarianism. Egalitarianism is likely to affect both the power balance and the emotional quality of the relationship, Risman and Johnson-Sumerford suggest, for the good.

Transitions out of Parenting: Empty Nests

Even without marital dissolution, transitions in family occur. Many families experience the empty nest, and increasing numbers of others may wish to. An empty nest, ideally, occurs when all the children grow up and move away. Children are still growing up, but they are moving away with less and less frequency. Findings from the 2001 Census of Canada show that an amazing 58 percent of

Finally, An Empty Nest.... Maybe

When our older son was little he used to say, "Mommy, when I grow up, I'm going to live with you forever."

He kept his word! Like so many in these times, he left home for a while, then came back and scotch-taped himself to the basement suite for 20 more years — and bought a dog!

But, truly, hope springs eternal... I looked forward to getting rid of Kid and Dog. I could foresee many joys in my life with him outta there... finally, Kid bought a house. He's gone! In case he ever

thinks of moving back, his old bedroom has been turned into my sewing room...

But he drops off Dog each day so she — and we! — won't be lonely... Now there is doggie doo in two backyards....On his way home from work, he picks up Dog. It smells good in here, he says — every day! He goes to the stove and lifts the lids of all the pots. He hangs around. He watches us eat...

But (other hand again!), he still mows the "old folks'" lawn. He still shovels our walk.

Source: Edith Kirby. 1998. "Finally—An Empty Nest," *The Edmonton Journal*, April 3: I5. Reprinted with express permission of "Edmonton Journal Company," a CanWest Partnership.

Figure 11.2 MORE YOUNG ADULTS LIVING IN THE PARENTAL HOME, CANADA

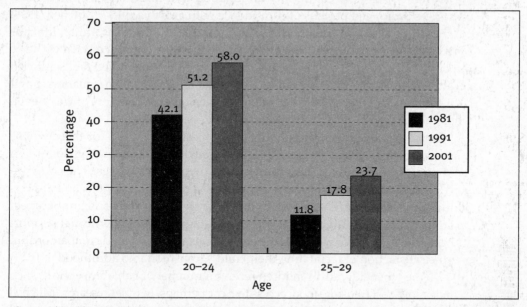

Source: Adapted from the Statistics Canada website. 2002. 2001 Census of Canada: Profile of Canadian Families and Households: Diversification Continues, Catalogue Number 96F0030XIE2001003, www.statcan.ca, accessed on October 22, 2002.

those aged 20 to 24 lived in their parental homes (Statistics Canada, 2002c). This is up from 47 percent in 1981. For young adults aged 25 to 29 in 2001, almost a quarter still lived in the family home. This, suggests Statistics Canada, is one reason for the overall decline in the proportion of households headed by people under age 30 in Canada.

Census data in Canada reveal that most people over age 65 live either alone or with a spouse only (Desjardins & Dumas, 1993: 67). So, empty nests are a reality for most Canadians. Among some elderly, there are a minority who feel that there is no one, or only one person, on whom they could rely for help (Moore & Rosenberg, 1997: 47). Among most, however, there are numbers of friends and family, both close and far, on whom they rely. Family networks are more geographically dispersed than are friends, so in essence family and friends may be reversed as older people build family-like relationships with networks of friends.

Sandwiched Families and Cluttered Nests

Recently, there has been a shift in living arrangements and family lives that in some ways constitutes a new kind of family. It takes two forms. One is the return to the family home of adult children, as well as the presence of adult children who never left in the first instance. This has become a very prevalent living arrangement, as indicated above by the 2001 Census data. In fact, some researchers argue that "[i]t is now commonly understood that midlife parenthood often comprises prolonged periods of coresidence with grown adults" (Mitchell, 1998: 2). The other is elders living with middle-aged children (Rosenthal, Martin-Matthews, & Matthews, 1996). People in midlife who live with or have responsibilities for both the young and the old are sometimes called the "sandwich generation." It is rare for three or more generations to share living quarters, but it is far from rare for them to be dependent on each other in a variety of ways, even when they maintain separate households.

Concerns have been raised that refilled nests are a crisis for those whose homes are being refilled, struggling as they are with work, caring for elders, and looking after themselves, their homes, and their communities. The common perception seems to be that young people are sponging off parents and are lay-abouts. Recent research by Mitchell (1998) shows that this is an incorrect presumption. Generations living together in families provide mutual support and generally get along well. Middle generations receive valued companionship and the satisfaction of facilitating their child's transition into adulthood.

On the other side, adult children receive a number of valuable services, such as free or low-cost housing, food, access to a car perhaps. In other research (Mitchell & Gee, 1996a), even marital satisfaction is unaffected by the presence at home of adult children, provided the kids do not leave and return home multiple times.

Young adults are more likely to leave the parental home when they live in stepfamilies than when they live in either single-parent or two-parent biological families (Mitchell, 1994). This raises the important question of long-term implications for social inequalities. If some young adults increase their disadvantage by leaving the family home earlier than others, then the ultimate outcome could be widening social inequalities. If combined with early pregnancies, early family starts, or leaving school to support oneself, the long-term consequences are magnified.

In terms of social policy, it seems that the family home is becoming a kind of safety net for youth who cannot establish themselves in independent residences (Mitchell & Gee, 1996b). Families that cannot afford, in economic or social terms, to take adult children into their homes may be forced to cut the net for their children. In times of sharp reductions in social transfers, this may force the young people to seek low-wage employment rather than education or training in order to support themselves. "Not being able to return to the security and comforts of home could have a devastating effect on the lives of young adults who are not psychologically prepared to be launched as adults" (Gee & Mitchell, 1996b: 68).

With respect to older relatives living with those in mid-life, the issues are remarkably similar. In Canada, with reductions in health-care dollars, those who are hospitalized return home "quicker and sicker." This often means, for elders, temporary or permanent reliance on their adult children for assistance.

Debate Box 11.1   CLUTTERED NESTS: LIVING AT HOME AS AN ADULT
Which side of the debate do you fall on?

I am AGAINST living at home as an adult

- The transition to adulthood is not successful until you are supporting yourself and living independently. Living at home in your twenties or thirties hinders your ability to become independent and to learn how to live in the adult world and function in adult situations. Basically, it turns you into an adult who cannot do adult things.

- If your parents are always taking care of you, how will you ever learn how to take care of yourself? The best way to learn is by doing.

- People in previous generations started out with nothing when they moved out. Kids today want too much, too fast. They have unrealistic expectations about how they will live when they first start out on their own. The problem is not the competitiveness of today's society, it is that kids do not want to work too hard, nor do they want to do without any of the material luxuries to which they are accustomed.

- Because they consider themselves to be grownups, adult children living at home do not want to have respect for their parents' wishes. They want to get all the benefits of living at home without following any of the rules. This creates friction and conflict between parents and children and makes for unhealthy family relations.

- The only person benefiting from living at home is the adult child. It is unfair to the parents, especially mom, who still has the extra work associated with having a kid living at home. Once in adulthood, kids should be taking care of themselves, not leaving it to mom. When does she get her life back?

- From a parent's perspective, having an adult child living at home is not enjoyable—it is nothing like having an underage child living at home. The adult child takes advantage of the comforts of home, but the parent has no authority. It is a completely unbalanced situation—like running a free hotel.

I am FOR living at home as an adult

- The transition to adulthood just takes longer in today's world. People marry later and go to school longer. Expecting kids to move out of the house at eighteen is an archaic idea that has no relevance in today's world.

- The home environment is a very good place to learn about budgeting, saving, and other financial skills. Typical family activities and responsibilities help prepare kids for the "real world." So, living at home longer just means you will be better prepared when you finally do move out.

- The world is much more competitive now. It is that much harder to get established. Staying at home until you are ready and well prepared is an important strategy. Otherwise, you'll just flounder and struggle. In this sense, living at home to save money, to go to school, to recover from an ended relationship, or for other reasons makes perfect sense.

- Your twenties and thirties can be very trying times, with big choices to make and major things happening. If your parents see what happens in your everyday life, they are better able to be a resource for you when you need help. Is that not what families are for, after all? Helping out and building closeness can strengthen family relations.

- Adult children are not teenagers, where parent–child conflict is common. Adult children can get along very well with their parents because they are old enough to appreciate them again. They become friends and equals with their parents. This makes for a cooperative home environment.

- From a parent's perspective, having an adult child at home is enjoyable. You get to share in their day-to-day life, the child helps out with the chores, and it is just one more person you get to see and visit with during the day. It is a good situation on both sides.

New Kinds of Close Relations

New ways to be close to those we care about are always emerging. The push may be shifting job situations, changing expectations of what a close relationship is, or a crisis of some sort.

In Chapter 3, we mentioned briefly that **"living apart together"** (LAT relationships) is of growing interest, mainly so far to European sociologists. This new kind of close relation may not be so new, as we saw in Chapter 2. In the fur trade in Canada, in the search for jobs, couples have often been separated by great distance in the past. What is new now is a change in expectations, at least by an increasing number of couples, that establishing a serious relationship means sharing a home.

When we think about living together apart, for the most part our minds turn to high powered jet-setting couples whose demanding jobs don't allow them to live in the same place. We also tend to imagine that couples such as this commute short distances to work, perhaps in a neighbouring city. Both of these images have some truth to them, but we shall see that there is more, much more, to living apart together in the 2000s.

"Shortly after my husband and I first met, I moved to London, England. He worked in Seattle and had an apartment in Vancouver" (Schmelke, 2002: n.p.).

"When Brett McQuade leaves for work each Monday morning, he kisses his wife, Katie, goodbye and heads for the airport in Columbus, Ohio, their hometown. His commute is a little longer than the average employee's—about 500 miles to New York City, where he puts in four 12-hour days until it's time to fly home again each Thursday night" (Franklin, 1999: n.p).

These couples defy the expectation that couples who are committed to each other live together happily ever after. These are couples together, living apart. They are part of a growing trend, as more women and men in couple relationships both have high-powered demanding careers, but not in the same place. What's good for one spouse's career, in terms of promotion or opportunity, may not benefit the other spouse's career. The compromise is commuting. Increasing numbers of corporate relocations involve commuter marriages or relationships. Linda Stroh, a professor of Industrial Relations at Loyola University in the U.S., estimates that about 7 percent of corporate relocations involve commuting relationships (Stroh, 2003). And, commuting couples are common among academics as well since it is difficult sometimes for two professors to find suitable jobs in the same university.

Living together apart certainly has its challenges. Among the greatest is maintaining the couple connection while being apart so much of the time. However, research shows that LATs are not all challenges. Work is concentrated into a work period, Stroh (2003) so that when the spouses are together they can focus more completely on each other and their relationship.

Not all LATs, however, are younger, high-powered couples. An interesting trend is for older couples to live in LATs. One study in Sweden (Borell & Carlsson,

2002) finds that the "young old" (those in their 60s and 70s) are actively involved in living together apart. It works for couples who may be lonely, who rely on each other for companionship and support, but who do not wish to marry or to set up housekeeping together on a permanent basis. What is interesting about this trend is that it is older people who are on forefront of inventing ways to be close in relationships without compromising their strong desires to live their own lives.

A crisis, such as a life-threatening illness, can challenge one's idea of family and precipitate new kinds of close relations. One study of the perceived families of persons living with HIV/AIDS reveals exciting new family options (Wong-Wylie & Doherty-Poirier, 1997). When a number of people with HIV/AIDS were asked who or what they considered to be family, the results were surprising.

For this group of respondents, family as process was paramount. To be considered family, an individual must have *a reciprocal relationship* with the defining person (the HIV/AIDS person), and must be *accepting, supportive,* a source of *health and wellness resources,* and an *inspirational influence.* What kinds of people met these criteria for the respondents? They listed seven categories of people as comprising their created families (not every respondent had family from each category): families of origin, health-care professionals, friends, other people with HIV/AIDS, deceased friends, family caregivers, and valued material objects.

Some specific examples fill in the human faces and the diversity of created family. One male respondent with HIV/AIDS saw his family as large and diverse. His closest family consisted of his partner (male), his daughter and his partner's daughter, and his ten good friends, both male and female (two of whom were deceased). Beyond that, family to him was members of the HIV/AIDS Society, his parents and their siblings and friends, numbering thirteen in all, and then his grandparents on both sides, three of whom were also deceased. Another respondent (female) saw her in-laws as being as important to her as family as her husband and father. Her many friends, both gay and straight (four of whom also had HIV/AIDS) were also part of her created family.

Another included his physician in his self-defined family in an equal place with his wife and son. In his case, all but one of the friends included in his family definition also had HIV/AIDS. Significantly, he specifically excluded some members of his blood family, such as his mother, from his family definition. Yet another person with HIV/AIDS defined his family as consisting of computers, bridge, his ex-partner, and the "gay world" writ large, only incidentally noting his mother, brother, and sister.

These findings emphasize the limitations of assuming we know what family is, or examining families by structure alone. Family processes matter, and we all possess the power to define family for ourselves. Most importantly, this study shows that family, however we define it, is becoming more rather than less important as this century and millennium draws to a close. This is a point we have made throughout this book in a variety of ways, and with numerous examples.

It need not take the crisis of HIV/AIDS for us to create new kinds of families. Many of us create families for ourselves—in a new land, in situations where we have lost our families through war or time, when we have irresolvable disputes with families, or when our memories of our families of origin are too horrid to forgive. In these cases, and endless others, we make families of our friends, our neighbours, our communities, those with whom we share something important, or even our pets, plants, work, computers, and sporting equipment.

Concluding Remarks

We have explored multiple and varied transitions and innovations in family in this chapter. With family being placed increasingly into the realm of ideology and politics, it sometimes seems as if different approaches to family are in competition for our hearts. The transitions and new kinds of close relations discussed here are not the full list of possible ways that family life changes and that we change family for ourselves. Nor are they arranged like a smorgasbord for us to choose what we like best. For most of us, the kinds of families we live in choose us. This is true for family change across the life course. It is also true for gay and lesbian families. And it is true in many single-parent families, because sometimes, as the old phrase has it, life happens. We do not necessarily make informed and deliberate choices about the ends of marriages or relationships. Sometimes the choice is not ours, but our partner's or spouse's. Sometimes, we flee from violence or an intolerable situation to something unknown but safer.

In our various kinds of families, however, we do make choices. We engage in and develop processes that define us as families. We try to do our best within the opportunities and constraints society offers. It is these choices that matter most to our outcomes and the outcomes of our children, and to our happiness. It is not the shape our families take.

In the contest over which kind of family is preferable or most sanctioned by society or religions, we can lose track of the reality that all of us in families are sharing and caring for each other. Single and two-parent families, for example, are not the great divide. Nor are heterosexual and gay/lesbian families. The similarities in daily family living far outweigh the differences.

CHAPTER SUMMARY

This chapter discusses transitions to different family situations of many sorts: singlehood, one-parent families, second relationship or remarriage, stepfamilies, empty nests, flights from family situations into new ones, and inventive and new kinds of families. We learn that some transitions can bring new ways to behave and to live in close relations, or fresh starts. Others could better be called stale starts, since they merely lead to a repetition of old patterns and of old relational problems.

Family transitions and new families are not new phenomena in human society. With large-scale immigration and high death rates in the past in North America, many single-parent families and orphans existed.

The perils of some transitions in family such as to single parenthood include high risks of poverty for single mothers and their children after separation and divorce. Similar risks exist for women who choose to have children on their own without partners, a phenomenon growing in popularity. At the same time, teens who become pregnant are much more likely to keep their babies rather than giving them up for adoption, as in the past, which creates risks of poverty and lifetime or long-term underachievement among young mothers. Adoption of children from other countries can have perils as well; the children face the cultural challenges of adapting to the new family's customs and the lingering effects of trauma experienced in early childhood.

Becoming a parent without a partner as a deliberate choice is a new kind of family, one which makes for multiple kinds of parenthood and families. Parenting arrangements on separation and divorce also create new kinds of parents, most notably in shared parenting situations in which a non-residential parent is involved in active parenting. The good news here is that families can extend beyond the walls of a household.

Remarriage is more common for men than for women; for both, the risks of divorce are higher with a second marriage. Social pressures toward remarriage are sometimes more ideological than material; people want to be like other couples in society and to avoid stigma. Cohabitation after divorce is growing as the family of choice in Canada, particularly in Quebec.

Blended families are increasing in Canada and pose challenges to the ways we think of families, for numerous reasons. New vocabularies to describe relationships must be invented. And the numbers of familial relationships both inside and outside the household multiply.

We learn that not all family transitions are choices. Some people flee from abuse, or from culturally sanctioned violence into new lives, in the process creating new families.

Living solo is a growing option for many people who maintain close family ties but not in their own households. Counter to this is the sandwich family, which involves both youth and elders living together with the middle generation, or cluttered nests, a variant on this theme where youth either never leave the family home or return home to live.

With aging, families change and family transitions are made. Changing times have enabled post-gender families to develop and some same-sex families to live more openly.

KEY TERMS

Artificial insemination A process of introducing semen into a woman's body without sexual intercourse; can be a medical process but may not be.

Binuclear family A term used to describe a blended family, or a family where the spouses each bring children and non-residential parents into a new family. This term enables the capturing of the concept of family as extending beyond household.

Blended family Typically describing a family comprising two previously married spouses, with children, who marry each other and bring their children together in a new family.

Custom of the country/ *à la façon de la pays* The long-standing practice among early fur traders in Canada to take Aboriginal wives, who were known as "country wives."

In vitro fertilization Generally known as test-tube fertilization; conception that occurs by bringing together ova and sperm in medical procedures.

Intergenerational contagion A process by which trends that begin in one generation may be adopted by other generations. An example is cohabitation, which was mostly a youthful phenomenon but has now been adopted by people of all generations.

Living apart together (LAT) Couples who are committed to each other but do not live together, previously called commuter relationships.

POSSLQ Person of the opposite sex sharing living quarters.

Post-gender families Families in which the division of labour is not based on gender.

PSSSLQ Person of the same sex sharing living quarters.

SNAF An acronym meaning standard North American family, or mother, father, two kids, and usually a dog or a cat.

Union libre Widely used term for common-law union in Quebec.

SUGGESTED READINGS

Castellano, Marlene Brant. 2002. *Aboriginal Family Trends: Extended Families, Nuclear Families, Families of the Heart.* Ottawa: The Vanier Institute of the Family www.vifamily.ca, accessed December 30, 2002. Written by an elder of the Mohawk Nation, former Chair of Native Studies at Trent University, this is a passionate and engaging look at resilience among Aboriginal families. It has stories of real people, among them Castellano's brother, Lloyd, father of six who struggled throughout his life with alcohol and drug problems but managed to endure, as well as trend data on Aboriginal families. An appendix has health trends.

Connidis, Ingrid Arnet. 2001. *Family Ties and Aging.* Thousand Oaks, CA: Sage. A book about family relationships in middle and later life. Changes in family structures over time and the life course, the extent of contact with family, family ties as avenues for exchanging support, and the quality of family life as families age are considered. Key in this book is the integration of theory with research findings.

Eichler, Margrit. 1997. *Family Shifts: Families, Policies and Gender Equality.* Toronto: Oxford. This book introduces and explores the various models of family. It reveals how complex families have become in their everyday lives and how many family relationships now exist. A key point, emphasized and demonstrated throughout the book, is that family and household are not synonymous.

Risman, Barbara J. 1998. *Gender Vertigo: American Families in Transition.* New Haven, Connecticut: Yale University Press. An examination of new kinds of families where gender is not the primary basis for family life. The concept of post-gender families enables us to see families in new light, with new possibilities.

REVIEW QUESTIONS

1. Give two examples of how immigration can produce new ways to be family.

2. Is it true that second families and ways to be family other than the nuclear family began largely in the 1970s?

3. Define the term "Quebec widow," common in Ontario earlier in this century.

4. Why is it expectable now that people will live in multiple kinds of families over their lives?

5. Which family members tend to maintain communications and ties among family members across households most?

6. Are men or are women better at living alone?

7. What are some of the problems with the way we measure single parenthood?

8. What are the reasons single mothers often experience poverty?

9. In what age group is childbearing outside marriage growing fastest?

10. What are some problems in comparing blended families with other nuclear families?

DISCUSSION QUESTIONS

1. In what ways were widows in the past similar to and different from single mothers today?

2. Are there other ways than those discussed here by which fresh starts in families can occur?

3. What are some of the challenges faced by families in which parents live separately but continue to be active in parenting?

4. What can all of us do to try to ensure that children from single-parent families are encouraged and not stigmatized?

5. What would happen if single mothers one day were no longer stigmatized? Would poverty among this group lessen?

6. Why are more women deliberately seeking to bear a child outside of marriage or a committed relationship?

7. Discuss some of the pressures to remarry after divorce. What implications they might have for second marriages?

8. What are the future implications of an increasing number of divorced older people?

9. Are changes in family part of family living or are they something new and different?

10. What are some insights gained into families and close relations by understanding more about gay and lesbian families? About post-gender families?

WEBLINKS

http://www.parentswithoutpartners.org/sup1.html
Parents without Partners
Facts about single-parent families.

http://nces.ed.gov/pubs97/97981.html
A U.S. article that shows that children in single-parent families are more likely to experience early school problems and are less likely to participate in early literacy activities than children in two-parent families.

http://www.ed.gov/PressReleases/10-1997/father.html
A U.S. article showing that children do better in school when their fathers are involved.

http://www.childtrends.org
Child Trends
A summary of key research findings on how social, economic, and cultural factors influence fathers' involvement with their children.

http://www.relationships.com.au/managing_sep/landing.asp
Relationship Australia
A discussion of managing separation for couples and families.

http://www.weber.edu/chfam/topics/nine.steps.html
Weber State University, Child and Family Services
Nine steps towards healthy stepfamilies.

CHAPTER TWELVE

A Glimpse into the Future:

Where Do Families Go From Here?

Chapter Outline

Introduction

We are nearing the end of a long and complex story about close relations. As we have said repeatedly, our close relations—especially our family relations—are intricate, varied, and always changing. We will finish by talking about likely changes to family life in the future, and the forces—especially, technological forces—behind those changes. In particular, the pace of technological change in the last decade has been daunting to even the most technologically aware people. This is captured well in *The Hitchhiker's Guide to Cybernomics* (1996: 8): "If cars had developed at the same pace as microprocessors over the past two decades, a typical car would now cost less than $5 and do 250 000 miles to the gallon."

This technological explosion is changing families in multifaceted ways. Reproductive technologies that let some people who are clinically infertile become parents raise basic questions. Equally challenging to many families are questions posed by medical technology that extends lives and close relations for longer than ever before. Marriages that have the potential to last 40, 50, or 60 years today must be nourished more carefully than marriages in the past, which for biological reasons could have lasted only 20 or 30 years.

Other questions arise from the cultural effects of technology. For example, routines such as family dinners—an important part of identity development—are becoming less common as families use microwave ovens and prepared, fast, or frozen foods to ease the time pressure that so many families experience today. Rather than sharing time together, family members may eat alone, standing in the kitchen, before racing off to the next activity. It might be many years before we will learn whether these changes have consequences for families, and what those consequences may be.

"Of all things, the future is the hardest to predict," Nobel Laureate John Polanyi said. Many predictions of the future—when reread years later—are more comical than accurate. Social scientists have had as little success as most others who have ventured guesses about the future. Demographers, for example, sometimes regarded as modern-day gurus because of their mathematical rigor, failed to predict both the baby boom and the subsequent baby bust. The Chief Statistician of Canada, Ivan Fellegi (1997: 28) notes, "High profile examples of misdiagnoses [of the future] abound." He then cites his personal favourite: "... the statement made by Lincoln Steffens, the American journalist, when he returned from a visit to the Soviet Union in 1919, 'I have seen the future; it works.'" Clearly, seeing the future, or at least seeing it with any precision is a major challenge.

Today, new technologies offer families new ways to start and prolong close relations, but they also pose new challenges to our relationships. We will explore some of these issues in this chapter. Trying to predict the long-term effects on families would be futile. However, it seems very likely that families will survive, as they have throughout the ages. Just as likely, technologies will transform them in fundamental ways.

In 50 or 100 years families will look the way we want them to look. As participants in the drama of human history, we will all have a say in creating families of the future. In another sense, that question is unanswerable, given the current state of sociological knowledge. All we can say for sure, at this point, is that certain factors that are larger than any of us are already changing family life. In this chapter, we focus on the new information technology as one example.

Just as earlier social inventions—the development of cities, factories, automobiles, telephones, and television—changed families in earlier times, information technologies—especially the computer, e-mail, and cyberspace—have already changed and will continue to change families within our own lifetimes. We cannot tell precisely how much or in what ways these technologies will impact family life. Nevertheless, we can make some educated guesses, based on available research findings.

Computers, and new information technology (from now on, IT) more generally, affect families in several ways (Hughes, Ebata, & Dollahite, 1999). First, they affect the culture as a whole and, thus, affect families indirectly. Second, IT affects the ways family members communicate with one another. Since

Table 12.1 INTERNET USERS: CROSS-COUNTRY PENETRATION: ADULTS USING INTERNET IN PAST 30 DAYS

COUNTRY	%	COUNTRY	%
USA	59	Urban Malaysia	23
Canada	56	France	22
Sweden	53	Urban Thailand	22
Australia	48	Urban Brazil	21
Switzerland	45	Urban Chile	20
Finland	44	Spain	18
Netherlands	40	Italy	16
Hong Kong	35	Urban Colombia	14
Japan	33	Turkey	14
Singapore	33	Urban Argentina	13
U.K.	33	Urban China	12
South Korea	31	Poland	11
Germany	29	Urban South Africa	9
Taiwan	29	Urban Egypt	8
Belgium	28	Philippines	8
Israel	27	Urban India	5
Urban Mexico	27	Urban Russia	5

Source: Angus Reid Group, Inc. The Face of the Web: Wave One. www.ipsos-reid.com/pdf/media/mr000322_ch.pdf.

communication is a central aspect of family life, as we saw in earlier chapters, new communication technology can change family lives appreciably. Third, IT is a means of teaching and therapy, giving people unequalled access to information and advice about family life. Finally, IT affects how and where we do our work. Let us consider each of these factors in turn.

The Connected Society

Today, we must recognize a new kind of community that is emerging due to new kinds of communications and, more importantly, an increase in global mobility and reduction in in-marriage. We must now consider *virtual communities*, especially close relations that exist in cyberspace. These close relations are characterized by infrequent face-to-face contact and regular contact through technology. Such virtual relations are becoming more common and will continue to do so.

Because of Canada's vast geography, its researchers have always been at the forefront of theorizing about long-distance communication technology and its effect on social organization. As a nation of vast distances and sparse population, Canada has always relied on transportation and communication technology to make social organization possible. The two key theorists in this area have been Harold Innis and Marshall McLuhan.

First, Innis (1958) argued that the transformation from oral to written cultures marked a transition from proximate, face-to-face governance to distant, imperial governance. Writing was the means by which laws were promulgated and enforced at a distance. Thus, writing supported global spread, empire-building, and cultural rationalization. A disciple of Innis, Marshall McLuhan (1962) argued that the transformation from written cultures to technologically mediated visual cultures (TV, movies, photographs) marked a transition from cool, reasoned, and inferential to "hot," compelling, and impressionistic information flow. Like writing, this information flow could cross great distances, so it was not out of line with empire building. What was different was the emotional, non-rational content.

"Modern" research on this topic began with the book *Network Nation* by Starr Roxanne Hiltz and Murray Turoff in 1978. Among other things, these authors predicted that by 1994 computerized conferencing would be a prominent form of communications in most organizations and as widely used in society as the telephone today. They also predicted that home recreational use of computer-mediated communication would make significant inroads into TV viewing patterns; psychologically and sociologically impact various group-communication objectives and processes; offer disadvantaged groups in the society opportunities to acquire the skills and social ties they need to become full members of the society; help individuals to form groups having common concerns, interests, or purposes; facilitate working at home; open the doors to new and unique types of services; and facilitate a richness and variability of human groupings and relationships.

Their writing provoked a great deal of comment and discussion by users of their pioneering EIES (Electronic Information Exchange System) in New Jersey. Such discussion continues today in the pages of *WIRED* magazine, among other places. Many have already commented on the addictive effects of computer-mediated communication on marriage and parenting ("Daddy spends all night on the computer talking to strangers and doesn't play with us any more"). Participants in EIES Peter and Trudi Johnson-Lenz went on to become experts on how electronic communications technologies can change interpersonal relations, especially in large organizations. The Lenzes have hundreds of useful publications on this and are major consultants in the area. By the 1990s, when a second edition of *Network Nation* was published, many of Hiltz and Turoff's predictions about e-mail use and computer-mediated communication had already come to pass.

In Canada, nearly all households have telephones, three out of four have cable television, one in seven has a cellular phone, and one of three have home computers (Dickinson and Sciadas, 1997), and these numbers are increasing quickly. (For purposes of comparison, a recent American survey estimates that 98 percent of American households have a television, 94 percent have a telephone, 81 percent have VCRs, 68 percent have cable television, and 44 percent have cellular phones. An estimated 37 percent have computers, and 19 percent are connected to the Internet (Hughes, Ebata, & Dollahite 1999: 5).) As a result, ever-speedier delivery of information, goods, and services has become a social fixation. Beepers, cell phones, and laptops connect ever more people, making them available around the clock. Quiet and privacy are nearly things of the past, no matter where a person is.

This electronic connectedness may turn out to be harmful: a guarantee of cultural homogeneity, preoccupation with information (*not* knowledge), faddishness, and dumbing down, or even a pathway to attention deficit disorder and outer-directedness. Electronic connectedness makes censorship and information management possible on a scale never before imaginable. Some researchers have associated frequent Internet use with less communication among members of one's household, declines in the size of one's social network, and increased depression and loneliness.

However, the connectedness may also be beneficial, as a means to weaken elite control over information and ensure that ordinary people can air their political, social, and cultural views more freely. Likely, this information revolution has both positive and negative effects: the two are not mutually exclusive.

Results of a three-year study by University of Toronto sociologists Barry Wellman and Keith Hampton reveal the daily social consequences of living in a highly wired, broadband neighbourhood. Their key finding is that living in a wired neighborhood with access to a high-speed local network encourages greater community participation, builds local relationships with neighbours and family, and helps maintain ties with friends and relatives living farther away. Wellman and Hampton refer to this combination of global and local activity as "glocalization."

They report that the Internet can encourage a growth in civic involvement that others have said is in decline in the Western world. Their work questions the view that people who spend more time on-line do so at the expense of contacts with their family and friends. Virtual relations, then, add to our social life; they do not distort or destroy it.

Unlike other studies that looked only at life on-line, Wellman and Hampton (see, for example Wellman and Hampton, 1999) looked at all people's relationships—in-person, by telephone, and on the Internet. They compared "wired" residents on a high-speed network, serving only their neighbourhood, with other "non-wired" residents living in the same neighbourhood. The community they studied, "Netville" (a pseudonym), is just outside greater Toronto. It was one of the world's first residential developments to be equipped with a broadband local network. Netville's local network gave participants more than 300 times the speed of ordinary dial-up modems and more than 10 times the speed of contemporary ADSL or cable modems. For two years, Netville residents enjoyed services that included high-speed Internet access, a videophone, an on-line jukebox, on-line health services, local discussion forums, and entertainment and educational applications.

Wellman and Hampton surveyed residents moving into and living in Netville. Residents there varied from beginner to expert in their degree of computer and Internet experience. Of the 109 homes that comprised Netville, 64 were connected to the local network while 45 remained unconnected.

The researchers found that residents with access to the high-speed local network recognize, talk to and visit with many more of their neighbours than do residents without this technology. Access to the local computer network introduces new methods of communication and increases communication with friends and relatives, and also with neighbours. More access to neighbours through the local network means that wired residents are much more likely to know neighbours living elsewhere in the suburb, not just those living right near them. A neighborhood e-mail list increases the amount of in-person socializing, as residents organize parties, barbecues, and other local events on-line. Besides more social activities with neighbours, wired residents also have more contact and exchange more help with friends and relatives living *outside* their neighbourhood.

Reflecting on the sheer increase in communication reveals the pluses and minuses of this new technology. On the one hand, increased connectedness provides more and easier opportunities to contact friends, neighbours, acquaintances, spouses, children, parents, and siblings. Whether this is a good thing is hard to say, because communication is itself a two-edged sword. It can please us or displease us, do us good or harm. Higher-frequency communication with someone we hate will not add to our well-being. Receiving dozens or hundreds of unwanted e-mail messages or faxes a day is a nuisance. The new connectedness may intrude on family life, disturbing family rituals and cohesion. So, communication technologies will have unpredictable effects, at least for a while.

Figure 12.1 PURPOSE OF INTERNET USE

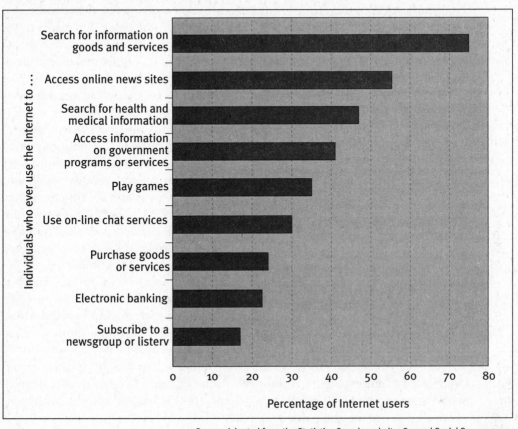

Source: Adapted from the Statistics Canada website, General Social Survey, 2000, www.statcan.ca/english/research/56F0006XIE/56F0006XIE2000001.pdf.

Intimacy and Technology

It is hard to say whether intimacy is decreasing as a result of the various changes described. Moreover, changes in intimacy that do occur depend on the *kind* of close relationship. Among lovers, it appears that serial intimacy has increased in the West, with easier divorce and easier cohabitation as an alternative to marriage. Among grown children, filial obligations towards aged parents appear to have weakened, although data continue to show children—especially, daughters—provide their parents with care and support. Among younger parents and their young children, it is unclear whether intimacy has weakened. Likewise, we do not know how the closeness of sibling relationships has changed in the last century. The changes may be greater for brothers than sisters, for half-siblings than for full-siblings, and so on. The research on this question has yet to be done.

What *is* known is relatively slight, especially in relation to the role of technological mediation of these trends. Haythornthwaite (2000, 2001) has shown, for example, that among strongly tied (i.e., closely related) people, easy, cheap technologies such as e-mail do not replace traditional, harder, and more expensive communication media, for example face-to-face meetings or telephone calls. Closely related communicators use a variety of technologies. They use new as well as old technologies, for example, and their frequency of communication by all means is high. A large amount of communication results; more, and more varied, communication strengthens a relationship. By contrast, weakly tied communicators rely on one medium and are less motivated to explore new technologies. Their relationships remain distant as a result.

Perhaps the most dangerous aspect of changes resulting from the new technology is what observers have called the "digital divide." Currently, access to and familiarity with much new communication technology that would assist close relations at a distance is distributed unequally by age, gender, education, income, neighbourhood (rural urban, rich poor), region, and country. Statistics Canada (1999) finds that people living in households with higher incomes typically have more access to computer communications. The socioeconomic status of a person's residential area also affects his or her access to computer communications, by affecting their availability in schools, libraries, and other public places. This conflation of household income effects with neighbourhood effects results in what Fong and Wellman (2000) have called a "double digital divide."

Such connectedness has a huge impact on people's futures. In a post-industrial, information-based economy, connectedness affects people's employability—their chance of getting a good job, or any job at all. The connectedness is also critical for participation in our dominant institutions—schools, workplaces, and public service organizations among others. Indirectly, this has an impact on family life, since as we have stressed in other chapters, the demands of work (including schoolwork) always influence the quality of close relations.

At present, we cannot predict how quickly the differences in technology access will shrink. They may shrink quickly, given the rapid spread in skills and steep decline in technology prices. Evidence from Australia (Stevenson, personal communication), for example, indicates that women in remote areas have taken to the Internet much more readily than men—mostly farmers and agricultural mechanics who are reluctant to go back to a classroom to learn computer literacy. Rural women often have to do the accounts and they seem more enthusiastic to learn, whether computers or anything else. Likewise, women seem much more inclined than men to use the Internet to build close relations. Men using the Internet see it as a functional tool, rather than a personal help.

So in the end, the computer may provide traditionally disadvantaged people with new opportunities to improve their social positions. This will improve family life, as well as changing the face of work and community life.

Technology and family development changes in technology that simplify contact among family and friends are likely to contribute to the quality and cohesion of relationships. Over the last 150 years, changes in communications

Table 12.2 INTERNET USE, 1997–2001

	1997	1998	1999	2000	2001
		ALL HOUSEHOLDS[1] %			
Purpose of use					
E-mail	13.3	19.3	26.3	37.4	46.1
Electronic banking	3.1	5.2	8.0	14.7	21.6
Purchasing goods/services	1.5	2.5	5.5	9.6	12.7
Medical/health information	...	9.6	15.6	22.9	30.1
Formal education/training	...	6.8	9.2	19.0	22.9
Government information	...	8.2	12.7	18.9	25.6
Search for employment	...	...	...	12.2	16.2
General browsing	13.6	17.6	24.3	36.2	44.3
Playing games	...	7.8	12.3	18.2	24.4
Chat groups	...	5.7	7.5	11.0	13.7
Obtaining/saving music	...	...	7.8	17.8	23.3
Listening to radio	...	...	5.0	9.3	12.3
Find sports-related information	...	...	...	17.3	22.1
Financial information	...	...	...	18.5	22.8
View the news	...	...	...	20.4	26.2
Travel information/arrangements	...	...	...	21.9	27.4
Other Internet services	2.2	2.6	10.0	17.7	21.1

... Not applicable.   1. The term "All households" refers to the population as a whole.

Source: Adapted from the Statistics Canada website, CANSIM II, Table 358-0006 and Catalogue Number 56F0004MIE. Last modified: April 17, 2002, www.statcan.ca/english/Pgdb/arts52a.htm.

and transportation technologies have made contact among kin and friends, whether they live near one another or great distances apart, less expensive, faster, and easier. As e-mail and Internet use become normal, everyday practices for the entire population, geographic constraints on social relationships continue to reduce. The spread of easy communication shrinks distances, and we can expect this shrinking of distance to continue.

Experts predict that one day the Internet could connect 600 million computer networks (Castells, 1996). Yet, despite the constant changes in the technological context of social relationships, most social theory bearing on the topic continues to assume that people form and maintain close relationships mainly through face-to-face interaction (Adams, 1998).

It was not until recently that people could travel or communicate with people who lived at a distance often enough to form a relationship with them. Accordingly, researchers who studied close relations focused on people who were geographically as well as emotionally close. Psychologists who studied interpersonal attraction, for example, focused on the importance of visual cues: how physical appearance plays a role in attraction, and what gestures and facial expressions people use to show involvement, for example (see Short, Williams, & Christie, 1976). Such stimuli are much less important in Internet chat rooms, where communicators cannot see each other. As a result, in the Internet age we need a new inventory of the ways people signal their characteristics, preferences, and qualities.

Comparing Communication Technologies

One strategy for studying the future of close relations and technology is by examining how technology has impacted close relations in the past. As we know from the history of the telephone, for example, new technologies have a way of rapidly crossing traditional social barriers and achieving wide adoption (Fisher, 1992). There may be no better way to predict the future effect of new technology on close relations at a distance than by reviewing the history of two recent communication technologies: the telephone and e-mail.

The Telephone

Social histories of the telephone (Pool, 1977; Fischer, 1992) show that, from the beginning, the telephone was used primarily for long-distance calling. Commercial interests advertised it as means to link family and friends, used largely by women for "kin-keeping." Like the automobile, the telephone was adopted rapidly throughout society. Despite some resistance, it quickly became a part of popular culture.

Compared with other means of conducting close relations at a distance, the telephone had many advantages. It was cheaper than distant travel. It enabled the speaker to avoid being seen by the listener, yet it created "symbolic proximity" for the two. It allowed escape from continued contact if one or both parties wished it. Beyond that, it allowed people to express their views in their own voices, was simple to use, and was as private as face-to-face communication. As a result, the telephone was adopted by everyone and used to maintain close relations, even at a distance. People quickly became dependent on the new communication instrument.

Surprisingly, despite its wide use, over the twentieth century the telephone's effects on social life were modest. There is no systematic evidence that the telephone has changed close relations. At most, the telephone facilitated them by keeping people in touch between face-to-face meetings.

Note, finally, that the telephone—like other forms of communication—has had both positive and negative effects on close relations. Researchers (Applewhite &

Segal, 1990) have studied the ways peacekeeping troops in the Sinai (in Israel) use telephones on the front lines. Using the telephone to talk to parents and spouses maintains social support systems while on duty. However, a large minority report negative experiences associated with their telephone calls. They report feeling sad after a phone call or angry about being in the Sinai, report getting phone calls they wish they had not received, or receiving disturbing news from home. Such experiences can be demoralizing and distract soldiers from their responsibilities. Yet, given the opportunity, people use telephones and other communication technology, all of which have the capacity to make them happy and to make them anxious or sad.

Likewise, survey data from nearby 500 civilian wives of soldiers who were posted in Somalia for Operation Restore Hope reveal that the mechanics of soldier–family communications affected spouses' adaptation to the stresses of the operation (Bell, Schumm, Knott, & Ender, 1999). Difficulty communicating with the soldier (particularly "connecting for the first time") was one of the most frequent problems that spouses experienced. Problems communicating during the mission not only predicted the level of spouse stress, but also affected either directly or through "spouse stress" several outcomes that are important to army planners. They included spouse support for the soldier remaining in the army, the soldier's intention to reenlist, spouse support for peacekeeping missions in general, and the family's adaptation to army life.

E-mail

In recent decades, we have all been exposed to a new means of communication over great distances—namely, e-mail. The advantages of e-mail are, in some cases, similar to those of the telephone. Like the telephone, e-mail is cheap—even cheaper than telephone communication and long-distance travel. It allows people to avoid being seen by the message recipient, yet it creates "symbolic proximity." Also like the telephone, e-mail allows escape from continued contact if that is desired.

Some of the advantages of e-mail are different from those of telephone. The sender can craft a message, as he or she can draft a letter but not a telephone conversation. Many phone conversations are chaotic, especially if they occur when not expected and we are in the middle of doing something else. E-mail, to the contrary, can be highly organized and to the point, systematic, and logical. E-mail gives one time to think and reflect. The sender can also distribute many copies of a message simultaneously, and await replies while carrying on with other tasks. E-mail is not as interruptive as the telephone, nor is it as dependent on both people being available at the same time.

However, e-mail is not without its disadvantages. Unlike the telephone, e-mail is a strictly print medium. The sender cannot express views in his or her own voice. It is a sensorily deprived or "cool" medium, permitting no touch, smell, sight, let alone sound. Relying on computer technology, e-mail is not as simple to use as the telephone, contributing to the "digital divide" we discussed earlier.

It's in the Mail

Hold onto your ballpoint pen Mr. Scrooge. Greeting cards are not the spirit of Christmas Past. Contrary to popular belief, the proliferation of e-mail has not yet managed to usurp greeting cards as the preferred mode of intimate communication during the annual holiday period.

A recent Ipsos-Reid survey revealed that receiving actual cards in the mail is a source of comfort to Canadians. E-mail just doesn't have the same personal touch.

Canada Post is as busy as ever picking up piles and piles of mail from boxes across the nation in time for Christmas delivery. Says Canada Post spokesman Chris Bartsch: "People have long said that greeting cards have faded in popularity because of the Internet, but we have never seen any evidence to support that."

In 2001, it peaked on Dec. 17 when more than 46 million pieces of mail entered the Canada Post mail stream. That high hasn't been hit yet this year, but Bartsch suspects it will happen this week.

So what are people sending? UNICEF Canada spokesman Jerry Seligman reports that old-master religious designs are big this year. Next up are cards featuring works of Canadian artists, especially art depicting Inuit life and retro imagery-cards depicting old-fashioned holiday scenes.

Source: *The Globe and Mail*, 2002. Saturday, December 14: Print Edition, p. L6. Reprinted with permission of The Globe and Mail.

Beyond that, e-mail carries a variety of dangers that are absent or controlled in other kinds of communication. For example, there is the danger of hasty, informal expression, called "**flaming**." This is encouraged by the absence of visual feedback from the message receiver. Faceless anonymity and the absence of the receiver lead to dangers of indiscretion, misunderstanding, and misquoting. The shield of visual and vocal anonymity may lead to non-conforming behaviour such as blunt disclosure, textual aggression, and self-misrepresentation, or can cause communicators difficulty in identifying or reaching shared opinions (see, for example, Kiester & Sproull, 1992). Other studies have found that the same shield of anonymity fosters greater self-disclosure and cancels out any negative outcomes.

The lack of temporal and spatial boundaries frees relationships and makes new relationships possible. This also makes relationships with on-line communicators possible for people formerly prevented from socializing—by a physical disability or agoraphobia, for example. However, the community feeling derived from cyber relations is, in many instances, illusory. At this time, we have no idea what net effect e-mail is having on close relations. On-line chat such as ICQ has become very popular and is used for a variety of types of communications. Because it is a real-time chat form of communication, it is presumably more active (or "hot") than e-mail.

Again surprisingly, despite its wide use the effects of e-mail on social life have been modest so far. There is no systematic evidence that e-mail has changed close relations. Like the telephone, e-mail has facilitated close relations by keeping people in touch between face-to-face meetings.

Some of this may be due to the lack of visual input, both on the telephone and on e-mail. Though many prefer the more anonymous e-mail, others await a technology that combines sound and sight. Such technology is currently in use, though it has not become commonplace. However, its weaknesses are already apparent and scientists are developing new technology that will provide more "natural" communication experiences in the form of three-dimensional tele-immersion.

The likely effects of communication technology on family life will vary with the stage in life cycle of the family and of particular family members. For example, families or family members who are particularly immobile—whether due to age, illness, or home caregiving responsibilities—will rely particularly heavily on new communication technology. Its availability will be particularly important in such cases. Yet, current studies of the Internet do not yet extend to all stages of family development. The elderly are almost absent from this literature, and there is little written about children. The most abundant information regarding children concerns parental fears about the on-line experiences their children might have and the resulting need to keep an eye on their computer use.

Research on relationships and Internet technology is just beginning. However, by applying the existing research, Adams (2002) is able to raise some basic questions about the likely effect of the new technology on family development. The basic premise of family development theory is that families continuously change with changes in social expectations, environmental constraints, and the demands of family members (e.g., biological, psychological, and social needs). As families change and restructure, they engage in *developmental tasks*, or activities that prepare them for upcoming stages.

Families are historical creatures, in the sense that the process of moving from one stage to another depends on earlier experiences (i.e., previous stages) and the length of time spent within a previous stage. Traditional "stages" include marriage without children, marriage with various aged children (e.g., infant, preschool, school age, adolescent, young adult), marriage with children that live outside the household, grandparenting, and marriage in late life. White (1991) has expanded these traditional stages to include divorce and remarriage, stages that people previously classified as "non-normative," or not widely accepted, but are now considered *"normative,"* or less deviant, family forms.

The growth of cohabitation and the rise of childbearing as a "discretionary option" have greatly increased the variety of family lives (Rowland, 1991). Even households with a married nuclear family structure often originate now in less traditional ways. With so many different kinds of family experiences, it makes no sense to speak of "the average family." Family development theory allows scholars to organize family experiences into specific categories while recognizing the dynamic nature of stage progression. This classification identifies different issues and opportunities likely to face families at distinct points of development. Individuals and families differ in their responses to IT, depending on their stage in the family life cycle.

A life-course approach helps us avoid some problems when thinking about the social effects of information technology. Extensive home use of the computer will likely affect some families more than others. For example, it could harm "early marriages"—newly formed couples and couples with no children or young children—more than post-retirement relationships that have been long established. Usually, "early marriages," particularly families with preschool children, need to invest a great deal of time in maintaining cohesion and solving new problems. They cannot afford to devote much time to computing (unless it is work-related and unavoidable), or marital quality could suffer. At this life stage, keeping in touch with aging parents who may have health problems may be less necessary too (cf. for example, White, 2001).

Busy working couples in established, loving relationships might rely on communication technologies to keep in touch with each other. They may send each other love notes while at work, communicate with each other while on work-related travel, even plan what to have for dinner. Communication technologies are also a means by which parents keep in touch with their children when they go to college or university. Increasingly, e-mail can be an important means of staying in touch with relatives in different parts of the world, as well as with aging parents.

As Adams (2002) points out, the primary research question offered by family development theory is, "How does technology influence family change over time?" More specifically, "How does the use of on-line communication influence the norms and roles of family members? How do families use technology in the developmental tasks that contribute to stage transitions? In what ways is the use of technology different across various stages of development and where is technology more influential? Does technology affect or contribute to the experience of off time, or non-normative stage transitions? How is the use of technology in early development qualitatively different from its use in later stages?"

Finally, "How does family development occur in families equipped with technology allowing continuous availability and how does this process compare to families without access to these tools?" Note that we could pose parallel questions about the development of friendship groups or networks—indeed, any networks of close relations. These are all questions we will have to answer before we can predict the future impact of IT on close relations, and we are not close to finding these answers yet.

Effects of New Communication Technology

We already know that the new technology affects how family members communicate with one another. However, researchers disagree about whether the overall effect of IT on family and community life is positive or negative. Early research has emphasized the tendency of computers and other IT to isolate families, individuate family members—to separate them from one another in individual activities—and even produce addictive behaviour.

In some quarters this debate continues (see, for example, the debate between Silverman, Rierdan, Shapiro, Kiesler, & Kraut in the pages of *American Psychologist*, September 1999 [780–84]). Among researchers who note a link between extensive Internet use and depression or loneliness, some argue that the Internet is to blame, by separating the user from sources of support and sociability. Here is an extreme example.

Young (1996) reports the case of a homemaker, aged 43, who is addicted to using the Internet. This non-technologically oriented woman with a reportedly happy home life and no prior addiction or psychiatric history would log in first thing in the morning, constantly check her e-mail throughout the day, and stay up late using the Internet, sometimes until dawn. She had an estimated average usage of 50 to 60 hours online per week. Significant family problems arose: her two teenage daughters felt ignored. Her husband of 17 years complained about the cost (up to $400 per month) and about his wife's loss of interest in their marriage. She, for her part, denied there was a problem and refused to seek treatment. She separated from her husband within a year after the purchase of her home computer, and remains estranged from her daughters.

Few cases of computer use are this extreme. We should not take this case as a model for all computer use and its effects on families. Some observers reverse the explanation, believing that depression and loneliness cause an extreme use of the Internet, as depressed lonely people look for new sources of support and sociability. Others still argue that the relationship is spurious: a third factor—call it "X"—causes some people both to feel depressed and to invest extreme amounts of time in the Internet. In the end, we cannot say whether excessive Internet use is a cause of depression, an effect, neither, or both. We cannot choose among these views without data that so far have been difficult to get, namely, longitudinal data on matched subjects. So the debate goes on.

Note, further, that there have been similar debates about the role of television. Some researchers have accused television too of producing isolation, loneliness, and depression when used extensively. Not surprisingly, since we assume that the two technologies feed similar needs, some have wondered whether computer usage will replace television viewing. Recent research (Coffey & Stipp, 2000) finds that, so far, it does not, and notes that television viewing often increases and modifies computer activity and Internet use.

Cybersex and Commitment

A special aspect of the family communication issue concerns computer-based dating and mating, cybersex, and what some call "emotional adultery" (Collins, 1999).

Cyberspace offers people unparalleled opportunities to meet and grow emotionally close to total strangers who may be at a considerable distance (Merkle & Richardson, 2000). This process completely reverses the usual practices of dating and mating. Usually, we meet people who are nearby and similar to us socially. Proximity and physical attraction are key in starting a relationship. We usually have a good opportunity to assess strangers physically, psychologically, and even morally before "falling in love" with them and revealing our intimate selves. However, in cyberspace, we meet people who are often faraway and sometimes unlike us socially. Physical attraction plays little if any part in our plunge into intimate, sometimes highly sexualized, and self-disclosing relationships. Our only means of assessing our "pen pals" is through the written word (or sometimes, pictures). This increases the likelihood that we will reveal our intimate selves early and "fall in love" without knowing the other person well.

The "self-disclosure" may be candid, masked, or downright devious. Many report adopting bogus names and identities for their interactions. Deception is part of the fun of cyberspace, a type of social gaming. Thus, some males take on the identities of females, and vice versa. The possibilities for play and deception are almost infinite. Interestingly, however, research (Kendall, 1998) on people's self-presentation in MUDDS (chat rooms organized for game playing) finds that gender continues to structure social interactions in remarkably conventional ways. At least in the early stages of contact, men in cyberspace tend to act in traditionally male ways, emphasizing the sexual aspects of their relations with women.

However, some relationships go beyond this, resulting in "virtual affairs" and "emotional adultery." Because of the inverted developmental sequence of a computer-mediated relationship, people often invest more time and reveal themselves more freely than they typically do in face-to-face relationships. Merkle and Richardson (2000) speculate that this greater investment may result in a stronger commitment to work through disagreements, to maintain the relationship. So, not only do Internet relationships develop more quickly but they are also more resistant to break-ups.

These cyber-relationships are alluring because they eliminate some of the difficulties we normally encounter interpersonally. A sense of distance and apparent anonymity reduces the anxiety people feel about showing their feelings or fears in face-to-face relationships. As a result, people reveal themselves fully only in the deepest and most intimate relationships—typically in those relationships that have survived a test of time. However, in computer-mediated relationships (CMRs), people come to know each other intimately much more quickly than they do in face-to-face relationships. Sometimes, they get to know each other as well as if they were having an intense sexual affair in person.

Collins (1999) asks "Should we regard cyber sexual affairs as a species of adultery, an impermissible form of sexual betrayal, and cyber-romances as a comparable species of emotional infidelity?" She concludes that, in the end, all that really matters is "practical fidelity." Collins (*op. cit.*: 254) defined a committed relationship as each participant being "devoted bodily to helping the other as much as s/he is able" and "enacting in the minutiae of everyday life a respectful concern for the other as an equal." From her point of view, we should not now regard virtual relationships as having the same significance as body-based relationships.

Not everyone would agree, however. In the view of some, computer-mediated relationships run the risk of producing emotional betrayal: a violation of the trust or expectations on which couples base an ongoing marital relationship. Some would argue that cybersex and cyber-romances run a real risk of establishing new relationships that can pass from being virtual to being "practical." (By now, many of us know people who met their mates, or left their spouses, because of cyber-romance.) In her classic work on divorce, Diane Vaughan (1985) emphasizes that a key stage in the breakdown of a marriage is the establishment, by one partner, of an alternate social world. Fantasy worlds sometimes become real worlds, and cyber-romances represent (for some) defects in a marital relationship that they had not previously noticed, or that they prefer to ignore. Their partners feel betrayed by Internet intimacy because they feel that all intimacy must remain within the boundaries of the marital relationship.

We need research to learn how people in computer-mediated relationships define the boundaries of betrayal and whether emotional infidelity against the computer partner is as destructive to these relationships as it is to face-to-face relationships. Computer-mediated relationships, by largely eliminating the sexual aspect of betrayal and emphasizing the emotional aspect, may largely redefine how our culture thinks about fidelity. For the time being, family therapists need to recognize that computer-mediated entry into rapid emotional intimacy may be a risk to any relationship where one or both partners are dissatisfied. If our culture views this as emotional betrayal, it will have the consequences of emotional betrayal. That is, it will contribute to the break-up of marriages and other close relations.

Technology for Caregiving

Cyberspace is not only a place for meeting and mating with strangers, or keeping in touch with family and friends. It is also a storehouse of useful information for people with problems. Increasingly, people look to cyberspace for the answers to questions about health, jobs, and family relations. Smith (1999) notes that "the new electronic frontier" has already changed family lives in important ways. For example, for caregivers who cannot get the support they need from doctors, support groups, or social networks, technology may play a greater role. In recent years, researchers have paid particular attention to the possible uses of the telephone and Internet as means of delivering social support.

In one study of caregivers to AD victims, researchers compared two programs. In one, four or five caregivers held regular supportive conversations with one another over the telephone. In the other, researchers provided taped informational lectures over the telephone. After three months, caregivers in *both* programs showed less psychological distress, more perception that they were receiving social support, and more satisfaction with the support they were receiving. After six months, the gains had levelled off or declined; caregiver burden and social conflict increased again (Goodman, 1990). As between the two programs, participants learned more by listening to the informational lectures.

Health professionals have sometimes set up telephone support groups for AIDS caregivers. Use of the telephone gives people a sense of confidentiality not afforded in face-to-face groups. It also supports people who are isolated because of the stigma associated with HIV/AIDS and the lack of support networks in their communities (Wiener, 1998). In one program, caregivers in semi-structured groups made eight conference calls to exchange information about resources and coping strategies. Participants report feeling satisfied with the group experience (Meier, Galinsky, & Rounds, 1995). However, results of the experiment were mixed. Participants felt less isolated and more personally effective, but their sense of social support and coping did not improve (Rounds, Galinsky, & Despard, 1995).

Like telephone-mediated groups, computer-mediated support groups have the potential to serve clients who are unable or unwilling to participate in traditional face-to-face support groups. Computer-mediated groups offer advantages. They include the elimination of time and distance barriers, lack of group size restrictions, increased variety and diversity of support, anonymity, pre- and post-group support, opportunity for expression through written communication, and potential training experiences for group leaders (Finn, 1995).

As a result, health professionals have adapted computer technology to a variety of self-help/mutual aid groups, including computer-based 12-step groups for problems with alcohol, narcotics, eating, gambling, compulsive sexuality, relationships, smoking, and others. Where addiction problems are concerned, the benefits of going on-line, besides those previously mentioned, include greater access to support, dispersal of dependency, meeting the needs of people with esoteric concerns, reduction of barriers related to social status cues, increased participation of reluctant members, improved relational communication, and better communication by people with interpersonal difficulties.

However, computer-mediated groups also have disadvantages. Potential disadvantages of going on-line include destructive interactions, lack of clear and accountable leadership, promoting social isolation, limited access to noncomputer-using populations, and lack of research about benefits and user satisfaction (Finn, 1996; Finn & Lavitt, 1994).

Here is how the computer-mediated process works, at its best: In one study, for three months six breast cancer patients used home computers to connect to a bulletin board on which they read messages from and posted messages to each other. They had no difficulty learning to use the computer and used it an average of one hour a week. The patients discussed their medical conditions, shared personal concerns, and offered one another support—as in traditional face-to-face support groups (Weinberg, Schmale, Uken, & Wessel, 1996). Participants in this study felt that the experience instilled hope, group cohesion, and universality (i.e., sisterhood). For all these reasons, the process was considered helpful overall (Weinberg, Uken, Schmale, & Adamek, 1995).

The success of computer-based communication in this area may account for the existence of an ongoing Breast Cancer List, a discussion group on the Internet. List members exchange information, social support, and personal empowerment (Sharf, 1997).

A great deal of information relevant to family life is available on-line. A survey of family life education sites on the Web (Elliott, 1999) reveals that many sites are already available in certain topic areas, such as parenting and human development. Fewer sites are to be found in other areas, such as family resource management. In time, people will fill these gaps. One area that deserves more attention is devoted to fathering skills, since men are disproportionately common users of the Internet, and men are known to play too small a role in their children's development (Morris, Dollahite, & Hawkins, 1999).

The Internet also has a role to play in family therapy, especially in treating families that are isolated or whose members are geographically separated. Consider the problems associated with home care, and how new information technology might help home caregivers. Again, we need to emphasize that, while all families have difficulty providing homecare, some families have more difficulty than others.

Consider the families of children who rely on ventilators to help them breathe. When they are discharged from hospital to home care, often because long-term institutional facilities are not available, their families suffer an enormous burden. Typically, one family member, usually the mother, bears most of the hardship. Poor, young, single mothers face an almost impossible responsibility here. Socially and economically marginal families can scarcely cope. Cohen (1999) writes "Prior to having a technology-dependent child at home, marginalized families may have had little sustained social contact with the world beyond their own family, neighbourhood, and church. Poverty, lack of transportation, limited education, and unemployment effectively isolate them from mainstream society."

Imagine, then, how difficult it is when a technology-dependent child comes home. The child on a ventilator, for example, needs a regular routine of care, bathing, dressing, meals, play, and naps. Families may require group and individual psychosocial support as well as nursing assistance to adapt to this situation. Computers and Internet-based facilities provide the information and support that such families will need.

Therapists continue to try new computerized methods in their areas of specialization. For example, CHESS is a promising health information and decision support for patients and families. It is a stand-alone, guided computer system that helps caregivers cope with conditions like Alzheimer's. With this system, caregivers use a personal computer at home to obtain brief answers to many standard health questions, and detailed articles and descriptions of services they may need (Gustafson, Gustafson, & Wackerbarth 1997). This might work in other situations—for example, with disabled children. However, its workability depends on the computer literacy of the caregiver.

Electronic bulletin boards can serve a similar function, helping cancer caregivers at home to develop skills in problem-solving and preventing physical, emotional, and social crises by offering services that are directly available at home for health education or counselling purposes (Bucher & Houts, 1999). For example, COPELINE allows the caregiver to connect (by telephone) with other caregivers and build a group identity focused on solving problems associated with caring for a patient at home. Again, the feasibility of the technology depends on the Internet literacy of the caregiver.

Use of the Internet for therapy has many of the same pros and cons as telephone use for this purpose. In using the Internet we must determine if this family can use e-mail, if they will benefit from it, and if the problems that this family faces will respond to innovative treatment. King, Engi, and Poulos (1998) predict an increased therapeutic use of electronic media, including interactive television, on-line chat groups, and Internet real-time video connections. However, they recognize that we need much more research on the benefits and costs of these approaches. Where people are going to rely on community education and support groups, we need to worry about issues of access, privacy, hostile communications, victimization, and legal issues (Finn, 2000).

The New Reproductive Technologies

Many social theorists think technological changes bring about social changes (i.e., Castells, 1996). In their theories, the presumed impacts of technological changes and innovations on societies, social institutions, and individuals give rise to a variety of ethical, cultural, and social concerns. People and societies are always in the position of having to react to, adjust to, or remedy a change caused by technology. Technology and innovation become reified as change agents, and are seen as forces like gravity by which they think us to be affected, largely for good, but with some bothersome negatives.

Researchers less often see technology as a social product textured by the conditions of its creation in society and its social uses. Marcuse (1968) prophetically argued that the science and technology project is a result of Western domination over both nature and humanity. However, to say so is to misunderstand the linkage between humans and technologies. Instead, they are sets of relations, for instance in networks. Technologies are not things; they are agents by which we make things happen—typically, things that we want to happen. By this reckoning, technology and humanity are linked in a dynamic relationship, with each changing the other and adjusting to the other. From this standpoint, technologies and families are co-producing each other, and social change is the outcome. Drawing out this plausibility opens doors to new analytical approaches to family change in a technological universe.

We have long known that a complex, dialectical relationship exists between scientific advances and social changes, although many of us may have forgotten or overlooked this in much contemporary sociological discussion. "The tools that rule" approach is brilliantly deconstructed by Canadian metallurgist Ursula Franklin with the example of the casting of Chinese bronzes in 1200 B.C. (Franklin, 1983). The design, the model building, the creation of the mould, and the casting of immense bronzes weighing hundreds of kilograms demands a large and highly coordinated work force. In this case, the technological achievement is possible only through a prior social achievement: an extension of human organization.

To take a more poignant example examined at length in the documentary movie *Shoah*, the destruction of European Jewry between 1935 and 1945 could not have been accomplished without new technologies such as the gas chamber. Far more important, however, were the new modes of human organization that made possible the massive collection and transportation of victims by rail, boat, truck, and otherwise. Prescriptive technologies, those that require intricate organization, coordination, and control, are always a major social invention. They create a culture of compliance, but technology does not drive the process; a society's quest for change does. Social change is the co-production of those products through technical and social inventions.

One of the most fundamental understandings to emerge from the new sociology of technology is that technology is more than hard wires and virtual buttons. Technologies embody ideas, dreams, visions, ideologies, practices, and procedures. Technologies have not transformed our families' communications and us. Instead, we use the technologies because social life in families has changed so much that direct communication is not as possible for many of us as it once was.

Technologies play a particular role within families, where they help us to extend and remember our histories. For example, generations of photographic images—produced by photographic technology—are the stuff of family narrative, sometimes more real than family life itself. The stories we tell ourselves about our families are scripted in our minds through these momentary images, becoming the framework for future action. As a result, the co-production of technologies and families is the means by which we preserve traditional families and invent new ones.

Electronic technologies have helped some rare individuals to jump off the so-called hamster wheel of work in order to work at leisure, at home, at a distance from the hubbub of commutes, office gossip, and the nine-to-five regime. Simultaneously, for some telework has meant an increased surveillance of family lives by technologies. Some employers closely monitor the work time and even the keystrokes of their home-working employees.

Figure 12.2 DISTRIBUTION OF INVESTMENTS BY TECHNOLOGY, CANADA, 2001

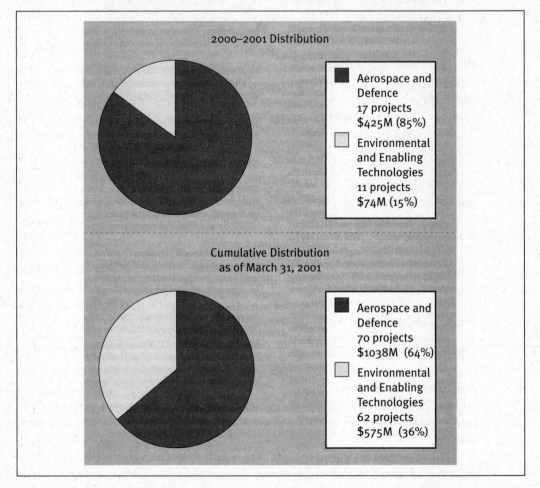

2000–2001 Distribution

- Aerospace and Defence
  17 projects
  $425M (85%)
- Environmental and Enabling Technologies
  11 projects
  $74M (15%)

Cumulative Distribution as of March 31, 2001

- Aerospace and Defence
  70 projects
  $1038M (64%)
- Environmental and Enabling Technologies
  62 projects
  $575M (36%)

Source: Technology Partnerships Canada Annual Report 2000–2001, strategis.ic.gc.ca/pics/tp/d658_tpc_2000_2001.pdf.

There is a kind of cyclicism in the duet of families and technologies, where domestic settings become free of paid work for a historical time. Then, domestic settings become workplaces again as they are now, with many home offices equipped with better laser printers, computers, and scanners than many workplaces. Petty bourgeois production of both services and goods has become common again in human history where the family as a unit works together to earn money for all members.

One prophetic contributor to our body of thought on technologies is Marshall McLuhan, discussed earlier. He describes in his early writings the motorcar as man's "mechanical bride" (see Franklin, 1990: 96; McLuhan, 1951). In time, the growing expense of cars and their necessity for life in suburbs moved the social relation of car and man from bride to "business partner" (Franklin, 1990: 97). Automobiles gave new generations of ordinary people mobility. It even gave them privacy; for many, the rear seats of automobiles became schools for learning about love and sex.

Cars aside, technology has even transformed sexuality, that most private of social activities, in a variety of ways. The social transformation of sexuality in marriages—towards better birth control and more pleasure—has led to the technologization of sexuality and the insatiable demand for pornography. The growth of contraceptive technology is a response to the demand for better contraception that goes back two centuries. Early prairie settlers coped with the problem of birth control as best they could, just as they struggled with the natural environment. They built sod houses, for example, when no logs existed and found ways to make them dry and warm, a necessity in the cold and long Canadian prairie winters. Likewise, they gave their contraceptive knowledge to each other, and Aboriginal women provided midwifery care to the homesteaders, a midwifery particularly invented for the harsh prairie climate.

The technological boom itself is created more by the demands of a changing society than by any inherent aspect of the technologies themselves (Brown & Lauder, 2001; McDaniel, 2000). Families pool and share their resources, and make contributions across generations to ensure that their members meet the new demands of society—financial, education, and technological. Often, technologies are used to advance traditional goals by traditional social means—through families, kinship networks, communities, churches, schools, and otherwise.

Research by Maureen Baker (2002), on the ways people use new reproductive technologies and what they have in mind when doing so, illustrates this point. Many cultures link heritage and status to "biological" children or children that are genetically related to their parents. Accordingly, in most parts of the world, "blood ties" are central to kinship. As a result, infertility causes people considerable anxiety, self-doubt, and depression, especially in societies that consider having children tantamount to entering normal adulthood. Such pronatalist ideas persist even in industrialized societies, such as Canada and New Zealand (where Baker is writing). There, fertility clinics increasingly offer hope to low-fertility couples.

Fertility treatments began in the 1960s and the first "test-tube" baby was born in Britain in 1978. Since then, a wide range of procedures have now become routine. Many studies have since found that fertility is important for social acceptance and the personal identity of both men and women. An inability to conceive contributes to feelings of guilt, anger, frustration, depression, and marital tension (Doyal, 1995).

Baker notes, for example, that one working-class married woman, who had experienced a still birth after her first in vitro fertilization six years ago, reported that all her friends were mothers and she felt left out when they talked about their children. Such concerns, and others, encourage some fertile couples to seek medical attention prematurely. Some become pregnant naturally before treatments begin or after they are finished.

Fertility clinics in Canada increasingly offer hope to low-fertility couples. They also help normalize medical intervention into reproduction and family life.

In New Zealand, public medical insurance will pay for one cycle of treatment for eligible couples and single women. New Zealand clinics will accept single and lesbian women if they qualify in other respects, and public insurance will pay for one sperm or egg donation and one cycle of IVF. Baker reports that the facilities established for this purpose treat patients as consumers. They provide basic medical information, and then ask the consumer to choose among several potential procedures. Consumers can even select their own sperm donor from a computerized data bank or find their own egg donor.

Many women who have undergone successful fertility treatment want to stay home from work to care for their child after spending so much time and effort trying to procreate. These couples come to focus especially strongly on the traditional aspects of family life. The fact that more low-fertility couples can now reproduce helps perpetuate the ideal of the traditional family with biological children and reinforces the social pressure on all couples to procreate.

Ironically, then, the desire to create a "normal" and socially accepted family unit remains strong in modern society. Parenthood is still closely aligned with maturity, normality, and gender identity. Women who remain voluntarily childfree continue to be perceived as deficient in important ways. Reproductive technology, then, merely helps modern women satisfy traditional goals and values. This supports our argument earlier that, at best, technology is a co-producer of social change. At worst, technology is the handmaiden of human aspirations, however forward or backward they may be.

If technology is to be understood in terms of social values and social organization, changes in family life must likewise be understood in those terms. As shorthand, we can think of recent changes in family life as a growth of individualization.

The Growth of Individualization

With industrialism and postindustrialism came a package of changes that had the net effect of letting people lead more separate yet interdependent lives. This has had a major impact on the definition and functioning of families. Let us focus on one aspect of this change—what we call the *individualization* of people's lives (Jones et al., 1990; also Beck-Gernsheim, 1983; Schultz, 1983; and Herlyn & Vogel, 1989). With individualization, there is more variety, fluidity, and idiosyncrasy in all of the major demographic processes: in migration, marriage, divorce, childbearing, family decision-making, and the relation of work life and family life. This is because, with individualization, we expect people to be self-sufficient actors in their economic, household, leisure, and intimate relationships.

Individualization of social roles means the empowerment of women, through higher levels of formal education and more participation in the paid labour force. The rise of a service economy creates more employment opportunities for women and, in this way, speeds up the process. Ultimately, a growth in jobs that free people from family dependency and control increases the variety, fluidity, and idiosyncrasy of people's private lives. Nevertheless, they still need and want the support, the emotional attachments of family lives. Given the choice, most North Americans still value and want marriage and children.

Intellectuals have always been quick to predict an end to "traditional," non-rational concerns like religion, ethnicity, and nationalism, among others; and they have usually have been wrong. None of these has disappeared and some have increased in strength and importance around the world, with both good and bad consequences. Repeatedly, they have changed form and resurfaced. Today, the forces of religion, ethnicity, and nationalism remain among the most potent factors in people's lives. Rational economic or political concerns do not diminish them, nor are they mere justifications for imperialism or responses to discrimination. Anyone who is religious, feels nationalistic, or has an ethnic identity knows better than that. These things have a reality and a meaning of their own both to individuals and to society.

Family life is similar in that it is, often, more emotional than rational. It, too, gives an important sense of belonging and identity. There is no sign that the human need for belonging is going to disappear. Yet there are also strong signs of *rationality*. People show signs of wanting to maximize their happiness by choosing their own destinies. When people have an opportunity to choose their own lives—

Debate Box 12.1 ARE THERE BETTER ALTERNATIVES TO FAMILY LIFE
Which side of the debate do you fall on?

YES	NO
• There are better ways of providing people with companionship than family life. A variety of friends and acquaintances, at work and elsewhere, can do far better.	• Family life provides a sense of intimacy and security that other forms of social organization cannot provide, largely through long-term shared experiences.
• There are better ways of providing people with sex than family life. Marital sex tends to become boring and routine with the passage of time. Variety is needed.	• Marital sex, though less frequent with the passage of time, is found to be more pleasing (on average) than casual sex with strangers, however pleasant.
• There are better ways of raising children in supervised groups than in families. Leaving aside neglect and abuse, families can be ill-informed and irrational about their children.	• Family life—including marriage and child-rearing—provides people with a sense of purpose and personal meaning that few other relationships can provide.
• There are better ways of providing for secure old age than in families. Increasingly, old people cannot rely on their children and need to rely on the state instead.	• There is no evidence that strangers do a better job of raising children than their parents do. Parents are more likely to provide love and affection than strangers.
• There are better ways of organizing social and economic life than in families. Families inject irrationality, stress, and home-based conflict into people's lives.	• Family life may be irrational, inefficient, and emotional. However, there is no reason why families need to be organized like businesses or armies.
• For these reasons, families are not likely to survive as a way of delivering "close relations" and intimacy in the future.	• For all of these reasons, families are likely to survive—in one form or another—as long as there are people.

for example, their mate, their living arrangement, or the number of children they will bear—they exercise this choice. In doing so they may ignore customary norms and expectations, or bend them to fit their own needs. This produces enhanced personal satisfaction but also social changes.

However, more personal choice also produces uncertainty and ambivalence about how, and when, to limit personal choice. Issues such as marriage of same-sex couples, birth control awareness among teenagers or abortions in the situation of sexual abuse or violent sexual assault but not in other situations when women seek it, have lines that are difficult to draw and it is not clear who is drawing them, or whether lines should be drawn at all.

Not surprisingly, there is a strong conservative reaction to this uncertainty. Traditionalists evoke emotion-laden images of current family arrangements—for example, the growing participation of men in family life—or of the pleasures of family life in the "old days." Whether or not these are solidly based arguments does not affect their power to sway public opinion. Supporting this conservative reaction is a part of the population spared much of the recent changes. For example, rural people are more likely to support resistance to contemporary family change.

The outcome of these struggles for and against change in family life is hard to predict. However, it seems likely that anything that (1) slows the growth of opportunities after an initial growth, or (2) increases the individualization of lives faster than the creation of new cultural meanings and norms, or (3) otherwise produces uncertainty (for example, a war or environmental disaster) will increase support for a backward-looking mythology of the family.

In order to cope with the ambivalence and uncertainty of intimacy and close relations these days, people typically develop new social forms and invent new lifestyles to deal with the uncertainties they face. The struggle to create new rules is especially important for women, who have been kept from a wide range of choices in the past. Solutions to the problem of uncertainty include both formal and informal changes. *Formal* changes include laws and policies, such as new legislation to define marriage and its rights and obligations, to support gender equity and affirmative action for women, to improve daycare, and to encourage fertility control. *Informal* changes include efforts people make in their own lives to negotiate new social roles and norms. For example, people work out new ways of disciplining the children of their spouse's first marriage, interacting with their mother's new boyfriend, or getting to know a co-worker's same-sex spouse.

A New Culture of Intimate Life

Out of all these efforts a new culture of intimate life emerges. Social and cultural changes, in turn, bring pressure for further structural changes by government and business. For example, the growth in part-time work, work sharing, and workplace childcare all reflect, in part, new ideas about the relationship between work and family life. So do pressures on employers to pay health, retirement, or death benefits to non-traditional "spouses." In turn these changes further increase choice, uncertainty, and cultural change, so the cycle of family change continues.

With few exceptions, this cycle works similarly in all societies. However, there are suppressers and enhancers at work. Bearing that in mind, what kinds of families are likely to result from this ongoing process of individualization? At least four main kinds of nuclear family are likely to appear; they differ along two main dimensions: (1) role separability and (2) personal interchangeability.

Role separability in families refers to the separation of being a spouse from being a parent. Many North American households are made up of cohabiting couples with children, or reconstituted or blended families, where spouses may or may not parent one another's children.

A second dimension, **personal interchangeability**, refers to the choosing of a spouse based on ability to do certain roles rather than for the individual's unique characteristics. People who marry for love choose a mate for his or her unique characteristics. People who marry for instrumental reasons are more interested in a mate who is a good provider, or who can produce healthy offspring. Personal interchangeability is well suited to societies with high rates of mortality. By contrast, purely romantic marriages are unpredictable and unstable. They are a luxury best enjoyed in prosperous times.

Now we can cross-classify nuclear families along these two dimensions. Doing so yields four possibilities: we call them the (1) corporate, (2) collected, (3) concatenated, and (4) cyclical family, respectively.

Inseparable family roles and personal interchangeability characterize the **corporate family.** In this kind of family people can come and go without changing the essential structure of the family. The husband serves as father to the younger generation in the household—children, apprentices, and household servants—and the wife serves as mother, whoever the natural parents of these children may be.

This type includes what Zimmerman called the Trustee Family and what Ogburn called the Multifunctional Autonomous Family (see Goldenberg, 1987: 131). It is only in a society dominated by this kind of family that people can think and speak of "the family," as a well-defined social institution. The state protects the institution of "the family," as does religion. In culture and by law, "the family" has social importance, enjoys its own resources, and commands its members' loyalties.

This kind of family emphasizes its members' duty to the group. As Sacks says, such families exist only because of choices people do *not* make:

> To be a child is to accept the authority of parents one did not choose.
> To be a husband or wife is to accept the exclusion of other sexual
> relationships. To be a parent is to accept responsibility for a future
> that I may not live to see. (Sacks, 1991: 56–57)

This kind of family is best suited to a theocratic, undifferentiated social structure. There, the state, the law, and religion are closely tied together and lean the same way on family matters. In societies where the corporate family dominates, competing models of life—for example, notions that individuals have rights and liberties—and competing institutions (like the secular school) hold little sway.

The "corporate family" existed among the nineteenth- and early twentieth-century European and North American middle classes. As we now know, its survival was aided by hypocrisy about the keeping of mistresses, involvements with prostitutes, visits to brothels, and carefully hidden homosexuality. It is a patriarchal family in which a double standard prevails and in which men are dominant. Today, the corporate family is still the dominant model in Western societies. However, it is gradually losing support in law and public opinion.

By contrast, separable roles and interchangeable performers characterize the **collected family**. It is similar to Duberman's (1975) "reconstituted" family, which follows the remarriage of partners who have children from previous unions. Like the corporate family, the collected family requires family members to conform to traditional notions of husband, wife, father, mother, and child. However, given the complexities of remarriage, family members concede the impossibility of compelling mates to be both good spouses *and* good parents to the resident children.

In these families, it is not the family as a whole but the component roles that are the locus of loyalty, meaning, and resources. Children are permitted to feel close to their mother, for example, without feeling obliged to love her spouse or call him "Daddy." Mothers can feel they are doing their duty as a "good mother" even if they select a partner who, they think, will not excel as a parent; and so on.

Societies like our own, with growing numbers of reconstituted families, are beginning to recognize the peculiar character and special needs of collected families. For example, the state increasingly delivers benefits to spouses *or* parents *or* children, not to the "family head" of earlier days. In this system, one cannot assume that the family has a "head." Nor is it thought proper to invent one for the purposes of dispensing state funds. The Census of Canada long ago changed from referring to "head of household" to simply calling one person in the household—whoever the person filling in the Census chooses—"Person 1." In 1988, the Canadian government began to send out family allowance cheques made payable to the custodial parent of a child, typically the mother. This change recognized the crucial difference between a corporate family and a collected family.

Such legal rethinking commanded a great deal of attention over the 1980s and it is still going on in many jurisdictions. However, people who live in, or idealize, corporate families oppose this change. After all, it concedes that corporate families are becoming less common. Opponents argue that accepting this change makes families normatively less important to people's lives than they once were.

A third kind of family, the **concatenated family**, is exactly opposite to the corporate family, since separable roles and unique performers characterize it. From the outside, the concatenated family looks like a chance event, a slow collision of individuals in time and space. The concatenated family is nothing more than a household at a particular moment in time. Here, they vest meanings, loyalties, and resources in individuals, not roles. Families exist only through the sharing of these meanings and resources. As a result, family members must constantly affirm and renegotiate the bases for this sharing.

Here, the meaning of *spouse* or *parent* is no longer certain. It is highly idiosyncratic from one person to another, and so from one household to another. Occasionally definitions will mesh for long periods. Sometimes, a shortage of alternatives will keep the household from dissolving despite a failure of definitions to mesh. In any event we cannot assume, in these families, that members will have a permanent commitment to "the family" or even to their current spouse and children.

The concatenated family is an extreme version of radical individualism. It assumes that people ought to have unlimited free choice in their living arrangements. This freedom is subject only to the legal protection of minors from the consequences of a family breakdown and the protection of all family members from household violence. They perceive family life as a lifestyle or individual choice—so far as the adults are concerned, a kind of supermarket for intimate relations.

In this system, mating is motivated mainly by considerations of the spouse's unique characteristics, which may not continue to allure. Childbearing is motivated by a biological drive to reproduce or by personal self-expression—a form of psychic consumption of children for personal pleasure. Under these conditions, marital dissolutions will likely be frequent, because of the high premium on varied experience. Childbearing continues, but at lower levels, because it is expensive, reduces marital satisfaction, and makes household dissolutions more difficult.

Not surprisingly, this family system creates many potential kinship connections (Gross, 1987). Along with this goes much confusion about parenting responsibilities and property rights. However, more mothers than fathers will remain with their children in case of a divorce. So in practice, concatenated families (with children) are more matrifocal. Women and children remain, while men come and go.

In North America and Europe, concatenated families are still far from the average. Yet they are common in certain subgroups (for example, the poorest and wealthiest classes, and among migrant or artistic communities). They may become an increasingly common though transient experience in many people's lives. That is, many people will spend a part of their lives in concatenated families (just as they spend a part of their lives in collected or corporate families).

Like the corporate family, the **cyclical (or recycled) family** features traditional (inseparable) roles. Still, unlike the corporate family, there is no interchangeability in the cyclical family. Instead, the performances of its members are unique. Each is a "return engagement" occurring *because of* the unique relationship of the members. This return engagement may be a second marriage of the same people, which is rare but occurs. More often, it is a second parenthood, during which people are called upon to parent their now-adult children (occasionally called "boomerang children") a second time.

For example, in Canada since 1981 the percentages of men and women between the ages of 20 and 34 years living with parents have risen significantly. The result is a complex household that *looks* like a corporate family but has none of the predictability or normative power of that older arrangement. Many reasons account for the return of adult children. They include unemployment, insufficient income for accommodation, or the need for additional education or babysitting help.

Unique family situations result from an interaction between the reasons for return and expectations of the children and parents. For example, the parents may expect their grown children to be tidy, follow curfews, and be independent. The children may expect to be looked after, even to receive an allowance. Yet they

Figure 12.3 MORE YOUNG ADULTS ARE LIVING WITH THEIR PARENT(S)

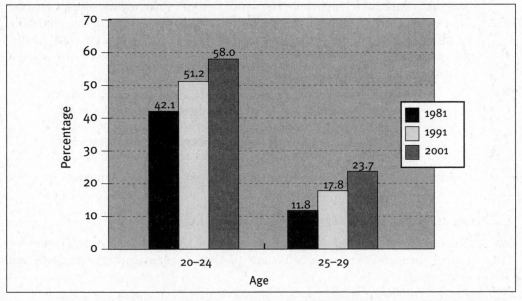

Source: Adapted from the Statistics Canada website,
www12.statcan.ca/english/census01/products/analytic/companion/fam/canada.cfm#young_adults.

violate household rules regarding the use of cars, stereo systems, home space, and so on. Naturally, conflicts can arise from these differences. There can also be mutual support and benefit for both generations.

Alongside these differences in expectations, problems also arise out of feelings of guilt or a desire to maintain good relations with one another (usually, parents trying to maintain good relations with their children). No one has yet established norms to guide behaviour in these circumstances, so we witness what amounts to a series of unique performances.

We can wonder whether the change from corporate families to collected, concatenated, and cyclical families is as inevitable as it seems. While we cannot be certain, the outcome seems clearer when we look at the process piece by piece: for example, ask what is the probability that women will leave the workforce to be financially dependent on husbands as they were in the past. Some wishful thinkers want (and some policymakers seem to be encouraging) mothers of preschool children to leave the workforce and devote their adult lives to family.

All answers are based on the best available data in the United States and Canada. Family incomes would drop 32 percent in the United States (*American Demographics*, 1997: 39), and 27 percent in Canada (Statistics Canada, 1997b: 3). Even after taking into consideration costs that they would not incur, such as for daycare and other work-related expenses, families would still suffer a net loss of income.

The loss would be greatest for those dual-income families in which the wife earns more than the husband (22 percent of dual-earner families in the U.S., 15 percent in Canada). There would be reduced overall spending too (except on food at home), which would slow the economy. Employers would lose valuable employees and suitable substitutes among men would be hard to find. Lastly, the editors of *American Demographics* mention what might happen to the women themselves who leave paid employment for family:

> We're talking about a generation of women for whom a job is much more than a paycheck... 63 percent of married women with children under age six work because it pays, one way or another. There's nothing to suggest they won't keep doing so. (*American Demographics*, 1997: 40).

There are no signs suggesting a return to old, restrictive family forms.

Problems to Solve in the Future

The vision statement of a research group at the University of Leeds, England—Care, Values and the Future of Welfare (CAVA)—states clearly the problem that is facing us:

> When the welfare state was set up, policies presumed that people would marry in their early twenties, that women would leave the labour market, that men would be primarily breadwinners and that women and children could rely on men's contributions to the insurance-based benefits system if they ever needed extra support. However, these presumptions are no longer valid, because there have been many changes—divorce has increased, men's and women's employment is very different, expectations of close relationships have changed. In addition, such changes have been different across ethnicity, class and family structure.

These changes have altered day-to-day life and perceptions of familial responsibilities as well as how they have affected the demands on social policies. The West is entering a period of major welfare resettlement—governments are seeking to restructure policy provision—and for this to be successful we, as a society, need to know how the changes in parenting and partnering are transforming the meanings and practices of care, intimacy, and obligation.

Research is needed to develop a new framework of values to underpin the social policies that support us in fulfilling our varied family responsibilities. The research would explore the different sets of beliefs, values, and moral frameworks that we all draw upon when trying to negotiate the sorts of dilemmas we are faced with in our everyday lives, for example:

- How do we find people to look after our children while we work?

- How do we decide who lives where after divorce?

- Whom do we turn to when we're in need?

In trying to find out more about how we sort these issues out, researchers will be asking:

- How far are these negotiations different in terms of class, gender, ethnicity, age, disability, local conditions, or personal biography?

- How should social policies support us in these negotiations? (www.leeds.ac.uk/cava)

When people today discuss family, they talk about two things. They stress that families, and what happens with families, matter to them. They also talk about the diversity of families today in comparison to the past. The diversity to which most people refer is a range of family forms, defined by legal and living arrangements of spouses, whether or not children are present, and even by the definition of who is a spouse. So, we hear about married couples with or without children, common-law or cohabiting couples with or without children, female- or male-headed single-parent families, adoptive families, foster families, empty nesters, gay or lesbian families, and the list goes on. At times the impression might be that a smorgasbord of choices about how to live in families exists. All one need do is pick the one that suits.

Yet this apparent diversity may be deceiving. People do not typically make informed choices about which family form they would prefer, matching their preferences with their personal characteristics and needs. Most people in families other than two-spouse families are there because of family life-cycle change, such as kids growing up and leaving home, or a marriage/relationship breakdown. Heterosexual people do not say, let us form a gay or lesbian family. The only family forms that involve true choice may be common-law couples or adoptive or foster families.

Viewing diverse families only as varied structures may be deceptive in other ways. We may overlook or underestimate diversity *within* various family forms, suggesting that families are more uniform than they are. This view diminishes the potential lessons that we might learn from looking at real families, whatever the form they take, and observing how the successful ones remain so. Form is not the key to living well in families, nor is it the key to maintaining close relations over the long term.

Innovations in Caring

The term *family* itself may be too restrictive, eliminating everyone to whom we are not related by blood or marriage. A student once told one author (McDaniel), on his return from a weekend family reunion, "If I weren't related to these people, I would likely have nothing to do with them!" Our restrictive idea of family takes away from us other ways to care for those we like. For example, we may parcel out our love and caring cautiously, thinking that family has a monopoly on caring. Yet, research by family sociologists on whom people turn to in crisis or need (McDaniel,

1994, for one example) shows that people see many non-family individuals as family. Researchers have called such individuals **fictive kin**, the idea being that they act like relatives though they are not. The curiosity in this term is the suggestion that the social distinction between family and friends is a clear one.

Children's survival and family continuity have always been major concerns, and individual interests have often been linked, if not subordinated, to family groups. There have been many different ways to carry forward assets and power in the framework of the family. In Europe, systems that stress the importance of patrimonial arrangements are generally associated with the Roman conception of property, whereas systems favouring egalitarian redistribution in enlarged kinship groups have an affinity with "barbarian" customs. In Japan and China, or on the Pacific atolls, other kinds of family systems are found, but in all of them, adoption, affiliation, or family recomposition give priority to family continuity and well-being, inventing solutions to conflict, penury, infertility, and death. No future could be imagined without children, and the succession of generations was secured by these practices, resulting in early geographical, social, and family mobility for children and sometimes young men and women (Fauve-Chamoux, 1998).

Men's family roles, as well as women's, are forever tied to changes in the economic structure, as well as important events such as mass immigration, recession or depression, and war. The diversity of men's roles today is not new, but reflects the historical variation that has always existed along racial, ethnic, class, and religious lines. Although men's family authority is historically rooted in material conditions, this component of male identity has lessened in the past generation, and men have responded with strategies that either enhance or negate their familial roles (Mintz, 1998).

African-American, single, female-headed families are inventing a new way to be familial. Stacey (1990) argues, from a study of working-class families in California, that it is *not* middle-class families with their well-aired problems of balancing work and family, deciding whether to have children, and struggling to raise quality children who are the innovators in family, but working-class families. White, middle-class families are more the beneficiaries than the creators of family change. African-American and Chicano working-class women are the postmodern family pioneers, who draw on traditional family networks while they create new ones to meet new needs. **Other-mothering** is one such family innovation, which permits extended relations or friends to mother children and moves beyond the nuclear, biological family. Other-mothering is

> ... revolutionary in American society because it takes place in opposition to the ideas that parents, especially mothers, should be the only child rearers... This kind of shared responsibility for child care can only happen in small community settings where people know and trust one another. It cannot happen in those settings if parents regard their children as their "property," their possession. (Hooks, 1984: 144)

Table 12.3 LABOUR PARTICIPATION RATES BY SEX, AGE, AND COUNTRY, 1999

	CANADA	UNITED STATES	JAPAN	AUSTRALIA	NEW ZEALAND
			1999		
			%		
LABOUR Participation rate					
Both sexes	**75.9**	77.2	72.4	72.9	75.2
Men	**82.0**	84.0	85.3	82.1	83.2
15–24	**65.3**	68.0	47.7	70.8	66.9
25–54	**91.1**	91.7	97.1	90.0	91.1
55–64	**60.7**	67.9	85.2	61.7	71.6
65 and over	**9.8**	16.9	35.5	9.2	10.8
Women	**69.8**	70.7	59.5	63.6	67.4
15–24	**61.7**	62.9	46.7	65.9	59.6
25–54	**78.2**	76.8	66.4	69.2	73.5
55–64	**39.4**	51.5	49.8	31.7	48.4
65 and over	**3.4**	8.9	14.9	2.9	4.0

Source: Data adapted from Statistics Canada website, www.statcan.ca/english/Pgdb/labor 23a.htm.

Thinking about the future as an extension of the present, for better or worse, takes us back to the beginning of this chapter and the idea that the future evolves from the present and the past. Several current trends are considered here as they move into the future. Of the many that could be selected, we will attempt to shed light on three: dual- or multiple-income families, refilled nests, and family diversity across the life course.

Dual-Income Families

Dual-income families are important carriers of family change. It is not that women in the past did not work—they did, many of them for pay in the workforce, and also at home. What is new since the late twentieth century in North America is the proportion of women with families who work outside the home. The fastest-growing labour-force participation rate between 1981 and 1991 in Canada occurred among mothers of preschool children. Maternal employment is no passing fad that will cease because some politicians or conservative forces try to push the clock back to the 1950s. The economy needs the wages and skills of women too much, and governments need the taxes women contribute.

That most couples will be working when they get together is a given these days. Career and job commitments may lead to postponed weddings and to more commuting relationships in the future. More husbands may follow their spouse's career or job opportunities in the future. Women may delay childbearing in the future but the emotional value placed on children will mean that most couples will have children at some point.

With children and dual incomes will come the challenge to both work and family for both men and women. It could be that with changes in the global marketplace, men's work may not be as privileged as it was in the past, when men were seen as *primary* family providers. Women increasingly are taking on the role of provider in the 1990s in families where a man is present, as men's work becomes more precarious and insecure. This means changes in the roles and expectations of spouses and in the ways children come to see what mothers and fathers are and do.

Recent research at the crossroads of work and family life suggests that an employee's relationship with his or her direct boss may be key to renegotiating the border between work and family. Research by Winfield and Rushing (2002) reports that employees perceive more supervisor support around problems in bridging the boundaries between work and family life when their immediate supervisor is the same race or the same sex as they are. This sense of organizational support is further enhanced when coworkers are similar in race and sex—an effect that is particularly strong for women. The same is not true for family responsibilities, however. Employees who have supervisors with similar family responsibilities are less likely to report that the supervisor is supportive of bridging the border between work and family.

Refilled Nests

What are *refilled nests* and what is the present and future trend for such nests? For a time it was the common pattern that children grew up and left the family home when they could make their own way in the world. Children still do this, but the age at which they can make their own way in the world has advanced considerably. Boyd and Pryor (1989) suggest that couples who thought that their children had grown up and "flown away" soon discover that the family home (nest) has been refilled with adult children who are returning to school (or have never left school), having trouble finding or keeping jobs, getting separated or divorced, or even having children of their own. Family nests can refill readily when adult children bring their own children and possibly spouses back to the family home.

What does this trend mean when developed into a future scenario? In some ways, it could be a harkening back to the past, when we presumed extended families to share one home. In fact, this seldom occurred in reality since life expectancy was lower and there were not many three-generation families around, or around for long. Also, many people did not prefer to live in multiple-generation families anyway and did so only when they had little choice (McDaniel & Lewis, 1997). The future may be, then, like the past: some families live in refilled nests only out of necessity and do not see themselves as creating anything new, merely pooling housing and resources to survive. Others, however, may see huge creative possibilities in refilled nests—childcare, for example, by grandparents while parents work; for sharing housework among more family members; for reducing environmental problems by having fewer accommodations; for developing new ways of intergenerational caring for elders. The probability is high that the range of options presented by and created in refilled nests will widen into the future, but that the phenomenon will not go away anytime soon.

Diversity Across the Life Cycle

A different take on family diversity than discussed thus far is to consider diversity across the life cycle. One useful way to examine this diversity is to look at families in midlife the period in which family diversity is widest. It could be, for example, that in midlife men are retiring early and women are beginning careers or education, some couples are having grandchildren, others having children for the first time. Some may be focusing on family as a priority for the first time in their lives, while others are focusing on work after a long time of attention to family. Some marriages may be breaking up, others just beginning.

The trend toward diversity in close relations across the life cycle reveals a clear pattern of individualization of family life. People live longer now than ever before. In the lifetime allotted to each of us, we can—and likely will—live in many kinds of family situations. This is true even if our family lives are stable and secure. Children grow up and leave home eventually—even if it takes them a longer time to do so! Couples find themselves in different family situations simply by living year after year. The longer we live, the more diversity of family we will face. Mix in other changes such as divorce, remarriage, possibly living common-law at some point, and we quickly realize that the various kinds of family forms that we have discussed in this book may take place for one person in his or her lifetime. The life-cycle perspective offers a different view of diversity and one well worth considering, if for no other reason than to promote tolerance of other ways of being close in families.

Policy Challenges

Societies are not particularly wise in anticipating the challenges that will face them in a few years time. Nor are they fully able to figure out what steps to take in policy to meet these challenges or even if policy is the way to meet challenges. Nonetheless, even in these times of government lessening in North America, policy, both public and private, matters to our plans. Business plans involve anticipating changes and, hopefully, developing in the directions of those trends, however approximately. We now recognize that society's ultimate objectives—good quality of life and long life for as many of its citizens as possible, with a productive and growing economy—do not lend themselves readily to direct intervention. Nevertheless, some issues and challenges are emerging out of the mists of the future, which we ignore at our peril. We will focus on a few of these as distinct family policy challenges.

Growing family inequalities pose one such challenge. Some interesting current trends have emerged in the last decade. The group with the highest incomes increased their family incomes most (Statistics Canada, 1997b: 20), while the group with the lowest family incomes lost most. The result is increasing family income inequality in Canada, a trend apparent since 1980. Since many more families in the lowest income groups depend on government sources for at least part of their income (about 59 percent in 1996 according to Statistics Canada (1997c: 18)), it is decreasing government contributions that account most for the growth in inequality. Meanwhile, government support and tax policies continue to reduce family income inequalities (Statistics Canada, 1997c: 21). The concern for the future is whether continuing declines in government support for low-income families will further increase family inequality in Canada. The unfortunate conclusion is that this is likely.

Some might wonder whether family inequality is a problem at all. Research evidence suggests that it is, and a significant problem, too—not only for those families with low income, but for all of society. In pioneering research, Wilkinson (1994) has shown that mortality rates and life expectancies in the industrialized world are more related to income inequality than to *per capita* income or *per capita* economic growth. What factors are involved here and how are they related to family?

The importance of relative income to health suggests that psychological factors related to deprivation and disadvantage are involved. That is to say, it is less a matter of the immediate physical effects of inferior material conditions than of the social meanings we attach to those conditions and how people feel about their circumstances and about themselves (Wilkinson, 1994: 70).

McDaniel (1998a) shows how meanings given to relative deprivation filter through families. Poor children in affluent societies feel negatively about themselves and often blame their families for the relative deprivation. This has severe implications for their life chances and potential to contribute to society. Cheal (1996: xv) adds that the higher risk of being poor while a child and the fact that government programs seem to do so little for low-income families with children is a huge cause for concern about families and society in the future. Poor children often grow up to be poor adults or adults whose early deprivation prevents them from catching up on growth, education, skills acquisition, or lost hope.

A second major emerging policy challenge is childcare. If mothers of young children continue to work for pay in the numbers they currently do, and if "mother work" remains a woman's domain primarily, some solution to caring for children while mothers work must be found. In the lengthy public deliberation on the pros and cons of daycare, children who need care while mothers work are not getting the kind of care they need. The capacity of all care facilities and options combined in both the U.S. and Canada represents only a fraction of the demand.

The large baby boom generation does not make this mismatch any easier. Pressures are likely to increase on businesses and on governments to provide childcare at the worksite or in the home neighbourhood, and also to continue to develop means to meet working people's family needs such as parental leaves, flexible work hours, recreational facilities for children, and after-school programs.

This issue is central to the future of families, since without some solution, couples may have little choice but to restrict their childbearing even further or forgo parenthood altogether. As with growing family inequality, all of the society would suffer as a result. Childcare is also crucial to gender equality, since without access to affordable childcare, women who become mothers may be forced to restrict themselves to lower-paying or part-time work rather than contribute to society in ways commensurate with their talents and education. This goes against deeply held values of equality of opportunity for all and the idea that education should pay off for individuals, who take advantage of its opportunities, and for society, which reaps the rewards of a creative, contributing educated workforce.

Reducing Family Violence: A Comprehensive Federal Approach

The federal government has renewed its commitment to reduce family violence in Canada. Because this is a long-term problem, the commitment is also long-term. The federal Initiative promotes public awareness of the risk factors of family violence and the need for public involvement in responding to it; strengthens the criminal justice system and housing systems to respond; and supports data collection, research and evaluation efforts to identify effective interventions.

This Initiative marks a new stage in federal efforts to reduce family violence. The issue of family violence has been integrated into ongoing programming in many government departments. We have learned that the best way to address family violence is to support a common vision and a coordinated approach.

With the long-term goal of reducing the occurrence of family violence in Canada, the federal government provides the Family Violence Initiative with $7 million permanent annual funding. This allocation supports and complements activities across seven departments and agencies: Health Canada, Canada Mortgage and Housing Corporation, Justice Canada, RCMP, Canadian Heritage, Status of Women Canada, and Statistics Canada. Additionally, Indian and Northern Affairs Canada, Human Resources Development Canada, Citizenship and Immigration Canada, Correctional Service of Canada and the Department of National Defence address family violence issues through existing departmental programs and activities.

On behalf of the federal government, Health Canada coordinates the Family Violence Initiative and operates the electronic information database of the National Clearinghouse on Family Violence and its 1-800 telephone line. The Clearinghouse synthesizes and disseminates information on best practices to prevent and treat family violence.

Source: National Clearinghouse on Family Violence website, www.hc-sc.gc.ca/hppb/familyviolence/initiative_e.html, Health Canada, 1999. Reproduced with the permission of the Minister of Public Works and Government Services Canada, 2003.

Family-policy challenges are complex and diverse but may be central to the future of families and of us all. We openly acknowledge the centrality of families to our individual lives and happiness and also to our collective futures and yet we seem reluctant to meet the needs of families in developing creative solutions. Lesemann and Nicol (1995: 124) argue, "It is paradoxical that the family seems simultaneously to be recognized and supported by the government... and abandoned by it."

The authors of a recent analysis of data from the National Longitudinal Survey of Children and Youth (NLSCY) end with a "blueprint for a family-enabling society." In this blueprint, four corner posts are identified.

First is **collaboration**: constructive collaboration is necessary among all levels of government to set the conditions for improving outcomes for children. Collaboration is also necessary among business and social agencies, schools, and other institutions within the communities. Cooperation is needed in four key areas: promoting healthy pregnancy, birth and infancy; improving parenting and family supports; strengthening early childhood development, learning and care; and strengthening community supports. The best way of supporting children is by supporting the families in which they are growing up.

Second is **investment in human capital**, based on life-long learning. An estimated one out of every four Canadian children is vulnerable, and this vulnerability is only weakly connected with family income. The effects of good parenting far outweigh the effects of income in longitudinal Canadian research using the NLSCY. Parental education, especially the mother's education, is particularly influential for good outcomes. At the same time, older children require ongoing educational and social supports to stay in school. Opportunities for continuing education should be available to every age group, so that the generations will reinforce one another's strengths and not weaknesses.

Third is **social inclusion**. Communities need to ensure that the most vulnerable, often isolated, children are included in school and community activities. To achieve this, we need to design programs and policies that integrate children of all backgrounds and abilities, rather than segregate them from one another. The longitudinal (NLSCY) evidence shows that children from low-income families appear to benefit most from daycare, for example. Schools also have an important part to play in developing a community's least advantaged children, by overcoming their disadvantages at home. When SES segregates children socially and educationally, the least advantaged children are made even more vulnerable.

Finally, we need an increased capacity for **program evaluation**, monitoring, and research. Good researchers will respect the children and families they study. In all good studies, children will be viewed as having inherent rights as human beings. Moreover, they will be recognized as individuals with a growing need for autonomy. In turn, successful communities will promote such research and support and protect the outcomes of their least-advantaged, most vulnerable children. We need to ensure that our research measures these outcomes, our social policies promote them, and our communities enforce them. (Willms, 2000b)

Concluding Remarks

Two views of history are directly useful for our glimpse into the future of families. First, there is the image of the present as the peak of progress, at least of progress thus far attained by humanity. We see ourselves emerging from a grim, dreary past into a bright present where we are smarter, wiser, and happier than our ancestors. The future holds more of the same improvements and advances over the present. A contrasting view, equally prevalent, is that we used to have, or be, something wonderful, but with time, what was good slipped away, replaced by a society with fewer clear values, more social problems, less stability, and less certainty.

It might be that these differing visions are not mutually exclusive. In all likelihood, the future holds new and unforeseen problems that will challenge many families and their members—in addition to all the problems we can already anticipate. However, it also seems likely that we will learn more about how healthy families operate and how to help other families do the same.

So far, no one has found a "technological fix" for the kinds of organizational, interpersonal, and emotional problems that normally arise in ordinary family life—indeed, in all close relations. We do not foresee an easy solution to the problems of family life through genetic engineering, artificial intelligence, faster computers, smarter houses, or better electrical appliances. Nor is the answer to our family problems likely to arrive in the form of little white pills that can satisfy our human needs for love, meaning, belonging, attachment, and meaningful communication. That leaves no one but people, and sociology, to work out our close relations in the future.

CHAPTER SUMMARY

In this chapter, we mull over the future of close relations, beginning with a clear understanding that social prediction is far from a perfect science or art. Contesting visions of families in the future are considered.

We begin with an examination of the new communication technologies, virtual communities, and the role of families in the "connected society." We note that new technologies increase the reach of family life, instead of limiting it, as critics had feared. While it is difficult to predict the likely effects of cyberspace on family life, we note that two major communication technologies—telephone and e-mail—did not transform family life as drastically as people had expected. On the contrary, they allowed people to pursue their most cherished goals more efficiently.

The new communication technology poses problems in relation to sexuality, specifically cybersex and the potential for on-line infidelity. Mating and dating on-line create new ethnic issues and may force families to re-think what they mean by commitment in the face of extended sexual opportunities. The same technology that extends the reach of mating and dating also extends the reach of caregiving. So, just as technology lures people away from their family, if they wish, it also allows them to pay closer attention to their family members' needs. The way technology will be used, and will affect society, depends on people's wishes and values.

The new reproductive technologies likewise illustrate the importance of human agency. Though these new technologies offer new opportunities, and new ethical challenges, they are currently being used to further traditional pronatalist agendas. There is no reason to expect they will do otherwise in the future.

The most dramatic future changes to family life are extensions of changes that have been in process for centuries: namely, the individualization of family life. More families are re-thinking spousal and parental roles and shifting away from uniform corporate family structures to a wide variety of collected, concatenated, and cyclical family structures.

KEY WORDS

Collected family The collected family requires family members to conform to traditional notions of husband, wife, father, mother, and child. However, given the complexities of remarriage, family members concede the impossibility of compelling mates to be both good spouses *and* good parents to the resident children.

Concatenated family Is exactly opposite to the corporate family, since separable roles and unique performers characterize it. From the outside, the concatenated family looks like a chance event, a slow collision of individuals in time and space. The concatenated family is nothing more than a household at a particular moment in time.

Corporate family In this kind of family people can come and go without changing the essential structure of the family. The husband serves as father to the younger generation in the household—children, apprentices, and household servants—and the wife serves as mother, whoever the natural parents of these children may be.

Cyclical families (or recycled) family Features traditional (inseparable) roles. Still, unlike the corporate family, there is no interchangeability in the cyclical

family. Instead, the performances of its members are unique. Each is a "return engagement" occurring *because of* the unique relationship of the members. This return engagement may be a second marriage of the same people, which is rare but occurs.

Fictive kin people see many non-family individuals as family. These people act like relatives though they are not.

Flaming A hasty, informal e-mail expression. This is encouraged by the absence of visual feedback from the message receiver.

Other-mothering Permits extended relations or friends to mother children and moves beyond the nuclear, biological family.

Personal interchangeability Refers to the choosing of a spouse based on ability to do certain roles rather than for the individual's unique characteristics.

Refilled nests Family nests can refill readily when adult children bring their own children and possibly spouses back to the family home.

Role separability Refers to the separation of being a spouse from being a parent.

REVIEW QUESTIONS

1. How do computers and IT affect families?

2. What are some of the benefits and downfalls of electronic connectedness?

3. What are the advantages and disadvantages of using telephone or e-mail with regards to conducting close relations at a distance?

4. What types of questions does the Family Development Theory seek to answer?

5. With regards to using technology for caregiving, what are some advantages and disadvantages of computer-mediated groups?

6. Although IVF can help those who struggle with infertility, it does have some negative side effects. What are they?

7. How do people cope with the ambivalence and uncertainty of intimacy and close relations these days?

8. Name the four types of families that result from the ongoing process of individualization. Briefly describe each.

9. Three family trends are becoming more prevalent today. These are dual-income families, refilled nests, and family diversity across the life cycle. Comment on each.

10. Name and discuss a few of the policy changes that face our society today.

DISCUSSION QUESTIONS

1. Although both the telephone and e-mail have greatly altered the way people communicate, each has its pros and cons. Which one of these has facilitated communication the most? Has one done as much harm as it has good? Discuss.

2. There's lots of debate surrounding the impact of the Internet with regards to social relations. Argue for or against the idea that the Internet is damaging the way we interact socially. Some even say it can cause addiction or depression, while others counter that depression might cause the addiction. What's your view on this?

3. Much has been made over "virtual affairs" and their importance with regards to commitment. Do you believe that, if you're in a committed relationship, that these types of relations over the net constitute a form of cheating, or "emotional adultery" if you will? Explain your reasoning for why or why not.

4. Some view "refilled nests" negatively, but others see huge creative possibilities. Give pros and cons for this emerging trend in our society today. Overall do you see this trend as positive or negative?

5. Given that the government promotes marriage and the nuclear family, what role and responsibilities should it have to people when marriage does not turn out "happily ever after"?

6. List possible policy changes that can help families deal with problems regardless of their composition. Do you think that policies today protect only the traditional family values?

ACTIVITIES

1. Investigate people's opinions regarding "cyber affairs." What is the general opinion? Does the opinion differ for men and women? What conclusions can you draw from your findings?

2. Consider gay/lesbian parents. Each group will be assigned one scenario to consider what federal/provincial policies need to be changed or created to help eliminate the discrimination against these and other "different families." Also, have each group consider the role of a police officer or social worker in each scenario if called in. How could this person help to resolve the situation? Reconvene the class and discuss possible solutions.

SUGGESTED READINGS

Dearnley, James and John Feather. 2001. *The Wired World: An Introduction to the Theory and Practice of the Information Society.* London: Library Association. Nowadays there is a prerequisite for everyone, a governmental official or a citizen, to operate with such notions as e-government, computers, Internet, information society. Most universities include courses on information sciences, theories of information society and information policy, courses for computer or information literacy, in study programs in mathematics, informatics, business, sociology, or some other discipline. Dearnley and Feather address their book to those who will be working in the field of information services or information management and they have defined the task of preparing a study guide for those who do not have methodically organized knowledge of information theory.

Furlong, Andy and Fred Cartmel. 1997. *Young People and Social Change: Individualization and Risk in Late Modernity.* Buckingham [England]; Philadelphia: Open University Press. Furlong and Cartmel consider whether traditional parameters, understood as structuring the life chances and experiences of young people, are still relevant. They argue that, although social structures such as class continue to shape life chances, these structures tend to become obscured as collectivist traditions weaken and individualist values intensify.

Hayden, Dolores. 2002. *Redesigning the American Dream: The Future of Housing, Work, and Family Life.* New York: W. W. Norton. This book is a great illustration of the changing American society. Hayden addresses issues concerning evolution of housing, rethinking of private and public life, and many other issues dealing with the future of housing, work, and family life.

Inhorn, Marcia C. and Frank van Balen (Eds.). 2002 May. *Infertility Around the Globe: New Thinking on Childlessness, Gender, and Reproductive Technologies.* CA: University of California Press. This collection of essays breaks new ground by examining the global impact of infertility as a major reproductive health issue, one that has profoundly affected the lives of countless women and men. Based on original research by seventeen internationally acclaimed social scientists, it is the first book to investigate the use of reproductive technologies in non-Western countries.

Risman, Barbara J. and Donette Johnson-Sumerford. 1998. Doing it fairly: study of postgender marriages. *Journal of Marriage and the Family 60*: 23–40. This article is an original study of what the authors see as a new kind of family in which gender roles are not the primary basis for deciding who does what.

WEBLINKS

http://www.childtrends.org/
Child Trends
A summary of key research findings on how social, economic, and cultural factors influence fathers' involvement with their children.

http://www.hsph.harvard.edu/grhf/
The Global Reproductive Health Forum @ Harvard (GRHF)
An Internet networking project that aims to encourage the proliferation of critical discussions about reproductive health and gender on the net. GRHF provides interactive electronic forums, global discussions, distributes reproductive health and rights materials from a variety of perspectives through their clearinghouse, as well as maintains an extensive, up-to-date research library.

http://www.cybersexualaddiction.com/
CybersexualAddiction.com
A timely look at the powerfully addictive mix of Internet use, sexuality, and romantic fantasy. This site offers information, self-tests, and help.

REFERENCES

Abbott, Douglas A., & Glenna Slater. 2000 Spring. Strengths and stresses of Omaha Indian families living on the reservation. *Great Plains Research* 10(1): 145–168.

Abrar, Stefania. 1996. Feminist intervention and local domestic violence policy. *Parliamentary Affairs* 49(1): 191–205.

Abu-Laban, Sharon McIrvin, & Susan A. McDaniel. 1998. Beauty, status and aging, pp. 78, 102. In Nancy Mandell (Ed.), *Feminist Issues: Race, Class and Sexuality* (2nd edition), Scarborough, ON: Prentice Hall Allyn and Bacon.

Ackerman, Marc J. 1996. *Does Wednesday Mean Mom's House or Dad's? Parenting Together While Living Apart.* Toronto: Wiley & Sons.

Adams, Gerald R., Thomas Gullotta, & Mary Anne Clancy. 1985. Homeless adolescents: A descriptive study of similarities and differences between runaways and throwaways. *Adolescence* 20: 715, 724.

Adams, Jeffrey M., & Warren H. Jones. 1997. The conceptualization of marital commitment: an integrative analysis. *Journal of Personality and Social Psychology* 72(5): 1177–1196.

Adams, Owen B., & Dhruva Nagnur. 1990. Marrying and divorcing: A status report for Canada. In Craig McKie & K. Thompson (Eds.), *Canadian Social Trends.* Toronto: Thompson Educational Press.

Adams, Rebecca G. 1998. The demise of territorial determinism: Online friendships, pp. 153–162. In Rebecca G. Adams and Graham Allan (Eds.), *Placing Friendship in Context.* UK: Cambridge University Press.

Adams, Rebecca G., & Michelle Stevenson. 2002. A lifetime of relationships mediated by technology. In F. Lang and K.L. Fingerman (Eds.), *Growing Together: Personal Relationships Across the Lifespan.* New York: Cambridge University Press.

Adelmann, Pamela K., Kirsten Chadwick, & Dana Royce Baerger. 1996. Marital quality of black and white adults over the life course. *Journal of Social and Personal Relationships* 13(3): 361–384.

Adlaf, Edward M., Yola M. Zdanowicz, & Reginald G. Smart. Alcohol and other drug use among street-involved youth in Toronto. *Addiction Research* 4(1): 11–24.

Aguilar, Rudy J., & Narina Nunez Nightingale. 1994 March. The impact of specific battering experiences on the self-esteem of abused women. *Journal of Family Violence* 9: 35–45.

Alberta Advisory Council on Women's Issues. 1996. *Breadmakers and Breadwinners... The Voices of Alberta Women.* Edmonton: Alberta Advisory Council on Women's Issues.

Alberta Government. 2002. Legislation addresses needs of *Albertans in committed interdependent relationships.* Alberta Government News Release, May 7, 2002. www.gov.ab.ca/just.

Aldarondo, Etiony, & David B. Sugarman. 1996 October. Risk marker analysis of the cessation and persistence of wife assault. *Journal of Consulting and Clinical Psychology* 64, 1010–1019.

Aldridge, Jo, & Saul Becker. 1999 August. Children as carers: The impact of parental illness and disability on children's caring roles. *Journal of Family Therapy* 21(3): 303–320.

Alexander, Christopher. 1997. Factors contributing to the termination of long-term gay male relationships. *Journal of Gay & Lesbian Social Services* 7(1): 1–12.

Alford-Cooper, Finnegan. 1993. Women as family caregivers: An American social problem. *Journal of Women and Aging* 5(1): 43–57.

Ali, Jennifer, & William R. Avison. 1997 December. Employment transitions and psychological distress: The contrasting experiences of single and married mothers. *Journal of Health and Social Behavior* 38(4): 345–362.

Allen, Katherine R. 2000. A conscious and inclusive family studies. *Journal of Marriage and the Family* 62(1): 4–17.

Allen, Mike, & Nancy Burrell. 1996. Comparing the impact of homosexual and heterosexual parents on children: Meta-analysis of existing research. *Journal of Homosexuality* 32(2): 19–35.

Allison, David B., Michael C. Neale, Melissa I. Kezis, & Vincent Alfonso. Assortative mating for relative weight: Genetic implications. *Behavior Genetics* 26(2): 103–111.

Allmendinger, Juta, Hannah Bruckner, & Erika Bruckner. 1992. Marital bonds and social pension: Or on the usefulness of individual analyses. *Soziale Welt* 43(1): 90–116

Amato, Paul R. 1994 Summer. The impact of divorce on men and women in India and the United States. *Journal of Comparative Family Studies* 25.

Amato, Paul R. 1996 August. Explaining the intergenerational transmission of divorce. *Journal of Marriage and the Family* 58.

Amato, Paul R., & Alan Booth. 1995 February. Changes in gender role attitudes and perceived marital quality. *American Sociological Review* 60.

Amato, Paul R., & Alan Booth. 1996 May. A prospective study of divorce and parent–child relationships. *Journal of Marriage and the Family* 58: 356–365.

Amato, Paul R., Laura Spencer Loomis, & Alan Booth. 1995. Parental divorce, marital conflict and offspring well-being during early adulthood. *Social Forces* 73(3): 895–915.

Amato, Paul R., & Sandra J. Rezac. 1994 June. Contact with nonresident parents, interparental conflict and children's behavior. *Journal of Family Issues 15*.

Amato, Paul R., & J.M. Sobolewski. 2001. The effects of divorce and marital discord on adult children's psychological well-being. *American Sociological Review* 66: 900–921.

Ambert, Anne-Marie. 2002. *Divorce: Facts, Causes, and Consequences*. Ottawa: The Vanier Instititute of the Family.

American Demographics Editors. 1997 December. What if...? *American Demographics*: 38–45.

Ammerman, Robert T., & Richard J. Patz. 1996 September. Determinants of child abuse potential: Contribution of parent and child factors. *Journal of Clinical Child Psychology* 25: 300–307.

Anderssen, Erin. 2002. The Mathematics of Divorce. *The Globe and Mail*, 17 August: F1, F2.

Andersson B.E. 1996. Children's development related to day-care, type of family and other home factors. *European Child & Adolescent Psychiatry 5*, supplement 1, 73–75.

Andrade, Chittaranjan, Kirstine Postma, & K. Abraham. 1999 Spring. Influence of women's work status on the well-being of Indian couples. *The International Journal of Social Psychiatry* 45(1): 65–75.

Angenent, Huub L., Balthasar M. Beke, & Paul G. Shane. 1991. Structural problems in institutional care for youth. *Journal of Health and Social Policy* 2(4): 83–98.

Angus Reid Group. 1994. *The State of the Family in Canada*. Angus Reid Group: Toronto.

Angus Reid Group. 1999. *Family Matters: A Look at Issues Concerning Families and Raising Children in Canada Today*. Angus Reid Group: Toronto.

Anstorp, Trine, & Kirsten Benum. 1988. Social network stimulation as preventive method among middle-aged women in a neighborhood in Oslo. *International Journal of Family Psychiatry Vol.* 6(2): 177–187.

Anthony, E.J. 1970. The impact of mental and physical illness on family life. *American Journal of Psychiatry* 127: 138–145.

Antill, John K., & Sandra Cotton. 1987. Self disclosure between husbands and wives: Its relation to sex roles and marital happiness. *Australian Journal of Psychology* 39(1): 11–24.

Applbaum, Kalman. 1995 Winter. "Marriage with the proper stranger: Arranged marriages in Metropolitan Japan," *Ethnology* 34 (Winter): 37–51.

Applewhite, Larry W., & David R. Segal. 1990 Fall. Telephone use by peacekeeping troops in the Sinai. *Armed Forces and Society* 17: 1, 117–126.

Arat-Koc, Sedef. 1990. Importing housewives: Non-citizen domestic workers and the crisis of the domestic sphere in Canada, pp. 81–104. In Meg Luxton, Harriet Rosenberg, & Sedef Arat-Koc (Eds.), *Through the Kitchen Window: The Politics of Home and Family* (2nd enlarged edition). Toronto: Garamond.

Arat-Koc, Sedef. 1992. In the privacy of our own home: Foreign domestic workers as a solution to the crisis of the domestic sphere in Canada, pp. 149–174. In M.P. Connelly & Pat Armstrong (Eds.), *Feminism in Action*. Toronto: Canadian Scholars Press.

Arber, Sara, & Jay Ginn. 1995. The mirage of gender equality: occupational success in the labour market and within marriage. *British Journal of Sociology* 46(1): 21–43.

Arditti, Joyce A. 1997. Women, divorce, and economic risk. *Family and Conciliation Courts Review* 35(1).

Arditti, Joyce A. 1999 April. Rethinking relationships between divorced mothers and their children: Capitalizing on family strengths. *Family Relations* 48(2): 109–119.

Arendell, Terry J. 1995. *Fathers in divorce: Best case scenarios*. American Sociological Association.

Armistead, Lisa, Rex Forehand, Steven R.H. Beach, & Gene H. Brody. 1995. Predicting interpersonal competence in young adulthood: The role of family, self and peer systems during adolescence. *Journal of Child and Family Studies* 4(4).

Armstrong, Pat, & Hugh Armstrong. 1994. *The Double Ghetto: Canadian Women and Their Segregated Work*, 3rd edition. Toronto: McClelland & Stewart.

Aronson, Jane. 1994. Women's sense of responsibility for the care of older people: But who else is going to do it? pp. 175–194. In Victor Marshall & Barry McPherson (Eds.), *Aging: Canadian Perspectives*. Peterborough, Ontario: Broadview Press.

Arroyo, Judith A., Tracy L. Simpson, & Alfredo S. Aragon. 1997. Childhood sexual abuse among Hispanic and non-Hispanic white college women. *Hispanic Journal of Behavioral Sciences* 19 (Feb): 57–68.

Aryee, Samuel, & Vivienne Luk. 1996. Balancing two major parts of adult life experience: Work and family identity among dual-earner couples. *Human Relations* 49(4): 465–487.

Aseltine, Robert H. Jr. 1996 June. Pathways linking parental divorce with adolescent depression. *Journal of Health and Social Behavior* 37.

Atienza Audie A., & Mary Ann Parris Stephens. 2000 September. Social interactions at work and the well-being of daughters involved in parent care. *Journal of Applied Gerontology* 19(3): 243–263.

Atwood, Joan D., & Madeline Seifer. 1997 Spring. Extramarital affairs and constructed meaning: A social constructionist therapeutic approach. *The American Journal of Family Therapy* 25.

Aube, Jennifer & Richard Koestner. 1995. Gender characteristics and relationship adjustment: Another look at similarity complementarity hypotheses. *Journal of Personality* 63(4).

Aveline, David Timothy. 2000 May. *"My Son, My Son!" How Parents Adapt to Having a Gay Son.* Dissertation Abstracts International, A: *The Humanities and Social Sciences* 60(11): 4195–A.

Averill, Patricia, & Thomas G. Power. 1995. Parental attitudes and children's experiences in soccer: Correlates of effort and enjoyment. *International Journal of Behavioral Development* 18(2): 263–276.

Axinn, William G., & Arland Thornton. 1993. Mothers, children, and cohabitation: The intergenerational effects of attitudes and behavior. *American Sociological Review* 58(2): 233–246.

Baer, Paul E., & James H. Bray. 1999 March. Adolescent individuation and alcohol use. *Journal of Studies on Alcohol* 60, Supplement 13, 52–62.

Bagley, Cherie A., & Juanita Elizabeth Carroll. 1998. Healing forces in African-American families, pp. 117–142. In Hamilton I. McCubbin, Elizabeth A. Thompson, Anne I. Thompson, & Jo A. Futrell (Eds.), *Resiliency in African-American Families.* Thousand Oaks, CA: Sage.

Bahr, Howard M., & Bruce A. Chadwick. 1980. Sex and social change in Middletown. In Stephen J. Bahr (Ed.), *Economics and The Family.* Lexington, Mass: Lexington Books.

Bakan, Abigail & Daiva K. Stasiulis. 1995. Making the match: Domestic placement agencies and the racialization of women's household work. *Signs* 20(2): 303–335.

Baker, David B., & Kevin McCall. 1995 March. Parenting stress in parents of children with attention deficit hyperactivity disorder and parents of children with learning disabilities. *Journal of Child and Family Studies* 4: 57–68.

Baker, Maureen. 1994. *Canada's Changing Families: Challenges to Public Policy.* Ottawa: Vanier Institute of the Family.

Baker, Maureen. 1995. *Canadian Family Policies: Cross-National Comparisons.* Toronto: University of Toronto Press.

Baker, Maureen. 1996a. Introduction to family studies: Cultural variations and family trends, pp. 3–34. In Maureen Baker (Ed.), *Families: Changing Trends in Canada* 3rd edition. Toronto: McGraw-Hill Ryerson.

Baker, Maureen. 1996b. The future of family life, pp. 299–317. In Maureen Baker, *Families: Changing Trends in Canada* 3rd edition. Toronto: McGraw-Hill Ryerson.

Baker, Maureen. 2001. *Families: Labour and Love, Family Diversity in a Changing World.* Vancouver: University of British Columbia Press.

Baker, Maureen. 2002. *Medically assisted fertility, gender and the future of family life.* International Sociology Association Paper, Brisbane July 7–13, 2001.

Baker, Maureen & Donna Lero. 1996. Division of labour: Paid work and family structure, pp. 78–103. In Maureen Baker (Ed.), *Families: Changing Trends in Canada.* Toronto: McGraw-Hill Ryerson.

Baker, Robin, Gary Kiger, & Pamela J. Riley. 1996. Time, dirt and money: The effects of gender, gender ideology and type of earner marriage on time, household-task and economic satisfaction among couples with children. *Journal of Behavior and Personality* 11(5):161–177.

Balakrishnan, T.R., Evelyne Lapierre-Adamcyk, & Karol J. Krotki. 1993. *Family and Childbearing in Canada: A Demographic Analysis.* Toronto: University of Toronto Press.

Bankston, Carl L. III, & Stephen J. Caldas. 1998 January-March. Race, poverty, family structure, and the inequality of schools. *Sociological Spectrum* 18(1): 55–76.

Barber, Bonnie L., & Janic M. Lyons. 1994 August. Family processes and adolescent adjustment in intact and remarried families. *Journal of Youth & Adolescence, Vol. 23*(4): 421–436.

Barnett, Mark A., Steven W. Quackenbush, & Christina S. Sinisi. 1996. Factors affecting children's, adolescent's, and young adult's perceptions of parental discipline. *Journal of Genetic Psychology* 157(4): 411–424.

Barnett, Ola W., Tomas E. Martinez, & Mae Keyson. 1996 June. The relationship between violence, social support, and self-blame in battered women. *Journal of Interpersonal Violence* 11: 221–233.

Barrett, Michele, & Mary McIntosh. 1980. *The Anti-Social Family.* London: Verso.

Basavarahappa, K.G., & Frank Jones. 1999. Visible minority income differences, pp. 230–257. In Shiva S. Halli & Leo Driedger (Eds.), *Immigrant Canada: Demographic, Economic, and Social Challenges.* Toronto: University of Toronto Press.

Bass, David M., & Linda S. Noelker. 1987 June. The influence of family caregivers on elder's use of in-home services: An expanded conceptual framework. *Journal of Health and Social Behavior* 28(2): 184–196.

Battle, Juan J., & Michael D. Bennet. 1997. African-American families and public policy: The legacy of the Moynihan Report, pp. 150–167. In Cedric Herring (Ed.), *African Americans and the Public Agenda: The Paradoxes of Public Policy.* Thousand Oaks, CA: Sage.

Beaujot, Rod. 2000. *Earning and Caring in Canadian Families.* Peterborough, Ontario: Broadview Press.

Beck, Ulrich, & Elisabeth Beck-Gernsheim. 2002. *Individualization: Institutionalized Individualism and its Social and Political Consequences*, p. 221. London: Thousand Oaks: Sage.

Beck-Gernsheim, Elisabeth. 1983. From living for others to a life of one's own: Structural changes in women's lives. *Soziale Welt 34*(3): 307–340.

Becker, Thomas, Graham Thornicroft, Morven Leese, Paul McCrone, Sonia Johnson, Maya Albert, David Turner. 1997 July. Social networks and service use among representative cases of psychosis in South London. *The British Journal of Psychiatry 171*, 15–19.

Behrers, Dean M. 1998. *Self-Isolation and Social Support.* International Sociological Association (ISA).

Bell, Bruce D., Walter R. Schumm, Benjamin Knott, Morten G. Ender. 1999 Spring. The desert fax: A research note on calling home from Somalia. *Armed Forces & Society 25*: 3, 509–521

Belsky, J. 1990. Parental and nonparental child care and children's socioemotional development: A decade in review. *Journal of Marriage and the Family 52*: 885–903.

Belsky, Jay, & David Eggebeen. 1991. Early and extensive maternal employment and young children's socioemotional development: Children of the National Longitudinal Survey of Youth. *Journal of Marriage and the Family 53*(4): 1083–1098.

Belsky, Jay & Michael Rovine. 1990. Patterns of marital change across the transition to parenthood: Pregnancy to three years postpartum. *Journal of Marriage and the Family 52*(1): 5–19.

Belsky, Jay, Sharon Woodworth, & Keith Crnic. 1996. Trouble in the second year: Three questions about family interaction. *Child Development 67*(2): 556–578.

Belt, William, & Richard Abidin. 1996 November. The relation of childhood abuse and early parenting experiences to current marital quality in a nonclinical sample. *Child Abuse and Neglect 20*: 1019–1030.

Ben-Ari, Adital. 1995. The discovery that an offspring is gay: Parents', gay men's, and lesbians' perspectives. *Journal of Homosexuality 30*(1): 89–112.

Ben-David, Amith, & Yoav Lavee. 1996 Winter. Between war and peace: Interactional patterns of couples under prolonged uncertainty. *The American Journal of Family Therapy 24*: 343–357.

Bennun, Ian. 1997. Systemic marital therapy with one partner: A reconsideration of theory, research and practice. *Sexual and Marital Therapy 12*(1).

Benoit, Cecilia. 2000. *Women, Work and Social Rights: Canada in Historical and Comparative Perspective.* Scarborough, ON: Prentice-Hall Allyn & Bacon Canada.

Berger, Brigitte, & Peter L. Berger. 1983. *The War over the Family: Capturing the Middle Ground.* London: Hutchinson.

Berger, Peggy S., Alicia Skinner Cook, Robert L. DelCampo, Ruth Herreras, Randy R. Weigel. 1994 Fall. Family/work roles' relation to perceived stress: Do gender and ethnicity matter? *Journal of Family and Economic Issues 15*(3): 223–242.

Bergmann, Barbara. 1987. *The Economic Emergence of Women.* New York: Basic Books.

Bernard, Jessie. 1973. *The Future of Marriage.* New York: Bantam.

Bernardes, Jon. 1993. Responsibilities in studying postmodern families. *Journal of Family Issues 14*(1): 35–49.

Bernier, C., S. Laflamme, & R.M. Zhou. 1996. Housework: Reductions in gender division and development of a complicated problem. *Canadian Review of Sociology and Anthropology 33*(1): 1–21.

Bernier, Leon, Anne Morisette, & Gilles Roy. 1992. A need for love, or feelings gone awry. *Revue internationale d'action communautaire 27*(67): 101–115.

Berry, Mary Frances. 1993. *The Politics of Parenthood: Child Care, Women's Rights and the Myth of the Good Mother.* New York: Viking.

Beyer, Sylvia. 1995. Maternal employment and children's academic achievement: parenting styles as mediating variable. *Developmental Review 15*(2): 212–253.

Bharat, Shalini, & P. Aggleton. 1999 February. Facing the challenge: Household responses to HIV/AIDS in Mumbai, India. *AIDS Care, Vol. 11*(1): 31–44.

Bibby, Reginald. 2001a. Canada's Teens: A National Reading on Family Life. *Transition Magazine,* Vol. 31, No.3. Ottawa: Vanier Institute of the Family. Accessed at www.vifamily.ca, August 15, 2002.

Bibby, Reginald. 2001b. *Canada's Teens: Today, Yesterday, And Tomorrow.* Toronto, ON: Stoddart.

Biegel, David E., David M. Bass, Richard Schulz, & Richard Morycz. 1993 November. Predictors of in-home and out-of-home service use by family caregivers of Alzheimer's disease patients. *Journal of Aging & Health Vol. 5*(4): 419–438.

Biggs, Simon, Chris Phillipson, & Paul Kingston. 1995. *Elder Abuse in Perspective.*

Bird Chloe E., & Michelle Rogers. 1998. *Parenting and depression: The impact of the division of labor within couples and perceptions of equity.* Society for the Study of Social Problems (SSSP).

Birenbaum-Carmeli, Daphna. 1998. Reproductive partners: Doctor-woman relations in Israeli and Canadian IVF contexts, pp. 75–92. In Nancy Scheper-Hughes, Carolyn Sargent (Eds.) *Small Mall Wars: The Cultural Politics of Childhood.* Berkeley: University California Press.

Bischoff, Richard J., McBride, Andrea. 1996. Client perceptions of couples and family therapy. *American Journal of Family Therapy 24*(2).

Black, Dan, Gary Gates, Seth Sanders, & Lowell Taylor. 2000. Demographics of the gay and lesbian population in the United States: Evidence from available systematic data sources. *Demography 37*(2): 139–154.

Blagg, Harry. 1997 Autumn. A just measure of shame? Aboriginal youth and conferencing in Australia. *British Journal of Criminology 37*(4): 481–501.

Blair, Sampson Lee. 2000. *Parents and Family Structure: An Examination of Ethnic-Based Variations in Children's Household Labor*. American Sociological Association (ASA).

Blair-Loy, Mary F. 1996. *Career and family patterns of executive women in finance: Evidence of structural and cultural change*. American Sociological Association, Association paper.

Block, Cindy Eileen. 1999 October. *The Role of Grandmothers and Stepgrandmothers in the Social Support Systems of Young Adult Grandchildren*. Dissertation Abstracts International, A: *The Humanities and Social Sciences 60*(4): 1345–A.

Blom, S. 1994. Marriage and cohabitation in a changing society: Experience of Norwegian men and women born in 1945 and 1960. *European Studies of Population* 10: 143–173.

Bodenmann, Guy, Andrea Kaiser, Kurt Hahlweg, Gabriele Fehm-Wolfsdorf. Communication patterns during marital conflict: A cross-cultural representation. *Personal Relationships Vol. 5*(3): 343–356.

Boje, Thomas P. 1995. Introduction to Part III. *International Journal of Sociology 25*(2): 1–8.

Bolte, Angela. 1998 Spring. Do wedding dresses come in lavender? The prospects and implications of same-sex marriage. *Social Theory and Practice 24*(1): 111–131.

Boney-McCoy, Sue, & David Finkelhor. 1996 December. Is youth victimization related to trauma symptoms and depression after controlling for prior symptoms and family relationships? A longitudinal, prospective study. *Journal of Consulting and Clinical Psychology 64:* 1406–1416.

Booth, Alan & Paul R. Amato. 1994 February. Parental marital quality, parental divorce and relations with parents. *Journal of Marriage and the Family 56*.

Borden, Bradley, & Dianne Googins. 1987 July-August. Vulnerability of working parents: Balancing work and home roles. *Social Work 32*(4): 295–300.

Borell, Klas, & Sofie Ghazanfareeon Karlsson. 2002. Reconceptualising intimacy and ageing: Living apart together. Paper presented at International Symposium, *Reconceptualising Gender and Ageing*, Centre for Research on Ageing and Gender, University of Surrey, 25–27 June.

Bornat Joanna, Brian Dimmock, David Jones, Shelia Peace. 1999 March. Stepfamilies and older people: Evaluating the implications of family change for an ageing population. *Ageing and Society 19*(2): 239–261.

Bosman, Rie. 1994. Educational attainment of children in mother-headed families: The impact of socialization. *Netherlands Journal of Social Sciences 30*(2): 148–169.

Boyd, Monica, & Susan McDaniel. 1996. Gender inequality in the Canadian policy context: A mosaic. *Revista Mundial de Sociologia 2:* 25–50.

Boyd, Monica, & Edward T. Pryor. 1989. The cluttered nest: The living arrangements of young adult Canadians. *Canadian Journal of Sociology 14*(4): 461–477.

Bracher, Micheal and Gigi Santow. 1998. Economic independence and union formation in Sweden. *Population Studies 52*: 275–294.

Bradbury, Bettina. 1984. Pigs, cows and boarders: Non-wage forms of survival among Montreal families, 1861–1891. *Labour/Le Travail 14:* 9–46.

Bradbury, Bettina. 1996. The social and economic origins of contemporary families, pp. 55–77. In Maureen Baker (Ed.), *Families: Changing Trends in Canada* 3rd edition. Toronto: McGraw-Hill Ryerson.

Brannen, Stephen J., & Allen Rubin. 1996. Comparing the effectiveness of gender-specific and couples groups in a court-mandated spouse abuse treatment program. *Research on Social Work Practice 6*(4): 405–424.

Bray, James H., & Ernest N. Jouriles 1995. Treatment of marital conflict and preventions of divorce. *Journal of Marital and family Therapy 21*(4).

Bray, Robert M., Carol S. Camlin, John A. Fairbank, George H. Dunteman, Sara C. Wheeless, 2001 Spring. The effects of stress on job functioning of military men and women. *Armed Forces & Society 27*(3): 397–417.

Brehl, Robert. 1998. Internet can be a home wrecker. *The Globe and Mail*, 23 February: A1, A5.

Breton, Raymond. 1972 September. Institutional completeness of ethnic communities and the personal relations of immigrants. *American Journal of Sociology 1964, 70*(2): 193–205.

Brinkerhoff, Merlin B., & Eugen Lupri. 1988. Interspousal violence. *Canadian Journal of Sociology* 13 (4): 407–434.

Bronstein, Phyllis, Paula Duncan, & Adele D'Ari. 1996 October. Family and parenting behaviors predicting middle school adjustment: A longitudinal study. *Family Relations 45*: 415–426.

Broude, Gwen J. 1996 Fall. The realities of daycare. *Public Interest 125*: 95–105.

Brown, Jennifer S.H., 1992. A Cree nurse in the cradle of Methodism: Little Mary and the Egerton R. Young family at Norway House and Berens River, pp. 93–110. In Bettina Bradbury (Ed.), *Canadian Family History: Selected Readings*. Toronto: Copp Clark Pitman.

Brown, Phillip, & Hugh Lauder. 2001. *Capitalism and Social Progress: The Future of Society in a Global Economy*, pp. xvi, 338. Basingstoke, Hampshire; New York: Palgrave.

Bruce, N. 1970. Delinquent and non-delinquent reactions to parental deprivation. *British Journal of Criminology 10*: 270–276.

Brown-Smith, Naima. 1998 January. Family secrets. *Journal of Family Issues 19*(1): 20–42.

Bruhn, J.G. 1977. Effects of chronic illness on the family. *Journal of Family Practice 4*: 1057–1067.

Brumberg, Joan Jacobs. 1998. *The Body Project*. New York: Random House.

Brunstein, Joachim C., Gabriele Dangelmayer, & Oliver C. Schultheiss. 1996. Personal goals and social support in close relationships: Effects on relationship mood and marital satisfaction. *Journal of Personality and Social Psychology 71*(5).

Bryant, H.D. et al. 1963. Physical abuse of children: An agency study. *Child Welfare 42*: 125–130.

Bucher, Julia A., Peter S. Houts, Arthur M. Nezu, Christine Maguth Nezu. 1996 January. The prepared family caregiver: A problem-solving approach to family caregiver education. *Patient Education & Counseling Vol. 27*(1), 63–73.

Buchmann, Marlis, & Maria Charles. 1995 Summer. Organizational and institutional factors in the process of gender stratification: Comparing social arrangements in six European countries. *International Journal of Sociology 25*(2): 66-95.

Bumpus, Matthew Franklin. 2001 February. *Mechanisms Linking Work-to-Family Spillover and Parents' Knowledge of Their Children's Daily Lives*. Dissertation Abstracts International, A: *The Humanities and Social Sciences 61*(8): 3368–A.

Bumpus, Matthew F., Ann C. Crouter, & Susan M. McHale. 1999 May. Work demands of dual-earner couples: Implications for parents' knowledge about children's daily lives in middle childhood. *Marriage and the Family 61*(2): 465–475.

Buntain-Ricklefs, Joanne J., Kathi J. Kemper, Michelle Bell, & Thomas Babonis. 1994. Punishments: What predicts adult approval? *Child Abuse and Neglect 18*(11): 945–955.

Burden, D., & B. Googins. 1986. *Boston University Balancing Job and Homelife Study: Managing Work and Family Stress in Corporations*. Boston: Boston University School of Social Work.

Burden, D., & B. Googins. 1987. Vulnerability of working parents: Balancing work and home roles. *Social Work 32*(4): 295–299.

Burnette, B.A. 1975. Family adjustments to cystic fibrosis. *American Journal of Nursing 75*, 1986–1999.

Burnholt Vanessa, & Clare G. Wenger. 1998 September. Differences over time in older people's relationships with children and siblings. *Ageing and Society 18*(5): 537–562.

Burstein, Paul, R. Marie Bricher, & Rachel L. Einwohner. 1995 February. Policy alternatives and political change: Work, family, and gender on the congressional agenda, 1945–1990. *American Sociological Review 60*: 67–83.

Burton, Roberta, & Michael McGee. 1996. The relational systems model: An analysis of Gottman's findings on marital success. *Journal of Family Social Work 1*(4): 3–17.

Busby, Dean M., 1991. Violence in the family, pp. 335–385. In Stephen J. Bahr (Ed.), *Family Research: A Sixty-Year Review, 1930–1990, Volume 1*. New York: Lexington Books, Maxwell Macmillan International.

Buss, David M., 1985. Human mate selection. *American Scientist 73*(1): 47–51.

Buss, David M., & Todd K.Shackelford. 1997. From vigilance to violence: Mate retention tactics in married couples. *Journal of Personality and Social Psychology 72*(2).

Bussell, Danielle A., 1995. A pilot study of African American children's cognitive and emotional reactions to parental separation. *Journal of Divorce and Remarriage 24*(3–4).

Butler, Ruth, and Nurit Ruzany. 1993. Age and socialization effects on the development of social comparison motives and normative ability assessment in kibbutz and urban children. *Child Development 64*(2): 532–543.

Call, Vaughn R.A., Susan Sprecher, & Pepper Schwartz. 1995 August. The incidence and frequency of marital sex in a national sample. *Journal of Marriage and the Family 57*.

Calliste, Agnes. 2001. Black families in Canada: Exploring the interconnections of race, class and gender. In Bonnie Fox (Ed.), *Family Patterns, Gender Relations*, 2nd edition. Don Mills, ON: Oxford.

Campbell, A. 1980. *The sense of well-being in America: Recent patterns and trends*. New York: McGraw-Hill.

Campbell, Jacquelyn C., Paul Miller, & Mary M. Cardwell. 1994 June. Relationship status of battered women over time. *Journal of Family Violence 9*: 99–111.

Campbell, Rebecca, Cris Sullivan, & William S. Davidson. 1995 June. Women who use domestic violence shelters: Changes in depression over time. *Psychology of Women Quarterly 19*: 237–255.

Canada. Department of Justice. 2002. Minister of Justice Announces the Child-Centred Family Justice Strategy, http://www.canada.justice.gc. ca/en/news/nr/; Accessed on December 21, 2002.

Canadian Council on Social Development. 1997. *The Progress of Canada's Children*. Ottawa: Canadian Council on Social Development.

Cancian, Francesca. 1987. *Love in America*. New York: Cambridge University Press.

Cannon, Bethany. 1999 December. Marriage and Cohabitation: A Comparison of Adult Attachment Style and Quality Between the Two Types of Relationships. Dissertation Abstracts International: Section B: *The Sciences & Engineering. 60*(5–B): 2332.

Caradec, Vincent. 1997. Forms of conjugal life among the young elderly. *Population: An English Selection* 9: 47–74.

Carlson, M.J., & M.E. Corcoran. 2001. Family structure and children's behavioral and cognitive outcomes. *Journal of Marriage and Family* 63: 779–792.

Caron Sandra L., & Marjorie Ulin. 1997 July-August. Closeting and the quality of lesbian relationships. *Families in Society* 78(4): 413–419.

Carr, Deborah. 1996. Two paths to self-employment? Women's and men's self-employment in the United States, 1980. *Work and Occupations* 23(1): 26–53.

Carroll, Grace. 1998 Summer. Mundane extreme environmental stress and African American families: A case for recognizing different realities. *Journal of Comparative Family Studies* 29(2): 271–284.

Carrier, Sylvie. 1995. Family status and career situation for professional women. *Work, Employment, and Society* 9(2): 343–358.

Carstensen, Laura L., John M. Gottman, & Robert W. Levenson. 1995 March. Emotional behavior in long-term marriage. *Psychology and Aging 10.*

Carswick, Kelly. 1997 Winter. Canadian caregivers. *Canadian Social Trends 2.*

Cascardi, Michele, K., Daniel O'Leary, & Erika E. Lawrence. 1995. Characteristics of women physically abused by their spouses and who seek treatment regarding marital conflict. *Journal of Consulting and Clinical Psychology* 63: 616–623.

Cashdan, Elizabeth. 1994. A sensitive period for learning about food. *Human Nature* 5(3): 279–291.

Castellano, Marlene Brant. 2002. *Aboriginal Family Trends: Extended Families, Nuclear Families, Families of the Heart.* Ottawa: The Vanier Institute of the Family www.vifamily.ca; accessed 30 December 2002.

Castells, Manuel. 1996 March. The net and the self: Working notes for a critical theory of the informational society. *Critique of Anthropology* 16(1): 9–38.

Cavan, R., & K.R. Ranck. 1938. *The Family and the Depression.* Chicago: University of Chicago Press.

CBC News. *The Family-Friendly Workplace: A Look at Two Companies,* 23 March 1994.

Cernkovich, S.A., & Peggy C. Giordano. 1987. Family relationships and delinquency. *Criminology* 25: 295–321.

Chadwick, B.A., & C.B. Chappell, 1980. The two-income family in Middletown, 1924–1978. In Stephen J. Bahr (Ed.), *Economics and The Family.* Lexington, Mass: Lexington Books.

Chafetz, Janet Saltzman, & Jaqueline Hagan. 1996 Summer. The gender division of labor and family change in industrial societies: A theoretical accounting. *Journal of Comparative Family Studies,* 27: 187–219.

Chan, Anna Y., & Ken. R. Smith. 1996. *A Comparison of the Marital Quality and Stability of Interracial and Same-Race Marriages.* American Sociological Association.

Chan, Yuk-Chung. 1994 March. Parenting stress and social support of mothers who physically abuse their children in Hong Kong. *Child Abuse and Neglect 18:* 261–269.

Chant, Sylvia. 2000 December. Men in crisis? Reflections on masculinities, work and family in North-West Costa Rica *European Journal of Development Research* 12(2): 199–218.

Chao, Ruth K. 1994. Beyond parental control and authoritarian parenting style: Understanding Chinese parenting through the cultural notion of training. *Child Development* 65(4): 1111–1119.

Chao, Ruth K. 1996. Chinese and European American mothers' beliefs about the role of parenting in children's school success, *Journal of Cross Cultural Psychology* 27(4): 403–423.

Chappell, Neena L. 1996 Fall. Editorial. *Canadian Journal on Aging/La Revue Canadienne du Vieillissement 15,* 3, 341–345.

Chappell, Neena L. 1997 Fall. Health care reform: Implications for seniors. *Journal of Aging Studies* 11(3): 171–175.

Chappell, Neena & Audrey Blandford. 1991 September. Informal and formal care: Exploring the complementarity. *Ageing and Society, 11*(3): 299–317.

Chappell, Neena L. & Susan A. McDaniel. 1999 March. Health care in regression: Contradictions, tensions and implications for Canadian seniors. *Canadian Public Policy/Analyse de Politiques,* 25(1): 123–132.

Chappell, Neena L. & Margaret Penning. 1996 January. Behavioural problems and distress among caregivers of people with dementia. *Ageing and Society* 16(1): 57–73.

Chatters, Linda M., Robert Joseph Taylor, & Rukmalie Jayakody. 1994 Autumn. Fictive kinship relations in black extended families. *Journal of Comparative Family Studies* 25(3): 297–312.

Cheal, David. 1991. *Family and the State of Theory.* Toronto: University of Toronto Press.

Cheal, David. 1993. Unity and difference in postmodern families. *Journal of Social Issues* 14(1): 3–19.

Cheal, David. 1996. *New Poverty: Families in Postmodern Society.* Westport, CT: Greenwood Press.

Cheal, David. 1997. Hidden in the household: Poverty and dependence at different ages. Paper presented at the Conference, Intergenerational Equity in Canada, 20–21 February. Statistics Canada, Ottawa.

Cheal, David. 2002. *Sociology and Family Life.* London: Palgrave.

Chekki, Dan A. 1996. Cultural dynamics and futuristic scenarios of the Virasaiva community in North America. *Research in Community Sociology* 6: 295–310.

Chen, Qin. 1999. *Development During Adolescence: Age, Family Support and Daily Experience.* American Sociological Association (ASA).

Cheng, Simon, H., & Wen H. Kuo. 2000 Autumn. Family socialization of ethnic identity among Chinese American pre-adolescents. *Journal of Comparative Family Studies* 31(4): 463–484.

Chenn, Chao-Nan. 1999 April. Change of living arrangement and its consequences among the elderly in Taiwan. Proceedings of the National Science Council, Republic of China, Part C: *Humanities and Social Sciences* 9(2): 364–375.

Cherry, Andrew. 1993. Combining cluster and discriminant analysis to develop a social bond typology of runaway youth. *Research on Social Work Practice* 3(2): 175–190.

Chilton, R.J., & G.E. Markle. 1972. Family disruption, delinquent conduct and the effect of subclassification. *American Sociological Review, 37*: 93–99.

Choi, Alfred & Jeffrey L. Edleson. 1996. Social Disapproval of Wife Assaults: A National Survey of Singapore. *Journal of Comparative Family Studies* 27(1): 73–88.

Choi, Namkee G. 1995. Long-term elderly widows and divorcees: Similarities and differences. *Journal of Women and Aging* 7(3).

Christensen, Donna-Hendrickson & Kathryn D. Rettig. 1995. The relationship of remarriage to post-divorce co-parenting. *Journal of Divorce and Remarriage 24:* 1–2.

Church, Elizabeth. 1996. Kinship and stepfamilies, pp. 81–106. In Marion Lynn (Ed.), *Voices: Essays on Canadian Families.* Scarborough, ON: Nelson.

Church, Elizabeth. 1998. Ottawa relaxes work rules on foreign spouses, *The Globe and Mail* 2 October 1998: B23.

Clark, Roger, & Terry Clifford. 1996. Towards a resources and stressors model: The psychological adjustment of adult children of divorce. *Journal of Divorce and Remarriage 25:* 3–4.

Clark, Susan M. 1993. Support needs of the Canadian single parent family, pp. 223–238. In Joe Hudson & Burt Galaway (Eds.), *Single Parent Families: Perspectives on Research and Policy.* Toronto: Thompson.

Clarkberg, Marin, & Phyllis Moen. 2001 March. Understanding the time-squeeze: Married couples' preferred and actual work-hour strategies. *American Behavioral Scientist* 44(7): 1115–1136.

Clarke, Sally, & Barbara Wilson. 1994 July. The relative stability of remarriage; a cohort approach using vital statistics. *Family Relations 43.*

Clarke-Stewart, K. Allison. 1991. Does day care affect development? *Journal of Reproductive and Infant Psychology* 9(2–3): 67–78.

Clifford, Janice Elizabeth. 1998 February. *The Effects of Single-Mother Families on Adult Children's Marital Stability.* Dissertation Abstracts International, A: *The Humanities and Social Sciences* 58(8): 3320–A.

Clifford, Terry, & Roger Clark. 1995. Family climate, family structure and self-esteem in college females: The physical versus psychological—wholeness divorce debate revisited. *Journal of Divorce and Remarriage* 23(3–4).

Climo, Jacob. 1992. *Distant Parents.* New Brunswick, NJ: Rutgers University Press.

Coffey, Steve, & Horst Stipp. 1997 March-April. The interactions between computer and television usage. *Journal of Advertising Research* 37(2): 61–67.

Cohan, Marsha H., 1999 September. The technology-dependent child and the socially marginalized family: A provisional framework. *Qualitative Health Research* 9(5): 654–668.

Cohan, Catherine L., & Stacey Kleinbaum. 2002 February. Toward a greater understanding of the cohabitation effect: Premarital cohabitation and marital communication. *Journal of Marriage and the Family* 64(1): 180–192.

Coleman, H.H., M.L. Weinman, & P.H. Bartholomew. 1980. Factors affecting conjugal violence. *Journal of Psychology* 105: 197–202.

Coleman, Jean U., & Sandra M. Stith. 1997 June. Nursing students' attitudes toward victims of domestic violence as predicted by selected individual and relationship variables. *Journal of Family Violence* 12: 113–138.

Coleman, Marilyn, Lawrence Ganong, & Susan M. Cable. 1997 February. Beliefs about women's intergenerational family obligations to provide support before and after divorce and remarriage. *Journal of Marriage and the Family* 59: 165–176.

Collier, Linda M., Juliet Dee, Douglas Fraleigh, & Joseph J. Hemmer. 1995. Interact: A symposium of responses to the Hate Speech Forum. *Howard Journal of Communications* 5(4): 317–330.

Collins, Louise. 1999 Summer. Emotional adultery: Cybersex and commitment. *Social Theory and Practice 25:* 2, 243–270.

Collins, Patricia Hill. 1990. Mammies, matriarchs and other controlling images, pp. 67–90. In *Black Feminist Thought: Knowledge, Consciousness and the Politics of Empowerment.* Boston: Union Hyman.

Collins, Randall. 1975. *Conflict Sociology: Toward an Explanatory Science.* New York: Academic Press.

Collins, Stephen. 1991. The transition from lone-parent family to step-family, pp. 156–175. In Michael Hardy & Graham Crow (Eds.), *Lone Parenthood: Coping with Constraints and Making Opportunities in Single-Parent Families.* Toronto: University of Toronto Press.

Collis, Marion. 1999 March. Marital conflict and men's leisure: How women negotiate male power in a small mining community. *Journal of Sociology* 35(1): 60–76.

Coltrane, Scott. 1998. *Gender and Families*. Thousand Oaks, California: Pine Forge Press.

Conger, Rand D., Xiaojia Ge, & Glen H. Elder, Jr., 1994 April. Economic stress, coercive family process, and developmental problems of adolescents. *Child Development* 65: 541–561.

Connidis, Ingrid. 1985 March. The service needs of older people: Implications for public policy. *Canadian Journal on Aging/La Revue Canadienne du Vieillissement* 4(1): 3–10.

Connidis, Ingrid. 1989 Fall. Contact between siblings in later life. *Canadian Journal of Sociology/Cahiers canadiens de sociologie* 14(4): 429–442.

Connidis, Ingrid Arnet. 2001. *Family Ties and Aging*. Thousand Oaks, CA: Sage.

Connidis, Ingrid Arnet, & Julie A. McMullin. 1994. Social support in older age: Assessing the impact of marital and parent status.*Canadian Journal on Aging/La Revue Canadienne du Vieillissement* 13(4): 510–527.

Connidis, Ingrid Arnet, Carolyn J. Rosenthal, & Julie Ann McMullin. 1996 December. The impact of family composition on providing help to older parents: A study of employed adults. *Research on Aging* 18(4): 402–429.

Conte, Anthony E. 1994. The discipline dilemma: Problems and promises. *Education* 115(2): 308–331.

Contreras, Raquel, Susan S. Hendrick, & Clyde Hendrick. 1996. Perspectives on marital love and satisfaction in Mexican American and Anglo-American couples. *Journal of Counseling and Development* 74(4).

Cook, Donelda A., & Michelle Fine. 1995. Motherwit: Childrearing Lessons from African-American Mothers of Low Income, pp. 118–142. In Beth Blue Swadener & Sally Lubeck (Eds.), *Children and Families At Promise: Deconstructing the Discourse of Risk*. Albany: State University of New York Press.

Cooksey, Elizabeth C., Elizabeth G. Menaghan, & Susan M. Jekielek. 1997. Life course effects of work and family circumstances on children. *Social Forces* 76(2): 637–667.

Cooney, Rosemary Santana. 1999 November. Primary family caregivers of impaired elderly in Shanghai, China. *Research on Aging* 21(6): 739–761.

Cooney, Teresa M., & Jane Kurz. 1996. Mental health outcomes following recent parental divorce: The case of young adult offspring. *Journal of Family Issues* 17(4).

Coontz, Stephanie. 1992. *The Way We Never Were: American Families and the Nostalgia Trap*. New York: Basic Books.

Corak, Miles. 1998. *Death and Divorce: The Long-Term Consequences of Parental Loss*. Paper presented at the 2nd CILN Conference, Burlington, Ontario, 27–28 September 1998.

Corak, Miles and Andrew Heisz. 1999. *Death and Divorce: The Long-Term Consequences of Parental Loss on Adolescents*. Analytical Studies Branch Research Paper Series. Ottawa: Statistics Canada, Catalogue number 11F0019MIE999135.

Corley, Charles J., Timothy S. Bynum, Angel Prewitt, & Pamela Schram. 1996 July. The impact of race on juvenile court processes: Quantitative analyses with qualitative insights.*Caribbean Journal of Criminology and Social Psychology* 1(2): 1–23.

Correa, Sonia. 1994. *Population and Reproductive Rights: Feminist Perspectives from the South*. London: Zed Books.

Cortex, J.B., & F.M. Gatti. 1972. *Delinquency and Crime: A Biopsychosocial Approach*. New York: Seminar Press.

Cote, Marguerite Michelle. 1992, A painful situation still crying out for a solution: Montreal's street youth. *Revue internationale d'action communautaire* 27(67): 145–152.

Cowan, Carolyn Pape & Philip A. Cowen. 1995 October. Interventions to ease the transition to parenthood: Why they are needed and what they can do. *Family Relations 44*.

Cowan, Philip, F.L. Jessica, & Carolyn Pape Cowan. 1995 September. Who's got the power? Gender differences in partners' perceptions of influence during marital problem-solving discussions. *Family Process* 34(3): 303–321.

Cox, Chante L., Michael O. Wexler, Caryl E. Rusbult, & Stanley O. Gaines, Jr. 1997. Prescriptive support and commitment processes in close relationships. *Social Psychology Quarterly* 60(1): 79–90.

Cox, Christine E. 2000. *The Contributions of Grandmothers to Perceived Competence in Young Children*. Southern Sociological Society (SSS).

Coxet, Martha J., Blair Paley, Margaret Burchinal, & Chris C. Payne. 1999 August. Marital perceptions and interactions across the transition to parenthood. *Journal of Marriage and the Family* 61(3): 611–625.

Creamer, Mark, & Ian M. Campbell. 1988. The role of interpersonal perception in dyadic adjustment. *Journal of Clinical Psychology* 44 (3): 424–430.

Crohan, Susan E. 1996 November. Marital quality and conflict across the transition to parenthood in African American and white couples. *Journal of Marriage and the Family 58*.

Cross, Gary & Richard Szostak. 1995. Women and work before the factory, pp. 37–51. In Gary Cross & Richard Szostak (Eds.), *Technology and American Society: A History*. Englewood Cliffs, NJ: Prentice Hall.

Crouter, Ann C., & Beth Manke. 1994 April. The changing American workplace: Implications for individuals and families. *Family Relations 43*: 117–124.

Crouter, Ann C. 1984. Spillover from family to work: The neglected side of the work-family interface. *Human Relations 37*(6): 425–441.

Currie, Dawn. 1988. Rethinking what we do and how we do it: A study of reproductive decisions. *Canadian Review of Sociology and Anthropology 25*(2): 231–253.

D'Emilio, John, & Estelle B. Freedman. 1988. *Intimate Matters: A History of Sexuality*. New York: Harper & Row.

Dahinten, V. Susan, & J. Douglas Willms. 2002. The effects of adolescent child-bearing on children's outcomes. Pp. 243–258 in J. Douglas Willms, ed. *Vulnerable Children: Findings from Canada's National Longitudinal Survey of Children and Youth*. Edmonton: University of Alberta Press, and Ottawa: Human Resources Development Canada, Applied Research Branch.

Dalla Zuanna, Gianpiero, Stefano Gavini, & Angela Spinelli. 1998 March. The effect of changing sexual, marital and contraceptive behaviour on conceptions, abortions, and births. *European Journal of Population/Revue europeenne de demographie 14*(1): 61–88.

Daly, Anne & Diane Sinuth. 1996 November. Policy challenges of the contemporary socio-economic status of indigenous Australian families. *Australian Journal of Social Issues 31*(4): 355–375.

Daly, Kerry J., & Michael P. Sobol. 1993 Fall. The adoption alternative for pregnant adolescents: Decision making, consequences, and policy implications. *The Journal of Social Issues 48*(3): 143–161.

Daly, Martin, & Margo Wilson. 1985. Child abuse and other risks of not living with both parents. *Ethology and Sociobiology 6*(4): 197–210.

Darroch, Gordon. 1981 February. Urban ethnicity in Canada: Personal assimilation and political communities. *La Revue Canadienne de Sociologie et d'Anthropologie/The Canadian Review of Sociology and Anthropology 18*(1): 93–100.

Dasgupta, Shamita Das, & Sujata Warrier. 1996. In the footsteps of Arundhati: Asian Indian women's experience of domestic violence in the United States. *Violence Against Women 2*(3): 238–259.

Davies, Lorraine, & Patricia Jane Carrier. 1998. The importance of power relations for the division of household labour. *Canadian Journal of Sociology 23*(4).

Davies, Lorraine, Julie Ann McMullin, William R. Avison, with Gale L. Cassidy. 2001. *Social Policy, Gender Inequality and Poverty*. Ottawa: Status of Women Canada.

Davis, Liane V., Jan L. Hagen, & Theresa J. Early. 1994. Social services for battered women: Are they adequate, accessible, and appropriate? *Social Work 39*: 695–704.

Davis, Phillip W. 1996. Threats of corporal punishment as verbal aggression: A naturalistic study. *Child Abuse and Neglect 20*(4): 289–304.

Davis, Robert C., & Barbara Smith. 1995 October. Domestic violence reforms: Empty promises or fulfilled expectations? *Crime and Delinquency 41*: 541–552.

Dawson, Pam & Carolyn J. Rosenthal. 1996. Wives of institutionalized elderly men: The first stage of the transition to quasi-widowhood. *Journal of Aging and Health*, 1991, 3, 3, 315–334.

Deal, James E., Karen Smith Wampler, & Charles F. Halverson Jr. 1992 December. The importance of similarity in the marital relationship. *Family Process 31*(4): 369–382.

DeBoer, Danelle D. 2002 December. *The Effect of Infertility on Individual Well-Being*. Dissertation Abstracts International, A: The Humanities and Social Sciences 62, 6, 2249–A.

Degliantoni, Lisa. 1997 March April. I love you just the way you are. *Psychology Today 30*.

Deimling, Gary T., Noelker, Linda S. & Aloen L. Townsend. 1989. *A Comparative Analysis of Family Caregivers' Health and Well-Being*. North Central Sociological Association (NCSA).

DeKeseredy, Walter S., & Katharine D. Kelly. 1995. Sexual abuse in Canadian university and college dating relationships: The contribution of male peer support. *Journal of Family Violence 10*(1): 41–53.

DeKeseredy, Walter S. & Katharine D. Kelly. 1993. The incidence and prevalence of woman abuse in Canadian university and college dating relationships. *Canadian Journal of Sociology 18*(2): 137–159.

DeKeseredy, Walter S., & Martin D. Schwartz. 1994. Locating a history of some Canadian woman abuse in elementary and high school dating relationships. *Humanity and Society 18*(3): 49–63.

DeLongis, Anita & Darrin R. Lehman. 1989 March. The usefulness of a structured diary approach in studying marital relationships. *Journal of Family Psychology 2*(3): 337–343.

DeMaris, Alfred, & Steven Swinford. 1996 January. Female victims of spousal violence: Factors influencing their level of fearfulness. *Family Relations 45*: 98–106.

Demi, Alice, Roger Bakeman, & Linda Moneyham. 1997 March. Effects of resources and stressors on burden and depression of family members who provide care to an HIV-infected woman. *Journal of Family Psychology 11*: 35–48.

Demo, David H., & Alan C. Acock. 1996. Singlehood, marriage and remarriage: The effects of family structure and family relationships on mothers' well-being. *Journal of Family Issues 17*(3).

Denton W.H., B.R. Burleson, B.V. Hobbs, M. Von Stein, & C.P. Rodriguez. 2001 October. Cardiovascular reactivity and initiate/avoid patterns of marital communication: a test of Gottman's psychophysiologic model of marital interaction. *Journal of Behavioral Medicine* 24(5): 401–421.

Desjardins, Bernard, & Jean Dumas. 1993. *Population Aging and the Elderly, Current Demographic Analysis.* Ottawa: Statistics Canada. Catalogue no.91–533E.

Desrosiers, Helene, Celine LeBourdais, & Benoit Laplante. 1995. The breakup of reconstituted families: The experience of Canadian women. *Recherches Sociographiques* 36(1): 47–64.

Devine, Danielle, & Rex Forehand. 1996 April. Cascading toward divorce: The roles of marital and child factors. *Journal of Consulting and Clinical Psychology* 64.

Devine, John. 1995. Can metal detectors replace the panopticon? *Cultural Anthropology* 10(2): 171–195.

Dickson, Paul & George Sciadas. 1997 February. Canadians connected: Household computer use. *Canadian Economic Observer.*

Diez-Bbolanos, A.M., & Perez Rodrigues. 1989 July. Effects of inequality on the female's marital adjustment and satisfaction. *Revista de psicologia General y Aplicada* 42(3): 395–401.

Dinkmeyer, Don, & Robert Sherman. 1989 March-June. Brief Adlerian family therapy. *Individual Psychology: Journal of Adlerian Theory, Research & Practice. Special Issue: Varieties of Brief Therapy* 45(1–2): 148–158.

Dixon-Mueller, Ruth. 1993. *Population Policy and Women's Rights.* Westport, CT: Praeger.

Doherty, William J. & Deborah S. Simmons. 1996. Clinical practice patterns of marriage and family therapists: A national survey of therapists and their clients. *Journal of Marital and Family Therapy* 22(1).

Donovan, Catherine. 2000 May. Who needs a father? Negotiating biological fatherhood in British lesbian families using self-insemination. *Sexualities* 3(2): 149–164.

Dooley, Martin. 1993. Recent changes in the economic welfare of lone mother families in Canada: The roles of market work, earnings and transfers, pp. 115–132. In Joe Hudson & Burt Galaway (Eds.), *Single Parent Families: Perspectives on Research and Policy.* Toronto: Thompson.

Dorow, Sara. 2002. China R us? Care, consumption and transnationally adopted children. In D. Cook, (Ed.), *Symbolic Childhood.* New York: Peter Lang.

Douglass, Frazier M., & Robin Douglass. 1995 July. The marital problems questionnaire (MPQ): A short screening instrument for marital therapy. *Family Relations* 44.

Downs, William R., & Joan F. Robertson. 1991. Random versus clinical samples: A question of inference. *Journal of Social Service Research, Vol.* 14(1–2): 57–83.

Doyal, L. 1995. *What Makes Women Sick: Gender and the Political Economy of Health.* New Jersey: Rutgers University Press.

Drakich, Janice. 1993. In whose best interest? The politics of joint custody, pp. 331–341. In Bonnie Fox (Ed.), *Family Patterns, Gender Relations.* Toronto: Oxford.

Drapeau, Sylvie, Marie Simard, Madeleine Beaudry, & Cecile Charbonneau. 2000 January. Siblings in family transitions. *Family Relations: Interdisciplinary Journal of Applied Family Studies* 49(1): 77–85.

Dronkers, Jaap 1996. *The effects of parental conflicts and divorce on the average well-being of pupils in secondary education.* American Sociological Association.

Dryburgh, Heather. 2001. Teenage pregnancy. *Health Reports* 12(1): 1–9. Ottawa: Statistics Canada, Catalogue number 82–003.

Dryler, Helen. 1998. *Educational Choice in Sweden: Studies on the Importance of Gender and Social Contexts.* Swedish Institute for Social Research Dissertation Series 31.

Dua, Enakshi. 1999. Beyond diversity: Exploring the ways in which the discourse of race has shaped the institution of the nuclear family, pp. 237–260. In Enaskshi Dua (Ed.), *Scratching the Surface: Canadian Anti-Racist Feminist Thought.* Toronto: Women's Press.

Duberman, Lucile. 1975. *The Reconstituted Family: A Study of Remarried Couples and their Children.* Chicago: Nelson-Hall Publishers.

Dubinsky, Karen. 1999. *The Second Greatest Disappointment: Honeymooning and Tourism at Niagara Falls.* Toronto: Between the Lines.

Ducibella, John, S. 1995. Consideration of the impact of how children are informed of their parents' divorce decisions: A review of the literature. *Journal of Divorce and Remarriage* 24 (3–4).

Dudley, James R., 1996. Noncustodial fathers speak about their parental role. *Family and Conciliation Courts Review* 34(3).

Dunne, G. 1997. *Lesbian Lifestyles: Women, Work and the Politics of Sexuality.* Toronto: University of Toronto.

Duong Tran, Quang, Serge Lee, & Sokley Khoi. 1996 December. Ethnic and gender differences in parental expectations and life stress. *Child and Adolescent Social Work Journal* 13: 515–526.

Duran-Aydintug, Candan. Former spouses exiting role identities. *Journal of Divorce and Remarriage* 24(3–4): 195.

Duran-Aydintug, & Marilyn Ihinger-Tallman. 1995. Law and stepfamilies. *Marriage and Family Review* 21(3–4): 169–192.

Durkheim, Émile. 1951. *Suicide, étude de sociologie.* (English Title) *Suicide: A Study in Sociology.* Translated by John A. Spaulding and George Simpson. Glencoe, Ill: Free Press.

Durkheim, Émile. 1957. *The Elementary Forms of the Religious Life*. New York: Free Press.

Durodoye, Beth A. 1997. Factors of marital satisfaction among African American couples and Nigerian male/African American female couples. *Journal of Cross-Cultural Psychology* 28(1).

Duvander, Ann Zofie E. 1999. The transition from cohabitation to marriage: A longitudinal study of the propensity to marry in Sweden in the early 1990s. *Journal of Family Issues* 20(5): 698–717.

Duxbury, Linda Elizabeth, Christopher Alan Higgins, & D. Roland Thomas. 1996. Work and family environments and the adoption of computer-supported supplemental work-at-home. *Journal of Vocational Behavior* 49(1): 1–23.

Dwyer, Diane C., Paul R. Smokowski, & John C. Bricout. Domestic violence research: theoretical and practice implications for social work. *Clinical Social Work Journal* 23 (summer): 185–198.

Easterlin, Richard, & Eileen Crimmins. 1991. Private materialism, personal self-fulfillment, family life and public interest: the nature, effects and causes of recent changes in the values of American youth. *Public Opinion Quarterly* 55: 499–533.

Easterlin, Richard, Christine Schaeffer, & Diane Macunovich. 1993. Will the baby boomers be less well off than their parents? Income, wealth, and family circumstances over the life cycle. *Population and Development Review*, 19(3): 497–522.

Eaton, Linda Carole. 2000 August. *A Study of the Correlation between the Coming-Out Process and the First Long-Term Homosexual Relationship between Gay Males*. Dissertation Abstracts International, A: The Humanities and Social Sciences 61, 2, 782–A–783–A.

The Economist. 1996. Let them wed. January 6 Issue.

Edit S. Molnar, & Pongracz Tiborne. 1998. Extramarital Births in Europe and Hungary in the 1990s. *Szociologiai Szemle* 3: 37–54.

Edleson, Jeffrey L. 1999 August. Children's witnessing of adult domestic violence. *Journal of Interpersonal Violence* 14(8): 839–870.

Eells, Laura Workman, & Kathleen O'Flaherty. 1996. Gender perceptual differences in relation to marital problems. *Journal of Divorce and Remarriage* 25(2).

Ehrenreich, Barbara. 2001, 2002. *Nickel and Dimed: On (Not) Getting by in America*, 1st Owl Books edition. New York: Henry Holt.

Ehrensaft, Mirian K., & Dina Vivian. 1996. Spouses' reasons for not reporting existing marital aggression as a marital problem. *Journal of Family Psychology* 10(4).

Eichler, Margrit. 1988. *Families in Canada Today: Recent Changes and Their Policy Consequences*, 2nd edition. Toronto: Gage.

Eichler, Margit. 1989 February. Reflections on motherhood, apple pie, the new reproductive technologies and the role of sociologists in society. *Society-Societe* 13(1): 1–5.

Eichler, Margrit. 1996. Lone parent families: An instable category in search of stable policies. In C.J. Richardson (Ed.) *Family Life: Patterns and Perspectives*. Toronto: McGraw-Hill Ryerson.

Eichler, Margrit. 1997. *Family Shifts: Families, Policies and Gender Equality*. Toronto: Oxford University Press.

Eichler, Margrit. 2001. Biases in Family Literature, pp. 51–66. In Maureen Baker (Ed.), *Families: Changing Trends in Canada, 4th edition*. Toronto: McGraw-Hill Ryerson.

Eichstedt, Jennifer L. 1996. Heterosexism and gay/lesbian/bisexual experiences: Teaching strategies and exercises. *Teaching Sociology* 24: 384–388.

Ek, Carl A., & Lala Carr Steelman. 1988. Becoming a runaway: From the accounts of youthful runners. *Youth and Society* 9(3): 334–358.

Elder, Glen H. Jr. 1992. Models of the Life Course, *Contemporary Sociology* 21: 632–635.

Elliot, M. 1999. Classifying family life education on the World Wide Web. *Family Relations* 48: 7–13.

Ellison, Christopher G. 1996. Conservative Protestantism and the corporal punishment of children: Clarifying the issues., *Journal for the Scientific Study of Religion* 35(1): 1–16.

Ellison, Christopher G., John P. Bartkowski, & Michelle L. Segal. 1996. Conservative Protestantism and the parental use of corporal punishment. *Social Forces* 74(3): 1003–1028.

Ellison, Nicole B. 1999 Fall. Social impacts: New perspectives on telework. *Social Science Computer Review* 17(3): 338–356.

Elmer, E. & G. Gregg. 1967. Developmental aspects of abused children. *Pediatrics* 50: 596–602.

Emanuels-Zuurveen, Lineke, & Paul M.G. Emmelkamp. 1996. Individual behavioral-cognitive therapy v. marital therapy for depression in maritally distressed couples. *British Journal of Psychiatry* 169(2).

Emanuels-Zuurveen, Lineke, & Paul M.G. Emmelkamp. 1997. Spouse aided therapy with depressed patients. *Behavior Modification* 21(1).

Emick Michelle A., & Bert Hayslip Jr. 1996. Custodial grandparenting: New roles for middle-aged and older adults. *International Journal of Aging and Human Development* 43(2): 135–154.

Engels, Frederick. 1972. *The Origin of the Family, Private Property and the State*. New York: Pathfinder.

Engle, Patrice L., Sarah Castle, & Purnima Menon. 1996. Child Development: Vulnerability and Resilience. *Social Science and Medicine* 43(5): 621–635.

Epstein, Rachel. 1996. Lesbian families, pp. 107–130. In Lynn, Marion (Ed.), *Voices: Essays on Canadian Families*. Toronto: Nelson Canada.

Erel, Osnat, & Bonnie Burman. 1995 July. Inter-relatedness of marital relations and parent-child relations: A meta-analytic review. *Psychological Bulletin 118.*

Erel, Osnat, Gayla Margolin, & Richard S. John. 1998. Observed sibling interaction: Links with the marital and the mother-child relationship. *Developmental Psychology 34*(2): 288–298.

Erickson, Rebecca J., Laura Nichols, & Christian Ritter. 2000 October. Family influences on absenteeism: Testing an expanded process model. *Journal of Vocational Behavior 57*(2): 246–272.

Erikson, Erik H. 1950. *Childhood and Society*. New York: Norton.

Estrada, Ana Ulloa, & Julianne M. Holmes. 1999 April-June. Couples' perceptions of effective and ineffective ingredients of marital therapy. *Journal of Sex & Marital Therapy 25*(2): 151–162.

Etaugh, Claire & Denise Folger. 1998 August. Perceptions of parents whose work and parenting behaviors deviate from role expectations. *Sex Roles 39*(3–4): 215–223.

Etaugh, Claire & Cara Moss. 2001 May. Attitudes of employed women toward parents who choose full-time or part-time employment following their child's birth. *Sex Roles 44*(9–10): 611–619.

Eyster, Sandra Lee. 2000 August. *Friends, Family and a Committed Relationship: Identity Theory and the Relationships of Married Heterosexual and Cohabiting Lesbian Couples*. Dissertation Abstracts International, A: The Humanities and Social Sciences 61(2): 783–A.

Ezra, Marni, & Melissa Deckman. 1996 March-April. Balancing work and family responsibilities: Flextime and child care in the federal government. *Public Administration Review 56*: 174–179.

Faludi, Susan. 1991. *Backlash: The Undeclared War Against American Women*. New York: Crown.

Farber, Naomi. 1999 November-December. Losing ground, gaining insight. *Society 37*, 1(243): 16–23.

Farhood, Laila, Huda Zurayk, Monique Chaya, Fadia Saadeh, Garbis Meshefedjian, & Thuraya Sidani. 1993. The impact of war on the physical and mental health of the family: The Lebanese experience. *Social Science and Medicine 36*(12): 1555–1567.

Farkas, Janice I., & Angela M. O'Rand. 1998 March. The pension mix for women in middle and late life: The changing employment relationship. *Social Forces 76*(3): 1007–1032.

Fast, Janet E., Norah C. Keating, Leslie Oakes, & Deanna L. Williamson. 1997. *Conceptualizing and Operationalizing the Costs of Informal Elder Care*. NHRDP Project No. 6609–1963–55. Ottawa: National Health Research and Development Program, Health Canada.

Fauve-Chamoux, Antoniette. 1998. Introduction: Adoption, affiliation, and family recomposition—inventing family continuity. *History of the Family 3*(4): 385–392.

Fawcett, Matthew. 1990. Taking the middle path: Recent Swedish legislation grants minimal property rights to unmarried cohabitants. *Family Law Quarterly 24*: 179–202.

Feerick, Margaret M., & Jeffrey J. Haugaard. 1999 December. Long-term effects of witnessing marital violence for women: The contribution of childhood physical and sexual abuse. *Journal of Family Violence 14*(4): 377–398.

Feldman, Shirley S., Lawrence Fisher, & Laura Seitel. 1997. The effect of parents' marital satisfaction on young adults' adaptation: A longitudinal study. *Journal of Research on Adolescence 7*(1): 55–80.

Fellegi, Ivan. 1997. *Statistical services: Preparing for the future*. Chief Statistician of Canada's presentation to the United Kingdom Statistics Users Conference, 11 November 1997, London.

Ferri, Elsa. 1993. Socialization experiences of children in lone parent families: Evidence from the British National Child Development Study, pp. 281–290. In Joe Hudson & Burt Galaway (Eds.), *Single Parent Families: Perspectives on Research and Policy*. Toronto: Thompson.

Field, B. 1972. The child with spina bifida: Medical and social aspects of the problems of a child with multiple handicaps and his family. *Medical Journal of Australia 2*: 1294–1287.

Fineman, Martha Albertson, & Roxanne Mykitiuk (Eds.) 1994. *The Public Nature of Private Violence: The Discovery of Domestic Abuse*. New York, NY: Routledge.

Finklehor, David, Nancy Asdigian, & Gerald Hotaling. 1996. New categories of missing children: Injured, lost, delinquent, and victims of caregiver mix-ups. *Child Welfare 75*(4): 291–310.

Finn, Jerry. 1995. Computer-based self-help groups: A new resource to supplement support groups. *Social Work with Groups. Special Issue: Support Groups, Current Perspectives on Theory and Practice, Vol. 18*(1): 109–117.

Finn, Jerry. 1996. Computer-based self-help groups: On-line recovery for addictions. *Computers in Human Services, Vol. 13*(1): 21–41.

Finn, Jerry, & Mary Banach. 2000 April. Victimization online: The downside of seeking human services for women on the Internet. *CyberPsychology & Behavior 3*(2): 243–254.

Finn, Jerry, & Mary Banach. 2000 October. Victimization online: The downside of seeking human services for women on the Internet. *CyberPsychology & Behavior 3*(5): 785–796.

Finn, Jerry, & Melissa Lavitt. 1994. Computer-based self-help groups for sexual abuse survivors. *Social Work with Groups 17*(1–2): 21–46.

Finnie, Ross. 1993. Women, men, and the economic consequences of divorce: Evidence from Canadian longitudinal data. *Canadian Review of Sociology and Anthropology 30*(2): 205–241.

Firestone, Juanita M., Linda C. Lambert, & William A. Vega. 1999, June. Intimate violence among women of Mexican origin: Correlates of abuse. *Journal of Gender, Culture, and Health 4*(2): 119–134.

Firestone, Juanita, & Beth Anne Shelton. 1988 December. An estimation of the effects of women's work on available leisure time. *Journal of Family Issues 9*(4): 478–495.

Fischer, Claude S. 1992. *America Calling: A Social History of the Telephone to 1940*. Berkeley, CA: University of California Press.

Fisher, H. 1992. *Anatomy of Love: A Natural History of Mating, Marriage and Why We Stray*. New York: Fawcett.

Fiske, Jo-Anne, & Rose Johnny. 1996. The Neduten family: Yesterday and today pp. 225–241. In Marion Lynn (Ed.), *Voices: Essays on Canadian Families*. Toronto: Nelson.

Flanagan, Constance A. 1988. *The Effects of Parents' Insecure Work Attachment on the Young Adolescent*. North Central Sociological Association (NCSA).

Flandrin, J-L. 1979. *Families in Former Times: Kinship, Household and Sexuality in Early Modern France*. Cambridge: Cambridge University Press.

Fligstein N., A. Hochschild, K. Voss, J. Schor, M. Burawoy. 1995. Roundtable Discussion: Overwork: Causes and consequences of rising work hours. *Berkeley Journal of Sociology: A Critical Review, Volume XXXXV*.

Flippen, Chenoa Anne. 2000 June. Racial and ethnic inequality in housing wealth: A multi-level approach. *Dissertation Abstracts International, A: The Humanities and Social Sciences 60*(12): 4619–A.

Flippen, Chenoa A. 2000. *Unequal Returns to Housing Investments? A Study of Real Housing Appreciation among Black, White, and Hispanic Households*. American Sociological Association.

Florsheim, Margaret J., & John J. Herr. 1990 Winter. Family counseling with elders. *Generations: Journal of the American Society on Aging. Special Issue: Counseling and Therapy for Elders, Vol. 14*(1): 40–42.

Follette, William C., Neil S. Jacobson, Dirk Revenstorf, Donald H. Baucom, Kurt Hahlweg, Gayla Margolin. 2000 June. Variability in outcome and clinical significance of behavioral marital therapy: A reanalysis of outcome data. *Prevention & Treatment Vol. 3*, np.

Follingstad, Diane R., Michael J. Brondino, & Kathryn J. Kleinfelter. 1996 September. Reputation and behavior of battered women who kill their partners: Do these variables negate self-defense? *Journal of Family Violence 11*: 251–267.

Fondacaro, Mark R., Michael E. Dunkle, & Maithilee K. Pathak. 1998 February. Procedural justice in resolving family disputes: A psychosocial analysis of individual and family functioning in late adolescence. *Journal of Youth and Adolescence 27*(1): 101–119.

Fong, Eric, Barry Wellman, Melissa Kew, & Rima Wilkes. 2001 June. *Correlates of the digital divide: Individual, household and spatial variation*. Report to Office of Learning Technologies, Human Resources Development Canada.

Formoso, Diana, Nancy A. Gonzales, & Leona S. Aiken. 2000 April. Family conflict and children's internalizing & externalizing behavior: Protective factors. *American Journal of Community Psychology 28*(2): 175–199.

Forsyth, Craig, & Robert Gramling. 1998. Socio-economic factors affecting the rise of commuter marriage. *International Journal of the Sociology of the Family, 28*(2): 93–106.

Forte, James A., David D. Franks, & Janett A. Forte. 1996 January. Asymmetrical role-taking: Comparing battered women. *Social Work 41*: 59–73.

Forthofer, Melinda S., Howard J. Markman, & Martha Cox. 1996 August. Associations between marital distress and work loss in a national sample. *Journal of Marriage and the Family 58*.

Fournier, Suzanne, and Ernie Crey. 1997. *Stolen From Our Embrace: The Abduction of First Nations Children and the Restoration of Aboriginal Communities*. Vancouver and Toronto: Douglas and McIntyre.

Fowers, Blaine J., Eileen M. Lyons, & Kelly H. Montel. 1996. Positive marital illusions: Self-enhancement or relationship enhancement? *Journal of Family Psychology 10*(2).

Fowers, Blaine J., Kelly H. Montel, & David H. Olson. 1996. Predicting marital success for premarital couple types based on PREPARE. *Journal of Marriage and Family Therapy 22*(1).

Fowers, B.J., & D.H. Olson. 1986. Predicting marital success with PREPARE: *A predictive validity study. Journal of Marital and Family Therapy 12*: 403–413.

Fox, Bonnie. 1993. The rise and fall of the breadwinner-homemaker family, pp.147–157. In Bonnie Fox (Ed.), *Family Patterns/Gender Relations*. Toronto: Oxford.

Fox, Bonnie. 2001 November. The formative years: How parenthood creates gender. *La Revue Canadienne de Sociologie et d'Anthropologie/The Canadian Review of Sociology and Anthropology 38*(4): 373–390.

Fox, Bonnie J. and Meg Luxton. 2000. Conceptualizing family, pp. 22–33. In Bonnie J. Fox (Ed.), *Family Patterns, Gender Relations*. Toronto: Oxford,

Fox, Greer-Litton, & Priscilla White Blanton. 1995. Noncustodial fathers following divorce. *Marriage and Family Review* 20(1–2).

Fox, Greer Litton, & Dudley Chancey. 1998 November. Sources of economic distress: Individual and family outcomes. *Journal of Family Issues* 19(6): 725–749.

Frame, Marsha Wiggins, & Constance L. Shehan. 1994 April. Work and well-being in the two-person career: Relocation stress and coping among clergy husbands and wives. *Family Relations* 43: 196-205.

Franklin, Mary Beth. 1999. Till a long-distance job do us part, *Kiplinger's Personal Finance Magazine* January, www.findarticles.com; accessed 31 December 2002.

Franklin, Ursula M. 1983, 1990. *The Real World of Technology.* Montreal, Toronto: CBC Enterprises.

Franks, Melissa M., & Mary Anne Paris Stephens. 1996 January. Social support in the context of caregiving: Husbands' provision of support to wives involved in parent care. *Journals of Gerontology Series B: Psychological Sciences and Social Sciences.*

Frederick, Judith, & Jason Hamel. 1998 Spring. Canadian attitudes to divorce. *Canadian Social Trends:* 6–11.

Fredriksen, Karen. 1996. Gender differences in employment and the informal care of adults. *Journal of Women & Aging* 8(2): 35–53.

Freedman, David, & David Hemenway. 2000 June. Precursors of lethal violence: A death row sample. *Social Science and Medicine* 50(12): 1757–1770.

Freiband, David M., 1996 June. *The Fulfillment of Marital Ideals: A Study of Marital Satisfaction and Personal Well-Being.* Dissertation Abstracts International: Section B: The Sciences & Engineering Vol. 56(12–B), pp. 7092.

Freidenberg, Judith, & Muriel Hammer. 1998 Spring. Social networks and health care: The case of elderly Latinos in East Harlem. *Urban Anthropology* 27(1): 49–85.

Freidrich, W.N. 1979. Predictors of the coping behavior of mothers of handicapped children. *Journal of Consulting and Clinical Psychology,* 47: 1140–1141.

French, Maggie. 1991. Becoming a lone parent, pp. 126–142. In Michael Hardy & Graham Crow (Eds.), *Lone Parenthood: Coping with Constraints and Making Opportunities in Single-Parent Families.* Toronto: University of Toronto Press.

Friedemann, Marie Louise, & Adele A. Webb. 1995. Family health and mental health six years after economic stress and unemployment. *Issues in Mental Health Nursing,* 16(1): 51–66.

Friendly, Martha. 1994. *Child Care Policy in Canada: Putting the Pieces Together.* Don Mills, ON: Addison-Wesley.

Furstenberg, Frank F. Jr. 1996 June. The future of housework the second. *American Demographics:* 34–40.

Furstenberg, Frank F. Jr., J. Brooks-Gunn, & P. Morgan. 1987. *Adolescent Mothers in Later Life.* New York: Cambridge.

Gadd, Jane. 1997. The drift to the bottom. *The Globe and Mail,* 21 June: D1, D2.

Gaines, Stanley O. Jr. 1996. Impact of interpersonal traits and gender-role compliance on interpersonal resource exchange among dating and engaged/married couples. *Journal of Social and Personal Relationships* 13(2).

Galambos, Nancy L., Heather A. Sears et al. 1995. Parents' work overload and problem behaviour in young adolescents. *Journal of Research on Adolescents,* 5(2): 201–223.

Galambos, Nancy L., & Heather A. Sears. 1998 November. Adolescents' perceptions of parents' work and adolescents' work values in two-earner families. *Journal of Early Adolescence* 18(4): 397–420.

Galinsky, E., & D. Hughes. 1986. *The Fortune Magazine Child-Care Study.* New York: Bank Street College.

Galinsky, Ellen, Diane Hughes, & Judy David. 1990. Trends in corporate family-supportive policies. *Marriage and Family Review* 15(3–4): 75–94.

Galin, Rita S., 1994. The intersection of class and age: Mother-in-law/daughter-in-law relations in rural Taiwan. *Journal of Cross Cultural Gerontology* 9(2): 127–140.

Galston, William A., 1996. Braking divorce for the sake of children, The American Enterprise 7 (May/June). *The Globe and Mail,* 2000, 49.

Galt, Virginia. Telework option boosts job satisfaction. *The Globe and Mail,* October 12, 2000.

Ganong-Coleman, Lawrence H. 1998 Fall. Attitudes regarding Filial Responsibilities to Help Elderly Divorced Parents and Stepparents. *Journal of Aging Studies* 12(3): 271–290.

Ganster, Daniel C., & Bart Victor. 1988 March. The impact of social support on mental and physical health. *The British Journal of Medical Psychology* 61(1): 17–36.

Gardiner, Greg. 1997 April. Aboriginal boys' business: A study of indigenous youth in Victoria in relation to educational participation and contact with the juvenile justice system. *Journal of Intercultural Studies* 18(1): 49–61.

Garnefski, Nadia, & Sjoukje Okma. 1996. Addiction risk and aggressive/criminal behaviour in adolescence: Influence of family, school and peers. *Journal of Adolescence* 19(6): 503–512.

Garnett, Gale. 1997. Joni Mitchell: Our sad-eyed lyricist of love. *The Globe and Mail,* 6 December: D19.

Garo Baca, Eleonora Celia. 1995 June. Some considerations about feminine subjectivity. *Revista IDEA de la Facultad de Ciencias de Humanas* 9(18): 109–114.

Gartner, Rosemary, & Bonnie J. Fox. 1993. Commentary and debate. *Canadian Journal of Sociology 18*(3): 313–324.

Gee, Ellen M. 1986. The life course of Canadian women: An historical and demographic analysis. *Social Indicators Research 18*: 263–283.

Gee, Ellen M. 1990. Preferred timing of women's life events: A Canadian study. *International Journal of Aging and Human Development 31*(4): 279–294.

Gee, Ellen M. 1993. Adult outcomes associated with childhood family structure: An appraisal of research and an examination of Canadian data, pp. 291–310. In Joe Hudson & Burt Galaway (Eds.), *Single Parent Families: Perspectives on Research and Policy.* Toronto: Thompson.

Gee, Ellen M. 1995. Contemporary diversities, pp. 79–110. In Nancy Mandell & Ann Duffy (Eds.), *Canadian Families: Diversity, Conflict and Change.* Toronto: Harcourt Brace.

Gee, Ellen M., & Meredith M. Kimball. 1987. *Women and Aging.* Toronto: Butterworths.

Gelles, Richard J. 1996. Constraints against family violence: How well do they work? pp. 30–42. In Eve S. Buzzawa, & Carl G. Buzzawa (Eds.), *Do Arrests and Restraining Orders Work?* Thousand Oaks, CA: Sage Publications.

Gelles, Richard J. 1994 Spring. Introduction: Part of a special issue on family violence. *Journal of Comparative Family Studies 25*: 1–6.

Gelles R., & D. Loseke (Eds.). 1993. *Current Controversies on Family Violence.* Newbury Park, CA: Sage.

Gerstel, Naomi. 1984. *Commuter Marriage: A Study of Work and Family.* New York: Guilford Press.

Gibbs, Ian, & Ian Sinclair. 1999 February. Treatment and treatment outcomes in children's homes. *Child & Family Social Work 4*(1): 1–8.

Gibson, Douglas M. 1998. Requiem for a master storyteller, *The Globe and Mail,* 28 February: C3.

Giele, Janet Zollinger. 1996. Decline of family: Conservative, liberal and feminist views. In David Popenoe, Jean Bethke Elshtain, and David Blankenhorn (Eds.), *Promises to Keep: Decline and Renewal of Marriage in America.* Lanham, MD: Rowman and Littlefield Publishers, Inc.

Giddens, Anthony. 1992. *The Transformation of Intimacy: Sexuality, Love, and Eroticism in Modern Societies.* Cambridge: Polity Press.

Giles-Sims, Jean. 1994. *Family structure and corporal punishment.* International Sociological Association, Association paper.

Gill, Gurjeet, & Ray Hibbins. 1996. Wives' encounters: Family work stress and leisure in two-job families. *International Journal of Sociology of the Family 26*(2): 43–54.

Gillmore, Mary Rogers, Steven M. Lewis, Mary Jane Lohr, Michael S. Spencer, & Rachelle D. White. 1997 August. Repeat pregnancies among adolescent mothers. *Journal of Marriage and the Family 59*: 536–550.

Ginn, Jay, & Jane Sandell. 1997 September. Balancing home and employment: Stress reported by social services staff. *Work, Employment and Society 11*(3): 413–434.

Glass, Jennifer, & Tetsushi Fujimoto. 1995. Employer characteristics and the provision of family responsive policies. *Work and Occupations 22*(4): 380–411.

Glenn, Evelyn Nagano. 1987. Gender and the family. In Beth B. Hess & Myra Marx Ferree (Eds.), *Analyzing Gender: A Handbook of Social Science Research.* Newbury Park: Sage.

Glenn, E. N. 1994. Social constructions of mothering, pp. 1–29. In E.N. Glenn, G. Chang, & L.R. Forcey (Eds.), *Mothering, Ideology, Experience and Agency.* New York: Routledge.

Glenn, Norval D. 1975. The contribution of marriage to the psychological well-being of males and females. *Journal of Marriage and the Family 37*(3): 594–601.

Glenn, Norval D. 1990. Qualitative research on marital quality in the 1980s: A critical review. *Journal of Marriage and the Family 52*: 818–831.

Glenn, Norval D. 1998. Closed hearts, closed minds: The textbook story of marriage. *Society 35*(3): 69–79.

Glick, Susan. 1997 April. *Examining the Relationship Between Perceived Emotional Expressiveness and Marital Adjustment.* Dissertation Abstracts International: Section B: The Sciences & Engineering Vol. 57(10–B), pp. 6648.

The Globe and Mail. 1993. Should governments try to make marriage more robust? 22 March: A17.

The Globe and Mail. 1997. Is it wrong to keep a promise? Editorial, 7 October: A20.

Gokalp, Catherine, & Henri Levidon. 1983 Fall-Winter. Effects of wives' employment on fathers' participation in family life. *The Tocqueville Review/La Revue Tocqueville 5*(2): 397–418.

Goldberg, Margaret E., Barbara W. Lex, & Nancy K. Mello. 1996 April. Impact of maternal alcoholism on separation of children from their mothers: Findings from a sample of incarcerated women. *American Journal of Orthopsychiatry 66*: 228–238.

Goldenberg, Sheldon. 1987. *Thinking Sociologically.* Belmont, CA: Wadsworth.

Goldstein, Marion Z. 1990. The role of mutual support groups and family therapy for caregivers of demented elderly. *Journal of Geriatric Psychiatry 23*(2): 117–128.

Goldstein, D., & A. Rosenbaum. 1985. An evaluation of the self-esteem of maritally violent men. *Family Relations 34*: 425–428.

Golombok, Susan, & Fiona Tasker. 1994. Children in lesbian and gay families: Theories and evidence. *Annual Review of Sex Research 5*: 73–100.

Gonzalez Almagro, Ignacio. 1993 January. Socialization: An Interactive Process RS. *Cuadernos de Realidades Sociales* 41–42 227–246.

Gonzalez, Ketty P., Tiffany M. Field, & David Lasko. 1995. Adolescents from divorced and intact families. *Journal of Divorce and Remarriage 23*(3–4).

Goode, William. 1993. *World Changes in Divorce Patterns*. New Haven: Yale University Press.

Goodman, Catherine. 1990 November. Evaluation of a model self-help telephone program: Impact on natural networks. *Social Work 35*(6): 556–562

Goodman, Lisa A., Mary Ann Dutton, & Maxine Harris. 1995 October. Episodically homeless women with serious mental illness: Prevalence of physical and sexual assault. *American Journal of Orthopsychiatry 65*: 468–478.

Goossens, Frits A., Geertruud Ottenhoff, & Willem Koops. 1991. Day care and social outcomes in middle childhood: A retrospective study. *Journal of Reproductive and Infant Psychology 9*(2–3): 137–150.

Gordon, Linda, & Sara McLanahan. 1991. Single parenthood in 1900. *Journal of Family History 16*(2): 97–116.

Gordon, Robert A. 1996. Parental licensure and its sanction. *Society 34*(1): 65–69.

Gordon, Sean, & Tony Sesku. 1997. Mom's side of family known for large numbers, *Edmonton Journal*, 21 November: A12.

Gorlick, Carolyne A., & D. Alan Pomfret. 1993. Hope and circumstance: Single mothers exiting social assistance, pp. 253–270. In Joe Hudson & Burt Galaway (Eds.), *Single Parent Families: Perspectives on Research and Policy*. Toronto: Thompson.

Gottlieb, Benjamin H. 1985 July-August. Assessing and strengthening the impact of social support on mental health. *Social Work 30*(4): 293–300.

Gottlieb, Benjamin H. 1985. Social support and community mental health, pp. 303–326. In Sheldon Cohen and Leonard S. Syme, *Social Support and Health*. San Diego, CA: Academic Press.

Gottlieb, Benjamin H. 1985 Spring. Social networks and social support: An overview of research, practice, and policy implications. *Health Education Quarterly 12*(1): 5–22.

Gottlieb, Benjamin H., E. Kevin Kelloway, & Anne Martin-Matthews. 1996. Predictors of work family conflict, stress, and job satisfaction among nurses. *Canadian Journal of Nursing Research 28*(2): 99–117.

Gottlieb, Benjamin H., E. Kevin Kelloway, & Maryann Fraboni. 1994 December. Aspects of eldercare that place employees at risk. *The Gerontologist*. 34: 815–821.

Gottlieb, Laurie N., Ariella Lang, & Rhonda Amsel. 1996. The long-term effects of grief on marital intimacy following an infant's death. *Omega 33*(1).

Gottman, J.M. 1979. *Marital Interaction: Experimental Investigations*. New York: Academic Press.

Gottman, John M. 1982 Summer. Emotional responsiveness in marital conversations. *Journal of Communication 3*: 108–120.

Gottman, J.M. 1994. *What Predicts Divorce? The Relationship between Marital Processes and Marital Outcomes*. Hillsdale, NJ: Lawrence Erlbaum Associates.

Gottman, John M, Howard Markman, & Clifford Notarius. 1977. The topography of marital conflict: A sequential analysis of verbal and nonverbal behavior. *Journal of Marriage and the Family 39*(3): 461–477.

Gottman, John M., & Albert L. Porterfield. 1981. Communicative competence in the nonverbal behavior of married couples. *Journal of Marriage and the Family 43*(4): 817–824.

Gove, W.R., & R.D. Crutchfield. 1982. The family and juvenile delinquency. *Sociological Quarterly 23*: 301–319.

Graham, Carolyn W., Judith L. Fischer, Duane Crawford, Jacki Fitzpatrick, Kristan Bina. 2000 October. Parental status, social support, and marital adjustment. *Journal of Family Issues 21*(7): 888–905.

Grandin, Elaine, & Eugen Lupri. 1997. Intimate violence in Canada and the United States: A cross-national comparison. *Journal of Family Violence 12*(4): 417–443.

Grant, Kathryn E., & Bruce E. Compas. 1995 December. Stress and anxious depressed symptoms among adolescents: Searching for mechanisms of risk. *Journal of Consulting and Clinical Psychology 63*: 1015–1021.

Grant, Travis R., Alan J. Hawkins, David C. Dollahite. 2001. Web-based education and support for fathers: Remote but promising, pp. 143–170. In Jay Fagan & Alan J. Hawkins (Ed.), *Clinical and Educational Interventions with Fathers*. Binghamton, NY: Haworth Clinical Practice Press.

Gray, John. 1996. Domesticity, Diapers and Dad. *The Globe and Mail*, 15 June: D1.

Gray-Little, Bernadette, Donald H. Baucom, & Sherry L. Hamby. 1996. Marital power, marital adjustment and therapy outcomes. *Journal of Family Psychology 10*(3).

Greaves, Kathleen Marie. 2001 May. *The Social Construction of Sexual Interaction in Heterosexual Relationships: A Qualitative Analysis*. Dissertation Abstracts International, A: The Humanities and Social Sciences 61, 11, 4565–A-4566-A.

Green, Gill, Stephen Platt, Susan Eley, & Stephen T. Green. 1996 January. "Now and again it really hits me": The impact of an HIV-positive diagnosis upon psychosocial well-being. *Journal of Health Psychology* 1(1): 125–141.

Greenstein, Theodore N., 1995. *Gender ideology and perceptions of the fairness of the division of household labor: Effects on marital quality.* American Sociological Association paper.

Greif, Geoffrey L. 1995. When divorced fathers want no contact with their children: A preliminary analysis. *Journal of Divorce and Remarriage* 23(1–2).

Griffin, Joan M., Rebecca Fuhrer, Stephen A. Stansfeld, & Michael Marmot. 2002 March. The importance of low control at work and home on depression and anxiety: Do these effects vary by gender and social class? *Social Science and Medicine* 54(5): 783–798.

Grimm-Thomas, Karen, & Maureen Perry-Jenkins. 1994 April. All in a day's work: Job experiences, self-esteem, and fathering in working class families. *Family Relations,* 43: 174–181.

Grindstaff, Carl F. 1990. *Long-term consequences of adolescent marriage and fertility.* In Report on the Demographic Situation in Canada 1988. Ottawa: Statistics Canada, Catalogue no. 91–209.

Gringeri, Christina. 1995. Flexibility, the family ethic, and rural home-based work. *Affilia* 10(1): 70–86.

Grissett, Barbara, & Allen L. Furr. 1994. Effects of parental divorce on children's financial support for college. *Journal of Divorce and Remarriage* 22(1–2).

Groat, H. Theodore, Peggy C. Giordano, Stephen A. Cernkovich, M.D. Pugh, & Steven P. Swinford. 1997. Attitudes toward childbearing among young parents. *Journal of Marriage and the Family* 59: 568–581.

Gross, Penny. 1987. Defining post-divorce remarriage families: A typology based on the subjective perceptions of children. *Journal of Divorce* 10(1,2): 205–217.

Groves, Melissa & Diane Horm-Wingerd. 1991. Commuter marriages: Personal, family and career issues. *Sociology and Social Research,* 75(4): 212–217.

Gustafson, D.H., R.E. Gustafson, S.B. Wackerbarth. 1997. CHESS: Health information and decision support for patients and families. *Generations* 21(3): 56–59.

Guttman, Joseph. 1993. *Divorce in Psychosocial Perspective: Theory and Research.* Hillsdale, NJ: Lawrence Erlbaum Associates.

Gwyn, Sandra. 1992. *Tapestry of War: A Private View of Canadians in the Great War.* Toronto: HarperCollins.

Haas, Stephen M., & Laura Stafford. 1998 December. An initial examination of maintenance behaviors in gay and lesbian relationships. *Journal of Social and Personal Relationships* 15(6): 846–855.

Haddad, Tony, & Lawrence Lam. 1994 Summer. The impact of migration on the sexual division of family work: A case study of Italian immigrant couples. *Journal of Comparative Family Studies* 25(2): 167–182.

Hall, David R. & John Z. Zhao. 1995. Cohabitation and divorce in Canada: Testing the selectivity hypothesis. *Journal of Marriage and Family* 57(2): 421–427.

Halli, Shiva, & Zachery Zimmer. 1991. Common-law unions as a differentiating factor in the failure of marriage in Canada. *Social Indicators Research* 24: 329–345.

Hamby Sherry L. 2000 October. The importance of community in a feminist analysis of domestic violence among American Indians. *American Journal of Community Psychology* 28(5): 649–669.

Haines Erica, & Kate Weiner. 2000 July. "Everybody's got a dad…". Issues for lesbian families in the management of donor insemination. *Sociology of Health and Illness* 22(4): 477–499.

Hallman, Bonnie C., & Alun E. Joseph. 1999 Winter. Getting there: Mapping the gendered geography of caregiving to elderly relatives. *Canadian Journal on Aging/La Revue Canadienne du Vieillissement* 18(4): 397–414.

Hannah, Mo Teresa, Wade Luquet, & Joan McCormick. 1997 Spring. COMPASS as a measure of the efficacy of couples therapy. *The American Journal of Family Therapy* 25.

Hanson, Barbara. 1992. *The Myth of Biological Time Clock.* International Sociological Association Paper.

Harker, Kathryn. 2000. *Immigrant Generation, Assimilation and Adolescent Psychological Wellbeing: The Importance of Mediating Factors.* Southern Sociological Society (SSS).

Harrell, W.A., 1995. Husbands' involvement in housework: Effects of relative earning power and masculine orientation, *Psychological Reports* 77(3): 1331–1337.

Harris, Kathleen Mullan. 1997. *Teen Mothers and the Revolving Welfare Door.* Philadelphia: Temple University Press.

Harris, Marvin. 1997. *Culture, People, Nature: an Introduction to General Anthropology,* 7th edition. New York: Longman.

Harris, Maxine. 1996. Treating sexual abuse trauma with dually diagnosed women. *Community Mental Health Journal* 32: 371–385.

Harris, Sarah B. 1996. For better or for worse. *Journal of Elder Abuse and Neglect* 8(1): 1–33.

Harrison, Kelley A., Gina S. Richman, Glenda L. Vittimberga. 2000 March. Parental stress in grandparents versus parents raising children with behavior problems. *Journal of Family Issues* 21(2): 262–270.

Harter, Stephanie Lewis, & Robert J. Vanecek. 2000 Winter. Family of origin environment and coping with situations which vary by level of stress intensity. *Journal of Social and Clinical Psychology* 19(4): 463–479.

Hartmann, Heidi, & Roberta Spalter-Roth. 1996. A feminist approach to public policy making for women and families. *Current Perspectives in Social Theory 16*: 33–51.

Hartos, Jessica L., Thomas G. Power. 2000 September. Relations among single mothers' awareness of their adolescents' stressors, maternal monitoring, mother-adolescent comunication, and adolescent adjustment. *Journal of Adolescent Research 15*(5): 546–563.

Hattar-Pollara, Marianne, Afaf Ibrahim Meleis, & Hassanat Nagib. 2000 June. A study of the spousal role of Egyptian women in clerical jobs. *Health Care for Women International 21*(4): 305–317.

Havens, Betty, & Judith Chipperfield. 1990. Does informal care relate to ethnic diversity or social isolation? *International Sociological Association (ISA)*.

Hayes, Donald P., & Margaret G. Ahrens. 1988. Vocabulary simplification for children: A special case of motherese? *Journal of Child Language 15*(2): 395–410.

Hays, Sharon. 1997. *The Cultural Contradictions of Motherhood*. New Haven: Yale University Press.

Hays, Sharon. 1998. Reconsidering the choice: Do Americans really prefer workplace over home? *Contemporary Sociology 27*(1): 28–32.

Haythornthwaite, Caroline. 2001 January. *Tie strength and the impact of new media*. Proceedings of the 24th Hawaii International Conference of System Sciences.

Haythornthwaite, Caroline. 2001 November. Introduction: The Internet in everyday life. *American Behavorial Scientist 45*(3): 363–382.

Haythornthwaite, Caroline, M.M. Kazmer, J. Robins, & S. Showmaker. 2000. Community development among distance learners: Temporal and technological dimensions. *Journal of Computer-Mediated Communication 6*(1).

Hernan, Deidre. 2000 March. Expectations and attitudes affecting patterns of informal care in farming families in Northern Ireland. *Ageing and Society 20*(2): 203–216.

Heinicke, Christopher M., & Donald Guthrie. 1996. Prebirth marital interactions and postbirth marital development. *Infant Mental Health Journal 17*(2).

Heitlinger, Alena. 1993. *Women's Equality, Demography and Public Policies*. New York: St. Martin's.

Heitritter, Dianne Lynn. 1999 November. Meanings of family strength voiced by Somali immigrants: Reaching an inductive understanding. *Dissertation Abstracts International, A: The Humanities and Social Sciences 60*, 5, 1782–A-1783–A.

Helms-Erikson, Heather. 2001 November. Marital quality ten years after the transition to parenthood: Implications of the timing of parenthood and the division of housework. *Journal of Marriage and the Family 63*(4): 1099–1110.

Henderson, A. J. Z., K. Bartholomew, & D.G. Dutton. He loves me; he loves me not: Attachment and separation resolution of abused women. *Journal of Family Violence 12* (June): 169–191.

Hendrick, C., & S. Hendrick. 1996. Gender and the experience of heterosexual love, pp. 131–148. In J.T. Wood (Ed.), *Gendered Relationships*. Mountain View, Colorado: Mayfield.

Hennessy, Ellis, & Edward C. Melhuish. 1991. Early day care and the development of school-age children: A review. *Journal of Reproductive and Infant Psychology 9*(2–3): 117–136.

Henripin, Jacques, & Yves Peron. 1971. Demographic transitions in the province of Quebec. In David Glass & Roger Revelle (Eds.), *Population and Social Change*. London: Edward Arnold.

Hensley, Robert 1996. Relationship termination and the Fisher divorce adjustment scale: A comparative study. *Journal of Divorce and Remarriage 25*(1–2).

Heriot, Jessica. 1996. Maternal protectiveness following the disclosure of intrafamilial child sexual abuse. *Journal of Interpersonal Violence 11*(2): 181–194.

Herlyn, Ingrid, & Ulrike Vogel. 1989 July. Individualization: A New Perspective on the Life Situation of Women. *Zeitschrift fur Sozialisationsforschung und Erziehungssoziologie 9*(3): 162–178

Hessing, Melody. 1994 Winter. More than clockwork: Women's time management in their combined workloads. *Sociological Perspectives 37*: 611–633.

Hetherington, E. Mavis, & John Kelly. 2002. *For Better or for Worse: Divorce Reconsidered*. New York: W. W. Norton.

Hidalgo, Nitza M. 1997 November. A layering of family and friends: Four Puerto Rican families' meaning of community. *Education and Urban Society 30*(1): 20–40.

Hier, Sally J., Paula J. Korboot, & Robert D. Schweitzer. 1990. Social adjustment and symptomatology in two types of homeless adolescents: Runaways and throwaways. *Adolescence 25*(100): 761–771.

Hibbard, Judith H. 1985 Spring. Social ties and health status: An examination of moderating factors. *Health Education Quarterly 12*(1): 23–34.

Higgins, Christopher, Linda Duxbury, & Catherine Lee. 1994 April. Impact of life-cycle stage and gender on the ability to balance work and family responsibilities. *Family Relations 43*: 144–150.

Higgins, Daryl J., & Marita P. McCabe. 1994. The relationship of child sexual abuse and family violence to adult adjustment: Toward an integrated risk-sequelae model. *The Journal of Sex Research 31*(4): 255–266.

Hill, R. 1949. *Families Under Stress: Adjustment to the Crises of War Separation and Reunion*. New York: Harper and Bros.

Hill, Jeffrey E., Alan J. Hawkins, Maria Ferris, Michelle Weitzman. 2001 January. Finding an extra day a week: The positive influence of perceived job flexibility on work and family life balance. *Family Relations* 50(1): 49–58.

Hill, Robert G., Geoff Shepherd, & Pollyanna Hardy. 1998 December. In sickness and in health: The experiences of friends and relatives caring for people with manic depression. *Journal of Mental Health (UK)* 7(6): 611–620.

The Hitchhikers Guide To Cybernomics, a survey of the world economy. 1996 Fall. *The Economist*, s. 19.

Hobart, Charles. 1996. Intimacy and family life: Sexuality, cohabitation, and marriage, pp. 143–173. In Maureen Baker (Ed.), *Families: Changing Trends in Canada* (3rd edition). Toronto: McGraw-Hill Ryerson.

Hobart, Charles, & Frank Grigel. 1992. Cohabitation among Canadian students at the end of the eighties. *Journal of Comparative Family Studies* 23: 311–337.

Hochschild, A. 1983. *The Managed Heart*. Berkeley: University of California Press.

Hochschild, Arlie Russell. 1997. *The Time Bind: When Work Becomes Home and Home Becomes Work*. New York: Metropolitan Books.

Hock, Ellen, Mary-Beth Schirtzinger, & Wilma J. Lutz. 1995 March. Maternal depressive symptomatology over the transition to parenthood: Assessing the influence of marital satisfaction and marital sex role traditionalism. *Journal of Family Psychology* 9.

Hoelter, Lynette. 2000 February. *Fair is Fair—or is it? Perceptions of Fairness in the Household Division of Labor*. Dissertation Abstracts International Section A: Humanities & Social Sciences, Vol. 62(7–A), pp. 2587.

Hoem, Britta, & Jan M. Hoem. 1988 September. The Swedish family: Aspects of contemporary developments. *Journal of Family Issues* 9(3): 397–424.

Hoem, Jan. 1997. Educational gradients in divorce risks in Sweden in recent decades. *Population Studies* 51(1): 19–27.

Hoem, B., & Hoem, J.M. 1992. The disruption of marital and non-marital unions in contemporary Sweden, pp. 61–93. In J. Trussell, R. Hankinson, & J. Tilton (Eds.) *Demographic Applications of Event History Analysis*. Oxford, UK: Clarendon Press for IUSSP.

Hofferth, Sandra L., & S.G. Deich. 1994 September. Recent U.S. child care and family legislation in comparative perspective. *Journal of Family Issues* 15: 424–448.

Hoffman, Charles D., & Debra K. Ledford. 1995. Adult children of divorce: Relationships with their mothers and fathers prior to, following parental separation, and currently. *Journal of Divorce and Remarriage* 24(3–4).

Hoffman, Martin L., 1979. Development of moral thought, feeling, and behavior. *American Psychologist* 34(10): 958–966.

Hoffman, Saul, & Greg Duncan. 1995 Winter. The effect of incomes, wages and AFDC benefits in marital disruption. *The Journal of Human Resources 30*.

Hoglund, Collete L., & Karen B. Nicholas. 1995 June. Shame, guilt, and anger in college students exposed to abusive family environments. *Journal of Family Violence* 10: 141–157.

Holdaway, Doris M., & JoAnn Ray. 1992. Attitudes of street kids toward foster care. *Child and Adolescent Social Work Journal* 9(4): 307–317.

Holman, Thomas B., & Bing Dao Li. 1997. Premarital factors influencing perceived readiness for marriage. *Journal of Family Issues* 18(2): 124–144.

Holmstrom, Lynda Lytle, Paul S. Gray, & David A. Karp. 1999. *Good-Bye Mom and Dad: College-Bound Seniors' Perceptions of Parental Letting Go*. American Sociological Association (ASA).

Holtzworth-Munroe, Amy, Jennifer Waltz, Neil S. Jacobson, Valerie Monaco, Peter A. Fehrenbach, & John M. Gottman. 1992. Recruiting nonviolent men as control subjects for research on marital violence: How easily can it be done? *Violence and Victims* 7(1): 79–88.

Honey, Maureen. 1997. Maternal welders: Women's sexuality and propaganda on the home front during World War II. *Prospects* 22: 479–519.

Hooks, Bell. 1984. *Feminist Theory: From Margin to Centre*. Boston: South End Press.

Hooks, Gwen. 1997. *The Keystone Legacy: Recollections of a Black Settler*. Edmonton, Alberta: Brightest Pebble.

Hopper, Joseph. 1993 November. The rhetoric of motives in divorce. *Journal of Marriage and the Family* 55: 801–813.

Horn, Janice D., Heidi M. Feldman, & Dianna L. Ploof. 1995. Parent and professional perceptions about stress and coping strategies during a child's lengthy hospitalization. *Social Work in Health Care* 21(1): 107–127.

Hornung, C.A., B.C. McCullough, & T. Sugimoto. 1981 August. Status relationships in marriage: Risk factors in spouse abuse. *Journal of Marriage and the Family* 43(3): 675–692.

Hornung, C.A., B.C. McCullough, & T. Sugimoto. 1982. Status relationships in marriage: Risk factors in spouse abuse. *Journal of Marriage and the Family* 42: 675–692.

Horowitz, Allan V., Julie McLaughlin, Helene Raskin White, 1998 June. How the negative and positive aspects of partner relationships affect the mental health of young married people. *Journal of Health & Social Behavior* 39(2): 124–136.

Horton, Hayward Derrick, & Melvin E. Thomas. 1998 Winter. Race, class, and family structure: Differences in housing values for black and white homeowners. *Sociological Inquiry* 68(1): 114–136.

House, James S., Debra Umberson, & Karl Richard Landis. 1988. Structures and processes of social support. *Annual Review of Sociology* 14: 293–318.

Howell, Nancy, with Patricia Albanese, & Kwaku Obosu-Mensah. 2001. Ethnic families, pp. 116–142. In

Maureen Baker (Ed.), *Families: Changing Trends in Canada*, 4th edition. Toronto: McGraw-Hill Ryerson.

Huang, I-Chiao. 1991. Family stress and coping, pp. 289–334. In Stephen J. Bahr (Ed.), *Family Research: A Sixty-Year Review, 1930–1990, Volume 1*. New York: Lexington Books, Maxwell Macmillan International.

Huck, Barbara. 2001 February/March. Love in another world. *The Beaver: Canada's History Magazine*: 12–19.

Hudson Joe, & Burt Galaway (Eds.), *Single Parent Families: Perspectives on Research and Policy*. Toronto: Thompson.

Huisman, Kimberly A. 1996. Wife battering in Asian American communities: Identifying the service needs of an overlooked segment of the U.S. population. *Violence Against Women* 2(3): 260–283.

Hull, Jeremy. 2001. *Aboriginal Single Mothers in Canada, 1996: A Statistical Profile*. Research and Analysis Directorate, Indian and Northern Affairs, Ottawa.

Iacovetta, Franca. 1992. From contadina to worker: Southern Italian immigrant working women in Toronto, 1947–1962, pp. 281–303. In Bettina Bradbury (Ed.), *Canadian Family History: Selected Readings*. Toronto: Copp Clark Pitman.

Illig, Diane S. 1999 October. *Instrument Development for Assessing the Task Allocation by Lesbian and Gay Couples with Regard to Household and Familial Tasks*. Dissertation Abstracts International, A: The Humanities and Social Sciences 60, 4, 1347–A.

Innus, Harold Adams. 1995, c1951. *The Bias of Communication*. University of Toronto Press.

International Labor Organization. 1998. Gap in employment treatment for men and women still exists, *ILO News*, 15 February.

Isralowitz, Richard E. 1993. The kibbutz in transition: The influence of child sleeping arrangements on work and leisure attitudes and behavior. *Israel Social Science Research* 8(1): 91–107.

Isralowitz, Richard E. & Michal Palgi. 1992. Work attitudes and behaviors of kibbutz parents with familial and communal child sleeping arrangements. *Journal of Social Psychology* 132(1): 121–123.

Istar, Arlene. 1996. Couple assessment: Identifying and intervening in domestic violence in lesbian relationships. *Journal of Gay and Lesbian Social Services* 4(1): 93–106.

Jackson, Nicky Ali. 1996. Observational experiences of intrapersonal conflict and teenage victimization: A comparative study among spouses and cohabitors. *Journal of Family Violence* 11(3): 191–203.

Jacobson, Bert H., & Steven G. Aldana et al. 1996 September-October. The relationship between perceived stress and self-reported illness-related absenteeism. *American Journal of Health Promotion* 11(1): 54–61.

Jacobson, Neil S. 1989. The politics of intimacy. *The Behavior Therapist* 12(2): 29–32.

Jacobson, Neil S., John M. Guttman, Eric Gortner, Sara Berns, & Susan Jacoby. 2002. Half at ease in splitsville: A social scientist's long-term findings on the consquences of divorce. *The New York Times Book Review* 19 May: 38.

James, Adrian L., 1995. Social work in divorce: Welfare, mediation and justice. *International Journal of Law and the Family* 9(3).

James, Simon. 1996. Female household investment strategy in human and non-human capital with the risk of divorce. *Journal of Divorce and Remarriage* 25(1–2).

James-Fergus, Sharon. 1999. Rebuilding the African-Caribbean family in Britain, pp. 247–256. In Geoff Dench (Ed.), *Rewriting the Sexual Contract*. New Brunswick, NJ: Transaction.

Janus, Mark David, Anne W. Burgess, & Arlene McCormack. 1987. Histories of sexual abuse in adolescent male runaways. *Adolescence* 22(86): 405–417.

Janus, Mark David, Francis X. Archambault, Scott W. Brown, & Lesley A. Welsh. 1995. Physical abuse in Canadian runaway adolescents. *Child Abuse and Neglect* 19(4): 433–447.

Jargowsky, Paul. 1998. Urban poverty, race, and the inner city: The bitter fruit of thirty years of neglect, pp. 79–94. In Fred R. Harris, Lynn A. Curtis (Eds.), *Locked in the Poorhouse: Cities, Race, and Poverty in the United States*. Lanham, MD: Rowman & Littlefield.

Jarrett, Robin L., 1997 Summer. African-American family and parenting strategies in impoverished neighborhoods. *Qualitative Sociology* 20(2): 275–288.

Jarrett, Robin L., 1997 June. *Resilience Among Low-Income African American Youth: An Ethnographic Perspective Ethos* 25(2): 218–229.

Jasinski, Jana L., Nancy L. Asdigian, Glenda Kaufman Kantor. 1997 December. Ethnic adaptations to occupational strain: Work-related stress, drinking, and wife assault among Anglo and Hispanic Husbands. *Journal of Interpersonal Violence* 12(6): 814–831.

Jekielek, Susan M., 1996. *The Relative and Interactive Effects of Parental Conflict and Parental Marital Disruption on Child Well-Being*. American Sociological Association.

Jex, Steve M., & Tina C. Elacqua. 1999 April-June. Time management as a moderator of relations between stressors and employee strain. *Work & Stress* 13(2): 182–191.

Johnson, Phyllis J. 1998 May. Performance of household tasks by Vietnamese and Laotian refugees: Tradition and change. *Journal of Family Issues* 19(3): 245–273.

Johnson, Sheri L., & Theodore Jacob. 1997. Marital interactions of depressed men and women. *Journal of Consulting and Clinical Psychology* 65(1).

Johnson, Sue. 1997. A critical review of marital therapy outcome. *Canadian Journal of Psychiatry* 42(3).

Johnson, Susan M., & E. Talitman. 1997. Predictors of success in emotionally focused marital therapy. *Journal of Marital and Family Therapy* 23(2).

Jones, Carol, & Gordon Causer. 1995. Men don't have families: Equality and motherhood in technical employment. *Gender, Work and Organization* 2(2): 51–62.

Jones, Charles, Linn Clark, Joan Grusec, Randle Hart, Gabriele Plickert, & Lorne Tepperman. 2002 March. *Poverty, Social Capital, Parenting and Child Outcomes in Canada, A Report to the Applied Research Branch.* Strategic Policy, Human Resources Development Canada.

Jones, Charles L., Lorna Marsden, Lorne Tepperman. 1990. *Lives of Their Own: The Individualization of Women's Lives.* Toronto: Oxford University Press.

Jones, Elise F., Jacqueline Darroch Forrest, Noreen Goldman, Stanley Henshaw, Richard Lincoln, Jeannie Rosoff, Charles F. Westoff, & Deidre Wulf. 1993. *Teenage Pregnancy in Industrialized Countries.*

Jones, Fiona, & Ben Fletcher. 1993. An Empirical study of occupational stress transmission in working couples. *Human Relations* 46(7): 881–903.

Jones-Webb, Rhonda, Lonnie Snowden, Denise Herd, Brian Short, Peter Hannan. 1997 September. Alcohol-related problems among Black, Hispanic and White men: The contribution of neighborhood poverty. *Journal of Studies on Alcohol* 58(5): 539–545.

Jordan, Karen M., & Robert H. Deluty. 2000. Social support, coming out, and relationship satisfaction in lesbian couples. *Journal of Lesbian Studies* 4(1): 145–164.

Joubert, Charles. 1995 April. Catholicism and indices of social pathology in the states. *Psychological Reports* 76.

Judge, Sharon Lesar. 1998 July. Parental coping strategies and strengths in families of young children with disabilities. *Family Relations: Interdisciplinary Journal of Applied Family Studies* 47(3): 263–268.

Julian, Teresa W. & Patrick C. McKenry. 1993. Mediators of male violence toward female intimates. *Journal of Family Violence* 8(1): 39–56.

Jurk, Imas, et al. 1980. Family responses to mechanisms of adjustment following death of children with cancer. *Australian Pediatric Journal:* 85–88.

Kahana, Eva, & Boaz Kahana, Jennifer Kinney. 1982. Coping among vulnerable elders, pp. 64–85. In Zev Harel, Phyllis Ehrlich et al. (Eds.), *The Vulnerable Aged: People, Services, and Policies.* New York: Springer Publishing Co.

Kalin, Rudolf, & Carol A. Lloyd. 1985. Sex role identity, sex-role ideology and marital adjustment. *International Journal of Women's Studies* 8(1): 32–39.

Kalnins, Ilze et al. 1980. Concurrent stresses in families with a leukemic child. *Journal of Pediatric Psychology* 5(1): 81–92.

Kamerman, Sheila B., & Alfred J. Kahn. 1988 Fall. What Europe does for single-parent families. *The Public Interest* 93: 70–86.

Kamerman, Sheila, & Alfred Kahn (Eds.). 1997. *Family Change and Family Policies in Great Britain, Canada, New Zealand, and the United States.* Oxford: Clarendon Press.

Kanof, A., B. Kutner, & N.B. Georeon. 1972. The impact of infantile amaurotic familial idiocy (Tay-Sachs disease) on the family. *Pediatrics* 49: 37–45.

Kanter, Rosabeth Moss. 1983. *The Change Masters: Innovations for Productivity in the American Corporation.* New York: Simon and Schuster.

Kaplan, D.M., A. Smith, R. Grobstein, & S. Fischman. 1980. Family mediation of stress, pp. 475–488. In P.W. Power, & A.E. Dello-Orto (Eds.), *Role of the Family in the Rehabilitation of the Physically Disabled.* University Park Press, Baltimore, MD.

Kaplan, Elaine Bell. 1997. *Not Our Kind of Girl: Unravelling the Myth of Black Teenage Motherhood.* Berkeley, CA: University of California Press.

Karasek, Robert, & Tores Theorell. 1990. *Healthy Work: Stress, Productivity, and the Reconstruction of Working Life.* New York: Basic Books.

Karney, Benjamin R., & Thomas N. Bradbury. 1995. Assessing longitudinal change in marriage: An introduction to the analysis of growth curves. *Journal of Marriage and the Family* 57(4): 1091–1108.

Kashani, J.H., R. Venzke, & E.A. Millar. 1981. Depression in children admitted to hospital for orthopedic procedures. *British Journal of Psychiatry* 138: 21–35.

Kashubeck, Susan, Sheila M. Pottebaum, & Nancy O. Read. 1994 January. Predicting elopement from residential treatment. *American Journal of Orthopsychiatry* 64(1): 126–135.

Katz, Jennifer, Ileana Arias, Steven R.H. Beach, Gene Brody, & Paul Roman. 1995. Excuses, excuses: Accounting for the effects of partner violence on marital satisfaction and stability. *Violence and Victims* 10(4).

Katzev, Aphra R., Rebecca L. Warner, & Alan C. Acock. 1994 February. Girls or boys? Relationship of gender to marital instability. *Journal of Marriage and the Family* 56: 89–100.

Keating, Norah, Janet Fast, Judith Frederick (Statistics Canada), Kelly Cranswick (Statistics Canada), & Cathryn Perrier. 1999. *Eldercare in Canada: Context, content and consequences.* Ottawa: Statistics Canada, Housing, Family and Social Statistics Division.

Keating, Norah, Karen Kerr, Sharon Warren, Michael Grace, et al. 1994 Summer. Who's the family in family caregiving? *Canadian Journal on Aging* 13(2): 268–287.

Keller, Diane W. 1999 October. *Dimensions of Parenting Stress of Mothers and Fathers of a School-Age Child with a Disability*. Dissertation Abstracts International, A: The Humanities and Social Sciences 60(4): 1347–A.

Kellogg, Nancy D., Thomas J. Hoffman, & Elizabeth R. Taylor. 1999 Summer. Early sexual experiences among pregnant and parenting adolescents. *Adolescence* 34(134): 293–303.

Kelly, Katharine D., & Walter S. DeKeseredy. 1994. Women's fear of crime and abuse in college and university dating relations. *Violence and Victims* 9(1): 17–30.

Kemp, Anita, Bonnie L. Green, & Christine Hovanitz. 1995 March. Incidence and correlates of post-traumatic stress disorder in battered women: Shelter and community samples. *Journal of Interpersonal Violence* 10: 43–55.

Kempe, C.H., F.N. Silverman, B.F. Steele, W. Droegmueller & H.K. Silver. 1962. The battered-child syndrome. *Journal of the American Medical Association* 181: 17–24.

Kendall, Lori. 1998 Summer. Meaning and identity in Cyberspace: The performance of gender, class, and race online. *Symbolic Interaction* 21(2): 129–153.

Kennedy, Cheryl-Ann, J.H. Skurnick, M. Foley, & D.B. Louria. 1995. Gender differences in HIV-related psychological distress in heterosexual couples. *AIDS Care* 7(suppl. 1): S33–S38.

Kermeen, Patricia. 1995 June. Improving postpartum marital relationships. *Psychological Reports 76*.

Kesner, John E. & Patrick C. McKenry. 2001 March–April. Single parenthood and social competence in children of color. *Families in Society* 82(2): 136–144.

Keyfitz, Nathan. 1986. The family that does not reproduce itself. *Population and Development Review* (suppl. 12): 139–154.

Keyfitz, Nathan. 1988. On the wholesomeness of marriage. In L. Tepperman & J. Curtis (Eds.), *Readings in sociology: An introduction*. Toronto: McGraw-Hill Ryerson.

Khandelwal, Ajay Kumar. 1999. *Narratives of Rise and Fall: Family, Memory and Mobility in Jaipur City*. Dissertation Abstracts International, C: Worldwide 60(3): 559–C.

Kheshgi-Genovese, Zareena, & Thomas A. Genovese. 1997. Developing the spousal relationship within stepfamilies. *Families in Society: The Journal of Contemporary Human Services* 78(3): 255–271.

Kiernan, Kathleen E., & Valerie Estaugh. 1993. *Cohabitation: Extra-marital Child-bearing and Social Policy*. London: Family Policy Studies Centre.

Kiester, Sara, Lee S. Sproull, John P. Walsh, & Bradford W. Hesse. 1992 Summer. Self-selected and randomly selected respondents in a computer network survey. *The Public Opinion Quarterly* 56(2): 214–244.

Kim, Jae Yop, & Kyu-taik, Sung. 2000 December. Conjugal violence in Korean American Families: A residue of the cultural tradition. *Journal of Family Violence* 15(4): 331–345.

King, Donna, & Carol E. Mackinnon. 1988. Making difficult choices easier: A review of research on day care and children's development. *Family Relations* 37(4): 392–398.

King, Storm A., Susan Engi, & Stephan T. Poulos. 1998 February. Using the Internet to assist family therapy. *British Journal of Guidance & Counselling* 26(1): 43–52.

King, Valerie, and Alan Booth. 2000. *Family Instability and Interpersonal Trust*. Paper presented at the Annual Meetings of the Population Association of America, Los Angeles. Located at www.gendercenter.org.

Kinnunen, Ulla, Jan Gerris, & Ad Vermulst. 1996 October. Work experiences and family functioning among employed fathers with children of school age. *Family Relations* 45: 449–455.

Kirchler, Erich. 1989 March. Everyday life experiences at home: An interaction diary approach to assess marital relationships. *Journal of Family Psychology* 2(3): 311–336.

Kirchmeyer, Catherine. 1993 May. Nonwork-to-work spillover: A more balanced view of the experiences and coping of professional women and men. *Sex Roles* 28(9–10): 531–552.

Kirk, H. David. 1984. *Shared Fate: A Theory and Method of Adoptive Relationships*. New York: Free Press.

Kirk, H. David. 1988. *Exploring Adoptive Family Life*. Port Angeles, Washington & Brentwood Bay, British Columbia: Ben-Simon Press.

Kirk, H. David, & Susan A. McDaniel. 1984. Adoption policy in Great Britain and North America. *Journal of Social Policy* 13(1): 75–84.

Kleban, Morton H., Elaine M. Brody, Claire B. Schoonover, & Christine Hoffman. 1989 May. Family help to the elderly: perceptions of sons-in-law regarding parent care. *Journal of Marriage and the Family* 51(2): 303–312.

Klein, David M., and James M. White. 1996. *Family Theories: An Introduction*. Thousand Oaks, California: Sage.

Klevens, Joanne, Maria Clara Bayon, & Margarita Sierra. 2000 March. Risk factors and context of men who physically abuse in Bogota, Colombia. *Child Abuse and Neglect* 24(3): 323–332

Klinger, Rochelle L. 1995. Gay violence. *Journal of Gay & Lesbian Psychotherapy* 2(3): 119–134.

Kluwer, Esther S., Jose Heesink, & Evert Van de Vliert. 1996 November. Marital conflict about the division of household labor and paid work. *Journal of Marriage and the Family 58*.

Kluwer, Esther S., Jose A.M. Heesink, & Evert Van De Vliert. 1997 August. The marital dynamics of conflict over the division of labor. *Journal of Marriage and the Family 59*: 635–653.

Knudson, Martin Carmen, & Anne R. Mahoney. 1996. Gender dilemmas and myth in the construction of marital bargains: Issues for marital therapy. *Family Processes 35*(2).

Kochanska, Grazyna. 1991. Socialization and temperament in the development of guilt and conscience. *Child Development 62*(6): 1379–1392.

Kochanska, Grazyna, Darcie L. Padavich, & Amy L. Koenig. 1996. Children's narratives about hypothetical moral dilemmas and objective measures of their conscience: Mutual relations and socialization antecedents. *Child Development 67*(4): 1420–1436.

Kogos, Jennifer L., & John Snarey. 1995. Parental divorce and the moral development of adolescents. *Journal of Divorce and Remarriage 23*(3–4).

Kohen, Dafna, Clyde Hertzman, & J. Douglas Willms. 2002. The importance of quality child care. Pp. 261–276 in J. Douglas Willms, ed. *Vulnerable Children: Findings from Canada's National Longitudinal Survey of Children and Youth*. Edmonton: University of Alberta Press, and Ottawa: Human Resources Development Canada, Applied Research Branch.

Kohli, Martin. 1986. Social organization and subjective construction of life course, pp. 271–292. In A.B. Sorenson, F.E. Weinhert, & L.R. Sharrod (Eds.), *Human Development and the Life Course*. Hillsdale, CA: Erlbaum.

Kolata, Gina. 1997. March of progress: Yesterday's never is today's why not. *Edmonton Journal*, 7 December: B4.

Kolbo, Jerome R., 1996. Risk and resilience among children exposed to family violence. *Violence and Victims 11*(2): 113–128.

Kolbo, Jerome R., Eleanor H. Blakely, & David Engleman. 1996 June. Children who witness domestic violence: A review of empirical literature. *Journal of Interpersonal Violence 11*: 281–293.

Kontos, Susan, & Loraine Dunn, 1989. Attitudes of care givers, maternal experiences with day care, and children's development. *Journal of Applied Developmental Psychology 10*(1): 37–51.

Kopiec, Kathleen M., 2000. *Witnessing Interparental Violence and Children's Adjustment*. American Sociological Association (ASA).

Kossek, Ellen Ernst, Parshotam Dass, & Beverly DeMarr. 1994 September. The dominant logic of employer-sponsored work and family initiatives: Human resource managers' institutional role. *Human Relations 47*: 1121–1149.

Kozuch, Patricia, & Teresa M. Cooney. Young adults' marital and family attitudes: The role of recent parental divorce, and family and parental conflict. *Journal of Divorce and Remarriage 23*(3–4): 1995.

Kposowa, Augustine. 1995. *Risk Factors for Divorce in the United States*. American Sociological Association.

Kruk, E. 1995. Grandparent grandchild contact loss: Findings from a study of grandparent rights members. *Canadian Journal on Aging 14*(4): 737–754.

Kufeldt, Kathleen, & Margaret Nimmo. 1987. Youth on the street: Abuse and neglect in the eighties. *Child Abuse and Neglect 11*(4): 531–543.

Kufeldt, Kathleen, & Philip E. Perry. 1989. Running around with runaways. *Community Alternatives 1*(1): 85–97.

Kulik Liat, & Haia Zuckerman Bareli. 1997 September. Continuity and discontinuity in attitudes toward marital power relations: Pre-retired versus retired husbands. *Ageing and Society, 17*(5): 571–595.

Kumar, Pramod, & Jayshree Dhyani. 1996. Marital adjustment: A study of some related factors. *Indian Journal of Clinical Psychology 23*(2).

Kunz, Jennifer, & Stephen J. Bahr. 1996. A Profile of Parental Homicide against Children. *Journal of Family Violence 11*(4): 347–362.

Kunz, Jennifer, & Phillip R. Kunz. 1995. Social support during the process of divorce: It does make a difference. *Journal of Divorce and Remarriage 24*(3–4).

Kurtz, Linda. 1995. The relationship between parental coping strategies and children's adaptive processes in divorced and intact families. *Journal of Divorce and Remarriage 24*(3–4).

Kurz, Demie. 1995. *For Richer or For Poorer: Mothers Confront Divorce*. New York: Routledge.

Kurz, Demie. 1996. Separation, divorce, and woman abuse. *Violence against Women 2*(1).

Kwan, Alex, Yui-huen. 1995. Elder abuse in Hong Kong: A new family problem for the Old East? *Journal of Elder Abuse and Neglect 6* (3–4): 565–580.

Lackey, Chad, & Kirk R. Williams. 1995. Social bonding and the cessation of partner violence across generations. *Journal of Marriage and the Family 57*: 295–305.

Lademann, A. 1980. The neurologically handicapped child. *Scandinavian Journal of Audiology 10* (suppl.): 23–26.

Laewen, Hans Joachim. 1989. A discussion of day care for children up to age three. *Zeitschrift fur Padagogik 35*(6): 869–888.

Lamb, Michael E. 1996. Effects of nonparental child care on child development: An update. *Canadian Journal of Psychiatry 41*(6): 330–342.

Lamba, Navjot K. 2003. The employment experiences of Canadian refugees: Measuring the impact of human and social capital on employment outcomes. *The Canadian Review of Sociology and Anthropology 40*(1), forthcoming.

Landale, Nancy S., & Nimfa B. Ogena. 1995. Migration and union dissolution among Puerto Rican women. *International Migration Review 29* (3): 671–692.

Landis, Kleine, Linda Foley, & Loretta Nall. 1995. Attitudes toward marriage and divorce held by young adults. *Journal of Divorce and Remarriage* 24(3–4).

Landolt, Monica A., Martin L. Lalumiere, & Vernon L. Quinsey. 1995. Sex differences in intra-sex variations in human mating tactics: An evolutionary approach. *Ethology and Sociobiology* 16(1): 3–23.

Landolt, Monica A., & Donald G. Dutton. 1997 September. Power and personality: An analysis of gay male intimate abuse. *Sex Roles* 37(5–6): 335–359.

Landry, Yves. 1992. Les filles du roi au xviie siécle: Orphelines en France. *Pioniéres au Canada*, Montreal: Lemeac.

Lapierre-Adamcyk, Evelyne. 1987 May. *Mariage et politique de la famille*. Paper presented at the Association des Demographiques du Québec, Ottawa.

Lapierre-Adamcyk, Evelyne, & Carole Charvet. 2000. Cohabitation and marriage: An assessment of research in demography. *Canadian Studies in Population* 27(1): 239–254.

Larcombe, E.S. 1978. A handicapped child means a handicapped family. *Journal of the Royal College of General Practice 28*, 46–52.

Larson, Jeffrey H., Stephan M. Wilson, & Rochelle Beley. 1994 April. The impact of job insecurity on marital and family relations. *Family Relations, 43*: 138–143.

Larson Reed W., & Sally Gillman. 1999 February. Transmission of emotions in the daily interactions of single-mother families. *Journal of Marriage and the Family* 61(1): 21–37.

LaSala, Michael C. 2000 Spring. Lesbians, gay men, and their parents: Family therapy for the coming-out crisis. *Family Process* 39(1): 67–81.

LaSala, Michael C., 2000. Gay male couples: The importance of coming out and being out to parents. *Journal of Homosexuality* 39(2): 47–71.

Laub, J.H., & R.J. Sampson. 1988. Unraveling families and delinquency: A reanalysis of the Glueck's data. *Criminology 26:* 355–380.

Lauer, Robert H., Jeanette C. Lauer, & Sarah T. Kerr. 1990. The long-term marriage: Perceptions of stability and satisfaction. *International Journal of Aging and Human Development* 31(3): 189–195.

Laumann, E.O, J.H.Gagnon, R.T. Michael, & S. Michaels. 1994. *The Social Organization of Sexuality: Sexual Practices in the United States*. Chicago: University of Chicago Press.

Lavee, Yoav, Shlomo Sharlin, & Ruth Katz. 1996. The effect of parenting stress on marital quality: An integrated mother-father model. *Journal of Family Issues 17.*

Lawrence, Elden Eugene. 2000 June. *Returning to Traditional Beliefs and Practices: A Solution for Indian Alcoholism*. Dissertation Abstracts International, A: The Humanities and Social Sciences 60, 12, 4611–A.

Laws, Judith Long, & Pepper Schwartz. 1977. *Sexual Scripts: The Social Construction of Female Sexuality.* Hindsdale, Illinois: Dryden.

Leavitt, Robin Lynn. 1991. Power and resistance in infant-toddler day care centers. *Sociological Studies of Child Development* 4: 91–112.

LeBourdais, Celine, G. Neil, and Pierre Turcotte. 2000. The changing face of conjugal relationships, *Canadian Social Trends 56*: 14–17.

LeBourdais, Celine, & Nicole Marcil-Gratton. 1994. Quebec's pro-active approach to family policy, pp. 103–116. In Maureen Baker (Ed.), *Canada's Changing Families: Challenges to Public Policy*. Ottawa: Vanier Institute of the Family.

LeBourdais, Celine, Ghyslaine Neill, and Pierre Turcotte. 2000 Spring. The changing face of conjugal relationships. *Canadian Social Trends:* 14–17.

Le Bourdais, Celine, & Nicole Marcil-Gratton. 1996. Family transformations across the Canadian/American border: When the laggard becomes the leader. *Journal of Comparative Family Studies* 27(3): 415–436.

Le Bourdais, Celine, Ghyslaine Neill, & Nathalie Vachon. 2000. Family disruption in Canada: Impact of the changing patterns of family formation and of female employment. *Canadian Studies in Population* 27(1): 85–105.

Lechner, Viola M. 1993. Support systems and stress reduction among workers caring for dependent parents. *Social Work* 38(4): 461–469.

Lechner, Viola M., & Masahito Sasaki. 1995. Japan and the United States struggle with who will care for our aging parents when caregivers are employed. *Journal of Gerontological Social Work* 24(1–2): 97–114.

Lehr, Valerie. 1999. *Queer Family Values: Debunking the Myth of the Nuclear Family*. Philadelphia: Temple University Press.

Leiper, Jean McKenzie. 1998 Fall. Women lawyers and their working arrangements: Time crunch, stress and career paths. *Canadian Journal of Law and Society/Revue canadienne droit et societe* 13(2): 117–134.

Leiter, Michael P., & Marie-Josette Durup. 1996. Work, home, and in-between: A longitudinal study of spillover. *Journal of Applied and Behavioural Science* 32(1): 29–47.

Lempert, Lora Bex. 1996a. Language obstacles in the narratives of abused women. *Mid-American Review of Sociology* 19(1–2): 15–32.

Lempert, Lora Bex. 1996b. Women's strategies of survival: Developing agency in abusive relationships. *Journal of Family Violence* 11(3): 269–289.

Leonard, Suzanne. 1995 November-December. Love stories. *Psychology Today 28.*

Lero, Donna S., & Lois M. Brockman. 1993. Single parent families in Canada: A closer look, pp. 91–114. In Joe Hudson & Burt Galaway (Eds.), *Single Parent*

Families: Perspectives on Research and Policy. Toronto: Thompson.

Lesemann, Frederic, & Roger Nicol. 1994. Family policy: International comparisons, pp. 117–125. In Maureen Baker (Ed.), *Canada's Changing Families: Challenges to Public Policy*. Ottawa: The Vanier Institute of the Family.

Letellier, Patrick. 1994 Summer. Gay and bisexual male domestic violence victimization: Challenges to feminist theory and responses to violence. *Violence and Victims 9*(2): 95–106.

Leung, A.K.C., W.L.M. Robson, H. Cho, & S.H.N. Lim. 1996. Latchkey children. *Journal of the Royal Society of Health 116*(6): 356–359.

Levan, Chris. 1998. Learning the rules on how to fight fairly, *Edmonton Journal* 31, January: F4.

Levine, Robert, Suguro Sato, Tsukasa Hashimoti, & Jyoti Verma. 1995 September. Love and marriage in eleven cultures. *Journal of Cross-Cultural Psychology 26*.

Levy, D.M. 1945. *The War and Family Life: Report for the War Emergency Committee, 1944*. Reprinted in American Journal of Orthopsychiatry, 15: 140–152.

Lewin, Alisa, & Yeheskel Hasenfeld. 1995. *Divorce: Does Warfare Policy Reduce the Gains from Marriage?* American Sociological Association.

Lewis, Jane. 1997 Summer. Gender and welfare regimes: Further thoughts. *Social Politics*.

Lewis, Suzan, & Cary L. Cooper. 1995. Balancing the work/home interface: A European perspective. *Human Resource Management Review 5*(4): 289–305.

Leyser, Yona. 1964 July. Stress and adaptation in Orthodox Jewish families with a disabled child. *American Journal of Orthopsychiatry 64*: 376–385.

Lieberman, Morton A., & Lawrence Fisher. 1995 February. The impact of chronic illness on the health and well-being of family members. *The Gerontologist 35*: 94–102.

Liebkind, Karmela. 1993. Self-Reported Ethnic Identity, Depression, and Anxiety among Young Vietnamese Refugees and Their Parents. *Journal of Refugee Studies 6*(1): 25–39.

Lillard, Lee, Michael Brien, & Linda Waite. 1995 August. Premarital cohabitation and subsequent divorce: A matter of self-selection? *Demography 32*.

Linden, E., & J.C. Hackler. 1973. Affective ties and delinquency. *Pacific Sociological Review 16*: 27–46.

Lindsey, Elizabeth W. 1998 July. The impact of homelessness and shelter life on family relationships. *Family Relations: Interdisciplinary Journal of Applied Family Studies 47*(3): 243–252.

Lipman, Ellen L., David R. Offord, Martin D. Dooley, & Martin H. Boyle. 2002. Children's outcomes in differing types of single-parent families. Pp. 229–242 in J. Douglas Willms, ed. *Vulnerable Children: Findings from Canada's National Longitudinal Survey of Children*

and Youth. Edmonton: University of Alberta Press, and Ottawa: Human Resources Development Canada, Applied Research Branch.

Lippman, S.B., W.A. James, R.L. Frierson. 1993. AIDS and the family: Implications for counseling. *AIDS Care 5*(1): 71–78.

Litwin, Howard. 1998 February-March. Social network type and health status in a national sample of elderly Israelis. *Social Science and Medicine 46*(4–5): 599–609.

Liu, Xiaoru, & Howard B. Kaplan. 2001 Fall. Role strain and illicit drug use: The moderating influence of commitment to conventional values. *Journal of Drug Issues 31*(4): 833–856.

Livingston, Mary J., Kim Burley, & Thomas P. Springer. 1996. The importance of being feminine: Gender, sex role, occupational and marital role commitment, and their relationship to anticipated work-family conflict. *Journal of Social Behavior and Personality 11*(5): 179–192.

Lobo, Francis, & Glen Watkins. 1995. Late career unemployment in the 1990s: Its impact on the family. *Journal of Family Studies 1*(2): 103–113.

Lockhart, Lettie L., Barbara W. White, & Vicki Causby. 1994 December. Letting out the secret: Violence in lesbian relationships. *Journal of Interpersonal Violence 9*: 469–492.

Lorber, Judith. 1996. Beyond the binaries: Depolarizing the categories of sex, sexuality and gender. *Sociological Inquiry 66*(2): 143–159.

Luker, Kristin. 1996. *Dubious Conceptions: The Politics of Teenage Pregnancy*. Cambridge, MA: Harvard University Press.

Lundgren-Gaveras, Lena. 1996. The work-family needs of single parents: A comparison of American and Swedish policy trends. *Journal of Sociology and Social Welfare 23*(1): 131–147.

Lupri, Eugen. 1993. Spousal violence: Wife abuse across the life course. *Zeitschrift fnr Sozialisationforschung und Erziehungssoziologie 13*(3): 232–257.

Lupri, Eugen, & James Frideres. 1981. The quality of marriage and the passage of time: Marital satisfaction over the family life cycle. *Canadian Journal of Sociology 6*: 283–305.

Lupri, Eugen, Elaine Grandin, & Merlin B. Brinkerhoff. 1994. Socioeconomic status and male violence in the Canadian home: A reexamination. *Canadian Journal of Sociology 19*(1): 47–73.

Lupri, Eugen, & Don Mills. 1987. The household division of labour in young dual-earner couples. *International Review of Sociology 2*: 33–54.

Luster, Tom, Harry Perlstadt, & Marvin McKinney. 1996 July. The effects of a family support program and other factors on the home environments provided by adolescent mothers. *Family Relations 45*: 255–264.

Luxton, Meg. 1986. Two hands for the clock, pp. 39–55. In Meg Luxton & Harriet Rosenberg (Eds.), *Through the Kitchen Window: The Politics of Home and Family.* Toronto: Garamond.

Luxton, Meg (Ed.). 1997. *Feminism and Families: Critical Policies and Changing Practices.* Halifax: Fernwood.

Luxton, Meg. 2001. Conceptualizing "families": Theoretical frameworks and family research, pp. 28–50. In Maureen Baker (Ed.), *Families: Changing Trends in Canada,* 4th edition. Toronto: McGraw-Hill Ryerson.

Luxton, Meg, & Ester Reiter. 1997. Double, double, toil and trouble. Women's experience of work and family in Canada, 1980–1995, pp. 197–221. In Patricia M. Evans, & Gerda R. Wekerle (Eds.), *Women and the Canadian Welfare State: Challenges and Change.* Toronto: University of Toronto Press.

Luxton, Meg, Harriet Rosenberg, & Sedef Arat-Koc (Eds.). 1990. *Through the Kitchen Window: The Politics of Home and Family.* Toronto: Garamond.

Luxton, Meg, & June Corman. 2001. *Getting By in Hard Times: Gendered Labour at Home and on the Job.* Toronto: University of Toronto Press.

Lye, Diane N., & Ingrid Waldron. 1997. Attitudes toward cohabitation, family and gender roles: Relationships to values and political ideology. *Sociological Perspectives* 40(2): 199–225.

Lykken, David. 1996. Psychopathy, sociopathy, and crime. *Society* 34(1): 29–38.

Maas, Ineke. 1995. Demography and aging: Long-term effects of divorce, early widowhood, and migration on resources and integration in old age. *Korea Journal of Population and Development* 24(2): 275–299.

MacDermid, Shelley M., Margaret Williams, & Stephen Marks. 1994 April. Is small beautiful? Work family tension, work conditions, and organisational size. *Family Relations,* 43: 159–167.

MacDonald, Andrea. 1998. Course looks at kids' lit from gay angle, *The Edmonton Journal,* 9 January 1998: H6.

MacEwen, Karyl E., & Julian Barling. 1994. Daily Consequences of Work Interference with Family and Family Interference with Work. *Work and Stress* 8(3): 244–254.

Mackay, Fiona. 1996. The zero tolerance campaign: Setting the agenda. *Parliamentary Affairs* 49(1): 206–220.

Mackey, Wade C. 1995. U.S. fathering behaviors within a cross-cultural context: An evaluation by an alternate benchmark. *Journal of Comparative Family Studies* 26(3): 445–458.

Macmillan, Ross, & Rosemary Gartner. 1996. *When She Brings Home the Bacon: Labour Force Participation and the Risk of Spousal Violence against Women,* unpublished mss. Toronto: Department of Sociology, University of Toronto.

Maeda, Naoko. 1999. Intergenerational relations of the elderly in an inner area of the metropolis. *Kazoku Shakaigaku Kenkyu/Japanese Journal of Family Sociology* 11: 83–94.

Mak, Anita S. 1996. Adolescent delinquency and perceptions of parental care and protection: A case control study. *Journal of Family Studies* 2(1): 29–39.

Malin, Maili, Elina Hemminki, Outi Raikkonen, Sinikka Sihvo, & M.L. Perala. 2002 July. What do women want? Women's experiences of infertility treatment. *Social Science and Medicine* 53(1): 123–133.

Man, Guida C. 1996. *Hong Kong Middle-Class Chinese Immigrant Women in Canada: An Inquiry in the Social Organization of Work.* American Sociological Association (ASA).

Man, Guida. 2001. From Hong Kong to Canada: Immigration and the changing family lives of middle-class women from Hong Kong, pp. 420–438. In Bonnie J. Fox (Ed.), *Family Patterns, Gender Divisions,* 2nd edition. Toronto: Oxford University Press.

Mandell, Deena. 1995a. Fathers who don't pay child support: Hearing their voices. *Journal of Divorce and Remarriage* 23(1–2).

Mandell, Deena. 1995b. Non supporting divorced fathers: The problem in context. *Canadian Social Work Review* 12(2).

Mann, Susan A., Michael D. Grimes, Alice Abel Kemp, & Pamela J. Jenkins. 1997. Paradigm shifts in family sociology? Evidence from three decades of family textbooks. *Journal of Family Issues* 18(3): 315–349.

Manning, W. & D.T. Lichter. 1996. Parental cohabitation and children's economic well-being. *Journal of Marriage and the Family* 58(4): 998–1010.

Marano, Hara-Estroff. 1997 March-April. Love lesson: Six new moves to improve your relationship. *Psychology Today 30.*

Marcenes, Wagner, & Aubrey Sheilham. 1996. The relationship between marital quality and oral health status. *Psychology and Health* 11(3).

Marcil-Gratton, Nicole. 1993. Growing up with a single parent: A transitional experience? Some demographic measurements, pp. 73–90. In Joe Hudson and Burt Galaway (Eds.), *Single Parent Families: Perspectives on Research and Policy.* Toronto: Thompson Educational Publishing.

Marcil-Gratton, Nicole, Céline Le Bourdais, & Évelyne Lapierre-Adamcyk. 2000 Autumn. The implications of parents' conjugal histories for children. *Isuma* 1(2): 32–40.

Marcuse, Herbert. 1991. *One-Dimensional Man: Studies in the Ideology of Advanced Industrial Society,* 2nd edition. Boston: Beacon Press.

Margolin, Gayla, & Richard S. John. 1997. Children's exposure to marital aggression: Direct and mediated effects, pp. 90–104. In Glenda Kaufman Kantor and Jana L. Jasinski (Eds.), *Out of Darkness: Contemporary*

Perspectives on Family Violence. Thousand Oaks, CA: Sage Publications.

Marks, Lynne. 1998. When in doubt, it seems, blame the mothers. *The Globe and Mail*, 26 January: A21.

Marks, N.F. 1996. Flying solo at mid-life: Gender, marital status and psychological well-being. *Journal of Marriage and the Family 58*(4): 917–932.

Marshall, Katherine. 1990 Spring. Household chores. *Canadian Social Trends*: 18–19.

Marshall, Katherine. 1993 Autumn. Employed Parents and the Division of Housework. *Perspectives on Labour and Income*: 23–30.

Martin-Matthews, Anne E., & David Ralph Matthews. 1994. *Patterns of Interaction and Support in the Social Worlds of Infertile Couples.* International Sociological Association (ISA).

Mason, Mary Ann, Arlene Skolnick, and Stephen D. Sugarman (Eds.). 2003. *All Our Families: New Policies for a New Century* 2nd edition. New York: Oxford University Press.

Mastekaasa, Arne. 1995. Divorce and subjective distress: Panel evidence. *European Sociological Review 11*(2).

Matthews, Anne Martin, & Lori D. Campbell. 1995. Gender roles, employment and informal care, pp. 129–143. In Sara Arber & Jay Ginn (Eds.), *Connecting Gender and Ageing: A Sociological Approach.* Buckingham, UK: Open U Press.

Matthews, Lisa S., Rand D. Conger, & K.A.S. Wickrama. 1996. Work-family conflict and marital quality: Mediating processes. *Social Psychology Quarterly 59*(1): 62–79.

Mattingly, Marybeth J., & Robert N. Bozick. 2001. *Children raised by same-sex couples: Much ado about nothing.* Southern Sociological Society (SSS).

Mattox, William R. Jr. 1996 May-June. Marital bliss. *The American Enterprise 7*.

Mattson, A. 1972. Long-term physical illness in childhood: A challenge to psychosocial adaptation. *Pediatrics 5*: 801–811.

Mauno Saijo, & Ulla Kinnunen. 1999 August. Job insecurity and well-being: A longitudinal study among male and female employees in Finland. *Community, Work & Family 2*(2): 147–171.

Maxwell, Judith. 1996. *The Social Dimensions of Economic Growth.* Eric J. Hanson Memorial Lecture. Edmonton: University of Alberta, Department of Economics.

McCarroll, Linda Diane. 2000 August. *Family Rituals: Promoting the Ethnic Identity of Preschoolers.* Dissertation Abstracts International, A: The Humanities and Social Sciences 61, 2, 783–A.

McCloskey, Laura A. 1996 August. Socioeconomic and coercive power within the family. *Gender and Society*: 449–463.

McCloskey, Laura A., Aurelio Jose Figueredo, & Mary P. Koss. 1995 October. The effects of systemic family violence on children's mental health. *Child Development 66*: 1239–1261.

McCormack, Arlene, Ann Wolbert Burgess, & Peter Gaccione. 1986. Influence of family structure and financial stability on physical and sexual abuse among a runaway population. *International Journal of Sociology of the Family 16*(2): 251–262.

McCormack, Arlene, Mark David Janus, & Ann Wolbert Burgess. 1986. Runaway youths and sexual victimization: Gender differences in an adolescent runaway population. *Child Abuse and Neglect 10*(3): 387–395.

McCubbin, Hamilton I., William Michael Fleming, Anne I. Thompson, Paul Neitman, Kelly M. Elver, Sue Ann Savas. 1998. Resiliency and coping in "at risk" African-American youth and their families, pp. 287–328. In Hamilton I. McCubbin, Elizabeth A. Thompson, Anne I. Thompson, & Jo A. Futrell (Eds.), *Resiliency in African-American families.* Thousand Oaks, CA: Sage.

McCurdy, Susan J., & Avraham Scherman. 1996. Effects of family structure on the adolescent separation-individuation process. *Adolescence 31*(122).

McDaniel, Susan A. 1988. Women's roles, reproduction, and the new reproductive technologies: A new stork rising. In Ann Duffy & Nancy Mandell (Eds.), *Reconstructing Canadian Families: Feminist Perspectives.* Toronto: Butterworths.

McDaniel, Susan A. 1989. Reconceptualizing the nuptiality/fertility relationship in Canada in a new age. *Canadian Studies in Population 16*(2): 163–186.

McDaniel, Susan A. 1993a. Single parenthood: policy apartheid in Canada, pp. 203–211. In Burt Galloway and Joe Hudson (Eds.), *Single Parent Families: Canadian Perspectives on Research and Policy.* Toronto: Thompson Educational Publishing.

McDaniel, Susan A. 1993b. The changing Canadian family: Women's roles and the impact of feminism, pp. 422–451. In Sandra Burt & Lorraine Code (Eds.), *Changing Patterns: Women in Canada* 2nd edition. Toronto: McClelland & Stewart.

McDaniel, Susan A. 1993c. Where the contradictions meet: Women and family security in Canada in the 1990s, pp. 163–180. *In Family Security in Insecure Times.* Ottawa: National Forum on Family Security.

McDaniel, Susan A. 1994. *Family and Friends 1990: General Social Survey Analysis Series.* Ottawa: Statistics Canada, Minister of Supply and Services. Catalogue No. 11-612E, No. 9, ISBN 0–660–15354–8.

McDaniel, Susan A. 1995. *Families Function: Family Bridges from Past to Future.* Occasional Paper Series, No. 19/1995. Vienna: United Nations Secretariat for the International Year of the Family.

McDaniel, Susan A. 1996a. Family/work challenges among older working Canadians, pp. 195–214. In Marion Lynn (Ed.), *Voices: Essays on Canadian Families.* Toronto: Nelson.

McDaniel, Susan A. 1996b. The family lives of the middle-aged and elderly in Canada, pp. 195–211. In Maureen Baker (Ed.), *Families: Changing Trends in Canada* 3rd edition. Toronto: McGraw-Hill Ryerson.

McDaniel, Susan A. 1996c. Toward a synthesis of feminist and demographic perspectives on fertility. *The Sociological Quarterly* 37(1): 83–104.

McDaniel, Susan A. 1997. Intergenerational transfers, social solidarity, and social policy: Unanswered questions and policy challenges. *Canadian Public Policy/Canadian Journal on Aging* (Joint issue): 1–21.

McDaniel, Susan A. 1998a. Towards Healthy Families, pp. 3–42. In *National Forum on Health, Determinants of Health: Settings and Issue*, Vol. 3. Ste.-Foy, Quebec: Editions Multimodes.

McDaniel, Susan A. 1998b. Families, feminism and the state. In Wayne Anthony & Les Samuelson (Eds.), *Power and Resistance: Critical Thinking About Canadian Social Issues*, 2nd edition. Toronto: Fernwood.

McDaniel, Susan A. 2002. Women's changing relations to the state and citizenship: Caring and intergenerational relations in globalizing western democracies. *Canadian Review of Sociology and Anthropology* 39(2): 1–26

McDaniel, Susan A., & Robert Lewis. 1998c. Did they or didn't they? Intergenerational supports in families past: A case study of Brigus, Newfoundland, 1920–1945, pp. 475–497. In Lori Chambers & Edgar-Andre Montigny (Eds.), *Family Matters: Papers in Post-Confederation Canadian Family History*. Toronto: Canadian Scholars Press.

McDaniel, Susan A. 1999. Untangling love and domination: Challenges of home care for the elderly in a reconstructing Canada. *Journal of Canadian Studies*, 34(3): 191–213.

McIlroy, Anne. 1998. One way to build better families, *The Globe and Mail*, 29 September: A1, A6.

McKenna, James J. 1996. Sudden infant death syndrome in cross-cultural perspective: Is infant-parent cosleeping protective? *Annual Review of Anthropology* 25: 201–216.

McKie, Craig. 1993. An overview of lone parenthood in Canada, pp. 53–72. In Joe Hudson & Burt Galaway (Eds.), *Single Parent Families: Perspectives on Research and Policy*. Toronto: Thompson.

McLanaham, Sara S., & Julia Adams. 1987, 1989. Parenthood and psychological well-being. *Annual Review of Sociology* 13: 237–257.

McLanahan, Sara, & Irwin Garfinkel. 1993. Single motherhood in the United States: Growth, problems, and policies, pp. 15–30. In Joe Hudson & Burt Galaway (Eds.), *Single Parent Families: Perspectives on Research and Policy*. Toronto: Thompson.

McLaren, Angus, & Arlene McLaren. 1986. *The Bedroom and the State: The Changing Practices and Politics of Contraception and Abortion in Canada, 1880–1980*. Toronto: McClelland & Stewart.

McLaren, Arlene Tigar. 1996. Coercive invitations: How young women in school make sense of mothering and waged labour. *British Journal of Sociology of Education* 17(3): 279–298.

McLeod, Jane D., Candace Kruttschnitt, & Maude Dornfeld. 1994. Does parenting explain the effects of structural conditions on children's antisocial behavior? A comparison of blacks and whites. *Social Forces* 73(2): 575–604.

McLeod, Jane D. & Michael J. Shanahan. 1993 June. Poverty, parenting, and children's mental health. *American Sociological Review* 58(3): 351–366.

McLuhan, Marshall. 1951, 1968. *The Mechanical Bride: Folklore of Industrial Man*, vii, 157. Boston: Beacon Press

McLuhan, Marshall. 1994. *Understanding media: The extensions of man. Extensions of Man*. Cambridge, MA: MIT Press.

McMahon, Martha. 1995. *Engendering Motherhood: Identity and Self-Transformation in Women's Lives*. New York: Guilford.

McMahon, Martha, & Ellen Pence. 1996 September. Replying to Dan O'Leary. *Journal of Interpersonal Violence 11*.

McManus, Michael J. 1996 May-June. The marriage-saving movement. *The American Enterprise 7*.

McMullin, Julie Ann, & Victor W. Marshall. 1996 Fall. Family, friends, stress, and well-being: Does childlessness make a difference? *Canadian Journal on Aging/La Revue Canadienne du Vieillissement* 15(3): 355–373.

Mcnamara, Paul E., & Christine K. Ranney. 1999. The distribution of income in New York state: Trends and implications for public policy. pp. 17–34. In Thomas A. Hirschl & Tim B. Heaton (Eds.), *New York State in the 21st Century*, Westport, CT: Praeger, 1999.

Mechanic, David. 1996. Changing medical organization and the erosion of trust. *The Milbank Quarterly* 74(2): 171–189.

Meeks, Suzanne, Diane B. Arnkoff, Carol R. Glass, & Clifford J. Notarius. 1986. Wives' employment status, hassles, communication and relational efficacy: Intra-versus extra-relationship factors and marital adjustment. *Family Relations* 35(2): 249–255.

Meier, Andrea, Maeda J. Galinsky, & Kathleen A. Rounds. 1995. Telephone support groups for caregivers of persons with AIDS. *Social Work with Groups. Special Groups: Current Perspectives on Theory and Practice* 18(1): 99–108.

Meil Landwerlin, Gerardo. 1992 January-April. Family policy: Content and meaning. *Revista Internacional de Sociología* 1: 173–191.

Meissner, Martin. 1986. *Estrangement from Sociability and the Work of Women in Canada*. International Sociological Association.

Meissner, Martin. 1975. On the division of labour and sexual inequality. *Sociologie du Travail* 17(4): 329–350.

Menaghan, Elizabeth G. 1993. *The Long Reach of the Job: Effects of Parents' Occupational Conditions on Family Patterns and Children's Well-Being*. American Sociological Association, Association paper.

Merkle, Erich R., & Rhonda A. Richardson. 2000 April. Digital dating and virtual relating: Conceptualizing computer- mediated romantic relationships. *Family Relations: Interdisciplinary Journal of Applied Family Studies. 49*(2): 187–192.

Merrill, Lex L., Linda K. Hervig, & Joel S. Milner. 1996. Childhood parenting experiences, intimate partner conflict resolution, and adult risk for child physical abuse. *Child Abuse and Neglect* 20(11): 1049–1065.

Merskin, D.L. & M. Huberlie. 1996. Companionship in the Classifieds: The adoption of personal advertisements by daily newspapers. *Journalism and Mass Communication Quarterly* 73(1): 219–229.

Meyerstein, Israela. 1997. The problem box ritual: Helping families prepare for remarriage. *Journal of Family Psychotherapy* 8(1): 61–65.

Millar, Nancy. 1999. *Once Upon a Wedding*. Calgary: Bayeaux Arts.

Millar, Wayne, & Surinder Wadhera. 1997. A perspective on Canadian teenage births, 1992–1994: Older men and younger women? *Canadian Journal of Public Health* 88: 333–336.

Miller, A. Therese, Colleen Eggertson-Tacon, & Brian Quigg. 1990. Patterns of runaway behavior within a larger systems context: The road to empowerment. *Adolescence* 25(98): 271–289.

Miller, David, & P. Gillies. 1996. Is there life after work? Experiences of HIV and oncology health staff. *AIDS Care* 8(2): 167–182.

Mills, Melinda. 2000. *The Transformation of Partnerships: Canada, The Netherlands, and the Russian Federation*. Amsterdam: Thela Thesis.

Minkler, Meredith, & Relda Robinson-Beckley, Jr. 1994. Raising grandchildren from crack-cocaine households: Effects on family and friendship ties of African-American women. *American Journal of Orthopsychiatry* 64(1): 20–29.

Minkler, Meredith, & Kathleen M. Roe. 1996 Spring. Grandparents as surrogate parents. *Generations, 20*: 34–38.

Minton, Carmelle, & Kay Pasley. 1996. Fathers' parenting role identity and father involvement: A comparison of non-divorced and divorced, nonresident fathers. *Journal of Family Issues* 17(1).

Mintz, Steven. 1998. From patriarchy to androgyny and other myths: Placing men's family roles in historical perspective, pp. 3–30. In Alan Booth & Ann C. Crouter (Eds.), *Men in Families: When do they Get Involved? What Difference Does it Make?* Mahwah, NJ: Lawrence Erlbaum Associates.

Mitchell, Barbara. 1994. Family structure and leaving the nest: A social resource perspective. *Sociological Perspectives* 37(4): 651–671.

Mitchell, Barbara. 1998. *The Refilled Nest: Debunking the Myth of Family-in-Crisis*. Paper presented at the 9th Annual John K. Friesen Conference, The Overselling of Population Aging, Simon Fraser University, 14–15 May 1998.

Mitchell, Barbara A. & Ellen M. Gee. 1996a. Boomerang kids and midlife parental marital satisfaction. *Family Relations* 45: 442–448.

Mitchell, Barbara A. & Ellen M. Gee. 1996b. Young adults returning home: Implications for social policy, pp. 61–71. In Burt Galaway & Joe Hudson (Eds.), *Youth in Transition: Perspectives on Research and Policy*. Toronto: Thompson Educational Publishing.

Mitchell, Barbara. 2000. The refilled nest: Debunking the myth of families in crisis, pp. 80–99. In Ellen M. Gee and Gloria Gutman (Eds.), *The Overselling of Population Aging: Apocalyptic Demography, Intergenerational Challenges and Social Policy*. Toronto: Oxford University Press.

Mitchinson, Wendy. 2002. *Giving Birth in Canada: 1900–1950*. Toronto: University of Toronto Press.

Moen Phyllis & Yan Yu. 2000 August. Effective work/life strategies: Working couples, work conditions, gender, and life quality. *Social Problems* 47(3): 291–326.

Mofina, Rick. 2003. Gay families no longer rejected, *The Edmonton Journal*, 3 January: A5.

Molassiotis, A., O.B.A. Van Den Akker, & B.J. Broughton. 1997 February. Perceived social support, family environment and psychosocial recovery in bone marrow transplant long-term survivors. *Social Science & Medicine, Vol. 44*(3): 317–325.

Molseed, Mari J. 1995. In loco parentis: An elaboration of the parental relationship form. *Symbolic Interaction*, 1995 18(3): 341–354.

Monahan, D.J., L. Kohman, & M. Coleman. 1996. Open-heart surgery: consequences for caregivers. *Journal of Gerontological Social Work* 25(3–4): 53–70.

Moncher, Frank J. 1995 September. Social isolation and child-abuse risk. *Families in Society* 76: 421–433.

Mongeau, P.A., & C.M. Carey. 1996. Who's wooing whom: An experimental investigation of date initiation and expectancy violation. *Western Journal of Communication* 60(3): 195–213.

Monk, Timothy H., Marilyn J. Essex, Nancy A. Snider, Marjorie H. Klein, et al. 1996. The impact of the birth of a baby on the time structure and social mixture of a couple's daily life and its consequences for well-being. *Journal of Applied Social Psychology*.

Moogk, Peter. 1982. Les petits sauvages: The children of eighteenth century New France. In Joy Parr (Ed.),

Childhood and Family in Canadian History. Toronto: McClelland and Stewart.

Mookherjee, H.N. 1997. Marital Status, Gender and Perception of Well-Being. *Journal of Social Psychology* 137(1): 95–105.

Moore Lappé, Frances. 1985. *What To Do After You Turn Off the TV? Fresh Ideas for Enjoying Family Time.* New York: Ballantine Books.

Moore, Dahlia. 1995. Role conflict: Not only for women? A comparative analysis of 5 nations. *International Journal of Comparative Sociology* 36(1–2): 17–35.

Moore, Eric G., & Mark W. Rosenberg, with Donald McGuiness. 1997. *Growing Old in Canada: Demographic and Geographic Perspectives.* Toronto & Ottawa: Nelson & Statistics Canada. Catalogue no. 96-321–MPE, no. 1.

Moral, Felix. 1999 April-June. The unemployed in the family unit: Providers and dependents. *Revista Espanola de nvestigaciones Sociologicas 86:* 153–184.

Morrison, Kati, & Airdrie Thompson-Guppy, with Patricia Bell. 1986. *Stepmothers: Exploring the Myth.* Ottawa: Canadian Council on Social Development.

Mortimer, Jeylan T. 1980. Occupation-family linkages as perceived by men in the early stages of professional and managerial careers. *Research in the Interweave of Social Roles 1:* 99–117.

Morton, Suzanne. 1992a. The June bride as the working-class bride: Getting married in a Halifax working-class neighbourhood in the 1920s, pp. 360–379. In Bettina Bradbury (Ed.), *Canadian Family History: Selected Readings.* Toronto: Copp Clark Pitman.

Morton, Suzanne. 1992b. Women on their own: Single mothers in working-class Halifax in the 1920s. *Acadiensis XXI(2):* 90–107.

Motohashi, S. 1978. A record of a mother of a handicapped child. *Japanese Journal of Nursing 42:* 968–970.

Motta, Robert W. 1994. Identification of characteristics and causes of childhood post-traumatic stress disorder. *Psychology in the Schools* 31(1): 49–56.

Mui, Ada C. 1995a February. Caring for frail elderly parents: A comparison of adult sons and daughters. *The Gerontologist 35:* 86–93.

Mui, Ada C. 1995b August. Multidimensional predictors of caregiver strain among older persons caring for frail spouses. *Journal of Marriage and the Family 57:* 733–740.

Mulhall, Peter F., Donald Stone, & Brian Stone. 1996. Home alone: Is it a risk factor for middle-school students? *Journal of Drug Education* 26(1): 39–48.

Mullen, Kenneth. 1996. Marital status and men's health. The *International Journal of Sociology and Social Policy* 16(3): 47–67.

Muller, Robert T., Ann E. Goebel-Fabbri, Terry Diamond, & David Dinklage. 2000 April. Social support and the relationship between family and community violence exposure and psychopathology among high-risk adolescents. *Child Abuse and Neglect* 24(4): 449–464.

Mullin, Walter Joseph. 2000. *The Impact of Depression on Marital Beliefs and Marital Communication.* Dissertation Abstracts International Section A: Humanities & Social Sciences Vol. 60(12–A), pp. 4606.

Munsch, Joyce, John Woodward, & Nancy Darling. 1995. Children's perceptions of their relationship with coresiding and non-coresiding fathers. *Journal of Divorce and Remarriage* 23(1–2).

Muramatsu, Mikiko. 2000 May. The life course expectations of women students in Japan. *Kyoiku-shakaigaku Kenkyu/The Journal of Educational Sociology 66:* 137–155.

Muransky, Jean M., Darlene DeMarie-Deblow. 1995. Differences between high school students from intact and divorced families. *Journal of Divorce and Remarriage* 23(3–4).

Murray, Sandra L., John G. Holmes, & W. Dale. 1996. The benefits of positive illusions: Idealization and the construction of satisfaction in close relationships. *Journal of Personality and Social Psychology* 70(1).

Myers, Hector F., & Sylvie Taylor. 1998 Spring. Family contributions to risk and resilience in African-American children. *Journal of Comparative Family Studies* 29(1): 215–229.

Myers, Scott M. & Alan Booth. 1996. Men's retirement and marital quality. *Journal of Family Issues* 17(3).

Nagai Akiko. 1992. Household work by dual-income couples. *Kazoku Shakaigaku Kenkyu/ Japanese Journal of Family Sociology 4:* 67–78.

Nakhaie, M.R. 1995. Housework in Canada: The national picture. *Journal of Comparative Family Studies* 26(3): 409–425.

Nathan, Michael, Aliza Schnabel-Brandes, & Harvey Peskin. 1981. Together and apart: Kibbutz children, twelfth grade graduates in 1969, after ten years: A follow-up study. *Kibbutz 8:* 105–115.

Nault, Francois, & Alain Belanger. 1996. *The Decline in Marriage in Canada, 1981–1991.* Ottawa: Statistics Canada. Catalogue no. 84–536-XPB.

Nazer, Nancy, & Janet Salaff. 1996. Telework and taking care: The elderly. *Society for the Study of Social Problems.*

Nelson, Fiona. 1996. *Lesbian Motherhood: An Exploration of Canadian Lesbian Families.* Toronto: University of Toronto Press.

Nelson, Geoffrey. 1994 January. Emotional well-being of separated and married women: Long-term follow-up study. *American Journal of Orthopsychiatry 64.*

Newell, Lloyd David. 1999 October. *A Qualitative Analysis of Family Rituals and Traditions*. Dissertation Abstracts International, A: The Humanities and Social Sciences 60, 4, 1348–A.

Nietfeld, Markus, & Rolf Becker. 1999 October. Hard times for families. Theory and empirical investigation about the impact of unemployment and socioeconomic deprivation on the quality of family relations. *Zeitschrift fur Soziologie der Erziehung und Socialisation 19*(4): 369–387.

Nippert-Eng, Christena. 1996. Calendars and keys: The classification of "home" and "work." *Sociological Forum 11*(3): 563–582.

Nobes, Gavin, & Marjorie Smith. 2002 April. Family structure and the physical punishment of children. *Journal of Family Issues 23*(3): 349–373.

Nock, Steven L. 1995 May. Commitment and dependency in marriage. *Journal of Marriage and the Family 57*.

Noelker, Linda S., & George Shaffer. 1985 Summer. Care networks: How they form and change. *Generations: Journal of the American Society on Aging 10*(4): 62–64.

Noivo, Edite. 1994. *Immigrant Families and Social Injuries: The Life-Worlds of Three Generations*. International Sociological Association (ISA).

Noller, Patricia. 1996. What is this thing called love? Defining the love that supports marriage and family. *Personal Relationships 3*(1): 97–115.

Norton, Pamela, & Clifford Drew. 1994 Spring. Autism and potential family stressors. *The American Journal of Family Therapy 22*: 67–76.

Notarius, Clifford I., & Jennifer S. Johnson. 1982. Emotional expression in husbands and wives. *Journal of Marriage and the Family 44*(2): 483–489.

O'Connor, Pat. 1995. Understanding/variations marital sexual pleasure: An impossible task? *Sociological Review 43*(2).

O'Donohue, William, & Julie L. Crouch. 1996 January. Marital therapy and gender-linked factors in communication. *Journal of Marital and Family Therapy 22*.

O'Farrell, Timothy J., & Christopher M. Murphy. 1995 April. Marital violence before and after alcoholism treatment. *Journal of Consulting and Clinical Psychology 63*: 256–262.

O'Farrell, Timothy J., & Michael Feehan. 1999 March. Alcoholism treatment and the family: Do family and individual treatments for alcoholic adults have preventive effects for children? *Journal of Studies on Alcohol. Special Issue: Alcohol and the family: Opportunities for prevention, Vol.* Supp 13, pp. 125–129.

O'Keefe, Maura. 1996. The differential effects of family violence on adolescent adjustment. *Child and Adolescent Social Work Journal 13*(1): 51–68.

O'Keefe, Maura. 1997 March. Incarcerated battered women: A comparison of battered women who killed their abusers and those incarcerated for other offenses. *Journal of Family Violence 12*(1): 1–19.

O'Leary, Micky, Janet Franzoni, & Gregory Brack. 1996. Divorcing parents: Factors related to coping and adjustment. *Journal of Divorce and Remarriage 25*(3–4): 85–103.

O'Neill, John. 1994. *The Missing Child in Liberal Theory: Towards a Covenant Theory of Family, Community, Welfare and the Civic State*. Toronto: University of Toronto Press.

Oakley, Ann. 1974. *The Sociology of Housework*. Bath: Martin Robinson.

Odegaard, Paul. 1996. Empathy induction in the couple treatment of depression: Shifting the focus from self to other. *Families, Systems and Health 14*(2).

Oerton, Sarah. 1997. Queer housewives? Some problems in theorising the division of domestic labour in lesbian and gay households. *Women's Studies International Forum 20*(3): 421–430.

Oerton, Sarah. 1998. Reclaiming the "housewife"? Lesbians and household work. *Journal of Lesbian Studies 2*(4): 69–83.

Oppenheim, David, Frederick S. Wamboldt, Leslie A. Gavin, Andrew G. Renouf et al. 1996. Couples co-construction of the story of their child's birth, associations with marital adaptation. *Journal of Narrative and Life History 6*(1).

Oppenheimer, Valerie Kincade. 1997. Women's employment and the gain to marriage: The specialization and trading model. *Annual Review of Sociology 23*: 431–453.

Orava, Tammy A., Peter J. McLeod, & Donald Sharpe. 1996 June. Perceptions of control, depressive symptomatology, and self-esteem of women in transition from abusive relationships. *Journal of Family Violence 11*: 167–186.

Orbuch, Terri L., James S. House, & Pamela S. Mero. 1996 June. Marital quality over the life course. *Social Psychology Quarterly 59*.

Orloff, Ann Shola. 1993. Gender and the social rights of citizenship: The comparative analysis of gender relations and welfare states. *American Sociological Review 58*(3): 303–328.

Orodenker, Sylvia Z. 1990 February. Family caregiving in a changing society: The effects of employment on caregiver stress. *Family & Community Health 12*(4): 58–70.

Osterman, Paul. 1995. Work/family programs and the employment relationship. *Administrative Science Quarterly 40*: 681–700.

Overstreet, Stacy & Shawnee Braun. 2000 April. Exposure to community violence and post-traumatic stress symptoms: Mediating factors. *American Journal of Orthopsychiatry 70*(2): 263–271.

Paden, Shelley, & Cheryl Buehler. 1995. Coping with the dual-income lifestyle. *Journal of Marriage and the Family 57*: 101–110.

Pal, Salmali. 1999 March. Looking for my Prince Charming. *Newsweek* 15 March 133(11):12.

Palacio-Quintin. 2000 Autumn. The impact of day care on child development. *Isuma*: 17–22.

Palgi, Michal. 1993. Kibbutz woman: Gender roles and status. *Israel Social Science Research 8*(1): 108–121.

Papps, Fiona, Michael Walker, Antonietta Trimboli, & Carmelina Trimboli. 1995. Parental discipline in Anglo, Greek Lebanese, and Vietnamese cultures. *Journal of Cross-Cultural Psychology 26*(1): 49–64.

Parcel, Toby L., & Elizabeth G. Menaghan. 1993. Family social capital and children's behavior problems. *Social Psychology Quarterly 56*(2): 120–135.

Paredes, Maceda Catherine. 1995 October-December. Filipino women and intermarriages. *Asian Migrant 8*(4).

Parker, Seymour, & Hilda Parker. 1992. Male gender identity in the Israeli kibbutz: Reflections on "protest masculinity." *Ethos 20*(3): 340–357

Parr, Joy (Ed.). 1990. *Childhood and Family in Canadian History*. Toronto: McClelland and Stewart.

Parr, Joy. 1999. *Domestic Goods: The Material, the Moral and the Economic in the Postwar Years*. Toronto: University of Toronto Press.

Pasch, Lauri A., & Thomas N. Bradbury. 1998. Social support, conflict, and the development of marital dysfunction. *Journal of Consulting and Clinical Psychology 66*(2): 219–230.

Pasupathi, Monisha, Laura L. Carstensen, Robert W. Levenson, John M. Gottman. 1999 Summer. Responsive listening in long-married couples: A psycholinguistic perspective. *Journal of Nonverbal Behavior. Special Issue: Aging and Nonverbal Behavior Vol. 23*(2), pp. 173–193.

Patterson, Thomas L., William S. Shaw, Shirley J. Semple, Mariana Cherner, et al. 1996 Winter. Relationship of psychosocial factors to HIV disease progression. *Annals of Behavioral Medicine 18*(1): 30–39

Paulson, Sharon E. 1996 April. Maternal employment and adolescent achievement revisited: An ecological perspective. *Family Relations 45*: 201–208.

Payne, Malcolm. 1995. Understanding going missing: Issues for social work and social services. *British Journal of Social Work 25*(3): 333–348.

Pearcey, Nancy R. 1995 September. Laboring at love. *The American Enterprise 6*(Sept.): 40–42.

Pecchioni, Loretta L. 2001 April. Implicit decision-making in family caregiving. *Journal of Social and Personal Relationships 18*(2): 219–237.

Peeples, Faith, & Rolf Loeber. 1994 June. Do individual factors and neighborhood context explain ethnic differences in juvenile delinquency? *Journal of Quantitative Criminology 10*(2): 141–157.

Peiser, Nadine C., & Patrick C.L. Heaven. 1996 December. Family influences on self-reported delinquency among high school students. *Journal of Adolescence*: 557–568.

Penhale, Bridget. 1993. The abuse of elderly people: Considerations for practice. *British Journal of Social Work 23*(2): 95–112.

Penning, Margaret J., & Neena L. Chappell. 1990 March. Self-care in relation to informal and formal care. *Ageing and Society 10*(1): 41–59.

Peressinc, Mauro. 1994 Spring. Utilitarian attachment and rejection of the ethnic game: Relationship with the host country in the life stories of a group of Italian immigrants in Montreal. *Revue internationale d'action communautaire/International Review of Community Development, 31*(71): 47–61.

Perez, J.F. 1978. *The Family Roots of Adolescent Delinquency*. New York: Van Nostrand.

Perreira, Krista M., & Frank A. Sloan. 2001 July. Life events and alcohol consumption among mature adults: A longitudinal analysis. *Journal of Studies on Alcohol 62*(4): 501–508.

Pescosolido, Bernice A. 1991. Illness careers and network ties: A conceptual model of utilization and compliance. *Advances in Medical Sociology 2*: 161–184.

Pescosolido, Bernice A. 1996. Bringing the "community" into utilization models: How social networks link individuals to changing systems of care. *Research in the Sociology of Health Care, 13*(Part A), 171–197.

Pescosolido, Bernice A., Eric Wright, & William Patrick Sullivan. 1995. Communities of care: A theoretical perspective on case management models in mental health. *Advances in Medical Sociology 6*: 37–79.

Peters, Alice. 1997. *Canadian Children in the 1990s: Selected Findings of the National Longitudinal Survey of Children and Youth*. Paper presented at the Canadian Population Society meetings, St. John's, Newfoundland.

Peters, John F. 1995. Canadian families into the year 2000. *International Journal of Sociology of the Family 25*(1): 63–79.

Peterson, Richard, R. 1996a. A re-evaluation of the economic consequences of divorce. *American Sociological Review 61*(3).

Peterson, Richard, R. 1996b. Statistical errors, faulty conclusions, misguided policy: Reply to Weitzman. *American Sociological Review 61*(3).

Pett, Marjorie A., Beth Vaughan-Cole, & Bruce E. Wampold. 1994 April. Maternal employment and perceived stress: Their impact on children's adjustment and mother-child interaction in young divorced and married families. *Family Relations 43*: 151–158.

Phillips, Andrew. 1997. Christian men on the march, *Maclean's* 6 October: 52–53.

Phillips, K.D., & R.D. Sowell. 2001 December. Cope and coping in HIV-infected African-American women of reproductive age. *Journal of National Black Nurses' Association: JNBNA, 11*(2): 18–24.

Phillips, Lisa. 1995. The family in income tax policy. *Policy Options/Options Politiques 16*(10): 30–32.

Phillips, Roderick. 1988. *Putting Asunder: The History of Divorce in Western Society.* New York: Cambridge University Press.

Philp, Margaret. 1998. Public day care pays off for whole society, *The Globe and Mail* 5 March: A8.

Phipps, Shelley. 1998. Comparing economic well-being of children in one-mother families in Canada, Norway and the United States. *Policy Options 19*(7): 10–13.

Pickett, Susan A., Judith A. Cook, & Bertram J. Cohler. 1994. Caregiving burden experienced by parents of offspring with severe mental illness: The impact of off-timedness. *Journal of Applied Social Sciences 18*(2): 199–207.

Pina, Darlene L., & Vern L. Bengston. 1995 June. Division of household labor and the well-being of retirement-aged wives. *The Gerontologist 35.*

Plass, Peggy S., & Gerald T. Hotaling. 1995. The intergenerational transmission of running away: Childhood experiences of the parents of runaways. *Journal of Youth and Adolescence 24*(3): 335–348.

Pogrebin, Letty C., 1983. *Family Politics.* New York: McGraw-Hill.

Polansky, Norman A., James M. Gaudin, & Allie C. Kilpatrick. 1992. Family radicals. *Children & Youth Services Review. Special Issue: Reforming Child Welfare through Demonstration and Evaluation 14*(1–2): 19–26.

Pomerleau, Andree, Gerard Malcuit, & Colette Sabatier. 1991. Child-rearing practices and parental beliefs in three cultural groups of Montreal: Québécois, Vietnamese, Haitian, pp. 45–68. In Marc H. Bornstein (Ed.), *Cultural Approaches to Parenting: Crosscurrents in Contemporary Psychology.*

Pool, Ithiel de Sola (Ed.). 1977. *The Social Impact of the Telephone.* Cambridge, MS: MIT Press.

Popenoe, David. 1988. *Disturbing the Nest: Family Change and Decline in Modern Societies.* New York: A. de Gruyter.

Popenoe, David. 1996a. Modern marriage: Revising the cultural script, pp. 247–270. In David Popenoe, Jean Bethke Elshtain, & David Blankenhorn (Eds.), *Promises to Keep: Decline and Renewal of Marriage in America.* Lanham, MD: Rowman and Littlefield Publishers, Inc.

Popenoe, David. 1996b. *Life Without Father.* New York: Free Press.

Powers, Jane Levine, John Eckenrode, & Barbara Jaklitsch. 1990. Maltreatment among runaway and homeless youth. *Child Abuse and Neglect 14*(1): 87–98.

Presser, Harriet B. 1995 November. *Job, family, and gender: Determinants of nonstandard work schedules among employed Americans in 1991.* 32: 577–598.

Price, Virginia Ann. 1989. Characteristics and needs of Boston street youth: One agency's response. *Children and Youth Services Review 11*(1): 75–90.

Promise Keepers. 1996. *Man of His Word: New Testament.* Colorado Springs, Colorado: International Bible Society.

Quirk, Gregory J., & Leonel Casco. 1994. Stress disorders of families of the disappeared: A controlled study in Honduras. *Social Science and Medicine 39*(12): 1675–1679.

Rabin, Claire, & Giora Rahav. 1995. Differences and similarities between younger and older marriages across cultures: A comparison of American and Israeli retired nondistressed marriages. *American Journal of Family Therapy 23*(3).

Radziszewska, Barbara, Jean L. Richardson, Clyde W. Dent, & Brian R. Flay. 1996. Parenting style and adolescent depressive symptoms, smoking and academic achievement: Ethnic, gender, and SES differences. *Journal of Behavioral Medicine 19*(3): 289–305.

Raitt, Fiona. 1996. Domestic violence and divorce mediation. *Journal of Social Welfare and Family Law 18*(1): 11–20.

Ram, Bali. 1990. *New Trends in the Family: Demographic Facts and Features.* Ottawa: Statistics Canada. Catalogue no. 91–535E.

Ram, Bali. 2000. Current issues in family demography: Canadian examples. *Canadian Studies in Population 27*(1): 1–41.

Rank, Mark, & Larry Davis. 1996 October. Perceived happiness outside of marriage among black and white spouses. *Family Relations 45.*

Rank & Hirschl, 1999 November. The economic risk of childhood in America: Estimating the probability of poverty across the formative years. *Journal of Marriage and the Family 61*(4): 1058–1067.

Rankin, Elizabeth Anne DeSalvo. 1993. Stresses and rewards experienced by employed mothers, *Health Care for Women International 14*(6): 527–537.

Ravanera, Zenaida R., & Fernando Rajulton. 1996. Stability and crisis in the family life course— findings from the 1990 General Social Survey, Canada. *Canadian Studies in Population 23*(2): 165–184.

Record, Ann Elise, & Marjorie E. Starrels. 1991. *Gender and Generational Divisions of Housework: Patterns and Explanations.* American Sociological Association (ASA).

Reimann, Renate. 1999 March. *Shared Parenting in a Changing World of Work: Lesbian Couples' Transition to*

Parenthood and Their Division of Labor. Dissertation Abstracts International, A: The Humanities and Social Sciences 59, 9, 3662–A.

Reimann, Renate. 1999. *Becoming Lesbian Mothers: Lesbian Couples' Transition to Parenthood.* American Sociological Association (ASA).

Reisner, Ellin. 2000 October. *Work/Family Spillover: A Qualitative Study of Public Transportation Operators.* Dissertation Abstracts International, A: The Humanities and Social Sciences, 61, 4, 1637–A.

Reitsma-Street, Marge. 1991. Girls learn to care: Girls policed to care. In Carol Baines, Patricia Evans, & Sheila Neysmith (Eds.), *Women's Caring: Feminist Perspectives on Social Welfare.* Toronto: McClelland & Stewart.

Reitz, Jeffrey G. 1983. *The Survival of Ethnic Groups.* Toronto: McGraw-Hill Ryerson, c1980.

Religious Tolerance.org. 2002. *Homosexual (Same-sex) Marriages in Canada,* located at www.religioustolerance.org/hom_marb0.htm, September 12, 2002.

Remennick, Larissa. 2000 December. Childless in the land of imperative motherhood: Stigma and coping among infertile Israeli women. *Sex Roles* 43(11–12): 821–841.

Ren, Xinhua Steve. 1997 January. Marital status and quality of relationships: The impact on health perception. *Social Science and Medicine* 44(2): 241–249.

Renaud, Marc. 1997. Statement to the Standing Committee on Industry, House of Commons, on behalf of the Social Sciences and Humanities Research Council of Canada, 11 December.

Renzetti, Claire M. 1996. The poverty of services for battered lesbians. *Journal of Gay and Lesbian Social Services* 4(1): 61–68.

Rettig, Kathryn D., Ronit D. Leichentritt, & Sharon M. Danes. 1999 Spring. The effects of resources, decision making, and decision implementing on perceived family well-being in adjusting to an economic stressor. *Journal of Family and Economic Issues* 20(1): 5–34.

Reynolds, Jeremy Edward. 2002 February. *You Can't Always Get the Hours You Want: A Cross-National Examination of Mismatches between Actual and Preferred Work Hours.* Dissertation Abstracts International, A: The Humanities and Social Sciences 62, 8, 2896-A-2897–A.

Richards, John. 1998. The case for subsidizing the Traditional Family, *The Globe and Mail,* 26 January: A21.

Richardson, C. James. 1996. Divorce and remarriage, pp. 215–248. In Maureen Baker (Ed.), *Families: Changing Trends in Canada* 3rd Edition. Toronto: McGraw-Hill Ryerson.

Richardson, C. James. 2001. Divorce and remarriage. In Maureen Baker (Ed.), *Families: Changing Trends in Canada,* 4th edition, pp. 206–237. Toronto: McGraw-Hill Ryerson.

Riches, Gordon, & Pamela Dawson. 1996. An intimate loneliness: Evaluating the impact of a child's death on parental self-identity and marital relationships. *Journal of Family Therapy* 18(1).

Richmond, Virginia P. 1995. Amount of communication in marital dyads as a function of dyad and individual marital satisfaction. *Communication Research Reports* 12(2): 152–159.

Riege, M. Gray. 1972. Parental affection and juvenile delinquency in girls. *British Journal of Criminology* 12: 55–73.

Risman, Barbara. 1998. *Gender Vertigo: American Families in Transition.* New Haven: Yale University Press.

Risman, Barbara, & Pepper Schwartz. 2002. After the sexual revolution: Gender politics in teen dating. *Contexts: Understanding People in their Social World* (a publication of the American Sociological Association) 1(1): 16–24.

Risman, Barbara J., & Danette Johnson-Sumerford. 1998. Doing it fairly: Study of postgender marriages. *Journal of Marriage and the Family* 60: 23–40.

Roberts, Albert R. 1996 September. Battered women who kill: a comparative study of incarcerated participants with a community sample of battered women. *Journal of Family Violence* 11: 291–304.

Roberts, Nicole A., & Robert W. Levenson. 2001 November. The remains of the workday: Impact of job stress and exhaustion on marital interaction in police couples. *Journal of Marriage and the Family* 63(4): 1052–1067.

Rodgers, Bryan. 1994 October. Pathways between parental divorce and adult depression. *The Journal of Child Psychology and Psychiatry and Allied Discipline* 35.

Rodrigues, James R., & Tricia L. Park. 1996. General and illness-specific adjustment to cancer: Relationship to marital status and marital quality. *Journal of Psychosomatic Research* 40(1).

Roesler, Thomasa A., & Tiffany Weissmann Wind. 1994. Telling the secret: Adult women describe their disclosures of incest. *Journal of Interpersonal Violence* 9: 327–338.

Rorty, Marcia, Joel Yager, & Elizabeth Rossotto. 1995. Aspects of childhood physical punishment and family environment correlates in bulimia nervosa. *Child Abuse and Neglect* 19(6): 659–667.

Roschelle, Anne R. 1999. Gender, family structure, and social structure: Racial ethnic families in the United States, pp. 311–340. In Myra Marx Ferree, Judith Lorber, & Beth B. Hess (Eds.) *Revisioning Gender.* Thousand Oaks, CA: Sage.

Rosenberg, Stanley D., Robert E. Drake, & Kim Mueser. 1996. New directions for treatment research on sequelae of sexual abuse in persons with severe mental illness. *Community Mental Health Journal* 32: 387–400.

Rosenthal, Carolyn J. 1997 Summer. The changing contexts of family care in Canada. *Ageing International* 24(1): 13–31.

Rosenthal, Carolyn. 1999. Changing families, lifecourse and aging. In Ellen M. Gee & Gloria Gutman (Eds.), *The Overselling of Population Aging: Apocalytic Demography and Intergenerational Challenges*. Toronto: Oxford University Press.

Rosenthal, Carol J., & Pam Dawson. 1991 August. Wives of institutionalized elderly men: The first stage of the transition to quasi-widowhood. *Journal of Aging and Health* 3(3): 315–334.

Rosenthal, Carolyn J., Sarah H. Matthews, & Victor W. Marshall. 1989 June. Is parent care normative? The experiences of a sample of middle-aged women. *Research on Aging* 11(2): 244–260.

Rosenthal, Carolyn J., Anne Martin Matthews, & Sarah H. Matthews. 1996. Caught in the middle? Occupancy in multiple roles and help to parents in a national probability sample of Canadian adults. *Journal of Gerontology* 51B(6): S274–S283.

Rosenthal, Carolyn J., Joanne Sulman, & Victor W. Marshall. 1992 Summer. Problems experienced by families of long-stay patients. *Canadian Journal on Aging/La Revue Canadienne du Vieillissement* 11(2): 169–183.

Ross, Susan M. 1996. Risk of physical abuse to children of spouse-abusing parents. *Child Abuse and Neglect* 20(7): 589–598.

Ross, Margaret M., Carolyn J. Rosenthal, & Pamela G. Dawson. 1997 Spring. Spousal caregiving in the institutional setting: Task performance. *Canadian Journal on Aging/La Revue Canadienne du Vieillissement* 16(1): 51–69.

Rotherham-Borus, Mary J., 1993. Suicidal behavior and risk factors among runaway youths. *American Journal of Psychiatry*, 150(1): 103–107.

Rotherham-Borus, Mary Jane, Karen A. Mahler, Cheryl Koopman, & Kris Langabeer. 1996. Sexual abuse history and associated multiple risk behavior in adolescent runaways. *American Journal of Orthopsychiatry* 3(July): 390–400.

Rounds, Kathleen A., Maeda J. Galinsky, & Mathieu R. Despard. 1995 October. Evaluation of telephone support groups for persons with HIV disease. *Research on Social Work Practice, Special Issue: A Festchrift in Honor of Edwin J.Thomas, Vol. 5*(4): 442–459.

Rout, Usha Rani, Sue Lewis, & Carolyn Kagan. 1999 January-June. Work and family roles: Indian career women in India and the West. *Indian Journal of Gender Studies* 6(1): 91–108.

Rowland, D.T., 1991 Spring. Family diversity and the life cycle. *Journal of Comparative Family Studies* 22(1): 1–14.

Roxburgh, Susan J., 1995a. *Job Stress and the Well-Being of Women in the Paid Labor Force: An Integration of the Job Stress Models of Kohn and Schooler and Robert Karasek*. American Sociological Association (ASA), Association paper.

Roxburgh, Susan J., 1995b. *The Effect of the Quality of Home and Work Roles on the Mental Health of Women in the Paid Labor Force*. American Sociological Association (ASA), Association paper.

Rwanpororo, Rosern Kobusingye. 2001 March. *Social Support: Its Mediation of Gendered Patterns in Work-Family Stress and Health for Dual-Earner Couples*. Dissertation Abstracts International, A: The Humanities and Social Sciences 61, 9, 3792–A-3793–A.

Ryan, Kristapher. 1990. *From We to Just Me, A Birth Mother's Journey: Decision-Making, Letting Go, Grieving, Healing*. Winnipeg, Manitoba: Freedom To Be Me Seminars.

Ryder, Norman B. 1992. Reproductive retrenchment in Canada and in the United States; Proceedings, The Peopling of the Americas. *International Union for the Scientific Study of Population*. 3: 155–170.

Sabourin, Teresa Chandler. 1995. The role of negative reciprocity in spouse abuse: A relational control analysis. *Journal of Applied Communication Research* 23(4).

Sabourin, Teresa Chandler, & Glen H. Stamp. 1995. Communication and the experience of dialectical tensions in family life: An examination of abusive and nonabusive families. *Communication Monographs* 62(3).

Sacks, Jonathan, 1991. *The Persistence of Faith: Religion, Morality and Society in a Secular Age*. The 1990 Reith Lectures. London: Weidenfeld and Nicolson.

Saffron, Lisa. 1998. Raising children in an age of diversity—advantages of having a lesbian mother. *Journal of Lesbian Studies* 2(4): 35–47.

Sagi, Abraham, Marinus H. Van-Ijzendoorn, Ora Aviezer, Frank Donnell, & Ofra Mayseless. 1994. Sleeping out of home in a kibbutz communal arrangement: It makes a difference for infant-mother attachment. *Child Development* 65(4): 992–1004.

Sagner, Andreas, & Raymond Z. Mtati. 1999 July. Politics of pension sharing in urban South Africa. *Ageing and Society* 19(4): 393–416.

Saha, Tulshi D. 1991. *Social Change, Women's Positions and Decision Making in the Family: A Micro Investigation for Bangladesh*. American Sociological Association (ASA).

Saintjacques, M.C. 1995. Role strain prediction in stepfamilies. *Journal of Divorce and Remarriage* 24(1–2): 51–72.

Salazar, Cruz & Eugenia Salazar. 1997 January-April. The use of free time and asymmetrical relations by gender and between generations. *Sociologica* 12(33): 19–137.

Samaan, Rodney A. 2000 February. The influences of race, ethnicity, and poverty on the mental health of children. *Journal of Health Care for the Poor and Underserved* 11(1): 100–110.

Sampson, Robert J. & Janet L. Lauritsen. 1997. Racial and ethnic disparities in crime and criminal justice in the United States. In Michael Tonry (Ed.), *Ethnicity, Crime, and Immigration: Comparative and Cross-National Perspectives*, pp. 311–374. Chicago, IL: University of Chicago Press.

Sanchez, Laura & Elizabeth Thomson. 1997. Becoming mothers and fathers: Parenthood, gender and the division of labour. *Gender and Society* 11(6): 747–772.

Sandefur, Gary, Martin Molly, & Thomas Wells. 1998. Poverty as a Public Health Issue: Since the Kerner Report of 1968. In Fred R. Harris, Lynn A. Curtis (Eds.), *Locked in the Poorhouse: Cities, Race, and Poverty in the United States*, pp. 33–56. Lanham, MD: Rowman & Littlefield.

Sanik, Margaret Mietus. 1993. The effects of time allocation on parental stress. *Social Indicators Research* 30(2–3): 175–184.

Sarantakos, Sotirios. 1996 October. Same-sex couples: Problems and prospects. *Journal of Family Studies* 2(2): 147–163.

Sarantakos, Sotirios. 1998. Sex and power in same-sex couples. *Australian Journal of Social Issues* 33(1): 17–36.

Sauve, Roger. 2002. *Job, family and stress among husbands, wives and lone parents 15–64 from 1990 to 2000.* Ottawa: The Vanier Institute of the Family www.vifamily.ca accessed 30 December 2002.

Savolainen, Jukka, Eero Lahelma, Karri Silventionen, & Anne Helene Gauthier. 2001 Winter. Parenthood and psychological well-being in Finland: Does public policy make a difference? *Journal of Comparative Family Studies* 32(1): 61–74.

Scanzoni, John. 2000. *Designing Families: The Search for Self and Community in the Information Age.* Thousand Oaks, CA: Pine Forge Press.

Scanzoni, John. 2001. From the normal family to alternate families to the quest for diversity with interdependence. *Journal of Family Issues*, 22(6): 688–710.

Schilit, Rebecca, Gwat-yong Lie, Marilyn Montagne. 1990. Substance use as a correlate of violence in intimate lesbian relationships. *Journal of Homosexuality* 19(3): 51–65.

Schlesinger, Benjamin 1998. *Strong families: A portrait.* Transition. Ottawa: The Vanier Institute of the Family, June: 4–7.

Schmelke, Jill. 2002. Commuter relationships: Dealing with the distance. *MochaSofa; Women Connecting for Solutions* www.mocha.sofa.ca accessed 31 December 2002.

Schmertman, Carl P., Monica Boyd, William Serow, & Douglas White. 2000 January. Elder-child coresidence in the United States: Evidence from the 1990 census. *Research on Aging* 22(1): 23–42.

Schneider, Carl E. 1996. The law and the stability of marriage: The family as a social institution, pp. 187–213. In David Popenoe, Jean Bethke Elshtain, & David Blankenhorn (Eds.) *Promises to Keep: Decline and Renewal of Marriage in America*, Lanham, MD: Rowman and Littlefield Publishers, Inc.

Schofield, Hilary, & Helen Herrman. 1993 May. Characteristics of carers in Victoria. *Family Matters* 34: 21–26.

Schor, J. Fligstein N., A. Hochschild, K. Voss, M. Burawoy. 1996. Roundtable Discussion: Overwork: Causes and consequences of rising work hours. *Berkeley Journal of Sociology: a Critical Review, Volume XXXXV.*

Schultz, Wolfgang. 1983. From the institution of the family to differentiated relationships between men, women, and children: On structural changes of marriage and the family. *Soziale-Welt 34*, 4 401–419.

Schumm, Walter R., Anthony P. Jurich, Stephan R. Bollman, & Margaret A. Bugaighis. 1985. His and her marriage revisited. *Journal of Family Issues* 6(2): 221–227.

Schwartz, Cowan, Ruth. 1992. Twentieth century changes in household technology, pp. 82–92. In Arlene Skolnick & Jerome Skolnick (Eds.), *Family in Transition*, 7th edition. New York: HarperCollins.

Schwartz, Pepper, & Virginia Rutter. 1998. *The Gender of Sexuality.* Thousand Oaks, California: Pine Forge Press.

Scott, Katherine. 1996. *The Progress of Canada's Children.* Ottawa: Canadian Council on Social Development.

Scott-Little, M. Catherine, & Susan D. Holloway. 1994. Caregivers' attributions about children's misbehavior in child-care centers. *Journal of Applied Developmental Psychology* 15(2): 241–253.

Seaver, Carol. 1996. Muted lives: Older battered women. *Journal of Elder Abuse and Neglect* 8(2): 3–21.

Seiffge-Krinke Inge. 1999 June. Families with daughters, families with sons: Different challenges for family relationships and marital satisfaction? *Journal of Youth and Adolescence* 28(3): 325–342.

Seltzer, Judith A. 1994. Consequences of marital dissolution for children. *Annual Review of Sociology* 20: 235–266.

Sever, Aysan. 1990. Mate selection patterns of men and women in personal advertisements. *Atlantis: A Women's Studies Journal* 15(2): 70–76.

Seyler, Dian L., Pamela A. Monroe, & James C. Garand. 1995 March. Balancing work and family: The role of employer-supported child care benefits. *Journal of Social Issues* 16: 170–193.

Shadish, William R., Kevin Ragsdale, & Renata R. Glaser. 1995. The efficacy and effectiveness of marital and family therapy: A perspective from meta-analysis. *Journal of Marital and Family Therapy* 21(4).

Shah, Bindi. 2000. *Reconstructing Ethnic Identity/Creating Belonging: A Case Study of the Role of Community Youth Programs in the Lives of Adolescent Laotian Girls.* American Sociological Association (ASA).

Shane, Paul G. 1989. Changing patterns among homeless and runaway youth. *American Journal of Orthopsychiatry* 59(2): 208–214.

Shane, Paul G. 1991. A sample of homeless and runaway youth in New Jersey and their health status. *Journal of Health and Social Policy* 2(4): 73–82.

Sharf, Barbara F. 1997. Communicating breast cancer on-line: Support and empowerment on the Internet. *Women & Health* 26(1): 65–84.

Shaver, Sheila, & Jonathan Bradshaw. 1995. The recognition of wifely labour by welfare states. *Social Policy and Administration* 29(1): 10–25.

Shavit, Yossi, Claude S. Fischer, & Yael Koresh. 1994. Kin and nonkin under collective threat: Israeli networks during the Gulf War. *Social Forces* 72(4): 1197–1215.

Shaw, Kevin, & Jack Dann. 1999 August. Work is sacred—the journey out of welfare. *Journal of Occupational Science: Australia* 6(2): 80–87.

Shaw Crouse, Janice (Ed.). 1999. *The State of Marriage in 20th Century America: Implications for the Next Millennium,* located at www.beverlylahaye institute.org, August 16, 2002.

Shek, Daniel T.L. 1995a June. Gender differences in marital quality and well-being in Chinese married adults. *Sex Roles 32.*

Shek, Daniel T.L. 1995b Marital quality and psychological well-being of married adults in a Chinese context. *Journal of Genetic Psychology* 156(1).

Shellenberger, Sylvia, Couch, Kathy Watkins, & Mary Anne Drake. 1989 Fall. Elderly family members and their caregivers: characteristics and development of the relationship. *Family Systems Medicine* 7(3): 317–322.

Sheridan, Michael J. A proposed intergenerational model of substance abuse, family functioning, and abuse/neglect. *Child Abuse and Neglect* 19(May): 519–530.

Shi,Liping. 2000 February. The communication structure of intercultural married couples and their marital satisfaction. *Soshioroji* 44(3): 57–73.

Shoham, Efrat. 1994 Fall. Family characteristics of delinquent youth in time of war. *International Journal of Offender Therapy and Comparative Criminology* 38(3): 247–258.

Short, James F. Jr. 1997. *Poverty, Ethnicity, and Violent Crime.* Boulder, CO: Westview.

Short, J., E. Williams, & B. Christie. 1976. *The Social Psychology of Telecommunications.* London; New York: Wiley.

Shortt, Joanne Wu. 1996. Psychological factors in the longitudinal course of battering: When do the couples split up? When does the abuse decrease? *Violence and Victims* 11(4): 371–392.

Shucksmith, J., L.B. Hendry, & A. Glendinning. 1995. Models of parenting: Implications for adolescent well-being within different types of family contexts. *Journal of Adolescence* 18(3): 253–270.

Shupe, Anson D., William A. Stacey, & Lonnie R. Hazlewood. 1987. *Violent Men, Violent Couples: The Dynamics of Domestic Violence.* Lexington: Lexington Books.

Shuval, Judith T., Diana Shye, & Rachel Javetz. 1990. *Gender Differences among Health Professionals Regarding Self-Care by Lay People.* International Sociological Association (ISA).

Silver, Hilary, & Frances Goldscheider. 1994 June. Flexible work and housework: Work and family constraints on women's domestic labor. *Social Forces* 72: 1103–1119.

Silverman, Eliane Leslau. 1984. *The Last Best West: Women on the Alberta Frontier 1880–1930.* Montreal: Eden Press.

Sim, Hee-Ong, & Samuel Vuchinich. 1996 May. The declining effects of family stressors on antisocial behavior from childhood to adolescence and early adulthood. *Journal of Family Issues 17.*

Simmons, Deborah S., & William J. Doherty. 1995. Defining who we are and what we do: Clinical practice patterns of marriage and family therapists in Minnesota. *Journal of Marital and Family Therapy* 21(1).

Simons, Ronald, & Les Whitbeck. 1991. Running away during adolescence as a precursor to adult homelessness. *Social Science Review* 65(2): 224–247.

Sitrin, Allison Gayle. 2001 September. *The Impact of the Quality of Marital Adaptation on Prenatal Maternal Representations and Postnatal Satisfaction with Social Support.* Dissertation Abstracts International: Section B: The Sciences & Engineering Vol. 62(3–B) pp. 1599.

Skirboll, Esther, & Rhoda Taylor. 1998. *Two Homes, Two Jobs, One Marriage: Commuter Spousal Relationships,* International Sociological Association Paper.

Skitka, Linda & Michele Frazier. 1995. Ameliorating the effects of parental divorce: Do small group interventions work? *Journal of Divorce and Remarriage* 24(3–4).

Skolnick, Arlene. 1991. *Embattled Paradise: The American Family in an Age of Uncertainty.* New York: Basic Books.

Skrypnek, Berna J., & Janet E. Fast. 1996. Work and family policy in Canada: Family needs, collective solutions. *Journal of Family Issues* 17(6): 793–812.

Smart, Carol, and Bren Neale. 1999. *Family Fragments?* Cambridge, U.K.: Polity Press.

Smith, Christine Biship, Margaret L. McLaughlin, Kerry K. Osborne. 1997 March. Conduct control on Usenet. *Journal of Computer-Mediated Communication* 2(4): np.

Smith, Dorothy. 1993. The Standard North American Family: SNAF as an ideological code. *Journal of Family Issues 14*(1): 50–65.

Smith, Jane E., V. Waldorf, & D. Trembath. 1990. Single white male looking for thin, very attractive.... *Sex Roles 23*(11&12): 675–683.

Smith, Richard B., & Robert A. Brown. 1997. The impact of social support on gay male couples. *Journal of Homosexuality 33*(2): 39–61.

Smock, Pamela J. 1994 September. Gender and the short-run economic consequences of marital disruption. *Social Forces 73*.

Snarey, John, & Linda Son. 1986. Sex-identity development among kibbutz-born males: A test of the Whiting hypothesis. *Ethos 14*(2): 99–119.

Snell, James G. 1983. The White life for two: The defence of marriage and sexual morality in Canada, 1890–1914. *Histoire sociale/Social History 16*(31): 111–128.

Snow, Catherine E. 1991. The language of the mother-child relationship, pp. 195–210. In Martin Woodhead, Ronnie Carr, & Paul Light (Eds), *Becoming a Person: Child Development in Social Context*, Vol. 1.

Snowdon, Anne W., Sheila Cameron, & Katherine Dunham. 1994. Relationships between stress, coping resources and satisfaction with family functioning in families of children with disabilities. *Canadian Journal of Nursing Research 26*(3): 63–76.

Snyder, D.K., & L.A. Fruchtman. 1981. Differential patterns of wife abuse: A data-based typology. *Journal of Consulting and Clinical Psychology 49*: 878–885.

Snyder, Robert A. 1995. One man's time warp is another (wo)man's treasure: The importance of individual and situational differences in shift work tolerance and satisfaction. *Human Resource Development Quarterly 6*(4): 397–407.

Sogner, Solvi. 1993. Historical features of women's position in society, pp. 145–184. In Nora Federici, K.O. Mason, & Solvi Sogner (Eds.), *Women's Position and Demographic Change*. Oxford: Clarendon.

Soley, Clive. 1999. The politics of the family, pp. 214–221. In Geoff Dench (Ed.), *Rewriting the Sexual Contract*. New Brunswick, NJ: Transaction.

Sommer, Dion. 1992. A child's place in society: New challenges for the family and day care. *Children and Society 6*(4): 317–335.

Song, Jung Ah, Betsy M. Bergen, & Walter Schumm. 1995. Sexual satisfaction among Korean-American couples in the Midwestern United States. *Journal of Sex and Marital Therapy 21*(3).

Song, Miri. 1995. *Children's Labor Participation in Chinese Take-Away Businesses in Britain*. American Sociological Association, Association paper.

South, S.J., K. Trent, and Y. Shen. 2001. Changing partners: Toward a macrostructural opportunity theory of marital dissolution. *Journal of Marriage and Family 63*: 743–754.

South, Scott. 1985. Economic conditions and the divorce rate: A time-series analysis of the children. *Journal of Marriage and the Family 47*(1): 31–42.

South, Scott. 1995 July. Do you need to shop around? Age at marriage, spousal alternatives and divorce. *Journal of Family Issues 16*.

South, Scott, & Kim Lloyd. 1995 February. Spousal alternatives and marital dissolution. *American Sociological Review 60*.

Spalter-Roth, Roberta M., Heidi I. Hartmann, Linda M. Andrews. 1990. *Mothers, children, and low-wage work: The ability to earn a family wage*. American Sociological Association (ASA).

Spanier, Graham B. 1979. The measurement of marital quality. *Journal of Sex and Marital Therapy 5*(3): 288–300.

Spillane-Grieco, Eileen. 1984. Characteristics of a helpful relationship: A study of empathic understanding and positive regard between runaways and their parents. *Adolescence 19*(73): 63–75.

Sprott, Julie E. 1994. One person's "spoiling" is another's freedom to become: Overcoming ethnocentric views about parental control. *Social Science and Medicine 38*(8): 1111–1124.

Stacey, Judith. 1990. *Brave New Families*. New York: Basic Books.

Stacey, Judith. 1996. *In the Name of the Family: Rethinking Family Values in the Postmodern Age*. Boston: Beacon.

Stacey, William A., Lonnie R. Hazlewood, & Anson D. Shupe. 1994. *The Violent Couple*. Westport, CN: Praeger.

Stanley, Sandra C., Janet G. Hunt, & Larry L. Hunt. 1986. The relative deprivation of husbands in dual-earner households. *Journal of Family Issues 7*(1): 3–20.

Stanton, Glenn T. 1996 May-June. The counter-revolution against easy divorce: New rumbling in the states. *The American Enterprise 7*.

Statistical Record of Women Worldwide. 1991. Detroit: Gale Research.

Statistics Canada. 1992. *Families, Number, Type and Structure*. Ottawa: Statistics Canada, Catalogue no. 93–312.

Statistics Canada. 1993. The violence against women survey. *The Daily*, 18 November.

Statistics Canada. 1995. *Households' Unpaid Work: Measuring and Valuation*. Ottawa: Statistics Canada. Catalogue no. 13–603E, no. 3.

Statistics Canada. 1996a. *Life Events: How Families Change, Labour and Income Dynamics* 5(1). Ottawa: Statistics Canada.

Statistics Canada. 1996b. Canadian families: Diversity and change. *The Daily*, 19 June.

Statistics Canada. 1996c. Dual-earner families. *The Daily*, 6 June.

Statistics Canada. 1997 Autumn. Divorce in the 1990s. *Health Reports, 9*(2):Catalogue No. 82–003–XPB.

Statistics Canada. 1997a. Formation of first common-law unions. *The Daily, 9* December.

Statistics Canada. 1997b. Earnings characteristics of two-partner families. *The Daily*, 26 August: 2–3.

Statistics Canada. 1997c. *Income Distributions by Size in Canada, 1996.* Ottawa: Statistics Canada. Catalogue no. 13–207–XPB.

Statistics Canada. 1998a. 1996 Census: Labour force activity, occupation and industry, place of work, mode of transportation to work, unpaid work. *The Daily*, 17 March.

Statistics Canada. 1998b. 1996 Census: Marital status, common-law unions and families. *The Daily*, 14 October.

Statistics Canada. 1998c. 1996 Census: Aboriginal data. *The Daily*, 13 January.

Statistics Canada. 1998d. 1996 Census: Private households, housing costs and social and economic characteristics of families. *The Daily*, 9 June.

Statistics Canada. 1998e. Earnings of men and women, 1996. *The Daily*, 23 March.

Statistics Canada. 1998f. Marriages and Divorces, 1996. *The Daily*, 29 January.

Statistics Canada. 1998g. Sterility. *The Daily*, 24 January.

Statistics Canada. 1998h. 1996 Census: ethnic origin, visible minorities. *The Daily*, 17 February.

Statistics Canada. 1999. *Age, Sex, Marital Status and Common-law Status.* Ottawa: Ministry of Industry, April. Catalogue No. 92–353–XIE.

Statistics Canada. 2001. Marriages, *The Daily*, Thursday, November 15.

Statistics Canada. 2001. Marriages, 1998. *The Daily*, 15 November.

Statistics Canada. 2002a. Changing conjugal life in Canada. *The Daily*, 11 July.

Statistics Canada. 2002a. 2001 Census: Profile of Canadian Families and Households: Diversification Continues. Census release 22 October 2002, www.statcan.ca.

Statistics Canada. 2002b. *General Social Survey–Cycle 15: Family History*. Ottawa: Statistics Canada. Catalogue number 89–575–XIE. www.statcan.ca available on 11 July 2002.

Statistics Canada. 2002b. Divorces, 1999 and 2000, *The Daily*, 2 December.

Statistics Canada. 2002. *Census 2001: Language composition of Canada.* Census Release, December 10, 2002.

Statistics Canada. 2002b. Cumulative earnings among young workers. *The Daily*, 19 November.

Statistics Canada. 2002c. *2001 Census of Canada: Profile of Canadian Families and Households: Diversification Continues.* Ottawa: Statistics Canada, Catalogue number 96F0030XIE2001003. www.statcan.ca accessed on 22 October 2002.

Statistics Canada. 2002c. Census family. *Census Dictionary*, 12 September 2002 www.statcan.ca/english/census2001/dict/fam003.html.

Statistics Canada. 2002d. Family income, 2000. *The Daily*, 30 October.

Steinberg, Laurence, Susie D. Lamborn, Nancy Darling, Nina S. Mounts, & Sanford M. Dornbusch. 1994. Over-time changes in adjustment and competence among adolescents from authoritative, authoritarian, indulgent, and neglectful families. *Child Development* 65(3): 754–770.

Steinhauer, et al. 1984 March. The process model of family functioning. *Canadian Journal of Psychiatry* 29: 77–88.

Steinmetz, S.K. 1977. *The Cycle of Violence: Assertive, Aggressive, and Abusive Family Interaction.* New York: Praeger.

Stephens, Linda S. 1996. Will Johnny see Daddy this week? An empirical test of three theoretical perspectives of post-divorce contact. *Journal of Family Issues* 12(4).

Stermac, Lana, Alison Davidson, & Peter M. Sheridan. 1995 Summer. Incidence of nonsexual violence in incest offenders. *International Journal of Offender Therapy and Comparative Criminology 39:* 167–178.

Stern, Phyllis. 1984. Stepfather family dynamics: An overview for therapists. *Issues in Mental Health Nursing* 6(1–2): 89–103.

Stern, Susan B., & Carolyn A. Smith. 1995. Family processes and delinquency in an ecological context. *Social Service Review* 69(4): 703–731.

Stiffman, Arlene Rubin. 1989a. Physical and sexual abuse in runaway youths. *Child Abuse and Neglect* 13(3): 417–426.

Stiffman, Arlene Rubin, 1989b. Suicide attempts in runaway youths. *Suicide and Life Threatening Behavior* 19(2): 147–159.

Stohs, Joanne Hovan. 1995. Predictors of conflict over the household division of labor among women employed full-time. *Sex Roles* 33(3–4).

Straus, M. 1992. Family violence. In Edgar F. Borgatta & Marie L. Borgatta (Eds.), *Encyclopedia of Sociology*, Vol. 2. New York: Macmillan Publishing Co.

Straus, Murray A. 1996. *Identifying Offenders in Criminal Justice Research on Domestic Assault.* Beverley Hills, CA: Sage Publications.

Straus, M.A., R.J. Gelles, & S.K. Steinmetz. 1980. *Behind Closed Doors: Violence in the American Family.* Garden City, NY: Doubleday.

Stroh, Linda K. 2003. A review of relocation: The impact on work and family. *Human Resource Management Review.*

Sugarman, David B., & Susan L. Frankel. 1996. Patriarchal ideology and wife-assault: A meta-analytic review. *Journal of Family Violence* 11(1): 13–40.

Suitor, Jill J. & Karl Pillemer. 1988 November. Explaining intergenerational conflict when adult children and elderly parents live together. *Journal of Marriage and the Family* 50(4): 1037–1047.

Suitor, J. Jill & Karl Pillemer. 1995. *Changes in Support and Interpersonal Stress in the Networks of Married Caregiving Daughters: Findings from a Two-Year Panel Study.* ASP Association paper.

Sullivan, Kieran T., & Thomas N. Bradbury. 1997. Are premarital prevention programs reaching couples at risk for marital dysfunctions? *Journal of Consulting and Clinical Psychology* 65(1).

Sullivan, Maureen. 1996 December. Rozzie and Harriet? Gender and family patterns of lesbian coparents. *Gender & Society* 10(6): 747–767.

Sulman, Joanne, Carolyn J. Rosenthal, Victor W. Marshall, & Joanne Daciuk. 1996. Elderly patients in the acute care hospital: Factors associated with long stay and its impact on patients and families. *Journal of Gerontological Social Work* 25(3–4): 33–52.

Susser, Ezra S., Shang P. Lin, Sarah A. Conover, & Elmer L. Struening. 1991. Childhood antecedents of homelessness in psychiatric patients. *American Journal of Psychiatry* 148(8): 1026–1030.

Sussman, Steve, & Clyde W. Dent. 2000. One-year prospective prediction of drug use from stress-related variables. *Substance Use & Misuse* 35(5): 717–735.

Swadener, Beth Blue, & Sally Lubeck. (Eds.). 1995. *Children and Families at Promise: Deconstructing the Discourse of Risk.* Albany, NY: State University of New York Press.

Sweeny, Megan. 1996. *The Decision to Divorce and Subsequent Remarriage: Does it Matter Which Spouse Chose to Leave?* American Sociological Association.

Sweet, James A., & Larry L. Bumpass. 1987. *American Families and Households.* New York: Russell Sage Foundation.

Sweezy, Kate, & Jill Tiefenthaler. 1996. Do state-level variables affect divorce rates? *Review of Social Economy* 54(1).

Sydie, Rosalind A. 1986. *Natural Women, Cultured Men: A Feminist Perspective on Sociological Theory.* Toronto: Methuen.

Szinovacz, Maximilian. 1996. Couples' employment/retirement patterns and perceptions of marital quality. *Research on Aging* 18(2).

Tannen, Deborah. 1993. *Gender and Conversational Interaction.* New York: Oxford University Press.

Tasker, Fiona, & Susan Golombok. 1995. Adults raised as children in lesbian families. *American Journal of Orthopsychiatry* 65(2): 203–215.

Tavecchico, Louis W.C., M.A.E. Thomeer, & W. Meeus. 1999. Attachment, social network and homelessness in young people. *Social Behavior and Personality* 27(3): 247–262.

Tayler, Lyn, Gordon Parker, & Kay Roy. Parental divorce and its effects on the quality of intimate relationships in adulthood. *Journal of Divorce and Remarriage* 24(3–4).

Taylor, Lorraine C., Ivora D. Hinton & Melvin N. Wilson. 1995. Parental influences of academic performance in African-American students. *Journal of Child and Family Studies* 4(3): 293–302.

Taylor, S.C. 1980 November-December. Siblings need a plan of care too. *Pediatric Nursing:* 9–13.

Teare, John F., Karen Authier, & Roger Peterson. 1994. Differential patterns of post-shelter placement as a function of problem type and severity. *Journal of Child and Family Studies* 3(1): 7–22.

Tennstedt, Sharon L., & John B. McKinlay. 1987. *Predictors of informal care: The role of social network characteristics.* American Sociological Association (ASA).

Tennstedt, Sharon L., & Judith G. Gonyea. 1994. An agenda for work and eldercare research: methodological challenges and future directions. *Research on Aging* 16(1): 85–108.

Tepperman, Barry, & G. Frydman. 1999. The Internet as a Support Medium in Cancer Care. In T. N. Arvantis, S.F. Keevil, and J. Woodall (Eds.), *Proceedings of the Third Annual World Congress on the Internet in Medicine, Mednet 98.* Birmingham, UK: The University of Birmingham: Educational Technology Research Papers Series.

Tepperman, Lorne. 1994. *Choices and Chances: Sociology for Everyday Life,* 2nd edition. Toronto: Holt-HBJ.

Testa, Mark, Nan Marie Astone, Marilyn Krogh, Kathryn M. Neckerman. 1989 January. Employment and marriage among inner-city fathers. *The Annals of the American Academy of Political and Social Science* 501: 79–91.

Theriault, C. & M. Cyr. 1996. Relation between satisfaction linked to three social roles and satisfaction with life among housewives. *Canadian Journal of Behavioural Sciences* 28(2): 79–85.

Thomas, Geoff, Garth J.O. Fletcher, & Craig Lange. 1997. On-line empathetic accuracy in marital interaction. *Journal of Personality and Social Psychology* 72(4).

Thomas, Linda Thiede, & Daniel C. Ganster. 1995 February. Impact of family-supportive work variables on work-family conflict and strain: A control perspective. *Journal of Applied Psychology 80*: 6–15.

Thomas, Nancy L. 1991. *The New in Loco Parentis 23*(5): 33–39.

Thomas, Tania N. 1995. Acculturative stress in the adjustment of immigrant families. *Journal of Social Distress and the Homeless 4*(2): 131–142.

Thomas, William Issac & Florian Znaniecki. 1925. *The Polish Peasant in Europe and America.* Edited and abridged by Eli Zaretsky. Urbana, IL: University of Illinois Press, c1984.

Thompson, Elizabeth A. 2000 April. Mothers' experiences of an adult child's HIV/AIDS diagnosis: Maternal responses to and resolutions of accountability for AIDS. *Family Relations: Interdisciplinary Journal of Applied Family Studies 49*(2): 155–164.

Thompson, Suzanne C., Louis J. Medvene, & Debra Freedman. 1995. Caregiving in the close relationship of cardiac patients: exchange, power and attribution perspectives on caregiver resentment. *Personal Relationships 2*(2).

Thornberry, Terence P., Carolyn A. Smith, & Gregory Howard. 1997 August. Risk factors for teenage fatherhood. *Journal of Marriage and the Family 59*: 505–522.

Thornton, Arland. 1977 August. Children and marital stability. *Journal of Marriage and the Family 39*(3): 531–540.

Thornton, Arland. 1996.Comparative and historical perspectives on marriage, divorce, and family life, pp. 69–87. In Popenoe, David, Jean Bethke Elshtain, & David Blankenhorn (Eds.), *Promises to Keep: Decline and Renewal of Marriage in America.* Lanham, MD: Rowman and Littlefield Publishers, Inc.

Thornton, Arland, & Linda Young-DeMarco. 2001. Four decades of trends in attitudes toward family issues in the Unites States: The 1960s through the 1990s. *Journal of Marriage and Family 63*(4): 1009–1037.

Tingey, Holly, Gary Kiger, & Pamela J. Riley. 1996. Juggling multiple roles: Perceptions of working mothers. *Social Science Journal 33*(2): 183–191.

Tirone, Susan, & Alison Pedlar. 2000 Spring. Understanding the leisure experiences of a minority ethnic group: South Asian teens and young adults in Canada. *Loisir et Societe/Society and Leisure 23*(1): 145–169.

Tocqueville-Review/Revue-Tocqueville; 1980–1981, 3, 1, fall-winter, 5–41.

Toliver, Susan Diane. 1998. *Black Families in Corporate America.* Thousand Oaks, CA: Sage Publications.

Tower, Roni-Beth, & Stanislav V. Kasl. 1996. Gender, marital closeness and depressive symptoms in elderly couples. *Journals of Gerontology, Series B, Psychological Sciences and Social Sciences 51B*(3).

Townsend, Nicholas W. 2002. *The Package Deal: Marriage, Work and Fatherhood in Men's Lives.* Philadelphia: Temple University Press.

Tran, Huong Hoai. 1994 November. The adaptation of Vietnamese refugees in American society. *Dissertation Abstracts International, A: The Humanities and Social Sciences 55*(5): 1389–A.

Trappe, Heike. 1995. *Women's Changing Life Courses in the German Democratic Republic (GDR).* American Sociological Association, Association paper.

Trost, Jan. 1988. Conceptualising the family. *International Sociology 3*(3): 301–308.

Trudel, Gilles, Lyne Landry, & Yvette Larose. 1997. Low sexual desire: The role of anxiety, depression and marital adjustment. *Sexual and Marital Therapy 12*(1).

Trute, Barry. 1995 October. Gender differences in the psychological adjustment of parents of young, developmentally disabled children. *The Journal of Child Psychology and Psychiatry and Allied Disciplines*: 1225–1242.

Tsang, Beryl. 2001. *Child Custody and Access: The Experiences of Abused Immigrant and Refugee Women.* Toronto: Education Wife Assault.

Turcotte, Pierre & Alain Belanger. 1997. Moving in together: The formation of first common-law unions. *Canadian Social Trends 47*: 7–10.

Turk, J. 1964. Impact of cystic fibrosis on family functioning. *Pediatrics 34*: 67–71.

Tzeng, Jessie, & Robert Mare. 1995 December. Labor market and socioeconomic effects on marital stability. *Social Science Research 24*.

United Nations. 1991. *Building the Smallest Democracy at the Heart of Society.* Vienna: United Nations International Year of the Family Secretariat.

United States Bureau of the Census. 1995. *Statistical Abstract of the United States.* Washington, D.C.: U.S. Department of Commerce.

Urquhart, Jane. 1997. *The Underpainter.* Toronto: McClelland and Stewart.

Valens, E.G. 1975. *The Other Side of the Mountain.* New York: Warner Books.

Valman, H.B. 1981. The handicapped child. *British Medical Journal 283*: 1166–1169.

Valpy, Michael. 1998. Out of the darkness of Cinderella. *The Globe and Mail*, 9 January: A21.

Van Crombrugge, Hans & Lieve Vandemeulebroecke. 1991. Family and center day care under three: The child's experience. *Community Alternatives 3*(2): 35–58.

Van Kirk, Sylvia. 1980. *"Many Tender Ties": Women in Fur-Trade Society, 1670–1870.* Winnipeg: Watson & Dwyer.

Van Kirk, Sylvia. 1992. The custom of the country: An examination of fur trade marriage practices, pp. 67–92. In Bettina Bradbury (Ed.), *Canadian Family*

History: Selected Readings. Toronto: Copp Clark Pitman.

Van Roosmalen, Erica, & Susan A. McDaniel. 1989. Peer group influence as a factor in smoking behavior of adolescents. *Adolescence XXIV* (96): 801–816.

Van Roosmalen, Erica, & Susan A. McDaniel. 1992. Adolescent smoking intentions: Gender differences in peer context. *Adolescence* 27 (105): 87–105.

Van Voorhis, P., F.T. Cullen, R.A. Mathers, & C. Chenoweth Garner. 1988. The impact of family structure and quality on delinquency: A comparative assessment of structural and functional factors. *Criminology* 26: 235–261.

Vangelisti, Anita, & Mary A. Banski. 1993 April. Couples' debriefing conversations: The impact of gender, occupation, and demographic characteristics. *Family Relations* 42.

Vanier Institute of the Family. 1994. *Profiling Canada's Families*. Ottawa: Vanier Institute of the Family.

Vanier Institute of the Family. 2002. *Profiling Canada's Families II*. Ottawa: Vanier Institute of the Family.

Vansteenwegen, Alfons. 1996a. Individual and relational changes seven years after couples therapy. *Journal of Couples Therapy* 6(1–2).

Vansteenwegen, Alfons. 1996b. Who benefits from couple therapy? A comparison of successful and unsuccessful couples. *Journal of Sex and Marital Therapy* 22(1).

Vansteenwegen, Alfons. 1997. Do marital therapists do what they say they do? A comparison between experiential and communication couples therapy. *Sexual and Marital Therapy* 12(1).

Vansteenwegen, Alfons. 1998 April-June. Divorce after couple therapy: An overlooked perspective of outcome research. *Journal of Sex & Marital Therapy* 24(2),: 123–130.

Vaughan, Diane. 1985. *Uncoupling: Turning Points in Intimate Relationships*. New York: Oxford University Press.

Veenhoven, Ruut. 1983. The growing impact of marriage. *Social Indicators Research* 12(1): 49–63.

Veevers. Jean E. 1980. *Childless by Choice*. Toronto: Butterworths.

Veevers, Jean E. 1975. The moral careers of voluntarily childless wives: Notes on the defense of a variant world view. *Family Coordinator* 24(4): 473–487.

Vergun, Pamela Bea, Sanford M. Dornbusch, & Laurence Steinberg. 1996. "Come all of you turn to and help one another": *Authoritative Parenting, Community Orientation, and Deviance Among High School Students*. American Sociological Association paper.

Vinokur, Amiran D., Richard H. Price, & Robert D. Caplan. 1996. Hard times and hurtful partners: How financial strain affects depression and relationship satisfaction of unemployed persons and their spouses. *Journal of Personality and Social Psychology* 71.

Volling, Brenda L., & Jay Belsky. 1991. Multiple determinants of father involvement during infancy in dual-earner and single-earner families. *Journal of Marriage and the Family* 53(2): 461–474.

Voss K., A. Hochschild, N. Fligstein, K. Voss, J. Schor, M. Burawoy. 2001. Roundtable Discussion: Overwork: Causes and consequences of rising work hours. *Berkeley Journal of Sociology: A Critical Review, Volume XXXXV.*

Wadsby, Marie, & Gunilla Sydsjoe. 2001 December. From pregnancy to parenthood: A study of couples' relationship. Frangraviditet till foeraeldraskap: En studie av parrelationen. *Nordisk Psykologi* 53(4): 275–288.

Waite, Linda. 1995. Does marriage matter? *Demography* 32(4): 483–507.

Waite, Linda J., & Maggie Gallagher. 2000. *The Case for Marriage*. New York: Doubleday.

Walczynski, Pamela Theresa. 1998 April. *Power, Personality, and Conflictual Interaction: An Exploration of Demand/Withdraw Interaction in Same-Sex and Cross-Sex Couples*. Dissertation Abstracts International: Section B: The Sciences & Engineering Vol. 58(10–B), pp. 5660.

Waldner, Lisa K., & Brian Magruder. 1999. Coming out to parents: Perceptions of family relations, perceived resources, and identity expression as predictors of identity disclosure for gay and lesbian adolescents. *Journal of Homosexuality* 37(2): 83–100.

Waldner-Haugrud, Lisa K., Linda Vaden Gratch, Brian Magruder. 1997 Summer. Victimization and perpetration rates of violence in gay and lesbian relationships: *Gender issues explored. Violence and Victims* 12(2): 173–184.

Waldron-Hennessey, Rebecca, & Ronald M. Sabatelli. 1997. The parental comparison level index: A measure for assessing parental rewards and costs relative to expectations. *Journal of Marriage and the Family* 59(4): 824–847.

Waldrop, Deborah P., Joseph A. Weber, Shondel L. Herald, Julie Pruett, Kathy Cooper, & Kevin Juozapavicius. 1999 March. Wisdom and life experiences: How grandfathers mentor their grandchildren. *Journal of Aging and Identity* 4(1): 33–46.

Walker, Karen E. & Frank F. Furstenburg. 1994. *Neighborhood Settings and Parenting Strategies*. American Sociological Association, Association paper.

Wallace, Jean E., 1997 April. It's about time: A study of hours worked and work spillover among law firm lawyers. *Journal of Vocational Behavior* 50(2): 227–248.

Wallerstein, Judith S. 1996 April. The psychological tasks of marriage: part 2. *American Journal of Orthopsychiatry 66.*

Wallerstein, Judith S., Julia Lewis, and Sandy Blakeslee. 2000. *The Unexpected Legacy of Divorce: A 25 Year Landmark Study.* New York: Hyperion.

Wallerstein, J., & S. Blakelee. 1990. *Second Chances: Men, Women, and Children A Decade After Divorce.* New York: Ticknor and Fields.

Walters, Karina L., & Jane M. Simoni. 1999 August. Trauma, substance use, and HIV risk among urban American Indian women.*Cultural Diversity & Ethnic Minority Psychology 5*(3): 236–248.

Walters, Suzanna Danuta. 1999. Sex, text and context: (In)between feminism and cultural studies. In Myra Marx Ferree, Judith Lorber, and Beth B. Hess (Eds.), *Revisioning Gender.* Thousand Oaks, CA: Sage.

Walters, Vivienne, Rhonda Lenton, et al. 1996. Paid work, unpaid work and social support: A study of the health of male and female nurses. *Social Science and Medicine 43*(11): 1627–1636.

Ward, Peter. 1990. *Courtship, Love and Marriage in Nineteenth Century English Canada.* Montreal & Kingston: McGill-Queen's University Press.

Waring, Edward M., Charles H. Chamberlaine, & Claudia Carver. 1995 Spring. A pilot study of marital therapy as a treatment for depression. *The American Journal of Family Therapy 23:* 3–10.

Waring, Marilyn. 1988. *If Women Counted: A New Feminist Economics.* San Francisco: Harper & Row.

Warren, Jennifer A., & Phyllis J. Johnson. 1995 April. The impact of workplace support on work-family role strain. *Family Relations 44:* 163–169.

Watkins, Susan C. 1993. If all we knew about women was what we read in Demography, what would we know? *Demography 30*(4): 551–577.

Watson, Jeffrey A. 1997 Winter. Factors associated with African American grandparents' interest in grandparent education. *The Journal of Negro Education 66*(1): 73–82.

Weaver, Terri L., & George A. Clum. 1996. Interpersonal violence: Expanding the search for long-term sequelae within a sample of battered women. *Journal of Traumatic Stress 9*(4): 783–803.

Webster, Pamela S., & Regula A. Herzog. 1995 January. Effects of parental divorce and memories of family problems on relationships between adult children and their parents. *Journal of Gerontology, Series B: Psychological Sciences and Social Sciences 50B.*

Webster, Pamela S., Terri L. Orbuch, & James S. House. 1995 September. *Effects of Childhood Family Background on Adult Marital Quality and Perceived Stability.* American Sociological Association 101.

Weinberg, Nancy, John Schmale, Janet Uken, & Keith Wessel. 1996 February. Online help: Cancer patients participate in a computer-mediated support group. *Health & Social Work, Vol. 21* (1), 24–29.

Weiner, Jennifer, Lisa Harlow, & Jerome Adams. 1995. Psychological adjustment of college students from families of divorce. *Journal of Divorce and Remarriage 23*(3–4).

Weinfeld, Morton. 2001. *Like Everyone Else...but Different: The Paradoxical Success of Canadian Jews.* Toronto: McClelland and Stewart.

Weisfeld, G.E., R.J.H. Russell, C.C. Weisfeld, & P.A. Wells. 1992. Correlates of satisfaction in British marriages. *Ethology and Sociobiology 13*(2): 125–145.

Weiss, Robert S. 1996. Parenting from separate households, pp. 215–230. In David Popenoe, Jean Bethke Elshtain, & David Blankenhorn (Eds.), *Promises to Keep: Decline and Renewal of Marriage in America.* Lanham, MD: Rowman and Littlefield Publishers, Inc.

Weitzman, Lenore. 1985. *The Divorce Revolution: The Unexpected Social and Economic Effects for Women and Children in America.* New York: Free Press.

Weitzman, Lenore J. 1996. The economic consequences of divorce are still unequal: Comment on Peterson. *American Sociological Review 61*(3).

Wellman, Barry, & Keith Hampton. 1999 November. Living networked on and offline. *Contemporary Sociology 28:* 6, 648–654.

Wells, L.E., & J.H. Rankin. 1988. Direct parental controls and delinquency. *Criminology 26:* 263–285.

Wells, Mona, & Harjit S. Sandhu, 1986. The juvenile runaway: A historical perspective. *Free Inquiry in Creative Sociology 14*(2): 143–147.

West, Carolyn M. 1998. Leaving a second closet: Outing partner violence in same-sex couples, pp. 163–183. In Jana L. Jasinski & Linda M. Williams (Eds.), *Partner Violence: A Comprehensive Review of 20 Years of Research.* Thousand Oaks, CA: Sage.

Weston, K. 1991. *Families We Choose: Lesbians, Gays, Kinship.* New York: Columbia University Press.

Wetle, Terrie. 1991. Successful aging: New hope for optimizing mental and physical well-being. *Journal of Geriatric Psychiatry 24*(1): 3–12.

Whalen, Dorothy M., Jerry J. Bigner, Clifton E. Barber. 2000. The grandmother role as experienced by lesbian women. *Journal of Women & Aging 12*(3–4): 39–57.

Wharton, Amy S., & Rebecca J. Erickson. 1995. The consequences of caring: Exploring the links between women's job and family emotion work. *Sociological Quarterly 36*(2): 273–296.

Wherry, Jeffrey N., John B. Jolly, John F. Aruffo, Greg Gillette, Lela Vaught, & Rebecca Methony. 1994. Family trauma and dysfunction in sexually abused female adolescent psychiatric and control groups. *Journal of Child Sexual Abuse 3*(1): 53–65.

Whisman, Mark A., & Neil S. Jacobson. 1989. Depression, marital satisfaction, and marital and personality measures of sex roles. *Journal of Marital and Family Therapy 15*(2): 177–186.

Whitbeck, Les B., Danny R. Hoyt, & Kevin A. Ackley. 1997. Families of homeless and runaway adolescents: A comparison of parent/caretaker and adolescent perspectives on parenting, family violence, and adolescent conduct. *Child Abuse and Neglect* 21(6): 517–528.

Whitbeck, Les B., & Ronald L. Simons. 1990. Life on the streets: The victimization of runaway and homeless adolescents. *Youth and Society* 22(1): 108–125.

White, James M. 1998. The normative interpretation of life course event histories. *Marriage and Family Review* 27(3–4): 211–235.

White, James M. & David Watt. 1999 Winter. Computers and the family life: A family development perspective. *Journal of Comparative Family Studies* 30: 1, 1–15.

White, James M. 1992. Marital status and well-being in Canada: An analysis of age group variations. *Journal of Family Issues* 13(3): 390–409.

White, Kimberly et al. 1984. Unstable diabetes and unstable families: A psychosocial evaluation of diabetic children with recurrent ketoacidosis. *Pediatrics, 73*(6): 749–755.

White, Lynn. 1990. Determinants of divorce: A review of research in the eighties. *Journal of Marriage and the Family 52*(4): 904–912.

Whitehead, Barbara Dafoe. 1990. The family in an unfriendly culture. *Family Affairs 3*: 1–2.

Whitehead, Barbara Dafoe. 1996. The decline of marriage as the social basis of childbearing, pp. 3–14. In David Popenoe, Jean Bethke Elshtain, & David Blankenhorn (Eds.), *Promises to Keep: Decline and Renewal of Marriage in America.* Lanham, MD: Rowman and Littlefield Publishers, Inc.

Wiener, Lori S., Nancy Heilman, Haven B. Battles. 1998. Public disclosure of HIV: Psychosocial considerations for children, pp. 193–217. In Valerian J. Derlega, & Anita P. Barbee (Eds.) *HIV and Social Interaction.* Thousand Oaks, CA: Sage.

Wiersma, Uco J. 1994 February. A taxonomy of behavioral strategies for coping with work-home conflict. *Human Relations* 47: 211–221.

Wilkinson, Richard G. 1994. From material scarcity to social disadvantage. *Daedalus: Journal of the American Academy of Arts and Sciences* 123(4): 61–77.

Wilkinson, Ross B. 1995. Changes in psychological health and the marital relationship through childbearing: Transition or process as stress? *Australian Journal of Psychology* 47(2).

Willen, Helena, & Henry Montgomery. 1996. The impact of wishing for children and having children on attainment and importance of life values. *Journal of Comparative Family Studies* 27(3): 499–518.

Williams, Lee, & Joan Jurich. 1995 April. Predicting marital success after five years: Assessing the predictive validity of FOCCUS. *Journal of Marital and Family Therapy* 21.

Williams, Lindy, Kalyani Mehta, & Hui-Sheng Lin. 1999 December. Intergenerational influence in Singapore and Taiwan: The role of the elderly in family decisions. *Journal of Cross-Cultural Gerontology* 14(4): 291–322.

Willms, J. Douglas (Ed.). 2002. *Vulnerable Children: Findings from Canada's Longitudinal Survey of Children and Youth.* Edmonton: University of Alberta Press.

Willms, J. Douglas. 2002a. Socioeconomic gradients for childhood vulnerability. Pp. 71–102 in J. Douglas Willms, ed. *Vulnerable Children: Findings from Canada's National Longitudinal Survey of Children and Youth.* Edmonton: University of Alberta Press, and Ottawa: Human Resources Development Canada, Applied Research Branch

Willms, J. Douglas. 2002b. Implications of the findings for social policy renewal. Pp. 359–377 in J. Douglas Willms, ed. *Vulnerable Children: Findings from Canada's National Longitudinal Survey of Children and Youth.* Edmonton: University of Alberta Press, and Ottawa: Human Resources Development Canada, Applied Research Branch.

Willoughby, Jennifer C., & Laraine Masters Glidden. 1995. Fathers helping out: Shared child care and marital satisfaction of parents of children with disabilities. *American Journal on Mental Retardation* 99(4).

Wilson, Paul A., Stephen T. Moore, Dana S. Rubin, Pamela K. Bartels. 1990. Informal caregivers of the chronically ill and their social support: A pilot study. *Journal of Gerontological Social Work* 15(1–2): 155–170

Wilson, S.J. 1996. *Women, Families and Work* (4th edition). Toronto: McGraw-Hill Ryerson.

Wilson, William J. 1987. *The Truly Disadvantaged: The Inner City, the Underclass, and Public Policy.* Chicago: University of Chicago Press.

Winch, Robert F. 1962. *The Modern Family.* New York: Holt

Wind, Tiffany-Weissmann, & Louise Silvern. 1994 May. Parenting and family stress as mediators of the long-term effects of child abuse. *Child Abuse and Neglect 18*: 439–453.

Windle, Michael, & Levent Dumenci. 1997 August. Parental and occupational distress as predictors of depressive symptoms among dual-income couples: A multilevel modeling approach. *Journal of Marriage and the Family* 59: 625–634.

Wissenstein, Michael. 1997. Is number of newborn killings rising? *The Gazette* (Montreal) 19 November: B1.

Wolak, Janis, & David Finklehor. 1998. Children exposed to partner violence, pp. 73–112. In Jana L. Jasinski & Linda M. Williams (Eds.), *Partner Violence: A Comprehensive Review of 20 years of research.* Thousand Oaks, CA: Sage.

Wolcott, Ilene & Helen Glezer. 1995 Winter. Impact of the work environment on workers with family responsibilities. *Family Matters 41*, 15–19.

Wolf, Diane L. (Ed.). 1996. *Feminist Dilemmas in Fieldwork. Boulder.* CO: Westview Press.

Wolf, Rosalie S. 1996. Elder abuse and family violence: Testimony presented before the U.S. Senate Special Committee on Aging. *Journal of Elder Abuse and Neglect 8*(1): 81–96.

Wong, Yin-Ling Irene, & Irving Piliavin. 1999. *Familial Support, Housing Resources, and Psychological Distress among Homeless Persons: A Longitudinal Analysis.* American Sociological Association (ASA).

Wong-Wylie, Gina, & Marianne Doherty-Poirier. 1997. *Created Families: Perspectives From Persons Living with HIV/AIDS.* Paper presented at the Canadian Home Economics Association, Victoria, B.C.

Worthington, Everett L., Michael E. McCullough, & Joanne L. Shortz. 1995 October. Can couples assessment and feedback improve relationships? Assessment as a brief relationship enrichment procedure. *Journal of Counseling Psychology 42.*

Wright, Eric Reaney. 1994 August. *Caring For Those Who "Can't": Gender, Network Structure, and the Burden of Caring for People with Mental Illness.* Dissertation Abstracts International, A: The Humanities and Social Sciences 55, 2, 380–A.

Wright, Mareena McKinley, & Sue Keir Hoppe. 1994. *Integrating Stress and Life Course Perspectives in the Study of Psychological Response to Job Loss.* An association paper for the Society for the Study of Social Problems.

Wu, Zheng. 1994. Remarriage in Canada: A social exchange perspective. *Journal of Divorce and Remarriage 21*(3–4): 191–224.

Wu, Zheng. 1995. Remarriage after widowhood: A marital history study of older Canadians. *Canadian Journal on Aging 14*(4): 719–736.

Wu, Zheng. 2000. *Cohabitation: An Alternative Form of Family Living.* Don Mills, ON: Oxford University Press.

Wu, Zheng, & T.R. Balakrishnan. 1995. The dissolution of premarital cohabitation in Canada. *Demography* 32: 521–532.

Wu, Zheng, & R. Hart. 2002. The effects of marital and nonmarital union transition on health. *Journal of Marriage and Family* 64: 420–432.

Wylie, Betty Jane. 1997. *Family: An Exploration.* Canada (no place of publication listed): Northstone.

Xiaohe, Xu, & Martin King Whyte. 1990. Love matches and arranged marriages. *Journal of Marriage and the Family, 52*(3): 709–722.

Yang, Kang-lin. 1999 November. *The Relationship among Family Dynamics, Interpersonal Competence and Psychological Adjustment in Late Adolescence and Young Adulthood: A Taiwanese Sample.* Dissertation Abstracts International, A: The Humanities and Social Sciences 60, 5, 1785–A.

Yelsma, Paul. 1996 June. Affective orientations of perpetrators, victims, and functional spouses. *Journal of Interpersonal Violence 11*: 141–161.

Ying Yu-Wen, & Lee Peter A. 1999 April. The development of ethnic identity in Asian-American adolescents: Status and outcome. *American Journal of Orthopsychiatry 69*(2): 194–208.

Yllo, K., & M.A. Straus. 1981. Interpersonal violence among married and cohabiting couples. *Family Relations 30*: 339–347.

York, Glyn Y. 1987 Summer. Religious-based denial in the NICU: Implications for social work. *Social Work in Health Care, Vol. 12*(4), pp. 31–45.

Young, K.S. 1996 December. Psychology of computer use: XL. Addictive use of the Internet: A case that breaks the stereotype. *Psychological Reports 70*(3 Pt. 1): 899–902.

Zachariah, Rachel. 1996. Predictors of psychological well-being of women during pregnancy; replication and extension. *Journal of Social Behavior and Personality 11*(1).

Zarit, Steven H., & Carol J. Whitlatch. 1993. The effects of placement in nursing homes on family caregivers: Short and long term consequences. *Irish Journal of Psychology 14*(1): 25–37.

Zetterlind, Ulla Marianne. 1999 Fall. *Relatives of Alcoholics: Studies of Hardship, Behaviour, Symptomatology and Methods of Intervention.* Dissertation Abstracts International, C: Worldwide, 60, 3, 560–C.

Zhan, Gao. June 1998. *The Sojourning Life as Problematic: Marital Crises of Chinese Students Who Are Studying in the U.S.* Dissertation Abstracts International, A: The Humanities and Social Sciences 58, 12, 4825–A.

Zhang, Sheldon X. 1995. Measuring shaming in an ethnic context. *British Journal of Criminology 35*(2): 248–262.

Zick, Cathleen D., & Jane L. McCullough. 1991 April. Trends in married couples' time use: Evidence from 1977–78 and 1987–88. *Sex Roles 24*, 7–8, 459–487.

Zill, Nicholas, & Christine Winquist Nord. 1994. Running in Place: How American Families are Faring in a Changing Economy and an Individualistic Society. *Child Trends.* Washington, D.C.

Zimmerman, Shirley. 1988. *Understanding Family Policy: Theoretical Approaches.* Beverly Hills, CA: Sage.

Zinsmeister, Karl. 1996 September-October. Family meltdown in the classroom. *The American Enterprise* 7: 42–45.

Zvonkovic, A.M., K.M. Greaves, C.J. Schmiege, & L.D. Hall. 1996. The marital construction of gender through work and family decisions: A qualitative analysis. *Journal of Marriage and the Family 58*: 91–100.

INDEX